THE COMPLETE BOOK OF Baking

THE COMPLETE BOOK OF
Baking

Photography by Ray Joyce

WINDWARD

THE CONTRIBUTORS

Betty Dunleavy
Betty has undertaken the lion's share of this book, which is appropriate since she has had huge experience in cooking and is particularly interested in cakes and desserts. For years cookery editor of a national women's magazine, Betty has also worked in industry and with advertising agencies as a food consultant and writer.

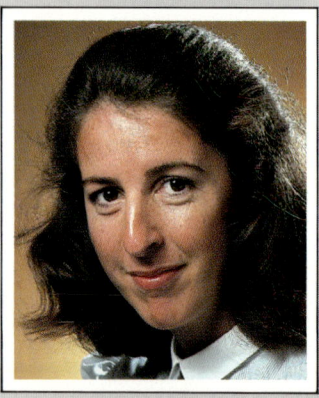

Janice Baker
Janice has a magic hand when it comes to making food look good. With the help of Sue Whitter, she prepared all the food for photography in this book. An experienced home economist, Janice is particularly interested in pies and home-made bread and that's what she's written about.

Ann Creber
Ann is a versatile lady indeed. She writes for a slimming magazine, is constantly in demand by the food industry (she has a number of industry-related cookbooks under her belt) and styles food for advertisements and for magazines.

Anne Marshall
Running her own cookery school, working as a consultant for the food industry and writing regular magazine articles keeps Anne Marshall pretty busy. She has already written a book on pies so was the obvious choice for the pastry and tarts chapters.

Michael Lawrence
Renowned for his expertise in the kitchen, Mike writes articles on both wine and food. Biscuits and cookies were what he opted for—not just sweet biscuits, he included a few of his favourite savoury biscuits too.

Mark Pearson
Mark has a special interest in health food cookery. But then Mark has many interests—he currently owns and runs an Italian restaurant. His chapter on tea cakes and breads is full of really interesting and different new recipes.

Susan Tomnay
Managing Editor of this book, Susan loves yeast cookery. It's the one branch of cookery she maintains, where you can't make mistakes by being too heavy-handed. Susan also writes food articles for magazines and newspapers.

THE PHOTOGRAPHER

Ray Joyce
Ray approached this book with enthusiasm and dedication. Not only did he patiently set up each shot, but he went out of his way to find locations and prowled around antique shops looking for just the right prop.

ACKNOWLEDGEMENTS

The Publishers would like to thank the following people for lending props for use in photography:
Doulton Tableware
Noritake
Village Living, Avalon
David Jones, Sydney
Giftmaker, Paddington
Accoutrement Cook Shops, Chatswood and Mosman
G. H. Hardy Antiques, Paddington
Melocco Ltd, Annandale
Georges of Collins Street
Crown Street Restoration Centre, Sydney
Inini, Neutral Bay
Gordon Smail of Pooters, Barossa Valley

We would like to particularly thank Appley Hoare Antiques, Mosman and Madeline Fyfe-Smith of Tee Jays Antiques, Willoughby for their generosity and Judy and David Gazzard for kindly allowing us to use their beautiful cottage as a backdrop for some of the photographs.

Windward

An imprint owned by WH Smith & Son Limited
Registered No 237811 England
Trading as WHS Distributors,
St John's House, East Street, Leicester, LE1 6NE.

All Rights Reserved

No part of this publication may be reproduced, stored in a retrieval system, or transmitted, in any form or by any means, electronic, mechanical, photocopying, recording or othewise without the prior permission of the publishers.

ISBN 0 7112 0364 4

Originated by Lansdowne Press, Australia
© Lansdowne Press 1984

Printed in Singapore
By Kyodo Printing Co. Ltd.

Contents

INTRODUCTION 8

BREAD 10

COOKING WITH YEAST 30

TEA CAKES & BREADS 46

LARGE CAKES 66

SMALL CAKES 110

ICINGS, FILLINGS & GLAZES 126

BISCUITS & COOKIES 150

PASTRY 178

PASTRIES 198

TARTS & TARTLETS 226

SWEET PIES 254

SAVOURY PIES 286

DESSERTS 314

INDEX 364

Introduction

I really enjoyed working on this book because baking is my favourite branch of cookery. Ever since I was a child I've been fascinated by its magic. I used to watch my mother beating the eggs and sugar to make one of her renowned sponge cakes and would hover around the oven until she said it was ready. She always looked pleased when she saw it had risen beautifully, I don't think she ever got over the magic of baking either.

When I baked my first loaf of bread, I was so amazed that it turned out well and I loved the smell and taste so much that I began baking a loaf every day. My big treat of the day was to make a tomato sandwich from the crust of the still-warm loaf. I did that for five years. I still bake my own bread, but now I make four loaves at a time and freeze them.

I think that modern technology explains in part why baking has become so popular again. Now we can bring a lost tradition back into our lives without having to spend huge amounts of time on it—because now we have electric mixers, food processors and freezers. We can fill our kitchens with the smell of home-baked cakes, pies and breads and still go to work, look after our children, read books.

In *The Complete Book of Baking* you'll find your favourite recipes as well as a lot of new ones and you'll see many of them in the beautiful colour photographs.

In the Pastry and Icing chapters, where we felt it was necessary, we've supplemented our instructions with step-by-step colour photographs.

The oven temperatures and cooking times specified in the book are those used by the people who tested the recipes. Gas and electric ovens differ slightly; gas ovens usually require a lower temperature than electric ovens. Convection ovens are different from both gas and electric, the temperature required is usually lower than a standard oven and it normally takes less time than stated. Naturally we couldn't go into all these factors with every recipe, so you will have to experiment with one or two recipes and alter them according to your oven's particular quirks.

There are other variables too: flours differ from country to country and even from area to area within countries. Some absorb more liquid than others and only you can be the judge of this. Try the amount of flour specified in a few recipes, but if the mixture is consistently too liquid or too dry, then adjust the flour accordingly.

Baking is a branch of cookery that responds well to instinct. The more experience you have in it, the more your instinct will work for you. You'll know when a mixture doesn't feel right. Most experienced bread makers can tell by the texture of the dough whether it will be good loaf or not, even before the dough has risen.

When commissioning the book we decided that rather than have one person write it all, we'd use an expert in each field. Every contributor has had vast experience in his or her sphere but more than that, they all share a love of baking and a great enthusiasm for their subject.

In fact the entire project has been an enthusiastic exercise. The photographer, Ray Joyce, and the food stylists, Janice Baker and Susan Whitter, approached their task with gusto. And judging by the number of people who just happened to be passing the test kitchen every afternoon, wondering if there was a little something for them to take home, the results of their labour were well appreciated.

Susan Tomnay

All flour is plain (all-purpose) flour unless otherwise specified.

Bread

There is something terribly rewarding about making your own bread. That mysterious transformation of the swelling dough into a crusty golden loaf, crackling as it cools down from the fierce oven. Possibly it is the creative reward, from gathering all those raw materials together and turning them into 'the staff of life'. Or is it the response from hoards of admirers who stamp into the kitchen after sniffing that unforgettable aroma of freshly baked bread? Whatever it may be, breadmaking is ever popular.

There are limitless forms bread dough can be turned into—whatever the imagination desires. A French Master Baker has gone as far as making a bread chandelier and carved loaves as wall hangings. We don't need to take it as far as that, but let's be imaginative with our loaves and experiment once the basic technique has been mastered. We don't have to rely on the 'white sliced loaf', thank goodness.

Here are just some of the basic points to good bread-making and a selection of well-tried and some new bread recipes.

Happy kneading.

Janice Baker

1. Milk Bread (see p. 16)
2. Wholemeal Bread (see p. 17)
3. Milk Bread (see p. 16)
4. Bread Knots (see p. 16)
5. French Bread (see p. 20)
6. Milk Bread ring (see p. 16)
7. Household Bread Plait (see p. 17)
8. Challah Braid (see p. 24)
9. Household Bread (see p. 17)
10. Household Bread (see p. 17)
11. Potato Bread (see p. 24)
12. Naan (see p. 25)
13. Cottage Loaf (see p. 18)
14. Cloverleaf Rolls (see p. 17)
15. Crescent Rolls (see p. 16)

THE INGREDIENTS
Flours
Most breads are made with plain wheat flour to some extent. Wheat flour has a high percentage of gluten—a protein in the wheat structure which stretches and will form that all-important network necessary for bread-making. The gluten is developed through stirring, beating and kneading the dough.

'Strong' flour has gluten added to it to give flour with a high percentage of gluten. This type of flour absorbs more liquid and will give a larger, lighter loaf.

'All-purpose' flour is a flour of medium strength (medium gluten percentage) and will give a very satisfactory loaf.

'Soft' flour is low in gluten and should be mixed with a stronger flour for bread-making, or be kept specially for cake-making.

Rye flour has a good gluten content, but the gluten is slightly different to that found in wheat flour. This flour is often difficult to handle as it becomes quite sticky. But if used in combination with wheat flour, it gives a very good dough.

Rice flour is high in starch and is excellent when used as a dusting flour when moulding a sticky dough. It dries the surface without altering the flour content of the dough.

Potato flour is also used for dusting. This will give a good shiny surface to the loaf when mixed with water and brushed over the loaf before baking.

Chick pea or lentil flour, buck wheat, soy, barley or millet flour may all be used in combination with plain wheat flour. But first master the art of bread-making, then let your head go and experiment with the different flours.

Gluten
In wheat flour and other flours, there are glutenous proteins which form gluten when the dough is made. Gluten is important firstly because when developed, it forms the skin of the tiny pockets that hold the gas given off from the yeast. Secondly the development or ripening of the gluten plays a major part in the flavour of the dough. Gluten is obtainable from most health food shops, and if you wish to increase the gluten content of your flour, add 1 teaspoon of gluten to 1 cup of all-purpose flour. Sift three times to distribute the gluten evenly through the flour.

Wheat germ
Apart from its nutritional value, wheat germ improves the dough, helps to produce a good open crumb in the bread and prolongs the keeping quality of the loaf.

Wheat germ, millet grain and cracked wheat may be added to the flour or kneaded into the surface of the dough. These ingredients give not only added value to the loaf but also interesting texture and flavour. Vary the bread by kneading the dough finally in sesame seeds (toasted or plain), poppy seeds, pumpkin seeds, sunflower seeds or rock salt, or a combination of these.

Yeast
Yeast is a living plant which produces tiny bubbles of carbon dioxide and, when combined with moisture, food (in the form of flour) and warmth, will expand the bulk of a dough. Like any plant it is particular about its environment. It loves a temperature of about 27°C (85°F). At a slightly lower temperature it works more slowly, and lower still it hibernates. At a high temperature of about 54°C (130°F) it expires.

Today's store-bought yeasts are reliable and work very quickly. Two forms are available: fresh compressed, and dried.

Fresh compressed yeast should be bought in reasonable quantities, about 125 g (4 oz) at a time. The yeast should be firm and moist in consistency, creamy beige in colour and sweet smelling.

Store the block in a plastic container or glass jar with a few ventilation holes pierced in the lid to allow the moisture in the yeast to circulate and not condense inside the container.

In hot climates the yeast should keep quite well in the refrigerator for about 2 to 3 weeks.

It may also be frozen. Cut the block into 30 g (1oz) pieces, wrap each separately, and store in a freezer bag or plastic box labelled and dated. Yeast in good condition will keep successfully for about 3 months. Allow the yeast about 15 minutes to thaw before using. If liked, it may be thawed in tepid water.

Dried yeast: After using fresh yeast it is difficult to comprehend that the creamy granules of dried yeast will raise a dough, and particularly such a small quantity of granules. For this reason most people tend to be heavy-handed when using dried yeast, with the result that the dough rises too quickly and the loaf, after baking, will quickly go stale.

Where the recipe calls for 30 g (1 oz) fresh compressed yeast, use only 7 g (¼ oz) dried yeast. For 15 g (½ oz) fresh compressed yeast, use only 1 teaspoon dried yeast. And for 7 g (¼ oz) fresh compressed yeast, use only ¼ teaspoon dried yeast.

To reactivate dried yeast, sprinkle it over a little warm water and leave for 10 to 15 minutes. Whisk for a few seconds and add to the dough in the normal way.

Butter
Fat is seldom added to everyday bread, other than in the form of oil or milk.

When a dough or batter is to be enriched with butter, the butter is usually worked in after the straight dough has risen for the first time. This is because the fat globules, in coating the flour grains, make them sticky and makes the action of the yeast more difficult in the dough. But once the yeast has done its work and spread evenly through the dough, the addition of fat presents less of a problem.

Oil
Oil added to the dough makes it exceptionally easy to handle, although only a very small portion is used.

Olive oil is by far the best to add, for the flavour is superb. But for an alternative oil and flavour, use peanut oil, sunflower seed oil or even sesame seed oil.

Milk
Milk added to dough (in the proportion of 1 part milk to 3 parts water) improves the quality of the

texture of the loaf and gives a softer crust—although oil or fat will do the same.

Salt

The addition of salt is all-important, for bread made without salt is really unpalatable. Salt retards the yeast action, slowing the process and preventing the dough from overfermenting or developing a sour taste if a slow rising is called for. If a fast rising is necessary it is quite possible to increase the quantity of yeast a little and keep the salt content constant. Salt helps the retention of moisture in the dough, but too much salt makes the crust very hard.

If coarse salt crystals are used, these must be dissolved in tepid water first, for once the crystals are mixed with the flour nothing will dissolve them. Fine cooking salt, of course, may be added to the flour. Rock salt kneaded into the surface of the dough gives a good crunchy crust.

Sugar

Sugar stimulates the yeast, where salt retards it. Always add the sugar to the yeast with the other ingredients, for if added directly it will overstimulate and exhaust the yeast.

THE PROCESS OF BREAD-MAKING

Sponging

The process of sponging speeds up the rising of the dough and gives a lighter dough. The yeast, warm liquid and flour are mixed together and allowed to 'sponge' in one of the following ways:

- A well is made in the weighed and sifted flour, and the yeast mixture is added to the centre. A light batter is formed then covered thickly with some of the flour. This is left to 'sponge'. When the foaming liquid breaks through the flour, the 'sponge' is ready.
- Yeast, flour and water are mixed together in a small bowl, left to 'sponge' until foaming, then added to the weighed flour.
- Yeast is mixed with a little warm liquid and flour and formed into a small ball. This ball is then dropped into a bowl of warm water. When the ball rises in the liquid, it is ready. This is then sifted out and added to the dough.

Kneading

The dough should be kneaded with a regular rhythmic action, using the heel of your hand to push, then the cupped hand to draw the dough back again. Your other hand turns the dough at the same time. This action distributes the yeast evenly throughout the dough and develops the gluten in the dough. The dough should be smooth and elastic—when a finger is pressed into the dough the depression should disappear quickly.

Rising

The dough is left in a warm draught-free place to 'rise' until doubled in bulk.

Shaping

The dough is turned out of the bowl onto a floured surface and kneaded lightly to the required shape.

Proving

When the dough has been shaped and placed into its tin (or onto a baking tray) it is allowed to 'prove' or rise until it is almost doubled in bulk.

It is then scored, brushed with a glaze and sprinkled with seeds, or is left natural.

Baking

Baking is usually done in a hot oven, to quickly kill the yeast and set the loaf. Some recipes require the temperature to be lowered after 15 minutes.

When cooked the crust should be a good rich colour, and when the base of the loaf is tapped with your knuckles it should sound hollow.

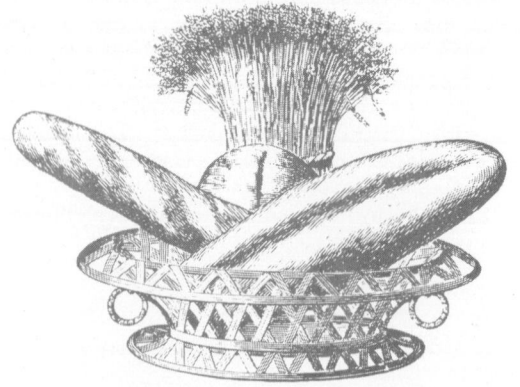

1. Sponging, well method

2. Sponging, ball method

3. Kneading

4. Rising

6. Proving

Milk Bread

Makes 1 loaf

4 cups (1 lb) flour

1 teaspoon salt

1½ cups (12 fl oz) milk

2 teaspoons sugar

15 g (½ oz) fresh compressed yeast

60 g (2 oz) butter

Sift the flour and salt into a large warmed bowl.

Warm half of the milk to 'blood heat' with the sugar.

Cream the yeast in a small bowl and pour it over the warm milk and sugar. Stir until the yeast has dissolved.

Make a well in the centre of the flour and pour in the milk-sugar and yeast mixture. Stir in sufficient surrounding flour to make a light batter. Sprinkle the top of the batter with a little flour. Leave the bowl to stand in a warm place until the batter looks spongy and is full of bubbles.

Warm the rest of the milk with the butter, and pour this onto the sponge in the bowl. Mix to a soft dough (using extra flour or extra warm milk if necessary). Place the dough on a lightly-floured surface and knead until the dough is smooth and elastic. Rinse out the bowl and lightly grease it with butter. Return the dough to the bowl. Turn the dough over so that the top is lightly greased, and cover loosely with a cloth or with cling film. Leave to rise in a warm place until doubled in bulk.

Preheat the oven to 230°C (450°F/Gas 8).

Punch the dough down with your fist and knead it lightly on a floured surface. Shape the dough into a loaf shape and place it on a lightly greased baking tray or in a greased bread tin. Leave to prove in a warm place for about 30 minutes or until the loaf has risen to almost the required shape.

Bake in the very hot oven for 45 minutes or until the crust resounds when tapped. If the base is slightly damp, leave it out of its tin and return it to the oven for a few minutes. Cool on a wire rack.

Bread Knots

Makes 12 knots

½ quantity Milk Bread dough (see recipe above)

1 egg, beaten

poppy seeds, sesame seeds, caraway seeds or little grated Cheddar cheese

Make Milk Bread dough according to the directions given in the recipe. Leave the dough to rise in the bowl until doubled in bulk.

Preheat the oven to 230°C (450°F/Gas 8).

Punch the dough down and knead it lightly on a floured surface. Divide the dough into 12 equal portions. Roll each into a sausage shape about 15 cm (6 in) long, and then tie each into a knot. Place apart on a greased baking tray. Leave in a warm place to prove into shape and double in size.

Brush with beaten egg to glaze, and sprinkle with poppy seeds, sesame seeds, caraway seeds or Cheddar cheese.

Bake for 10 to 15 minutes or until golden brown.

Crescent Rolls

Makes 8

½ quantity Milk Bread dough (see recipe above)

soft butter

1 egg, beaten

sesame seeds or caraway seeds

Make Milk Bread dough according to the directions given in the recipe. Leave the dough to rise in the bowl until doubled in bulk.

Preheat the oven to 230°C (450°F/Gas 8).

Punch the dough down and knead it lightly on a floured surface. Roll the dough into a circle 5 mm (¼ in) thick, and spread the top with soft butter. Cut into eight wedges. Roll up each wedge, rolling from the wider edge towards the point. Shape each into a crescent, stretching the dough gently. Place on a greased baking tray and leave in a warm place to prove.

Brush with beaten egg to glaze, and sprinkle with sesame seeds or caraway seeds.

Bake for 10 to 15 minutes or until golden brown.

Wholemeal Bread

Makes 1 loaf

2 cups (8 oz) plain flour
2 cups (8 oz) wholemeal flour
2 teaspoons salt
15 g (½ oz) fresh compressed yeast
1⅔ cups (13 fl oz) lukewarm water
sesame seeds or poppy seeds

Mix the flours together in a large warmed bowl and add the salt.

Cream the yeast and add a little of the lukewarm water. Sprinkle with a little flour and leave to stand in a warm place until it becomes frothy.

Make a well in the flour, and add the yeast mixture and the remaining water. Mix with a wooden spoon until the dough comes cleanly away from the sides of the bowl. Turn out onto a lightly-floured surface and knead for about 10 minutes. Return the dough to the rinsed-out bowl. Cover with a damp cloth or cling film, and set aside in a warm place until doubled in bulk.

Preheat the oven to 220°C (425°F/Gas 7).

Punch the dough down and knead lightly for about 3 minutes, then place in a greased 23 × 12 × 8 cm (9 × 5 × 3 in) bread tin. Cover with a cloth and leave to stand in a warm place to prove.

Brush the top of the loaf with lukewarm water and score the surface in two or three places with a sharp knife. Sprinkle with sesame or poppy seeds.

Bake for 35 to 45 minutes or until the bottom of the loaf sounds hollow when you turn the loaf out of its tin and tap it with your knuckles. Cool on a wire rack.

Household Bread

Makes 4 loaves

2 kg (4 lb) plain flour (or a mixture of wholemeal flour with wheat germ or rye flour)
1½ tablespoons salt
1 tablespoon sugar
30 g (1 oz) fresh compressed yeast
5 cups (1.25 litres) tepid water

Sift the flour, salt and sugar into a large warmed bowl.

Cream the yeast with the tepid water. Make a well in the centre of the flour and pour the water-yeast mixture into this. Mix until a fairly liquid batter has formed. Sprinkle the surface of the batter thickly with some of the surrounding flour.

Leave the bowl covered in a warm place until the frothing batter breaks through. This 'sponging' should take about 30 minutes.

Beat in the surrounding flour, first using a wooden spoon, then your hands. Lift the dough out onto a floured surface and knead the dough until smooth and elastic (about 10 to 15 minutes). Return the dough to the rinsed-out bowl and cut a cross in the top of the dough. Cover and place in a warm place for about 2 hours, or leave overnight in a cool place.

Preheat the oven to 200°C (400°F/Gas 6).

Punch the dough down and knead it lightly. Divide the dough into four, and form into the required shapes—place into four greased bread tins, or if cottage loaves or plaits place on greased baking trays. Leave the loaves to prove.

Bake in the hot oven until a deep golden brown, for about 40 minutes to 1 hour. Cool on a wire rack.

Cloverleaf Rolls

Makes 24

1 quantity Milk Bread dough (see recipe page 16)
melted butter
poppy seeds

Make Milk Bread dough according to directions given in the recipe. Leave the dough to rise in the bowl until doubled in bulk.

Preheat the oven to 230°C (450°F/Gas 8).

Punch the dough down, turn out onto a lightly-floured surface and knead until smooth. Divide the dough evenly into 24 pieces. Then divide each piece into three and form into small balls.

Lightly grease muffin trays that have 24 cavities. Into each cavity place three balls, forming a three-leafed clover pattern. Leave the trays in a warm place until the rolls prove and double in bulk.

Brush with melted butter to glaze, and sprinkle with poppy seeds if liked.

Bake for 15 to 18 minutes or until golden brown.

Farmhouse Loaves

Makes 2 loaves

30 g (1 oz) fresh compressed yeast
2 cups (16fl oz) tepid water
2 tablespoons honey
3 cups (12 oz) plain flour
3 cups (12 oz) wholemeal flour
1 tablespoon salt
grated Cheddar cheese plus caraway seeds for sprinkling

Mix the yeast with about half a cup of the tepid water. Stir the honey into the remaining 1½ cups of tepid water.

Sift the flours together with the salt into a large warmed bowl. Make a well in the centre of the flour and into this pour the yeast mixture and the honey and water. Gradually draw in the surrounding flour and mix until it is a smooth dough (add extra water, if necessary, to make a manageable dough). Turn the dough out onto a lightly-floured surface and knead until smooth and elastic (about 7 minutes).

Rinse the bowl clean and lightly grease it with a little butter or oil. Return the dough to the bowl and turn it once so that the top surface is oiled. Cover and leave in a warm place until doubled in bulk.

Preheat the oven to 200°C (400°F/Gas 6).

Punch the dough down and leave it to rest for 10 minutes.

Turn the dough out onto a lightly-floured surface and knead lightly. Divide the dough in half and form into two loaves of the shapes required—place into two greased bread tins, or if cottage loaves or plaits place on greased baking trays. Leave the loaves in a warm place to prove until doubled in bulk.

Sprinkle with grated cheese and caraway seeds if liked.

Bake for 40 to 45 minutes or until the crust is golden brown and the loaf sounds hollow when tapped with the knuckles. Leave to cool on a wire rack.

Cottage Loaf

Makes 2 loaves

1 quantity Farmhouse dough (see recipe above)
extra flour (rice flour, if desired) for dusting

Make the dough according to the directions given in the recipe for Farmhouse Loaves. Leave the dough to rise and double in bulk.

Preheat the oven to 200°C (400°F/Gas 6).

Punch the dough down and knead it lightly on a floured surface. Divide the dough in half. From each of these two pieces, break off about a quarter of the dough. Knead each piece into a round shape, two large and two small.

To assemble each cottage loaf, place a small round of dough ontop of a larger round, using a little milk or water to stick. Then briefly plunge a floury wooden spoon handle or finger right down into the centre of the dough.

Place the shaped bread on a greased baking tray and cover with a large bowl inverted, or with a cloth. Leave to rise for about 30 minutes or until well risen. Just before baking, dust with extra flour.

Bake for 45 minutes or until the bread sounds hollow when tapped with the knuckles.

Cracked Wheat Bread

Makes 2 loaves

1 cup (4 oz) finely ground cracked wheat
3 cups (24fl oz) boiling water
60 g (2 oz) butter
1 tablespoon salt
3 tablespoons honey
1 tablespoon molasses
¾ cup (6fl oz) milk
30 g (1 oz) fresh compressed yeast
¼ cup (2fl oz) water
4 cups (1 lb) plain flour
2 cups (8 oz) wholemeal flour

Mix the cracked wheat and boiling water together in a saucepan and cook for about 10 minutes, or until most of the moisture is absorbed. Stir in the butter, salt, honey, molasses and milk.

Cream the yeast with the water until dissolved.

Sift the flours into a large warmed bowl and stir in the cracked wheat mixture. Mix, using your hands, until thoroughly combined. Stir in the yeast mixture, and add more warm water if necessary to form a manageable dough. Lift the dough out onto a floured surface and knead until smooth.

Rinse out the bowl and lightly oil it. Return the dough to the bowl and turn once so that the surface is lightly greased. Cover and leave in a warm place until doubled in bulk.

Preheat the oven to 200°C (400°F/Gas 6).

Punch the dough down and knead it lightly. Divide the dough into two and place in lightly-greased deep bread tins. Leave to prove until well risen.

Bake for 40 minutes or until crusty golden brown. Remove each loaf from its tin, and if the base is slightly damp return the bread to the oven for 5 minutes. Cool on a wire rack.

Right: **Farmhouse Loaves** (see above).

Country Oatmeal Bread

Makes 1 loaf

¾ cup (6fl oz) boiling water

½ cup (1½ oz) rolled oats

45 g (1½ oz) butter

¼ cup (2fl oz) molasses

2 teaspoons salt

15 g (½ oz) fresh compressed yeast

½ cup (4fl oz) warm water

2¾ cups (11 oz) strong white flour

1 egg

1 egg white, slightly beaten

¼ cup (1 oz) rolled oats for sprinkling

¼ teaspoon coarse salt for sprinkling

Combine the boiling water with the rolled oats, butter, molasses and salt. Allow to cool to lukewarm.

Cream the yeast and dissolve it in the ½ cup of warm water.

Sift the flour into a large warmed bowl and make a well in the centre. Stir in the dissolved yeast, then the egg, then the cooled rolled oats mixture. Using a wooden spoon, stir to thoroughly combine. Turn out onto a lightly-floured surface and knead until smooth.

Return the dough to a rinsed-out bowl and leave covered in a warm place until doubled in bulk (about 1 to 1½ hours).

Preheat the oven to 190°C (375°F/Gas 5).

Punch the dough down and lightly knead it into a round. Grease the inside of a deep round cake tin or a large 1 kg (2 lb) fruit can, and place the dough in the tin. Brush its surface with the beaten egg white and sprinkle with the remaining ¼ cup of rolled oats and salt. Leave in a warm place until almost doubled in bulk.

Bake for 1 hour or until the crust is brown and the loaf sounds hollow when you turn it out of the tin and tap it with your knuckles. If browning too quickly, cover with a piece of brown paper or aluminium foil. When cooked, remove the loaf from the tin and cool on a wire rack.

French Bread

French bread is made with a high percentage of soft low-gluten flour from French home-grown wheat and a small portion of high-gluten imported wheat. The maturing of the dough is a lengthy process and the baking is very elaborate. Steam is injected into the ovens by means of pipes for the first 15 minutes, causing the bread to expand to its utmost capacity unhindered by the formation of a hard crust. The second half of the baking—with dry heat—turns the crust golden and crisp.

It is therefore not surprising that any 'French' bread we might try to make has little resemblance to the original. But we have included this recipe for those who wish to make French bread sticks.

Makes 2 long loaves

15 g (½ oz) fresh compressed yeast

15 g (½ oz) butter, softened

1 teaspoon sugar

1¼ cups (10fl oz) warm water

4 cups (1 lb) flour

1 teaspoon salt

Place the yeast, butter and sugar into a bowl. Stir in the warm water until the butter melts and the yeast is liquified.

Sift flour and salt into a large warmed bowl. Stir in the liquid ingredients. Gather the dough into a mass and turn it out onto a floured surface. Knead for 3 to 4 minutes, until the dough is smooth and elastic.

Grease the rinsed-out mixing bowl with a little butter or oil, and place the dough in the bowl. Turn the dough over so that the top is smeared with butter or oil. Cover with a sheet of cling film and leave in a warm place for about 1 to 1½ hours. The dough will rise to two and a half times its original bulk and should be light and spongy.

Preheat the oven to 190°C (375°F/Gas 5).

Punch the dough down and turn it out onto a floured surface. Roll it out to an oblong shape 30 × 20 cm (12 × 8 in). Check during rolling to make sure the dough is not sticking—flouring the surface again if necessary. Using a very sharp knife, cut the dough cleanly in half lengthways; do not drag the knife through the dough. Roll up each loaf tightly from the long side. Seal the ends and roll lengths slightly to make a good shape. Place the loaves on a greased baking tray, and leave to prove in a warm place for about 20 minutes.

Make slashes across the loaf at intervals and brush the surface with water. Bake for 40 minutes or until golden brown and crisp. Remove from the baking tray and cool on a wire rack.

Sourdough Bread

The term Sourdough brings to mind a sour flavoured dough—but really it refers to the fermenting process the flour goes through to form the starter for the dough.

In kitchens where yeast baking has been going on for years sourdough starters were made from flour, salt, sugar and potato water and success was assured because the yeast organisms were in the air. But today, to achieve the flavour and be assured of success, a commercial yeast is added to start the fermenting off.

Sourdough Starter

1 sachet or 2 teaspoons active dry yeast
2 cups (16fl oz) lukewarm water
2 cups (8 oz) flour

Dissolve the yeast in warm water in a large glass bowl. Gradually stir in the flour, then beat until smooth. Cover the bowl with a tea towel and leave to stand overnight in a warm place. Bubbles should appear on the surface, but if after 24 hours none have appeared, discard and start again.

Stir the mixture well and cover with cling film, and return to a warm draught-free place. Leave to stand until foamy (about 2 to 3 days).

When the sourdough starter has become foamy, stir it well and pour into a clean glass jar. Cover well and store in the refrigerator. When a clear liquid has risen to the top, the starter is ready to use. Stir before using.

The starter can be stored in the refrigerator for several weeks and used for several batches of bread. To replenish your supplies, discard all but 1 cup of the starter, because any excess (unless reactivated) may become rancid. Add 1 cup of starter to 1 cup of flour and 1 cup of lukewarm water, then proceed as before.

Always allow the starter to warm to room temperature before adding it to dough.

Makes 2 loaves

4 cups (1 lb) flour
2 teaspoons salt
1 cup Sourdough Starter (see above)
1½ cups (12fl oz) warm water
2 teaspoons molasses, honey or golden syrup
Next morning:
1½-2 cups (6-8 oz) flour
30 g (1 oz) butter
2 small eggs

Sift the flour and salt into a large warmed bowl. Make a well in the centre of the flour and stir in 1 cup of sourdough starter, the water, and molasses, honey or golden syrup. Mix thoroughly and leave to stand overnight uncovered in a warm place.

Next morning: Preheat the oven to 200°C (400°F/Gas 6).

Stir down any crust that may have formed and add the 1½-2 cups of flour.

Soften the butter and incorporate it into the dough with the eggs.

Turn the dough out onto a well-floured surface and knead until smooth and elastic. Shape the dough into two loaves and place on greased baking trays or in greased bread tins. Brush lightly with a little extra butter. Leave the loaves to prove until almost doubled in bulk.

Bake for 45 to 50 minutes. Cool on a wire rack.

Quick Sourdough Rye Bread

Makes 2 loaves

4 cups (1 lb) rye flour
6 cups (1½ lb) strong wheat flour
¾ teaspoon salt
2½ cups (20fl oz) water
22 g (¾ oz) fresh compressed yeast
1 teaspoon caraway seeds

Measure out half of the wheat flour, half of the rye flour and half of the salt, and mix together in a large bowl. Mix in enough of the warm water to make a soft dough, at first using a wooden spoon, then your hand. Place the dough in a clean bowl and leave to stand in a warm place for about 12 to 16 hours or until it gives an agreeably sour smell.

Mix together the remaining flours and salt. Dissolve the yeast in some of the remaining water and stir into the flour, adding more warm water to make a soft dough.

Incorporate the soured dough with the new dough, and knead until it is smooth and elastic. Return the dough to a clean warmed bowl. Leave in a warm place for about 1½ hours or until doubled in bulk.

Preheat the oven to 200°C (400°F/Gas 6).

Punch the dough down and turn it out onto a floured surface. Knead the caraway seeds into the dough and shape it into two cigar or torpedo shapes. Place on a greased baking tray and leave to prove for 1½ hours or until well-risen and well-shaped.

Prick the loaves with a fork in four or five places before placing in the oven. Bake for about 1 hour in the hot oven, reducing the temperature after 20 minutes or so to moderately hot, 190°C (375°F/Gas 5). Cool on a wire rack.

Note: If you wish to have the characteristic shiny crust of rye bread; mix a little potato flour or rice flour with boiling water, and brush this over the loaves just before baking and again about half-way through baking.

Rye Bread

Makes 2 loaves.

30 g (1 oz) fresh compressed yeast
1½ cups (12 fl oz) warm water
¼ cup (3 fl oz) molasses
⅓ cup (3 oz) sugar
1 tablespoon fennel seeds
1 tablespoon anise seed
2½ cups (10 oz) rye flour
2½ cups (10 oz) plain flour
30 g (1 oz) butter

Cream the yeast with the warm water in a large bowl. Stir in the molasses, sugar, fennel seeds and anise seeds. Sift the rye flour over and beat until a smooth dough. Gradually add the plain flour and mix to a smooth dough, holding back some of the flour if the dough is getting too stiff. Soften the butter and work into the dough. Turn the dough out onto a floured surface and knead until smooth.

Rinse out the bowl and return the dough to the bowl. Leave to rise in a warm place until doubled in bulk. This will be slower than normal, as the dough is quite a heavy one.

Preheat the oven to 190°C (375°F/Gas 5).

Punch the dough down and knead the dough into a round. Divide it in two and knead each into a long oval shape—the shape of a cigar. A sprinkling of rice flour or potato flour will help if the dough is sticky.

Place the shaped loaves onto greased baking trays and leave to prove until almost doubled in bulk.

Make four diagonal slashes in the tops of the loaves and bake for 30 to 35 minutes. Cool on a wire rack.

Corn Bread

Makes 2 loaves

30 g (1 oz) fresh compressed yeast
2 cups (16 fl oz) warm water
2 teaspoons salt
½ cup (5 fl oz) golden syrup, light corn syrup or molasses
4 tablespoons oil or melted butter
1 cup (5 oz) corn meal, Polenta
5–5½ cups (1 lb 4 oz – 1 lb 6 oz) flour

Cream the yeast and dissolve it in the warm water in a large mixing bowl. Add the salt, golden syrup (or corn syrup or molasses), oil (or melted butter), corn meal and half of the flour. Beat using a wooden spoon until smooth and combined. Add more of the remaining flour, if required, to produce a manageable dough.

Turn the dough out onto a floured surface and knead until smooth and elastic, about 10 minutes. Rinse out the bowl and lightly grease it with oil or butter. Return the dough to the bowl and turn it to grease the top. Cover and set in a warm place until doubled in bulk.

Preheat the oven to 190°C (375°F/Gas 5).

Punch the dough down and turn it out onto a lightly-floured surface. Knead lightly and divide the dough in half. Shape each into a round, or into a loaf shape if baking in bread tins. Place on greased baking trays or in two greased bread tins, and leave to prove for about 30 minutes.

Bake for 35 to 40 minutes or until the loaves sound hollow when tapped. Turn out onto a wire rack to cool.

Flower Pot Loaves

Home-made bread baked in terracotta flower pots, casseroles or ovenware serving dishes looks irresistible when brought to the table. It is a novel way of serving bread. Cracked Wheat Bread or Farmhouse Loaves (see page 18) are both suitable for baking in flower pots.

Use new terracotta flower pots. Scrub them clean but don't use detergent, just hot clean water. Leave the pots upside down to dry well.

When it is time to bake the loaves, oil the inside of each pot well or line it with aluminium foil. Fill the pot (whether it be a flower pot, casserole or serving dish) more than half-full with the dough. Leave to prove in a warm place until the dough has risen well.

Brush the top of the dough with beaten egg glaze, or with water or milk warmed to room temperature, or leave it lightly-floured. Score the surface if liked. Sprinkle with poppy seeds, sesame seeds or caraway seeds if liked.

Bake in a preheated oven at 200°C (400°F/Gas 6) for about 45 minutes depending on the size of the pot, until the loaf sounds hollow when you turn it out of the pot and tap it with your knuckles. Cool on a wire rack, then return the bread to the pot to serve.

Right: **Clockwise from right: Olive and Feta Cheese Bread (see p. 28); Bacon Loaf (see p. 26); Flower Pot Loaves (see above).**

Challah Braid

Makes 2 loaves

---
22 g (¾ oz) fresh compressed yeast

1⅓ cups (11fl oz) lukewarm water
---
3 eggs
---
1 tablespoon sugar
---
1 tablespoon sea salt
---
5 cups (1¼ lbs) flour
---
60 g (2 oz) butter, softened
---
1 egg yolk, mixed with a little water
---
poppy seeds, if liked, for sprinkling

Cream the yeast and dissolve it in the lukewarm water. Beat the eggs, sugar and sea salt together until combined.

Sift the flour into a large warmed bowl. Make a well in the centre and pour over the yeast and egg mixtures. Add the softened butter. Beat, gradually drawing in the surrounding flour, until the dough is smooth.

Turn the dough out onto a floured surface and knead until smooth and elastic, adding more flour if necessary; kneading should take about 5 to 7 minutes.

Rinse out the bowl and lightly grease with a little butter or oil. Return the dough to the bowl and turn it over so that the greased surface is ontop. Cover and set in a warm place until doubled in bulk.

Preheat the oven to 200°C (400°F/Gas 6).

Punch the dough down and divide into six equal portions. Roll each portion into a long sausage shape about 2.5 cm (1 in) thick. Plait three of the strands together and then the other three. Pinch the ends to seal. Place the two loaves on lightly-greased baking trays and leave in a warm place to prove.

Brush the surface with egg yolk mixed with a little water and sprinkle with poppy seeds if liked. Bake for 35 to 40 minutes or until the bottom of the loaf sounds hollow when tapped. Cool on a wire rack.

Potato Bread

Potato bread is one of my favourites, for it is light in texture and yet still very moist. It keeps well and the loaf makes excellent light toast or croûtons.
The rolls may be brushed with a little egg glaze, if liked, to give them a glistening top, and a sprinkling of sesame seeds before baking.
Makes 16 rolls or 1 loaf

---
2 medium-sized potatoes, to yield ¾ cup (4 oz) when mashed
---
4 cups (1 lb) flour
---
1 tablespoon salt
---
15 g (½ oz) fresh compressed yeast

1¼ cups (10fl oz) milk and water mixed

Peel and cook the potatoes in boiling salted water until tender. Drain and set over heat to dry the potatoes. Mash or sieve the potatoes until smooth.

Sift the flour and salt into a large warmed bowl.

Cream the yeast and stir in the warm milk and water until the yeast has dissolved.

Rub the mashed potatoes while still warm into the flour (as you would rub butter in), until well mixed. Make a well in the centre and add the yeast mixture. Stir until a soft dough. Turn out and knead the dough until smooth and elastic.

Rinse the bowl out and lightly butter it. Return the dough to the bowl and turn it to grease the top. Cover and set in a warm place until doubled in bulk. This will take a little more time than usual with other bread recipes.

Preheat the oven to 200°C (400°F/Gas 6).

Punch the dough down and turn it out onto a working surface. Knead lightly and, if making rolls, divide into 16 portions. Knead each into a smooth ball, pulling the dough into itself to make a smooth top. Place on a lightly-greased baking tray, cover loosely with a cloth, and leave to prove.

When well-risen and well-shaped, bake for 15 to 20 minutes or until golden brown. Cool on a wire rack.

For the loaf: Shape the dough into the required shape and place in a deep straight-sided tin. Cover with a damp cloth or a piece of cling film and leave to prove for about an hour.

Bake for 45 minutes or until the crust is a good brown and the loaf sounds hollow when tapped. Take care not to let the crust get too brown and harden. Cool on a wire rack.

Pocket Bread

This Middle Eastern bread is delicious served warm with Hummus or Taramosalata, or simply split open and served with a variety of fillings.
Makes 6

15 g (½ oz) fresh compressed yeast
1⅓ cups (11 fl oz) warm water
3–3½ cups (12–14 oz) flour
1 teaspoon salt
pinch sugar
1 tablespoon olive oil
cornmeal for dusting

Dissolve the yeast in a little of the warm water.

Sift half of the flour into a warmed bowl. Stir in the salt, sugar, oil, the remaining warm water and the dissolved yeast. Beat until smooth, adding enough of the remaining flour to make a soft dough.

Turn the dough out onto a lightly-floured surface and knead until smooth and elastic (about 10 minutes).

Rinse out the bowl and lightly grease it. Return the dough to the bowl and turn it once so that the greased surface is uppermost. Cover and leave in a warm place until doubled in bulk (about 1 hour).

Preheat the oven to 260°C (500°F/Gas 10).

Punch the dough down and divide it into six equal parts. Shape into balls and leave in a warm place to rise (about 30 minutes).

Sprinkle the working surface with cornmeal and on this roll out each ball into a circle about 3 mm (⅛ inch) thick. Place on ungreased baking trays and leave to prove for 15 minutes.

Bake for 10 minutes or until puffed and lightly browned.

Cool on wire trays and keep in a sealed plastic bag until ready to use.

Naan

This leavened Indian bread baked in the deep Tandoori ovens is delicious. The baker pats the bread out into an oval shape and places the bread straight onto the wall of the oven. To remove it, the baker uses a curved metal poker to hook the bread and lift it from the oven.
For our recipe we have adapted the method and the Naan is baked on heavy flat baking trays.
Makes 8

30 g (1 oz) fresh compressed yeast
¾ cup (6 fl oz) warm water
1 tablespoon sugar
¼ cup yoghurt or buttermilk
1 egg
60 g (2 oz) butter or ghee, melted
3½ cups (14 oz) plain flour
2 teaspoons salt

Cream the yeast and stir in the warm water.

Mix together the sugar, yoghurt (or buttermilk), egg, and melted butter (or ghee).

Sift the flour and salt into a warm mixing bowl and make a well in the centre. Stir in the yeast and water mixture, then the yoghurt and sugar mixture. Use a wooden spoon at first then, as the dough gets stiffer, use your hands. Turn the dough out of the bowl onto a lightly-floured surface and knead until smooth and elastic.

Rinse out the bowl and lightly oil it. Return the dough to the bowl and cover it loosely with a cloth. Leave in a warm place until doubled in bulk.

Preheat the oven to 230°C (450°F/Gas 8).

Punch the dough down and leave it to rest for 10 minutes.

Divide the dough into eight balls. Pat each into a round shape and then pull the dough to form an oval shape which is slightly thinner in the centre than at the edges. Each oval should be about 18 cm (7 in) long and about 10 cm (4 in) wide.

Place the heavy flat baking trays in the hot oven to heat them. When very hot, carefully remove them, place two loaves on each and quickly return to the oven. Bake for about 10 minutes or until golden and puffed. Serve warm with Tandoori Chicken or as an accompaniment to curries.

Variation: The Naan may be brushed with a little melted butter or ghee and sprinkled with poppy seeds, if liked, before baking.

Bacon Loaf

Makes 1 loaf.

250 g (8 oz) bacon or 125 g (4 oz) speck
15 g (½ oz) fresh compressed yeast
¼ cup (2fl oz) warm water
¼ cup (2fl oz) warm milk
1½ teaspoons sugar
1 teaspoon salt
2 eggs
3 cups flour
1 tablespoon olive oil
½ cup (2 oz) diced Emmenthaler cheese

Chop the bacon or speck coarsely. Fry until crisp, reserving the fat.

Cream the yeast with the warm water and milk.

Mix the sugar, salt and eggs together.

Sift the flour into a large warmed bowl and make a well in the centre. Stir in the yeast mixture, then the egg mixture and then the reserved bacon fat and the olive oil. Gradually draw in the surrounding flour until it forms a manageable dough, adding more liquid if necessary. Knead the dough in the bowl until smooth and elastic. Cover and leave in a warm place until doubled in bulk.

Preheat the oven to 200°C (400°F/Gas 6).

Punch the dough down and gently work in the diced cheese and the fried bacon. Shape into a smooth round and place in a shallow 20 cm (8 in) cake tin. Leave in a warm place until almost doubled in bulk.

Bake for 30 minutes or until golden brown. Serve warm.

Onion Bread

Makes 1 loaf.

15 g (½ oz) fresh compressed yeast
1 cup (8fl oz) warm water
3 cups (12 oz) flour
1 teaspoon sugar
2 teaspoons salt
3 tablespoons olive oil
3 large Spanish or brown onions
pinch of salt and sugar to season the onions

Cream the yeast with the warm water.

Sift the flour into a warm bowl with the sugar and salt. Stir in the dissolved yeast and water. Gradually draw in the surrounding flour to form a soft dough, adding a little more liquid if necessary. Turn the dough out onto a floured surface and knead until smooth.

Rinse out the bowl and return the dough to the bowl. Cover and leave in a warm place until doubled in bulk.

Preheat the oven to 200°C (400°F/Gas 6).

Punch the dough down and knead in 2 tablespoons of the olive oil.

Halve, peel and slice the onions thinly. Sauté them gently in the remaining tablespoon of olive oil until they are soft. Season to taste with salt and a little sugar. Set aside to cool.

Turn the dough out of the bowl and knead into a long sausage shape. Coil it into a ring and place on a baking tray. Secure the ends together. Leave to rise until almost doubled in bulk.

Spread over the cooled sautéed onions and bake in the hot oven for 15 minutes, then lower the heat to moderately hot, 190°C (375°F/Gas 5), and continue baking for a further 20 minutes or until golden brown. Serve bread hot or cold, sliced and with a pat of butter.

Garlic Bread

Garlic bread should be crisp and crusty on the outside and juicy and garlicky on the inside. So please don't skimp on the butter, and always use a good French loaf.

1 long loaf of French bread
4 cloves garlic, peeled
pinch of salt
185–250 g (6–8 oz) butter

Preheat the oven to 190°C (375°F/Gas 5). Slash the bread diagonally at 2 cm (¾ in) intervals, almost through to the base of the loaf.

Crush the garlic with a good pinch of salt, until a smooth paste. Soften the butter in a small bowl and add the crushed garlic. Mix well, using a metal spoon or plastic spatula, as garlic will taint a wooden spoon.

Spread the garlic butter between the slices of bread, smearing any remaining butter on the top. Wrap the bread in aluminium foil.

Place in the moderately hot oven for 15 minutes. Open the foil for the last 5 minutes to allow the crust to crisp.

Anchovy Loaf
In place of the garlic in the butter, use 6 mashed anchovy fillets which have been soaked in milk for a few minutes to remove excess salt. Mix the anchovy with 185–250 g of butter, then proceed as above.

Right: **Garlic Bread** (see above); **Melba Toast** (see p. 29); **Herb Bread** (see p. 29).

Cheese Bread

Makes 2 loaves.

30 g (1 oz) fresh compressed yeast
½ cup (4fl oz) warm water
1½ cups (12fl oz) warm milk
1 tablespoon salt
2 tablespoons sugar
¼ cup (2fl oz) olive oil
1 egg
6 cups (1½ lb) flour
1½ cups (6 oz) grated cheddar cheese
1 teaspoon caraway seeds
extra grated cheese for sprinkling

Cream the yeast with the warm water.

Mix together the milk, salt, sugar, oil and egg.

Sift the flour into a large warmed bowl and stir in the yeast and water, and then the milk mixture. Sprinkle over the grated cheese and caraway seeds, and add a little more liquid if necessary to form a manageable dough. Turn the dough out onto a lightly-floured surface and knead until smooth and elastic.

Rinse the bowl clean and lightly oil it. Return the dough to the bowl and turn it once to oil the surface. Cover and leave in a warm place until doubled in bulk.

Preheat the oven to 200°C (400°F/Gas 6).

Punch the dough down and knead it lightly. Divide the dough in half and shape into the required shape—place in greased bread tins or onto greased trays. Leave to prove in a warm place until well risen.

Bake for 40 minutes or until golden brown. If liked, the loaves may be sprinkled with extra cheese and returned to the oven for 5 minutes until the cheese has melted. Cool the loaves on a wire rack.

Olive and Feta Cheese Bread

Makes 1 loaf.

2 cups (8 oz) plain flour
2 cups (8 oz) wholemeal flour
1 teaspoon salt
15 g (½ oz) fresh compressed yeast
1⅔ cups (13fl oz) lukewarm water
60 g (2 oz) feta cheese, crumbled
⅓ cup (2 oz) black olives, stoned and sliced
1 tablespoon olive oil

In a large warmed bowl, mix together the flours and salt.

Cream the yeast with a little of the water and flour, and set it aside for about 10 minutes or until it becomes frothy.

Make a well in the flour and add the yeast mixture, then the remaining water. Mix with a wooden spoon until the dough comes away from the sides of the bowl, then knead with your hands for about 10 minutes or until the dough is smooth and elastic. Cover the bowl with a cloth and set it aside in a warm place until the dough doubles in bulk.

Preheat the oven to 220°C (425°F/Gas 7).

Punch the dough down and add the feta cheese, olives and oil. Knead until they are well distributed throughout the dough. Oil a 23 × 12 × 8 cm (9 × 5 × 3 in) bread tin and put the dough into it. Cover with a cloth and leave to rise to the top of the tin. Depending upon the warmth in the room, this will take 30 minutes to 1 hour.

Bake the bread in the hot oven for 25 minutes, then reduce the temperature to moderately hot, 190°C (375°F/Gas 5), and bake for a further 20 minutes.

Remove the loaf from the tin and tap the base with your knuckles. If it sounds hollow, the loaf is cooked. If it is soft, return it to the oven for a further 5 minutes without the tin. Cool on a wire rack.

Herb Bread

*If fresh herbs are available, triple the amounts suggested for the dried herbs.
Makes 2 loaves.*

30 g (1 oz) fresh compressed yeast
2 cups (16fl oz) warm water
6 cups (1½ lb) flour
3 teaspoons salt
3 teaspoons sugar
1 tablespoon olive oil
1 teaspoon dried marjoram
½ teaspoon dried thyme
4 tablespoons fresh chopped parsley

Cream the yeast with the water.

Sift the flour into a large warmed bowl with the salt and sugar. Make a well in the centre and add the dissolved yeast and water. Pour over the olive oil and sprinkle over the herbs. Gradually draw in the surrounding flour, first with a wooden spoon then with your hands. Turn the dough out onto a floured surface and knead until smooth and elastic.

Rinse out the bowl and lightly oil it. Return the dough to the bowl and turn it once to oil the top surface of the dough. Cover and leave in a warm place until doubled in bulk.

Preheat the oven to 200°C (400°F/Gas 6).

Punch the dough down and lightly knead. Divide it in half and shape into required shapes—place into greased bread tins or onto greased baking trays. Leave in a warm place until nearly doubled in bulk.

Brush the top surfaces with milk or egg glaze and sprinkle with extra herbs or poppy seeds. Bake for 40 minutes or until the loaf sounds hollow when tapped with the knuckles. Cool on a wire rack.

Variations: In place of the herbs use 2 teaspoons of caraway seeds and dill seeds; or 2 teaspoons of grated nutmeg, 2 teaspoons of dill and 1 tablespoon of fresh sage.

Flat Armenian Bread

Makes 10 large rounds.

22 g (¾ oz) fresh compressed yeast
2½ cups (20fl oz) lukewarm water
6 cups (1½ lb) plain flour
125 g (4 oz) unsalted butter
3 teaspoons sugar
2½ teaspoons salt
1½ tablespoons sesame seeds

Cream the yeast and dissolve it in about ½ cup of the lukewarm water. Sprinkle with a little flour and leave in a warm place until bubbling.

Melt the butter and add sugar and salt, stirring until dissolved. Allow it to cool a little.

Sift the flour into a large warmed bowl and make a well in the centre. Pour the yeast mixture into the well in the flour then the melted butter mixture and then gradually the remaining lukewarm water. Not all of the water may be needed. Beat, gradually incorporating the flour until the dough is smooth and soft. Beat for about 10 minutes. Cover loosely and leave in a warm place to rise, until doubled in bulk.

Preheat the oven to 180°C (350°F/Gas 4).

Turn the dough out onto a floured surface and divide into 10 equal parts. Knead each lightly into a ball, then roll out each ball into a circle as thinly as possible. Place two on a greased baking tray. Sprinkle with a little water and then sprinkle with a pinch or two of sesame seeds.

Bake in the coolest part of the oven for about 20 minutes or until the bread is a pale golden brown. Transfer to a wire rack.

Sprinkle and bake the remaining eight rounds, two at a time, as above.

Melba Toast

Escoffier invented these wafer-thin crisp toasts for Dame Nellie Melba after learning that she was dieting. But diet or no diet, these toasts are lovely served with pâté, terrine or caviar, or just simply with a pat of unsalted butter. Once made, the toasts will keep for quite some time in an air-tight container.

Place slices of bread in a toaster or under a grill and lightly toast on both sides.

Cut off the crusts and then slice the toast in half diagonally. Slice each triangle of toast horizontally through the soft centre. Place the pieces of toast soft side up on a baking tray and bake in a preheated moderate oven, 180°C (350°F/Gas 4), for 15 minutes or until pale golden and crisp. Allow to cool and store in an air-tight container.

Cooking with Yeast

If your cakes never rise, if your pastries are leathery and your puddings stodgy, if you despair of ever being able to bake, try cooking with yeast.

Yeast cookery is for the heavy-handed. The more you knead the dough, the more you slap it down and stretch it out, the lighter will be the result.

Bread and cakes made with yeast often scare people off. They think of yeast cookery as being the domain of professional bakers and therefore not within their own capabilities. But yeast cookery is one of the easiest and least-complicated branches of baking. Hardly anything can go wrong. And even though the start-to-finish time is generally longer with yeast cookery than with other types of baked goods, you don't have to be there all the time: you can mix a dough in the morning, leave it to rise through the day and bake it that night. Or you can mix it in the evening, leave it to rise overnight and bake it the next morning. If you want the dough to rise quickly, you can put it in a very warm environment; if you want it to rise slowly, you can refrigerate it. Yeast-leavened dough is very accommodating and will fit into most people's routines.

The one thing you have to be careful of with yeast dough is that the yeast is not mixed with hot liquid. It will kill the yeast and the dough won't rise. Always make sure you use tepid liquid in any yeast recipe.

Because yeast dough can be treated roughly, it lends itself to all kinds of imaginative presentations. You can push it out flat, spread it with fruit purée or a dried fruit and spice mixture, roll it up, Swiss (jelly) roll fashion and bake it either whole or cut into slices. You can plait it, you can form it into a ring, you can bake it in a mould. You can mix it with fruit or nuts or both.

And home-made yeast cooking is so delightfully unexpected. Imagine being served home-made pretzels at a cocktail party, or finishing off a dinner party with home-made fruit bread served with brie or camembert.

Susan Tomnay

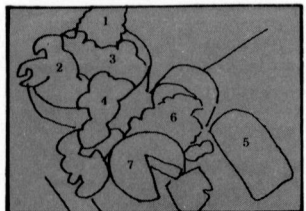

1. Bagels (see p. 36)
2. Croissants (see p. 36)
3. Brioche (see p. 37)
4. Almond and Orange Buns (see p. 41)
5. Cranberry Bread (see p. 41)
6. Chelsea Buns (see p. 44)
7. Sally Lunn (see p. 44)

Spiced Plaited Loaf

Makes 2 loaves

30 g (1 oz) fresh yeast or 15 g (½ oz) dried yeast
⅓ cup (3 oz) sugar
¾ cup (6fl oz) warm water
1 tablespoon salt
60 g (2 oz) butter, softened
1¼ cups (10fl oz) warm milk
1 tablespoon ground cinnamon, or a mixture of cinnamon nutmeg and allspice
6 cups (1½ lb) flour
Glaze: 1 egg yolk, beaten with 1 tablespoon water

Dissolve the yeast and sugar in the warm water and set aside. Add the salt and butter to the warm milk and when the butter has melted, stir in the yeast mixture. Pour this liquid into a warmed bowl and add the spices.

Add the flour, a cup at a time, beating well between each addition (you may not need all the flour). Knead the dough until it is smooth and elastic—this will take about 8 minutes. Form the dough into a ball and put it back into the rinsed-out and buttered bowl. Cover with a thick towel and leave in a warm place until it has doubled in bulk.

Punch down the dough and knead it for a couple of minutes. Then divide the dough into six pieces. Shape each piece into a ball and then into a long sausage shape with tapered ends. Press the ends of three strands together and plait them, finishing off neatly by pressing the ends together. Do the same with the remaining three strands.

Place the loaves, with a space between them, on a buttered baking tray, cover loosely with a towel, and leave them to rise for 30 minutes or until they have doubled in bulk.

Preheat the oven to 220°C (425°F/Gas 7). Paint the loaves with the egg yolk and water mixture—which should be no colder than room temperature. Bake them for 15 minutes, then reduce the oven temperature to 180°C (350°F/Gas 4) for a further 20 to 25 minutes or until the loaves are golden brown and the base sounds hollow when rapped with the knuckles. Allow to cool on wire racks.

Fruit and Nut Bread

Makes 1 loaf

3 cups (12 oz) flour
⅓ cup (2 oz) brown sugar
pinch of salt
1 teaspoon mixed spice (I use ground cinnamon, grated nutmeg, powdered ginger and allspice)
15 g (½ oz) fresh yeast or 7 g (¼ oz) dried yeast
⅔ cup (5fl oz) tepid milk
60 g (2 oz) butter, melted and cooled
½ cup (3 oz) sultanas
½ cup (2½ oz) currants
⅓ cup (2 oz) candied peel
1 cup (4 oz) chopped Brazil nuts
Glaze: ⅔ cup (5fl oz) milk
6 tablespoons sugar

Put the flour, sugar, salt and spices in a large bowl. Make a well in the centre. Dissolve the yeast in a little of the milk and pour it into the flour. Add the butter and the remaining milk and mix together.

Knead the dough until it feels soft and elastic, adding more flour or warm water if necessary. Put the dough back into the bowl, cover with a cloth, and leave in a warm place until the dough has doubled in bulk (about 1½ hours).

Add the fruit and nuts and knead again until well mixed. Grease a small loaf tin with butter, and put the dough into it, pressing it down well. Cover with a cloth and leave it in a warm place until the dough comes to the top of the tin (about 30 minutes).

Preheat the oven to 200°C (400°F/Gas 6). Bake for 35 to 45 minutes or until the loaf has shrunk slightly in the tin and it is brown on top. Remove from the tin, turn it upside down and tap it lightly with your knuckles. If it feels soft, return it to the oven, upside down, without the tin, for a further 5 minutes.

To make the glaze: Put the milk and sugar into a saucepan and bring to the boil, stirring constantly until the sugar has dissolved. Boil for 3 to 5 minutes or until the glaze has thickened slightly.

As soon as the loaf is cooked, paint it with the sugar and milk glaze and leave it on a wire rack to cool.

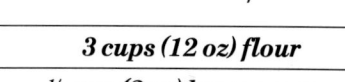

Hot Cross Buns

Makes 20

1¼ cups (10fl oz) milk

30 g (1 oz) fresh yeast or 15 g (½ oz) dried yeast

4 cups (1 lb) flour

2 teaspoons salt

⅓ cup (2 oz) brown sugar

2 teaspoons mixed spice (ground cinnamon, nutmeg, ginger, allspice, coriander)

60 g (2 oz) butter, melted and cooled

2 eggs

2 tablespoons currants

1 tablespoon candied peel

Glaze:
2 tablespoons milk (taken from the 1¼ cups above)

2 tablespoons caster (powdered) sugar

Cross:
small quantity shortcrust pastry (see page 182)

or
4 tablespoons self-raising flour

2 tablespoons cold water

First warm the milk to tepid and put a tablespoon of it into a cup with the yeast and a pinch of sugar. Give it a stir and leave it for 15 minutes, by which time it will be frothy.

Put the flour, salt, sugar and spices together in a bowl and mix well. Make a well in the centre and pour in the yeast mixture, the melted butter, the eggs and a little of the milk. Knead the dough, adding more milk if necessary, until you have a smooth, rather stiff dough which comes away easily from the sides of the bowl. You may not need all the milk to achieve this (and 2 tablespoons of it will be required later for the glaze).

Now add the dried fruit and knead well so that it is evenly distributed. Cover the bowl with a towel and leave in a warm place for at least 2 hours or until it has doubled in bulk.

Knead the dough again until it feels elastic. Divide the dough into 20 even portions and form each portion into a ball. Place them on well-greased baking sheets, cover with a towel and leave in a warm place until they have doubled in bulk. In warm weather this will take about 30 minutes.

Preheat the oven to 190°C (375°F/Gas 5).

To make a cross in the top of each bun, use one of three methods.

- Score a cross with a sharp pointed knife.
- Cut shortcrust pastry into short strips, moisten one side with water and stick the strips in a cross shape on the top of the buns.
- Mix the self-raising flour with the water, beating until smooth. Put the mixture into a small funnel made with greaseproof paper and pipe a cross on top of each bun.

Place the buns on a buttered baking tray and bake in the preheated oven for 15 to 20 minutes, turning the tray around once during cooking.

Meanwhile, make the glaze. Boil the milk and caster sugar together until it starts to become thick and syrupy. Take the buns out of the oven and brush them immediately with the glaze, giving them two coats.

Devonshire Splits

These are buns which, in Devon, are split in half and spread with strawberry jam and thick Devonshire cream. They may be served hot or cold.

Makes 16 buns

15 g (½ oz) fresh yeast or 7 g (¼ oz) dried yeast

pinch of sugar

2 tablespoons lukewarm water

4 cups (1 lb) flour

¼ teaspoon salt

1¼ cups (10fl oz) lukewarm milk

2 tablespoons melted butter

Put the yeast, water and a pinch of sugar into a bowl and set aside in a warm place until it is puffed up and frothy.

Sift the flour and salt into a large warmed bowl, make a well in the centre and pour in the yeast mixture, the milk and the melted butter. Using your hands, gradually draw the flour into the liquid and continue mixing until the dough comes away cleanly from the sides of the bowl.

Turn the dough out onto a floured board and knead for 5 minutes. Return it to the rinsed-out and dried bowl, cover with a thick towel, and set aside in a warm place for 1½ hours or until the dough has doubled in bulk.

Knead again for 2 minutes, then divide the dough into 16 equal pieces. Form the pieces into balls, place them on a floured baking sheet, cover with a towel and set them aside for 20 minutes.

Preheat the oven to 220°C (425°F/Gas 7). Bake the buns for 15 minutes, turning them once during cooking. Eat them straight from the oven, or allow to cool on wire racks.

Right: **Clockwise from bottom left: Hot Cross Buns (see above); Fruit and Nut Bread (see p. 33); Spiced Plaited Loaf (see p. 33).**

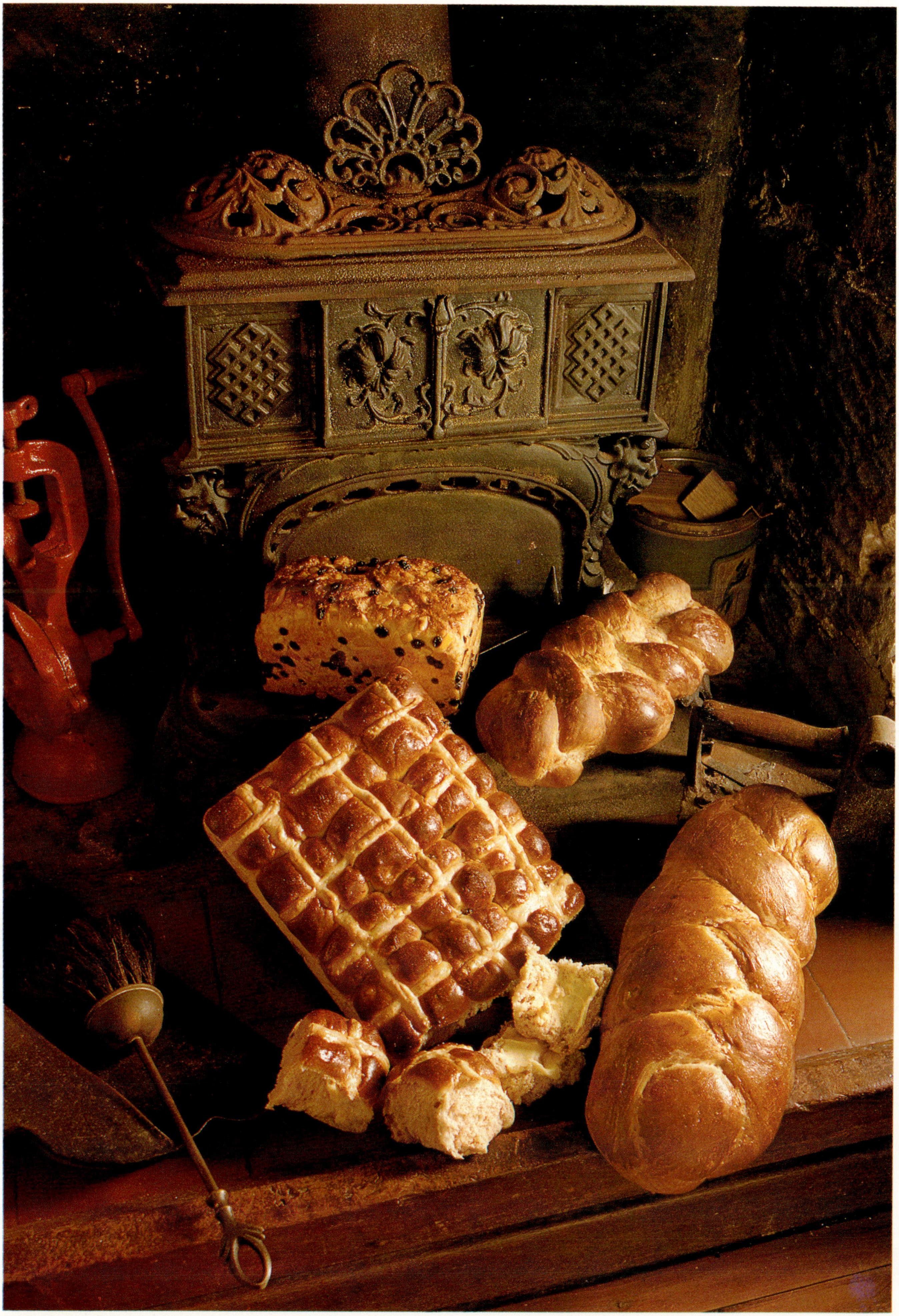

Croissants

Croissants take a very long time to prepare and, to be quite honest, I'd much rather buy them. But if you live far away from a good baker, here's how to make them at home. This recipe is an adaptation of Julia Child's recipe from her book, Mastering the Art of French Cooking, Vol. 2 (Penguin)—*it's the recipe I've had my best results with.*

There are a few points I'd like to stress: Don't attempt to make croissants in hot humid weather—the dough becomes too sticky to work with, no matter how many times you refrigerate it. You will need a marble slab or board, at least 50 × 25 cm (20 × 10 in). At almost every stage of the preparation of croissants, you can refrigerate the dough and leave it until you are ready to begin the next stage. You can freeze them once they're baked, too, and thaw them in a preheated oven at 200°C (400°F/Gas 6) for about 5 minutes.

Makes 12

7 g (¼ oz) fresh yeast
3 tablespoons tepid water
3 teaspoons sugar
2 cups (8 oz) flour
1½ teaspoons salt
⅔ cup (5 fl oz) tepid milk
2 tablespoons vegetable oil
125 g (4 oz) unsalted butter
Glaze:
1 egg
1 teaspoon water

Put the yeast, water and 1 teaspoon of sugar into a bowl and set aside until it is puffed up and frothy.

Sift the flour into a bowl. Dissolve the remaining sugar and the salt in the milk. Make a well in the flour and pour in the yeast mixture, the milk mixture and the oil. Blend together with your hands, scraping all the dough from the sides of the bowl and knead it on a lightly-floured board for about 5 minutes. It will be very sticky.

Rinse and dry the bowl and return the dough to it covering with a towel. Set it aside in a warm place until it has risen to about three times its original volume. Depending upon the temperature, this will take 3 to 4 hours.

Knead it slightly on a lightly-floured board, then press it out into a rectangle about 30 × 20 cm (12 × 8 in). Fold it into three horizontally, return it to the bowl, cover again and leave it to rise until double in bulk.

Remove the dough from the bowl and place it on a lightly-floured plate. Cover the dough and plate with cling film and refrigerate for 30 minutes.

Meanwhile, put the butter into a bowl of cold water and knead it with your hands (in the water), until it is soft and spreadable—but not oily.

Put the dough on a lightly-floured board and push it out into a rectangle about 35 × 20 cm (14 × 8 in); it is easiest to have one of the shorter sides nearest you. Using your hands, spread the butter over the far two-thirds of the dough, leaving a 6 mm (¼ inch) border all round; fold the unbuttered third of the dough up to the middle, then fold the top third down over it.

Lightly flour the surface of the dough. Swivel it around 90° so that the shortest side is nearest you. Roll it out carefully into a rectangle about 35 × 15 cm (14 × 16 in) and again fold one third over, then the other third. If the butter starts to become oily, refrigerate the dough immediately.

Sprinkle the dough lightly with flour, wrap it in greaseproof paper and chill it in the refrigerator for 1 hour.

Remove from the fridge and leave to rest for about 10 minutes. Then roll into a rectangle 35 × 15 cm (14 × 6 in) and fold it again into three. Once more, turn the dough, roll it out again and fold it again. Wrap it in greaseproof paper and chill it for 2 hours.

Remove the dough from the fridge and leave to rest for 10 minutes. Roll the dough out into a rectangle about 50 × 12 cm (20 × 5 in), cut in half and chill one half. Cut the other half into three pieces, roll out each piece into a square and cut it in half diagonally, making two triangles. Starting with the base of the triangle, roll it up towards the point, stretching the point slightly as you do so. Curve the roll into a crescent shape and place on a buttered baking tray. Do the same with the remaining dough.

Cover the dough crescents with cling film and set aside in a warm place until they have risen to double their original size.

Preheat the oven to 240°C (475°F/Gas 9). Beat the egg with the water and brush this glaze over the croissants. Bake for 12 to 15 minutes until they are golden brown. Cool slightly on a wire rack before serving.

Bagels

Makes about 24

1 cup (8 fl oz) milk
60 g (2 oz) butter
5 teaspoons caster (powdered) sugar
15 g (½ oz) fresh yeast or 7 g (¼ oz) dried yeast
1 egg, separated
½ teaspoon salt
3½ cups (14 oz) flour
poppy seeds, for sprinkling

Bring the milk to the boil, remove it from the heat and add the butter and sugar, stirring until the butter has melted and the sugar has dissolved. Set the milk mixture aside until it has cooled to tepid.

Add the yeast to the cooled milk mixture and set it aside in a warm place until it starts to froth.

Add the egg white (unbeaten) and the salt to the milk mixture, stirring well. Then add the flour, a little at a time, stirring constantly until the dough is smooth. Knead the dough on a floured board for about 15 minutes or until it is smooth and elastic. Put it into a greased bowl, cover with a towel and set aside for 1 to 1½ hours or until it has doubled in bulk.

Punch down the dough and divide it into 24 equal pieces. Form each piece into a ball and place your finger in the middle of it to make a hole. Widen the hole with your finger until it makes up about one-third of the ball's diameter. Set the bagels aside, covered with cling wrap, for about 10 minutes or until they start to rise.

Meanwhile, bring a large pan of water to the boil. When boiling, add the bagels, a few at a time; cook for about 15 seconds until they puff up, and then remove them immediately with a slotted spoon and place them on a greased baking sheet. Continue cooking the rest of the bagels in the same way.

Preheat the oven to 200°C (400°F/Gas 6). Mix the leftover egg yolk with a little cold water and paint it over the tops of the bagels. Sprinkle with poppy seeds and bake for about 20 minutes or until brown and crisp. Remove from the oven and allow to cool on wire racks.

Brioche

This is not the traditional method for making brioche—in fact, purists might be outraged at the thought of mixing the dough with a food processor. But I have found it quite difficult to make by hand. The large amounts of butter and eggs produce a very sticky dough which is hard to work with, particularly in hot weather. If your prefer to make it in the traditional way, or do not own a food processor, use the same ingredients but knead by hand. The dough may need to be refrigerated from time to time to prevent the butter from becoming oily.

Makes about 12

---
3 tablespoons lukewarm water
---
15 g (½ oz) fresh yeast or 7 g (¼ oz) dried yeast
---
1 teaspoon sugar
---
2 cups (8 oz) flour
---
additional 2 teaspoons sugar
---
1 teaspoon salt
---
3 large eggs, beaten
---
185 g (6 oz) unsalted butter

Glaze:
1 egg, beaten with 1 teaspoon of water

Pour the warm water into a small bowl and add the yeast and 1 teaspoon of sugar. Set the bowl aside until the yeast dissolves.

Put the flour, 2 teaspoons of sugar and the salt into the bowl of a food processor and add the yeast mixture and eggs. Process for a few minutes, stopping the machine and scraping down the sides when necessary. The dough will start out very sticky, but will become more elastic the longer you process it.

Put the butter into a bowl of cold water and squeeze it in your hands until it is soft. Divide it into six pieces and drop them one by one into the food processor, adding each piece only after the previous piece has been absorbed by the dough. By the time all the butter has been added, the dough should be elastic, though it will still be a bit sticky.

Put the dough into a clean bowl and cover with a towel. Set it aside to rise to triple its bulk. If the butter starts to melt and the dough looks oily, put the bowl in the refrigerator from time to time. It will take about 4 hours to rise.

Turn the dough out onto a lightly-floured board and form it into a rectangle about 25 × 12 cm (10 × 5 in). Fold it into three, as if you were making puff pastry, then press it out again, and again fold it into three. Put the dough back into the bowl, cover, and leave it to rise to double its bulk. This will take about 1½ hours.

Form the dough into a round, put it on a plate and cover it with foil. Put it in the fridge for about 30 minutes—if you don't do this, the dough will be too sticky to form into balls.

Grease individual brioche moulds or patty pan tins with butter. Take three-quarters of the dough and form little balls, each of which will half-fill a mould. Using two fingers, make a hole in the centre of each ball of dough, wider at the top than at the bottom.

Make smaller balls with the remaining dough and form each one into a tear-drop shape. Put the pointed end into the prepared hole so that each brioche has a little top-knot in the centre. Set aside for the dough to rise again, until it has doubled in volume.

Preheat the oven to 240°C (475°F/Gas 9). Just before baking, brush the surface of each brioche with the egg glaze. Using scissors, clip at intervals under the small ball of dough (this will ensure that it rises properly in the oven).

Bake for 15 minutes. Allow to cool on wire racks.

If you wish to freeze them, allow to cool then wrap carefully in plastic or foil and put in the freezer. Thaw for 10 minutes or so in an oven preheated to 180°C (350°F/Gas 4).

Fan Tans

These are little rolls made from layers of sweet dough. They're particularly good for breakfast split and spread with butter and jam (jelly).

Makes about 15

---
15 g (½ oz) fresh yeast or 7 g (¼ oz) dried yeast

¾ cup (6fl oz) warm milk

4 cups (1 lb) flour

¼ cup (2 oz) sugar

¼ teaspoon salt

90 g (3 oz) butter, melted

2 eggs, lightly beaten

Glaze:
1 egg, beaten with 1 tablespoon milk

Put the yeast in a bowl with a pinch of sugar and 2 tablespoons of the warm milk. Set the bowl aside until the mixture is puffed up and frothy.

Sift the flour into a large warmed bowl with the sugar and salt. Make a well in the centre and add the yeast mixture, the remaining milk, two-thirds of the melted butter and the eggs.

Using your hands, mix the flour into the liquid until the dough comes away cleanly from the sides of the bowl. Add more milk if the dough is too stiff. Turn out onto a floured board and knead for about 5 minutes or until it is smooth and elastic.

Rinse and dry the bowl and grease it lightly. Form the dough into a ball and return it to the bowl. Cover it with a towel, and set it aside in a warm place for 2 hours or until it has doubled in bulk.

Knead the dough again for a few minutes and leave it to rest for 10 minutes. Then roll out the dough into a rectangle about 3 mm (⅛ in) thick. Using a pastry brush, brush the dough with the remaining melted butter. Cut the dough into strips about 4 cm (1½ in) wide. Pile five strips on top of each other and press down lightly so that they stick together. Cut the strips into pieces about 5 cm (2 in) long.

Place the pieces on a greased baking tray, cover with a towel and leave in a warm place until they have doubled in bulk.

Preheat the oven to 220°C (425°F/Gas 7). Brush the top of each Fan Tan with the glaze. Bake for 20 to 25 minutes or until they are golden brown. Allow to cool on a wire rack before serving.

Pretzels

Makes 48

---
15 g (½ oz) fresh yeast or 7 g (¼ oz) dried yeast

¼ teaspoon sugar

1 cup (8fl oz) lukewarm milk

30 g (1 oz) butter, melted and cooled

3 cups (12 oz) flour

½ teaspoon salt

1 tablespoon caraway seeds (optional)

1 egg, lightly beaten

2 teaspoons coarse sea salt

Dissolve the yeast and sugar in 2 tablespoons of the lukewarm milk. Set it aside until it froths. Stir the melted butter into the remaining milk.

Sift the flour and salt into a warmed bowl (add half the caraway seeds, if using them) and make a well in the centre. Pour in the yeast mixture and the milk-butter mixture and stir with a wooden spoon until well mixed. Then turn out onto a floured board and knead with your hands until the dough is smooth and elastic. This will take 8 to 10 minutes.

Return the dough to the rinsed-out and lightly-greased bowl, cover with a towel and leave it in a warm place for about an hour or until it has doubled in bulk.

Punch the dough down and knead again, this time for about 4 minutes. Using your hands, form the dough into a sausage, about 30 cm (12 in) long. Cut the dough into 48 equal pieces and roll each piece out into a sausage about 15 cm (6 in) long.

To form them into pretzels, hold one end of the dough strip in each hand and form into a circle. Make a knot in the dough, and press the ends back on to the circle of dough (see photograph on page 39).

Preheat the oven to 190°C (375°F/Gas 5). Half-fill a large saucepan with water and bring to the boil. Add the pretzels, a few at a time so that you don't crowd the pan, and cook them until they rise to the surface (this will take about 1 minute). Remove them from the pan with a slotted spoon and drain them in a colander. Cook the remaining pretzels in the same way.

Place the pretzels on greased baking sheets and brush them with beaten egg. Sprinkle with coarse sea salt, and, if you desire, the remaining caraway seeds. Bake the pretzels for 15 minutes or until they are golden brown and crisp. Allow to cool on wire racks.

Right: **Pretzels** (see above).

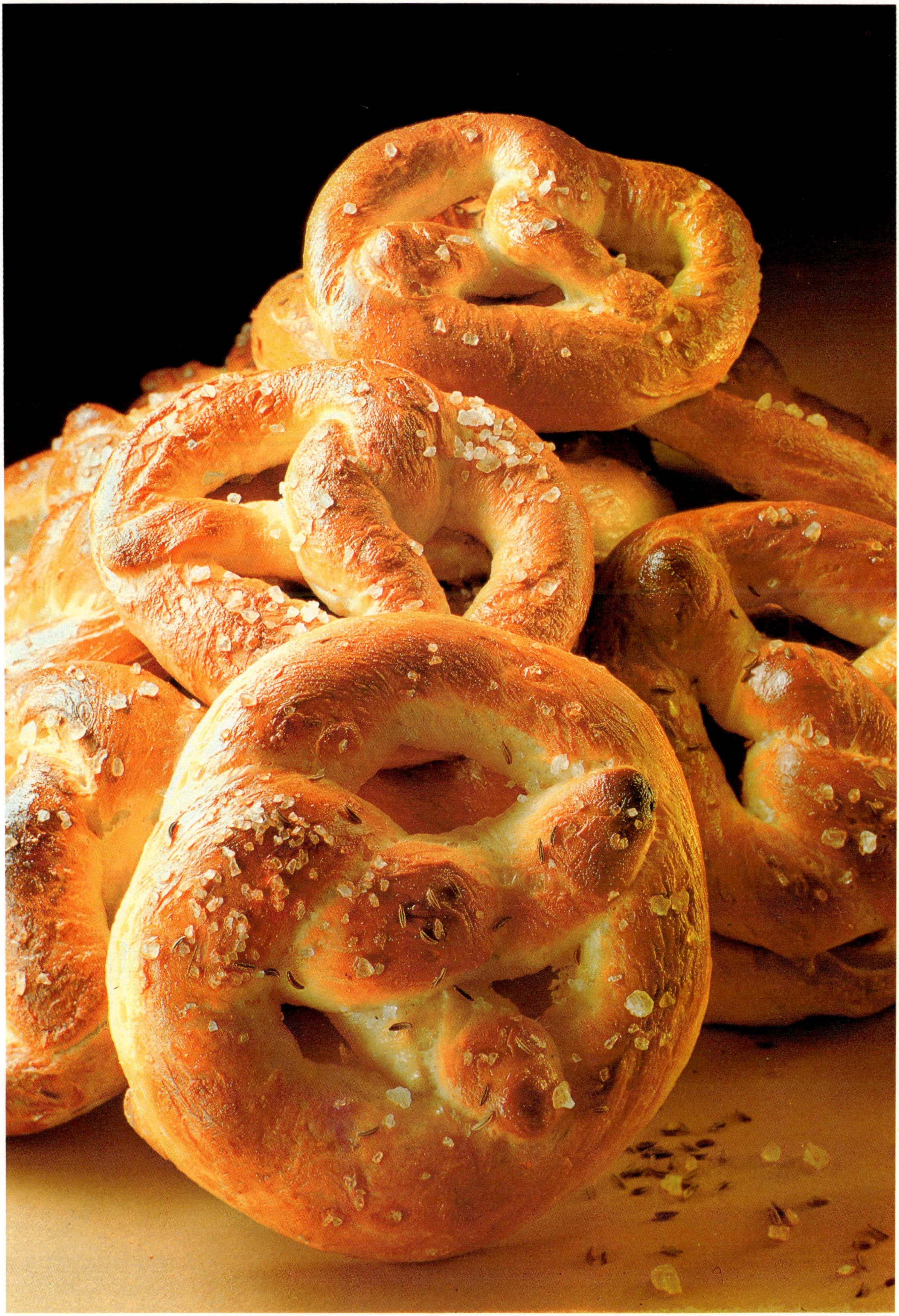

Tsoureki

This is a Greek bread, traditionally eaten on Easter Sunday. It is sweet and light, and makes a nice change from Hot Cross Buns.

Makes 1 large loaf

30 g (1 oz) fresh yeast or 15 g (½ oz) dried yeast
¼ cup (2fl oz) warm water
½ cup (4fl oz) lukewarm milk
½ teaspoon sugar
1 cup (4 oz) flour
3 eggs
additional ¾ cup (6 oz) sugar
grated rind of 1 lemon or ½ teaspoon caraway seeds
additional 4 cups (1 lb) flour
½ cup melted butter, cooled
sesame seeds
1 extra egg, for glaze

In a large warmed bowl, dissolve the yeast in the warm water. Add the milk, the ½ teaspoon of sugar and the cup of flour. Stir the batter well, cover the bowl with a thick towel and set it aside in a warm place to rise for about 1 hour.

Beat the eggs with the ¾ cup of sugar and lemon rind or caraway seeds in an electric mixer or over a pan of hot water until the mixture is quite thick.

Add the egg mixture to the batter, and add the 4 cups of flour and the butter. Mix until the dough comes away from the sides of the bowl, adding more flour if it is too sticky.

Knead it on a floured board until it is smooth and elastic—this will take about 5 minutes. Put the dough back into the rinsed-out and dried mixing bowl, cover with the towel and set aside in a warm place until it has doubled in bulk. This can take 2 or 3 hours, because the dough is so rich.

Punch the dough down, knead it again and divide it into three pieces. Roll each piece out on a floured board into a long, thin sausage. Sprinkle the sesame seeds on a plate, roll the sausages in them loosely.

Generously grease a baking sheet. Place the dough on it, cover and leave to rise to double its bulk.

Preheat the oven to 200°C (400°F/Gas 6). Beat the egg with a little cold water and brush this over the dough. Bake for 15 minutes, then reduce the temperature to 180°C (350°F/Gas 4) and bake for a further 30 to 35 minutes.

The bread emerges from the oven brown and shiny. Cool it on a wire rack.

Panettone

This sweet fruit bread, is a speciality of Milan, although it is sold all over Italy. It is cooked in a tall cylindrical tin about 15 cm (6 in) in diameter and 18 cm (7 in) high. A 1 kg (2 lb) coffee tin is a suitable substitute.

Makes 1 large loaf

90 g (3 oz) butter, softened
15 g (½ oz) fresh yeast or 7 g (¼ oz) dried yeast
¼ cup (2fl oz) lukewarm water
4 cups (1 lb) flour
⅓ cup (3 oz) sugar
1½ teaspoons salt
¾ cup (6fl oz) lukewarm milk
3 eggs, lightly beaten
½ cup (3 oz) candied peel
¾ cup (4 oz) sultanas (seedless raisins)
2 teaspoons grated lemon rind
2 tablespoons melted butter

Grease the tin generously with some of the softened butter. Line the bottom and sides with greaseproof paper, allowing it to extend above the top of the tin by about 2.5 cm (1 in). Grease the paper well and place the tin on a baking sheet.

Put the yeast, a pinch of sugar and the water into a bowl and set it aside in a warm place until it is puffed up and frothy.

Sift the flour, sugar and salt into a large warmed mixing bowl, make a well in the centre and pour in the yeast mixture and the milk. Using your hands, gradually draw the flour into the liquid and continue mixing until the dough comes away cleanly from the sides of the bowl.

Turn the dough out onto a floured board and knead it well until it is smooth and elastic. Place the dough in the rinsed-out and dried bowl, cover with a thick towel and set aside in a warm place until the dough has doubled in bulk.

Add the remaining softened butter, the eggs, candied peel, sultanas and lemon rind and knead again for about 5 minutes. Put the dough back into the bowl, cover and set aside in a warm place for about 1 hour.

Preheat the oven to 200°C (400°F/Gas 6). Put the dough into the prepared tin, cover and leave for 30 minutes or until it has risen slightly. Using a pastry brush, coat the top of the dough with some of the melted butter.

Bake the Panettone for 30 minutes, then reduce the temperature to 180°C (350°F/Gas 4) and bake for a further 30 minutes. Take the bread out of the oven and brush the top with the remaining melted butter. Allow it to cool in the tin for 20 minutes, then remove, peel off the paper and cool the Panettone completely on a wire rack.

Almond and Orange Buns

Makes about 8

7 g (¼ oz) fresh yeast
¼ cup (2 oz) sugar
1 tablespoon lukewarm water
½ cup (4 fl oz) milk
60 g (2 oz) butter, cut into small pieces
3 cups (12 oz) flour
¼ teaspoon salt
1 egg, lightly beaten
½ cup (3 oz) sultanas
¼ cup (2 fl oz) orange juice
2 teaspoons olive oil
3 tablespoons blanched almonds, chopped
1 tablespoon grated orange rind
1 egg yolk, beaten with 2 tablespoons milk

Dissolve the yeast and a pinch of sugar in the lukewarm water and set it aside for 15 minutes until it becomes frothy.

Put the milk in a saucepan, add the butter, and heat until the butter dissolves. Set it aside to cool to lukewarm.

Sift the flour and salt into a mixing bowl and add the remaining sugar. Make a well in the flour and add the yeast mixture, the beaten egg and the milk-butter mixture. Stir with a wooden spoon until the dough comes away from the sides of the bowl, then knead with your hands until the dough is smooth and elastic—this will take about 10 minutes. Rinse and dry the bowl, return the dough to it, cover with a towel and leave in a warm place for about 1½ hours or until the dough has doubled in bulk.

Meanwhile, macerate the sultanas in the orange juice for about 15 minutes or until they are plumped up.

When the dough has risen sufficiently, punch it down and add the olive oil, the drained sultanas, the almonds and orange rind. Knead the dough for a few minutes, long enough to evenly distribute the fruit and nuts, then divide it into eight equal pieces. Form each piece of dough into a ball, place them on a greased baking sheet, cover with a towel and set aside in a warm place for 30 to 40 minutes or until the dough has doubled in bulk.

Preheat the oven to 200°C (400°F/Gas 6). Brush the dough balls with the egg and milk mixture, and bake them for 20 to 25 minutes or until they are golden brown. Allow to cool on wire racks.

Cranberry Bread

Makes 1 large loaf

185 g (6 oz) fresh or canned cranberries
⅓ cup (3 oz) sugar
1 cup (4 oz) finely-chopped walnuts
grated rind of 1 orange
15 g (½ oz) fresh yeast or 7 g (¼ oz) dried yeast
1 cup (8 fl oz) lukewarm milk
4 cups (1 lb) flour
1 teaspoon salt
½ teaspoon grated nutmeg
½ teaspoon ground cinnamon
125 g (4 oz) butter
1 egg
Glaze:
2 tablespoons sugar
1 tablespoon milk

If you are using canned cranberries, drain them. Chop the cranberries in a blender or food processor; do not purée them. Put them into a bowl with the sugar, walnuts and orange rind.

Put the yeast into a small bowl with a pinch of sugar and 2 tablespoons of the warmed milk and set it aside in a warm place until it starts to become frothy.

Sift the flour, salt, nutmeg and cinnamon into a large warmed bowl. Make a well in the flour and add the yeast mixture, cranberry mixture, melted butter, egg, and the remaining milk. Using your hands, draw the flour into the liquid and continue mixing until the dough comes away from the sides of the bowl.

Turn it out onto a floured board and knead for 8 to 10 minutes or until the dough is smooth and elastic. Return the dough to the rinsed-out bowl, cover with a towel and leave in a warm place for 1 to 1½ hours or until it has doubled in bulk.

Punch the dough down and knead again for 3 or 4 minutes, then form it into a rectangle and place it in a greased 1 kg (2 lb) loaf tin. Cover with a towel and leave in a warm place for 35 minutes or until the dough has risen to the top of the tin.

Preheat the oven to 200°C (400°C/Gas 6). Bake for 15 minutes, then reduce the temperature to 180°C (350°F/Gas 4) and bake for a further 35 minutes. Remove the bread from the tin and rap the underside of the loaf with your knuckles. If it feels soft, return it to the oven, upside down—and without the tin, for a further 5 minutes.

To make the glaze, combine the sugar and milk in a small saucepan and cook over low heat, stirring constantly, until the sugar dissolves. Simmer for a few minutes to thicken the glaze slightly. As soon as the bread is cooked, paint the top and sides with the glaze and cool on a wire rack.

Crumpets

Although crumpets are cooked on a griddle and so perhaps should not be included in a book about baking, they are so good and so different from the store-bought kind, that a chapter on cooking with yeast wouldn't be complete without them.

Makes about 12

4 cups (1 lb) flour
15 g (½ oz) fresh yeast or 7 g (¼ oz) dried yeast
2½ oz tablespoons powdered milk
2 teaspoons salt
2¾ cups (22fl oz) tepid water
1 teaspoon bicarbonate of soda (baking soda) mixed with 4 tablespoons tepid water

Put the flour in a large heat-proof bowl and warm it in a low oven.

Dissolve the yeast in 2 tablespoons of the tepid water. Add the powdered milk and salt to the flour in the bowl and make a well in the centre. Add the yeast mixture and the remaining water, and beat until the mixture is very smooth and elastic. This will take about 5 minutes by hand, less time in an electric beater or food processor.

Cover the bowl with plastic wrap and leave in a warm place for about 1½ hours or until the batter has doubled in bulk and the surface is bubbly.

Add the bicarbonate of soda mixture and beat well. Leave the dough to stand for a further 15 minutes.

Grease a griddle or electric frying pan lightly with butter and grease four crumpet or egg rings lightly. Heat the griddle until very hot and place the rings on it. Using a large spoon, ladle the batter into the rings, filling to about half their depth (the mixture will be quite difficult to pour, since it is very rubbery). They should rise immediately and holes should start to appear on the surface. If no holes appear, add a little more water to the batter. As soon as the surface of the crumpets start to look dry—this will take 3 to 4 minutes—turn the crumpets over and cook on the other side for 30 seconds. Set them aside while you make the rest of the crumpets.

Toast them lightly and spread with butter.

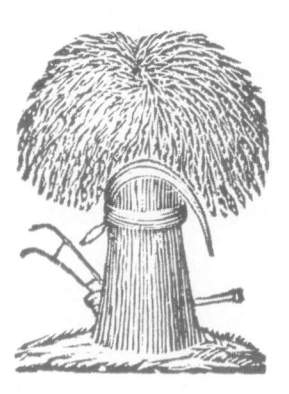

English Muffins

Makes about 12

1 egg
1¼ cups (10fl oz) tepid milk
30 g (1 oz) butter, melted and cooled
15 g (½ oz) fresh yeast or 7 g (¼ oz) dried yeast
4 tablespoons tepid water
4 cups (1 lb) flour
1 teaspoon salt

Beat the egg in a bowl and add the milk and butter. Cream the yeast with the tepid water and set aside.

Put the flour and salt into a bowl and warm it in a low oven. Make a well in the centre and pour in the yeast mixture and then the egg-milk-butter mixture. Mix well and then knead thoroughly, adding more flour or warm water if necessary. The dough should be soft and smooth. Cover the bowl with a thick towel and leave it in a warm place for about 1½ hours or until it has doubled in bulk.

Preheat the oven to 230°C (450°F/Gas 8). Roll the dough out on a floured board into a circle about 1 cm (½ in) thick and cut into rounds with a biscuit cutter about 5 cm (2 in) in diameter.

Place the muffins on a floured baking tray and bake for 8 minutes, then turn them over and bake the other side for a further 6 or 7 minutes, until they are well risen.

Traditionally, muffins are toasted on the outside, then they are pulled apart and buttered.

Right: **Crumpets (see above) and English Muffins (see above).**

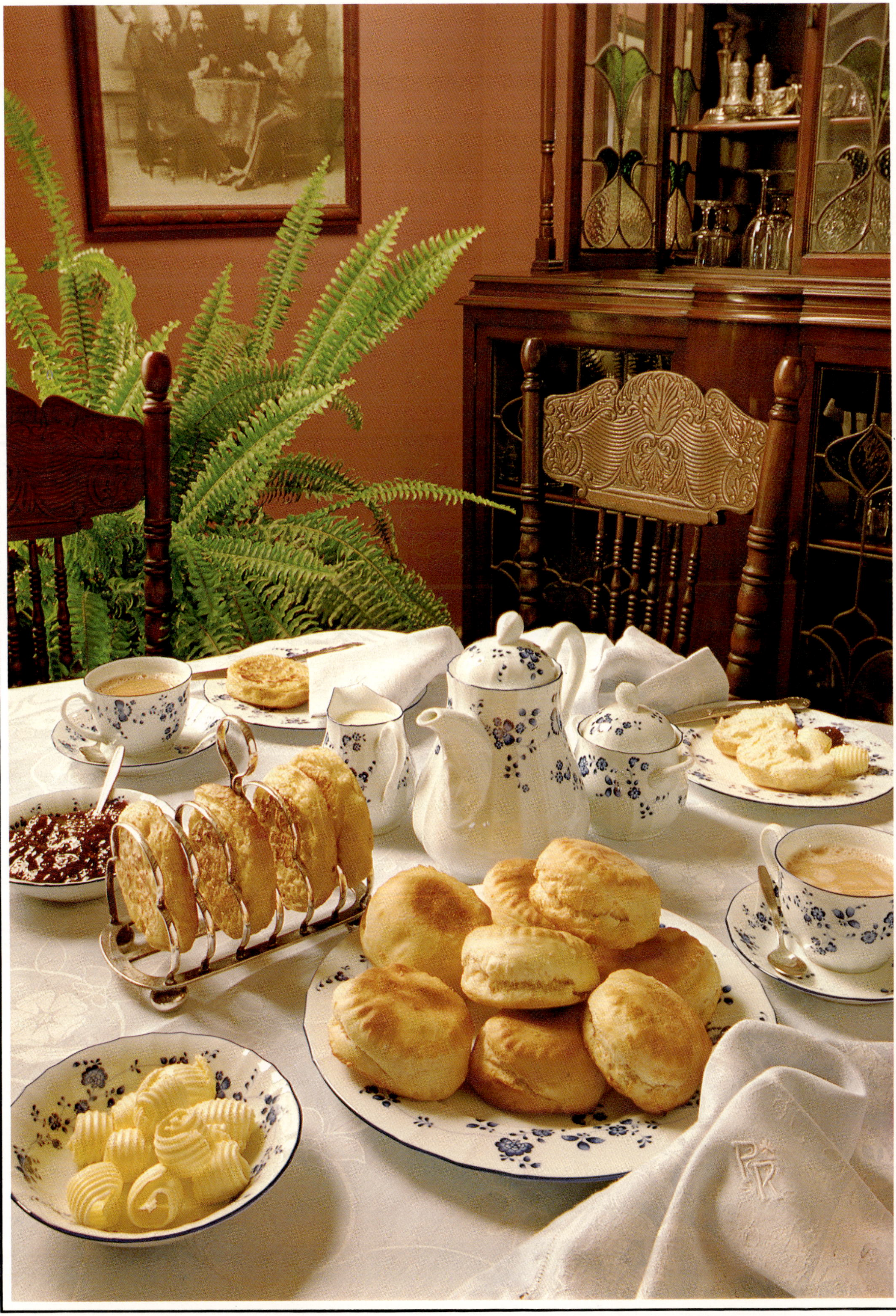

Sally Lunns

When I was a little girl my mother would buy tea cakes from the local cake shop and we would have them, spread thickly with butter, for afternoon tea on Saturdays. They always had thick white or pink icing on them and I loved them.

Recently I tried my hand at making them and discovered that not only was the result about 100 times better than the store-bought kind, but also they were simple to make and needed only half an hour's rising. The whole job, from start to finish, took an hour.

The tea cakes I made are called Sally Lunns, named after the woman who invented them, which must have been sometime in the early nineteenth century.

Below is the basic recipe, but it lends itself to many variations. You can add sultanas or any type of dried fruit; spices such as cinnamon, nutmeg and allspice can be mixed into the flour; grated orange or lemon rind can be added, with a tablespoon of the juice replacing the same quantity of milk. Grated or finely-sliced apple gives the cakes an interesting texture and flavour.

You can serve Sally Lunns warm from the oven, split in half and spread generously with butter, or you can cut wedges in half, toast them and spread with butter. They need either a thick milk and sugar glaze or lemon icing.

Makes two cakes

3 cups (12 oz) flour
½ teaspoon salt
1 cup (8 fl oz) milk
30 g (1 oz) butter
10 g (⅓ oz) dried yeast or 20 g (⅔ oz) fresh yeast
1 teaspoon sugar
1 egg
Glaze: *2 tablespoons sugar*
1 tablespoon milk

Sift the flour and salt into a heatproof bowl and put it in a low oven to warm it. Put two 18 cm (7 in) cake tins in the oven at the same time to warm them.

Heat the milk and butter together until the butter melts, then allow it to cool to tepid.

Put the yeast and sugar into a bowl and add a little of the tepid milk-butter mixture to it. Set aside for 5 minutes until it dissolves.

Beat the egg and add it to the milk-butter mixture, then add the yeast mixture. Make a well in the flour and pour in the milk mixture. Beat well with a wooden spoon, adding more flour if the mixture is too sticky. With floured hands, knead the dough for about 4 minutes, until it feels smooth and elastic.

Divide the dough into two, butter the warm cake tins and put half the dough into each, pressing down well around the edge. Cover the tins with a towel and leave them in a warm place to rise—it should only take half an hour for the dough to rise to the top of the tins.

Preheat the oven to 200°C (400°F/Gas 6). Bake the cakes for 15 to 20 minutes or until they are light brown on top and a skewer inserted into the centre comes out clean.

While they are cooking, make the glaze. Put the sugar and milk into a small saucepan and heat gently, stirring constantly, until the sugar dissolves. Let it simmer for a minute or two to thicken it slightly.

As soon as you take the cakes from the oven, turn them out onto wire racks and spread them with the glaze. Or you can ice them, once they've cooled, with lemon or pink icing.

Chelsea Buns

Makes about 36

1 tablespoon milk, warmed
pinch of sugar
15 g (½ oz) fresh yeast or 7 g (¼ oz) dried yeast
2½ cups (10 oz) flour
½ teaspoon salt
1 tablespoon sugar
grated rind of 1 lemon
½ teaspoon ground cinnamon
125 g (4 oz) butter
1 egg, beaten
additional ⅓ cup (2½ fl oz) milk, at blood heat
Filling: *45 g (1½ oz) butter, cut into small pieces*
¼ cup (1½ oz) brown sugar
1 cup (6 oz) dried fruit
1 tablespoon caster (powdered) sugar
Glaze: *2 tablespoons sugar*
1 tablespoon milk

Put the tablespoon of warmed milk (blood heat) into a cup with a pinch of sugar. Sprinkle the yeast into it and leave it in a warm place to rise and bubble—this will take about 15 minutes

In a warmed bowl, mix together the flour, salt, sugar, lemon rind and cinnamon. Cut the butter into small pieces and rub it into the flour mixture as if you were making pastry. If you have a food processor, make the dough in that. Add the yeast mixture, the egg and remaining milk and mix well. Knead until the dough is smooth and elastic—if it feels sticky, add more flour.

Cover the bowl with a cloth and leave the dough in a warm place to rise—near a fire or heater, or on top of a crock pot—but make sure it's not too hot or it will kill the yeast.

When the dough has doubled in bulk, knead it again and divide into four equal pieces (or six pieces if you want very small buns). Roll each piece out into a rectangle about 3 mm (1/8 in) thick. Dot each rectangle with a quarter of the butter, and sprinkle with a quarter of the brown sugar and dried fruit.

Fold in the two narrow ends of the rectangle to make a square. Turn the dough around and roll out again into a rectangle the same size. Roll the dough up—Swiss (jelly) roll fashion—and seal the edge with water. Cut the roll into slices 2.5 cm (1 in) thick and arrange them on buttered baking sheets, leaving a space between each one. Cover them with a cloth and leave them to rise again.

Preheat the oven to 220°C (425°F/Gas 7). When the dough buns are almost touching each other, sprinkle with the caster sugar. Bake for 15 minutes or until they are golden brown.

To make the glaze, heat together the 2 tablespoons of sugar and 1 tablespoon of milk. Paint the buns as soon as they are removed from the oven.

Variation:
Instead of using the sugar-milk glaze, allow the buns to cool on wire racks, then spread them with a thin lemon glacé icing—made from 1 tablespoon of lemon juice mixed with sifted icing (confectioners') sugar.

Stollen

Stollen is a sweet fruit bread, traditionally served in Germany at Christmas.

Makes 1 large loaf

15 g (1/2 oz) fresh yeast or 7 g (1/4 oz) dried yeast
1 tablespoon lukewarm water
125 g (4 oz) butter
3/4 cup (6 fl oz) milk, scalded
4 cups (1 lb) flour
3/4 cup (6 oz) sugar
1 teaspoon salt
1/2 teaspoon ground cinnamon
1/4 teaspoon ground mace
1/4 teaspoon ground cardamom
2 eggs, lightly beaten
1 cup (6 oz) chopped candied peel
1/2 cup (3 oz) sultanas (seedless raisins)
1/2 cup (2 1/2 oz) chopped walnuts

Icing:
2 tablespoons butter, melted
1 1/2 cups (8 oz) icing (confectioners') sugar
2 tablespoons water
1/4 teaspoon vanilla essence
walnut halves, for decoration

Put the yeast, a pinch of sugar and the water into a bowl, stir it and set it aside in a warm place until it is puffed up and frothy.

Stir the butter into the scalded milk until it has melted, then set aside to cool to lukewarm.

Sift the flour, sugar, salt and spices into a large warmed bowl, make a well in the centre and pour in the yeast mixture, the milk-butter mixture and the eggs.

Using your hands, gradually draw the flour into the liquid and continue mixing until the dough comes away cleanly from the sides of the bowl. Add more flour or milk as necessary. Turn the dough out onto a floured board and knead well until it is smooth and elastic.

Rinse out and dry the bowl and return the dough to it, sprinkling flour lightly over the top. Cover with a thick towel and set it aside in a warm place until the dough has doubled in bulk. This will take 1 to 1 1/2 hours.

Knead the dough again for a few minutes, then add the dried fruit and nuts and continue kneading until they are evenly distributed throughout the dough. Shape the dough into an oval and place it on a greased baking sheet. Cover with the towel and set aside in a warm place for about 45 minutes or until it has risen by about half.

Preheat the oven to 200°C (400°F/Gas 6). Bake the Stollen for 15 minutes, then reduce the temperature to 180°C (350°F/Gas 4) and bake for a further 30 minutes. Remove the bread from the oven and rap the underside with your knuckle. If it is hard and sounds hollow, the Stollen is cooked. If not, return it to the oven, upside down, and bake for another 5 minutes. Leave it to cool on a wire rack.

To make the icing, beat the butter, sugar and water together until they are well blended, then add the vanilla essence.

When the Stollen is cool, spread the icing generously over the top and sides, and decorate with walnut halves. Serve sliced and spread with butter.

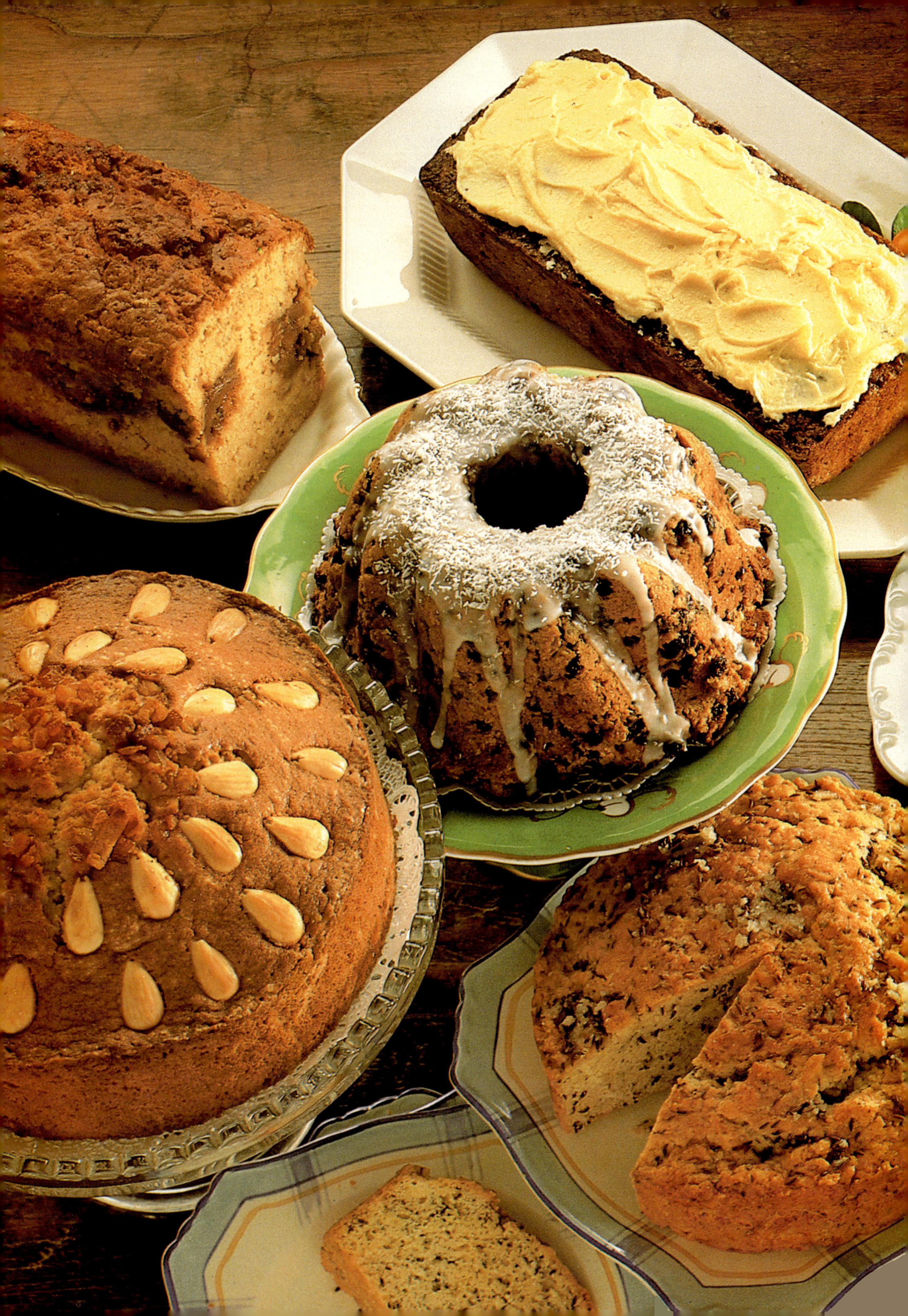

Tea Cakes & Breads

Tea Cakes & Breads

Rich images are evoked from the names 'tea cakes' and 'tea breads'. Afternoon sunlight, a crisp breeze, a mug of hot coffee, and the aroma of a fruit loaf warm from the morning bake. Or perhaps the special lace cloth, the fine china, the refreshing first sip of tea, a moment of closeness as the shadows lengthen, grandmother's scones and her favorite spice cake.

The recipes in this section all use baking powder—on its own or in the self-raising flour—as the rising agent. Some of the recipes recommend a topping for the cake of glazes or icings from a later chapter.

Sometimes when I'm baking, if I'm tense and worried about the results, perhaps working in a rush, the cake may be beautifully done but I am left undone. Follow the suggestions here, and relax—enjoy the planning, measuring and mixing, and that special feeling of fulfilment as you lift the cake from the oven.

Suggestions
- Get the oven ready first. Set the shelves at the right height, and preheat the oven.
- Have the ingredients at room temperature, particularly butter and milk.
- Tins or baking trays usually need some preparation beforehand. Use greaseproof paper to spread cake tins with butter. Sprinkle scone trays with flour.
- Measure ingredients with care.
- Open and close the oven door gently and infrequently.
- Brown paper may be placed over cakes that have browned but are not quite cooked.
- A cake is cooked if it shrinks from the side of the tin and is elastic to touch.
- Always cool the cake or bread before storing. Store in an airtight container.

Mark Pearson

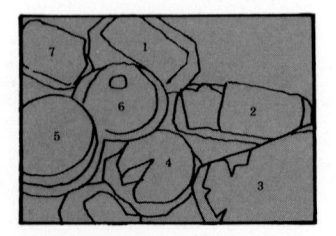

1. Wholemeal Pound Cake with Orange Frosting (see p. 60)
2. Glazed Banana Bread (see p. 65)
3. Gingerbread with lemon icing and glacé ginger (see p. 53)
4. Caraway Seed Cake (see p. 52)
5. Madeira Cake (see p. 50)
6. Rosewater Currant Ring (see p. 58)
7. Turkish Fig Bar (see p. 57)

TEA CAKES & BREADS

Basic Rich Butter Cake

Three eggs ensure a rich, moist cake with good keeping qualities. The straightforward taste complements a delicately spiced or perfumed tea.
Makes 1 cake

2 cups (8 oz) flour
1½ teaspoons baking powder
185 g (6 oz) butter
1 cup (7 oz) caster (powdered) sugar
3 eggs, beaten
3 tablespoons milk
½ teaspoon vanilla essence

Preheat the oven to 180°C (350°F/Gas 4). Grease a deep-sided cake tin 20 cm (8 in) round, and line it with greaseproof paper.

Sift the flour and baking powder together.

In a large bowl, cream the butter and sugar until light and fluffy. Add the eggs gradually, beating well after each addition. Mix in half the flour and half of the milk; combine well. Add the remaining flour and milk and the vanilla essence, and mix well. Turn into the cake tin and level the top.

Bake for 1 hour in the moderately hot oven. It is great served warm with a little butter.

Chocolate Butter Cake:
To the batter for Basic Rich Butter Cake, add 2 tablespoons of cocoa and mix in well.

Butter Cake with Peaches:
To the batter for Basic Rich Butter Cake, add 2 tablespoons of fresh wheatgerm and ½ cup (2 oz) of chopped dried peaches.

The peaches should be soaked in boiling water for 15 minutes, then drained and patted dry with a paper towel before being added to the mixture.

Walnut Butter Cake
To the batter for Basic Rich Butter Cake, add ½ cup (2 oz) of finely and freshly chopped walnuts and ½ teaspoon of grated nutmeg.

When baked, brush the hot cake with melted butter.

Then sprinkle the hot cake with a mixture of 2 teaspoons of brown sugar, 2 tablespoons of finely crushed walnuts, (or walnut meal) and a pinch of grated nutmeg.

Orange Butter Cake:
In the preparation of the batter for Basic Rich Butter Cake substitute orange juice for the milk and add the grated rind of 1 orange.

When baked, top the cake with Warm Glacé Icing (see recipe, page 130). Serve with clove-spiced tea.

Butter Cake with Crumble Topping
Before baking the batter for Basic Rich Butter Cake, cover it with crumble topping. Rub together ¼ cup (1 oz) wholemeal flour, 2 tablespoons butter, 2 tablespoons brown sugar, ¼ cup (1 oz) oatmeal, 1 tablespoon desiccated coconut, 1 teaspoon ground cinnamon. Lightly pat this mixture onto the batter. Then proceed with baking, as above.

Sand Cake

This cake is named after the texture, which comes from the ground rice. Ground rice can be purchased from your health food store, or easily made with a strong electric blender. Rice flour will not substitute.
Makes 1 cake

125 g (4 oz) butter
1 teaspoon grated lemon rind
1 cup (8 oz) sugar
3 eggs
1 cup (4 oz) flour
½ cup ground rice
1 teaspoon baking powder
¼ teaspoon grated nutmeg
4 tablespoons dry sherry
2 teaspoons lemon juice
icing (confectioners') sugar, for sprinkling

Preheat the oven to 180°C (350°F/Gas 4). Grease a 20 × 10 cm (8 × 4 in) loaf tin, and line it with greaseproof paper.

In a large bowl, beat together the butter and lemon rind, then gradually beat in the sugar. Add the eggs, one at a time, beating well after each.

Sift together the flour, ground rice, baking powder and nutmeg, and add this to the butter-sugar-eggs mixture. Mix well. Fold in the sherry and lemon juice. Turn into the tin.

Bake for 45 to 50 minutes. When cooked, remove from tin and cool on a wire rack. When cool, dust the surface with sifted icing sugar. Serve at the 'English' tea time, 5 p.m., with strong tea or black coffee enriched with a few drops of sweet sherry.

Madeira Cake

Makes 1 cake

---
250 g (8 oz) butter
---
grated rind of ½ lemon

½ teaspoon ground cinnamon

1¼ cups (10 oz) caster (powdered) sugar
---
5 eggs

3¼ cups (13 oz) flour
---
2 teaspoons baking powder
---
pinch of salt

½ cup (4 fl oz) milk

½ cup (2 oz) slivered blanched almonds
---
2 tablespoons (1 oz) glacé citron peel

Preheat the oven to 180°C (350°F/Gas 4). Grease a deep-sided cake tin 20 cm (8 in) round, and line it with greaseproof paper.

Cream the butter with the lemon rind and cinnamon, and add sugar gradually. Beat until the mixture is light and soft.

In a separate bowl, beat the eggs one at a time with some of the flour, then sift in the remaining flour with the baking powder and salt. Fold this into the butter-sugar mixture with the milk. Turn into the tin, and arrange the almonds and glacé peel on the top.

Bake for 1 hour, then reduce the heat to 160°C (325°F/Gas 3) and bake for another 15 minutes. Turn out onto a wire rack to cool.

I used to think that this cake was once made with real Madeira, the robust fortified wine. For a change, try substituting Madeira (or port) for half of the milk.

Coconut Cake

Makes 1 cake

3½ cups (14 oz) flour
---
pinch of salt
---
4 teaspoons baking powder
---
250 g (8 oz) butter

1¼ cups (10 oz) caster (powdered) sugar

½ cup (2 oz) desiccated coconut

⅓ cup grated solidified coconut milk
---
4 eggs, beaten

¾ cup (6 fl oz) milk

Preheat the oven to 180°C (350°F/Gas 4). Grease a 20 cm (8 in) cake tin, and line it with greaseproof paper.

Sift the flour, salt and baking powder into a large bowl. Rub in the butter until mixture resembles fine breadcrumbs. Stir in the sugar, coconut and grated solidified coconut milk. Gradually mix the eggs and milk into the flour mixture. Turn it into the cake tin and smooth the top.

Bake for 1½ to 1¾ hours. Turn out onto a wire rack to cool. The cake can be decorated with Warm Glacé Icing (see recipe, page 130), sprinkled with shredded coconut.

Pineapple Coconut Cake
To the batter for Coconut Cake, add ½ cup (3 oz) of chopped glacé pineapple and ¾ teaspoon of ground clove.

Cinnamon Tea Cake

Makes 1 cake

---
1 egg, separated

½ cup (4 oz) sugar

½ teaspoon vanilla essence

½ cup (4 fl oz) milk
---
1 cup (4 oz) self-raising flour
---
125 g (4 oz) butter, melted

Topping:
6 teaspoons (1 oz) melted butter

½ teaspoon ground cinnamon
---
1 tablespoon sugar

Preheat the oven to 190°C (375°F/Gas 5). Grease an 18 cm (7 in) cake tin.

Beat the egg white until stiff, then add the yolk. Gradually beat in the sugar.

In a small bowl, add the vanilla to the milk, then add this a little at a time to the egg and sugar mixture. Lightly stir in the sifted flour and the melted butter. Pour into the cake tin.

Bake for 20 to 25 minutes. Remove from the tin and, while still hot, brush with melted butter and sprinkle with sugar and cinnamon.

Serve warm or (just as good) cold, spread with unsalted butter. We recommend it served with a little fig jam and with black tea.

Right: **Clockwise from top: Light Fruit Cake (see p. 53); Coconut Cake (see above); Fresh Apple Cake (see p. 54); Cinnamon Tea Cake (see above).**

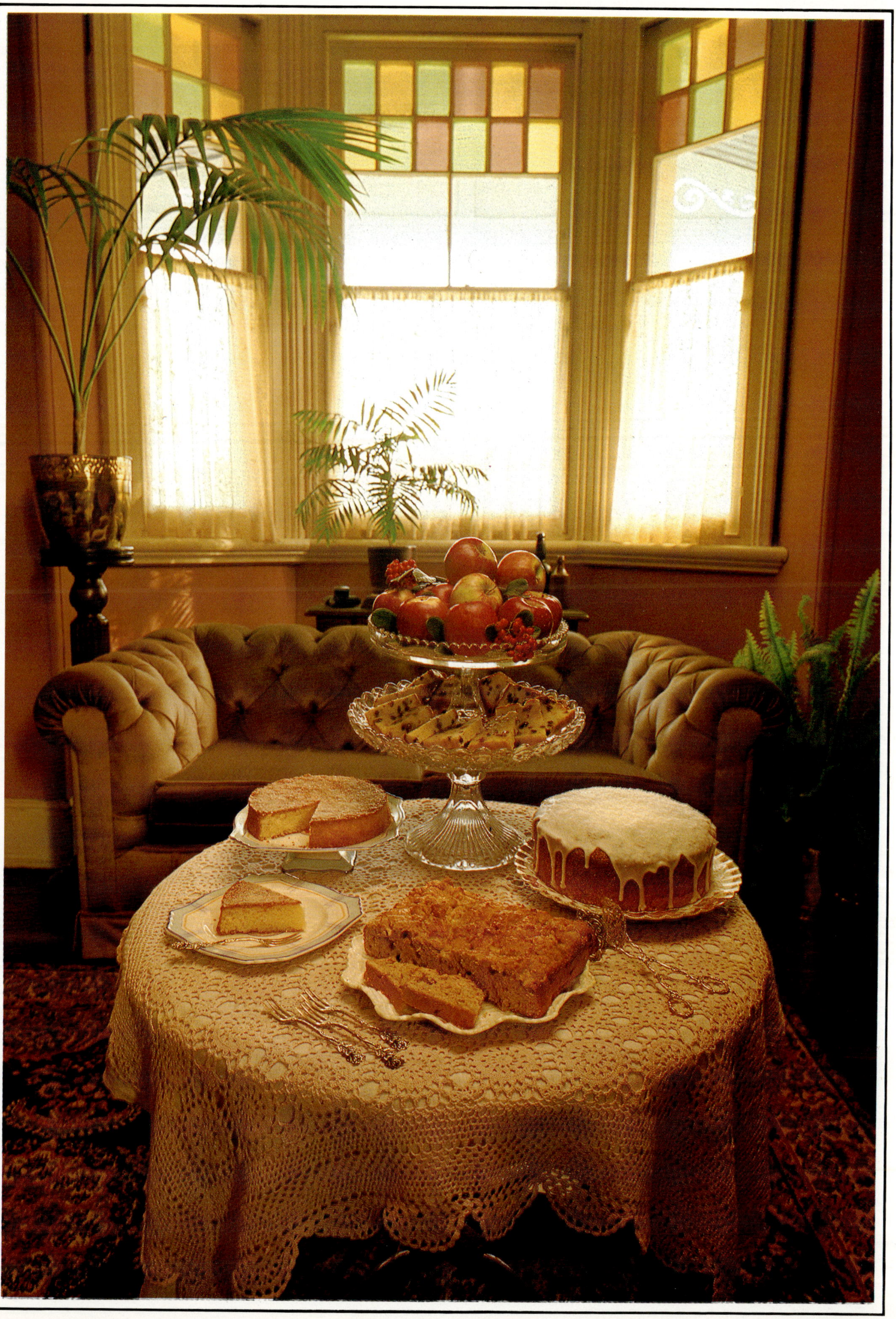

Caraway Seed Cake

Some love it, some hate it. Regrettably, many children do not like it.
Makes 1 cake

185 g (6 oz) butter

¼ cup (2 oz) caster (powdered) sugar

4 eggs

1¾ cups (7 oz) self-raising flour

2 tablespoons caraway seeds (they must be fresh)

2½ tablespoons ground almonds (or almond meal)

Topping:
60 g (2 oz) butter

2 tablespoons sugar

½ teaspoon ground caraway

finely grated rind of ½ lemon

Preheat the oven to 160°C (325°F/Gas 3). Grease a cake tin 18 cm (7 in) round, and place a disc of greaseproof paper on the base. Dust the paper and sides of the tin lightly with flour and shake out the excess.

Cream the butter until soft, add the sugar and beat until light and fluffy. Add the eggs one at a time, beating each in well.

In a separate bowl, mix the flour and caraway seeds together, then stir this into the creamed mixture along with the ground almonds. Mix well. Turn into the cake tin.

Bake for 1 hour and 10 minutes.

To prepare the topping, melt the butter in a saucepan and stir in the sugar, ground caraway and lemon rind.

Simmer for a few minutes, then when the cake is removed from the oven and turned out of its tin, spread the topping over it.

Sultana Cake

Makes 2 cakes

125 g (4 oz) butter

½ cup (4 oz) sugar

2 eggs

1 tablespoon grated citrus (orange or lemon) rind

1 cup (6 oz) sultanas

2 cups (8 oz) self-raising flour

⅔ cup (5fl oz) milk

Preheat the oven to 180°C (350°F/Gas 4). Grease two 25 × 8 cm (10 × 3 in) bar tins and line the base with greaseproof paper.

Cream the butter and sugar, until light and creamy. Add eggs one at a time, beating well after each addition. Beat in the citrus rind, then mix in the sultanas. Add the sifted flour alternately with the milk, and mix well. Turn into the tins.

Bake for 30 to 35 minutes. Turn out, and cool on rack. We sometimes put the cakes together with thick lemon frosting.

Sultana Cake Variations:
Try this with sliced dried apricots and a few slivered almonds mixed in before baking.

Another variation is to flavour the milk with vanilla. Simmer a chopped vanilla bean in about 1⅓ cups (10½fl oz) of milk until the flavour has been absorbed (about 15 minutes). Before adding the milk to the cake mixture, allow it to cool. Check that you have ⅔ cup (5½fl oz) of milk remaining after evaporation, and discard the vanilla bean.

Coffee Cake

Makes 1 cake

1¾ cups (7 oz) flour

1 teaspoon baking powder

½ teaspoon bicarbonate of soda (baking soda)

½ teaspoon salt

¼ teaspoon grated nutmeg

¾ cup (6 oz) sugar

125 g (4 oz) butter

½ cup (2 oz) oatmeal

⅓ cup (1 oz) wheatgerm

1 egg

¾ cup (4 oz) raisins, chopped a little

⅔ cup (5fl oz) milk

3 tablespoons instant coffee powder

icing (confectioners') sugar, for sprinkling

Preheat the oven to 180°C (350°F/Gas 4). Grease a 20 cm (8 in) square cake tin.

Sift together the flour, baking powder, bicarbonate of soda, salt, nutmeg and sugar.

In a separate bowl, rub the butter into the oatmeal and wheatgerm, then add this to the flour mixture. Add the egg and raisins, and mix well.

Warm the milk a little and dissolve the coffee in it. Blend this into the mixture and stir well. Pour into the cake tin.

Bake for about 35 minutes. Serve warm, cut into squares and dusted with sifted icing sugar.

A Light Fruit Cake

In this recipe, sultanas, currants and mixed peel are specified. But if you're feeling adventurous, try other dried fruits such as sliced or chopped figs, peaches or Californian dates.
Makes 1 cake

2½ cups (10 oz) flour
1 teaspoon baking powder
250 g (8 oz) butter
1 cup (7 oz) caster (powdered) sugar
4 eggs, beaten
½ cup (3 oz) sultanas
½ cup (2½ oz) currants
¼ cup (1½ oz) mixed peel
2 tablespoons milk

Preheat the oven to 160°C (325°F/Gas 3). Grease a deep-sided cake tin 20 cm (8 in) round, and line it with greaseproof paper.

Sift together the flour and baking powder.

In a large bowl, beat together the butter and sugar until light and fluffy. Add the beaten eggs gradually, beating well after each addition. Mix in the fruit, then the flour and then the milk. Turn out into the cake tin.

Bake for 1 hour 45 minutes. Remove from the tin and cool on a wire rack.

Poppy Seed Cake

Makes 1 cake

1 cup (6 oz) poppy seeds
6 eggs, separated
12 tablespoons honey
⅔ cup (5fl oz) vegetable oil
1 cup (4 oz) dry breadcrumbs
2 teaspoons baking powder
¼ teaspoon salt
1 teaspoon vanilla essence

Preheat the oven to 160°C (325°F/Gas 3). Grease a 20 cm (8 in) loaf tin.

Simmer poppy seeds for 15 minutes in a saucepan with enough water to cover. Drain, and allow to cool.

Beat the egg whites until stiff. Gradually add 3 tablespoons of honey and continue beating until stiff again. Set aside.

In a large bowl, beat the egg yolks till lemon coloured. Gradually beat in the remaining 9 tablespoons of honey and then the oil. Add the poppy seeds.

In a third bowl, combine the breadcrumbs, baking powder and salt, then blend this into the egg yolks mixture. Fold in the stiff egg whites and fold in the vanilla. Pour out into the tin.

Bake for 1 hour. Turn out onto a wire rack to cool.

Gingerbread

This is really a gingerbread cake. It has a dense, slightly sticky texture, and keeps well. In fact, it must be kept for a few days to be at its best.
Makes 1 cake

4 cups (1 lb) flour
3 level teaspoons ground ginger
3 teaspoons baking powder
1 teaspoon bicarbonate of soda (baking soda)
1 teaspoon salt
1½ cups (8 oz) brown sugar
185 g (6 oz) butter
½ cup (6 oz) treacle (or molasses)
½ cup (6 oz) golden syrup (light corn syrup)
2½ cups (20fl oz) milk
1 large egg, beaten

Preheat the oven to 180°C (350°F/Gas 4). Grease a deep-sided cake tin 20 cm (8 in) square, and line it with greaseproof paper.

Sift the dry ingredients, except the sugar, into a large bowl.

Warm the sugar, butter, treacle and syrup in a saucepan over low heat until the butter has just melted. Stir this into the dry mixture, together with the milk and beaten egg. Beat thoroughly and pour into the cake tin.

Bake in the centre of the oven for 1½ hours. Remove from the oven and allow to cool in the tin for 15 minutes. Then turn out onto a wire rack. When cold, wrap in foil without removing the paper. Store for 4 or 5 days before cutting into squares.

Serve with a hot mug of cocoa. It tastes even better with a thin lemon icing.

Fresh Apple Cake

Apple cakes are a family favorite. Even the children enjoy making this quick, easy and healthy recipe, using fresh raw apples. I never peel the apples for this cake.
Makes 1 cake

1 cup (6 oz) brown sugar
2 eggs
½ cup vegetable oil
1 teaspoon vanilla essence
3 tablespoons milk
3 cups diced fresh apple (about 4 apples, cored)
2 cups (8 oz) wholemeal flour
1 teaspoon baking powder
½ teaspoon salt
½ teaspoon ground cinnamon
½ teaspoon grated nutmeg

Preheat the oven to 180°C (350° F/Gas 4). Grease and flour a 22 cm (9 in) square cake tin.

Beat together the sugar and eggs until thick and light. Beat in the oil and vanilla and milk. Stir in the diced apple (allow for amounts that are slipped into the mouths of hungry onlookers!).

In a separate bowl sift together the flour, baking powder, salt, and spices, then fold this into the apple mixture. Pour into the cake tin.

Bake for 45 minutes. Serve warm, perhaps with hot custard or with a yoghurt and honey mix.

Chocolate Prune Cake

The moist fruit gives this cake good keeping qualities and a soft texture.
Makes 1 cake

1 cup (7 oz) whole prunes
125 g (4 oz) butter
1 cup (6 oz) brown sugar
2 eggs
1 cup (4 oz) self-raising flour
1 cup (4 oz) self-raising wholemeal flour
½ cup (2 oz) cocoa
½ teaspoon ground clove
½ cup (4fl oz) prune-cooking water

Preheat the oven to 180°C (350°F/Gas 4). Grease a 20 × 15 cm (8 × 6 in) square tin.

Gently simmer the prunes in 2 cups of water for 8 minutes. Cool, and drain, saving the liquid. Remove the stones.

Beat the butter and sugar until creamy. Add the eggs, and beat until well combined. Sift in the flours, cocoa and ground clove. Add the prunes and stir in, adding ½ cup of the prune-cooking liquid. Pour into the tin.

Bake for 40 minutes. Allow to cool in the tin.

The cake can later be iced with a chocolate icing (see recipe, page 130).

Chocolate Prune Cake with Walnuts
To the batter for Chocolate Prune Cake, add ½ cup (2 oz) of chopped walnuts.

Ice with a coffee icing (see recipe, page 130) and sprinkle with walnut meal.

Orange Blossom Cake

The haunting scent of springtime orange blossoms waft through your kitchen from this memorable invention.
Makes 1 cake

125 g (4 oz) butter
1¼ cups (7 oz) brown sugar
1 cup (8fl oz) milk
3 egg yolks
3 teaspoons orange blossom water
2 cups (9 oz) wholemeal flour
2 teaspoons baking powder
½ teaspoon salt
½ teaspoon ground clove
1 cup slivered blanched almonds
1 cup (5 oz) currants
2 tablespoons coarsely grated orange rind
3 egg whites, stiffly beaten

Preheat the oven to 180°C (350°F/Gas 4). Grease a large loaf tin.

Blend the butter and sugar together well. Add the milk, egg yolks and orange blossom water.

Into a separate bowl, sift together the flour, baking powder, salt and ground clove, then add this to the mixture and beat well. Add the almonds, currants and orange rind; mix well. Fold in the stiffly beaten egg whites. Spread into the tin.

Bake for 35 to 45 minutes. Turn out of the tin onto a wire rack.

The cake can be glazed while it is hot (see recipe, page 149). Or after it has cooled it can be coated with a thin simple icing and sprinkled with finely chopped mixed peel. Serve with black China tea.

Right: **Clockwise from top right: Chocolate Prune Cake (see above); Orange Blossom Cake (see above); Lemon Yoghurt Cake (see p. 56).**

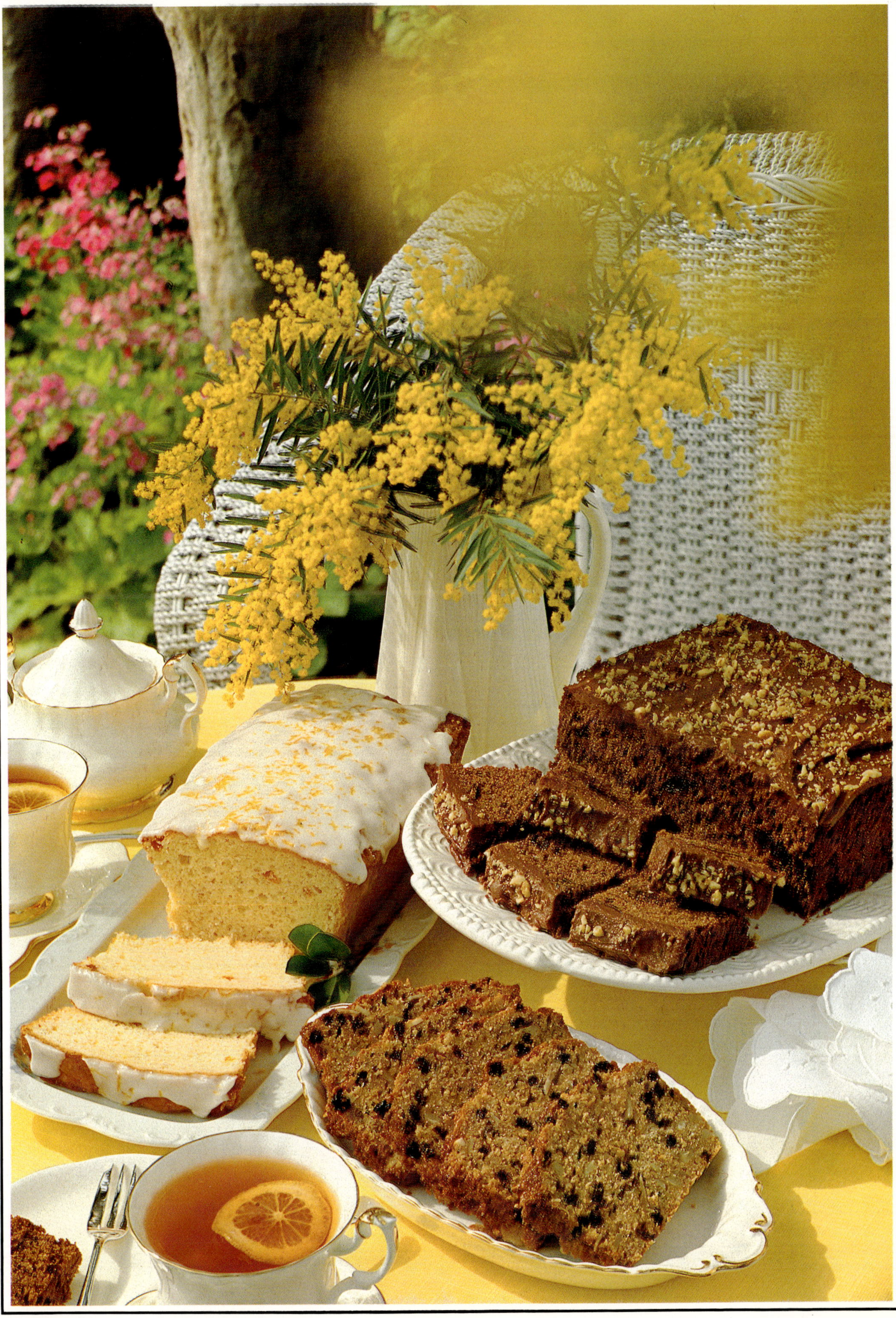

Walnut Crumble Apricot Cake

Makes 1 cake

125 g (4 oz) butter
⅔ cup (5 oz) caster (powdered) sugar
2 eggs
2 cups (8 oz) self-raising flour, sifted
½ cup (4fl oz) milk
16 dried apricots
Topping:
½ cup (2 oz) self-raising wholemeal flour
¼ cup (2 oz) raw sugar
¼ cup (1 oz) chopped walnuts
½ teaspoon ground cardamom
4 tablespoons butter

Soak the apricots in boiling water for 20 minutes. Preheat the oven to 180°C (350°F/Gas 4). Grease a 20 cm (8 in) springform tin.

Cream the butter and sugar until light and fluffy. Add the eggs one at a time, beating between each addition. Gently fold in the flour one-third at a time, alternately with the milk. Pour the batter into the cake tin.

Drain the apricots thoroughly, then arrange them ontop of the batter.

To prepare the crumble topping, mix all the dry indgredients together and then rub in the butter. Spread the crumble mixture over the apricots. Cover with foil.

Bake for 40 minutes. Gently remove the foil and bake for about 30 minutes more. Serve warm or cold.

Lemon Yoghurt Cake

Makes 1 cake

125 g (4 oz) butter
¾ cup (6 oz) caster (powdered) sugar
3 eggs
finely grated rind of 1 lemon
¾ cup (6fl oz) natural yoghurt
2 cups (8 oz) self-raising flour, sifted
½ cup (2 oz) sliced dried apricots

Preheat the oven to 160°C (325°F/Gas 3). Grease a 20 × 15 cm (8 × 6 inch) loaf tin.

Cream the butter and sugar until light and fluffy. Add the eggs one at a time, beating well between each. Gently fold in the lemon rind, yoghurt, sifted flour and dried apricot slices. Spoon the mixture into the tin.

Bake for 1¼ hours. Turn out onto a wire rack to cool.

The cake is made even more delicious by topping with a yoghurt icing. Mix 1 tablespoon of natural yoghurt with ½ cup (3 oz) of icing (confectioners') sugar, spread this over the cake, and sprinkle with finely grated lemon rind.

Coffee and Peppermint Cake

The strong coffee taste with a hint of peppermint makes this an ideal afternoon tea or supper cake.
Makes 1 cake

185 g (6 oz) butter
1 cup (7 oz) caster (powdered) sugar
2 cups (8 oz) flour
1½ teaspoons baking powder
3 eggs
3 tablespoons milk
4 tablespoons instant coffee powder
5 drops peppermint essence
¼ cup chopped glacé angelica (optional)

Preheat the oven to 180°C (350°F/Gas 4). Grease a deep-sided cake tin 20 cm (8 in) round, and line it with greaseproof paper.

Cream the butter and sugar until light and fluffy.

Into a separate bowl, sift the flour and baking powder together. To the butter and sugar, add the eggs gradually, beating after each.

Warm the milk and dissolve the coffee in it.

To the butter-sugar-egg mixture, add half of the flour and half of the coffee-milk. Combine well. Add the remaining flour and milk and the peppermint essence, mix well, then stir in the angelica. Turn into the cake tin and smooth over the top.

Bake for 1 hour. Turn out onto a wire rack to cool. Serve with hot chocolate or a chocolate liqueur.

TEA CAKES & BREADS

Turkish Fig Bar

*A rich cake of Oriental influence.
Makes 1 cake*

125 g (4 oz) butter

1 cup (6 oz) brown sugar

½ cup (4 fl oz) milk

1 teaspoon vanilla essence

3 egg yolks

2 cups (8 oz) self-raising flour

¾ teaspoon baking powder

pinch of salt

1 teaspoon grated nutmeg

3 egg whites, stiffly beaten

Fig Filling:
1 cup (6 oz) chopped dried figs

2 tablespoons honey

1 tablespoon finely grated lemon rind

2 cups water

2 teaspoons cornflour (cornstarch)

Prepare the filling first. Simmer the figs, honey and lemon rind in water for 10 minutes. Mix the cornflour with a little cold water to dissolve it, then add it to the simmering figs. Cook until it becomes very thick.

Preheat the oven to 180°C (350°F/Gas 4). Lightly grease a large loaf tin.

Blend the butter and sugar together well. Add the milk, vanilla and egg yolks and mix well. Sift in the flour, baking powder, salt and nutmeg, beating well. Fold in the stiffly beaten egg whites.

Spread half of the batter in the tin. On this, spread the filling, then cover with the rest of the batter.

Bake for 35 to 45 minutes. Turn out of the tin onto a wire rack to cool.

Fresh Pear and Bran Cake

Makes 1 cake

½ cup (2 oz) finely chopped walnuts

¾ cup (6 oz) raw sugar

1 teaspoon ground cinnamon

2 teaspoons wheat bran

1½ cups thinly sliced pear

½ teaspoon lemon juice

125 g (4 oz) butter

2 eggs

1¼ cups (5 oz) wholemeal flour

1½ teaspoons baking powder

½ cup (4 fl oz) sour cream

½ teaspoon milk

Preheat the oven to 180°C (350°F/Gas 4). Grease a deep loaf tin. Four bowls are needed for the preparation.

Combine the walnuts, ¼ cup of sugar, cinnamon, bran, pear slices and lemon juice.

In a large bowl, cream the butter and remaining ½ cup of sugar together well. Beat in the eggs, one at a time.

Sift together the flour and baking powder.

Combine the sour cream and milk together.

Into the butter-sugar-eggs mixture, stir the sifted dry ingredients alternately with the sour cream mixture. Pour half of this batter into the tin. Spread the fruit and nut mixture over this, then spread the rest of the batter.

Bake for 50 minutes. Turn out of the tin onto a wire rack to cool.

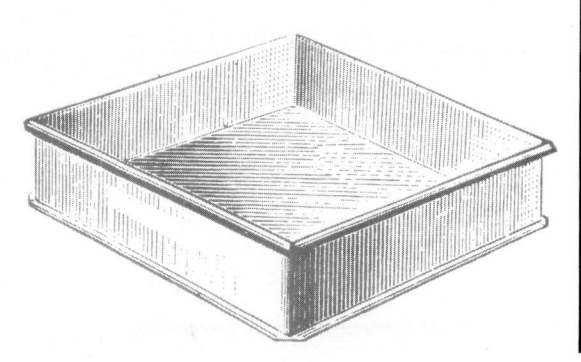

Rosewater Currant Ring

This exotic cake has a moist, thick texture and keeps extremely well.
Makes 1 cake

1 cup (6 oz) brown sugar
2 eggs
½ cup vegetable oil
3 tablespoon confectioners' rosewater
2 cups (10 oz) currants
1 cup (3 oz) desiccated coconut
2 cups (8 oz) wholemeal flour
1 teaspoon baking powder
½ teaspoon ground cinnamon
½ cup (4fl oz) currant-soaking water

Soak the currants in boiling water for 20 minutes. Preheat the oven to 180°C (350°F/Gas 4). Grease a deep ring tin.

Beat together the sugar and eggs then beat in the oil and rosewater. Drain the currants (reserve the currant-soaking water) and add the currants to the mixture. Stir in the coconut.

Into a separate bowl, sift the flour, baking powder and cinnamon together, then fold this into the sugar-egg-mixture, with ⅓-½ cup (3-4fl oz) of the currant-soaking water. Pour into the tin and level the top.

Bake for 45 minutes. Allow to cool before turning out of the tin.

For extra flavour the cake can be spread with thin simple icing (see page 130). Serve with strong black—preferably Turkish—coffee.

Pumpkin Nut Bread

Makes 1 loaf

1½ cups (12 oz) pumpkin purée
½ cup (6 oz) honey
½ cup (3 oz) brown sugar
½ cup (4fl oz) vegetable oil
½ cup (2½ oz) chopped dates
½ cup (2 oz) chopped walnuts
½ teaspoon salt
½ teaspoon ground cinnamon
½ teaspoon ground clove
2 teaspoons baking powder
1 cup (4 oz) plain flour
1¼ cups (5 oz) wholemeal flour
2 tablespoons wheat germ

Peel, chop and cook the pumpkin, then mash or purée sufficient of it to produce 1½ cups of purée.

Preheat the oven to 180°C (350°F/Gas 4). Grease a deep loaf tin.

In a large bowl, combine the honey, brown sugar, vegetable oil, pumpkin purée, dates, walnuts, salt, cinnamon, cloves and baking powder. Mix well.

Stir in the remaining ingredients, then pour the mixture into the tin.

Bake for about 1 hour. Cool in the tin for 20 minutes, then turn out onto a wire rack.

Lemon and Apricot Bread

Makes 1 Loaf

90 g (3 oz) butter
1 cup (8 oz) sugar
2 eggs
1½ cups (6 oz) flour
1½ teaspoons baking powder
¼ teaspoon salt
½ cup (4fl oz) milk
1 tablespoon grated lemon rind
1 tablespoon lemon juice
½ cup (3 oz) sultanas
½ cup (2 oz) chopped dried apricots
Topping: 2 tablespoons lemon juice
½ cup (4 oz) sugar

Preheat the oven to 190°C (375°F/Gas 5). Grease a large loaf tin.

Melt the butter, and mix it in a bowl with the sugar. Add the eggs one at a time and beat well. Add the sifted flour, baking powder and salt, alternately with the milk. Mix well. Fold in the lemon rind, lemon juice, sultanas and apricots. Pour into the tin and level the surface.

Bake for 50 to 60 minutes.

To prepare the topping, stir the lemon juice and sugar in a saucepan over low heat until the sugar dissolves. While the bread is still hot, spoon the topping over it. Allow to cool in the tin.

Right: Clockwise from top: Pumpkin Nut Bread (see above); Lemon and Apricot Bread (see above); Butter Cake with Crumble Topping (see p. 49).

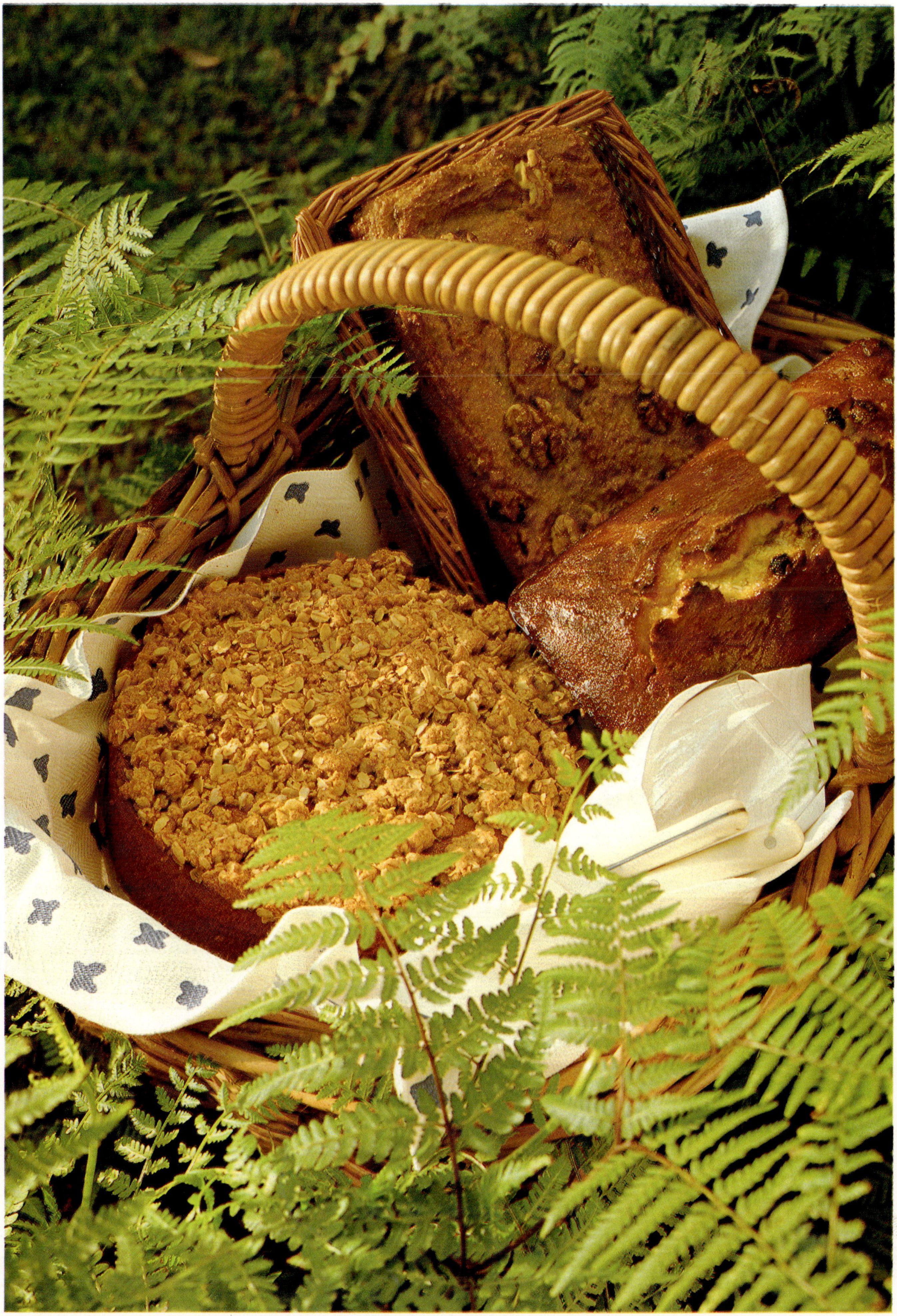

Wholemeal Pound Cake

A tradition that fell from favour but is very popular now is whole-grain baking—using wholemeal flour. Don't be afraid of a heavy result. If you haven't used wholemeal before, try using half plain (all-purpose) flour and half wholemeal flour.
Makes 1 cake

250 g (8 oz) butter

2 cups (10 oz) brown sugar

3 eggs, lightly beaten

1 teaspoon grated lemon rind

2¼ cups (9 oz) sifted wholemeal flour

1 teaspoon baking powder

½ teaspoon salt

1 cup (8fl oz) natural yoghurt with
1 teaspoon vanilla essence mixed in

Preheat the oven to 160°C (325°F/Gas 3). Grease a 25 cm (10 in) loaf tin. Dust with flour and shake out the excess.

Cream the butter until light and gradually beat in the sugar. Add the beaten eggs and mix thoroughly. Mix in the lemon rind, then the flour, baking powder, salt and yoghurt. Spread into the cake tin.

Bake for 65 minutes. Allow to cool in the tin for 15 minutes, then transfer to a wire rack.

Good with thick lemon frosting (see recipe, page 134).

Wholemeal Date Scones

Makes 15 scones

1 cup (4 oz) self-raising flour

1½ cups (6 oz) self-raising wholemeal flour

2 teaspoons fresh wheatgerm

pinch of salt

¼ teaspoon grated nutmeg

1 teaspoon ground cinnamon

½ teaspoon grated lemon rind

60 g (2 oz) butter

125 g (4 oz) dates, chopped

2 tablespoons honey

½ cup (4fl oz) milk

1 egg

Preheat the oven to 230°C (450°F/Gas 8). Grease a baking tray.

Sift the dry ingredients into a large bowl and add the lemon rind. Rub in the butter until the mixture resembles fine breadcrumbs. Add the chopped dates, mix lightly. Make a depression in the centre.

In a separate bowl combine the honey, egg and milk, and then pour this into the well in the larger bowl. Mix to a soft dough. Turn onto a floured surface and knead lightly. Pat out to 2 cm (¾ in) thickness and cut into 15 rounds. Place close together on the baking tray. Brush the tops with extra milk.

Bake for 12 to 15 minutes. Serve warm, or allow to cool on a wire rack.

Ginger Fig Scones

Makes 10–12 scones

2 cups (8 oz) self-raising flour

pinch of salt

1 teaspoon dry ground ginger

45 g (1½ oz) margarine

1 cup (6 oz) thinly sliced dried figs

4 tablespoons water, mixed with
4 tablespoons milk

milk for glazing

Preheat the oven to 230°C (450°F/Gas 8). (Do not grease the baking tray.)

Sift the flour, salt and ginger together into a bowl. Rub in the margarine. Add the sliced figs and then the milk/water mix to make soft dough. Turn out onto a floured surface and knead lightly. Pat out to 2 cm (¾ in) thickness and cut into 10–12 rounds. Set the rounds close together on the baking tray. Brush with milk.

Bake near the top of the oven for about 10 minutes. Allow to cool on a wire rack.

Caraway Muscatel Scones
Using the basic recipe for Ginger Fig Scones (above), try replacing the ginger with 2 teaspoons of caraway seeds and ½ teaspoon of ground caraway.

Replace the figs with 1 cup (6 oz) muscatels. These should be soaked in boiling water for 15 minutes, then drained and dried a little before they are added to the mixture.

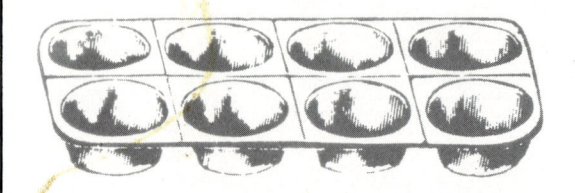

Paprika Scone Round

A savoury taste to share in the late afternoon.
Makes 1 loaf

½ cup (2 oz) flour
1⅓ cup (6 oz) wholemeal flour
3 level teaspoons baking powder
1 teaspoon salt
1 teaspoon paprika
sprinkle of ground dried chillies
1 teaspoon dried marjoram
¼ cup (2 oz) margarine
¼ cup (2 oz) brown sugar
⅔ cup (5fl oz) milk

Preheat the oven to 230°C (450°F/Gas 8). Lightly flour the baking tray.

Sift all the dry ingredients together into a bowl. Rub in the margarine until the mixture resembles breadcrumbs. Mix in enough of the milk to give a light dough. Mix with a broad knife blade so as not to remove the air between the particles—which would result in a heavy scone.

Turn out onto a floured surface, knead lightly. Shape into a round. Mark the top surface with a knife blade into, say, six equal triangles.

Bake near the top of an oven for about 15 minutes. Serve warm, cut into the six pieces and butter each liberally. Good with Romano cheese and a five o'clock sherry.

Gem Scones

Well known, well loved, especially at family gatherings.
The traditional rounded shape comes from the heavy 'iron'—usually made of cast aluminium today. Patty cake tins can be used—but reduce the oven temperature a little.
Makes 10 scones

30 g (1 oz) butter
2 tablespoons (2 oz) sugar
1 egg
pinch of salt
½ cup (4fl oz) milk
1 cup (4 oz) self-raising flour

Preheat the oven to 200°C (400°F/Gas 6). Heat the gem irons in the oven

Cream the butter and sugar. Add the egg, salt and milk, and combine well. Lightly fold in the sifted flour.

Grease the hot gem irons. Spoon the batter into them, to three-quarters fill each cavity.

Bake for 10 to 15 minutes. Serve warm.

Gem Scones Variations

The basic batter for gem scones is simple to make, and the flavour can be varied in many ways. These are just a few—why not create your own?

The first is to add ½ cup (3 oz) of sultanas to the batter.

The second gives a delicious savoury flavour. Add 2 tablespoons of chopped fresh dill, ½ teaspoon of paprika, 2 tablespoons of grated Parmesan cheese, and about 1 extra tablespoon of milk. Mix well into the batter.

For the third variation, add 2 tablespoons of desiccated coconut to the batter. And then, when filling the gem irons with batter, place 1 drop of marmalade in the centre of each scone before baking.

Soda Bread

Makes 1 loaf

4 cups (1 lb) flour
4 level teaspoons baking powder
1 teaspoon salt
30 g (1 oz) margarine
2 teaspoons caster (powdered) sugar
1 cup (8fl oz) buttermilk
¼ cup (2fl oz) milk

Preheat the oven to 200°C (400°F/Gas 6). Flour a baking tray.

Sift the flour, baking powder and salt into a bowl. Rub in the margarine until the mixture resembles breadcrumbs.

Mix in the sugar. Make a depression in the centre and add the buttermilk and milk. Mix to a soft dough with a broad-bladed knife (add a little more milk if necessary). Turn out onto a floured surface and knead lightly. Shape into a round and flatten slightly. Place on the baking tray, and mark the top with a knife into, say, six equal triangles for easy breaking when baked.

Bake for about 30 minutes. Cool on a wire rack, and serve fresh with butter and/or cream cheese.

Damper

Australian Damper surely must have originated from the Irish Soda Bread (using soda for leavening), as yeast would have been difficult to keep alive in the hot Australian outback. Damper is often baked in a lidded baking tin and placed in the glowing white coals of a camp fire.

Makes 1 loaf

4 cups (1 lb) self-raising flour
2 teaspoons salt
30 g (1 oz) butter
1 tablespoon sugar
1½ cups (12fl oz) water
1 egg yolk
1 tablespoon milk

Preheat the oven to 190°C (375°F/Gas 5).

Sift the flour and salt into a bowl. Rub in the butter. Then mix in the sugar. Make a well in the centre of the mixture, pour in the water and, using your hand, mix to a soft dough. Turn out onto a floured surface and knead until smooth.

Grease a 6–8 cup casserole dish well with butter (it may be pottery, cast iron or tin). Place the dough in the casserole rounded side up and cut a cross in the top. Beat the egg yolk and milk together, then brush this over the dough; it will give the damper a beautiful golden glaze. Cover with a well-greased lid or a buttered piece of aluminium foil.

Bake for about 45 minutes. Uncover for the last half of the cooking. Leave for a few minutes before turning out of the dish. Serve in thick slices.

Spiced Banana Scones

Makes 12 scones

2 cups (8 oz) self-raising flour
pinch of salt
90 g (3 oz) butter
⅔ cup (5fl oz) milk
an additional 30 g (1 oz) butter, melted
1 ripe banana
2 tablespoons raw sugar
½ teaspoon ground cinnamon
½ teaspoon grated nutmeg

Preheat the oven to 220°C (425°F/Gas 7). Lightly grease a baking tray.

Sift the flour and salt into a bowl. Rub in the butter until the mixture resembles fine breadcrumbs. Add the milk, and mix to a soft dough. Turn out onto a floured surface, knead lightly, and then roll out to about 5 mm (¼ in) thick. Cut into 12 rounds and brush the surface of each with melted butter.

Peel and mash the banana with a little brown sugar, and spread this over half of each round. Fold over and press the edges together firmly. Brush the tops with melted butter and sprinkle thickly with the sugar, cinnamon and nutmeg. Place on the baking tray, sugar side up.

Bake for 10 to 15 minutes. Serve warm, and don't allow them to dry out.

Right: **Clockwise from top right: Gem Scones (see p. 61); Soda Bread (see above); Wholemeal Date Scones (see p. 60); Spiced Banana Scones (see above).**

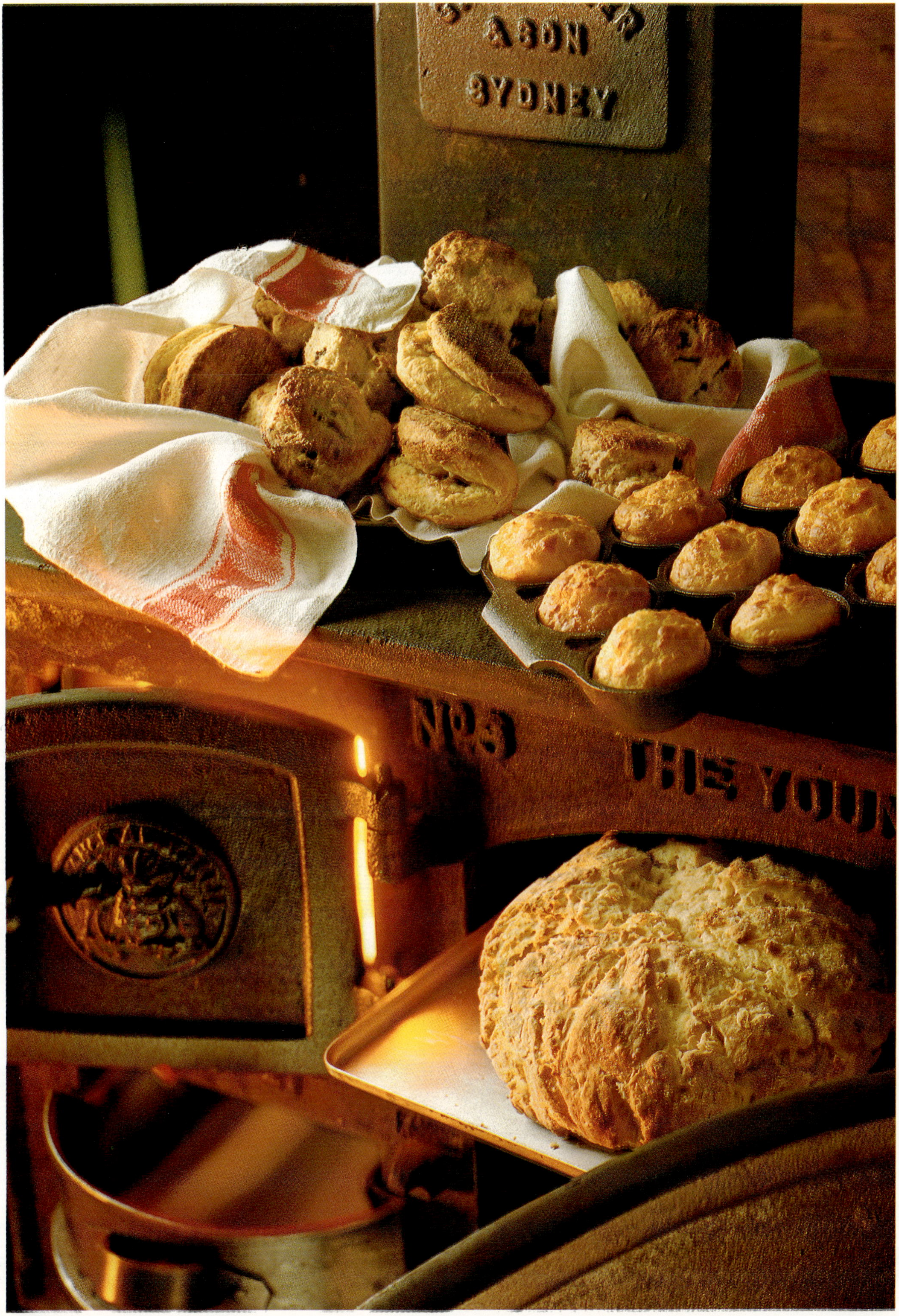
&SON
SYDNEY

Greek Coconut Cake

This cake keeps well, but must be stored in a well-sealed container.
Makes 1 cake

125 g (4 oz) butter
1 cup (8 oz) sugar
4 eggs, beaten
2 cups (6 oz) desiccated coconut
1 cup (4 oz) self-raising flour
Syrup:
1½ cups (12 oz) sugar
1¼ cups (10 fl oz) water
fresh grated rind of ½ lemon

Preheat the oven to 230°C (450°F/Gas 8). Grease a deep-sided cake tin 20 cm (8 in) square.
   Cream the butter and sugar until light and fluffy. Add well-beaten eggs; beat in well. Fold in the coconut and sifted flour; mix well. Spread the mixture in the cake tin.
   Bake for 15 minutes or until the top is golden brown, then reduce the heat to 150°C (300°F/Gas 2) and bake for a further 25 minutes.
   Allow to cool for 5 minutes in the tin, then pour over the prepared syrup. Allow the cake to become cold in the tin before turning it out.
Syrup: Stir the sugar, water and lemon rind in a saucepan over low heat until the sugar has dissolved. Increase the heat to bring it to the boil, then reduce the heat and simmer for 5 minutes. Pour hot over cake.
Variations: For fun, add 2 teaspoons of rosewater, or orange blossom water or crème de menthe essence to the syrup.

Prune Health Loaf

Makes 1 Loaf

60 g (2 oz) butter
¾ cup (4 oz) brown sugar
200 g (6½ oz) cottage cheese
finely grated rind of 1 lemon
2 eggs
½ cup (3 oz) halved and pitted prunes
1 tablespoon lemon juice
2 cups (9 oz) self-raising wholemeal flour
2 tablespoons wheatgerm
1 teaspoon mixed spice

Preheat the oven to 160°C (325°F/Gas 3). Grease a 20 × 15 cm (8 × 6 in) loaf tin.
   Cream together the butter and sugar until light and fluffy. Blend in the cottage cheese and lemon rind. Add the eggs one at a time, beating well between each addition. Fold in the remaining ingredients, and pour the mixture into the tin.
   Bake for 1 hour. Turn out of the tin and allow to cool on a wire rack. Serve sliced, with butter.

Easy Fruit Bread

Makes 1 loaf

4 cups (1 lb) self-raising flour
1 teaspoon grated nutmeg
60 g (2 oz) butter
1 cup (6 oz) brown sugar
1½ cups (8 oz) raisins
1⅔ cups (8 oz) currants
⅓ cup (2 oz) mixed peel
1 egg
1½ cups (12 fl oz) milk
1 cup (8 fl oz) golden syrup (light corn syrup)

Preheat the oven to 190°C (375°F/Gas 4). Grease a large loaf tin.
   Mix all the ingredients together very well with an electric beater. Pour the mixture into the tin.
   Bake for 1 hour. Turn out onto a wire rack to cool.

Malt Fruit Loaf:
Replace 3 tablespoons of the golden syrup with malt extract and continue as above.

TEA CAKES & BREADS

Glazed Banana Bread

Makes 1 loaf

2 cups (9 oz) self-raising wholemeal flour

2 tablespoons wheatgerm

½ teaspoon bicarbonate of soda (baking soda)

3 tablespoons butter

¾ cup (6 oz) caster (powdered) sugar

200 g (6½ oz) cottage cheese

2 eggs

1 cup (8 oz) mashed bananas (very ripe bananas!)

Preheat the oven to 180°c (350°F/Gas 4). Grease a 20 × 15 cm (8 × 6 in) loaf tin.

Sift the flour, wheatgerm and bicarbonate of soda together into a bowl, adding any coarser bits left in the sieve.

In a separate bowl, cream the butter, sugar and cottage cheese together. Add the eggs, one at a time, beating between each addition. Fold in the flour mixture and the mashed banana alternately. Pour into the tin.

Bake for 1 hour. Turn out onto a wire rack to cool.

If you like, spread warm glacé icing (see recipe, page 130) over the loaf and top it with a few slices of fresh banana cut diagonally and brushed with lemon juice. With or without icing, it is wonderful with mint tea.

Pineapple Bread

Makes 1 loaf

2 cups (9 oz) wholemeal flour

1 teaspoon baking powder

½ teaspoon salt

1 cup (6 oz) raisins

1 cup (4 oz) chopped walnuts

1 egg

½ cup (6 oz) honey

2 tablespoons vegetable oil

1 tablespoon vanilla essence

1 cup finely chopped pineapple

1 teaspoon bicarbonate of soda (baking soda)

Preheat the oven to 180°C (350°F/Gas 4). Grease a loaf tin.

Sift the dry ingredients into a bowl. Add the raisins and walnuts.

In a separate bowl beat together the egg, honey, oil and vanilla, then add this to the flour mixture.

Dissolve the bicarbonate of soda with the pineapple, and stir it in well into the batter. Pour into the tin.

Bake for 1 hour. Turn the bread out onto a wire rack to cool.

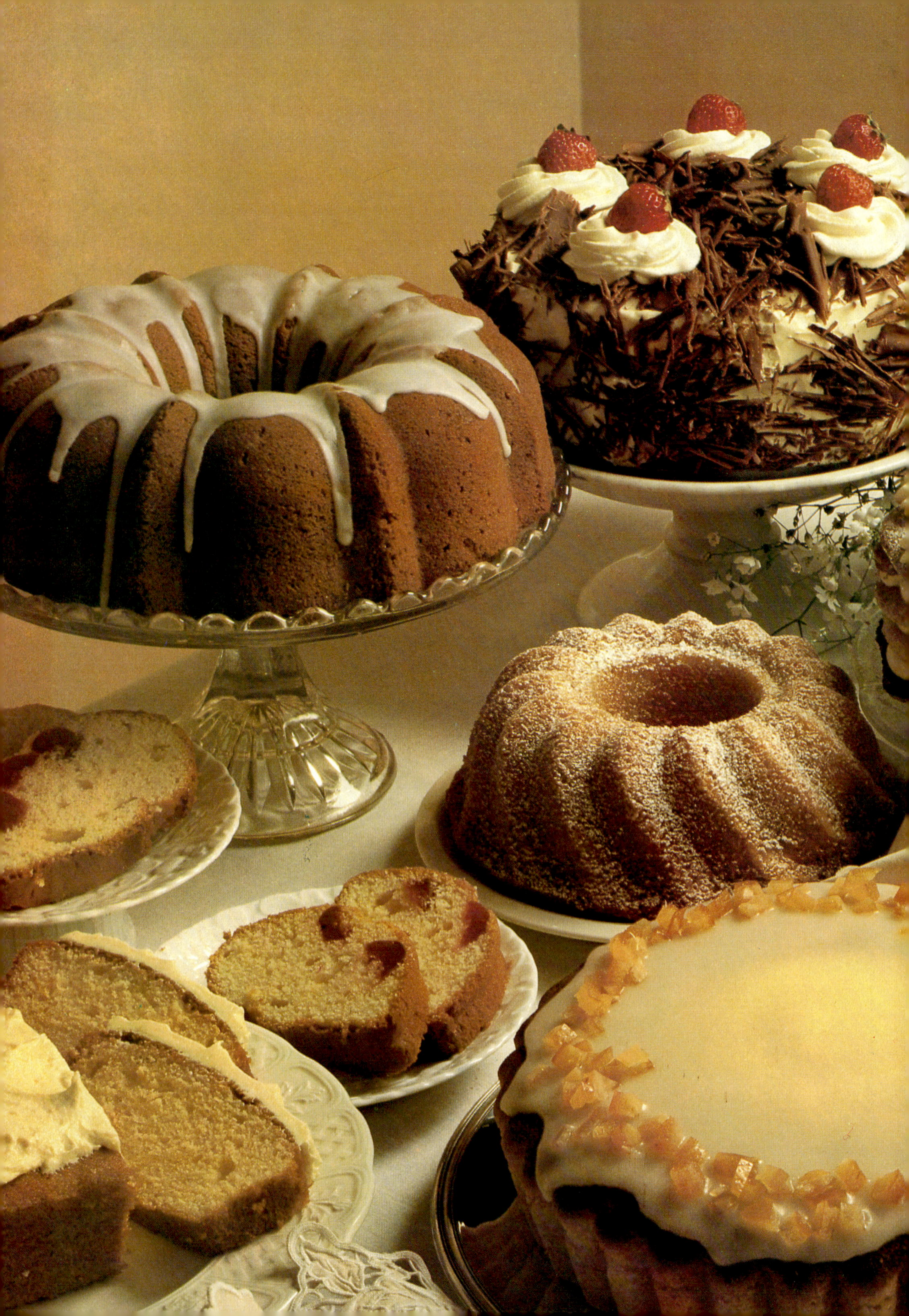

Large Cakes

Large Cakes

1. Coconut Butter Cake Ring (see p. 76)
2. Chocolate Fudge Cake (see p. 84)
3. Ginger Layer Cake (see p. 73)
4. Dundee Cake (see p. 105)
5. Swiss (Jelly) Roll (see p. 73)
6. Orange Butter Cake (see p. 76) with Orange Glacé Icing (see p. 130)
7. Orange Butter Cake (see p. 76) with Citrus Vienna Butter Cream (see p. 144)
8. Cherry Almond Butter Cake (see p. 76)
9. Foundation Butter Cake Ring (double quantity—see p. 76)

Few foods are more sought after, or more satisfying, than a home-baked cake... just as few skills are more sought after, or more satisfying, than those of the successful cake-maker. The magic words 'home-made' have carried an unswerving yardstick of quality for many centuries, since cake-making first began.

Ancient writings from Egypt mention the flat rounds of unleavened dough which were placed on hot stones to bake on either side until they were hard and brown... then to be eaten by dipping pieces in a mixture of honey and spices on special or sacrificial feast days when other foods were forbidden. Soon, other types of sweet flavours were added to the dough, and special hot stone ovens were built for cake-baking. As the cultures of Mesopotamia and Egypt spread throughout the then-known world, so the art of cake-making progressed and developed along with the general art of cookery itself.

Leavening or raising agents were introduced to produce a lighter, more acceptable product and then it was not long before grain sugar was known, opening up a whole new field for firstly the professional and later the domestic sweets cook.

Great chefs from the Italian and French Royal Courts vied with each other to extract the secrets of the monastery bakers and then to expand upon these to create dessert masterpieces for Royal approval and delight.

At this stage, except for the egg white–sugar meringue confections, most cakes were still being made with yeast ferments. It was not until the early half of the seventeenth century that science began to make an impact on cookery in general, and soon other ingredients were produced as raising agents which were more stable and took less time.

To this day many of the interchangeable names of Continental cakes—Gâteau, Torte, Küchen, Kake, etc—have symbolic significance, originally being eaten only at certain times of the year, but now often served at other special occasions.

Many of the modern butter cakes have their origin in the traditional 'Pound' cake. Scales were not commonly available in household kitchens, so that the only method of judging the weight of ingredients for cake-making was to use a store-bought pound of flour as the weighing medium. Also many old recipes used the egg as the measure of weight and thus evolved the still-used recipes specifying 'the weight of four eggs' in butter, or flour, and so on.

Modern cake-making techniques have advanced tremendously and no doubt will continue to advance as adventurous cooks find new and exciting ways to present their creations.

Betty Dunleavy

Modern Cake-making Techniques

With few exceptions, the method used for the mixing of the various types of cakes fall into one of the following categories.

- *Rubbing* the shortening through the dry ingredients—this method produces a fairly dry, coarse cake which is usually used for the inexpensive luncheon loaves and slices.
- *Creaming* the shortening and sugar together before the addition of the eggs and other ingredients—this method is used for light, medium and rich butter cakes, with or without added fruits, nuts, etc., as desired.
- *Beating* of the eggs (or egg whites) and sugar until thickened and increased in volume before folding in the dry ingredients—this method makes the light-textured sponge varieties with little or no shortening addition.
- *Mixing* of the melted shortening (or oil) with the other liquid or moist ingredients before the addition of the flour—this is an extremely popular quick-and-easy method for a large number of modern cakes suitable for all occasions.

Differences in texture and appearance are mainly due to the method chosen for combining the balanced ingredients before the cake is baked.

Packaged Cake Mixes

There is a great variety of prepared or semiprepared packaged cake mixes available for the busy homemaker who has not the time to prepare and mix ingredients for a home-baked cake. All types of cakes—butter cakes, fruit loaves, gingerbreads, sponges, orange and lemon cakes, chocolate and coffee cakes—may be made from these packages with the simple addition of 1 or 2 eggs and water or milk to produce successful results with very little time and effort.

Packaged cake mixes are usually of high quality with good keeping qualities. Busy homemakers often take advantage of the speed and convenience of a good cake mix, spending what little time is available for the filling or frosting to produce that 'home-made' personal touch.

Secrets of Success

When it comes to turning out a blue-ribbon cake every time, creative instinct is not enough. The straight and narrow path of correct proportions, careful attention to techniques and a reliable baking oven are of the utmost importance.

Here is a list of the basic steps to be considered for successful cake-making.

- Use a recipe from a reliable source.
- Weigh or measure ingredients accurately.
- Use the size of cake tin recommended.
- Line and/or grease the cake tin as instructed.
- Check the oven manufacturer's instructions to ensure the correct oven temperature, shelf position, etc.
- Follow the steps in the recipe carefully—beating, whisking, folding, etc., as instructed.
- Avoid opening the oven door during at least the first three-quarters of the baking time. Then open it only sparingly to ascertain the final baking time required.
- Allow the cake to 'settle' in the pan before turning it out onto a wire cake rack to cool away from any draughts.
- Do not ice the cake until it is completely cold.

Greasing Cake Tins

Most cake tins—even the so called non-stick cake tins—need to be lightly greased on the inside before adding the cake mixture so that the baked cake will turn out easily onto a rack or cooler without leaving part of the base, corners or sides adhering to the tin. Greasing should be done by evenly brushing or spreading a light layer of softened or melted shortening over the inside surface of the tin. Heavily salted shortenings should be avoided as the salt content may cause sticking problems. Allow the shortening to reset before spooning in the cake mixture.

Note: some cakes, particularly the light 'chiffon' or 'angel' cake varieties require to be baked in ungreased or oiled tins but this will always be mentioned in the recipe instructions.

Flouring Cake Tins

An extra precaution against sticking may be taken by lightly dusting the freshly greased surface of the cake tin with flour. Sprinkle 1 to 2 teaspoons of flour into the base of the tin and, slightly tilting the tin to all sides gently tap the outside to distribute the flour. Tip out any excess and allow the shortening to reset before use.

A second method is to spread a mixture of softened shortening and flour lightly over the inside surface of the tin and allow it to set before adding the cake mixture.

Lining Cake Tins

The precaution of lining cake tins before using for baking cakes can have two purposes.

1. To ensure that cakes—particularly high ratio sugar cakes—do not stick in the tins and break whilst turning out. Using greaseproof (not wax coated) paper, cut strips to neatly fit the sides and/or base of the tin, press over the freshly greased inside surface and grease again. When cooked and turned out the paper will adhere to the cake and may be carefully peeled away.

2. Two, three or even four layers of paper—or 1 to 2 layers of aluminium foil with an inner layer of greaseproof—may be used for large, heavily fruited cakes which require long, slow, baking. This thicker lining is allowed to protrude above the top of the tin for 2.5 to 5 cm (1–2 in) and acts as an insulator so that the outside of the cake does not become too browned and hard before the centre is cooked. Very large cakes may also be further protected by a sheet of foil or paper being placed loosely over the top, for the first half or two-thirds of the baking time so that the top does not become too hard and crusted.

Testing During Baking

Browned cakes are not necessarily cooked cakes. Test carefully to avoid disappointment.

- Firm yet springy to the touch—a gentle pressure with 1 or 2 fingertips on the surface will give a good indication for the lighter cakes.
- Slight shrinkage from the sides of the cake pan—again, this applies to lighter cakes and sponges.

- Insertion of a very fine skewer through the thickest section of the cake—no moist cake mixture should remain on the skewer on removal from firmer or larger cakes. Note that cake mixture on the skewer is not to be confused with particles of dried fruits, etc., from the richer cakes and loaves.

If in doubt, leave a little longer. A slightly overcooked cake is better than one that sinks in the middle after removal from the oven.

Reasons for Unsuccessful Cakes
- *Cakes sinking in the middle*

Too much sugar, too little flour. Too much raising agent, too much liquid. Incompletely cooked.
- *Surface cracking on cakes*

Too much flour, too little liquid. Too high an oven temperature. Too small a cake pan.
- *Excessively moist or 'soggy' cakes*

Too much liquid, too much sugar. Ingredients insufficiently mixed. Too slow an oven temperature. Incompletely cooked.
- *Coarse cake texture*

Undermixing or overmixing of ingredients. Too much raising agent. Too much shortening (butter, margarine, etc).
- *Rising and sinking whilst in the oven*

Too much liquid, too much raising agent. Too frequent/too soon opening of the oven door. Slamming the oven door to close it.
- *Hard, crusty top and sides*

Oven temperature too hot. Cake is overbaked.
- *Sticky, moist top*

Cake is underbaked. Contains too much sugar. Paper or foil placed on top creates steaming.
- *Heavy, compact texture*

Too little raising agent. Too much mixing after flour addition. Ingredient balance needs adjustment.

Note: that apart from the above-mentioned problems which may account for unsuccessful cake-baking, there are two more points of utmost importance.
- Ingredient processing methods vary from country to country. For example, the method of chlorination of flour in America produces a product which is capable of absorbing more sugar and liquids than that of Australian flour. Sugar and shortening moisture ratios can differ and so cause cake-making failures, particularly in the sweeter chocolate cakes, etc.
- In some parts of America and Europe, the high altitude can affect the action of certain agents in cake-making. In such areas, the quantities of some ingredients may need to be altered—such as additional liquids, less raising agents, etc.

If in doubt as to whether a particular cake recipe in this book will be successful in your country and in your area, without alteration, experiment first with the Basic or Foundation Butter Cake (see page 76), rather than one of the more elaborate mixtures.

Cake-making Ingredients
Only the best-quality, fresh ingredients can make a good quality cake:
- Butter or margarine should not show any signs of rancidity or foreign odours or flavours from incorrect storage.
- Eggs should be fresh to produce the utmost volume. Store them in the refrigerator if necessary, but allow them time to warm to room temperature before use in cake-making.
- Sugars should have been correctly stored and not allowed to absorb extra moisture. Use the specified type for best results.
- Flours that are freshly packaged retain their correct moisture content. Self-raising flours kept too long lose some of their raising quality.
- Liquids, such as water, milk, fruit juices and wines, should be used at room temperature unless otherwise stated. Use accurate measures.
- Flavouring ingredients, such as ground spices, dried fruits, coffee, chocolate or cocoa, should be as fresh as possible. Experienced cake-makers can sometimes alter a recipe by varying these ingredients, being sure to substitute others of a similar type and texture.

All ingredients should be assembled, cake tins prepared and ovens set for preheating, if required, before commencing to mix a cake.

Freezing Cakes
Before the advent of the freezer, the life of a cake was limited to the time it was able to be kept fresh when stored in an airtight container. Storage in the home freezer has increased that life to 3 to 6 months or more, depending on the type of cake and its filling and/or frosting.

For most practical purposes it is easier to freeze and store unfilled and undecorated cakes. However, there are times when to freeze the complete cake is more convenient, such as the period before entertaining a large number of people.

Unfilled, undecorated cakes should be packaged whilst fresh (but not hot) in plastic film or freezer bags or good-quality aluminium foil, excluding as much air as possible before sealing, and frozen quickly so as to avoid the formation of too many ice crystals which may cause the cake to become overmoist on thawing.

Filled, frosted and decorated cakes should be placed uncovered in the freezer to freeze quickly; then, once firm, removed from the freezer, wrapped and sealed securely and returned to the freezer as quickly as possible for storage.

Uncooked cake batters may be frozen already prepared in the greased cake tin. To cook, unwrap the cake tin and place it in the refrigerator to partially defrost before baking in the oven.

Defrosting Frozen Cakes
Plain cakes should be unsealed and left at room temperature, with the wrapping loosened but not completely removed, for 1 to 3 hours according to size.

Filled and decorated cakes may be unwrapped and allowed to thaw in the refrigerator for several hours or overnight.

Microwave ovens, with a defrosting versatility, are extremely handy for the quick and easy

---

Right: Clockwise from top: Mediterranean Semolina Cake (see p. 97); Rich Mocha Cream Gâteau (see p. 100); Continental Cream Sponge (see p. 74).

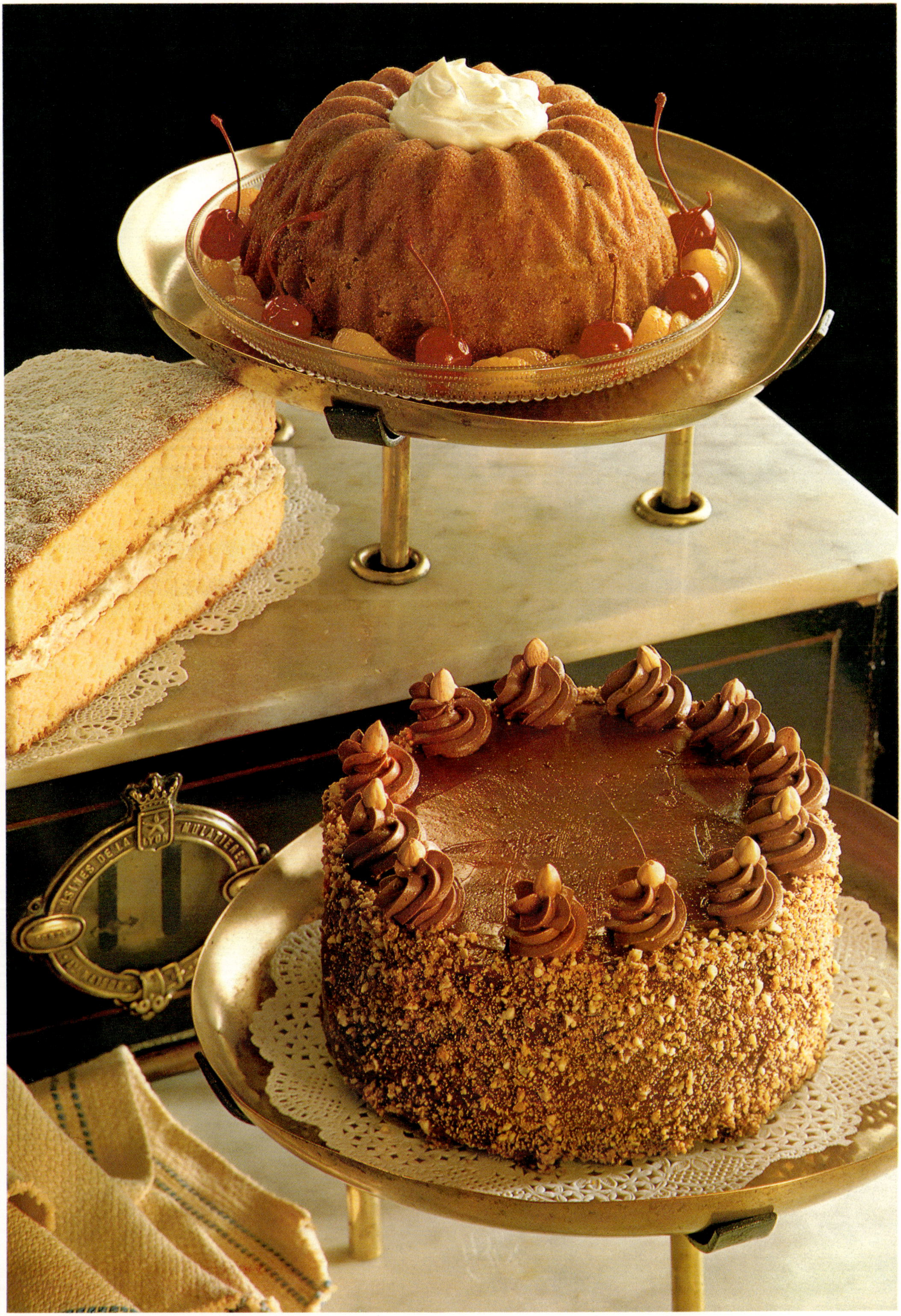

thawing of cakes. However, these are then likely to become stale more quickly unless eaten reasonably soon.

The most successful fillings and icings or frostings for freezer cakes are those with a reasonably high content of shortening (butter, margarine, etc.). Water icings tend to become brittle on thawing and unless properly thawed may cause moistness to develop immediately under the surface.

Quantity cake-baking, coupled with the use of a freezer for storing, is the most convenient and economical way to keep a supply of home-made confections on hand for use at short notice.

Covering the Cake with Icing

Rich fruit cakes made for various celebrations, such as weddings, birthdays, christenings and anniversaries, are usually covered with two types of icing:

- Almond or Mock Almond Paste (see recipes, page 133)—this undercoat or foundation icing not only provides the basic shape for the cake but also assists in adding flavour and longer keeping qualities.
- Fondant Covering Paste (see recipe, page 142)—

the outer or final covering icing is of primary importance, not only giving a professional finish to the cake but also providing a smooth, attractive background for the applied decorations. For those who prefer to dispense with the almond paste because of cost or personal taste, a double thickness (or one thicker layer) of fondant paste may be used. It is preferable to allow the undercoat to become firm and dry—a period of 2 to 3 days—before applying the final fondant covering.

After the cake has been stored, it is necessary for the following steps to be taken before covering:

- Carefully peel away the paper lining from the cake, taking particular care not to damage corners or edges.
- If the cake has risen slightly in a dome, cut it off with a sharp knife to level it and turn it upside down onto a board. The cake must sit firm and straight.
- Brush over the top and sides to remove any loose cake crumbs.
- Using small pieces of the almond paste (or fondant undercoat), patch up any cracks, holes or broken edges so that a good shape is produced for the final covering.
- Brush over the entire surface of the cake with lightly-beaten egg white, let it stand for 20 to 30 minutes, then brush over again and lift the cake onto a clean sheet of aluminium foil or greaseproof paper. The Almond or Mock Almond Paste and the Fondant Covering Paste can be made beforehand. Make up the mixture, adjusting the quantity as required. Keep almond paste and fondant paste in well-sealed airtight containers to prevent the surface drying. Just before use, knead until soft and pliable again.

The techniques for covering the cake apply to both almond paste and fondant paste:

- Measure the exterior of the cake with a ruler or flexible tape measure in one motion going up one side of the cake, across the top and down the other side, thus giving an approximate size for the covering.
- Roll out the paste to a round or square shape slightly smaller than the measurement obtained—the paste will stretch slightly when it is placed on the cake. Lift the paste continually from the board so that it does not stick underneath. If using sifted icing (confectioners') sugar on the board, use as little as possible because it may make the paste too firm and dry.
- Carefully lift the paste onto the prepared cake, using a rolling pin for assistance in centering the paste so that it falls evenly down the sides of the cake.
- Dust the palms of each hand with icing sugar. Commencing on the top of the cake, smooth the paste over the cake with a light swirling motion.
- Cup the palms and smooth the paste over the edge and sides, paying particular attention to the corners of square cakes. Avoid putting too much pressure on the paste, as this will cause it to stretch and handmarks to become visible (lengthy fingernails and heavily-ringed fingers can cause problems!).
- Trim away any excess paste at the base of the cake with a large sharp knife. Brush away any excess icing sugar and paste crumbs from around the base (not over the cake).
- Set aside to dry for 2 to 3 days before applying the final coating.

The techniques above apply to both almond paste and fondant paste. Extra points for fondant covering:

- After rolling out the paste on a lightly-coated board, carefully prick any air bubbles in the surface with a very fine needle. Smooth over gently.
- Once the fondant paste has been lifted on to the cake, a light dusting of cornflour on the palms of the hands before smoothing over will give an extra smoothness and shine to the surface.
- After the fondant paste has dried sufficiently, remove the cake from its foil or paper base and lift it onto its final plate or foil-covered board ready for decoration. To prevent slipping during movement and/or transport, spread a little Royal Icing under the cake (see recipe, page 130).

Decorations for Celebration Cakes

Decorations on celebration cakes are a matter of choice, depending mainly on the availability and expertise of professional or amateur assistance.

For hand-made decorations two types of icing can be used:

- Modelling Fondant (see recipe, page 142)—
A smooth pliable dough-paste used for hand-modelling flowers, leaves, etc., to be used as the decorative feature on the cake.
- Royal Icing (see recipe, page 130)—
The thin smooth icing which is filled into a piping bag with shaped nozzles for simple or elaborate pipework, and small flower and leaf designs.

SPONGES

Ginger Layer Cake

1 cup (4 oz) flour
pinch salt
4 eggs
¾ cup (5 oz) caster (powdered) sugar
5–6 lumps loaf sugar
2 oranges
1½ cups (12fl oz) cream
½ cup glacé ginger, thinly sliced

Prepare baking trays by brushing with oil then dusting with flour. Mark a 20 cm (8 inch) circle on each, using a plate or saucepan lid as a guide. Set oven temperature at 190°C (375°F/Gas 5).

Sift the flour with the salt. Break the eggs into a bowl and beat in the sugar gradually. Continue whisking until the mixture is thick and mousse-like. Using a large metal spoon cut and fold the sifted flour into the mixture.

To make the six layers of cake, spread equal amounts of the mixture over each of the six circles on the prepared trays. Bake for 5 to 8 minutes or until the cakes are pale golden in colour. Ease off the trays with a spatula onto wire racks. The trick is to be quick before the mixture sets on the trays.

Rub the loaf sugar over the skin of the oranges until well impregnated. Squeeze the oranges. Pound the sugar to a syrup with 1 to 2 tablespoons of the juice. Whip the cream and sweeten with orange syrup. Sandwich together the layers of cake with orange cream and sliced ginger. Decorate with extra whipped cream and ginger slices.

Swiss (Jelly) Roll

¾ cup (3 oz) self-raising flour
pinch salt
3 eggs
¾ cup (4½ oz) caster (powdered) sugar
1 tablespoon hot water
3–4 tablespoons warm jam
caster (powdered) sugar for dredging
whipped cream

Grease a 38 × 28 × 2.5 cm (15 × 11 × 1 in) Swiss (jelly) roll tin and line with greased greaseproof paper. Set oven temperature at 200°C (400°F/Gas 6). Sift the flour with the salt. Place the eggs and sugar in a bowl and stand over a pan of gently simmering, not boiling water. Whisk well until the mixture is very thick and creamy.

Remove the bowl from the heat and continue whisking until the mixture is cool. Fold in the flour as lightly as possible then the hot water. Pour the mixture into the prepared tin. Bake for 7 to 10 minutes until pale golden. Do not overcook as it makes rolling up difficult.

Quickly turn the sponge out onto a tea towel, well sprinkled with caster sugar. Trim off the crisp edges, roll in the towel, cool then unroll.

Spread with jam and whipped cream. roll up. Sprinkle with a little more caster sugar before serving.

Spiced Honey Sponge

Makes 1 layered sponge cake

3 eggs, separated
½ cup (4 oz) caster (powdered) sugar
1 teaspoon vanilla essence
¾ cup (3 oz) self raising flour
2 tablespoons cornflour (cornstarch)
1 teaspoon mixed spices
¼ teaspoon salt
¼ cup (2fl oz) milk, scalding hot
1 tablespoon (1 oz) honey
15 g (½ oz) butter
whipped sweetened cream, for filling
icing (confectioners') sugar, for topping
mixed spices, for topping

Preheat the oven to 180°C (350°F/Gas 4). Grease and flour two 18 cm (7 in) sandwich tins.

Beat the egg whites until stiff peaks form; gradually add the sugar, beating well after each addition, Then fold the egg yolks and vanilla essence through.

Sift the dry ingredients twice. Then sift this again over the egg mixture, and fold through very lightly.

Combine the milk, honey and butter. Slowly pour this down the side of the bowl into the egg-flour mixture, folding in very lightly. Pour into the prepared sandwich tins.

Bake for 22 to 25 minutes. Remove from the oven and allow to stand for 1 to 2 minutes before carefully turning out onto a fine mesh cake rack to cool.

When cold, join the two layers with the whipped cream, and dust the top with sifted icing sugar and mixed spices in desired proportions.

Blue Ribbon Sponge Sandwich

Makes 2 sponge layers

---
3 eggs

½ cup (4 oz) caster (powdered) sugar
---
1 cup (4 oz) flour
---
1 tablespoon cornflour (cornstarch)
---
2 teaspoons baking powder

¼ teaspoon salt
---
2 teaspoons butter or margarine

¼ cup (2fl oz) very hot water

½ teaspoon vanilla essence

Preheat the oven to 180°C (350°F/Gas 4). Grease two deep 18 cm (7 in) sandwich tins and dust lightly with flour.

Separate the eggs and place the whites in a clean, dry, preferably glass bowl; beat with an electric beater, hand-beater or egg whisk to stiff white foam. Add the caster sugar, 1 tablespoon at a time and beat well after each addition—the sugar must be completely dissolved. Fold in the egg yolks lightly and gently.

Sift the flour with the cornflour, baking powder and salt twice. Then sift this again over the egg mixture. (Don't mix it in yet.)

Melt the butter in the hot water, add the vanilla essence, and carefully pour down the side of the bowl into the egg mixture. Now, using a metal spoon and with a gentle folding motion, mix the dry ingredients and the liquid through the eggs and sugar. Pour the mixture gently into the two sandwich tins, being careful to avoid harshly knocking or banging either the bowl or the tins. Spread lightly to even the surface.

Bake for 22 to 25 minutes, preferably both tins on the same oven shelf so that both sponges will be evenly cooked and browned. Remove from the oven and allow to stand for 1 minute—out of a draught—then turn carefully onto a fine mesh cake rack or a tea towel over a cake rack to cool.

Topping and Filling Variations:
Plain Sponge: Fill with raspberry jam and dust the top with sifted icing (confectioners') sugar.

Cream Sponge: Fill with fresh whipped cream or Mock Cream (see recipe, page 140) and dust the top with icing sugar.

Lemon Sponge: Fill with Lemon Butter Cream (see recipe, page 145) and dust the top with icing sugar.

Toffee Sponge: Fill and top the sponge with fresh whipped cream and decorate with Toffee Topping (see recipe, page 138).

Strawberry Sponge: Fill and top with fresh whipped cream and decorate the top with whole or sliced strawberries.

Passionfruit: Fill with Mock Cream (see recipe, page 140) and cover the top with Passionfruit-flavoured Warm Glacé Icing (see recipe, page 130).

Continental Cream Sponge

Makes 1 layered cake

---
2 eggs
---
1 cup (8 oz) caster (powdered) sugar, slightly warmed
---
1 teaspoon vanilla essence
---
2 cups (8 oz) flour
---
2 teaspoons baking powder

¼ teaspoon salt
---
300 ml (10fl oz) thick cream, lightly whipped

Hungarian Hazelnut Filling (see recipe, page 140)
---
icing (confectioners') sugar, for topping

Preheat the oven to 160°C (325°F/Gas 3). Grease and flour a slab tin 23 cm (9 in) square.

Beat the eggs until very frothy. Gradually add the warmed caster sugar, beating each addition until well dissolved and then add the vanilla essence with the last addition of sugar.

Sift the flour, baking powder and salt together. Sift about half of this over the egg-sugar mixture and fold through gently. Add about half of the lightly-whipped cream and fold through gently. Repeat the flour and cream addition with the remaining mixtures—do not overmix. Spoon into the slab tin.

Bake for 55 to 60 minutes. Turn out carefully onto a cake rack to cool.

When cold, cut in half and sandwich together with the Hungarian Hazelnut Filling between the layers; dust sifted icing sugar over the top. Chill slightly, before serving in slices.

Right: **Blue Ribbon Sponge Sandwich** (see above).

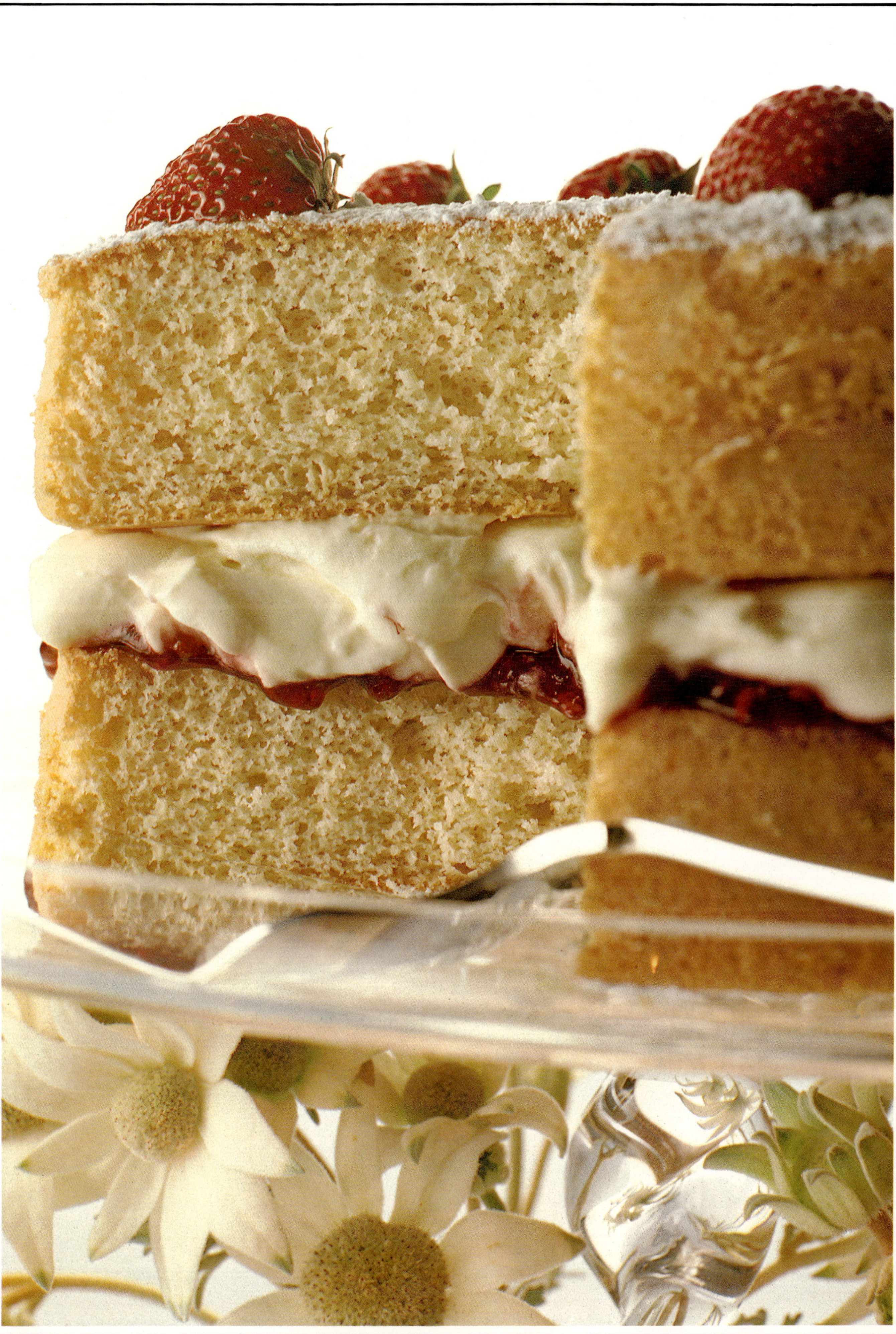

BUTTER CAKES

Basic or Foundation Butter Cake

The basic butter cake has a standard list of ingredients. However, by varying the proportions of the ingredients, different textures can be achieved.

Commonly known as the 4, 4, 8 cake, this makes a firm cake which is ideal for cutting into shapes for novelty cakes, patty cakes, fruit additions, etc.

125 g (4 oz) butter or margarine, softened
½ cup (4 oz) sugar
1 teaspoon vanilla essence
2 eggs
2 cups (8 oz) self-raising flour
¼ teaspoon salt
½ cup (4fl oz) milk

Commonly known as the 4, 6, 8 cake, this makes a softer cake more suited to larger cakes, loaves, layer cakes, etc., which require longer keeping qualities.

125 g (4 oz) butter or margarine, softened
¾ cup (6 oz) caster (powdered) sugar
1 teaspoon vanilla essence
3 eggs
2 cups (8 oz) self-raising flour
¼ teaspoon salt
¼ cup (2fl oz) milk

The mixing methods are the same. Either can be made for the following sized cake tins, and the baking temperatures and times vary according to the size (and depth) of cake and added flavouring ingredients.

Two 18 cm (7 in) sandwich tins:
  180°C (350°F/Gas 4) for 25 to 30 minutes.
One 28 × 18 cm (11 × 7 in) or 23 cm (9 in) slab tin:
  180°C (350°F/Gas 4) for 40 to 45 minutes.
One 18–20 cm (7–8 in) ring tin:
  180°C (350°F/Gas 4) for 35 to 40 minutes.
Two 24 × 6 cm (9½ × 2½ in) bar tins:
  180°C (350°F/Gas 4) for 30 to 35 minutes.
One 23 × 12 cm (9 × 4½ in) deep-sided loaf tin:
  160°C (325°F/Gas 3) for 55 to 60 minutes.
One 20 cm (8 in) deep-sided cake tin:
  160°C (325°F/Gas 3) for 55 to 60 minutes.
Twenty-four small or twenty large patty pans:
  190°C (375°F/Gas 5) for 15 to 17 minutes.

Preheat the oven to the temperature specified for the size of the cake tin. Grease the cake tin(s) well.

Beat the butter and sugar with the vanilla until light and creamy. Add the eggs one at a time, beating well after each addition.

Sift the flour and salt together. Sift and fold into the butter-sugar-eggs mixture in alternate batches with the milk, adding about a third of each at a time; mix lightly but thoroughly.

Spoon into the greased cake tin(s) and bake in the preheated oven according to temperature and times above. Remove from the oven and allow to stand for 3 to 7 minutes before turning out onto a cake rack to cool.

Flavoured Variations:
Chocolate:
Before mixing, heat the milk and add 2 tablespoons of cocoa to it. Allow to cool before use.
Mocha:
Before mixing, heat the milk and add 2 tablespoons of cocoa and 1 teaspoon of instant coffee powder (or coffee essence). Allow to cool before use.
Sultana:
Add ⅓–½ cup (2-4 oz) sultanas and 1 teaspoon mixed spices with the flour.
Cherry Almond:
Add 2 tablespoons of chopped glacé cherries and 2 tablespoons of slivered almonds with the flour.
Date:
Add ⅓–½ cup (2-4 oz) of chopped dates and 1 teaspoon grated lemon rind with the flour.
Banana:
Add ¾–1 cup (6-8 oz) of mashed banana with the flour and 1 teaspoon of bicarbonate of soda (baking soda) dissolved in the milk.
Orange:
Add 2 teaspoons of grated orange rind with the flour and substitute orange juice for the milk.
Coconut:
Add ⅓–½ cup (2-4 oz) of desiccated coconut with the flour and an extra 1–2 tablespoons of milk.

Marble Cake:
Divide the cake mixture into three portions. Add 2 tablespoons of melted chocolate to one portion; colour the second portion with pink food colouring; and leave the third portion plain.

Spoon alternate portions into the prepared deep-sided cake tin and swirl lightly with a skewer or fine knife blade to produce a marbled effect. Bake as above.

Rainbow Cake:
Prepare 2 quantities of cake mixture. Grease three 20 cm (8 in) sandwich tins.

Divide the cake mixture into three portions. To one portion, add 2 tablespoons of cocoa which has been dissolved in 3 tablespoons of hot milk or water and allowed to cool; colour the second portion with pink food colouring and add 1 teaspoon of strawberry essence; and leave the third portion plain.

Place each portion into one of the prepared cake tins and bake as above.

When cold, sandwich together in chocolate, pink and white formation, using jams (jelly) as the filling. Ice with Warm Glacé Icing (see recipe, page 130).

Continental Butter Ring Cake

Makes 1 fluted ring cake

250 g (8 oz) unsalted butter, chopped
3 eggs, separated
1 cup (8 oz) sugar, very slightly warmed
1½ tablespoons brandy
⅞ cup (7 fl oz) milk
2 cups (8 oz) flour
3 teaspoons baking powder
½ cup (2 oz) drinking chocolate powder
icing (confectioners') sugar, for topping

Preheat the oven to 160°C (325°F/Gas 3). Grease and flour a 20 cm (8 in) fluted ring tin.

Heat the butter until fully melted and commencing to colour slightly; remove from the heat and set aside to cool.

Beat the egg whites in a clean dry bowl, preferably glass, until stiff peaks form. Beat the egg yolks and fold them in, then add the sugar and brandy and beat for 5 to 6 minutes.

Sift the flour and baking powder together, then sift again over the egg mixture and fold through very lightly—do not overmix. Spoon half of the mixture into the fluted ring tin.

Sift the drinking chocolate over the remaining mixture and fold through very lightly. Spoon this into the ring tin; and with a fine skewer, swirl the two mixtures to produce a marbled effect.

Bake for about 1¼ hours. Remove from the oven and allow to stand for 3 to 4 minutes; then turn onto a cake rack to cool.

Dust liberally with sifted icing sugar before serving.

Classic Madeira Butter Cake

Makes 1 cake

250 g (8 oz) butter or margarine, softened
1 cup (8 oz) caster (powdered) sugar
1 teaspoon vanilla essence
4 eggs
2 cups (8 oz) flour
1½ teaspoons baking powder
2 tablespoons (1 oz) chopped mixed peel
extra 1 tablespoon sugar, for topping

Preheat the oven to 160°C (325°F/Gas 3). Line the base of a deep-sided 20 cm (8 in) cake tin and grease it well.

Beat the butter and sugar with the vanilla essence until very light and fluffy. Add the eggs one at a time, beating well between each addition. Sift the flour and baking powder over the mixture and stir gently to mix through. Spoon into the cake tin, and scatter the chopped peel and extra sugar evenly over the top.

Bake for 1¼ to 1½ hours. Remove from the oven and allow to stand for 8 to 10 minutes before turning out onto a wire cake rack to cool.

Note: Some recipes instruct that the mixed peel should be scattered over the surface of the cake about 30 minutes before the cake is finished baking. If this is desired, care must be taken to do this quickly without removing the cake from the oven, or there is a considerable risk of the cake sinking in the centre.

One Bowl Butter Cake Supreme

Makes 1 cake

1 cup (4 oz) self-raising flour
¼ cup (1 oz) custard powder
¼ teaspoon salt
1 cup (8 oz) caster (powdered) sugar
2 eggs
½ cup (4 fl oz) milk
1 teaspoon vanilla essence
125 g (4 oz) butter, softened

Preheat the oven to 160°C (325°F/Gas 3). Line and grease a deep-sided 18 cm (7 in) cake tin.

Sift the flour, custard powder, salt and caster sugar into a large bowl; make a well in the centre and break in the eggs. Add the milk, vanilla essence and butter, and beat for 8 to 10 minutes (if using an electric mixer, set on medium speed) until the mixture is very smooth. Pour into the cake tin.

Bake for 1¼ hours. Remove from the oven and allow to stand for 3 to 4 minutes before turning out carefully onto a cake rack to cool. When cold, ice and decorate as desired.

Variations:
Citrus: Add 2 teaspoons of grated orange or lemon rind to the dry ingredients.
Choc-Coffee: Add 2 tablespoons of cocoa and 1 teaspoon of instant coffee powder to the dry ingredients, plus 1 extra tablespoon of milk.

Rich Chocolate Butter Cake

Makes 1 cake

---
5 cm (2 in) strip of vanilla pod

½ cup (4fl oz) milk, hot
---
185 g (6 oz) pure cooking chocolate, chopped
---
185 g (6 oz) butter, softened

¾ cup (6 oz) caster (powdered) sugar
---
4 eggs, separated
---
1 cup (4 oz) flour

½ cup (2 oz) cornflour (cornstarch)
---
1 teaspoon baking powder

½ teaspoon bicarbonate of soda (baking soda)

Frosting:
1 block (4 oz) fruit and nut chocolate
---
30 g (1 oz) butter

¼ cup evaporated milk

½ cup (3 oz) icing (confectioners') sugar, sifted

Infuse the vanilla pod in the hot milk for 30 minutes. Preheat the oven to 180°C (350°F/Gas 4). Line the base of a deep-sided 20 cm (8 in) cake tin, and grease it well.

Discard the vanilla pod, and add the chocolate to the now vanilla-flavoured milk. Over a very low heat, stir in 30 g (1 oz) of the butter until well blended. Allow to cool.

Beat the remaining butter with the sugar until light and fluffy. Add the cooled chocolate mixture and beat well. Add the egg yolks one at a time and mix in lightly.

Sift the dry ingredients together, then sift them over the butter-chocolate mixture and fold in lightly. Beat the egg whites until they form stiff peaks then gently fold into the mixture—do not overmix. Turn into the cake tin.

Bake for 60 to 80 minutes. Remove from the oven and allow to stand for 5 to 6 minutes before carefully turning out onto a cake rack to cool.

When cold, wrap a 'collar' of greaseproof paper around the cake, allowing the top edge of the paper to stand about 2.5 cm (1 in) above the surface of the cake.

Frosting: Chop the block of chocolate into small pieces, and melt it with the butter in a heatproof basin placed over hot—not boiling—water. Remove from the heat, and stir in the evaporated milk and icing sugar. Quickly pour onto the top of the cake. Allow the frosting to set before removing the greaseproof paper. Stand overnight before cutting into slices.

Almond Butter Ring

Makes 1 fluted ring cake

¼ cup (1 oz) flaked almonds, for coating
---
250 g (8 oz) butter, softened

2½ cups (16 oz) caster (powdered) sugar
---
1 teaspoon vanilla essence

½ teaspoon almond essence
---
5 eggs

2½ cups (10 oz) flour

½ teaspoon baking powder

½ teaspoon bicarbonate of soda (baking soda)

¼ teaspoon salt

¾ cup (6fl oz) sour cream.

Preheat the oven to 160°C (325°F/Gas 3). Well grease a 23 cm (9 in) fluted ring cake tin and scatter the almonds over the surface, pressing on lightly; dust a little flour over all, shaking out all surplus.

Beat the butter, caster sugar, vanilla essence and almond essence until very light and frothy. Add the eggs one at a time, beating well after each addition

Sift the dry ingredients together, then sift over the butter-egg mixture and fold in. Add the sour cream and fold through lightly but thoroughly. Spoon the cake mixture into the prepared cake tin.

Bake for 1½–1¾ hours. Remove from the oven and allow to stand for 5 to 6 minutes before turning out onto a cake rack to cool.

If desired dust the cake lightly with sifted icing (confectioners') sugar before serving.

Right: Clockwise from top right: Almond Butter Ring (see above); Rich Chocolate Butter Cake (see above); Frosted Banana Cream Cake (see p. 80).

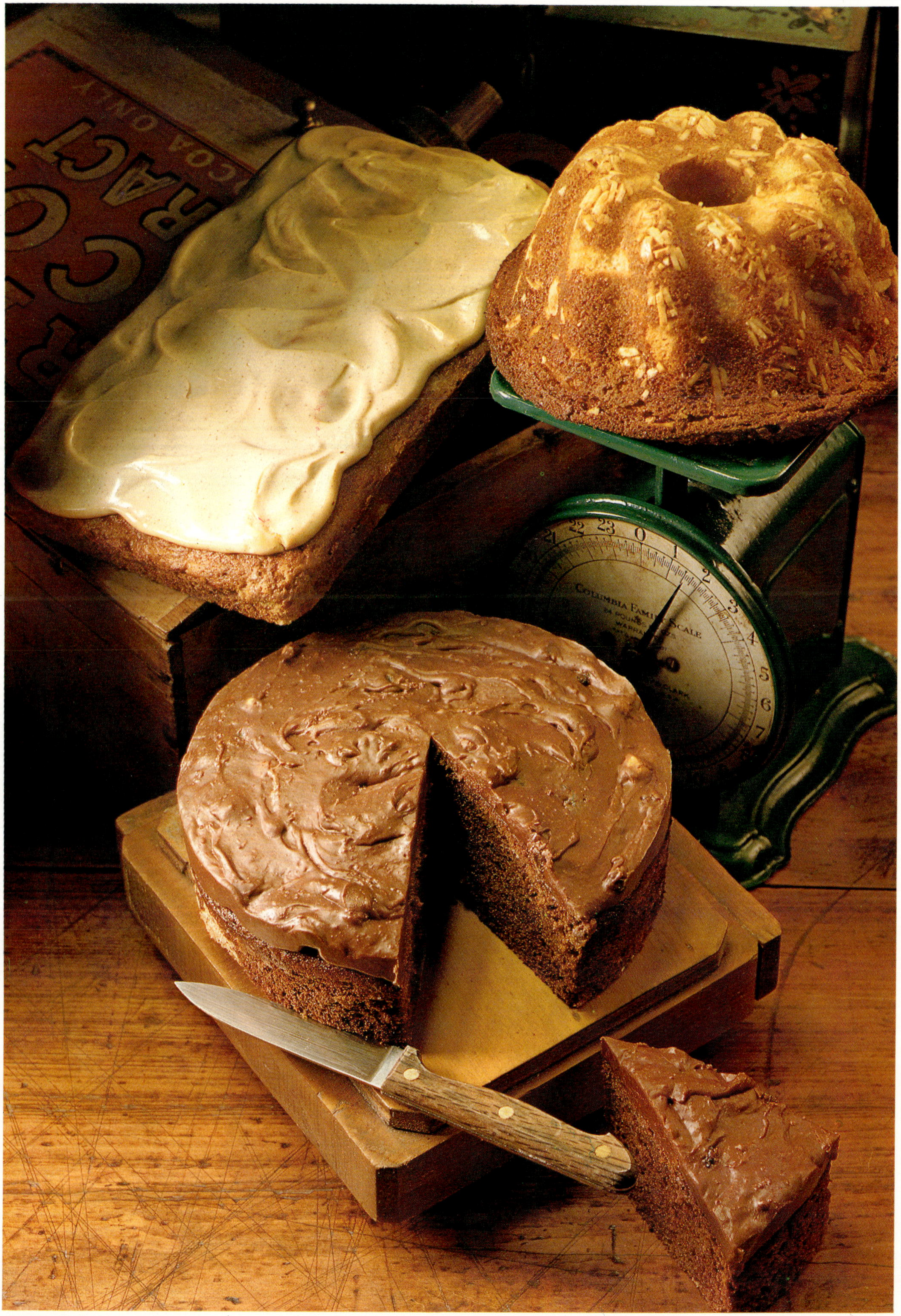

Cherry Crystal Ring

Makes 1 ring cake

---
90 g (3 oz) butter or margarine, softened

½ cup (4 oz) sugar
---
2 eggs

1½ cups (6 oz) self-raising flour, sifted

½ packet (2 oz) cherry-flavoured jelly crystals

½ cup (4fl oz) milk

Warm Glacé Icing (see recipe, page 130)

¼ cup (1½ oz) sliced glacé cherries

¼ cup (1½ oz) desiccated coconut, coloured pink

Preheat the oven to 180°C (350°F/Gas 4). Thoroughly grease a 20 cm (8 in) ring tin.

Beat the butter and sugar until creamy. Add the eggs one at a time, beating well after each addition. Fold in alternate batches of sifted flour, jelly crystals and milk, about a third of each at a time; mix lightly but thoroughly. Spoon into the ring tin.

Bake for 35 to 40 minutes. Remove from the oven and allow to stand for 2 to 3 minutes, then turn out onto a cake rack to cool.

When cold, ice with the Warm Glacé Icing and decorate with the cherry slices and coconut. If desired, the remaining ½ packet of cherry-flavoured jelly crystals may be used instead of the pink coconut.

Cherry Seed Cake

Makes 1 fluted ring cake

---
250 g (8 oz) butter or margarine, softened

¼ teaspoon salt (optional)

1½ cups (6 oz) flour
---
4 eggs, separated
---
1 cup (8 oz) caster (powdered) sugar

1–2 tablespoons caraway seeds

⅔ cup (4 oz) glacé cherries
---
extra ⅔ cup (2½ oz) flour
---
1 teaspoon baking powder

Warm-Glacé Icing (see recipe, page 130)

Preheat the oven to 160°C (325°F/Gas 3). Thoroughly grease and flour a 20–23 cm (8–9 in) fluted ring tin.

In a large bowl, beat the butter until creamy, adding the salt if desired. Gradually add the sifted flour, beating well after each addition.

Beat the egg whites until stiff, gradually add the sugar, beating well. Add the egg yolks and caraway seeds and beat for 1 to 2 minutes. Very lightly and gently, combine this into the butter-flour mixture. Slice the cherries into 3–4 rings, and fold through.

Sift the extra flour with the baking powder, then sift over the mixture in the bowl and fold in carefully. Spoon into the well-greased and floured fluted ring tin.

Bake for 75 to 80 minutes. Remove from the oven and allow to stand for 4 to 5 minutes before turning onto a wire cake rack to cool.

When cold, drizzle the Warm-Glacé Icing over, allowing it to run down between the flutes or grooves in the cake.

Frosted Banana Cream Cake

Makes 1 cake

---
125 g (4 oz) butter or margarine, softened
---
1 cup (8 oz) sugar
---
1 teaspoon vanilla essence

½ teaspoon ground cinnamon (or nutmeg)
---
2 eggs, beaten
---
1 cup mashed ripe banana

¼ cup (2fl oz) milk
---
2 cups (8 oz) flour

1½ teaspoons baking powder
---
1 teaspoon bicarbonate of soda (baking soda)

¼ teaspoon salt

¼ cup (1 oz) chopped walnuts

Cinnamon Cream Frosting:
1 cup (8fl oz) sour cream

¼ cup (1½ oz) brown sugar

½–1 teaspoon ground cinnamon (or nutmeg)

Preheat the oven to 180°C (350°F/Gas 4). Line and grease a slab tin 28 × 18 cm (11 × 7 in).

Beat the butter, sugar, vanilla essence and cinnamon (or nutmeg) until light and fluffy. Add the eggs, then the mashed banana and milk, beating well between each addition.

Sift the dry ingredients together, then sift over the butter-banana mixture and fold in. Add the walnuts and mix through. Turn into the slab tin.

Bake for 35 to 40 minutes. Remove from the oven and allow to stand for 5 to 6 minutes before turning out onto a cake rack to cool.

Frosting: Combine all the ingredients, beating well. Spread over the cake and allow to firm before slicing.

California Orange Cake

Makes 1 cake

125 g (4 oz) butter or margarine, softened
1 cup (8 oz) sugar
1 egg, beaten
½ teaspoon vanilla essence
2 cups (8 oz) flour
1 teaspoon baking powder
1 teaspoon bicarbonate of soda (baking soda)
¼ teaspoon salt
1 teaspoon ground cinnamon
1 cup (8fl oz) sour milk
1 large orange, just ripe
1 cup (4 oz) chopped walnuts or pecans
1 cup (5 oz) sultanas
½–¾ cup (1½–2 oz) flaked or desiccated coconut, for topping

Preheat the oven to 180°C (350°F/Gas 4). Line the base of a cake tin 23 cm (9 in) square, and grease well.

Beat the butter and sugar until creamy. Add the egg and vanilla essence, and beat well.

Sift the dry ingredients together, then sift again over the butter cream and fold in, alternately with the sour milk.

Peel the orange, removing as much of the white pith as possible; chop very finely and mix in a bowl with the chopped nuts and sultanas. With a slotted spoon, spoon out one-quarter to one-third of this mixture and mix it into the cake mixture, folding lightly. To the remaining orange-nuts-sultana mixture, add the coconut, and set aside until after baking.

Spoon the cake mixture into the cake tin, and bake for 40 to 45 minutes. Remove from the oven and allow to stand for 5 minutes.

Preheat the griller (broiler). Carefully spread the reserved orange-nuts-sultanas mixture over the top of the cake, and place under the griller to toast lightly. Remove from heat and allow to stand for a further 5 minutes. Then carefully turn out onto a cake rack which has been covered with greaseproof paper; reverse the cake to top side uppermost and allow to cool.

CHOCOLATE AND COFFEE CAKES

The name Coffee Cake can have two interpretations.
1. A butter-cake mixture which is flavoured with coffee: strong coffee liquid prepared from grains or instant coffee powder; liquid coffee essence available in bottles or coffee flavoured essence which may replace vanilla essence.
2. A simple butter-cake or tea bread which is finished with a crumbly topping made from a mixture of butter, flour, brown sugar and spices. This combination is coarsely sprinkled over the cake mixture before baking and forms an attractive flavoursome 'ready-made icing'.

Because this style of cake was quickly and easily made it was considered ideal to serve with morning coffee, so it became known as Coffee Cake.

Aunty Mary's Chocolate Roll

In this recipe, the ingredients list employs a very old system of measurement. The weight of the butter, the sugar, and the flour should each equal the weight of the two eggs used.

Makes 1 roll

2 eggs
equal their weight in: butter (or margarine), sugar, flour
1 teaspoon baking powder
1 tablespoon cocoa
1 teaspoon vanilla essence
2 tablespoons warm water
sugar and cocoa, for rolling and topping
Mock Cream Filling (see recipe, page 140)

Preheat the oven to 200°c (400°F/Gas 6). Line and grease a 30 × 25 cm (12 × 10 in) swiss roll tin (jelly roll pan).

Separate the eggs. Beat the butter and sugar to a cream, add the egg yolks and beat well.

Sift the flour, baking powder and cocoa three times; add to the butter cream and fold in. Then add the combined vanilla essence and warm water, and fold this in also.

Whisk the egg whites to soft peaks and fold very gently through the cake mixture—do not overmix. Turn into the prepared tin. Bake for 17 to 20 minutes.

Immerse a clean cloth in boiling water, wring it out and lay it on the work bench. Cover it with greaseproof paper, then sprinkle sugar over the surface of the paper. Turn the chocolate roll out of the tin onto the paper and peel away the lining. Carefully roll the cake in the paper; cover it loosely with the hot cloth and allow to cool.

When cold, unroll it and discard the paper. Spread the Mock Cream Filling, re-roll and dust with combined sugar and cocoa.

Sherried Chocolate Ring

(Photograph below)

Makes 1 fluted ring cake

½ cup (4 fl oz) boiling water

½ cup (2 oz) chopped dried apricots

½ cup (3 oz) chopped raisins

¼ cup (2 fl oz) sweet sherry

125 g (4 oz) butter or margarine, softened

¾ cup (6 oz) caster (powdered) sugar

2 eggs

90 g (3 oz) pure cooking chocolate, melted

2 cups (8 oz) self-raising flour

¼ teaspoon salt

¼ teaspoon bicarbonate of soda (baking soda)

½ cup (4 fl oz) milk

Honeyed Chocolate Frosting (see recipe, page 137)

Pour the boiling water over the apricots in a bowl; allow to stand a few minutes, then pour off the liquid. Add the raisins and sweet sherry to the apricots, and set aside for 1 hour.

Preheat the oven to 160°C (325°F/Gas 3). Thoroughly grease and flour a 20 cm (8 in) fluted ring tin.

Beat the butter and sugar until creamy. Add the eggs one at a time, beating well after each addition, then beat the cooled chocolate through. Sift the dry ingredients over the butter-chocolate mixture; fold through lightly. Then add the apricot-raisin mixture and the milk, and fold in lightly but thoroughly to combine. Spoon into the fluted ring tin.

Bake for 55 to 60 minutes. Remove from the oven and allow to stand for 5 to 6 minutes before turning out onto a cake rack to cool.

When cold, drizzle the Honeyed Chocolate Frosting over the top and allow it to run unevenly down the flutes or grooves in the cake.

LARGE CAKES

Whisked Chocolate Slice

Photograph (below)

Makes 1 cake

1½ cups (6 oz) flour
2 tablespoons (½ oz) cocoa
¾ cup (6 oz) sugar
¼ teaspoon salt
1 teaspoon baking powder
⅓ cup maize oil
1 tablespoon vinegar
1 teaspoon vanilla essence
1 cup (8 fl oz) water, just lukewarm
Chocolate Butter Cream (see recipe, page 144)

Preheat the oven to 180°C (350°F/Gas 4). Line and grease a 23 cm (9 in) slab tin.

Sift the flour, cocoa, sugar, salt and baking powder twice, then sift into the mixing bowl and make a well in the centre.

Mix the oil and vinegar with the vanilla essence and water, and beat to combine. Pour into the flour-cocoa mixture. Using a flat egg whisk, beat as quickly and lightly as possible to combine—do not 'overbeat'. Turn into the prepared slab tin.

Bake for 30 to 35 minutes or until springy to the touch. Remove from the oven and allow to stand for 5 to 6 minutes before turning out onto a cake rack to cool.

Cover with Chocolate Butter Cream and, when set, cut into slices or shapes for serving.

Special Crusted Chocolate Cake

(Photograph below)

Makes 1 deep cake

125 g (4 oz) butter or margarine, softened
1⅔ cup (9 oz) brown sugar
2 eggs, separated
125 g (4 oz) pure cooking chocolate, melted
1 cup (6 oz) chopped raisins
2½ cups (10 oz) flour
3 teaspoons baking powder
½ teaspoon cinnamon
½ cup (4 fl oz) sour milk
¼ cup (2 fl oz) brandy, warmed
1–2 tablespoons white sugar, for topping

Preheat the oven to 180°C (350°F/Gas 4). Line and grease a deep-sided 20 cm (8 in) cake tin.

Beat the butter and 1⅓ cups (7 oz) of the sugar until light and fluffy.

Beat the egg yolks with the remaining ⅓ cup (2 oz) of sugar, then beat the two mixtures together. Add the cooled chocolate and the raisins, and mix thoroughly.

Sift the dry ingredients together.

Combine the sour milk and brandy. Add alternate batches of the milk-brandy and flour mixtures to the butter-chocolate mixture.

Beat the egg whites until soft peaks form, and fold very lightly into the cake mixture—do not overmix. Spoon into the cake tin and sprinkle the white sugar over the top.

Bake in the preheated oven for 40 minutes, then lower the temperature slightly and bake for a further 40 to 45 minutes. Remove from the oven and allow to stand for 8 to 10 minutes before carefully turning out onto a cake rack to cool.

Carribean Coffee Cake

Makes 2 filled cakes

1½ cups (12 oz) sugar
¾ cup (6fl oz) boiling water
185 g (6 oz) butter or margarine, softened
1 teaspoon rum essence
3 eggs, separated
3 cups (12 oz) flour
3 teaspoons baking powder
¼ teaspoon salt
2 tablespoons (½ oz) full-cream milk powder
½ cup water, just lukewarm
whipped sweetened cream, for filling
icing (confectioners') sugar, for topping

Preheat the oven to 180°C (350°F/Gas 4). Line and grease two 20 cm (8 in) cake tins.

In a small, heavy-based saucepan, place ½ cup (4 oz) of the sugar and heat slowly, stirring constantly until the sugar has dissolved; discontinue stirring and allow the sugar to heat until a rich brown syrup forms and begins to smoke. This will take 7 to 10 minutes.

Remove from the heat and carefully, very gradually stir the boiling water through; set aside to cool and measure out ½ cup (4fl oz), discarding the remainder.

Beat the butter with the remaining 1 cup (8 oz) of sugar and the rum essence until creamy. Add the egg yolks one at a time, beating well after each addition.

Sift the flour, baking powder and salt together. Into the butter-sugar-egg mixture, fold in alternate batches of the flour mixture and the cooled syrup-water.

Beat the egg whites until soft peaks form, and gently fold into the cake mixture. Spoon into the two cake tins.

Bake for 25 to 30 minutes. Remove from the oven and allow to stand for 1 to 2 minutes before carefully turning out onto fine mesh cake racks to cool. When cold, cut each cake in half horizontally. Rejoin with a whipped cream filling, and dust sifted icing sugar over the top.

Chocolate Fudge Cake

Makes 1 layered cake.

90 g (3 oz) pure dark cooking chocolate, chopped
185 g (6 oz) butter or margarine, softened
1½ cups (8 oz) brown sugar
1 teaspoon vanilla essence
3 eggs
1 cup (8fl oz) sour cream
2 tablespoons (½ oz) cocoa
½ cup (4fl oz) hot water
1 tablespoon plum jam (plum jelly)
2½ cups (10 oz) self-raising flour
2½ cups (20fl oz) cream, whipped
Chocolate Caraque (see below)

Preheat the oven to 180°C (350°F/Gas 4). Base-line two 23 cm (9 in) sandwich tins, and grease them well.

Melt the chocolate in a bowl over hot—not boiling—water. Allow to cool.

Beat the butter, brown sugar and vanilla essence until very creamy. Add the eggs one at a time, beating well after each addition, then beat in the sour cream.

Blend the cocoa with the hot water and plum jam, and add to the butter cream with the melted chocolate. Beat well to combine. Sift the flour over the top and fold through lightly but thoroughly—do not overmix. Spoon into the two sandwich tins.

Bake for 30–35 minutes before turning out onto cake racks to cool.

When cold, fill with the whipped cream, sandwich together, and cover the top and sides with whipped cream, sweetened if desired with a little sugar. Decorate with Chocolate Caraque and rosettes of whipped cream and allow to firm before slicing.

Chocolate Caraque: Melt 100 g (3½ oz) dark chocolate over a pan of simmering water. Leave to cool and thicken then melt again. Spread it very thinly over a marble slab, a laminated bench-top or the back of a flat baking tray. Leave until just beginning to harden, then, using a sharp flexible knife, curl off splinters of chocolate.

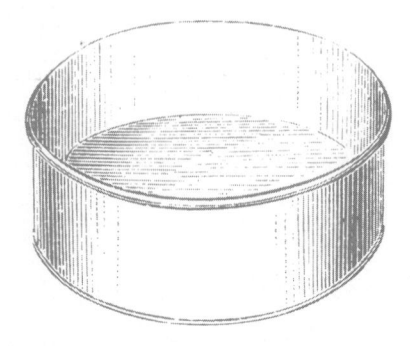

Ginger Chocolate Cake

Makes 1 slab cake

---
1 cup (5 oz) chopped crystallised ginger
---
1 cup (5 oz) brown sugar
---
125 g (4 oz) butter or margarine, chopped
---
1 tablespoon cocoa

¾ cup (6 fl oz) water
---
1 teaspoon bicarbonate of soda (baking soda)

¼ cup (2 fl oz) milk
---
2 cups (8 oz) flour
---
1 teaspoon baking powder
---
1 teaspoon ground ginger
---
1 egg, beaten

Chocolate Warm Glacé Icing (see recipe, page 130)
---
extra ⅓ cup (2 oz) chopped ginger, for topping

Preheat the oven to 180°C (350°F/Gas 4). Line the base of a 23 cm (9 in) slab tin, and grease it well.

Place the ginger, brown sugar, butter, cocoa and water into a small saucepan; bring slowly to the boil, simmer for 3 to 4 minutes, then set aside to cool.

Turn the mixture into a bowl. Dissolve the bicarbonate of soda in the milk and add to the bowl. Sift the dry ingredients over the top and fold in lightly. Add the egg and mix thoroughly. Spoon into the prepared slab tin.

Bake for 35–40 minutes. Remove from the oven and allow to stand for 4 to 5 minutes before turning out onto a cake rack to cool.

When cold, cover the top with the Chocolate Warm Glacé Icing, and scatter the extra chopped ginger over the surface.

Date and Nut Slice

Makes 1 cake

⅔ cup hot black coffee
---
1 cup (5 oz) chopped and stoned dates
---
1 packet chocolate cake mix
---
1 egg

½ cup (3 oz) salted peanuts, finely chopped

Coffee Vienna Butter Cream (see recipe, page 144)

Preheat the oven to 190°C (375°F/Gas 5). Line the base of a 20 cm (8 in) cake tin, and grease and flour it well.

Pour the hot coffee over the dates in a bowl and set aside until cooled.

Turn the packet of cake mix into a bowl. Add the egg and the coffee-date mixture, and beat for 2 to 3 minutes with a wooden spoon. Scatter the peanuts over and beat for a further 2 to 3 minutes (beating must be rapid and continuous). Spoon into the cake tin.

Bake for 35 to 40 minutes. Remove from the oven and let stand for 4–5 minutes before turning out onto a cake rack to cool.

When cold, cover with the Coffee Butter Cream and allow the icing to firm before cutting into slices.

Chocolate Velvet Cake

Makes 1 slab cake

2¼ cups (9 oz) flour
---
2 teaspoons baking powder

½ teaspoon bicarbonate of soda (baking soda)
---
3 eggs
---
1 teaspoon vanilla essence

1¼ cups (10 oz) sugar
---
1 cup (8 fl oz) egg-oil mayonnaise
---
125 g (4 oz) pure cooking chocolate, melted

Chocolate Peppermint Gloss (see recipe, page 137)

Preheat the oven to 180°C (350°F/Gas 4). Line the base of a 28 × 18 cm (11 × 7 in) slab tin, and grease it well.

Sift the flour, baking powder and bicarbonate of soda together 2 or 3 times.

Combine the eggs, vanilla essence and sugar in the bowl of an electric mixer and beat at high speed until thick and fluffy. Add the egg-oil mayonnaise and the cooled chocolate, and beat at half speed until well blended through. Remove from the mixer stand, add the sifted dry ingredients, and fold in using a metal or wooden spoon. Pour into the slab tin.

Bake for 50–55 minutes. Remove from the oven and allow to stand for 8 to 10 minutes before turning out onto a cake rack to cool. When cold, ice with the Chocolate Peppermint Gloss.

Crumble Top Coffee Cake

Makes 1 cake

1 egg
½ cup (4 oz) sugar
⅓ cup (2½ fl oz) maize oil
1 teaspoon vanilla essence
1½ cups (6 oz) flour
3 teaspoons baking powder
¼ teaspoon salt
½ cup (2 oz) minute (quick-cooking) oats, finely crushed
½ teaspoon mixed spices, optional
1 cup (5 oz) sultanas
Topping: *⅓ cup (2 oz) brown sugar*
½ cup (2 oz) self-raising flour
1 teaspoon mixed spices
60 g (2 oz) butter or margarine, melted and cooled

Preheat the oven to 190°C (375°F/Gas 5). Base-line and grease a cake tin 20 cm (8 in) square.

Combine the egg, sugar, maize oil and vanilla essence in a bowl and beat briskly for 2 to 3 minutes. Sift the flour, baking powder, salt, crushed oats and spices over the egg-oil mixture (including the residue oats from the sifter) and fold in lightly—do not overmix. Turn into the cake tin and scatter the sultanas evenly over the top.

Topping: Combine all the topping ingredients and press through the holes of a colander or coarse strainer over the top of the cake mixture.

Bake in the preheated oven for 15 minutes, then reduce the oven temperature to 180°C (350°F/Gas 4) and bake for a further 30 to 35 minutes. Remove from the oven and allow to stand for 3 to 4 minutes before turning out, then reverse the cake carefully onto a cake rack to cool.

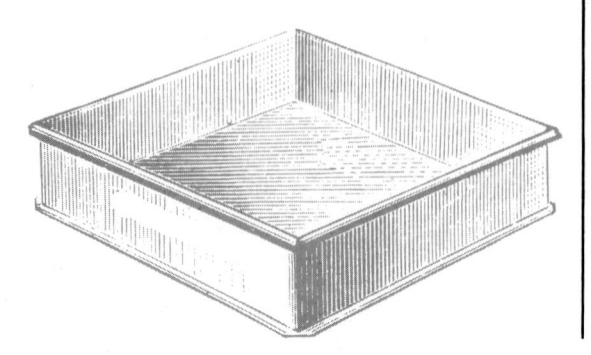

Hazelnut Coffee Cake

Makes 1 cake

185 g (6 oz) butter or margarine, softened
¾ cup (6 oz) caster (powdered) sugar
1 teaspoon instant coffee powder
1 tablespoon (1 oz) honey
4 eggs
1 tablespoon whiskey coffee cream liqueur
1¼ cups (4 oz) ground hazelnuts
1 cup (4 oz) self-raising flour
Coffee Fudge Frosting (see recipe, page 135)

Preheat the oven to 180°C (350°F/Gas 4). Grease and flour a deep-sided 20 cm (8 in) springform cake tin or fluted ring tin.

Beat the butter and sugar until creamy. Add the instant coffee powder and the honey, and beat until light and fluffy. Add the eggs one at a time, beating well after each addition. Beat the liqueur in well, and fold the hazelnuts through.

Sift the flour, then sift again over the butter-hazelnut mixture and fold through lightly. Spoon into the springform tin.

Bake for 45 to 50 minutes. Remove from the oven and allow to stand for 5 to 6 minutes before loosening the cake tin ring. When cold, place the cake on a serving platter and cover with the Coffee Fudge Frosting.

Right: **Hazelnut Coffee Cake (see above).**

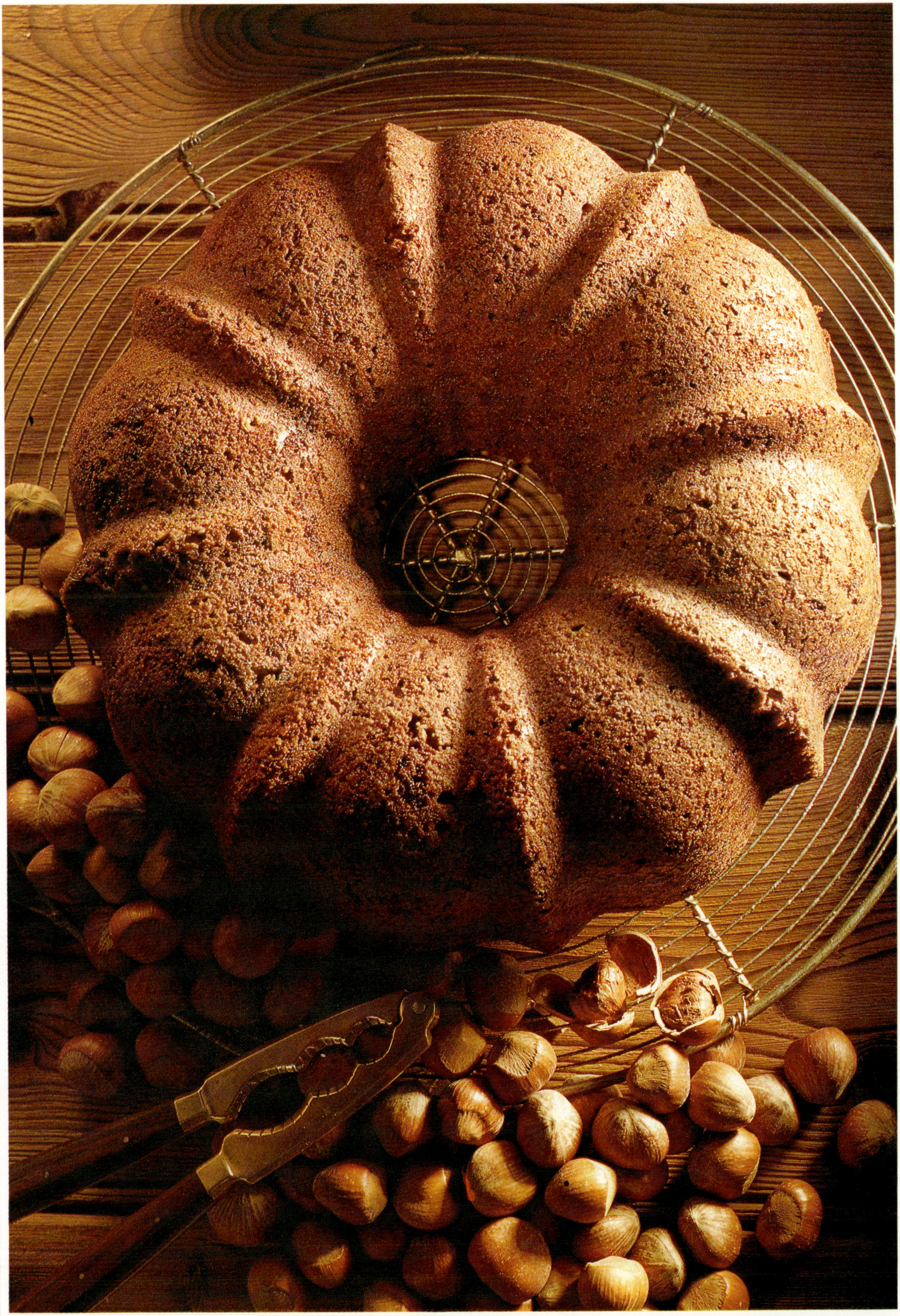

LUNCHEON CAKES AND LOAVES

Tomato Raisin Loaf

Makes 1 loaf cake

125 g (4 oz) butter or margarine, softened
¾ cup (6 oz) caster (powdered) sugar
1 teaspoon grated lemon rind
2 eggs
1 cup (8fl oz) skinned, chopped tomatoes
½ cup (3 oz) chopped raisins
¼ cup (1 oz) chopped nuts
1½ cups (6 oz) self-raising flour
½ cup (2 oz) wholemeal flour
1 teaspoon mixed spices
¼ teaspoon salt

Preheat the oven to 180°C (350°F/Gas 4). Line the base of a 23 × 10 cm (9 × 4 in) loaf tin, and grease it well.

Beat the butter, sugar and lemon rind until creamy. Add the eggs one at a time, beating well after each addition.

Press the tomatoes through a sieve to remove the seeds; add the pulp to the butter-cream, and add the raisins and nuts. Sift the dry ingredients over the butter-tomato mixture and fold through. Spoon into the loaf tin.

Bake for 35 to 40 minutes. Remove from the oven and allow to stand for 5 to 6 minutes before carefully turning out onto a cake rack to cool. Store in an airtight container for 2 to 3 days before slicing.

Note: Other similar recipes to this use canned tomato purée or soup. If using either of these in place of the fresh tomatoes, add a little more mixed spice to counteract the bland flavour.

Three Way Luncheon Cake

This moist ring cake may be baked in the oven of your choice: conventional (standard), convection (fan-forced) or microwave.
Makes 1 ring cake.

1¼ cups (5 oz) flour
1 teaspoon bicarbonate of soda (baking soda)
1 teaspoon baking powder
1 teaspoon mixed spices
1 cup (5 oz) brown sugar
⅔ cup (5½fl oz) maize oil
2 eggs
2 teaspoons grated lemon rind
1 tablespoon lemon juice
½ cup (3 oz) well-drained crushed pineapple
1 cup (3 oz) shredded carrot
¼ cup (1 oz) chopped salted nuts
Cream Cheese Frosting: 60 g (2 oz) packaged cream cheese, softened
1 cup (6 oz) icing (confectioners') sugar, sifted
2–3 tablespoons sweet sherry
½–1 teaspoon mixed spices

First check the oven manufacturer's instructions for baking time and temperature for the appliance to be used. If baking in a conventional oven or in a convection (fan-forced) oven, preheat the oven to the recommended temperature; grease and flour an 18–20 cm ring tin. If baking in a microwave oven, prepare the baking dish recommended below.

Sift the flour with the other dry ingredients into a bowl; add the brown sugar and toss through, then form a well in the centre. Add the maize oil, eggs, lemon rind and lemon juice, then the pineapple, carrot and chopped nuts, and beat all together with a flat egg whisk for 2 to 3 minutes.

Beat the cream cheese until smooth. Gradually add the icing sugar, beating well. Add sufficient sweet sherry to produce a spreading consistency; flavour with mixed spices, as desired.

When the ring cake is cool, spread the Cream Cheese Frosting roughly over the top. Allow the frosting to become firm before cutting.

Conventional Oven: Pour the mixture into a greased and floured 18–20 cm (7–8 in) ring tin, and bake in the preheated oven at 180°C (350°F/Gas 4) for 35 to 40 minutes. Remove from the oven and allow to stand for 2 to 3 minutes before turning out onto a cake rack to cool.

Orange Raisin Loaf

Makes 1 loaf cake

1 cup (6 oz) chopped raisins
1/4 cup (1 oz) chopped walnuts or pecans
2 teaspoons grated orange rind
1/3 cup (2 1/2 fl oz) orange juice
1 1/4 cups (5 oz) self-raising flour
1 cup (4 oz) self-raising wholemeal flour
1/2 teaspoon bicarbonate of soda (baking soda)
1/4 teaspoon salt
125 g (4 oz) butter or margarine, softened
1 cup (5 oz) brown sugar
1 cup (8 fl oz) natural yoghurt
2 eggs, beaten

Combine the raisins, walnuts and orange rind with the orange juice and set aside for 20 minutes, stirring occasionally.

Preheat the oven to 160°C (325°F/Gas 3). Line and grease a 23 × 12 cm (9 1/2 × 4 in) loaf tin.

Sift the flours, bicarbonate of soda and salt together, returning the wholegrain pieces from the sieve.

Cream the butter and brown sugar well. Add the yoghurt and eggs, and mix all together. Fold in alternate batches of the flour and raisin-walnut mixtures, about a third of each at a time; mix lightly but thoroughly to combine. Turn into the loaf tin.

Bake for 55 to 60 minutes. Remove from the oven and allow to stand for 5 to 6 minutes before carefully turning out onto a cake rack. When cold, store in an airtight container for 1 to 2 days before cutting into slices.

Currant Tea Loaf

Makes 1 loaf cake

1/2 cup (4 oz) sugar
1 cup (5 oz) currants
1 cup (8 fl oz) warm strong tea
2 1/2 cups (10 oz) self-raising flour
1 teaspoon mixed spices
1/4 teaspoon salt
1–2 teaspoons grated lemon (or orange) rind

Combine the sugar and currants in a large bowl; pour the tea over the top and set aside, stirring occasionally, for at least 1 hour.

Preheat the oven to 180°C (350°F/Gas 4). Line and grease a 20 × 8 cm (8 × 3 in) loaf tin.

Sift all the remaining ingredients together, then sift again over the currant mixture and stir until well mixed through—do not overmix. Spoon the mixture into the loaf tin.

Bake in the preheated oven for 20 minutes, then reduce the temperature to slow, 150°C (300°F/Gas 2), and bake for a further 40 to 45 minutes. Remove from the oven and allow to stand for 8 to 10 minutes before turning out onto a cake rack to cool.

Store in an airtight container for 1 day before cutting into slices and serving, buttered if desired.

Apricot Nut Loaf

Makes 1 loaf cake

1/2 cup (2 oz) chopped dried apricots
sweet sherry
1 egg
1 cup (8 oz) sugar
90 g (3 oz) butter or margarine, melted
2 cups (8 oz) flour
3 teaspoons baking powder
1/2 teaspoon bicarbonate of soda (baking soda)
1/4 teaspoon salt
1/2 cup (4 fl oz) orange juice
1 cup (4 oz) chopped walnuts

Soak the dried apricots in sufficient sweet sherry to cover for 1 hour.

Preheat the oven to 160°C (325°F/Gas 3). Line and grease a 20 × 10 cm (8 × 4 in) loaf tin. Drain the apricots well, and reserve 1/4 cup (2 fl oz) of the liquid.

Beat the egg until frothy. Gradually add the sugar, beating until well mixed. Stir the cooled butter through. Sift the flour, baking powder, bicarbonate of soda and salt over the egg-sugar mixture, and fold through in alternate batches with the orange juice and reserved apricot liquid. Add the walnuts and fold through lightly. Turn into the prepared loaf tin.

Bake for 75 to 80 minutes. Remove from the oven and allow to stand for 5 to 6 minutes before turning out onto a cake rack to cool. Store in an airtight container for 1 to 2 days before cutting into slices.

Pecan Prune Roll

Makes 2 nut roll cakes

1¼ cups (8 oz) prunes, stones removed
1 cup (8 fl oz) water
125 g (4 oz) butter or margarine, softened
1 cup (8 oz) sugar
2 tablespoons grated orange rind
2 cups (8 oz) flour
2 teaspoons baking powder
¼ teaspoon salt
½ teaspoon bicarbonate of soda (baking soda)
¼ cup (2 fl oz) orange juice or milk
½ cup (2 oz) chopped pecan nuts

Preheat the oven the 180°C (350°F/Gas 4). Thoroughly grease and flour two 20 × 8 cm (8 × 3 in) nut roll tins with perforated lids (or some perforated aluminium foil to cover the tops).

Simmer the prunes in the water for 3 to 4 minutes. Set aside to cool, then remove the prunes and chop finely, reserving ½ cup (4 fl oz) of the prune liquid.

Beat the butter, sugar and orange rind until light and fluffy. Gradually add the ½ cup (4 fl oz) of prune liquid, beating thoroughly. Sift the dry ingredients over the butter cream and fold through lightly. Add the prunes, orange juice and pecan nuts, and mix well. Spoon the mixture into the two tins and attach the perforated lids—or cover each with a rectangle of perforated aluminium foil.

Stand the nut roll tins upright in the oven and bake for 35 to 40 minutes. Remove from the oven, remove the lids and allow to stand for 5 to 6 minutes before carefully turning out onto cake racks to cool.

Walnut Date Roll: Substitute dates and walnuts for the prunes and pecans, and use grated lemon rind instead of the orange rind.

Cider Honey Luncheon Cake

Makes 1 loaf cake

1 cup (4 oz) flour
1 cup (4 oz) wholemeal flour
1 teaspoon mixed spices
¼ teaspoon salt
¼ teaspoon ground ginger
½ cup (3 oz) sultanas
2 tablespoons (1 oz) chopped mixed peel
¼ cup (1½ oz) brown sugar
125 g (4 oz) butter or margarine, melted
⅔ cup (7 oz) honey
1 teaspoon bicarbonate of soda (baking soda)
150 ml (5 fl oz) sparkling cider
1 egg, beaten

Preheat the oven to 160°C (325°F/Gas 3). Line and grease a 23 × 12 cm (9 × 4½ in) loaf tin.

Sift the flours with the spices, salt and ground ginger, returning the wholegrain pieces from the sieve. Combine with the sultanas, peel and brown sugar in a bowl, making a well in the centre.

Combine the hot melted butter with the honey, and pour into the well in the flour mixture.

Dissolve the bicarbonate of soda in the cider, and quickly add this and the beaten egg to the bowl. Beat all the ingredients together with a flat egg whisk until mixed thoroughly. Turn into the loaf tin.

Bake for 55 to 60 minutes. Remove from the oven and allow to stand for 5 to 6 minutes before carefully turning out onto a cake rack. When cold, store in an airtight container for 1 to 2 days before slicing.

Spread slices with honey and lemon-flavoured butter, if desired.

Right: **Cider Honey Luncheon Cake** (see above).

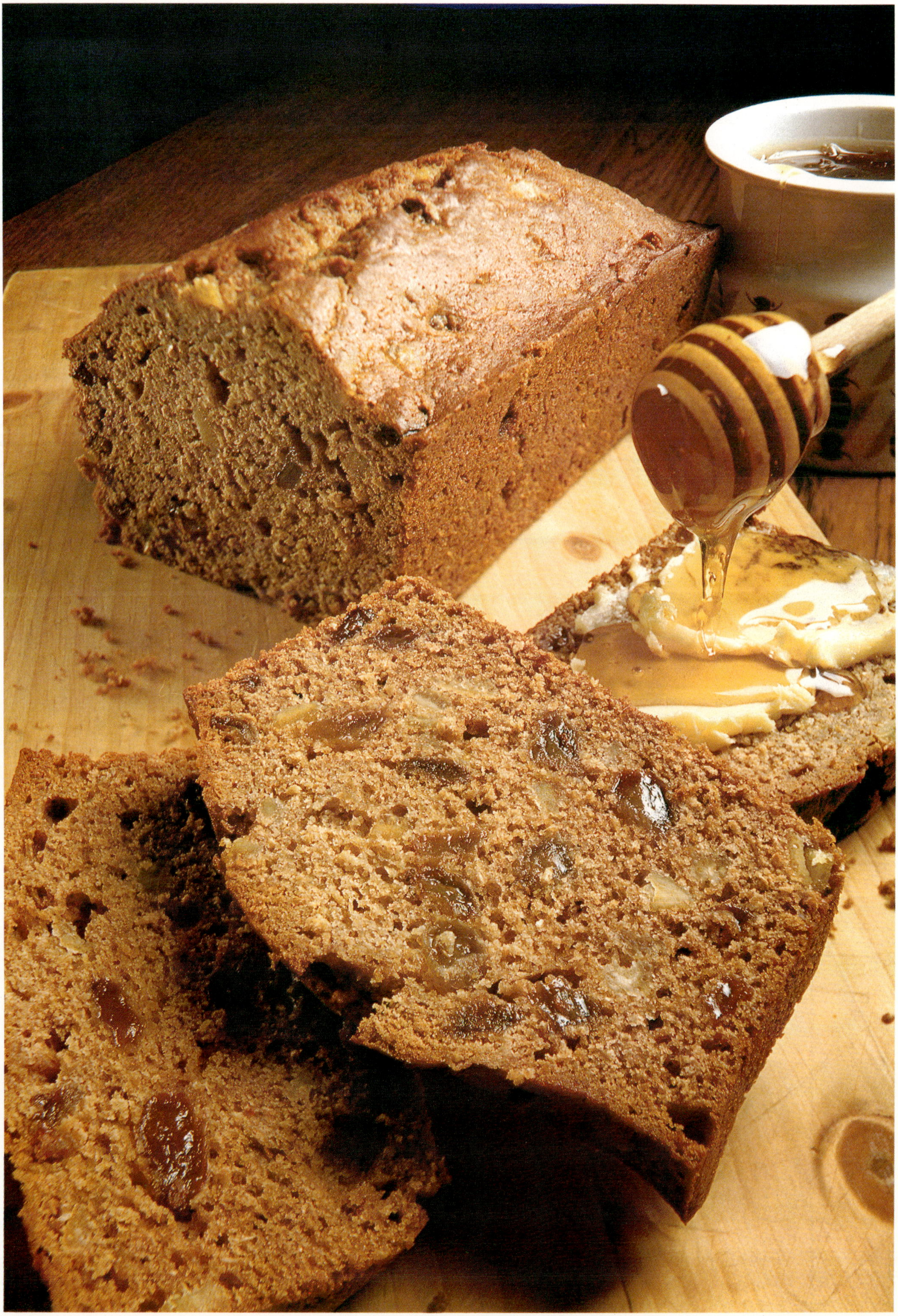

Buttermilk Fruit Loaf

Makes 1 loaf cake

½ cup (3 oz) brown sugar
¼ cup (3 oz) honey
60 g (2 oz) butter or margarine, softened
1 egg, beaten
1½ cups (6 oz) flour
1 teaspoon baking powder
½ teaspoon bicarbonate of soda (baking soda)
¼ teaspoon salt
¾ cup (4 oz) sultanas
1 cup (8 fl oz) buttermilk
¾ cup (2½ oz) minute (quick-cooking) oats

Preheat the oven to 160°C (325°F/Gas 3). Line and grease a 23 × 12 cm (9 × 4½ cm) loaf tin.

Combine the brown sugar, honey and butter in a bowl and beat until soft and creamy. Add the beaten egg and mix well. Sift the flour, baking powder, bicarbonate of soda and salt over the butter mixture and fold in. Add the sultanas and stir through.

Mix the buttermilk and oats together, and fold this into the mixture in the bowl; fold thoroughly to combine. Spoon into the loaf tin.

Bake for 55 to 60 minutes. Remove from the oven and allow to stand for 10 to 12 minutes before turning out onto a cake rack to cool. Store in an airtight container for 1 to 2 days before cutting into slices.

Raspberry Peanut Squares

Makes 1 slab in a 23 cm (9 in) tin

2 cups (8 oz) self-raising flour
¼ teaspoon salt
1 cup (7 oz) caster (powdered) sugar
125 g (4 oz) butter or margarine, chopped
1 cup (5 oz) chopped peanuts
3 tablespoons (3 oz) raspberry jam (raspberry jelly)
2 eggs, beaten
2 teaspoons lemon juice
¾ cup (6 fl oz) milk
icing (confectioners') sugar, for topping

Preheat the oven to 180°C (350°F/Gas 4). Line the base of a 23 cm (9 in) slab tin, and grease it well.

Place the flour, salt and sugar in the bowl of a food processor using the cutting blade; add the butter and process for a few seconds, then tip the mixture into a bowl. Add the peanuts, raspberry jam, beaten eggs, lemon juice and milk, and beat with a flat egg whisk for 1 to 2 minutes. Pour into the slab tin.

Bake for 40 to 45 minutes. Remove from the oven and allow to stand for 3 to 4 minutes before turning out carefully onto a cake rack to cool.

Sift a little icing sugar over the top and cut into squares for serving.

Granny's Apple Cake

Makes 1 cake

2 large green cooking apples, peeled and cored
½ cup (5 oz) golden syrup (light corn syrup)
90 g (3 oz) butter or margarine, softened
½ cup (3 oz) brown sugar, loosely packed
1 egg
½ teaspoon bicarbonate of soda (baking soda)
½ cup (4 fl oz) sour milk
2 cups (8 oz) flour, sifted
1 teaspoon mixed spices
½ cup (2½ oz) chopped dates

Slice the apples thinly and place with the golden syrup in a small non-stick saucepan; cover and cook over very low heat until the apples are soft, then set aside to cool.

Preheat the oven to 180°C (350°F/Gas 4). Line the base of an 18–20 cm (7–8 in) cake tin, and grease it well.

Beat the butter and sugar until creamy. Add the egg and beat well. Dissolve the bicarbonate of soda in the sour milk, and beat this in too. Fold in alternate batches of sifted flour and spices, cooked apple mixture and chopped dates, about a third of each at a time. Spoon into the cake tin.

Bake for 55 to 60 minutes. Remove from the oven and allow to stand for 5 to 6 minutes before turning out onto a cake rack to cool. Serve freshly baked, cut in slices and spread with butter, if desired.

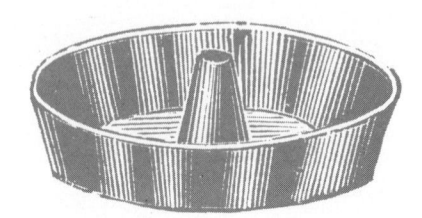

Spiced Buttermilk Cake

Makes 1 cake

---
125 g (4 oz) unsalted butter, softened
---
1 cup (7 oz) caster (powdered) sugar
---
1 egg

2¼ cups (9 oz) flour
---
1 teaspoon bicarbonate of soda (baking soda)
---
1 teaspoon ground cinnamon
---
1 teaspoon ground cardamom
---
1 teaspoon ground cloves

½ cup (3 oz) chopped raisins
---
1 cup (8 fl oz) buttermilk

Preheat the oven to 180°C (350°F/Gas 4). Base-line and grease a cake tin 23 cm (9 in) square.

Beat the butter until very white. Gradually add the sugar, beating well after each addition. Add the egg and beat well.

Sift the dry ingredients together, then sift again over the raisins and toss to mix through.

Add alternate batches of the flour-raisin mixture and the buttermilk to the butter cream, about a third of each at a time; fold in lightly but thoroughly—do not overmix. Spoon the mixture into the cake tin, spreading evenly.

Bake for 50 to 55 minutes. Remove from the oven and allow to stand for 5 to 6 minutes before turning out onto a cake rack to cool. When cold, cut into slices or squares for serving.

Cherry Lemon Ring

Makes 1 ring cake

1¾ cups (7 oz) self-raising flour

¼ cup (1 oz) cornflour (cornstarch)
---
1 tablespoon (¼ oz) full-cream milk powder

2–3 teaspoons grated lemon rind
---
1 cup (8 oz) sugar
---
125 g (4 oz) butter or margarine
---
3 eggs

½ cup (4 fl oz) water, lightly flavoured with lemon juice

⅔ cup (4 oz) chopped glacé cherries
---
lemon-flavoured Warm Glacé Icing (see recipe, page 130)

Preheat the oven to 180°C (350°F/Gas 4). Thoroughly grease a fluted 20 cm (8 in) ring tin.

Sift the dry ingredients into a bowl, add the lemon rind and sugar and toss to mix through; make a well in the centre.

Heat the butter until just melted and allow to cool.

Combine the eggs and water and beat well; add to the flour mixture, then add the cooled butter, and beat with a flat egg whisk for 4 to 5 minutes.

Scatter the chopped glacé cherries over the base and sides of the greased ring tin; press on lightly. Pour the cake mixture into the tin.

Bake for 45 to 50 minutes. Remove from the oven and allow to stand for 5 to 6 minutes before turning out carefully onto a cake rack.

When cold, drizzle lemon-flavoured Warm Glacé Icing over the top, allowing it to run into the flutes down the sides. When set, cut into slices.

Town and Country Loaves

Makes 2 loaf cakes

---
125 g (4 oz) butter or margarine, softened
---
1 cup (8 oz) sugar
---
2 eggs
---
2 tablespoons lemon juice
---
1 cup (5 oz) chopped and stoned dates

½ cup (2 oz) walnuts, chopped coarsely

3½ cups (14 oz) self-raising flour, sifted

½ cup (2 oz) cornflour (cornstarch)

½ teaspoon salt
---
1 cup milk

Topping:
3 tablespoons (3 oz) honey
---
3 tablespoons lemon juice

½ cup (3 oz) coarse sugar crystals

Preheat the oven to 180°C (350°F/Gas 4). Base-line and grease two 20 × 8 cm (8 × 3 in) loaf tins.

Beat the butter and sugar until creamy. Add the eggs one at a time, beating well after each addition, then add the lemon juice and beat well.

Combine the dates and walnuts with half the flour and toss well. Sift the other half of the flour with the cornflour and salt, and add both mixtures to the butter cream, folding in lightly. Add the milk and mix gently through. Spoon into the two loaf tins.

Bake for 35 to 40 minutes. Remove from the oven and allow to stand for 2 to 3 minutes, then turn out onto cake racks. Whilst still hot, brush each loaf with the combined honey and lemon juice and scatter the coarse sugar crystals over the surface.

One Egg Gingerbread

(Photograph below)
Makes 1 slab cake

4 cups (1 lb) flour
4 teaspoons baking powder
5 teaspoons ground ginger
¼ teaspoon salt
1 teaspoon bicarbonate of soda (baking soda)
1 cup (10 oz) treacle or golden syrup
185 g (6 oz) butter or margarine, chopped
1½ cups (8 oz) brown sugar
1 egg, beaten
300ml (10fl oz) milk, warmed
lemon-flavoured Warm Glacé Icing (see recipe, page 130)
⅓ cup (2 oz) chopped crystallised ginger

Preheat the oven to 180°C (350°F/Gas 4). Line and well grease a 28 × 25 cm (11 × 10 in) tin.
 Sift the flour, baking powder, ground ginger, salt and bicarbonate of soda into a bowl.
 Place the treacle, butter and brown sugar in a saucepan and heat slowly until the sugar is dissolved—do not overheat; cool and stir well.
 When barely warm, add to the flour mixture and fold through, lastly add the beaten egg and milk, and beat lightly to combine—do not overmix. Pour into the baking tin.
 Bake for 50 minutes, then lower oven temperature slightly and bake for a further 30 to 35 minutes. Stand cake for 8 to 10 minutes before cooling.
 When cold, ice with the lemon-flavoured Warm Glacé Icing and decorate with the chopped ginger.

Buttered Cottage Twists

(Photograph right)
Makes 2 bar cakes

2 eggs
1 cup (8 oz) sugar
½ cup (4 oz) cottage cheese
½ cup (4fl oz) maize oil
1 teaspoon grated lemon rind
1 teaspoon vanilla essence
4 cups (1 lb) flour, sifted
1 teaspoon bicarbonate of soda (baking soda)
½ cup (4fl oz) milk
2–3 tablespoons sesame seeds
butter or margarine, for spreading

Preheat the oven to 200°C (400°F/Gas 6). Grease a 24 × 6 cm (9½ × 2½ in) bar tin.
 Reserve one egg white for glazing. Combine the other egg white and the yolks with the sugar, and beat until fluffy. Add the cottage cheese, oil, lemon rind and vanilla, and beat well. Fold in the sifted flour and bicarbonate of soda, add the milk and mix to a soft dough—use a little extra milk if the mixture seems too firm.
 Turn onto a lightly-floured board; divide the dough into four and knead each to a thin strip about 30 cm (12 in) long. Taking two of the strips, twist loosely together and lift into the prepared bar tin. Repeat with the other two strips. Allow space between the two twists—the mixture will rise during baking. Lightly beat the reserved egg white and brush this over the twists; sprinkle the sesame seeds on top.
 Bake for 8 to 10 minutes, then reduce the temperature to moderate, 180°C (350°F/Gas 4), and bake for a further 25 to 30 minutes. Turn out and serve warm in buttered slices.

LARGE CAKES

Wholemeal Carrot Cake

(Photograph below right)
Makes 1 cake

1 cup (8 oz) sugar, very slightly warmed
¾ cup (6 fl oz) maize oil
2 eggs
1½ cups grated carrot
1 cup (4 oz) wholemeal flour
1 teaspoon baking powder
½ teaspoon ground ginger
½ teaspoon grated nutmeg
¼ teaspoon salt
¾ cup (4 oz) chopped raisins
½ cup (2 oz) chopped walnuts
1 teaspoon grated orange rind
Cream Cheese Frosting (see page 136)

Preheat the oven to 180°C (350°F/Gas 4). Line and grease a 20 × 12 cm (8 × 4½ in) loaf tin.

Beat the sugar and maize oil together until well mixed. Add the eggs one at a time, beating well after each addition; then add the grated carrot and mix well.

Sift the dry ingredients together. Place the raisins, walnuts and orange rind in another bowl, and sift the flour mixture over them; toss well to mix. Fold this into the sugar-carrot mixture, mixing lightly but thoroughly. Spoon into the loaf tin.

Bake for 35 to 40 minutes. Remove from the oven and allow to stand for 3 to 4 minutes before turning out onto a cake rack to cool.

Cream Cheese Frosting: Make according to the recipe on page 136, substituting orange rind for lemon rind.

Apricot Cream Bars

Makes 2 bar cakes

1½ cups (12fl oz) canned apricot nectar
½ cup (2 oz) chopped dried apricots
1⅓ cups (7 oz) chopped raisins
30 g (1 oz) butter or margarine
2 teaspoons grated lemon rind
¾ cup (6 oz) sugar
1 egg
⅓ cup (2½fl oz) fresh cream
2¾ cups (11 oz) flour
2 teaspoons bicarbonate of soda
¼ teaspoon salt
1–2 tablespoons lemon juice, as required

Preheat the oven to 180°C (350°F/Gas 4). Line the bases of two 25 × 8 cm (9 × 3 in) bar tins.

Combine the apricot nectar, dried apricots and raisins in a saucepan and bring slowly to the boil; simmer for 2 to 3 minutes, then add the butter and lemon rind and allow to cool.

Beat the sugar and egg together until the sugar is well dissolved. Add the cream and beat lightly.

Sift the dry ingredients over the egg-cream mixture, and fold this in lightly, alternately with the cold apricot-raisin mixture. Add sufficient lemon juice to make a moist cake mixture. Turn into the two bar tins.

Bake for 40 to 50 minutes. Remove from the oven and allow to stand for 5 to 6 minutes before turning out onto cake racks to cool. Store in an airtight container for 2 to 3 days before slicing.

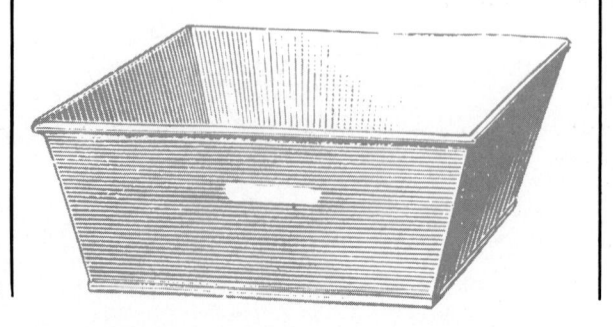

LAYER CAKES AND DESSERT GÂTEAUX

Grapefruit Cream Cake

Makes 1 recess cake

90 g (3 oz) butter or margarine, softened
¾ cup (6 oz) caster (powdered) sugar
⅓ cup (4 oz) grapefruit marmalade
2 teaspoons grated orange rind
½ cup (2 oz) chopped nuts
2 eggs, separated
2 cups (8 oz) flour
2 teaspoons baking powder
2 teaspoons full cream milk powder
¼ teaspoon salt
⅓ cup (2½fl oz) water
Filling: 1 cup (8fl oz) thick cream, whipped
2–3 teaspoons icing (confectioners') sugar
2–3 teaspoons grated orange rind
¼ cup (1 oz) chopped nuts

Preheat the oven to 180°C (350°F/Gas 4). Thoroughly grease and flour a 20 cm (8 in) recess tin.

Beat the butter and sugar until creamy. Gradually beat in the marmalade and orange rind, then add the chopped nuts and mix well. Mix the egg yolks into the butter cream. Then fold in the sifted dry ingredients and the water.

Beat the egg whites to a soft foam, and fold lightly through the cake mixture. Spoon into the recess tin.

Bake for 50 to 55 minutes. Remove from the oven and allow to stand for 4 to 5 minutes before turning out onto a cake rack to cool.

When the cake is cold, combine the ingredients for the filling and fill the recess; decorate as desired. Chill before cutting into slices.

Meringue Genoise

Makes 1 layered cake

Cake Mixture:
2 cups (8 oz) flour

¼ teaspoon salt

1 teaspoon baking powder

125 g (4 oz) butter or margarine

8 eggs at room temperature

1 cup (8 oz) sugar

1 teaspoon almond essence

Syrup:
½ cup (4fl oz) water

1 cup (8 oz) sugar

2–3 tablespoons apricot brandy liqueur

Meringue:
¼ cup (2fl oz) water

¾ cup (6 oz) sugar

4 egg whites

Filling and Topping:
¾ cup (8 oz) apricot jam (apricot jelly)

½ cup (2 oz) flaked almonds

¼ cup (2 oz) caster (powdered) sugar

Cake: Sift the flour, salt and baking powder three times onto a sheet of kitchen paper.

Heat the butter in a small saucepan until just melted; set aside to cool. Break the eggs into a large heatproof bowl, add the sugar and essence and place the bowl over a large saucepan containing gently simmering water; lift the saucepan off the heat and whisk the egg-sugar mixture briskly until thick, foaming and at least doubled in bulk (approximately 8 minutes). Lift the bowl off the saucepan and beat for a further 3 to 4 minutes; scatter the flour lightly over the surface and fold in very lightly.

Drizzle the butter around the edge of the mixture and fold in gently—do not overmix.

Carefully spoon equal portions of the mixture into two greased and floured 20 cm (8 in) cake tins; bake in a moderately hot oven 190°C (375°F/Gas 5) for 35 to 40 minutes.

Allow the cakes to remain in the tins for 3 to 4 minutes before turning onto a rack to cool.

Syrup: Place the water and sugar in a small heavy-based saucepan and bring slowly to the boil, stirring to dissolve the sugar; allow to boil, without stirring, for 2 to 3 minutes, then remove from heat. Allow to cool and add the liqueur.

Meringue: Bring the water and sugar to the boil in a small saucepan; boil for 1 minute, then allow to cool.

Beat the egg whites to a stiff foam. Slowly add the sugar syrup, beating constantly to a thick, white meringue.

To Assemble: Preheat the oven to 220°C (425°F/Gas 7).

Sandwich the two cakes together with about half the apricot jam. Spread the remainder over the top.

Place the cake on an ovenproof platter and cover all over with the meringue; scatter the almonds over the surface and then sprinkle liberally with the sugar.

Place in the preheated oven for 7 to 8 minutes to form a crust on the meringue. Remove from the oven and allow to cool before serving.

Mediterranean Semolina Cake

Makes 1 baba cake

250 g (8 oz) unsalted butter

1½ cups (12 oz) sugar

4 eggs, well beaten

1½ cups (6 oz) flour

1½ cups (8 oz) fine semolina

½ cup (2 oz) coarsely chopped almonds

½ teaspoon almond essence

¼ cup (2fl oz) orange juice

extra almonds, finely chopped for coating

Syrup:
½ cup (4 oz) sugar

1 cup (8fl oz) water

½ teaspoon ground cinnamon

½ teaspoon ground cloves

whipped sweetened cream, for topping

Preheat the oven to 180°C (350°F/Gas 4). Grease a 20 cm (8 in) baba mould or fluted ring tin.

Beat the butter and sugar until light and fluffy. Gradually add the beaten eggs, beating well.

Sift the flour; mix it with the semolina and almonds to combine. Fold into the butter cream in alternate batches with the almond essence and orange juice.

With the extra almonds (or use dried breadcrumbs), lightly coat the greased baba mould (or ring tin). Spoon the cake mixture over.

Bake for 50 to 60 minutes. Remove from the oven, allow to stand for 4 to 5 minutes, then carefully turn onto a deep-sided serving plate.

Syrup: In a small heavy-based saucepan dissolve the sugar in the water over low heat. Add the cinnamon and cloves, bring to the boil, then boil steadily for 5 minutes to form a syrup.

Slowly spoon over the cake, allowing the syrup to be absorbed. Cool and chill.

Serve in slices with whipped sweetened cream.

Genoise Gâteau

Makes 1 layered cake

Cake:
4 eggs

½ cup (4 oz) sugar

½ teaspoon vanilla essence

1 cup (4 oz) flour

½ teaspoon baking powder

¼ teaspoon salt

60 g (2 oz) butter or margarine, melted

Meringues:
3 egg whites

½ cup (4 oz) sugar

1 cup (3 oz) desiccated coconut

2 teaspoons cornflour (cornstarch)

Filling:
300 ml (10 fl oz) thick cream, chilled

2 tablespoons icing (confectioners') sugar

1–2 tablespoons brandy

Cake: Preheat the oven to 190°C (375°F/Gas 5). Well grease a 20 cm (8 in) cake tin.

Beat the eggs, sugar and vanilla in a heatproof bowl over a saucepan which contains hot—not boiling—water, for only 1 minute; remove the saucepan from the heat and continue to beat the mixture, using an electric hand beater or rotary whisk, until the mixture is pale, thick and foamy (about 6 to 8 minutes). Remove the bowl from the saucepan and continue beating for 2 to 3 minutes until the mixture cools to warm.

Sift the flour, baking powder and salt together, then sift again over the egg mixture; fold about half through. Drizzle the cooled butter over, and fold very lightly and gently until just combined—do not overmix. Pour into the cake tin.

Bake for 25 to 30 minutes or until springy to the touch. Remove from the oven and allow to stand for 4 to 5 minutes before carefully turning out onto a fine mesh cake rack to cool.

Meringues: Preheat the oven to 150°C (300°F/Gas 2). Grease two scone trays and dust lightly with cornflour.

Beat the egg whites in a clean dry bowl—preferably glass—until a stiff white foam. Gradually add the sugar, beating well after each addition so that the sugar is dissolved. Combine the coconut and cornflour and fold into the mixture. Spread in two 20 cm (8 in) circles on the prepared scone trays.

Bake for 35 to 40 minutes. Remove from the oven and allow to cool on the trays, then carefully run a broad knife or metal spatula underneath to loosen.

Filling: Beat the chilled cream until softly foaming; then add the icing sugar and brandy and beat until thick. Chill well before using.

To assemble: Carefully cut the cake in half horizontally. On the bottom half, spread one quarter of the filling. Place one meringue circle on this and spread another quarter of the filling over the meringue.

Place the second cake layer on this and spread the remaining filling over. Placing the second meringue circle on the top; press down very gently to adhere all layers. Chill before cutting into slices.

Variation: Add chopped, well-drained fresh or dried fruits through the filling.

Poppy Seed Layer Cake

Makes 1 four-layer cake

⅓ cup poppy seeds

⅓ cup (2½ fl oz) milk

60 g (2 oz) butter or margarine, softened

1 cup (8 oz) sugar

3 eggs, separated

⅓ cup evaporated milk

2 cups (8 oz) flour

3 teaspoons baking powder

¼ teaspoon salt

Mocha Custard Filling (see recipe, page 141)

icing (confectioners') sugar, for topping

Preheat the oven to 180°C (350°F/Gas 4). Base-line and grease two 20 cm (8 in) sandwich tins. Soak the poppy seeds in the milk to soften slightly.

Beat the butter until creamy; gradually add the sugar, beating well. Add the egg yolks, then the evaporated milk and the poppy seed-milk mixture, beating constantly. Fold in the sifted flour, baking powder and salt, mixing lightly. Spoon the mixture into the two sandwich tins.

Bake for 35 to 40 minutes or until springy to the touch. Remove from the oven and allow to stand for 3 to 4 minutes before turning out onto cake racks to cool.

When cold, cut each cake in half—horizontally—for filling. Reassemble the cakes, spreading with the Mocha Custard Filling between the layers. Dust sifted icing sugar over the top, and chill until the filling is firm enough for cutting.

Right: Clockwise from top: Passionfruit Snow Cake (see p. 101); California Orange Cake (see p. 81); Poppy Seed Layer Cake (see above).

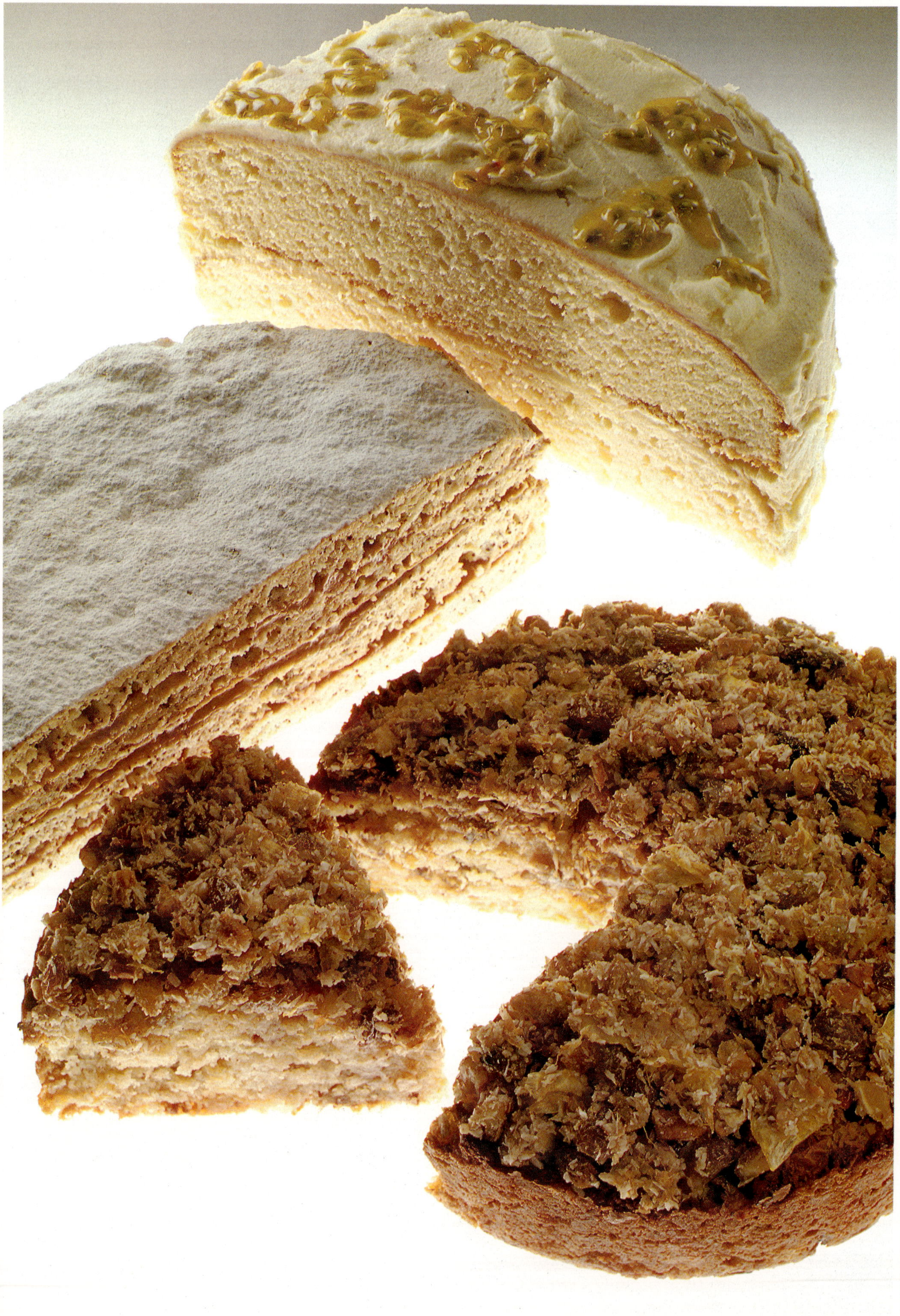

Chocolate Cream Torte

Makes 1 layered torte

Meringues:
6 egg whites
1½ cups (12 oz) sugar
¼ teaspoon salt
½ teaspoon cream of tartar
1 teaspoon almond essence
1 cup (2 oz) flaked or long-chip coconut
Filling:
185 g (6 oz) semi-sweet chocolate pieces
1 cup (2 oz) marshmallows, chopped
¾ cup (6fl oz) evaporated milk
¾ cup (6fl oz) thick cream, chilled

Preheat the oven to 150°C (300°F/Gas 2). Grease three scone trays and lightly dust with cornflour.

Beat the egg whites in a clean, dry bowl—preferably glass—until a stiff white foam. Gradually add half the sugar, beating well after each addition so that the sugar is dissolved.

Combine the remaining sugar with the salt and cream of tartar; scatter this over the egg white mixture and fold in very gently, adding the almond essence for flavour. Spread in three 18 cm (7 in) circles on the prepared scone trays. Scatter the coconut over each circle.

Bake for 30 to 35 minutes. Carefully loosen on the trays with a broad knife or metal spatula and set aside to cool.

Filling: Combine the chocolate pieces with the marshmallows and evaporated milk in a heatproof bowl placed over hot—not boiling—water; heat, stirring frequently until well blended. Remove from the heat and allow to cool.

Whip the cream until thickened and fold into the chocolate mixture. Chill, before using.

To assemble: Place one of the meringues on a serving plate and spread half of the chocolate filling over; top with a second meringue and again spread with filling.

Arrange the third meringue on the top and gently press down to adhere, being careful not to crack the crisp layers. Chill for at least 6 hours before serving.

Variation: Use finely chopped nuts in place of the coconut, and flavour the filling with rum or brandy essence or a little concentrated liqueur.

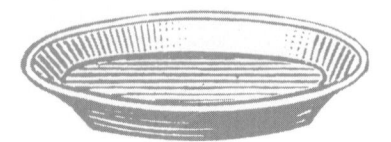

Rich Mocha Cream Gâteau

Makes 1 layered cake

375 g (12 oz) pure dark cooking chocolate, chopped
1 cup (8fl oz) milk
60 g (2 oz) butter or margarine, softened well
1¾ cups (7 oz) flour
1 teaspoon baking powder
2 teaspoons instant coffee powder
½ teaspoon bicarbonate of soda (baking soda)
¼ teaspoon salt
1 cup (8 oz) caster (powdered) sugar
3 eggs, beaten
2 teaspoons rum or brandy essence
Filling:
300 ml (10fl oz) thick cream, chilled
1 tablespoon icing (confectioners') sugar
Frosting:
185 g (6 oz) pure dark cooking chocolate, chopped
250 g (8 oz) unsalted butter, softened
2 egg yolks
1 teaspoon instant coffee powder
1 teaspoon rum or brandy essence
1¼–1½ cups (7–8 oz) icing (confectioners') sugar, sifted

Preheat the oven to 180°C (350°F/Gas 4). Line the bases of two 23 cm (9 in) sandwich tins, and grease well.

Place the chocolate in a heatproof bowl over hot—not boiling—water and allow to melt; set aside to cool slightly. When cool, combine with the milk and softened butter.

Sift the dry ingredients, including the sugar, into a large bowl and make a well in the centre; add the combined chocolate, milk and butter and beat for 1 to 2 minutes. Add the beaten eggs and essence, and beat for 2 minutes. Spoon into the sandwich tins.

Bake for 25 to 30 minutes. Remove from the oven and allow to stand for 2 to 3 minutes, then carefully turn out onto cake racks to cool. When cold, slice each cake in half horizontally—making four layers.

Filling: Whip the cream and icing sugar until thickened. Chill well.

Frosting: Melt the chocolate in a heatproof bowl over hot—not boiling—water. Allow to cool to room temperature.

Gradually blend the cooled chocolate into the creamed butter, then add the egg yolks and coffee powder and beat well. Flavour with the essence, and gradually add sufficient icing sugar to mix to a smooth spreading consistency.

To Assemble: Spread the whipped cream between the four cake layers and re-form into a gâteau, pressing gently to adhere. Spoon half the frosting onto the top of the gâteau and use the remainder for decoration in swirls or rosettes, as desired. Chill before serving, particularly in warm weather.

Caramel Layer Cake

Makes 1 layered cake

1½ cups (12 oz) caster (powdered) sugar
½ cup (4fl oz) hot black coffee—plus water, as required
2 cups (8 oz) flour
3 teaspoons baking powder
½ teaspoon salt
125 g (4 oz) butter or margarine, softened
2 eggs, beaten
Caramel Frosting: 2 tablespoons (1½ oz) sugar
90 g (3 oz) butter or margarine
100 ml (3fl oz) evaporated or creamy milk
1 teaspoon vanilla essence
3 cups (15 oz) icing (confectioners') sugar, sifted
Mock Cream (see recipe, page 140)

Preheat the oven to 180°C (350°F/Gas 4). Base-line and grease two 20–23 cm (8–9 in) sandwich tins.

Spoon ¼ cup (2 oz) of the sugar into a small heavy-based saucepan and dissolve over low heat, without stirring; allow to boil to a rich brown caramel (smoke fumes will appear).

Remove from the heat and slowly but very carefully add the hot coffee, stirring until all the toffee lumps dissolve. Return to a low heat if the mixture cools before the lumps dissolve. Allow the liquid to cool, then pour into a 250 ml cup measure and add sufficient water to make 225 ml (7½fl oz).

Sift the flour, baking powder and salt together twice and set aside.

Beat the butter with the remaining 1¼ cups of caster sugar until creamy. Add the beaten eggs and beat thoroughly; then beat in about half of the caramel liquid. Fold in the sifted flour alternately with the remaining caramel liquid, mixing lightly to combine. Spoon into the sandwich tins.

Bake for 25 to 35 minutes until springy to the touch. Remove from the oven and allow to stand for 1 to 2 minutes before turning out onto fine mesh cake racks to cool.

Caramel Frosting: Place the sugar in a small heavy-based saucepan and heat to form a caramel (as for the cake mixture, above).

Heat the butter and milk until just commencing to boil; then carefully stir into the caramel until the toffee lumps dissolve (as above). Add the vanilla essence. Pour into a heatproof bowl and allow to cool. Gradually add the icing sugar, beating until the mixture obtains a creamy spreading consistency.

To Assemble: Spread the Mock Cream filling onto one of the cake layers. Place the second layer on top, and press gently to adhere.

Spread half the Caramel Frosting over the top layer. Place the remaining Caramel Frosting in a cream bag with a rose tube, and pipe rosettes around the outer edge to decorate.

In warm weather, chill slightly before cutting into slices.

Passionfruit Snow Cake

Makes 2 cakes

90 g (3 oz) butter or margarine, softened well
1 cup (8 oz) caster (powdered) sugar
1 teaspoon vanilla essence
1¾ cups (7 oz) flour
2 teaspoons baking powder
¼ teaspoon salt
½ cup (4fl oz) milk
2 egg whites
Vienna Butter Cream (see recipe, page 144)
2–3 ripe passionfruit

Preheat the oven to 180°C (350°F/Gas 4). Line the bases of two 18 cm (7 in) sandwich tins, and grease well.

Place the butter, sugar and vanilla essence into a bowl; sift in the flour, baking powder and salt and add the milk. Beat for 1 to 2 minutes with a flat egg whisk.

Beat the egg whites until soft peaks form; very gently fold into the cake mixture. Spoon into the two sandwich tins.

Bake for 25 to 30 minutes or until springy to the touch. Remove from the oven and allow to stand for 1 to 2 minutes before turning out onto a cake rack to cool.

When cold, frost each cake with the Vienna Butter Cream. Cut the passionfruit in half and spoon the pulp over the top.

Frosted Peanut Butter Cake

Makes 1 layered cake

90 g (3 oz) butter or margarine, softened

1½ cups (12 oz) sugar

1 teaspoon vanilla essence

⅓ cup (3 oz) peanut butter—creamy type

2 eggs

2¼ cups (9 oz) flour

3 teaspoons baking powder

¼ teaspoon salt

1 cup (8fl oz) milk

Filling and Frosting:
90 g (3 oz) butter or margarine, softened

½ cup (4 oz) peanut butter—crunchy type

1 teaspoon vanilla essence

½ cup (4fl oz) evaporated milk

2–2½ cups (12–15 oz) icing (confectioners') sugar

2 tablespoons cocoa

Preheat the oven to 180°C (350°F/Gas 4). Base-line and grease two 20 cm (8 in) sandwich tins.

Beat the butter and sugar until creamy. Add the vanilla essence and peanut butter and beat well, then beat in the eggs one at a time.

Sift the flour, baking powder and salt together. Add to the butter-sugar-eggs mixture by sifting and folding in alternate batches of the flour and the milk, about a third of each at a time; mix lightly but thoroughly. Spoon the mixture into the sandwich tins.

Bake for 25 to 30 minutes. Remove from the oven and allow to stand for 2 to 3 minutes before turning out onto cake racks to cool. When cold, slice each cake in half horizontally, to make four layers.

Filling and Frosting: Beat the butter, peanut butter and vanilla essence until creamy. Add the evaporated milk and beat thoroughly, then gradually add the sifted icing sugar and cocoa, beating until a soft spreading consistency is obtained.

To Assemble: Use about two-thirds of the filling and frosting mixture for filling. Spread the mixture between the four cake layers, re-forming the cake, and gently pressing to adhere. Spread the remaining mixture ontop of the cake, swirling or roughing it to an attractive design. Chill before cutting, especially in warm weather.

Latticed Apple Cake

Makes 1 cake

185 g (6 oz) butter or margarine, softened

¾ cup (6 oz) sugar

1 teaspoon grated lemon rind

4 eggs

2¼ cups (9 oz) flour

2 teaspoons baking powder

Topping:
1 cup (6 oz) drained cooked (or canned) apples

1–2 tablespoons sugar (optional)

¼ quantity Almond Paste (see recipe, page 133)

½ cup apricot jam (apricot jelly)

1–2 tablespoons icing (confectioners') sugar

Preheat the oven to 180°C (350°F/Gas 4). Grease and flour a 20 cm (8 in) springform tin.

Beat the butter and sugar with the lemon rind until creamy. Add the eggs one at a time, beating well after each addition. Sift the flour and baking powder over the cream mixture and fold through. Spread into the springform tin and level the surface.

Bake for 35 to 40 minutes. Remove from the oven and leave in the tin for 5 to 6 minutes before adding the topping.

Topping: Sweeten the apples with the sugar, if desired. Roll out the Almond Paste to about 5 mm (¼ in) thickness and cut into 2 cm (¾ in) strips.

Carefully spread the apples over the still-warm cake and arrange a lattice pattern of Almond Paste strips ontop. Drop a little apricot jam between the lattice pieces.

Return to the oven for a further 15 to 20 minutes. Remove from the springform tin and allow to cool; dust with icing sugar before serving.

Right: Clockwise from top right: Latticed Apple Cake (see above); Golden Oat Cake (see p. 108); Aunty Mary's Chocolate Roll (see p. 81); Apricot Nut Loaf (see p. 89).

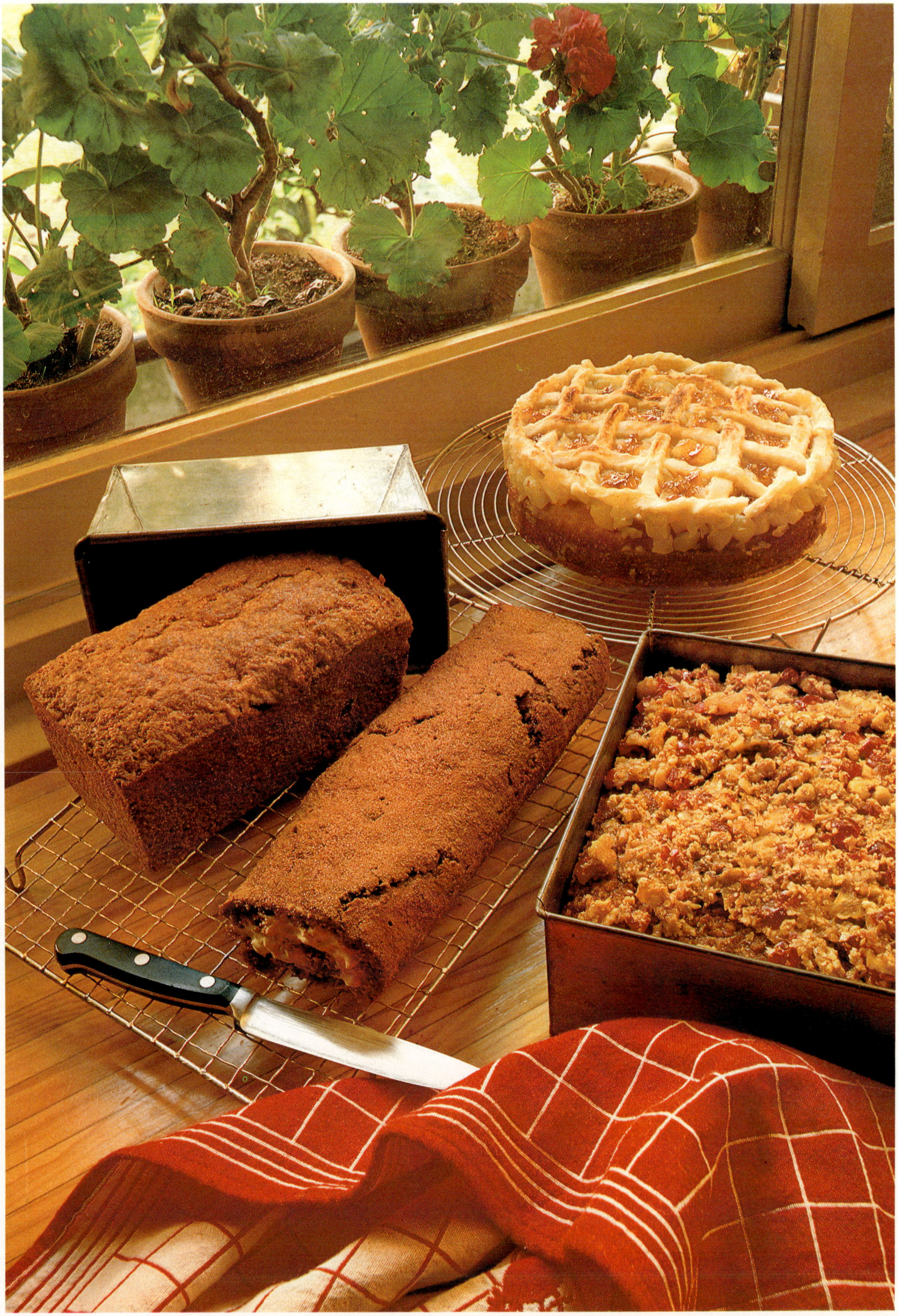

CELEBRATION AND CHRISTMAS CAKES

Rich Fruit Cake

This recipe is ideal for a special-occasion cake to celebrate a Christening, debutante party, graduation, coming of age, bon voyage, engagement, wedding anniversary, retirement or as an elaborate Christmas/New Year cake. After baking it should be stored for 2 to 3 weeks before icing and decorating.

For hints on lining the cake tin, baking and icing, see page 106.

Makes 1 25-28 cm (10–11 in, deep cake).

---

750 g (1½ lb) raisins

750 g (1½ lb) sultanas

375 g (12 oz) currants

250 g (8 oz) mixed peel

250 g (8 oz) glacé cherries

125 g (4 oz) dried apricots

125 g (8 oz) stoned dates

or use 2.75 kg (5¼ lb) mixed dried fruits (instead of above ingredients).

⅔ cup (5½ fl oz) port, Marsala or sweet sherry

125 g (4 oz) blanched almonds, chopped

500 g (1 lb) butter, softened

2⅔ cups (14 oz) brown sugar

2 tablespoons (2 oz) golden syrup (light corn syrup)

1 teaspoon glycerine (optional)

2 teaspoons grated lemon rind

8 eggs

5 cups (1¼ lb) flour

1 cup (4 oz) self-raising flour

½ teaspoon ground dried ginger

½ teaspoon ground cinnamon

½ teaspoon grated nutmeg

½ teaspoon bicarbonate of soda (baking soda)

½ teaspoon salt

extra port, Marsala or sweet sherry, as required

Combine the fruits in a non-metal bowl, chopping those that require it into small pieces (or put all the fruits in batches through a food processor and chop coarsely). Add the liquor and stir well to mix. Set aside for 10 to 12 hours, stirring from time to time.

Preheat the oven to 150°C (300°F/Gas 2). Line a deep-sided 25–28 cm (10–11 in) cake tin, and grease it thoroughly.

Add the almonds to the fruit and stir through.

In a very large bowl, beat the butter and brown sugar until creamy. Add the golden syrup, glycerine (optional) and lemon rind, and beat thoroughly. Add the eggs one at a time, beating well after each addition. At this stage it will be more practical to dispense with the beating implement and use a clean hand for further mixing.

In a separate bowl, sift the flours with the spices, bicarbonate of soda and salt. Sift half of this into the butter-egg mixture; add half the fruit mixture, and mix through. Add the remaining flour and fruit mixtures and fold in, mixing lightly but thoroughly to blend all the ingredients together. Add extra liquor if required.

Spoon the mixture into the lined and greased cake tin and smooth the surface with a wetted hand.

Place in the preheated oven and bake for 1 hour. Then reduce the temperature to 120–140°C (250°–275° F/Gas ½–1) and continue baking for about 4 more hours, depending on the size and depth of the cake.

Remove from the oven, cover loosely and allow to cool slowly in the cake tin. When quite cold, turn out carefully and wrap for storing.

Festive Fruit Wreath

Makes 1 fluted ring cake

---

1 cup (4 oz) chopped dried apricots

1 cup (4 oz) chopped walnuts or pecans

1½ cups (8 oz) chopped raisins or sultanas

1½ tablespoons brandy

1½ tablespoons orange juice

125 g (4 oz) butter or margarine, softened

¾ cup (6 oz) caster (powdered) sugar

3 eggs, separated

1 cup (3 oz) desiccated coconut

½ cup (4 oz) crushed and drained pineapple

1 cup (4 oz) self-raising flour

1 cup (4 oz) flour

Combine the apricots, walnuts and raisins with the brandy and fruit juices and set aside for 5 to 6 hours, stirring occasionally.

Preheat the oven to 160°C (325°F/Gas 3). Thoroughly grease and flour a 23 cm (9 in) fluted ring tin.

Beat the butter and sugar until creamy. Add the egg yolks and beat well; then mix in the coconut and drained pineapple.

Sift the flours together over the butter-coconut mixture and lightly fold in. Beat the egg whites until stiff and add with the dried fruit mixture. Mix lightly—do not overmix. Turn into the fluted ring tin and stand it on a scone tray.

Bake in the preheated oven for 1 hour, then reduce the temperature to 140°C (275°F/Gas 1) and bake for a further 50 to 60 minutes, covering the top of the cake with a sheet of aluminium foil to avoid overbrowning. Leave to cool in the tin.

Golden Fruit Cake

Makes 1 cake

½ cup (4 oz) caster (powdered) sugar
½ cup (4 oz) light brown sugar
2 eggs
½ cup (4 fl oz) maize oil
1 cup cooked and mashed pumpkin (about 375 g (12 oz) when raw)
2 tablespoons (2 oz) golden syrup (light corn syrup)
1 cup (4 oz) self-raising flour
1 cup (4 oz) flour
½ teaspoon ground cinnamon
¼ teaspoon grated nutmeg
¼ teaspoon ground ginger
1 tablespoon full-cream milk powder
1½ cups (8 oz) chopped raisins or sultanas
¼ cup (2 fl oz) water

Preheat the oven to 180°C (350°F/Gas 4). Base-line and grease an oblong cake tin 23 × 13 cm (9 × 5 in).

Combine the sugars, eggs and oil in a large bowl and beat with an electric hand mixer or rotary whisk for 2 minutes. Add the pumpkin and golden syrup and beat for a further 2 minutes; then remove the beaters or whisk.

Sift the flours, spices and milk powder together, then sift again over the sugar-pumpkin mixture; using a wooden spoon, fold through lightly. Then add the raisins and water and fold again. Turn into the cake tin.

Bake for 1 hour, then reduce the temperature slightly and bake for a further 20 to 30 minutes. Remove from the oven and allow to stand for 8 to 10 minutes before turning out onto a cake rack to cool. Let it stand overnight before slicing.

Dundee Cake

250 g (8 oz) butter
1 cup (6 oz) caster (powdered) sugar
2 oranges
5 eggs
2½ cups (10 oz) flour
1 teaspoon baking powder
pinch salt
½ cup (3 oz) almonds
1 cup (5 oz) sultanas
1 cup (5 oz) currants
½ cup (3 oz) chopped mixed peel
extra blanched almonds

Grease a 20 cm (8 in) round cake tin. Line tin with one thickness of brown and one thickness of greaseproof paper. Set oven temperature at 150°C (300°F/Gas 2).

Cream the butter and sugar with the grated rind of the oranges. Beat in the eggs, one at a time. Sift the flour, baking powder and salt. Blanch and chop the almonds. Mix into the flour with the fruit. Stir into the creamed mixture with 1 tablespoon orange juice. Turn into the prepared tin. Smooth the top and arrange extra blanched almonds in a pattern on the top. Bake for about 2 to 2½ hours or until a skewer inserted in centre come out clean. Cool in the tin.

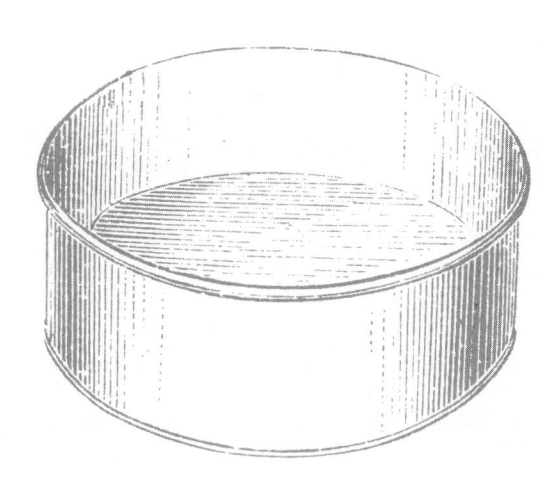

For a Perfect Fruit Cake

Cake tin linings, oven temperatures and baking times are most important to the overall result of the rich fruit cake and deserve the care and attention that the expensive ingredients demand.

Cake Tin Linings

The larger and richer the cake, the longer is the baking time. Greater protection is therefore needed to prevent the outsides of the cake from overcooking, overbrowning and drying out.

- For a 15–20 cm (6–8 in) cake tin, line with one layer of good quality thick aluminium foil, then line again with one to two layers of greaseproof paper and grease well.
- For a 23–28 cm (9–11 in) cake tin, line with two layers of good quality thick aluminium foil, then line again with two layers of greaseproof paper and grease well.
- For the very large cake tin, line as above but place another layer of aluminium foil around the outside of the tin and secure it, then stand the tin on a double thickness of foil on the actual oven shelf for baking.

Larger cakes may also require a sheet of foil over the top of the cake for the first 1 to 3 hours to prevent overbrowning, but care should be taken not to lay it too close onto the cake surface or steaming may cause a moist or soggy top layer.

The final shape of the baked cake depends upon the careful lining of the cake tin, particularly in square corners and around the base edges.

Cake, Size and Quantities

Cake Required	Rich Fruit Cake	Cake Tin Size
Single tier:		
Small	1 quantity	25–28 cm (10–11 in)
Large	1¼ quantities	30 cm (12 in)
Two tiers:		
Small	1¼ quantities	15–17 cm (6–6½ in) 25 cm (10 in)
Large	1¾ quantities	18–20 cm (7–8 in) 30 cm (12 in)
Three tiers:		
Small	1¾–2 quantities	17–18 cm (7–8¼ in) 23–24 cm (9–9½ in) 30–33 cm (12–13 in)

Note that square cake tins require slightly more mixture to fill than round ones. And for better visual balance, square cakes should be slightly deeper, especially for tiered and decorated varieties.

Cake Size, Baking Temperature, Time

Oven temperature thermostats are not always accurate, so unless you are sure of the correctness of your oven it may be wise to have it checked before embarking on the mammoth task of cooking a very large fruit cake for a special occasion. Also, be sure to check that the temperatures for baking stated below do coincide with those in your appliance instruction book. Check the oven position recommended in the manufacturer's instructions.

Cake Size	Oven Temperature	Baking Time
15–17 cm (6–6½ in)	160°C (325°F/Gas 3)	2–2½ hours
19–20 cm (7½–8 in)	150°C (300°F/Gas 2) then turn to 140°C (275°F/Gas 1)	2 hours + 1½–2 hours
24–25 cm (9½–10 in)	150°C (300°F/Gas 2) then turn to 140°C (275°F/Gas 1)	2½ hours + 2–2½ hours
29–30 cm (11½–12 in)	150°C (300°F/Gas 2) then turn to 140°C (275°F/Gas 1)	3 hours + 3–3½ hours
32–33 cm (12½–13 in)	150°C (300°F/Gas 2) then turn to 140°C (275°F/Gas 1)	3 hours + 3½–4 hours

Note that deep cakes will take longer to cook.

Do not disturb the cake for at least half to three-quarters of the baking time, then check the cake's progress, without holding the oven door open any longer than is necessary.

Start testing for doneness about 10 minutes before the minimum stated baking time. A very fine skewer pierced diagonally through the cake centre (preferably into a crack if visible) should be clear of moist cake mixture upon removal, though do not confuse dried fruits with uncooked cake mixture.

The cooked cake mixture should be firm to the touch of a finger in several surface spots. Some experienced cake bakers say there is a distinct humming sound from an uncooked rich fruit cake. If in doubt, leave for a further 5 to 10 minutes or turn off the oven and leave for 10 to 15 minutes.

Upon removal from the oven, if the surface of the cake appears a little dry, a brushover with a little extra liquor before covering will be of benefit; brush again if required after cooling and before final wrapping for storage.

1. Cut greaseproof strips to line sides of tin

2. Brush strips with melted butter

3. Line tin with buttered greaseproof

4. Cream butter and sugar, beat in eggs

5. Smooth top of cake mixture

6. Rich Fruit Cake (see p. 104)

Malted Sultana Cake

Makes 1 slab cake

3 cups (12 oz) flour
1 teaspoon baking powder
½ teaspoon bicarbonate of soda (baking soda)
¼ teaspoon salt
½ cup (4fl oz) milk, heated
⅓ cup (4 oz) golden syrup (light corn syrup)
½ cup (5fl oz) malt extract
1 tablespoon lemon juice
1½ cups (8 oz) sultanas
½ cup (2 oz) chopped walnuts
2 eggs, beaten

Preheat the oven to 150°C (300°F/Gas 2). Line the base of a 30 × 20 cm (12 × 8 in) baking tin, and grease well.

Sift the dry ingredients into a large bowl.

Into the hot milk, stir the golden syrup and malt extract, add the lemon juice and mix well to blend.

Toss the sultanas and walnuts through the flour mixture. Add the malt-milk mixture and the beaten eggs, and beat until thoroughly combined—do not overmix. Turn into the baking tin.

Bake for 1¼ hours. Remove from the oven and stand for 8 to 10 minutes before turning out onto a cake rack to cool. When cold, store overnight in an airtight container before cutting into slices and spreading with butter or margarine, if desired.

Fruit and Vegetable Cake

Makes 1 cake

2 eggs
½ cup (4 oz) raw sugar
¼ cup (3 oz) honey
100 ml (3fl oz) maize oil
1½ cups (6 oz) flour
3 teaspoons baking powder
1 teaspoon mixed spices
¼ teaspoon salt
¾ cup (4 oz) sultanas
¼ cup (1 oz) chopped walnuts
1 cup (4 oz) shredded raw zucchini (courgette) or choko

Preheat the oven to 180°C (350°F/Gas 4). Line and grease a 22 × 13 cm (8½ × 5 in) cake tin.

Place the eggs in the small bowl of an electric mixer and beat until thick and frothy. Add the sugar, honey and maize oil, and continue beating for 2 to 3 minutes.

Sift the flour, baking powder, spices and salt into a large bowl and make a well in the centre. Add the egg-sugar mixture and stir through lightly with a wooden spoon. Add the sultanas, walnuts and shredded vegetable, and fold through to combine thoroughly. Turn into the cake tin.

Bake for 55 to 60 minutes. Remove from the oven and allow to stand for 8 to 10 minutes before carefully turning out onto a cake rack to cool. Store in an airtight container for 1 to 2 days before cutting into slices.

Note: Small, young zucchini or chokoes can be shredded with their skins intact. Larger, older vegetables should be peeled and have their seeds removed first.

Golden Oat Cake

Makes 1 cake

1½ cups (6 oz) self-raising flour
½ teaspoon salt
⅔ cup (4 oz) brown sugar
2 teaspoons grated orange rind
1¼ cups (6 oz) minute oats
2 eggs
1 cup (8fl oz) milk
1 cup (5½fl oz) maize oil
Topping:
⅓ cup (2 oz) brown sugar
2 tablespoons (1 oz) minute oats
1 tablespoon maize oil
½ cup (4 oz) crushed and drained pineapple
2 tablespoons chopped glacé cherries
2 tablespoons chopped walnuts

Preheat the oven to 180°C (350°F/Gas 4). Line the base of a cake tin 23 cm (9 in) square, and grease well.

Sift the flour and salt into a bowl; add the brown sugar, orange rind and oats and toss to mix thoroughly.

Beat the eggs; add the milk and maize oil and mix well. Pour onto the flour-oats mixture and stir to combine all ingredients thoroughly—do not overmix. Turn into the cake tin.

Bake for 45 to 50 minutes. Combine the topping ingredients and, briefly removing the cake from the oven, quickly but carefully scatter over the top of the cake; lower the oven temperature to 160°C (325°F/Gas 3) and bake for a further 15 to 20 minutes. Serve warm.

Brandied Ale Fruit Cake

Makes 1 cake

---
1 kg (2 lb) mixed dried fruits

1 teaspoon grated orange rind

2½ cups (20fl oz) ginger ale—soft drink

60 g (2 oz) almonds

315 g (10 oz) butter or margarine, softened

1½ cups (8 oz) brown sugar

1 tablespoon glycerine

6 eggs

2½ cups (10 oz) flour

1 cup (4 oz) self-raising wholemeal flour

½ teaspoon ground cinnamon

½ teaspoon grated nutmeg

2–3 tablespoons brandy, for topping

Cut the mixed dried fruits into small pieces, add the orange rind, turn into a non-metal bowl and pour the ginger ale over. Let it stand overnight; stir occasionally. Before mixing the cake, fold the chopped almonds through.

Preheat the oven to 150°C (300°F/Gas 2). Line a 23 cm (9 in) cake tin with one layer of heavy-quality aluminium foil, allowing it to stand about 6 cm (2½ in) higher than the pan all around. Place lining of greaseproof paper inside the tin in a similar fashion smoothing out the corners evenly.

Spoon the fruit cake mixture into a prepared pan, pressing down firmly to level the surface with wetted palm of the hand. Carefully 'bang' the pan on the work bench to settle the mixture. Rest a sheet of aluminium foil across the lining of the cake tin.

Bake in the preheated oven for 1 hour; then remove the foil, decrease the oven temperature to 140°C (275°F/Gas 1) and bake for a further 3 to 3½ hours. Test with a fine metal skewer to ascertain whether the centre of the cake is completely cooked (see page 106). If the top of the cake appears to be drying or browning excessively, replace the foil over the cake tin during the last hour or so of baking.

Remove from the oven and brush the brandy over the top of the cake whilst it is hot and then again when cooled. Wrap and store the cake for 1 to 2 weeks before use.

Note: If the dried fruit mixture is very moist, decrease the ginger ale by about 3 tablespoons. However, it may need to be added at a later stage with the flour to give a good moist consistency.

Fruitmince Pecan Ring

Makes 1 ring cake

---
60 g (2 oz) butter or margarine, softened

½ cup (4 oz) caster (powdered) sugar

¼ teaspoon lemon essence

1 egg

¾ cup (5 oz) prepared fruitmince

¼ cup (1 oz) pecans, chopped

1½ cups (6 oz) flour

2 teaspoons baking powder

½ teaspoon bicarbonate of soda (baking soda)

¼ teaspoon salt

½ cup (4fl oz) milk

Pecan Butter Cream Topping:
Vienna Butter Cream (see recipe, page 144)

½ cup (2 oz) chopped pecan nuts

¼ teaspoon lemon essence

Preheat the oven to 180°C (350°F/Gas 4). Thoroughly grease an 18 cm (7 in) ring tin. Cream the butter and sugar until light and fluffy. Add the lemon essence and egg, and beat well. Stir the fruitmince and chopped pecans through the mixture. Sift the dry ingredients over and fold through, adding the milk in 2 or 3 batches. Spoon into the ring tin.

Bake for 45–50 minutes. Remove from the oven and allow to stand for 5 minutes before turning out onto a cake rack to cool.

Topping: Whilst the Vienna Butter Cream is still soft, fold in the pecan nuts and flavour with lemon essence.

When the cake is cold, spread the butter cream topping over and swirl or 'rough up' to an attractive design. Allow to set before cutting.

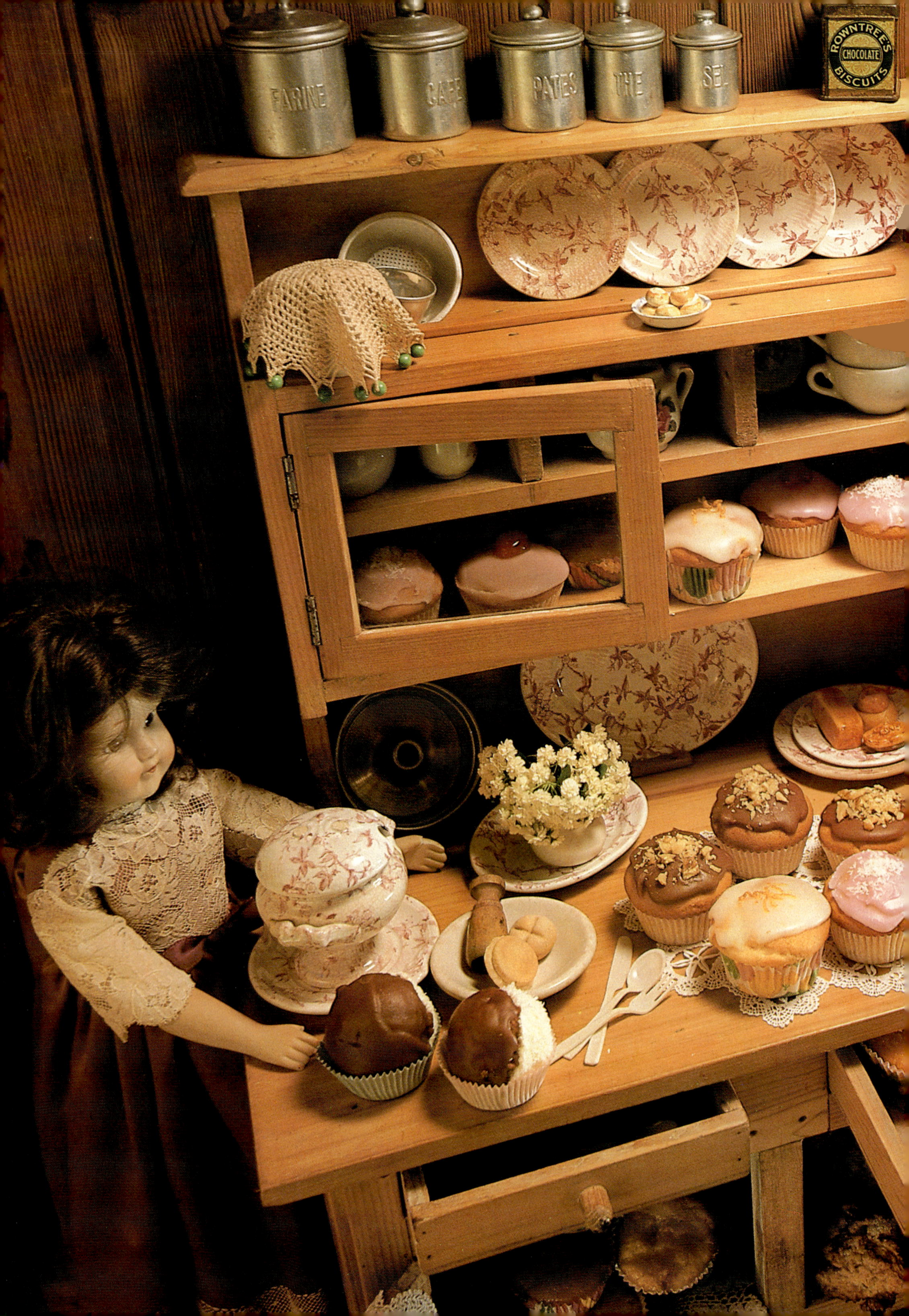
FARINE
CAFE
PATES
THE
SEL
ROWNTREE'S
CHOCOLATE
BISCUITS

Small Cakes

Small Cakes

1. Lamingtons (see p. 116)
2. Patty Cakes (see p. 114)
3. Butterfly Cakes (see p. 114)
4. Crusted Date Squares (see p. 124)
5. Chocomallows (see p. 121)
6. Rock Cakes (see p. 113)
7. St Clements Cakes (see p. 124)

The small cakes in this chapter are one-portion pieces of cake made for individual serving, whether made in separate containers or made as a larger cake and cut after baking.

The quantities of ingredients used, the preparation methods and the decoration for small cakes are not so very different from those of the larger cakes. Small or large cakes can be made from the same recipe—the best example being the Basic or Foundation Butter Cake mixture as described on page 76.

The mixture for small cakes may be a little firmer or sturdier in texture, particularly the varieties that are baked as one large cake and then cut into smaller pieces for individual serving. Small cakes that are individually made and baked are not usually as elaborate in finish or decoration as the larger ones, nor as time-consuming for the cook.

Little cakes for little people—apart from the ease of handling for tiny fingers, the more substantial mixture used for children's cakes means less breaking and crumbling. Children love to be given a cake of their very own, and with a little ingenuity and imagination you can prepare a whole host of little cakes, each one individual in simple decoration, for party times or other special occasions.

Small cakes can be attractive, dainty sweetmeats for special occasions—an idea probably originating in the meals known as 'High Tea' and 'Afternoon Tea'.

During the nineteenth century it became the custom in the stately homes of England to serve elaborate many-coursed meals both at midday and in the evening. In order for the diners to do full justice to both meals, the time between was lengthened and early lunch and a late dinner became the vogue.

This then left a long period without food, so an interim small meal became the sensible answer, particularly for the very young or elderly who were not expected to stay awake until late in the evening. This became known as 'High Tea' and always contained plates of little cakes in place of a more substantial or elaborate dessert.

Ladies of the period, reputedly headed by the Duchess of Bedford, also commenced the fashion of entertaining in the late afternoon. It was at about this time that tea was introduced as a beverage to drink at times other than after the evening meal or in places other than the tea houses which were well established in the larger cities. So 'Afternoon Tea' became the vogue, and ladies of society searched endlessly for unusual and exciting dainties to tempt their guests.

Betty Dunleavy

ABOUT SMALL CAKES

Freezing:
Little cakes—and large cakes—freeze well. They can be stored in a freezer plain or iced and decorated. However, careful freezing is required to preserve the shape of the cake. In freezing decorated cakes it is better to open freeze (on a plate without any covering) until very firm, then pack and seal in containers with rigid support to avoid damage whilst in the freezer compartment. With conservation of fuel and energy of vital importance, the wise cook will do as our grandmothers used to do—have a baking day every so often, filling the oven to capacity, but then wrapping and freezing those cakes that are not required for current use.

From the host of recipes for small cakes in this chapter, no doubt you'll find a treat to suit the occasion and your enthusiasm at the moment.

Small Cake Patty Tins:
There are many different varieties of shaped tins which are suitable for baking small cakes.

These generally are grouped in 6, 12 or 18 varying-sized indentations in the one mould, enabling the cake maker to bake a reasonable number at the one time. Material is of sheet aluminium, tin or similar metal alloy and the indentations for each small cake are approx. 5 cm (1¾ in) diameter and 2 cm (¾ in) in depth.

There is also a variety of tins with smaller, fancy-shaped indentations for specialty use, i.e. Petit Fours, etc. These shapes are often also used as setting moulds for cold savouries, tiny sweetmeats and other iced confections.

Convenience patty pans are also available in firm, fluted, greaseproof paper or aluminium foil. The containers can be placed separately inside each metal indentation, having the advantage of eliminating the necessity of greasing and later cleansing the metal tins. Another advantage of these loose containers is that they provide ideal protection for small cakes which are to be transported and/or handled by small children. Containers for baking gem cakes were originally made of cast iron and so required considerable preheating before use in order that the small cake would rise and cook quickly. These containers are now also available in thinner, lighter metals which can be heated more quickly and do not rust on storing.

Individual, deeper metal containers, known as muffin tins are also available for particular recipe use. These may be stacked on flat baking trays for convenience of baking in batches as required.

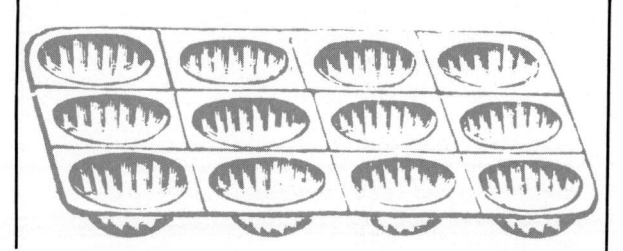

Rock Cakes

Makes 24–26 small cakes

2 cups (8 oz) self-raising flour

¼ teaspoon salt

½ teaspoon mixed spices

90 g (3 oz) butter or margarine, chopped

⅓ cup (3 oz) caster (powdered) sugar

2 tablespoons (1 oz) mixed dried fruits

1 tablespoon (½ oz) chopped dried peel

1 egg, beaten

2–3 tablespoons milk

extra butter, for spreading

Preheat the oven to 190°C (375°F/Gas 5). Prepare biscuit trays by greasing them well.

Sift the flour, salt and spices into a bowl; add the butter and rub through with the fingertips until fine. Then mix the sugar through.

Combine the dried fruits and peel with the egg; add this to the mixture, with sufficient milk to mix to a stiff consistency. Pile in heaped spoonfuls about 5 cm (2 in) apart on the biscuit trays.

Bake for 15 to 17 minutes. Turn onto cake racks to cool. Before serving, split each rock cake and spread with butter if desired.

Variations:
Sugar Tops: Before baking, sprinkle the tops with sugar or coffee crystals.

St Clements: Add 2 teaspoons of grated orange rind and 1 teaspoon of grated lemon rind instead of the dried peel.

Wholemeal: Substitute half of the white flour with wholemeal flour, and use raw sugar instead of caster sugar.

Patty Cakes

Makes 24–30 little cakes (depending on the size of the patty pans)

125 g (4 oz) butter or margarine, softened
½ cup (4 oz) caster (powdered) sugar
1 teaspoon vanilla essence
2 eggs, separated
¼ cup (2fl oz) milk
1½ cups (6 oz) self-raising flour
1 tablespoon cornflour (cornstarch)
¼ teaspoon salt
Warm Glacé Icing (see recipe, page 130)

Preheat the oven to 190°C (375°F/Gas 5). Grease the patty pans.

Beat the butter, sugar and vanilla essence until light and fluffy. Add the egg yolks and then the milk, and beat thoroughly.

Sift the flour, cornflour and salt together and fold this into the butter-egg mixture.

Beat the egg whites until white and foamy, and carefully fold in the mixture. Two-thirds fill each cavity in the patty pans.

Bake for 17 to 20 minutes. Turn out onto cake racks to cool. Ice with Warm Glacé Icing.

Variations:

Banana: Add 1 cup (8 oz) of mashed banana and 1 teaspoon of grated lemon rind to the mixture, and reduce the quantity of milk by 2 teaspoons.

Colour the icing pale lemon, using food colouring.

Cherry: Colour the cake mixture pale pink with food colouring, and add 2 tablespoons of chopped glacé cherries.

Colour the icing pale pink.

Choc-nut: Add 1 tablespoon of cocoa to the dry ingredients, and increase the quantity of milk by 2 teaspoons.

Ice with melted chocolate and sprinkle with chopped walnuts.

Sultana Spice: Add 1 teaspoon of ground mixed spices to the dry ingredients, and fold in ¼–½ cup (3–5 oz) of sultanas with the milk. Do not ice.

Date Surprise: Half fill the patty pans with the cake mixture, place half a date on top of each, and cover with remaining mixture to two-thirds fill. Colour the icing pale orange.

Passionfruit: Colour the cake mixture with a little orange food colouring.

Flavour the icing with passionfruit pulp.

Marble Cakes: Divide the cake mixture into three portions; colour one portion pink, colour the second portion chocolate, and leave the third portion natural. Drop spoonfuls of each mixture alternately into the patty pans before baking.

Use chocolate icing.

Cornflake Crisps: Spread 1 cup of cornflakes on to a plate; drop 1 tablespoon of cake mixture on to the cornflakes and lightly toss to coat it. Place in an individual greased paper container ready for baking. Do not ice.

Princess Cakes: Half fill the patty pans with the cake mixture, drop ½ teaspoon of raspberry jam on top, then cover with extra mixture.

Dust with icing sugar.

Butterfly Cakes: Using a sharp pointed knife, cut out a circle from the top of each cake to a depth of about 1 cm (½ in). Remove the top and cut it in half. Fill the well with jam and whipped cream, replace the tops on the cream so that they point upwards like little wings. Sprinkle with icing (confectioners') sugar.

Strawberry Sparklets

Makes 20–24 little cakes

125 g (4 oz) butter or margarine, softened
½ cup (4 oz) caster (powdered) sugar
½ teaspoon vanilla essence
2 eggs
1 packet (3½ oz) strawberry-flavoured jelly crystals (gelatin crystals)
2 cups (8 oz) self-raising flour
½ cup (4fl oz) milk
strawberry jam (jelly)
pastel pink glacé icing (see recipe, page 130)

Preheat the oven to 190°C (375°F/Gas 5). Prepare deep-sided patty pans by greasing them well.

Beat the butter and caster sugar until creamy. Flavour with the vanilla essence. Add the eggs one at a time, beating well between each addition. Stir in three-quarters of the jelly crystals. Fold in alternate batches of sifted flour and milk, about a third of each at a time.

Spoon ½ tablespoon of cake mixture into each patty pan cavity. Add about 1 teaspoon of strawberry jam, being careful not to touch the sides of the pan. Top with more cake mixture to two-thirds fill each cavity.

Bake for 15 to 17 minutes, until just firm to the touch. Turn out onto cake racks to cool. When cold, ice with pink glacé icing and sprinkle the remaining jelly crystals on top for decoration.

Right: **Strawberry Sparklets** (see above); **Jaffa Gems** (see p. 120); **Choc-Coffee Rounds** (see p. 116).

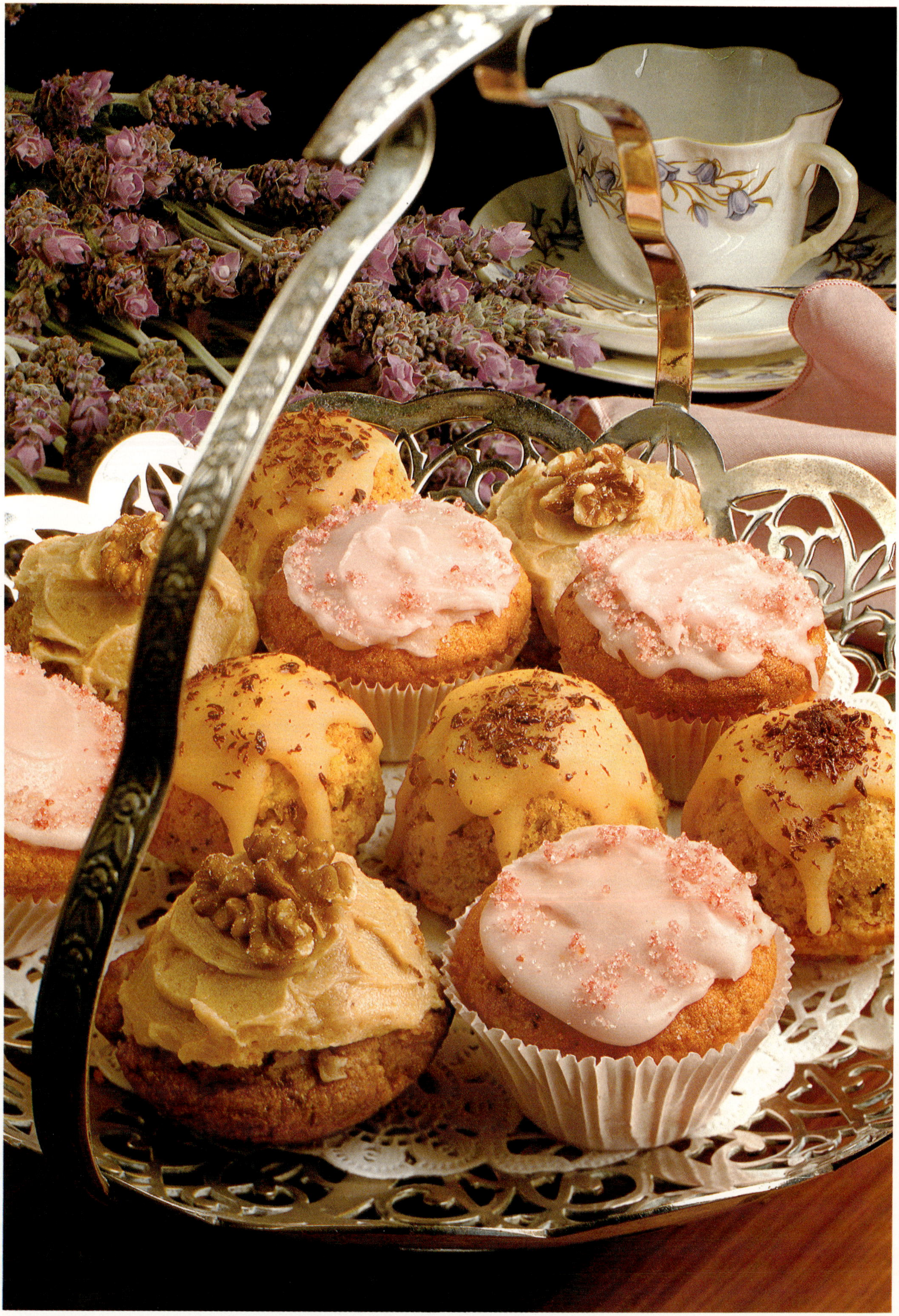

Spiced Sultana Patties

Makes 20–24 little cakes

2 cups (8 oz) self-raising flour
1/4 teaspoon salt
1 teaspoon mixed spices
1/4 cup (1 1/2 oz) brown sugar
1/2 cup (3 oz) sultanas
30 g (1 oz) butter or margarine
1 tablespoon golden syrup (light corn syrup)
2 eggs, beaten
3/4 cup (6fl oz) milk

Preheat the oven to 200°C (400°F/Gas 6). Grease deep-sided patty pans.

Sift the flour, salt and spices into a bowl. Add the brown sugar and sultanas, and mix through.

Melt the butter and blend with the golden syrup; beat into the eggs and add the milk to blend. Stir into the flour-sultana mixture quickly and lightly until just combined. Spoon into the deep patty pans to two-thirds fill.

Bake for 17 to 20 minutes. Turn out onto cake racks to cool. Store in an airtight container until ready for use.

Choc-Coffee Rounds

Makes 24–26 little cakes

125 g (4 oz) butter or margarine, softened
3/4 cup (4 oz) brown sugar
2 eggs, beaten
1 teaspoon vanilla essence
60 g (2 oz) cooking chocolate, melted
2 cups (8 oz) flour
1/2 teaspoon bicarbonate of soda (baking soda)
1/4 teaspoon salt
1 teaspoon baking powder
3/4 cup (6fl oz) sour cream
1/2 cup (2 oz) chopped walnuts
Choc-Coffee Cream (see recipe, page 144)

Preheat the oven to 190°C (375°F/Gas 5). Prepare shallow round-based patty pans by greasing well.

Cream the butter and sugar until light and fluffy. Beat the eggs and vanilla through, and then stir in the cooled chocolate.

Sift the flour, bicarbonate of soda, salt and baking powder together. Add to the chocolate mixture in alternate batches with the sour cream. Lightly fold the walnuts through. Spoon into the patty pans to two-thirds fill.

Bake for 15 to 17 minutes. Carefully turn out onto cake racks to cool.

Frost with the Choc-Coffee Cream and allow to set.

Lamingtons

Makes 16 little square cakes

125 g (4 oz) butter or margarine, softened
3/4 cup (6 oz) caster (powdered) sugar
1 teaspoon vanilla essence
2 eggs
1/2 cup (4fl oz) milk
2 cups (8 oz) self-raising flour
1/4 teaspoon salt
Icing:
2 cups (12 oz) icing (confectioners') sugar
2 tablespoons (1/2 oz) cocoa
30 g (1 oz) butter or margarine
3–4 tablespoons boiling milk or water
2 2/3 cups (8 oz) desiccated coconut

Preheat the oven to 180°C (350°F/Gas 4). Thoroughly grease a 20–23 cm (8–9 in) slab tin.

Beat the butter, sugar and vanilla essence until light and fluffy. Add the eggs one at a time, beating well after each addition. Beat as much of the milk into the mixture as possible with it beginning to 'curdle', then lightly fold in the sifted flour and salt and the remaining milk. Spoon into the slab tin.

Bake for 35 to 45 minutes. Allow to stand in the tin for 2 to 3 minutes, then turn out onto a cake rack. When cold, cut into 16 squares and set aside for several hours before icing.

Icing: Sift the icing sugar and cocoa into a bowl. Combine the butter and boiling milk, and pour this into the icing sugar mixture to form a creamy consistency. Stand the bowl over a container of hot water to keep the icing from setting too quickly.

Using a long-pronged fork for holding each cake square, dip each piece into the chocolate icing and twist to coat all sides. Place the desiccated coconut on a flat plate, and toss each iced square in it to coat thoroughly. Lift onto a cake rack to set; and store in an airtight container until ready for use.

Note: A packet butter cake mix may replace the above cake recipe, if desired.

Raisin Munchies

Makes 20–24 muffins

1 cup (4 oz) self-raising flour

¼ teaspoon salt

½ teaspoon mixed spices

1¼ cups (6 oz) prepared muesli mixture

¼ cup (1½ oz) brown sugar

½ cup (3 oz) chopped raisins

½ teaspoon bicarbonate of soda (baking soda)

¾ cup (6 fl oz) milk

1 tablespoon maize oil

1 egg beaten

1 tablespoon honey or golden syrup (light corn syrup), warmed

Preheat the oven to 190°C (375°F/Gas 5). Place patty cases made of foil in the cavities of deep-sided patty pans or muffin pans.

Sift the flour into a bowl with the salt and spices; add the muesli mixture, sugar and raisins, and mix well.

Dissolve the bicarbonate of soda in the milk; add the oil, beaten egg and honey or golden syrup, and stir into the flour-muesli mixture to make a soft dough. Two-thirds fill the foil patty cases with the cake mixture.

Bake for 15 to 17 minutes. Turn onto cake racks to cool. Store in an airtight container.

Coco-Lemon Cakes

Makes 20–24 little cakes

2 cups (8 oz) self-raising flour

¼ teaspoon salt

90 g (3 oz) butter or margarine, chopped

⅓ cup (3 oz) caster (powdered) sugar

⅓ cup (1 oz) desiccated coconut

2 teaspoons grated lemon rind

1 egg

2 tablespoons milk

1 teaspoon vanilla essence

extra desiccated coconut, for topping

Preheat the oven to 190°C (375°F/Gas 5). Grease the patty pans.

Sift the flour and salt into a bowl; rub in the butter with the tips of the fingers until fine. Then add the sugar, coconut and lemon rind, and mix thoroughly.

Beat the egg with the milk and vanilla essence, and mix into the flour-coconut mixture. (Should the coconut be dry, a little extra milk may be required.) Spoon into the patty pans to two-thirds fill; sprinkle a little extra coconut over the top.

Bake for 20 to 22 minutes. Turn out onto cake racks, and serve warm or freshly cold.

Spicy Apple Drops

Makes 20–24 little cakes

1 packet cake mix for butter cake

1 egg

water or milk

½–¾ cup (4–6 oz) cooked apple pulp

½ teaspoon ground cinnamon

½ teaspoon grated nutmeg

melted butter or margarine

1 tablespoon sugar

extra 1 teaspoon mixed cinnamon and nutmeg

Preheat the oven to 190°C (375°F/Gas 5). Prepare round-based patty pans by greasing them well.

Make up the cake mix according to directions on the packet, using the egg and slightly less water or milk than required to give a firmer batter.

Flavour the apple pulp with the combined cinnamon and nutmeg.

Spoon about 2 teaspoons of cake mixture into each patty pan cavity. Add about 1 teaspoon of the spiced apple pulp, being careful not to touch the sides of the pan. Top with more cake mixture to two-thirds fill each cavity.

Bake for 12–15 minutes, until golden brown and just firm to the touch. Remove from the patty pans and, while still warm, brush the tops with melted butter; quickly sprinkle with the combined sugar and extra spices. Allow to cool.

Peaches

Makes 10–12 little double-layer cakes

125 g (4 oz) butter or margarine, softened
½ cup (4 oz) sugar
3 eggs
½ cup (4 fl oz) milk
orange food colouring
2 cups (8 oz) self-raising flour
Decoration:
strawberry jam (strawberry jelly)
Mock Cream (see recipe, page 140)
strawberry and orange jelly (gelatin) crystals
boiling water

Preheat the oven to 200°C (400°F/Gas 6). Place small-cavity gem irons in the oven to heat them. Cream the butter and sugar well. Add the eggs one at a time, beating well after each addition; then add the milk with a little food colouring and beat thoroughly. Fold the sifted flour through lightly.

Quickly grease the heated gem irons and two-thirds fill each cavity with the cake mixture.

Bake for 14 to 16 minutes. Turn out onto cake racks to cool.

Decoration: From the top of each gem cake, scoop out a little mixture; fill with strawberry jam. Join two cakes together with the Mock Cream, then chill well.

Dissolve ¼ cup (1½ oz) of jelly crystals in ½ cup (4 fl oz) of boiling water; cool until thickening, then brush over the joined cakes.

Toss the joined cakes lightly in combined strawberry and orange jelly crystals to coat all over. Chill to set. Serve on a plate, with fresh peach tree leaves for decoration.

Petits Fours

According to Câreme, the famous French chef and pastry-maker of the early nineteenth century, Petits ('small') Fours ('oven' or 'bakehouse') were small cakes baked in the oven when it was cooling down at the end of a day's baking. These little cakes, of varying shapes, were then coated all over with left-over fondant icings and decorated with bits and pieces also left over from gâteaux and dessert cake masterpieces—candied angelica, glacé cherries, nuts, crystallised or piped flowers, and so on.

Most great restaurants who serve their foods in the Classic French style still present a plate of Petits Fours Riches or Petits Fours Glacé on the table with coffee—a collection of tiny cakes, meringues, pastries, marzipans, etc., cut into fancy shapes.

Home-style baking now interprets the name to mean a plate of small cakes cut into squares, diamonds, rounds, etc., coated with glacé icing and decorated delicately in pastel colours. Some enthusiastic cooks also coat the sides of the little cakes with finely chopped nuts, coloured coconut or crumbled cakecrumbs after spreading with a rich butter cream.

Cake Mixtures:
Foundation Butter Cake (see recipe, page 76)
Genoise (see recipe, page 98)
One Bowl Butter Cake Supreme (see recipe, page 77)

Icings:
Warm Glacé Icing (see page 130)
Royal Icing (see page 130)
Apricot Glaze (see page 149)

Decorations:
Glacé fruits, piped or crystallised flowers, marzipan fruits, piped rosettes, scrolls, etc.

Ginger-Pine Patties

Makes 10–12 little cakes

1¼ cups (5 oz) flour
2 teaspoons baking powder
¼ teaspoon salt
60 g (2 oz) butter or margarine
⅓ cup (3 oz) caster (powdered) sugar
1 egg, beaten
¼ cup (2 fl oz) milk
2 tablespoons crushed and drained pineapple
1 tablespoon chopped crystallised ginger
lemon flavoured Glacé Icing (see recipe page 130)

Preheat the oven to 180°C (350°F/Gas 4). Prepare deep-sided patty pans by greasing them well.

Sift the flour, baking powder and salt into a bowl; add the butter and rub through with the fingertips until the mixture is fine. Add the sugar. Combine the beaten egg with the milk and add, mixing to a soft dough. Fold in the pineapple and chopped ginger gradually. Two-thirds fill the patty pan cavities.

Bake for 17 to 20 minutes. Turn out onto cake racks to cool.

When cold, ice the tops with Lemon Glacé Icing.

Right: **Clockwise from top: Peaches (above); Petits Fours (above).**

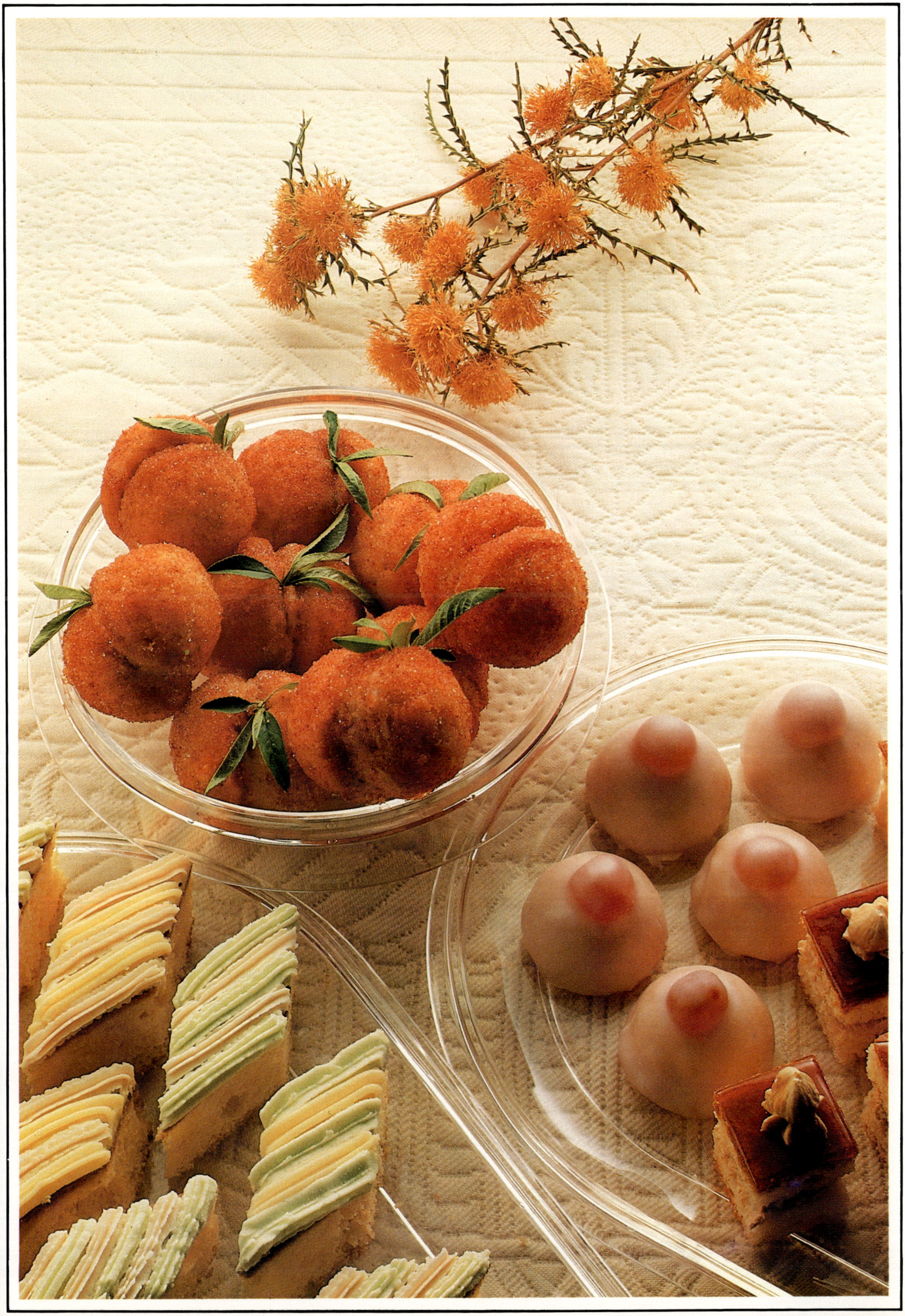

Sultana Bran Cakes

Makes 28–30 little cakes

125 g (4 oz) butter or margarine, softened
½ cup (4 oz) sugar
1 egg
1 cup (4 oz) bran cereal
1 cup (8fl oz) milk
1 cup (4 oz) self-raising flour
1 teaspoon mixed spices
¼ teaspoon salt
½–¾ cup (3–4 oz) sultanas

Preheat the oven to 190°C (375°F/Gas 5). Prepare deep-sided patty pans by greasing well.

Beat the butter and sugar to a cream; and add the egg, beating thoroughly.

Soak the bran cereal in the milk until well absorbed; then mix with the butter-egg mixture. Sift the flour, spices and salt together and fold into the butter-bran mixture with the sultanas. Spoon into the patty pans to two-thirds fill.

Bake for 12 to 15 minutes or until cooked and golden brown. Turn out onto a cake rack to cool.

Coffee Nut Cakes

Makes 26–30 little cakes

3 cups (12 oz) self-raising flour
¼ teaspoon salt
¾ cup (4 oz) brown sugar
½ cup (2 oz) chopped walnuts
¼ cup (1 oz) chopped dates or raisins
1 egg
45 g (1½ oz) butter or margarine, melted
1¼ cups (10fl oz) black coffee, cold

Preheat the oven to 190°C (375°F/Gas 5). Prepare deep-sided patty pans or muffin pans by greasing well.

Sift the flour and salt into a bowl, mix the sugar, walnuts and dates through, and make a well in the centre.

Beat the egg, cooled butter and black coffee together; pour this into the flour-fruit mixture and beat lightly but thoroughly to combine. Two-thirds fill the patty pan cavities.

Bake for 20 to 22 minutes. Turn out onto cake racks to cool, then serve freshly baked—with or without icing, as desired.

Jaffa Gems

Makes 24–30 gem cakes

125 g (4 oz) butter or margarine, softened
½ cup (4 oz) sugar
60 g (2 oz) coarsely grated chocolate
3 teaspoons grated orange rind
2 eggs
2 cups (8 oz) self-raising flour
¼ teaspoon salt
⅓ cup milk
Orange flavoured Glacé Icing (see recipe, page 130)
coarsely grated chocolate, for topping

Preheat the oven to 190°C (375°F/Gas 5). Heat the gem irons in the oven.

Beat the butter and sugar to a cream. Add the grated chocolate and orange rind, and beat well; then beat in the eggs one at a time.

Sift the flour and salt together, and fold into the butter-chocolate mixture alternately with the milk.

Quickly grease the heated gem irons and two-thirds fill the cavities with cake mixture.

Bake for 15 to 17 minutes. Turn out onto a cake rack to cool.

Ice the tops with Orange Glacé Icing and sprinkle with grated chocolate for decoration.

Thistledowns

Makes 38–40 small gem cakes

2 cups (8 oz) flour
3 teaspoons baking powder
¼ cup (2 oz) caster (powdered) sugar
¼ teaspoon salt
⅓ cup (3fl oz) maize oil
1 egg, beaten
2 tablespoons (½ oz) non-fat milk powder
1 cup (8fl oz) water
icing (confectioners) sugar for topping

Preheat the oven to 200°C (400°F/Gas 6). Heat the gem irons in the oven.

Sift the flour with the baking powder, caster sugar and salt twice, then sift into a bowl and make a well in the centre.

Combine the maize oil with the egg. Beat the milk powder into the water. Then beat the two mixtures together. Pour into the flour mixture and mix very lightly with a flat egg whisk until just smooth. Allow to stand for 15 to 20 minutes, undisturbed.

Quickly grease and flour the heated gem irons, and half fill each cavity with the cake mixture—use one movement for the filling, without 'topping up' with extra mixture.

Bake for 12 to 15 minutes. Carefully turn out onto cake racks, dust the tops with sifted icing sugar and serve very fresh.

Chocomallows

Makes 16–18 gem cakes

90 g (3 oz) butter or margarine, softened
⅓ cup (3 oz) caster (powdered) sugar
2 eggs, beaten
1½ cups (6 oz) self-raising flour
2 tablespoons (½ oz) cocoa
¼ teaspoon salt
½ teaspoon ground cinnamon
2 tablespoons evaporated milk
2 teaspoons lemon juice
Chocolate Glacé Icing (see recipe, page 130)
Marshmallow: *1 cup (8 fl oz) orange juice*
1 cup (8 oz) sugar
¼ teaspoon cream of tartar
1 tablespoon (½ oz) gelatine
2 teaspoons lemon juice
about 1 cup (3 oz) desiccated coconut

Preheat the oven to 200°C (400°F/Gas 6). Heat the gem irons in the oven.

Beat the butter and sugar until light and fluffy. Add the eggs and beat well. Into a separate bowl, sift the flour, cocoa, salt and cinnamon together. Combine the evaporated milk and lemon juice in a small bowl and set aside for 5 minutes.

Fold the dry ingredients into the butter mixture in alternate amounts with the soured milk.

Quickly grease the well-heated gem irons and two-thirds fill with the cake mixture.

Bake for 14 to 16 minutes. Turn out onto cake racks, and when cold level the tops and coat all over with Chocolate Glacé Icing; allow to set.

Marshmallow: Have clean gem irons on hand. Combine the orange juice, sugar, cream of tartar and gelatine in a small heavy-based saucepan, bring slowly to the boil, then allow to boil for 10 minutes.

Remove from the heat and allow to cool; turn into a large bowl and add the lemon juice. When the mixture is about the consistency of unbeaten egg whites, commence beating with an electric mixer or rotary whisk until the mixture is thickened well and increased greatly in volume.

Quickly fill into wetted gem irons, and chill until set. Unmould, and coat the rounded surface with the coconut, leaving the level tops uncoated.

To Assemble the Chocomallows: To join the chocolate and marshmallow rounds, slowly pass a heated metal spatula over the uncoated marshmallow surface to slightly dissolve, then quickly press the marshmallow against the level chocolate surface of the little cake to adhere. Allow to set before serving.

Golden Ginger Gems

Makes 16–18 gem cakes

60 g (2 oz) butter or margarine, softened
1¼ cup (2 oz) sugar
1 teaspoon ground ginger
2 tablespoons golden syrup   *(light corn syrup)*
1 egg
1½ cups (6 oz) flour
2 tablespoons (1 oz) chopped crystallised ginger
1 teaspoon bicarbonate of soda   *(baking soda)*
½ cup (4 fl oz) milk

Preheat the oven to 190°C (375°F/Gas 5). Place large-cavity gem irons (or foil patty cases) in the oven to heat them.

Beat the butter and sugar with the ground ginger until light and fluffy. Add the golden syrup, then the egg and beat well. Fold in the sifted flour and chopped ginger. Dissolve the bicarbonate of soda in the milk, and add to the mixture to make a soft dough.

Quickly grease the heated gem irons and two-thirds fill each cavity.

Bake for 12 to 15 minutes. Turn out onto cake racks, and serve warm or freshly cold.

Nut Pumpkin Gems

Makes 18–20 gem cakes

60 g (2 oz) butter or margarine, softened
¼ cup (2 oz) caster (powdered) sugar
½ teaspoon cinnamon
¾ cup (6 oz) cooked (or canned) mashed pumpkin, cold
1 egg
2½ cups (10 oz) self-raising flour
½ cup (2 oz) chopped walnuts
½ cup (4fl oz) milk
extra butter or margarine, for spreading

Preheat the oven to 220°C (425°F/Gas 7). Heat the gem irons in the oven.

Beat the butter and sugar until light. Add the cinnamon, pumpkin and egg and beat thoroughly. Fold in alternate batches of sifted flour, walnuts and milk, about a third of each at a time, to make a soft dough.

Quickly grease the heated gem irons and two-thirds fill with the mixture.

Bake for 12 to 15 minutes. Turn out onto cake racks and serve warm or cool, split and spread with butter.

Apricot Crunchies

Makes 20–24 little cakes

½ cup (1 oz) lightly crushed cornflakes
2 cups (8 oz) self-raising flour
½ teaspoon salt
3 tablespoons sugar
30 g (1 oz) butter or margarine, melted
1 egg, beaten
½ cup (4fl oz) milk
½ cup (2 oz) chopped dried apricots
extra 60 g (2 oz) butter or margarine, melted
3 tablespoons (1½ oz) brown sugar
½ cup (2 oz) chopped nuts

Preheat the oven to 200°C (400°F/Gas 6). Grease small patty pans well, and lightly coat the insides with the cornflakes.

Sift the flour, salt and sugar into a bowl.

Combine the melted butter, egg, milk and apricots, and add to the flour mixture; mix into a soft dough. Turn onto a lightly-floured board, pat out to 2.5 cm (1 in) thickness, and cut into 20 to 24 pieces. Dip each piece in the extra melted butter, then toss in a mixture of the combined brown sugar and nuts. Place one piece into each patty pan cavity.

Bake for 17 to 20 minutes. Turn out to cool on cake racks and eat whilst very fresh.

Spice 'n' Sugar Swirls

Makes 10–12 little swirls

250 g (8 oz) self-raising flour
½ teaspoon salt
1 tablespoon sugar
60 g (2 oz) butter or margarine
⅔ cup (5½fl oz) milk
1 egg, beaten
Filling:
30 g (1 oz) butter or margarine, melted
2 tablespoons brown sugar
1 teaspoon ground cinnamon
¾ cup (3 oz) chopped walnuts
Topping:
60 g (2 oz) butter or margarine, melted
2 tablespoons brown sugar
2 tablespoons chopped walnuts

Preheat the oven to 220°C (425°F/Gas 7). Grease the patty pans.

Sift the flour, salt and sugar into a bowl. Melt the butter, add the milk and beaten egg, and stir into the flour mixture with a knife blade to mix to a soft dough. Turn onto a lightly-floured board and pat out into a rectangle about 2.5 cm (1 in) thick.

Combine the filling ingredients and sprinkle over the dough. Roll the rectangle of dough up loosely, and cut into 10–12 slices. Into each patty pan cavity, place one slice—on its side so that the swirl is showing. Drizzle the melted butter over, and sprinkle with brown sugar and walnuts.

Bake for 15 to 17 minutes. Turn out onto cake racks, and serve warm.

Right: **Clockwise from top: Date and Peanut Ragamuffins (see p. 124); Apricot Crunchies (see above); Spice 'n' Sugar Swirls (see above); Nut Pumpkin Gems (see above).**

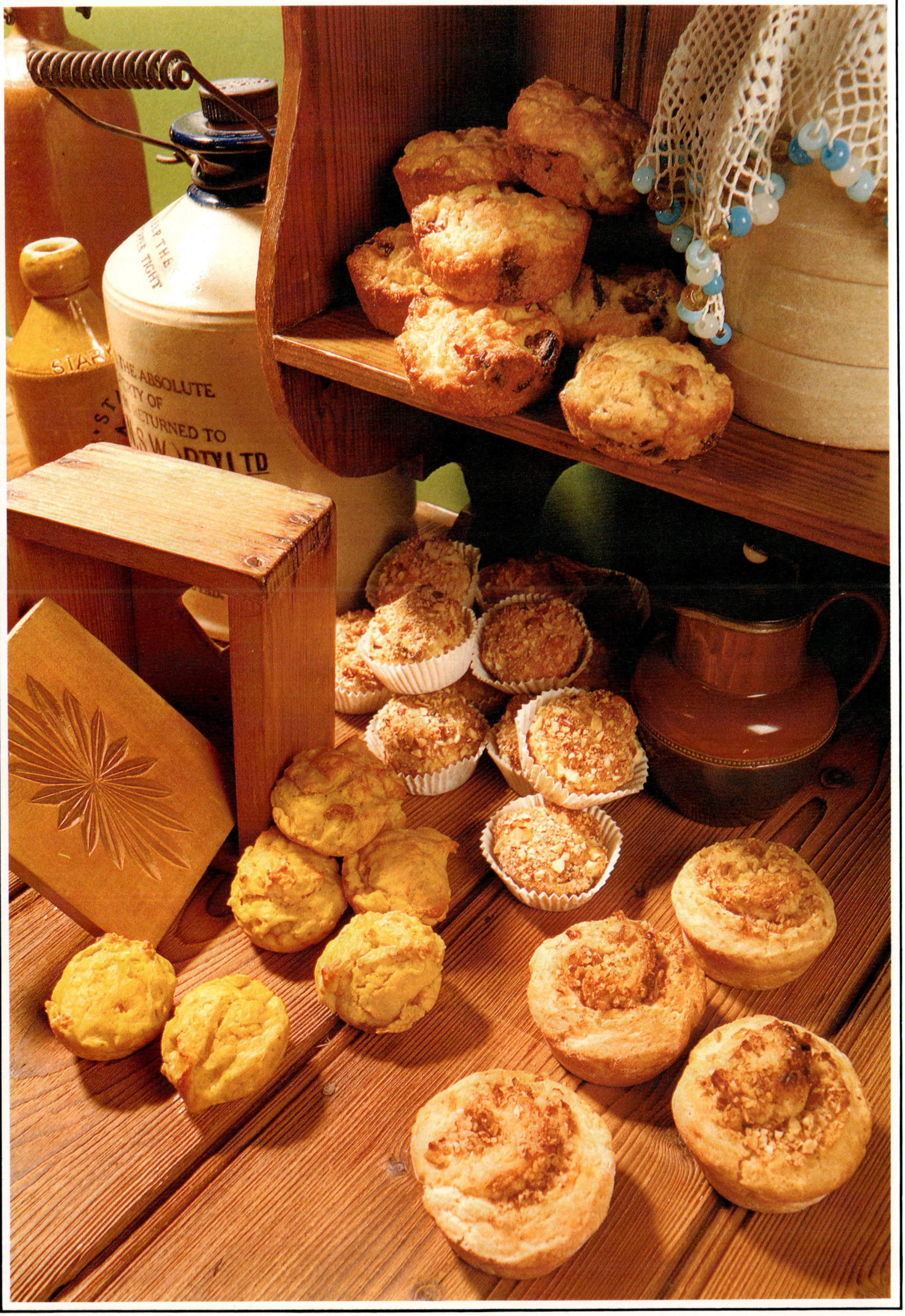
THE ABSOLUTE

Date and Peanut Ragamuffins

Makes 10–12 muffins

---
60 g (2 oz) butter or margarine, softened

¼ cup (2 oz) sugar
---
1 egg
---
1 cup (4 oz) self-raising flour

½ cup (2½ oz) chopped dates
---
2 tablespoons (1 oz) salted peanuts, chopped

1½ tablespoons orange juice

½ teaspoon bicarbonate of soda (baking soda)
---
1 tablespoon boiling water

Preheat the oven to 190°C (375°F/Gas 5). Well grease deep-sided patty pans (or muffin pans).

Beat the butter and sugar until creamy. Add the egg and mix thoroughly, then fold in the sifted flour.

Combine the dates, peanuts and orange juice in a bowl and mix well to separate the dates. Add to the butter mixture and fold through.

Dissolve the bicarbonate of soda in the boiling water, quickly sprinkle over the mixture and mix through lightly but thoroughly. Spoon into the patty pans to two-thirds fill.

Bake for 17 to 20 minutes. Turn out onto cake racks to cool, and serve whilst very fresh.

St Clements Cakes

Makes 20–24 little cakes

---
125 g (4 oz) butter or margarine, softened

⅔ cup (5 oz) caster (powdered) sugar
---
2 teaspoons grated orange rind

1½ cups (6 oz) self-raising flour
---
2 eggs, beaten
---
3 tablespoons milk

Syrup:
½ cup (4 oz) caster (powdered) sugar
---
2 tablespoons orange juice
---
2 tablespoons lemon juice

Preheat the oven to 190°C (375°F/Gas 5). Place individual paper patty cases in the patty pan cavities.

Beat the butter and sugar with the orange rind until light and fluffy. Add alternate batches of the sifted flour, eggs and milk, about a third of each at a time. Two-thirds fill the patty cases. Bake for 17 to 20 minutes. Remove from the oven and top with the syrup.

Syrup: Combine the sugar with the orange juice and lemon juice in a small saucepan, and heat slowly until the sugar is dissolved; then boil for 5 minutes.

Slowly spoon the syrup over each of the little cakes whilst they are still hot; set aside to cool on cake racks.

Crusted Date Squares

Cuts into 16 squares

---
60 g (2 oz) butter or margarine, softened

⅓ cup (3 oz) caster (powdered) sugar
---
1 egg
---
1 cup (4 oz) flour
---
1 teaspoon baking powder

¼ teaspoon bicarbonate of soda (baking soda)

¼ teaspoon salt

2–3 tablespoons orange juice

Filling:
¾ cup (4 oz) chopped, stoned dates

2–3 teaspoons grated orange rind
---
1 teaspoon grated lemon rind

¼ teaspoon mixed spices

⅔ cup (5 fl oz) combined orange and lemon juice

Topping:
1 cup (1 oz) cornflakes, lightly crushed

⅔ cup (2 oz) desiccated coconut

1–2 tablespoons brown sugar

Preheat the oven to 190°C (375°F/Gas 5). Thoroughly grease a 23–25 cm (9–10 in) slab tin.

Beat the butter and sugar to a cream. Add the egg and beat well. Sift the dry ingredients together, and then fold into the butter cream with sufficient orange juice to make a fairly firm mixture. Spread into the slab tin.

Filling: Combine the dates with the fruit rinds, spices and fruit juices in a small saucepan and heat slowly, stirring constantly, until the mixture forms a paste; remove from the heat and allow to cool. When cool, spread onto the cake mixture as evenly as possible.

Topping: Mix the cornflakes, desiccated coconut and brown sugar together and sprinkle over the date filling; pat down lightly with a broad knife or spatula.

Bake for 20 to 25 minutes. Mark into squares whilst hot, and allow to cool in the pan. Turn out and store in an airtight container until ready for use.

SMALL CAKES

Candy Cups

A recipe especially for microwave baking
Makes 12 little cakes

125 g (4 oz) butter or margarine, softened
½ cup (4 oz) sugar
1 egg
1 cup (8 fl oz) milk
2 cups (8 oz) self-raising flour.
1 tablespoon cocoa
peppermint candy stick, crushed, for topping

Combine the butter, sugar, egg, milk and sifted flour and cocoa in a bowl, and whisk with a rotary beater or flat egg whisk until all ingredients are blended well—do not overmix.

Place six double-thickness paper patty cases into individual small custard cups or similar non-metal dishes; spoon in the cake mixture to three-quarters fill each container (set the remaining mixture aside for the second batch). Arrange on the glass tray or base of a microwave oven and heat for 4 to 5 minutes—according to directions given in individual instruction booklets.

Remove from the oven and allow to stand for 4 to 5 minutes, then liberally sprinkle the top of each little cake with crushed peppermint candy. Allow to cool before use.

Repeat the heating procedure with the remaining mixture.

Note: A packet of chocolate cake mix may replace the above cake recipe, if desired.

Fairy Cakes 1.2.3

These Fairy Cakes may be baked in the oven of your choice: conventional (standard), convection (fan-forced) or microwave.
Makes 48 little cakes.

250 g (8 oz) butter or margarine, softened
1 cup (8 oz) sugar
2 teaspoons vanilla essence
4 eggs, beaten
4 cups (16 oz) self-raising flour
¼ teaspoon salt
1 tablespoon skim milk powder
1 cup (8 fl oz) water

If baking in a conventional oven or in a convection (fan-forced) oven, preheat to the recommended temperature.

Beat the butter and sugar to a cream. Add the vanilla essence and beat well. Add the eggs gradually and beat thoroughly.

Sift the flour, salt and milk powder, then sift again over the butter-egg mixture and fold in lightly; add the water and fold through.

Conventional Oven: Spoon the mixture into paper patty cases placed in patty pans, to two-thirds fill. Bake one or two dozen at a time in a moderately hot oven, 190°C (375°F/Gas 5), for 17 to 20 minutes.

Convection (Fan-forced) Oven: Spoon the mixture into paper patty cases placed in patty pans, to two-thirds fill. Bake all four dozen at a time in a moderately hot oven, 190°C (375°F/Gas 5), for 15 to 17 minutes.

Microwave Oven: Spoon the mixture into double-thickness paper patty cases, to half-fill; place the patty cases into small custard cups or similar non-metal dishes. (Or use the special microwave patty cake pans.) Heat-cook in batches of 6 to 9 according to manufacturer's instructions, for 2 to 2½ minutes – do not overcook.

Icing and Decoration: When cold, ice the tops of the little cakes with pastel-coloured Warm Glacé Icing (see recipe, page 130) and sprinkle pastel nonpareil ('hundreds and thousands') over the surface.

Micro Minis

A recipe especially for microwave baking
Makes 14–18 little cakes

¾ cup (3 oz) self-raising flour
1 tablespoon (½ oz) drinking chocolate
1½ tablespoons (½ oz) custard powder
1 teaspoon milk powder
⅓ cup (3 oz) sugar
1 egg
1 tablespoon water
90 g (3 oz) butter or margarine, melted
Toppings: *desiccated coconut, chocolate sprinkles, finely chopped nuts, or crushed chocolate rice cereal*

Sift the dry ingredients (including sugar) into a bowl and make a well in the centre; add the egg, water and cooled butter, and beat with a flat egg whisk for 2 minutes.

Place double-thickness paper patty cases into small custard cups or similar non-metal dishes (or use the special microwave patty cake pans) and barely half fill each with the cake mixture. Sprinkle one of the the above toppings over each container of mixture and heat-cook in batches of 6 to 8 according to manufacturer's instruction, for 2 to 2½ minutes—do not overcook.

Sprinkle a little more topping over each cake whilst the surfaces is still moist, if desired, and set aside to cool.

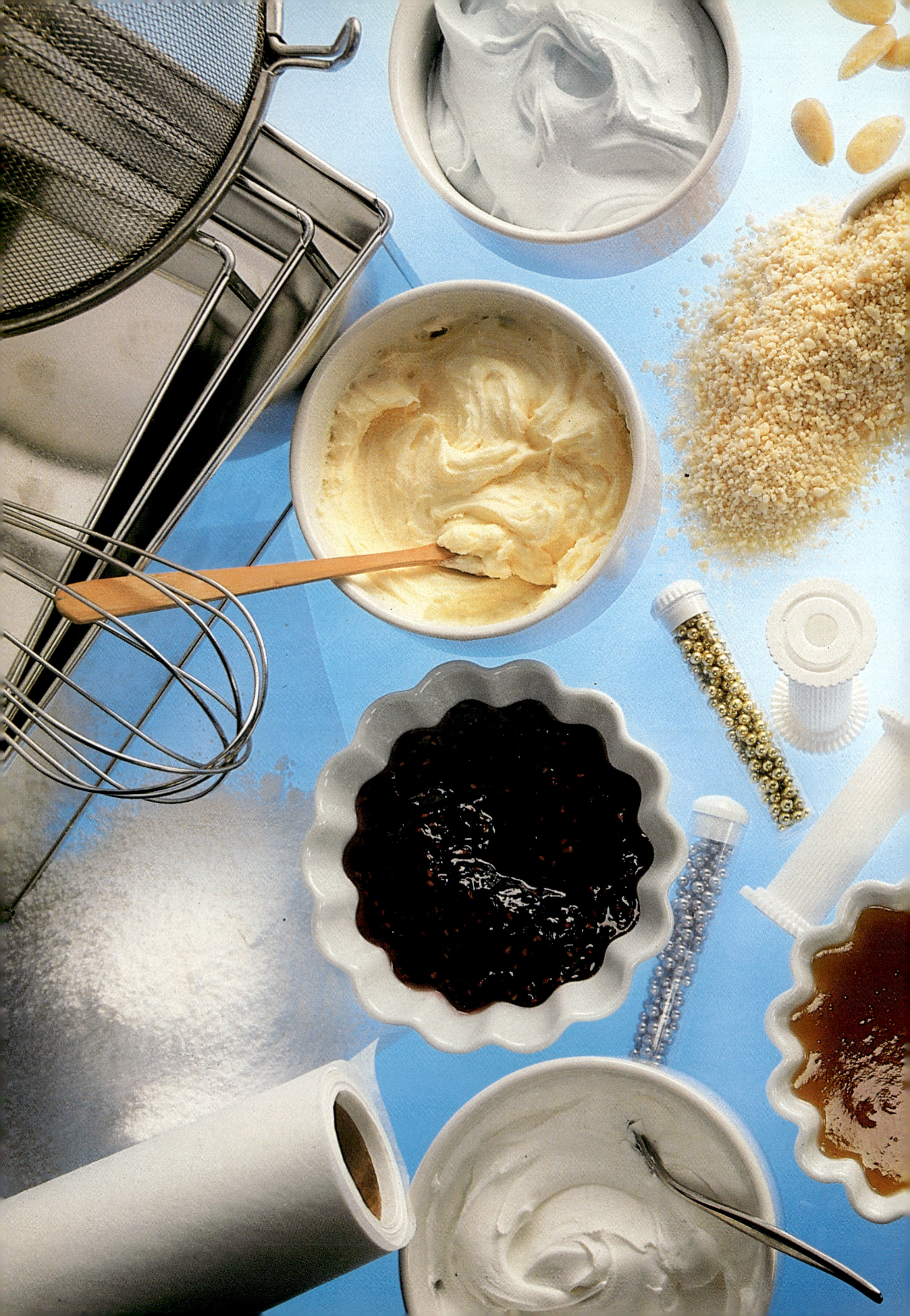

Icings, Fillings & Glazes

Icings, Fillings & Glazes

Icings, frostings and fillings help provide the final touch that adds so much to the appearance and taste of a cake. They also help to retain moisture in the cake by preventing the surface areas from drying, thus keeping it fresh and full-tasting for much longer.

Many types of coverings and fillings for cakes are especially applied to provide not only additional flavour but also texture contrast.

The icings, frostings, glazes, creams, fillings, toppings and pastes listed in this section have been especially chosen to tempt and please all tastes.

Beautiful icing and decoration of cakes requires patience, some experience and the wish to produce an attractive sweetmeat to delight your family and friends.

For general purposes, the following categories may be helpful to the new and enthusiastic cake-maker.

Betty Dunleavy

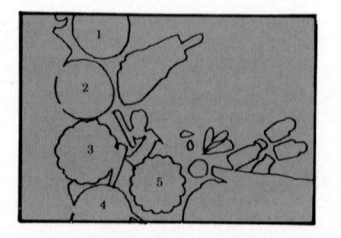

1. Coloured Royal Icing (see p. 130)
2. Vienna Butter Cream (see p. 144)
3. Raspberry Jam
4. Royal Icing (see p. 130)
5. Brandied Apricot Glaze (see p. 149)

Icings:
These are an icing (confectioners') sugar and liquid covering of a thinnish consistency which sets smoothly in a thin layer on the top of the cake. Varying degrees of hardness may be obtained, depending on the mixing method or the amount and use of a shortening in the ingredients.

Suitable for sponges, butter cakes, etc., where a simple coating is required, with flavouring and colouring as desired.

Frostings:
Frostings are thicker sugar-based mixtures which are beaten to produce a soft, fluffy or meringue-like consistency, to be applied in thicker roughened or swirling patterns for a more luscious special-occasion effect. Flavourings and colourings, with a minimum of feature ingredients may be added as desired.

Suitable for layered sponges, butter cakes, 'shaped' ring cakes, etc., for more elaborate or special-occasion use.

Creams:
Overlapping slightly in both ingredients and mixing methods, most creams have a larger proportion of shortening or cream content. With added flavourings and colourings, plus small amounts of extra ingredients, they may also be used as a filling because they do not set too hard.

Suitable for sponges, butter cakes, layered tortes or gâteaux. Many need refrigeration storage, particularly during warmer weather.

Glazes:
Glazes are heated mixtures of sugar and liquid, thin enough to be spooned or drizzled over the surface of the cake and absorbed. The sugar content is often supplied by the addition of jam, jelly or honey. A flavoured liqueur addition to the liquid is popular.

Suitable for dessert-style cakes which are served moist and for Continental layer cakes, etc.

Fillings:
These are thick, creamy mixtures whose main purpose is to hold together the layers of sponges, butter cakes and the richer, more special-occasion and dessert-style confections. A filling may also be made from a frosting recipe with added fruits, nuts, marshmallows, chocolates, creams, liqueurs or flavourings. Many need refrigeration storage.

Suitable for all types of sponges, butter cakes, rolled cakes, etc., to provide flavour and texture contrast.

Toppings:
Crunchy or crumble-style toppings are usually used on the simple luncheon cakes and loaves, sprinkled over the surface before or after baking. Care must be taken in turning out these cakes from their baking tins, to prevent damaging the textured surface.

Suitable for the firmer plain-style cakes to provide extra flavour and contrast interest.

Pastes and Fondants:
These are firmer coverings of a dough-like consistency—rolled out flat and lifted onto the cake, then hand-moulded into shape to set firmly for further finishing and decoration.

Suitable for the rich fruit cakes used for weddings, birthdays or other celebrations.

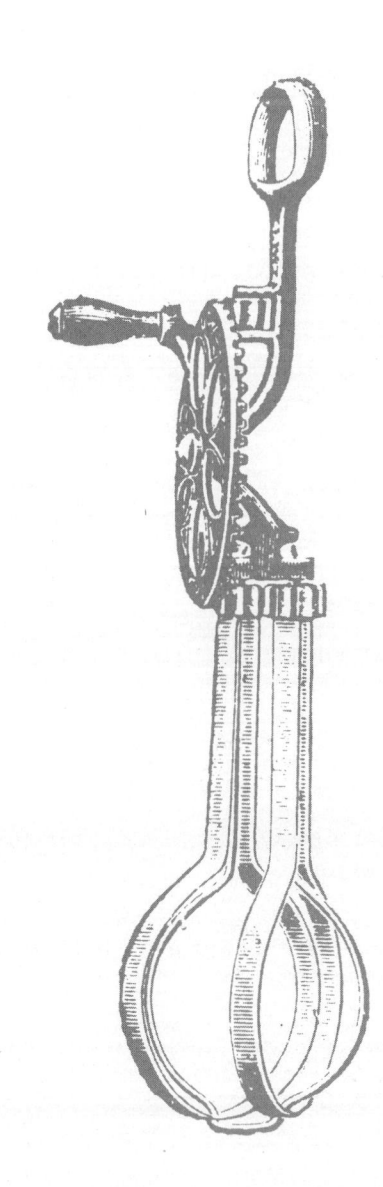

ICINGS

Warm Glacé Icing

Covers the top of an 18–20 cm (7–8 in) cake

1½ cups (8 oz) icing (confectioners') sugar

15 g (½ oz) butter or margarine

1–2 tablespoons water, boiling

Method 1
Sift the icing sugar into a bowl; make a well in the centre.

Melt the butter in about 1½ tablespoons of boiling water. Add this to the icing sugar, and stir to smooth consistency. Add drops of boiling water, as required, to blend to creamy consistency. Pour at once onto the cake, and smooth over with a broad knife or spatula.

Allow to set before cutting.

Method 2
Sift the icing sugar into a bowl; make a well in the centre. Add the butter and 1½ tablespoons of boiling water, and stir to a paste. Place the bowl over hot water and stir until the butter melts and the icing is warmed. Add drops of boiling water, if required, to produce a creamy consistency. Pour at once onto the cake, and smooth over with a broad knife or spatula.

Allow to set before cutting.

Note: To smooth the icing on the cake more easily, dip a broad knife or spatula into boiling water to heat, shake off excess water, and lightly wipe the whole blade over the icing to even out. Do not wipe again, as blemishes would remain on the quickly setting surface.

Variations

Citrus: Use orange juice or lemon juice instead of water and add drops of orange or yellow food colouring.

Passionfruit: Substitute passionfruit pulp for the water in Method 2.

Chocolate: Add 1–2 tablespoons of cocoa or drinking chocolate to the icing sugar.

Coffee: Blend 1–2 teaspoons of instant coffee powder or coffee essence into the boiling water in Method 1.

Mocha: add 1 tablespoon of cocoa and 1 teaspoon of instant coffee powder to the icing sugar in Method 2.

Pastel: Colour the icing with a few drops of pink, green or blue food colouring.

Royal Icing

Makes ½–¾ cup

1 egg white

1¼ cups (7 oz) icing (confectioners') sugar, finely sifted

½ teaspoon lemon juice, strained, or 2–3 drops weak-strength acetic acid

Place the egg white in a clean, dry basin (preferably glass) and beat lightly with a dry wooden spoon to break up but not become frothy.

Gradually add the icing sugar 1–2 tablespoons at a time, beating thoroughly after each addition to dissolve the sugar; as the mixture commences to thicken, add the icing sugar in smaller and smaller quantities.

When the mixture reaches the consistency of thick cream, add the lemon juice (or acetic acid) and continue beating for 1 to 2 minutes before adding more icing sugar as required—depending on size of egg white used.

Beat until the mixture will stand in short stiff peaks; cover the bowl with a damp—not wet—cloth until ready for use, re-beating again to smooth out if necessary. Use as required for pipe decoration work. Store tightly covered.

Note: Although the hand beating is tiresome, it produces a better icing than that made with electric mixers, which tend to incorporate too much air and produce a soft 'marshmallow' result.

1. Brush sides and top of cake with lightly beaten egg white. Roll out two-thirds of the Almond Paste into a long strip and use to cover sides of cake.

2. Roll out remaining Almond Paste into a square the size of the top of the cake and carefully lift onto cake.

3. Smooth top and sides of cake, sealing edges by pressing Almond Paste together, using a little egg white if necessary. Brush Almond Paste with egg white.

4. Sprinkle a work surface liberally with sifted icing sugar or cornflour. Roll out Covering Fondant and use to cover cake.

5. Smooth Covering Fondant over top and sides of cake, rubbing corners and edges well. Cut off excess fondant.

6. Place a spoonful of Royal Icing on the centre of a covered cake board. Centre the cake on the board. Leave fondant to set for at least 24 hours before decorating.

1

2

3

4

5

6

Mock Maple Icing

Covers the top of a 20–23 cm (8–9 in) cake

2 teaspoons butter or margarine
3 teaspoons golden syrup (light corn syrup)
1½ cups (8 oz) icing (confectioners') sugar, finely sifted
1–2 tablespoons lemon juice

Combine the butter and golden syrup in a heatproof bowl and melt over boiling water. Remove from the heat.

Gradually add three-quarters of the icing sugar, beating well. Add alternate batches of the remaining icing sugar and the lemon juice until the desired consistency is obtained.

Quickly pour over the cake and smooth around the top edge; or allow it to drizzle down the sides, if desired. Allow to set before cutting.

Rich Mocha Icing

Covers the top of a 20–23 cm (8–9 in) cake

90 g (3 oz) butter or margarine, softened
1½ cups (8 oz) icing (confectioners') sugar, sifted
4 tablespoons drinking chocolate
2 tablespoons cocoa
2 teaspoons instant coffee
2 tablespoons boiling water
1 teaspoon vanilla essence or brandy essence

Cream the butter with half of the icing sugar.

Combine the drinking chocolate, cocoa and instant coffee in a small bowl; add the boiling water and blend to a soft paste, adding the vanilla or brandy essence.

Gradually beat the chocolate mixture into the buttered cream, then add the remaining icing sugar and beat well.

Quickly pour over the cake and smooth around the top edge; or allow it to drizzle down the sides, if desired. Allow to set before cutting.

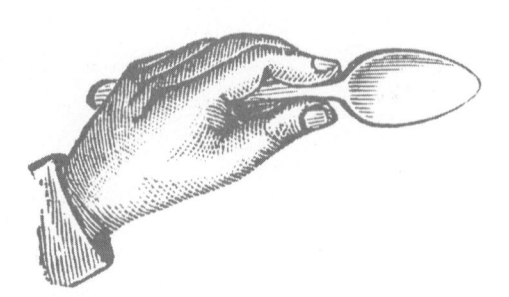

Satin Icing

Covers the top of a slab cake 25 cm (10 in) square

¼ cup (2 oz) sugar
¼ cup evaporated milk
1 teaspoon liquid glucose or light corn syrup
15 g (½ oz) butter or margarine
1½ cups (8 oz) icing (confectioners') sugar, sifted
1 teaspoon almond essence

Combine the sugar, evaporated milk, liquid glucose and butter in a heatproof bowl; stir over boiling water until the butter has melted and all ingredients are well blended. Remove from the heat.

Gradually add the icing sugar, beating well after each addition. Flavour with the almond essence, and spread over the cake. Allow to set before cutting.

Note: Should the icing seem a little thin, add an extra spoonful of icing sugar and beat well before using.

Boiled White Icing

Covers the tops and sides of two 20 cm (8 in) cakes

2 cups (1 lb) sugar
1 cup (8 fl oz) water
2 egg whites
pinch of salt
few drops lemon juice
1 teaspoon vanilla essence

Put the sugar and water into a saucepan over low heat and stir until the sugar has dissolved. Bring to the boil and cook until the syrup measures 120°C (240°F) on a sugar thermometer or until a spoonful of the mixture forms a soft ball when dropped into iced water. Remove from the heat.

Beat the egg whites with the salt until they are frothy. Pour the hot but not boiling syrup into the egg white, beating constantly. (The easiest way to do this is in an electric mixer.) Add the lemon juice and vanilla essence.

Set the icing aside for a few minutes so that it begins to harden, then use immediately.

PASTES

Almond Paste—Marzipan

Covers the top and sides of a 20 cm (8 in) fruit cake

4½ cups (1½ lb) pure icing (confectioners') sugar
2¼ cups (8 oz) ground almonds or almond meal
3 egg yolks
2 tablespoons sweet sherry
1 tablespoon lemon juice

Sift the icing sugar into a bowl and add the ground almonds; mix thoroughly and make a well in the centre.

Beat the egg yolks, sweet sherry and lemon juice together; pour into the icing sugar mixture and gradually work into a firm smooth paste with one hand, kneading well.

Lightly sprinkle a board or work bench with a little extra icing sugar, lift the mixture onto the board, and knead with both hands to a firm smooth dough—do not add too much extra icing sugar unless the dough is very soft. Cover tightly until ready for use, then re-knead gently before rolling out and applying to the cake as required.

Mock Almond Paste

This covering paste is useful as an economical base for a decorated celebration cake and also for those who do not like the rich almond taste of the authentic mixture.
Covers the top and sides of a 20 cm (8 in) fruit cake

3 cups (1 lb) pure icing (confectioners') sugar
2⅔ cups (8 oz) desiccated coconut
2 egg whites, lightly beaten
2 tablespoons liquid glucose, warmed to soften it
1 teaspoon glycerine
flavouring essence (almond, vanilla, peppermint)

Sift the icing sugar into a bowl and add the coconut; mix thoroughly and make a well in the centre.

Add the egg whites, glucose and glycerine and 1–2 teaspoons of the desired flavouring, and beat with a wooden spoon until as much of the icing sugar mixture is incorporated as possible before the paste becomes too thick to handle. Remove the spoon and work with one hand to form a firm, smooth paste.

Lift onto a board that is lightly sprinkled with icing sugar, and knead with both hands to a firm pliable dough—do not add too much icing sugar unless the dough is very soft. Cover tightly until ready for use, then re-knead gently before rolling out and applying to the cake as required.

FROSTINGS

Snow Frosting

This recipe is perhaps more commonly known as Seven-minute Frosting because the one-egg quantity takes seven minutes to cook.
Covers the top and sides of an 18–20 cm (7–8 in) cake

---
2 egg whites
---
4 tablespoons water

1⅓ cups (1 oz) sugar

½ teaspoon baking powder

Place the unbeaten egg whites and the water into a heatproof glass bowl and sprinkle the sugar over the top. Place the bowl over a saucepan containing boiling water, and beat constantly until the mixture foams and commences to thicken—approximately 12 minutes.

Scatter the baking powder over the surface and continue beating until the mixture thickens further and commences to 'crust' in the base of the bowl.

Remove from the heat and beat whilst cooling, for 1 to 2 minutes. Spoon over the top of the cake, allowing the mixture to fall over the sides; spread quickly all over the cake, and swirl into an attractive design with a knife or spatula. Allow to set before cutting.

Note: This frosting does need a little care in preparation: first to beat to the correct consistency before spooning over the cake and then to work quickly to swirl attractively before the frosting commences to harden.

Variations

Citrus: Substitute half the amount of water with orange juice or lemon juice, and colour with orange or yellow food colouring.

Chocolate Marble: *(Photograph below)* Drizzle 2–3 tablespoons of melted chocolate over the completed frosting on the cake and swirl through with a fine knife or skewer for a marbled effect.

Coffee: *(Photograph below)* Blend 1–2 teaspoons of instant coffee powder into the water before cooking, plus a little brandy or rum essence for flavour.

Nut Crunch: Quickly fold ½ cup (2 oz) of finely chopped almonds or desiccated coconut through the frosting before spooning over the cake. Or scatter nuts over the frosting on the cake before it commences to harden.

Cherry: Quickly fold ½ cup (3 oz) of chopped glacé cherries through the completed frosting and colour it pale pink with food colouring, just before spooning it over the cake.

Butter Nut Frosting

Covers the top of a 28 × 18 cm (11 × 7 in) slab cake

---
125 g (4 oz) cream cheese

⅓ cup (3 oz) peanut butter, crunchy style
---
1 teaspoon vanilla essence

1¼ cups (7 oz) icing (confectioners') sugar, sifted

Allow the cream cheese to soften at room temperature for about 30 minutes. Place in a bowl with the peanut butter, and mix to combine. Add the vanilla essence, and gradually beat in the icing sugar to form a thick spreading cream. If the mixture seems too stiff, a little milk or cream may be added and blended through. Spread onto the cake and allow to become firm before cutting.

Coffee Fudge Frosting

Covers the top and partially covers the sides of a 20–23 cm (8–9 in) fluted ring cake

---
⅔ cup (5½ fl oz) evaporated milk
---
1 cup (8 oz) sugar
---
60 g (2 oz) butter or margarine
---
1 teaspoon coffee essence
---
2 teaspoons whiskey–coffee cream liqueur

Place the evaporated milk, sugar, butter and coffee essence in a non-stick saucepan and heat slowly until the sugar is dissolved; stir gently to blend.

Bring to the boil; then boil steadily until, when a teaspoon of mixture is dropped into a glass of cold water, a soft ball is formed—about 5 minutes.

Take the saucepan from the heat and stand it in a large (heatproof) bowl containing iced water, to immediately retard further cooking. Beat constantly with a wooden spoon until the mixture commences to thicken. Remove the saucepan from the bowl.

Add the liqueur, and continue beating to a soft whipped-cream consistency. Pour onto the cake, allowing the frosting to drizzle down the sides. Allow to set before cutting.

Note: Cooking to the correct stage and the constant beating are the keys to success in making this creamy frosting.

Right: **Clockwise from top left: Snow Frosting (above); Coffee Frosting (above); Chocolate Marble Frosting (above).**

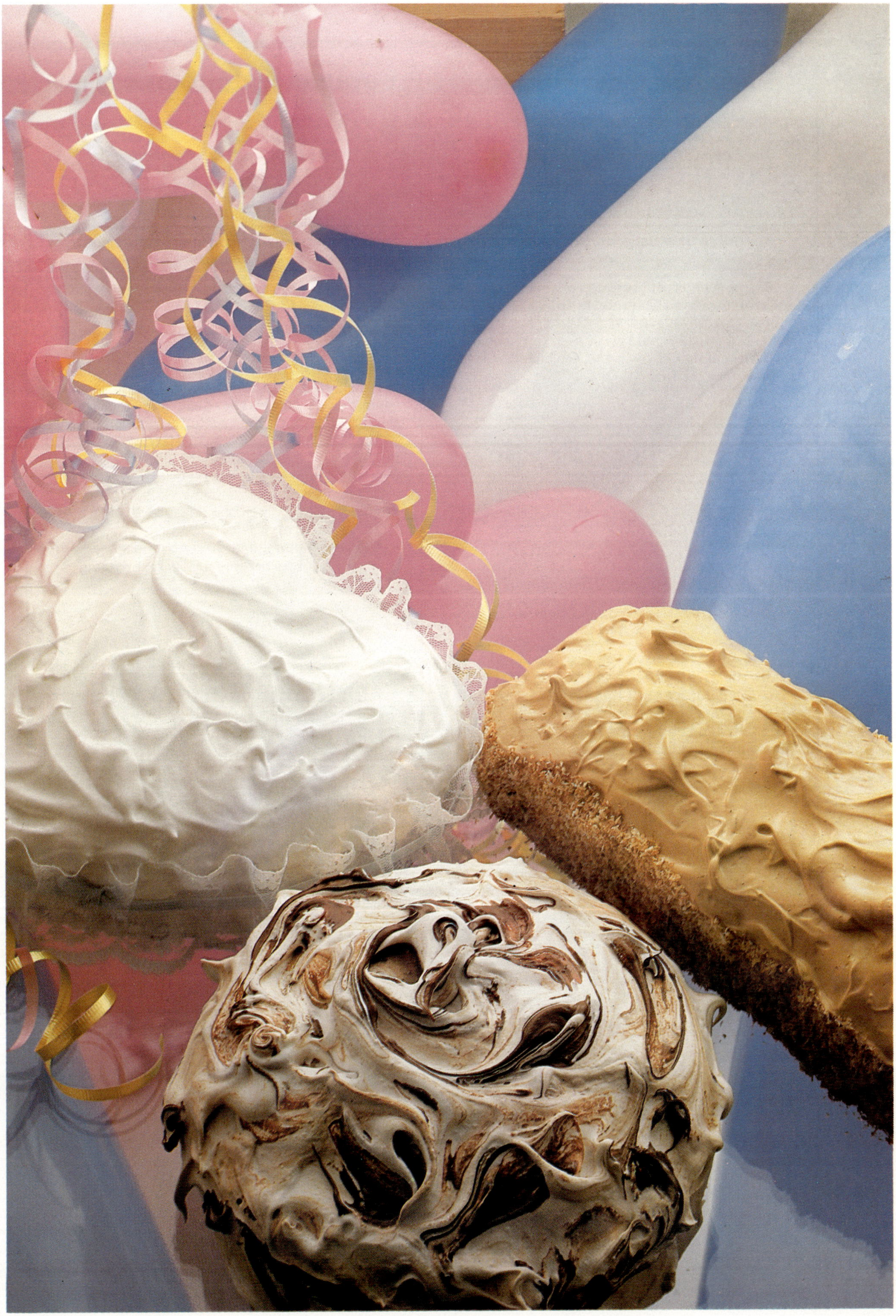

Sour Cream Frosting

Covers the top of a 30 × 18 cm (12 × 7 in) slab cake

1 cup (8 fl oz) sour cream, chilled
1 tablespoon lemon juice
¼ cup (1½ oz) brown sugar, firmly packed
1–2 teaspoons ground cinnamon

Beat the sour cream and lemon juice together, and chill for 10 to 15 minutes to thicken.

Beat the brown sugar through. Spoon onto the cake, and swirl or mark with a knife to decorate; sprinkle cinnamon over the top. Chill, to firm again before cutting.

Cream Cheese Frosting

Covers the top of a 20–23 cm (8–9 in) cake

125 g (4 oz) package cream cheese
60 g (2 oz) butter or margarine
1 teaspoon grated lemon rind
1½ cups (8 oz) icing (confectioners') sugar, sifted

Allow the cream cheese and butter to stand at room temperature until softened. Place in a bowl with the lemon rind and beat until creamy. Gradually add the icing sugar, beating well between each addition.

Spread onto the cake, using a knife to swirl into an attractive design. Allow to become firm before cutting.

Variations:

Cinnamon:
Add ½ teaspoon of ground cinnamon to the butter-cheese mixture. Or sprinkle the cinnamon over the frosting on the cake.

Chocolate:
Melt 60 g (2 oz) cooking chocolate and blend into the butter-cheese mixture; and flavour with vanilla essence before covering the cake.

Carrot:
Fold ½ cup (4 oz) of freshly grated carrot through the mixture before covering the cake

Sherry Nut:
Beat 1½ tablespoons of sweet sherry into the butter-cheese mixture; and fold in ½ cup (2 oz) of ground hazelnuts after adding the icing sugar.

Strawberry:
Fold 1 cup (4 oz) of chopped strawberries through the completed mixture, taking care not to break up the fruit pieces.

Caramel Walnut Frosting

Covers the top of a 20–23 cm (8–9 in) cake

90 g (3 oz) butter or margarine
½ cup (3 oz) brown sugar
3 tablespoons milk
1 cup (6 oz) icing (confectioners') sugar, sifted
½ cup (2 oz) coarsely chopped walnuts

Melt the butter in a small non-stick saucepan. Add the sugar, and stir carefully to blend so that the mixture does not come too far up the sides of the pan. Remove the spoon and bring to a full rolling boil. Lower the heat and cook, again stirring constantly but carefully, for 2 minutes.

Add the milk and cook, stirring until the mixture once again comes to the boil. Remove from the heat, and cool to lukewarm.

Gradually beat the icing sugar into the mixture, beating until the mixture is smooth and starts to thicken.

Add the walnuts, fold through, and spread onto the cake. Allow to become firm before cutting.

Crunchy Butterscotch Frosting

Covers and fills a 20–23 cm (8–9 in) double-layer cake

125 g (4 oz) packaged cream cheese
2 tablespoons cream or evaporated milk
¼ teaspoon salt
3 cups (1 lb) icing (confectioners') sugar, sifted
1 cup crushed butterscotch or toffee

Allow the cream cheese to stand at room temperature until softened. Beat until creamy; gradually add the cream and salt and beat well.

Add the icing sugar in three or four batches, beating well after each addition. Fold the crushed toffee or butterscotch through.

Use as a filling between the layers and to cover the cake. Decorate the top with extra toffee pieces, if desired.

Note: As the crushed toffee may soften on prolonged contact with the moist frosting, the cake will need to be kept refrigerated or chilled unless eaten within a day or two.

ICINGS, FILLINGS & GLAZES

Honeyed Chocolate Frosting

Covers the top of a 25 cm (10 in) slab cake

30 g (1 oz) butter or margarine
1 tablespoon honey
90 g (3 oz) cooking chocolate, grated
1½ cups (8 oz) icing (confectioners') sugar, sifted
2–3 teaspoons lemon juice

Combine the butter, honey and chocolate in a heatproof basin and heat over hot—not boiling—water until well blended. Remove from the heat and allow to cool slightly.

Gradually add the icing sugar, beating well; flavour with lemon juice.

Spoon over the cake and swirl or mark into an attractive design. Allow to set before cutting.

Chocolate Peppermint Gloss

Covers the top and sides of a 23 cm (9 in) ring cake

½ cup (4 oz) sugar
2 tablespoons cornflour (cornstarch)
1 cup (8 fl oz) hot milk
60 g (2 oz) pure chocolate, coarsely grated
¼ teaspoon salt
45 g (1½ oz) unsalted butter, chilled
½–1 teaspoon peppermint essence

Mix the sugar and cornflour in a small non-stick saucepan. Stir in the hot milk and add the grated chocolate, beating briskly to form a smooth sauce. Cook over a low heat, stirring constantly, until the sauce thickens. Add the salt, and remove from the heat.

Cut the butter into small chunks and add to the sauce gradually, beating well between each addition. Flavour with drops of the peppermint essence, as desired.

Spread onto the cake whilst icing is hot; smooth over where required and allow to set before cutting.

Rocky Road Frosting

Covers the top of a 23–25 cm (9–10 in) slab cake

125 g (4 oz) unsweetened cooking chocolate
1 packet (24–26) marshmallows, halved
60 g (2 oz) butter or margarine, chopped
¼ cup (2 fl oz) water or sweet sherry
1½ cups (8 oz) icing (confectioners') sugar, sifted
½ cup (3 oz) glacé cherries, halved
½ cups (3 oz) walnuts, halved or quartered

Coarsely chop the chocolate and place in a heavy-based saucepan with half the quantity of marshmallows, the butter and water; place over low heat and stir slowly but constantly until well blended. Remove from the heat and allow to cool to lukewarm.

Gradually add the icing sugar, folding in lightly. Fold the cherries and walnuts through and fold in the remaining marshmallows.

Spoon onto the cake and 'rough up' the surface with a knife. Allow to set before cutting.

Halving the marshmallows: Dip the blades of kitchen scissors frequently in either hot water or a bland-flavoured oil to prevent marshmallows constantly sticking whilst cutting.

TOPPINGS

Pine Nut Topping

This quickly made topping is spread on the cake and grilled (broiled) until bubbly and browned, producing a pleasant caramel flavour. It gives an interesting finish to a simple packet cake mix.
Covers the top of a slab cake 25 cm (10 in) square

60 g (2 oz) butter or margarine

60 g (2 oz) peanut butter

1 cup (6 oz) brown sugar

1½ cups (8 oz) finely chopped, salted peanuts

½ cup (4 oz) crushed, well-drained pineapple

Melt the butter and peanut butter in a saucepan over low heat. Add the sugar, peanuts and pineapple and mix all together. Spread over the top of the cool—not cold—cake, and place on the rack of the griller pan. Grill under low heat until the topping is bubbling and commencing to brown. Remove from heat and allow to cool before cutting.

Toffee Topping

Decorates the top of a 20 cm (8 in) cake

1 cup (8 oz) sugar

⅓ cup (3 fl oz) water, boiling

Dissolve the sugar in the water in a small saucepan over a very low heat; bring to the boil, then increase the heat and allow to boil rapidly until the syrup commences to colour a pale gold.

Meanwhile grease the base of a 20 cm (8 in) shallow cake tin.

When the syrup colours to a little lighter than desired, remove from the heat and allow the bubbles to subside; quickly but carefully pour into the prepared cake pan. Set aside, undisturbed until the toffee commences to set.

Decoration 1: As the toffee sets, mark into serving-sized wedges (eight to ten wedges) with a well-greased round-ended knife. When completely set, carefully lift the wedges out and decorate, cartwheel fashion, on a cream-topped sponge or light butter cake.

Decoration 2: Allow the toffee to completely set in the cake tin. With the handle of a knife, sharply tap the toffee surface to shatter into pieces, then lift out and scatter over a cream-topped sponge or light butter cake.

Coconut Topping

Covers the top of a 23 cm (9 in) slab cake

⅔ cup (4 oz) brown sugar

90 g (3 oz) butter or margarine, melted

¼ cup (2 fl oz) cream or evaporated milk

1½ cups (3 oz) flaked coconut

1 teaspoon vanilla essence

Combine all the ingredients in a basin and mix well. Spread over the top of the warm cake, and place on the rack of a griller (broiler) pan. Grill under low heat until the topping surface is bubbling and commencing to brown. Remove from the heat and allow to cool before cutting.

Note: Should the flaked coconut be unavailable, substitute 1 cup (3 oz) of desiccated coconut or 1½ cups (2½ oz) of chopped, shredded coconut.

Streusel Topping

Covers the top of a 20 cm (8 in) cake

90 g (3 oz) butter or margarine, softened

1 tablespoon brown sugar

1 cup (4 oz) chopped walnuts

1 teaspoon ground cinnamon

1 teaspoon grated orange rind

½ cup (3 oz) chopped glacé cherries

orange juice

Beat the butter and brown sugar until creamy. Add the walnuts, cinnamon and orange rind, and beat through. Fold the cherries through, and add sufficient orange juice to form a firm yet crumbly mixture.

Quickly sprinkle over the top of a half-baked, firm-textured cake without removing it from the oven; close the oven door and continue baking for the required time.

Remove the cake from the oven and allow to stand for 5 to 7 minutes in the tin; turn out onto a rack covered with a clean cloth, then turn back onto another rack and allow to cool before cutting.

Right: From top: Streusel Topping (see above); Pine Nut Topping (see above); Coconut Topping (see above).

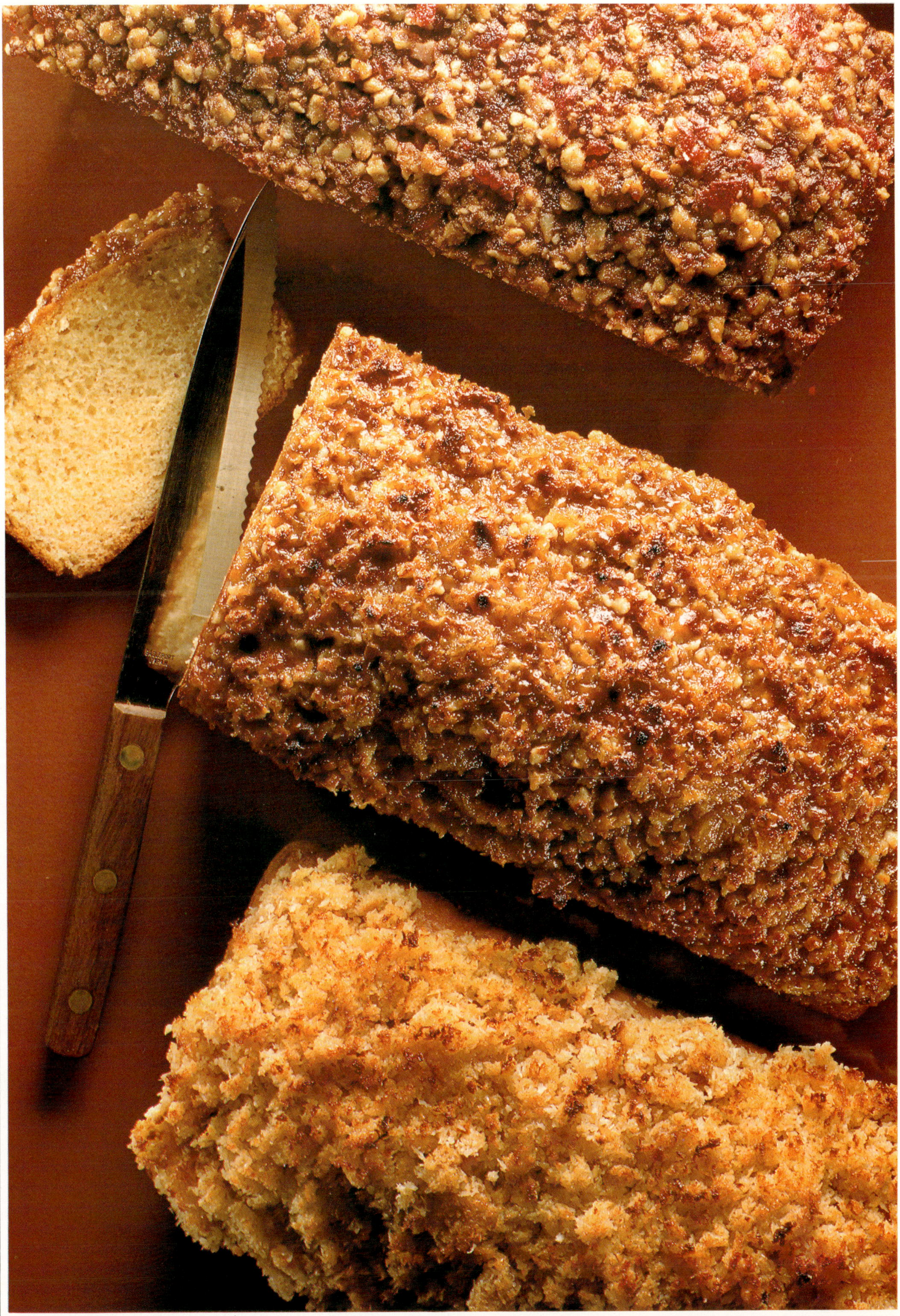

FILLINGS

Chocolate Liqueur Filling

Fills a 4-egg chocolate sponge roll

¾ cup (6fl oz) cream

60 g (2 oz) butter or margarine

375 g (12 oz) pure cooking chocolate, chopped

2 tablespoons coffee rum liqueur

Place the cream and butter in a non-stick saucepan and heat until boiling rapidly. Add the chocolate and stir until the chocolate has melted and is blended through. Remove from the heat and allow to cool.

Beat the mixture vigorously with an electric hand beater until it commences to thicken. Add the liqueur and continue beating until the filling is sufficiently thick to spread onto the sponge roll. Roll up and chill before cutting.

The richness of the chocolate filling requires no other covering to the roll than a light dusting of icing (confectioners') sugar or a whipped unsweetened cream.

Hungarian Hazelnut Filling

Fills a 20 cm (8 inch) cake, sliced into three layers

300 ml 1¼ cups (10fl oz) cream

½ cup (4 oz) caster sugar

¾ cup (3 oz) finely chopped hazelnuts

6 egg yolks

2–3 teaspoons brandy or rum

Place the cream, sugar and hazelnuts in a small non-stick saucepan; bring slowly to the boil, then simmer over low heat until the mixture is thick—approximately 10 minutes.

Remove from the heat, pour the mixture into a heatproof bowl (warmed slightly), and stir until cold.

Add the egg yolks one at a time and beat in thoroughly; flavour with brandy or rum. Spread onto the layers of cake, rejoin the layers and cover the outside of the cake as desired.

A simple chocolate-flavoured Vienna Butter Cream would compliment the richness of this filling (see recipe, page 144).

Lemon Sauce Filling

Makes 1½–1¾ cups (12–14fl oz)

½ cup (4 oz) sugar

2 tablespoons cornflour (cornstarch)

⅔ cup (5fl oz) water

2 egg yolks (optional)

30 g (1 oz) butter or margarine, chopped

3 teaspoons grated lemon rind

½ cup (4fl oz) lemon juice

Combine the sugar and cornflour in a small, non-stick saucepan; gradually blend in the water. Heat slowly until boiling, stirring constantly. Lower the heat and simmer for 1 to 2 minutes, stirring frequently.

(If a richer mixture is desired, add the egg yolks at this stage and beat in briskly.)

Remove from the heat and add the butter; stir until melted through. Then stir in the lemon rind and lemon juice.

Mock Cream Filling—Boiled

Makes 1½–1¾ cups (12–14fl oz)

300 ml/1¼ cups (10fl oz) milk

2 tablespoons cornflour (cornstarch)

60 g (2 oz) butter or margarine

1 teaspoon vanilla essence

2 tablespoons icing (confectioners') sugar

Blend 3 tablespoons of the milk with the cornflour.

Heat the remaining milk in a small, non-stick saucepan, until boiling. Gradually add the blended cornflour and stir briskly until smooth. Lower the heat and simmer for 1 to 2 minutes, then remove from the heat and allow to cool.

Beat the butter, vanilla essence and icing sugar until creamy. Gradually add the milk mixture, beating well between each addition.

Use as a filling for sponges or light layer cakes.

Note: A richer cream may be made by substituting half the milk with cream or evaporated milk.

Variations:

Chocolate:
Beat 2 tablespoons of grated chocolate into the hot milk mixture before cooling.

Mocha:
Add 1 tablespoon of cocoa and 1 teaspoon of instant coffee powder to the cornflour whilst blending with the milk.

Mock Cream Filling—Washed

This rich cream mixture derives its name from the method of covering the butter and sugar with water and pouring off between beatings—'washing'
Makes 1 cup

125 g (4 oz) butter, softened
½ cup (4 oz) sugar
1 tablespoon hot milk
vanilla essence

Beat the butter and sugar together until the mixture is very white and fine; care should be taken to constantly incorporate any mixture clinging up the sides of the bowl so that all the creaminess is of the same consistency.

Carefully pour ice-cold water over the mixture, let it stand for 1 minute, then pour it off and beat thoroughly. Repeat this 'washing' process two or three times until the mixture is very smooth and no sugar crystals remain undissolved.

Add the hot milk and vanilla essence, and beat through. Use to fill sponges, sponge rolls and light layer cakes.

Mocha Custard Filling

Makes 1¾–2 cups (14–16fl oz)

3 tablespoons custard powder
2 tablespoons cocoa
1 teaspoon instant coffee powder
4 tablespoons sugar
¼ teaspoon salt
1½ cups (12fl oz) milk
30 g (1 oz) butter or margarine
vanilla essence or brandy essence

Combine the custard powder, cocoa, instant coffee powder, sugar and salt in a small non-stick saucepan; gradually blend the milk through. Heat slowly, stirring constantly, until bubbling. Remove from the heat, and beat in the butter. Flavour as desired, cover and chill. Use to fill recess sponges, pie crusts, meringues, etc.

Note: Extra richness may be added to this filling by doubling the quantity of butter—to 60 g (2 oz).

Pineapple Ginger Filling

Makes 2½–3 cups (20–24fl oz)

1 tablespoon custard powder
¼ teaspoon ground ginger
300 ml/1¼ cups (10fl oz) milk
4 egg yolks
1 tablespoon golden syrup (light corn syrup)
1 tablespoon lemon juice
30 g (1 oz) butter or margarine, chopped
60 g (2 oz) crystallised ginger, chopped
1 cup (8 oz) crushed, well-drained pineapple

Combine the custard powder and ground ginger in a non-stick saucepan; blend the milk through and bring slowly to the boil, stirring constantly.

Beat the egg yolks, golden syrup and lemon juice together, then beat into the milk mixture with the butter pieces. Stir over low heat for 1 to 2 minutes until of a thick custard consistency. Allow to cool.

Fold the ginger and pineapple through, and chill before using. Use to fill meringues, pie crusts, layer tortes, etc.

Date and Walnut Filling

Makes 1½ cups (12 oz)

1½ cups (8 oz) pitted, chopped dates
½ cup (4fl oz) lemon juice
1 teaspoon grated lemon rind
¼ cup (1 oz) chopped walnuts
1 tablespoon brown sugar

Combine the dates and lemon juice in a small non-stick saucepan and stir over low heat until the dates have softened and the mixture is thick. Remove from the heat, add the lemon rind, walnuts and brown sugar and stir through. Allow to cool before using to fill spiced or fruited layer cakes, etc.

Note: This filling may be extended in volume with the addition of 60–90 g (2–3 oz) cream cheese, Ricotta cheese or natural yoghurt.

FONDANTS

Covering Fondant

Covers the top and sides of a 20 cm (8 in) fruit cake

| 30 ml (1 fl oz) water |
| 2 teaspoons gelatine |
| 10 g (⅓ oz) Copha (white vegetable shortening) |
| 1 tablespoon liquid glucose |
| 1 teaspoon glycerine |
| 3 cups (1 lb) pure icing (confectioners') sugar |
| food colouring (optional) |

Combine the water and gelatine in a heatproof bowl and place over boiling water until well blended. Add the Copha and liquid glucose and stir to combine, then add the glycerine.

Sift all but ½ cup (3 oz) of the icing sugar into a bowl, and make a well in the centre. Add the lukewarm gelatine mixture; stir with a wooden spoon until as much of the icing sugar is incorporated as possible before the paste becomes too thick to handle. Remove the spoon and work with one hand to form a soft, smooth paste. Add drops of food colouring to obtain desired pastel shade, if required.

Lift onto a board that is liberally sprinkled with the reserved ½ cup (3 oz) of icing sugar, and knead with both hands until smooth and pliable without stickiness. Cover tightly until ready for use, then re-knead gently before rolling out and applying to the cake as required.

Modelling Fondant

Makes about 750 g (1½ lb) mixture

| ½ cup (4 oz) sugar |
| 1 tablespoon liquid glucose |
| 40 ml (1⅓ fl oz) water |
| ¼ teaspoon cream of tartar |
| ½ teaspoon glycerine |
| 2½ teaspoons gelatine |
| extra 30 ml (1 fl oz) water, warmed |
| 30 g (1 oz) Copha (white vegetable shortening), chopped |
| 2½ cups (14 oz) pure icing (confectioners') sugar |
| food colouring (optional) |

Place the sugar, glucose, water, cream of tartar and glycerine in a small, heavy-based saucepan and heat slowly until the sugar is dissolved; bring slowly to the boil.

Boil the sugar syrup until it registers 115–116°C (240°F) on a sugar thermometer—or when a little dropped into a glass of cold water forms a soft ball. Remove from the heat.

Dissolve the gelatine in the warmed water, and add to the sugar mixture when the bubbles subside; allow the mixture to cool for 5 to 6 minutes, then add the chopped Copha and allow it to melt through.

Turn into a large bowl and gradually beat in three-quarters of the sifted icing sugar to form a thick paste. Cover with a damp—not wet—cloth and set aside for at least 12 hours.

Turn onto a board and knead in the remaining icing sugar. Add drops of food colouring, as desired.

---

1. To make hyacinths, colour Modelling Fondant with food colouring. Using cornflour lightly on fingertips, take a small piece of Modelling Fondant about the size of a pea and roll between the fingers to form a cone shape. Insert knitting needle (dipped in cornflour) and hollow centre out finely. Using scissors, cut to form six petals. Cut petals to a point and curl backwards.

2. Insert moistened hooked wire through the flower and secure at base using thumb and forefinger. One bud and two flowers may be twisted together to form a spray.

3. To make frangipani, roll out sufficient Modelling Fondant thinly to cut five petals at the same time with a petal cutter. Moisten petals and press them together to form a fan. Pick up petals and with the back of the flower facing you, lap right side over left and press firmly to join flower. Twist base with fingers.

4. Place flower in egg carton and curl each petal by placing small pieces of foil between them. Leave to dry. Make a green cone and when completely dry, place a small amount of Royal Icing inside cone to attach flower. To colour flower, use non-toxic chalk powder (mixture of lemon and light orange) and lightly dust with dry brush.

5. Extension Work. Using a No. 3 pipe and Royal Icing, pipe scallops around the base of the cake, allowing each row to dry before piping the next. You will need 4 or 5 rows of scallops to support the bridgework. Change to No. 00 pipe and drop threads from the top to the scallops. Make sure each line is straight and evenly spaced.

6. For lace pieces and embroidery work, Royal Icing is used with a No. 00 pipe.

1
2
3
4
5
6

CREAMS

Chocolate Butter Cream

Covers and fills a 20–23 cm (8–9 in) double-layer cake

90 g (3 oz) butter or margarine

1 cup (6 oz) semi-sweet chocolate pieces

½ cup (4 fl oz) sour cream

1 teaspoon vanilla essence or rum essence

2½–2¾ cups (14–16 oz) icing (confectioners') sugar

Combine the butter and chocolate pieces in a heatproof bowl over hot—not boiling—water, and stir until blended. Remove from the heat and allow to cool slightly.

Stir in the sour cream and vanilla, and gradually work in the sifted icing sugar to form a soft, spreading consistency; beat well.

Use as a filling between the layers and to cover the cake; swirl or peak the top into an attractive design. Allow to become firm before cutting.

Choc-Coffee Cream: Add 2 teaspoons of coffee essence to the melted chocolate mixture before adding the sour cream. Or add 2 teaspoons of instant coffee powder which has been blended to a paste with a little hot water.

Brandied Coffee Cream

Covers and fills a 23 cm (9 in) double-layer cake

250 g (8 oz) butter, softened

1 tablespoon instant coffee powder

3 tablespoons milk, heated

¼ teaspoon salt

3 cups (1 lb) icing (confectioners') sugar, sifted

1–2 tablespoons brandy

Beat the butter until creamy. Dissolve the instant coffee powder in the heated milk and add to the butter, beating well. Add the salt; and gradually beat in 2 cups of the icing sugar, beating well after each addition. Beat the brandy through; and continue adding the remaining icing sugar until the desired consistency is obtained.

Allow the coffee cream to stand for 10 minutes for the flavours to blend. Fill and cover the cake, and allow to set before cutting.

Vienna Butter Cream

Covers the top of an 18–20 cm (7–8 in) cake

60 g (2 oz) butter or margarine, softened

½ teaspoon vanilla essence

1 tablespoon milk

1¼ cups (7 oz) icing (confectioners') sugar

Beat the butter and vanilla in a bowl until creamy. Add the milk, and beat to blend in. Gradually add the sifted icing sugar, beating well after each addition.

Whilst still soft, spread onto the top of the cake; swirl or 'rough up' into an attractive design. Allow to firm before cutting.

As a Filling:
This soft cream may be used as a filling for cakes if made to a moister consistency. Use a little extra liquid or add such ingredients as crushed pineapple, apricot jam (apricot jelly), chopped canned fruits, fruitmince, etc.

Variations:

Citrus:
Add 1 teaspoon of grated orange rind or lemon rind to the creamy butter, and substitue fruit juice for milk.

Passionfruit:
Omit the vanilla, and use passionfruit pulp instead of the milk.

Chocolate Rum:
Use rum essence with the butter, and add 1–2 tablespoons of drinking chocolate to the icing sugar.

Coffee:
Blend 1–2 teaspoons of instant coffee with the milk, before adding it to the mixture.

Mocha:
Add 1 tablespoon of cocoa and 1 teaspoon of instant coffee powder to the icing sugar.

Honey Spice:
Add 1 tablespoon of honey to the creamy butter, use lemon juice instead of the milk, and add ¼ teaspoon of ground cinnamon with the icing sugar.

Nut Crunch:
Fold ½ cup (2 oz) finely chopped nuts (walnuts, hazelnuts, pecans, etc.) into the creamy mixture.

Sherry Cream:
Omit the vanilla essence. Add 1 tablespoon of sweet sherry with 1 egg yolk to the creamy butter.

Lemon Butter Cream

Makes 1–1¼ cups (8–10fl oz)

3 egg yolks
60 g (2 oz) butter or margarine, chopped
2 teaspoons cornflour (cornstarch)
⅓ cup (3 oz) sugar
2 teaspoons grated lemon rind
½ cup (4fl oz) lemon juice
1½ cup (4fl oz) whipped cream

Combine the egg yolks, butter, cornflour, sugar, lemon rind and lemon juice in the top half of a double boiler (double saucepan); blend well. Place over simmering water and cook, stirring frequently, until the mixture is of a thick custard consistency. Remove from the heat and allow to cool.

Fold the whipped cream through. (For a perfectly smooth Lemon Butter Cream, press the mixture through a fine sieve to remove any tiny pieces of lemon rind remaining.) Use as a filling for sponge cakes or meringues.

Variations

Passionfruit:
Omit the lemon rind; and substitute passionfruit pulp for two-thirds of the lemon juice.

Orange:
Use orange rind and juice instead of lemon rind and juice; and omit 2 teaspoons of the sugar.

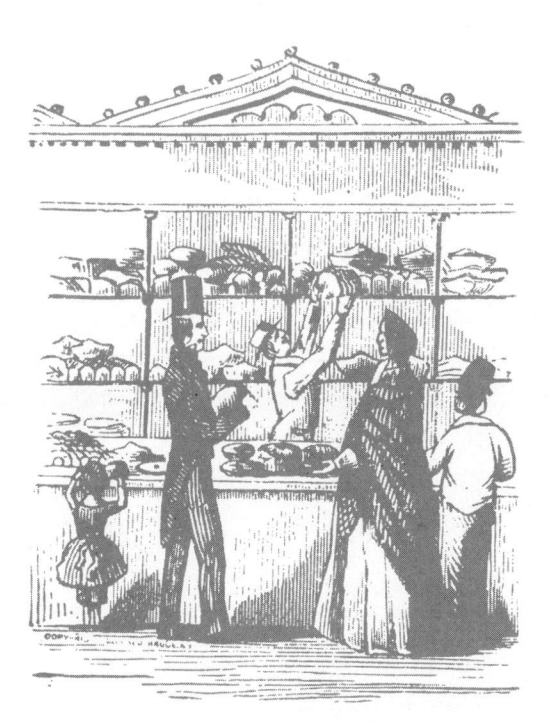

Lemon Ginger Cream

Covers or fills a slab cake 23 cm (9 in) square

4 eggs, separated
1¼ cups (10 oz) sugar
4 tablespoons lemon juice
1–2 teaspoon grated lemon rind
⅓ cup (2 oz) chopped crystallised ginger

Combine the eggs whites, sugar, lemon juice and lemon rind in a heatproof glass basin; beat to mix well. Place the basin over a saucepan containing boiling water, and cook, beating with a rotary or electric hand beater until thickened—approximately 5 minutes.

Beat the egg yolks in a small bowl until lemon coloured; quickly add about 3 tablespoons of the hot mixture and beat briskly to combine. Turn the egg yolk mixture into the hot mixture over the boiling water, and continue beating slowly for a further 5 minutes. Remove from the heat and allow to cool.

Fold the chopped ginger through; chill slightly. Stir again before use.

Variations

Orange Jaffa:
Substitute orange juice and rind for the lemon juice and rind; and substitute coarsely chopped chocolate for the ginger.

Pine Ginger:
Use pineapple juice instead of the lemon juice and rind; and add ½ cup (4 oz) of crushed well-drained pineapple with the ginger.

Coco-Pine:
Omit the ginger, and substitute ¼ cup (2 oz) of crushed well-drained pineapple and ¼ cup (½ oz) of desiccated coconut.

Lemallow:
Omit the ginger, and fold 8–10 marshmallows, quartered, into the cooled mixture.

Almond Pastry Cream

May be prepared and stored in the refrigerator for up to a week. A richer variation of Crème Pâtissière. Makes 2 cups (16fl oz)

½ cup (4fl oz) vanilla pastry cream (see recipe below)
90 g (3 oz) soft unsalted butter
⅔ cup (3 oz) ground almonds
¾ cup (4 oz) icing (confectioners') sugar
1 egg
1 tablespoon cornflour (cornstarch)
2 teaspoons rum

Make and chill the vanilla pastry cream according to the recipe.

Cream the butter until soft, then add the ground almonds and icing sugar and beat well, using either a wooden spoon or an electric mixer. Add the egg, and beat well. Add the cornflour and rum, and beat at medium speed until evenly combined.

Add the vanilla pastry cream, a tablespoon at a time, beating at medium speed, until it is all combined. Cover and store in the refrigerator until required.

Vanilla Pastry Cream

Makes 1 cup (8fl oz)

1 cup (8fl oz) milk
1 vanilla bean (or pod), split lengthways
3 large egg yolks
⅓ cup (2½ oz) sugar
2 tablespoons plain flour, or cornflour (cornstarch)

Place the milk and vanilla bean in a saucepan and bring to the boil; cover, and keep hot. Beat the egg yolks and sugar together with an electric mixer or a wire balloon whisk, until the mixture is thick enough to fall as a ribbon when the beater is lifted. Stir in the flour with a whisk.

Strain the hot milk into the mixture, beating continuously with the whisk. Return the mixture to the saucepan and bring to the boil, stirring continuously with a wooden spoon. Boil for 1 minute to thicken, stirring vigorously, then pour into a bowl and rub the surface with a knob of butter to prevent a skin forming while cooling. Use when cold, or cover and store in the refrigerator for up to a week.

Crème Pâtissière

Makes 1½–2 cups (12–16fl oz) filling

1¼ cups (10fl oz) milk
2 egg yolks
¼ cup (2 oz) sugar
2 tablespoons cornflour (cornstarch)
¼ teaspoon salt
extra ¼ cup (2fl oz) milk
1 teaspoon vanilla essence
60 g (2 oz) unsalted butter (optional)

The second and subsequent stages in preparing this mixture require a double boiler (double saucepan) with preheated water in the bottom half.

Heat the 1¼ cups of milk in a small saucepan until scalding; set aside.

Combine the egg yolks, sugar, cornflour and salt in the top half of a double boiler (double saucepan); gradually blend in the extra ¼ cup of milk. Add one-quarter of the scalded milk and stir through quickly; gradually beat in the remaining milk.

Heat, beating constantly, over hot water until the mixture thickens. Simmer a few minutes, then remove from the heat and flavour with vanilla.

For a particularly rich cream, add the chopped butter and beat until smooth.

Pour into a small bowl and allow to cool. Chill before use.

Right: Rich Fruit Cake (see p. 104), iced and decorated with Frangipani, Hyacinth and Lily of the Valley (see p. 143 for instructions).

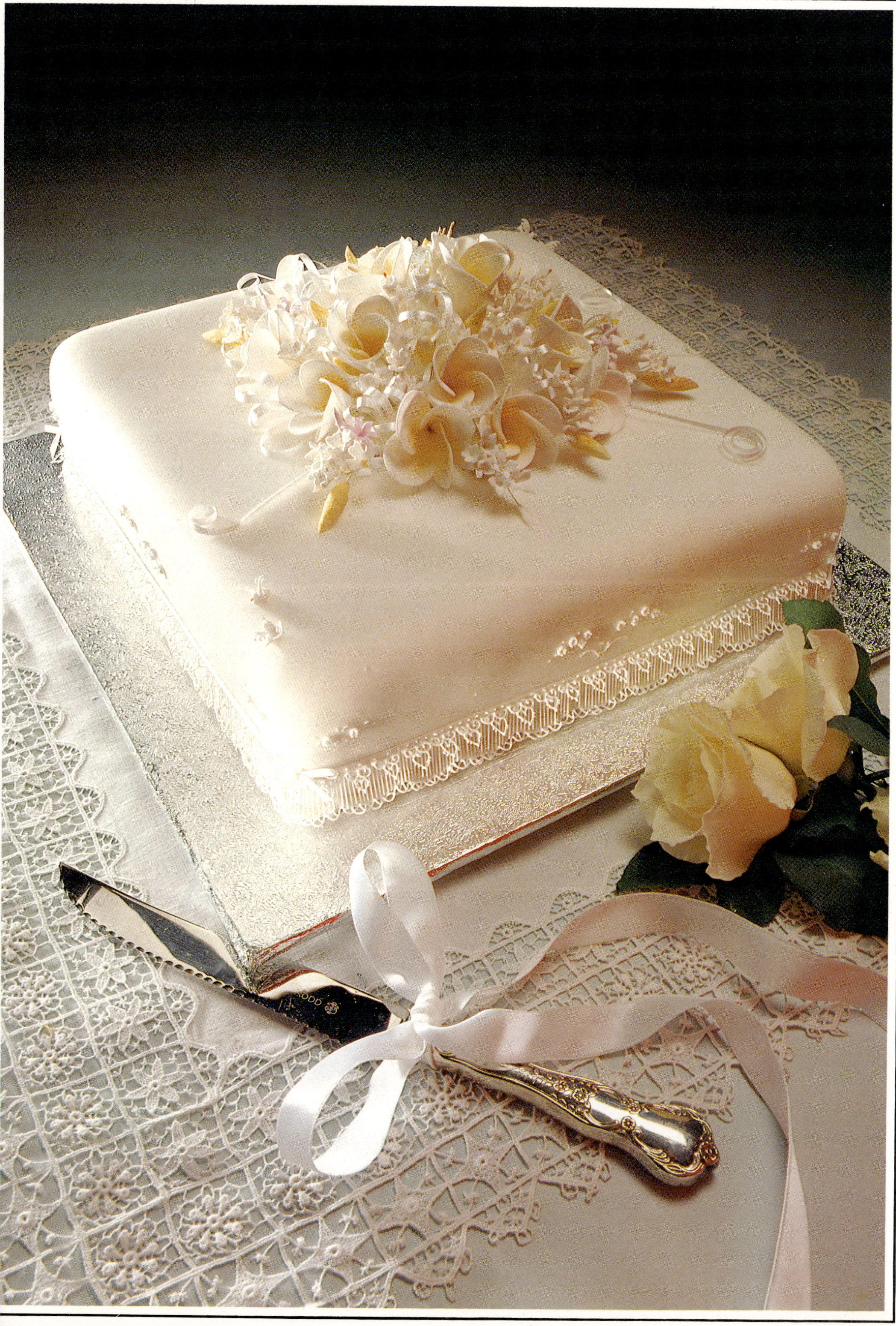

Hazelnut Custard Cream

Fills and covers the top of an 18–20 cm (7–8 in) double-layer cake

| 3 egg yolks |
| 1/3 cup (3 oz) sugar |
| 1 teaspoon cornflour (cornstarch) |
| 1/3 cup (3 fl oz) cream or evaporated milk |
| 1 tablespoon sweet sherry |
| 185 g (6 oz) unsalted butter, softened |
| 60 g (2 oz) hazelnuts, grated or ground coarsely |

In the top half of a double boiler (double saucepan), place the egg yolks and sugar. Beat until thick and lemon coloured—a small electric hand beater is ideal.

Scatter the cornflour over the surface, and beat again; gradually add the cream. Place over hot—not boiling—water and cook, stirring constantly with a wooden spoon, until thickened to custard consistency.

Remove from the heat and stir the sweet sherry through. Allow to cool, and chill.

Beat the butter in a bowl, again with the electric hand beater, until white and creamy; add the hazelnuts and mix through.

Gradually add spoonfuls of the chilled custard, beating gently with each addition. Remove the beater, place the bowl over a large basin containing iced water, and beat with a wooden spoon until the mixture is firm enough to spread onto the cake.

After spreading, chill the cake until the cream is firm before cutting.

Chocolate Almond Cream

Covers or fills 23 cm (9 in) cake

| 1/2 cup (2 oz) slivered, blanched almonds |
| 60 g (2 oz) butter or margarine |
| 1/2 cup (3 oz) semi-sweet chocolate pieces |
| 1 cup (8 fl oz) thickened or heavy cream, chilled |
| 1 tablespoon icing (confectioners') sugar |

Sauté the almonds in heated butter in a small pan until golden brown. Drain off (and discard) any excess butter, and set the almonds aside.

Melt the chocolate pieces over hot—not boiling—water; cool to just warm.

Beat the cream and icing sugar until thickened and standing in soft peaks. Gradually fold in the warm chocolate, allowing the chocolate to break off into hardened flecks. Fold the almonds through. Use to fill or cover light sponge cakes or chocolate cakes.

To Melt Chocolate: Mould a 'basin' to fit over a small saucepan, using heavy or double-thickness aluminium foil. Quarter fill the saucepan with hot water, place the foil 'basin' over and crimp the edges to secure. Place the chocolate on the foil and allow to melt.

Lift the foil 'basin' off the saucepan, spread open slightly and scrape out the melted chocolate with a pliable spatula. Discard the foil.

Brazilian Butter Cream

Fills (or covers the top of) a 23 cm (9 in) cake

| 185 g (6 oz) butter, softened |
| 1 cup (8 oz) sugar |
| 185 g (6 oz) pure unsweetened cooking chocolate, melted and cooled |
| 2 tablespoons rum |
| 1 tablespoon coffee-rum liqueur |
| 5 eggs, beaten |

Cream the butter and sugar in a bowl; add the chocolate and beat well. Beat in the rum and coffee liqueur. Add the beaten eggs and whisk thoroughly until the mixture commences to thicken.

Chill for about 1 hour, then whisk again before using to fill the cake. Chill the cake thoroughly to set the filling before cutting.

GLAZES

Brandied Apricot Glaze

Covers the top of 20 cm (8 in) sponge cake

| 1½ cups (1 lb) apricot jam (jelly) |
| ¾ cup (6 fl oz) water |
| 2–3 thin strips lemon peel |
| 2 tablespoons brandy or brandy liqueur |

Chop or mash the apricot jam to break up any pieces; push through a coarse sieve if necessary. Place in a non-stick saucepan with the water and lemon peel, and heat slowly until just commencing to boil; reduce the heat and simmer for 5 minutes.

Add the brandy, simmer for a further 5 minutes; remove the lemon peel and allow to cool.

Spoon over the cake, allowing the glaze to be partially absorbed into the surface. Chill.

Variations:
Apple or redcurrant jelly and port wine.
Raspberry jam (jelly) and sweet vermouth.
Marmalade and orange brandy liqueur.
Cherry jam (jelly) and Kirsch liqueur.

Chocolate Glaze

Covers the top of a 20 cm (8 in) cake

| 125 g (4 oz) pure semi-sweet chocolate |
| 60 g (2 oz) butter, chopped |
| 1 tablespoon golden syrup (light corn syrup) |

Grate the chocolate coarsely and place in a heatproof basin with the butter and golden syrup; place over hot—not boiling—water and stir occasionally until the chocolate and butter are melted and blended.

Remove from the heat and stir until the mixture cools slightly and thickens to the desired consistency. Pour over the cake, and when almost set mark into cutting sections. Allow to set before cutting.

Notes: Heat over hot—not boiling—water so that the cocoa fats will not separate in the chocolate and cause a dull finish to the glaze.

Stir—don't beat—whilst the mixture cools slightly; beating will incorporate air which will form bubbles in the glaze.

Mark the glaze into sections before fully set, as this will help to prevent unsightly cracks forming on the top when final cutting is performed.

If the cake is chilled before covering with the glaze, setting time will be shortened considerably.

Cherry Liqueur Glaze

Covers the top of a 20 cm (8 in) cake

| 1 can 450 g (15 oz) red cherries—approximate amount |
| water or lemon juice |
| 1 tablespoon arrowroot |
| 1 tablespoon cherry brandy liqueur |

Drain the canned cherries well and set them aside; measure the syrup, and add water or lemon juice to make ¾ cup (6 fl oz).

Blend the arrowroot with a little of the cherry syrup. Place the remaining syrup in a small saucepan; heat slowly until boiling.

Meanwhile arrange the seeded (pitted) cherries over the top of a sponge or light butter cake in a single layer.

Stir the blended arrowroot into the boiling syrup and cook, stirring constantly, for 1 minute. Add the cherry brandy liqueur, quickly blend through, and drizzle immediately over the cherries on the cake. Allow to set and chill before cutting.

Variations:
Canned strawberries and orange brandy liqueur.
Canned apricots and apricot brandy liqueur.
Canned sliced pears and crème de menthe liqueur with green food colouring.

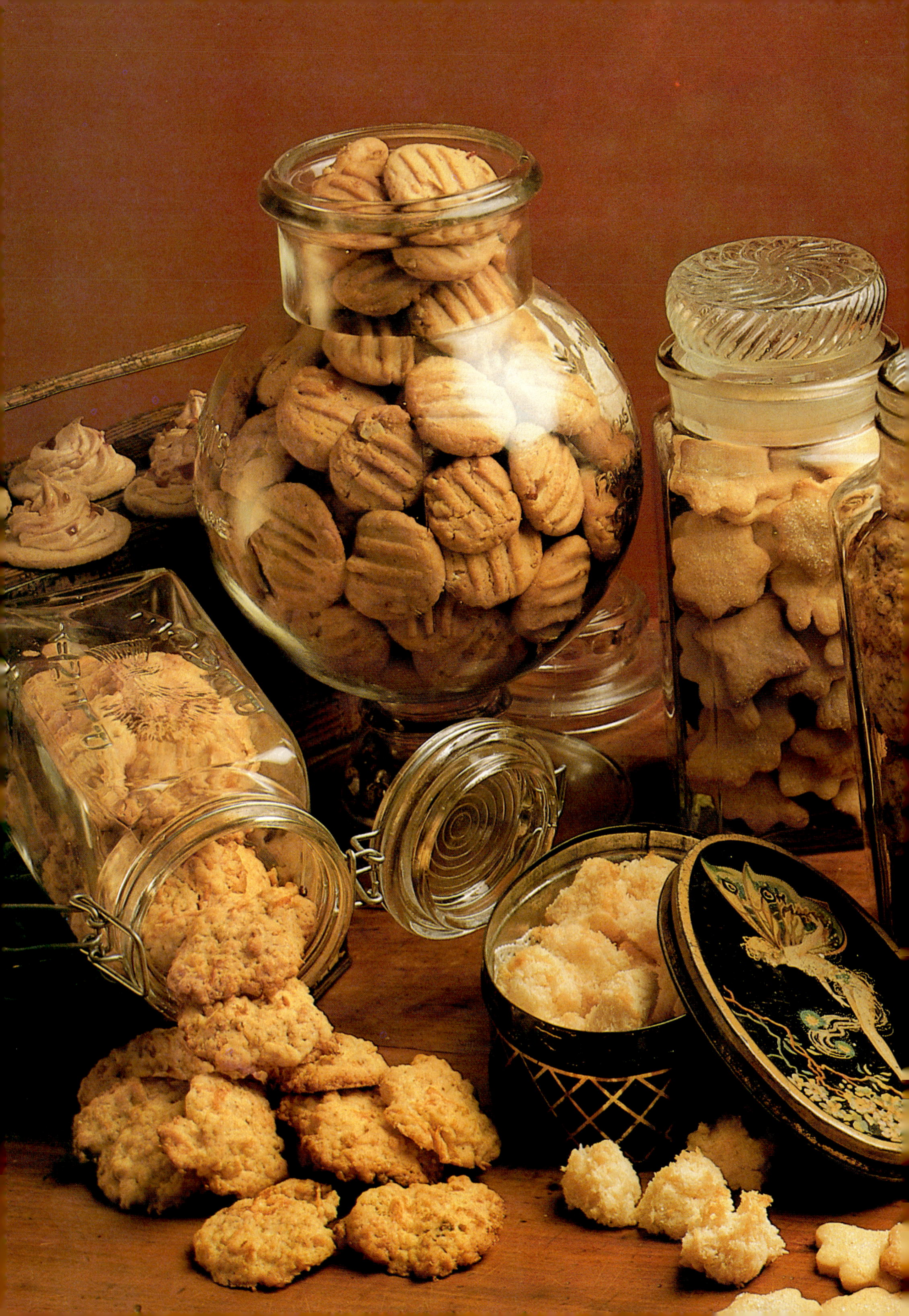

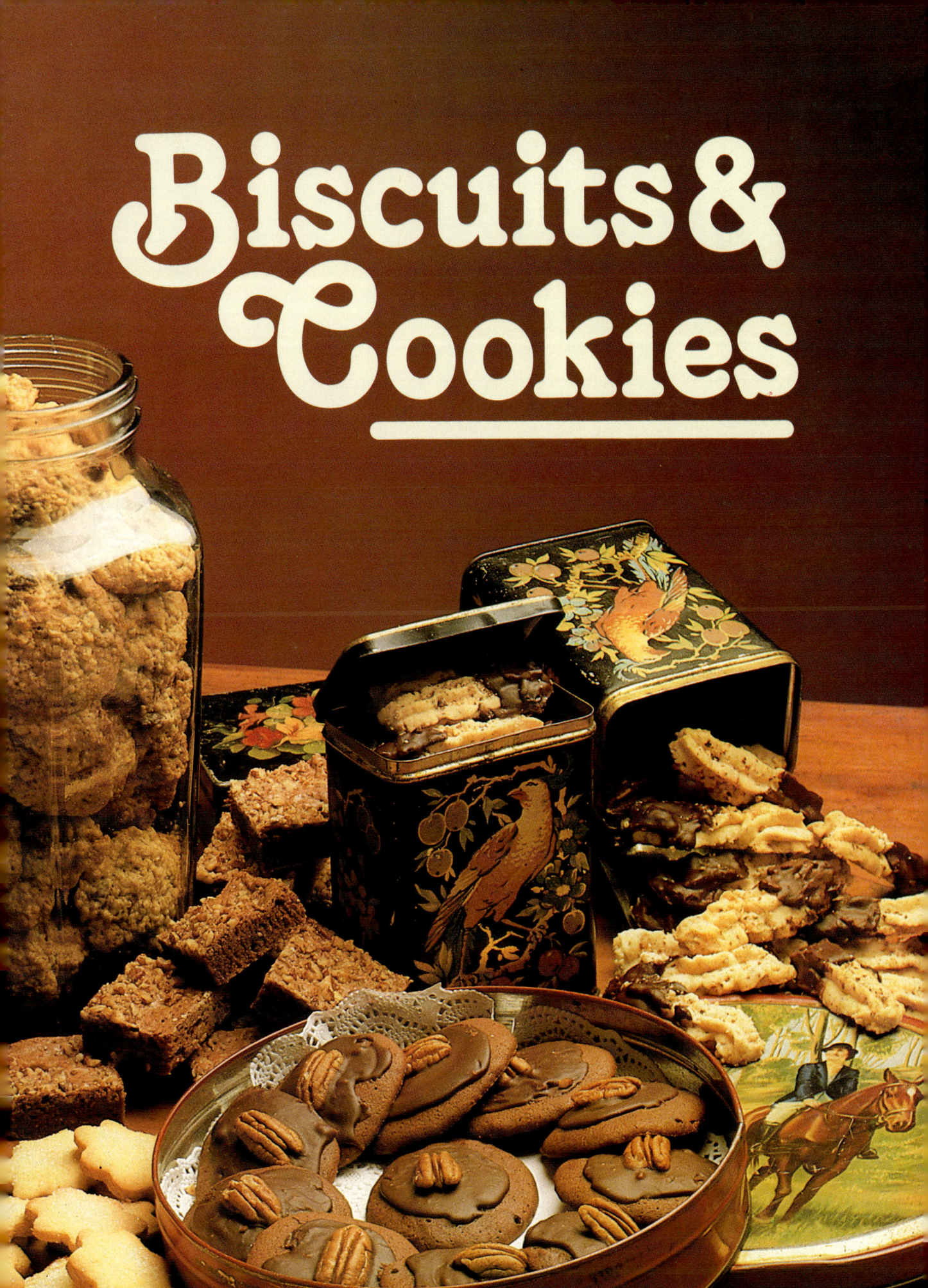

Biscuits & Cookies

Biscuits & Cookies

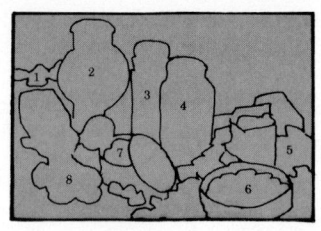

1. Raspberry Meringue Twirls (see p. 172)
2. American Peanut Butter Cookies (see p. 176)
3. Sugar Cookies (see p. 176)
4. Chocolate Chip Cookies (see p. 177)
5. Mixed Nut Bars (see p. 173)
6. Old Fashioned Chocolate Cookies (see p. 177)
7. Coconut Macaroons (see p. 160)
8. Oatmeal Carrot Cookies (see p. 177)

Anyone who has had children or had anything to do with them knows you need a bottomless biscuit jar. Today many good commercial biscuits are on the market, but the pleasure of making your own and the economic advantage produce more satisfying results. This section provides a wide selection of recipes for you to try.

The word 'cookie' (cooky or cookey), in wide use in North America, came from the Dutch word *koekje*, the diminutive of *koek*, which means 'cake'. 'Cookie' was in use in eighteenth-century England, but 'biscuit' is more common now. This word comes from the Old French *bescuit*, which was a flat cake of unleavened bread, made from fats, flours and eggs. In fact, the original French meaning inferred 'double baking', as the early biscuits were those 'ship's biscuits' or 'army biscuits' ('hard tack'), being bone-hard, dry and long-lasting. No wonder the art of dunking biscuits developed, because if you didn't dunk those biscuits you would probably break a tooth. The Italian was *biscotto*, Spanish *bizscho* and German *Zwieback*, all originally implying a rusk-like biscuit. They were sweet or savoury, also. The U.S. word 'cracker' is reserved for cookies that are unsweetened dry and crisp.

Hence, they are small cakes of various shapes (mostly round), with or without sweetening, which tend to be rather dry, hard and brittle more often than not. They may be a single shape, or two may be joined together with a filling; they are plain or decorated with fruit, nuts, coloured sugar, various icings or frostings. Initially they were sound, simple food whose plainness reflected the economic situation of the majority of the people several hundred years ago. Festive seasons always brought with them fancier biscuits and today's affluence ensures such cookie delights are always available.

In Europe, particularly the U.K., biscuits were an integral part of the afternoon imbibing of tea or coffee. Hence they tended to be plain so as to remain a part of the repast and not to dominate and satiate the palate with too much sweetness. Times changed and now they are of a richer style. As early immigrants brought their favourite biscuit recipes to the New World lands, their cooking was at first simple because there were usually many hardships to overcome, and these pioneers yearned for much they had left behind in their homelands.

The French petits fours are a member of the biscuit family, too. Before the advent of the electric oven, these were baked after the big cakes had been cooked and as temperature in the oven (*four*) was falling. They were of two types: the macaroons, shortbreads and other little fancy biscuits; and the sponge-cake fondant-coated ones. The latter group will not be treated at length here (see page 118).

Michael Lawrence

Types of Biscuits

There are both sweet and savoury biscuits, but their recipes are usually of two basic types: one uses butter and the other (the sponge type) uses eggs. As well, there are three methods of forming the biscuits: one where the dough is chilled or frozen (either in round logs or fancy shapes) before slicing off biscuits for baking; another where the dough is simply rolled out thinly and cut into shapes; and the third where the dough is poured or dropped and flattened with a knife—a thinner batter will actually flow over and fill a shallow tray, for cutting after baking into bars or shapes whilst warm. Biscuits can be filled in various ways with different fillings for variety.

The North American cookie-maker tends to favour quick baking at 230°C (450°F/Gas 8) so that they don't dry out. If a harder cookie is desired, after they are baked reduce the oven to 120°C (250°F/Gas ½) for a short period to dry out. The northern European favours slow baking to obtain a harder, crisper biscuit. Their oven temperature is usually 140–180°C (275–350°F/Gas 1–4).

Some Handy Hints

The amount of liquid required in a recipe to make a dough will vary depending upon the size of the eggs, the moisture in the flour and the general humidity and weather prevailing. Measure the flour before sifting.

All ingredients, especially eggs, must be at room temperature before making a biscuit dough. Eggs enrich a dough and make a crumblier biscuit.

Approximately double the amount of flour to fat and sugar is used for biscuits spooned directly onto trays or for rolled out and stamped out biscuits.

Minimise kneading the biscuit dough after addition of flour—otherwise they will toughen. And only lightly flour the work surface that dough is to be rolled upon.

Keep the dough chilled and covered before use, and dust the cutters with flour.

If greasing biscuit trays, use polyunsaturated oil only, as butter causes biscuits to stick, but butter in the mixture gives the best flavour.

Always use a shallow biscuit tray or one with a raised edge only on one side (except for bars and slices) so that they cook evenly. Make sure it is cold before use so that biscuits won't loose their shape. Leave space between biscuits for spreading (especially with drop biscuits).

Always preheat your oven and if cooking more than one tray of biscuits, space them well apart. Rotate the trays as well as reversing the top and bottom shelves towards the end of the cooking time for even browning.

After removing the tray from the oven, immediately lift off the biscuits with a spatula (to prevent further cooking) and place onto a rack to cool. Do not pile them on top of one another.

Do not store soft and crisp biscuits together. To keep soft biscuits moist, store in a cool place preferably in a stoneware jar fitted with a tight lid, and even place a clove-studded lemon or a piece of bread in with them. If crisp biscuits are stored in a jar or tin with a loose-fitting cover, they should not soften. If necessary, restore crispness by giving them 5 minutes in a slow oven, 150°C (300°F/Gas 2).

The number of biscuits made depends upon the thickness of the dough, the cutter or spoon size and whether or not you use the leftover pastry. The amount of flour used is also a guide. Generally 15 biscuits 4 cm (1½ in) in diameter are made for each cup of flour used.

SAVOURY BISCUITS

Cheese Straws

Makes about 30 savoury sticks

| 2 cups (8 oz) self-raising flour |
| 1 teaspoon salt |
| ¼–½ teaspoon cayenne pepper (to taste) |
| 125 g (4 oz) cheddar cheese, finely grated |
| 90 g (3 oz) Copha (white vegetable shortening), melted and cooled |
| 2 tablespoons cold water |

Preheat the oven to 230°C (450°F/Gas 8). Lightly grease the baking trays with polyunsaturated oil.

Sift together the flour, salt and cayenne pepper and thoroughly mix in the grated cheese.

Add the water to the melted Copha and pour it over the flour-cheese mixture, mixing to form a firm dough. Roll it thinly, cut into strips ½ cm × 10 cm (¼ in × 4 in) and twist each strip slightly.

Bake for 10 minutes. Turn onto wire racks to cool.

Sesame Seed Cheese Buttons

Makes about 30 little biscuits

| 1½ cups (6 oz) flour |
| 1 teaspoon salt |
| 1 teaspoon ground paprika |
| pinch of chilli powder |
| 1½ cups (6 oz) finely grated cheddar cheese |
| ½ cup (2 oz) finely grated Parmesan cheese |
| 185 g (6 oz) butter, cut into 1 cm (½ in) cubes |
| 2 tablespoons freshly toasted white sesame seeds |

Preheat the oven to 180°C (350°F/Gas 4). Grease the baking trays.

Sift together the flour, salt, paprika and chilli powder.

Cream together the cheese, butter and sesame seeds. Combine both mixtures to make a dough, and roll it into four 'logs' 2–3 cm (1–1¼ in) in diameter. Wrap each log in aluminium foil and chill in the refrigerator until firm. Then slice into rounds 5 mm (¼ in) thick.

Bake for 10 minutes. Turn onto wire racks to cool.

Sri Lankan Curry Crisps

Makes about 24

| 60 g (2 oz) finely grated cheddar cheese |
| 60 g (2 oz) butter |
| 1¼ cups (5 oz) self-raising flour, sifted |
| 1 teaspoon Sri Lankan (Ceylonese) curry powder |
| 1 teaspoon onion salt |
| 3 tablespoons milk |
| milk for brushing biscuits |
| ¼ cup (¼ oz) cornflake crumbs |
| 1 tablespoon dessicated coconut |
| 1 teaspoon garam masala (ground spices) |

Preheat the oven to 200°C (400°F/Gas 6). Grease the baking trays.

Cream the cheese and butter together. Add alternate batches of sifted flour/onion salt/curry powder and the milk, until a firm dough is formed. Turn out onto a floured board and knead lightly; roll out to a thickness of 5 mm (¼ in) and cut into small rounds. Top with a mixture of cornflake and coconut crumbs; sprinkle the garam masala over the topping.

Bake for 10 to 12 minutes until they are crisp and brown. These biscuits may be served hot or cold.

Right: **Clockwise from bottom right: Russian Caraway Triangles (see p. 156); Sri Lankan Curry Crisps (see p. 154); Bizcochos (see p. 156); Cheese Straws (see above); Kipferl (see p. 157).**

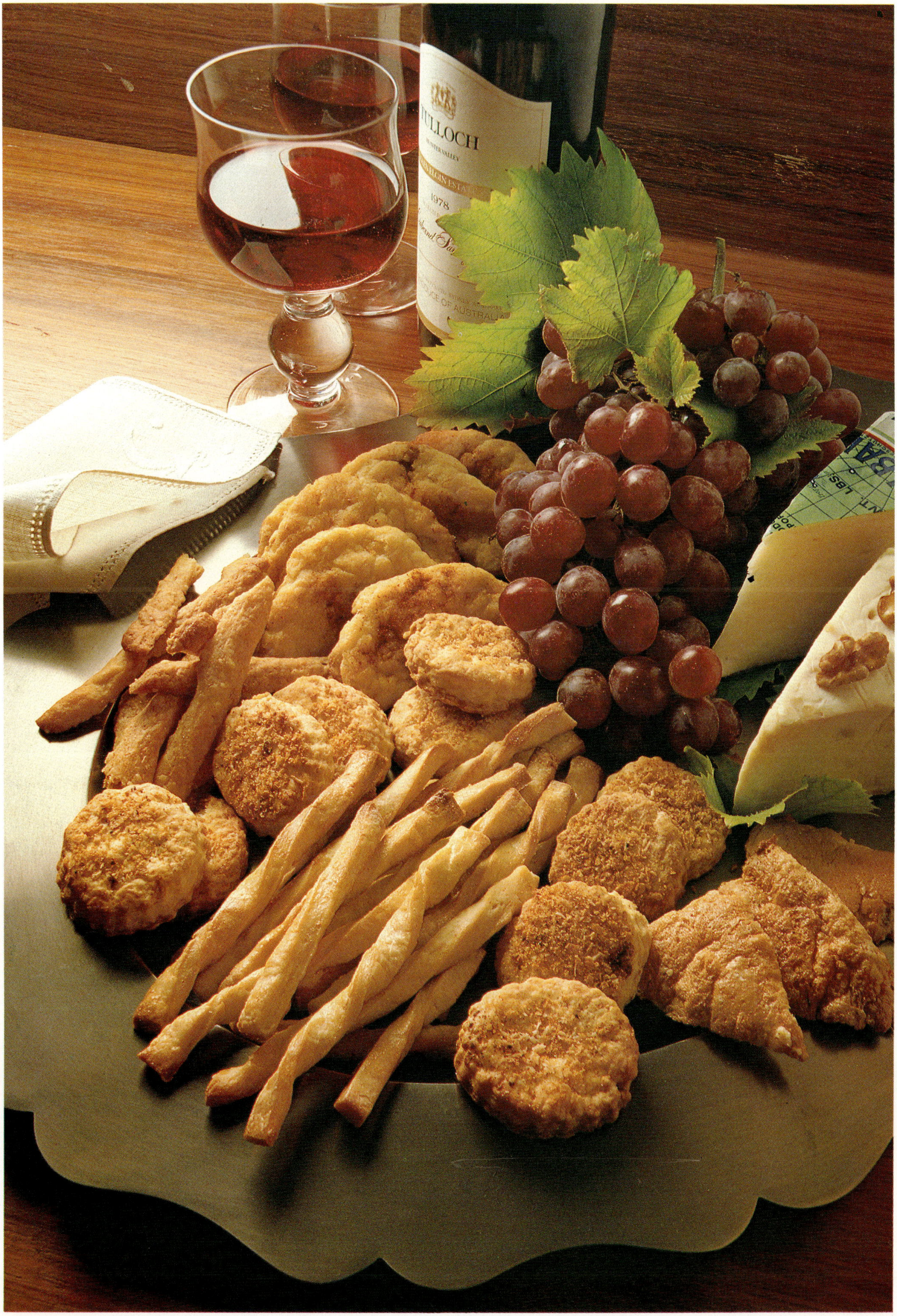
1978

Hungarian Onion Ham Slice

Cuts into 28 pieces

500 g (1 lb) 'Jatz' biscuits (salted crackers)
125 g (4 oz) ham, finely chopped
1 large onion, finely grated
½ green capsicum (pepper), finely chopped
1 clove garlic, minced
1 teaspoon dry English mustard powder
2 large eggs, lightly beaten
⅓ cup (3 fl oz) milk
¼ teaspoon salt
⅛ teaspoon ground black pepper
½ cup (2 oz) finely grated cheddar cheese
dried ground paprika, for garnish

Preheat the oven to 200°C (400°F/Gas 6). Thoroughly grease a shallow-sided 28 × 18 cm (11 × 7 in) slab tin.

Crush the cracker biscuits finely with a rolling pin, or make fine biscuit crumbs in a food processor. Combine with the ham, onion, capsicum, garlic and mustard, mixing well.

In a separate bowl, beat together the eggs, milk and salt and pepper, then pour this into the crumb mixture and mix thoroughly. Turn into the slab tin and press in well. Sprinkle the cheese evenly over the top, and dust with paprika, to taste.

Bake for 15 to 20 minutes until golden. Cut into 2 cm × 9 cm (1 in × 4 in) fingers and serve hot.

Bizcochos (Spanish Sherry Twists)

Makes about 36 twists

6 egg yolks, unbeaten
3 teaspoons finely grated orange zest
1 teaspoon finely grated lemon zest
1 tablespoon Amontillado sherry
1 teaspoon salt
125 g (4 oz) butter, softened
3 cups (12 oz) flour, sifted
beaten egg wash (1 egg, beaten with 1 tablespoon water)

Preheat the oven to 190°C (375°F/Gas 5). Grease the baking trays.

Cream together the egg yolks, zest, sherry, salt and butter. Gradually add the flour, kneading to make a smooth dough. Mould into twists and brush each twist with lightly beaten egg wash.

Bake for about 10 minutes or until golden brown. Turn onto wire racks to cool.

Russian Caraway Triangles

Makes about 50

3 eggs, separated
½ cup (4 oz) sugar
¼ teaspoon salt
1 teaspoon vanilla essence
¾ cup (3 oz) flour
½ tablespoon caraway seeds

Preheat the oven to 220°C (425°F/Gas 7). Grease a Swiss roll cake tin (jelly roll pan).

Beat the egg whites until stiff.

In a separate bowl, beat the egg yolks until lemon coloured; combine with the sugar, salt and vanilla essence.

Sift the flour three times, then mix in the caraway seeds. Combine the flour with the egg yolk mixture, mixing well. Gradually fold in the stiffly beaten egg whites, then pour the mixture into the cake tin.

Bake for 10 minutes, remove from the oven and cut into triangles then into half, horizontally; return to the oven and reduce the temperature to 150°C (300°F/Gas 2), for 5 minutes to dry out. Turn out onto wire racks to cool.

Kipferl (Austrian Potato Crescents)

Makes about 30

Dough:
2 cups (8 oz) self-raising flour, sifted

½ teaspoon salt

250 g (8 oz) butter, softened

2 cups (16 oz) mashed and sieved boiled potato, cold

Filling:
60 g (2 oz) butter, softened

¼ cup (1½ oz) brown sugar

¼ cup (1 oz) finely ground walnuts

ground paprika, for dusting

Preheat the oven to 200°C (400°F/Gas 6). Grease the baking trays.

Mix together the flour, salt and butter until it resembles coarse meal, adding more flour if necessary. Blend in the mashed potatoes, kneading well to make a smooth dough. Roll out on a lightly-floured surface, fold over and roll again. Repeat four times, refrigerating the dough from time to time if it becomes too sticky to handle. Finally, roll out thinly and cut into 5 cm (2 in) squares.

Blend together the filling ingredients until a smooth paste is formed. Place a small amount in the centre of each dough square and flatten it out. Roll up the dough, starting at a corner, then bend into a crescent shape.

Place the crescents on the baking trays, well spaced to allow for spreading. Bake for 20 minutes. Cool on wire racks, and sprinkle with paprika.

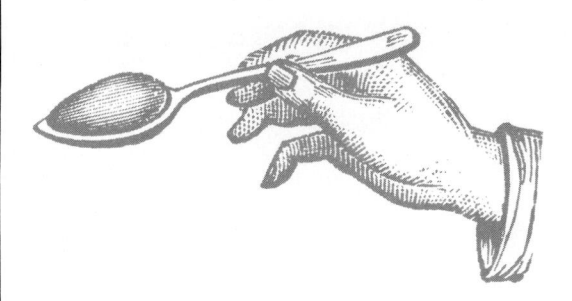

Mexican Tomato Biscuits

Makes about 30

2 cups (8 oz) self-raising flour, sifted

1 teaspoon chilli powder

1 teaspoon garlic salt

1 tablespoon finely chopped spring onions (scallions)

60 g (2 oz) butter

¾ cup (3 oz) coarsely grated matured cheddar cheese

½–¾ cup (4–6fl oz) 'V-8' or tomato juice

Preheat the oven to 200°C (400°F/Gas 6). Thoroughly grease the baking trays.

Sift together the flour, chilli powder and salt, then rub in the butter until the mixture resembles breadcrumbs. Mix in the cheese, then add sufficient 'V-8' juice to make a firm dough. Turn onto a floured board, knead lightly, and roll out to 5 mm (¼ in) thickness. Cut out rounds or other shapes with a cookie cutter.

Bake for 10 to 12 minutes. Turn onto wire racks and allow to cool before serving.

For an Indian version, substitute hot curry powder for the chilli powder.

Italian Wine Crackers

Makes about 30

1 cup (4 oz) flour

generous pinch of ground black pepper

¼ cup (2fl oz) dry red wine—a variety such as Shiraz

¼ cup (2fl oz) dry white wine—a variety such as Semillon

1 cup (8fl oz) water

1 egg yolk

Preheat the oven to 150°C (300°F/Gas 2). Grease the baking trays.

Sift the flour and pepper together twice. Heat the wine and water in a saucepan, bring to the boil, then gradually mix in the flour until the dough that is formed comes away from the sides of the saucepan in a ball. Allow it to cool.

Beat in the egg yolk. Turn onto a lightly floured board, and knead well. Roll the dough out thinly and cut into shapes.

Bake for about 15 minutes or until crisp and dry. Turn onto wire racks to cool.

SWEET BISCUITS

Almond Macaroons

Makes about 40

| 7 egg whites |
| 500 g (1 lb) caster (powdered) sugar, sifted |
| 500 g (1 lb) finely ground blanched almonds, sifted |
| 2 tablespoons rose water or orange water |

Preheat the oven to 120°C (250°F/Gas ½). Thoroughly grease the baking trays.

Beat the egg whites until dry, then gradually add sugar until it is all incorporated. Add the rose water to the ground almond, mixing well; then gradually incorporate this into the egg white-sugar mixture. Drop spoonfuls onto the trays, allowing room for spreading.

Bake for 30 minutes. Allow to cool on the tray.

Note: If making your own almond powder, thoroughly chill the almonds (to reduce oiliness) before chopping in a food processor. Sieve and re-crush coarser fragments.

Scottish Shortbread

Cuts into 8 wedges

| 1½ cups (6 oz) plain flour, sifted |
| ¼ cup (2 oz) caster (powdered) sugar |
| 125 g (4 oz) butter |
| ¼ teaspoon vanilla essence |
| caster (powdered) sugar, for dusting |

Preheat the oven to 150°C (300°F/Gas 2). Grease a baking tray.

Combine all the shortbread ingredients in the bowl of a food processor and mix until it forms a ball of dough. (Or cream the butter and sugar together before adding the sifted flour to make a smooth dough.) Turn it onto the baking tray and press it into a round flat cake about 1 cm (less than ½ in) thick. Crimp the edges with the fingertips, and prick all over with a fork. If desired, shallow cuts may be made to mark it into eight wedges.

Bake for about 1 hour, until firm and pale golden. Slide onto a wire rack to cool, and dust the top with caster sugar. When cold, cut into wedges.

Swedish Christmas Cookies

Makes about 36

| 2 yolks from hard-boiled eggs |
| 90 g (3 oz) butter |
| ⅓ cup (3 oz) caster (powdered) sugar |
| ⅓ cup (3 fl oz) thick sour cream |
| zest from ½ lemon |
| zest from ½ orange |
| 1 raw egg yolk |
| 1 cup (4 oz) flour (more if required), sifted |
| ⅛ teaspoon bicarbonate of soda (baking soda) |
| ⅛ teaspoon salt |
| *Topping:* 1 egg white, well beaten |
| 1 tablespoon caster (powdered) sugar |
| 1 tablespoon ground almonds |

Preheat the oven to 160°C (325°F/Gas 3). Grease the baking trays.

Mash the hard-boiled egg yolks with the butter until a smooth paste is formed. Blend in the sugar, mixing well. Add the sour cream, lemon and orange zest and raw egg yolk.

Sift the flour, bicarbonate of soda and salt together and add to the other ingredients, mixing well and adding more flour (if necessary) to obtain a firm, rollable dough. Roll out to 5 mm (¼ in) thickness and press out fancy shapes, such as stars or the shapes of animals. Brush with beaten egg white, and sprinkle with sugar-nut mixture.

Bake for 15 to 20 minutes. Turn onto wire racks to cool.

Right: Clockwise from top: Scottish Shortbread (see above); Canadian Fruit and Nut Drops (see p. 165); Swedish Christmas Cookies (see above); Almond Macaroons (see above).

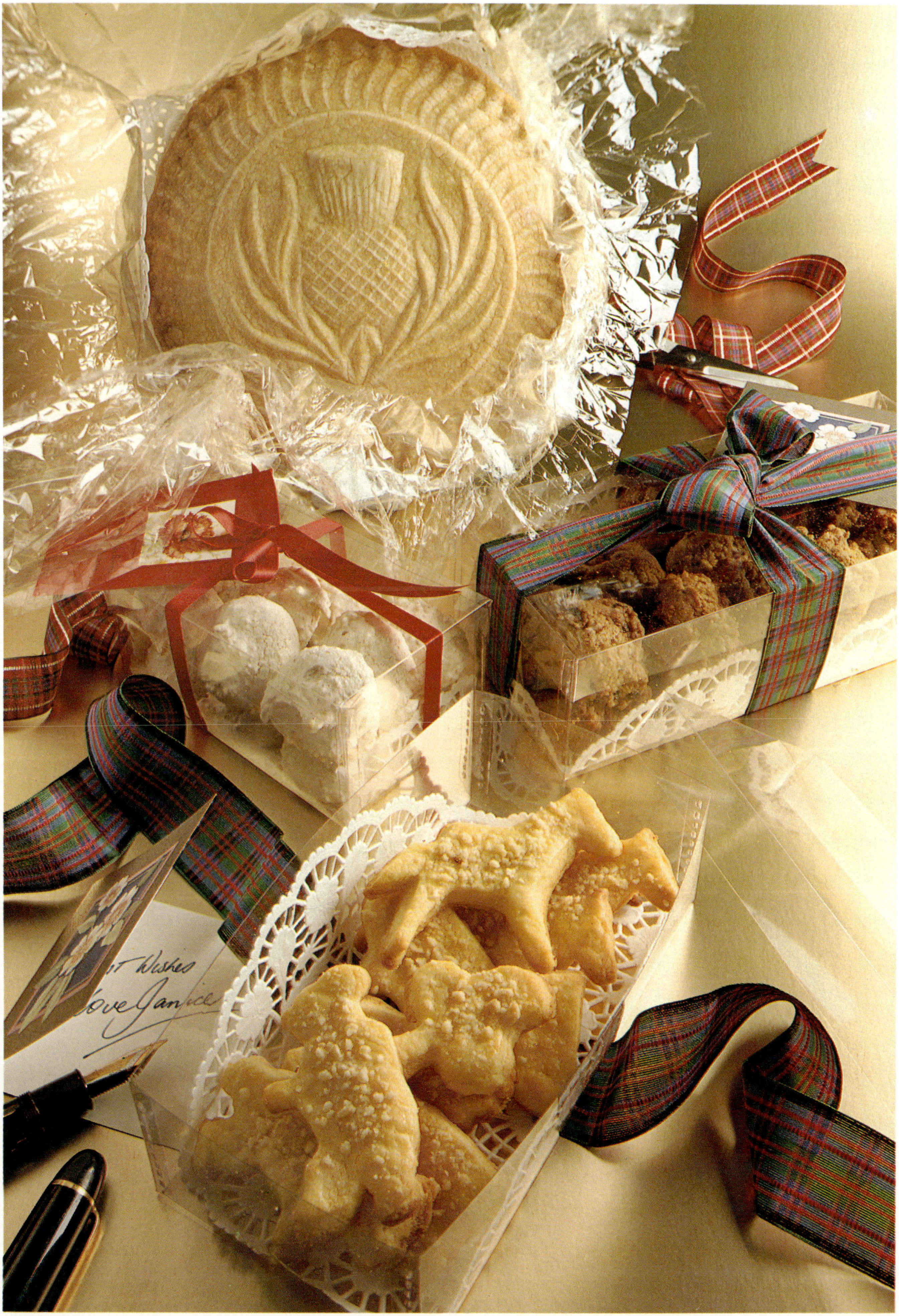
Wishes

Coconut Macaroons

Makes 20-24

2 cups (6 oz) desiccated coconut

1 teaspoon cream of tartar

3 teaspoons cornflour (cornstarch)

4 egg whites, at room temperature

1⅓ cups (10 oz) caster (powdered) sugar

1 teaspoon vanilla essence

Combine the coconut, cream of tartar and cornflour in a bowl; toss lightly to mix.

Whisk the egg whites in a clean glass bowl until frothy and soft peaks form; gradually add the sugar, beating well after each addition.

Add the vanilla then quickly but lightly fold in the coconut mixture—do not overmix.

Place in rough teaspoonfuls onto greased trays which have been lightly dusted with cornflour.

Place in a pre-heated very cool oven 120°C (250°F/Gas ½) and bake for 40 to 45 minutes, until dry and crisp.

Open the oven door and allow to cool in the oven for 30 minutes; remove and when cold lift into airtight containers to store.

Note: For rougher textured macaroons use 1 cup (3 oz) desiccated coconut and 1 cup (2 oz) flaked or chopped shredded coconut.

German Aniseed Cookies

Makes about 15

3 eggs

1 cup (7 oz) sugar

1 cup (4 oz) flour, sifted

1½ tablespoons anise seeds

Preheat the oven to 180°C (350°F/Gas 4). Grease the baking trays.

Beat the eggs and sugar together for 10 minutes with an electric mixer (for 30 minutes by hand). Then gradually add flour and anise seeds and mix until well incorporated. Drop spoonfuls on to greased baking trays, allowing room for spreading. Allow to stand overnight. A hard crust will form on each (the crust will puff up to resemble icing when they are baked) and bake for 10 minutes.

Banana-Bender's Biscuits

Makes about 25

60 g (2 oz) butter

1 cup (7 oz) sugar

2 cups (12 oz) mashed ripe banana

1½ cups (6 oz) flour, sifted

1 teaspoon bicarbonate of soda (baking soda)

½ teaspoon salt

2 eggs, well beaten

1½ cups (6 oz) chopped pecan nuts

Preheat the oven to 150°C (300°F/Gas 2). Grease the baking trays.

Cream together the butter and sugar. Sift the flour, bicarbonate of soda and salt together and fold into the butter-sugar mixture. Mix in the beaten eggs, banana and nuts. Spoon drops of the mixture onto the baking trays, allowing space around each biscuit.

Bake for 20 to 25 minutes. Turn onto wire racks to cool. Being rich and moist, they do not keep for very long.

Queensland Crunchies

Makes about 25

½ cup (2 oz) flour, sifted

¼ teaspoon salt

1 teaspoon baking powder

¼ cup (1 oz) fine cake crumbs

⅓ cup (3 oz) sugar

1 egg, lightly beaten

¼ cup (1 oz) finely chopped macadamia nuts

¼ cup (2 oz) crushed pineapple, well drained and dried

caster (powdered) sugar, for dusting

Preheat the oven to 180°C (350°F/Gas 4). Thoroughly grease and flour the baking trays.

Sift together the flour, salt and baking powder, then mix with the sugar and cake crumbs. Mix in the egg, nuts and pineapple to make a thick batter. Drop spoonfuls onto the trays, allowing space between each.

Bake for 10 minutes. Dust with caster sugar and allow to cool on the trays.

Coconut Butterscotch Cookies

Makes about 30

| 1 cup (5 oz) brown sugar |
| 170 g (5½ oz) butter, softened |
| 4 egg yolks, lightly beaten |
| 2 cups (8 oz) flour, sifted |
| 2 teaspoons baking powder |
| ½ cup (1½ oz) dessicated coconut |
| ¼ cup (2 fl oz) milk |

Preheat the oven to 180°C (350°F/Gas 4). Grease the baking trays thoroughly.

Cream the sugar and butter together. Beat in the egg yolks. Sift the flour and baking powder together and add to the mixture in alternate batches with the milk. Incorporate the coconut. Drop teaspoonfuls onto the baking trays, allowing space for spreading.

Bake for 10 to 12 minutes. Turn onto wire racks to cool.

Sweet Shrewsbury Coriander Cakes

Makes about 60

| 185 g (6 oz) butter, softened |
| 1 cup (7 oz) sugar |
| 3 eggs, unbeaten |
| 4 cups (1 lb) flour, sifted |
| ¼ teaspoon bicarbonate of soda (baking soda) |
| 2 teaspoons ground coriander seed |
| ½ cup (4 fl oz) milk |

Preheat the oven to 230°C (450°F/Gas 8). Grease the baking trays.

Cream the butter and sugar together. Add the eggs, mixing well. Sift the flour, bicarbonate of soda and coriander seed together. Add alternate batches of the flour mixture and the milk to the butter-egg-sugar mixture, about a third of each at a time, and mix well until a dough is made. Knead it until smooth. Roll it out, then cut into 5 cm (2 in) circles.

Bake for about 15 minutes or until light brown. Turn onto wire racks and allow to cool.

Lemon Honey Crackers

Makes about 25

| 2 cups (8 oz) flour, sifted |
| pinch of salt |
| 1 teaspoon bicarbonate of soda (baking soda) |
| ½ teaspoon dried ground thyme |
| 2 eggs, lightly beaten |
| finely grated rind of ½ lemon |
| 2 tablespoons honey |

Preheat the oven to 180°C (350°F/Gas 4). Grease the baking trays.

Sift the dry ingredients together; then beat in the eggs, lemon rind and honey, mixing well. Roll out thinly and cut into rounds or fancy shapes.

Bake for 15 minutes. Turn onto wire racks to cool.

Hazelnut-Popcorn Macaroons

Makes about 15

| 1 large egg white |
| pinch of salt |
| ⅓ cup (3 oz) caster (powdered) sugar |
| ½ teaspoon vanilla essence |
| 1 cup (2 oz) popped corn |
| ⅓ cup (1½ oz) finely chopped hazelnuts |

Preheat the oven to 150°C (300°F/Gas 2). Thoroughly grease the baking trays.

Beat the egg white and salt until it holds stiff peaks. Gradually beat in the caster sugar, making sure it is beaten for long enough to dissolve the sugar. Add the vanilla essence, then fold in the popcorn and hazelnuts. Drop teaspoonfuls onto the baking tray, allowing room for spreading.

Bake for about 15 minutes or until brown.

Variations:
Cornflakes or puffed wheat could be used instead of popcorn, and other nuts could replace the hazelnuts for variation.

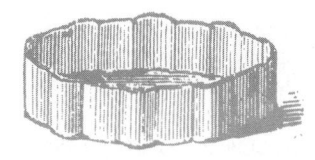

Apple Surprises
(Photograph below)

Makes about 40

2½ cups (10 oz) flour, sifted
1 teaspoon bicarbonate of soda (baking soda)
½ teaspoon salt
1 teaspoon ground cinnamon
1 teaspoon ground cloves
1½ cups (8 oz) brown sugar
125 g (4 oz) butter, softened
1 large egg, lightly beaten
¼ cup (2 fl oz) apple juice
½ cup (2 oz) finely chopped walnuts
1 cup (4 oz) peeled, cored, coarsely grated apple
1 cup (5 oz) raisins, finely chopped

Preheat the oven to 200°C (400°F/Gas 6). Thoroughly grease the baking trays.
  Sift the flour, bicarbonate of soda, salt, cinnamon and cloves together. In a large bowl, cream the sugar and butter together. Beat in the egg. Gradually fold in alternate batches of the flour mixture and the apple juice. Then add the walnuts, grated apple and raisins. Drop teaspoonfuls onto the baking tray.
  Bake for 8 to 10 minutes. Turn onto wire racks to cool.

Pecan Nut Buttons
(Photograph below)

Makes about 20

2 eggs, lightly beaten
½ cup (4 oz) caster (powdered) sugar
¾ cup (3 oz) self-raising flour, sifted
1 cup (4 oz) finely chopped pecans

Preheat the oven to 180°C (350°F/Gas 4). Grease and flour the baking trays.
  Beat the eggs and sugar together until light and creamy. Fold in the flour and the pecans. Form the mixture into small balls and place on the trays; slightly flatten with a fork.
  Bake for 12 to 15 minutes. Allow to cool on wire racks.

Val's Anzac Biscuits

(Photograph below)

Makes about 30

1 cup (3 oz) rolled oats
1 cup (5 oz) brown sugar, firmly packed
1 cup (3 oz) desiccated coconut
1 cup (4 oz) flour, sifted
2 teaspoons dried ground ginger
¼ teaspoon salt.
125 g (4 oz) butter
1 tablespoon golden syrup (light corn syrup)
1 teaspoon bicarbonate of soda (baking soda)
2 tablespoons boiling water

Preheat the oven to 180°C (350°F/Gas 4). Grease the baking trays.

Place the oats, sugar and coconut into a bowl; sift the flour, ginger and salt over, and mix thoroughly.

Melt the butter in a saucepan; remove from the heat and add the golden syrup. Dissolve the bicarbonate of soda in the boiling water and add to the saucepan, stirring well; pour over the flour mixture and blend well. Drop spoonfuls onto the greased trays, allowing room for spreading.

Bake for 10 to 12 minutes. Remove from the oven and allow to cool on the tray.

Date Pillows

(Photograph below)

Makes about 20

250 g (8 oz) Philadelphia Cream Cheese, softened
125 g (4 oz) butter
1 teaspoon vanilla essence
2 cups (8 oz) flour
Filling: 1 tablespoon sugar
¼ cup (2 fl oz) hot water
1 teaspoon lemon juice
½ cup (2½ oz) finely chopped dates

Cream together the cheese and butter until smooth. Add the vanilla essence and flour, and mix well to form a dough. Cover, and chill for several hours.

To prepare the filling, dissolve the sugar in the hot water in a saucepan. Add the lemon juice and dates, and simmer until thickened, stirring often. Allow to cool.

Preheat the oven to 220°C (425°F/Gas 7). Roll the dough out thinly and cut into 8 cm (3 in) squares. Spoon a little filling along the centre of each square, and fold over each side to seal, pressing with a floured fork. Prick the top and place on a greased baking tray.

Bake for 12 to 15 minutes. Turn onto a wire rack to cool.

Low Calorie Energy Biscuits

Cuts into 36 squares

155 g (5 oz) margarine
2 tablespoons honey
1 cup (4 oz) dried apricots
1 cup (5 oz) dried dates
1 cup (4 oz) finely chopped mixed nuts
2½ cups (10 oz) wholemeal flour
1 teaspoon baking powder
3 tablespoons skim milk powder
1½ cups (12fl oz) water

Preheat the oven to 180°C (350°F/Gas 4). Thoroughly grease a swiss roll tin (jelly roll pan).

Melt the margarine in a saucepan; remove from the heat and add the honey. Transfer the mixture to a bowl, and mix in the fruits and nuts.

Sift the flour with the baking powder, then add any residue left in the sieve; combine with the fruit and nut mixture. Dissolve the milk powder in the water and combine with all the other ingredients, mixing well. Press into the Swiss roll tin.

Bake for 30 minutes, allow to cool in the tin, cut into squares and serve cold.

Coconut Chocolate Drop Cookies

Makes about 40

125 g (4 oz) dark cooking chocolate
2 cups (6 oz) desiccated coconut
1 teaspoon vanilla essence
pinch of salt
3 tablespoons flour
1⅓ cups (10fl oz) condensed milk

Melt the chocolate in a double boiler. Mix in the other ingredients, and chill the mixture.

Preheat the oven to 180°C (350°F/Gas 4). Drop teaspoonfuls of the mixture onto a greased and floured baking tray and bake for about 15 minutes until just browned. Allow to cool on wire racks.

Coffee Nut Cookies

Makes about 30

2 cups (8 oz) flour
1 teaspoon baking powder
⅛ teaspoon salt
125 g (4 oz) butter
1 cup (7 oz) sugar
1 tablespoon instant coffee powder
1 tablespoon hot water
1 large egg
½ cup (3 oz) finely chopped walnuts

Sift the flour, baking powder and salt together into a bowl.

In a separate bowl, cream the butter and sugar together. Dissolve the coffee powder in the hot water and allow to cool.

Beat the egg and coffee together with the butter and sugar, combine this with the flour mixture and add the walnuts to make a dough. Divide the mixture in half and roll into two cylinders, 5 cm (2 in) in diameter. Wrap in foil and chill. Preheat the oven to 190°C (375°F/Gas 5). Grease the baking trays. Cut the chilled rolls into 5 mm (¼ in) rounds and bake for 8 to 10 minutes. Turn onto wire racks to cool.

Pennsylvanian Buttermilk Cookies

Makes about 35

2 cups (14 oz) sugar
2 cups (500 g) lard (pork fat)
1 egg, lightly beaten
1 teaspoon grated nutmeg
¼ teaspoon salt
2 cups (16fl oz) buttermilk
1 teaspoon bicarbonate of soda (baking soda)
enough flour for rolling dough

Preheat the oven to 180°C (350°F/Gas 4). Grease the baking trays.

Cream the sugar and lard together. Beat in the egg, nutmeg and salt.

Combine the buttermilk with the bicarbonate of soda, and add this to the mixture. Add sufficient flour to make the mixture into a rollable dough. Roll out to 5 mm (¼ in) thickness, and cut into shapes.

Bake for 10 to 12 minutes. Allow to cool on wire racks.

BISCUITS & COOKIES

Canadian Fruit and Nut Drops

Makes about 50

250 g (8 oz) butter
1½ cups (8 oz) brown sugar, firmly packed
½ cup (3 oz) currants
1 cup (5 oz) chopped dates
1 cup (4 oz) chopped blanched almonds
3 cups (12 oz) flour
1 teaspoon bicarbonate of soda (baking soda)
½ teaspoon salt
1 teaspoon ground cloves
1 teaspoon ground cinnamon
1 teaspoon ground nutmeg
3 eggs, well beaten
3 tablespoons maple syrup
1 teaspoon grated lemon zest

Preheat the oven to 180°C (350°F/Gas 4). Grease the baking trays.

Cream together the butter and sugar, then mix in the currants, dates and almonds.

Sift the flour, bicarbonate of soda, salt and spices together, then incorporate this into the first-made mixture. Add the beaten eggs, maple syrup and lemon zest, blending well. Drop spoonfuls onto the tray, allowing room for spreading.

Bake for 15 to 20 minutes. Turn onto wire racks to cool.

Honey Strips

Makes about 50

3¾ cups (15 oz) flour, sifted
2 teaspoons baking powder
¼ teaspoon salt
⅓ cup (3 oz) sugar
125 g (4 oz) butter
1 large egg
2 tablespoons lemon juice, strained
1 cup (10 oz) clear aromatic honey, warmed
⅔ cup (3 oz) blanched chopped almonds

Preheat the oven to 180°C (350°F/Gas 4). Grease the baking trays.

Sift the flour, baking powder and salt together into a bowl. In a separate bowl, cream the sugar and butter together; then add the egg, and beat in well. Mix in the lemon juice and honey; then thoroughly blend in the flour mixture and the nuts, to make a dough. Roll out on a lightly floured board to 5 mm (¼ in) thickness and cut into strips.

Bake for 10 to 12 minutes until brown. Turn onto wire racks to cool.

Greek Honey Fig Biscuits

Makes about 50

¾ cup (6 oz) caster (powdered) sugar
125 g (4 oz) butter
2 large eggs, well beaten
1 teaspoon lemon extract
½ cup (5 oz) honey, warmed
2⅔ cups (11 oz) flour, sifted
1½ teaspoons baking powder
3 tablespoons milk
1 cup (5 oz) finely chopped dried figs
2 tablespoons finely chopped orange zest
½ cup (2 oz) dessicated coconut

Preheat the oven to 180°C (350°F/Gas 4). Grease the baking trays.

Cream the sugar and butter together. Add the beaten eggs, lemon extract and honey, mixing well. Sift in the flour and baking powder together; then add the milk. Mix in the figs, orange zest and coconut. Drop spoonfuls onto the baking tray, allowing room for spreading.

Bake for 10 to 15 minutes. Remove from the oven and allow to cool on the tray.

Brazil Nut Stars

Makes about 40

2 large eggs, well beaten
2 cups (10 oz) brown sugar, firmly packed
1½ teaspoons vanilla essence
1¾ cups (7 oz) flour
½ teaspoon baking powder
500 g (1 lb) Brazil nuts, finely chopped
caster (powdered) sugar, for dusting

To the well-beaten eggs, add the sugar and vanilla and beat until light and foamy.

In a separate bowl, sift the flour and baking powder together, then mix in the nuts. Combine the two mixtures, mixing well to form a dough. Cover the bowl and refrigerate for several hours.

Preheat the oven to 180°C (350°F/Gas 4). Grease the baking trays.

Roll out the dough between two sheets of greaseproof paper; and stamp out fancy shapes such as stars.

Bake for 12 to 15 minutes until they are lightly browned. Turn onto wire racks to cool and then dust with caster sugar.

Scandinavian Sour Cream Biscuits

Makes about 25

2 cups (14 oz) caster (powdered) sugar
250 g (8 oz) thick sour cream
250 g (8 oz) butter, softened
2 large eggs, well beaten
1 teaspoon bicarbonate of soda (baking soda)
1½ teaspoons vanilla essence

Preheat the oven to 160°C (325°F/Gas 3). Thoroughly grease the baking trays.

Mix together all the ingredients in the order listed, to make a dough. Roll the dough out to 5 mm (¼ in) thick, then cut into fancy shapes with a cookie cutter. Bake for 10 to 12 minutes. Turn onto wire racks to cool.

Cinnamon Shapes

Makes about 30

6 egg whites
pinch salt
2½ cups (1 lb) caster (powdered) sugar
finely grated rind of 1 lemon
1 teaspoon ground cinnamon
500 g (1 lb) ground almonds

Preheat the oven to 180°C (350°F/Gas 4). Grease the baking trays thoroughly.

Beat the egg whites and salt until stiff. Gradually add the sugar, and continue beating until stiff peaks are formed. Beat in the lemon rind, then reserve a quarter of the mixture for covering the shapes.

To the larger quantity of mixture, add the cinnamon and ground almonds, mixing well. Sprinkle the work bench with a little additional caster sugar to minimise sticking, and roll the mixture out thinly. Cut into shapes with biscuit cutters and spread a small amount of the reserved mixture on the top of each shape.

Bake for about 20 minutes or until light brown. Turn onto wire racks to cool.

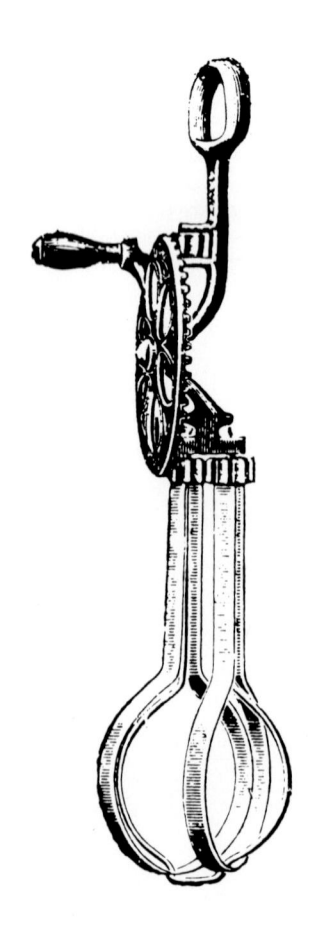

Right: Brazil Nut Stars (see above); Cinnamon Shapes (see above).

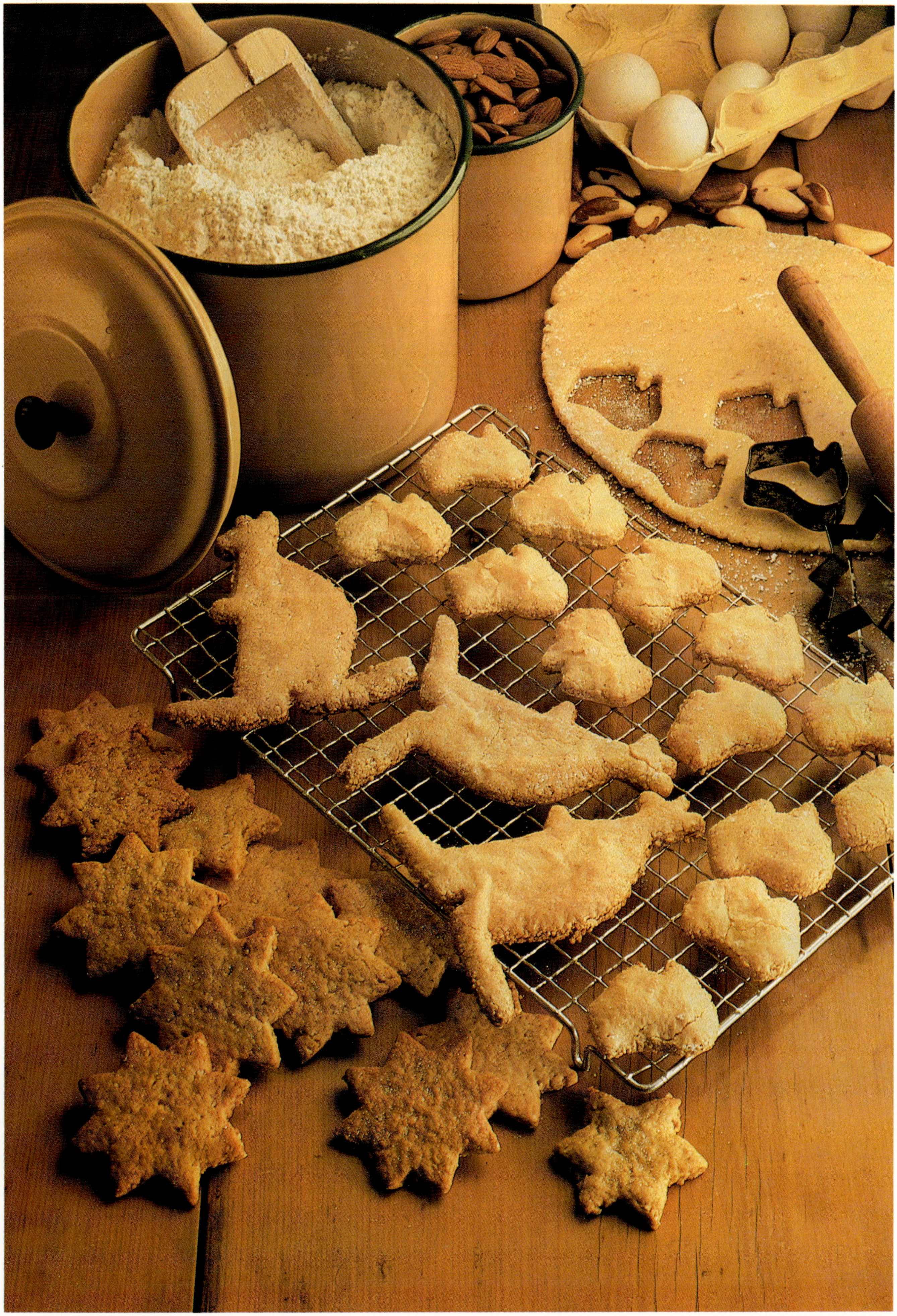

Orange Almond Biscuits

Makes about 30

125 g (4 oz) butter, melted
½ cup (4 oz) sugar
1 tablespoon finely grated orange rind
1 tablespoon finely grated lemon rind
2 teaspoons lemon juice
2 teaspoons orange juice
1 large egg, separated
2 cups (8 oz) flour
1 teaspoon baking powder
pinch of salt
1 cup (4 oz) finely chopped almonds
candied peel or glacé cherry, for garnish

Preheat the oven to 180°C (350°F/Gas 4). Thoroughly grease the baking trays.

Cream the butter and sugar together. Add the citrus rinds and juices, plus the egg yolk, and mix well. Sift the flour, baking powder and salt together and add this to the mixture; mix well to form a stiff dough. Make small balls, dip into the beaten egg white, and roll in the chopped almonds. Place on the baking tray and flatten with a fork. Decorate with candied peel or glacé cherry.

Bake for 12 to 15 minutes. Allow to cool on wire racks.

Citrus Biscuits

Makes about 30

1 cup (7 oz) sugar
125 g (4 oz) butter, softened
1 egg, well beaten
1 tablespoon lemon juice
½ teaspoon finely grated lemon rind
1 teaspoon orange rind
2 cups (8 oz) flour, sifted
1 teaspoon baking powder
pinch of salt

Cream the sugar and butter together. Beat in the egg, lemon juice and lemon and orange rind. Sift together the dry ingredients, and carefully mix together with the other ingredients to form a dough. Work into a cylindrical shape and chill thoroughly.

Preheat the oven to 220°C (425°F/Gas 7). Slice off thin rounds of dough and place them on well-greased baking trays. Bake for 10 minutes. Turn onto wire racks to cool.

Peanut-Peach Cookies

An easy recipe prepared with a food processor
Makes about 25

125 g (4 oz) dried peaches
500 g (1 lb) shelled peanuts
2 tablespoons lemon juice
1½ cups (12fl oz) condensed milk

Soak the dried peaches in hot water for at least 30 minutes. Very finely chop the peanuts in a food processor (or grind them in a mill) and set aside.

Drain the peaches, then mince or finely chop in a food processor. Add the ground peanuts, lemon juice and condensed milk, and blend well.

Drop spoonfuls onto greased baking trays and bake in a preheated oven at 180°C (350°F/Gas 4) for 20 minutes. Remove immediately from the tray and cool on wire racks.

Apricot Tang Slice

Cuts into 28 pieces

125 g (4 oz) dried apricots, soaked
½ cup (4 oz) caster (powdered) sugar
125 g (4 oz) butter, softened
1 egg, lightly beaten
¼ teaspoon ground cinnamon
2 tablespoons (1 oz) finely chopped preserved ginger
½ cup (2 oz) finely chopped blanched almonds
1¼ cups (5 oz) self-raising flour, sifted
½ cup (2 oz) cornflour (cornstarch), sifted
pinch of salt
1 teaspoon cocoa
¼–½ cup (2–4fl oz) milk
60 g (2 oz) dark cooking chocolate, finely grated

Preheat the oven to 200°C (400°F/Gas 6). Thoroughly grease a shallow 28 × 23 cm (11 × 9 in) baking tin.

Chop the soaked apricots and set aside. Cream the sugar and butter together, then beat in the egg and cinnamon. Stir in the reserved apricots, and the ginger and almonds. Sift the flour, cornflour, salt and cocoa together; blend this into the butter-sugar-fruit mixture in alternate batches with the milk and chocolate, about a third of each at a time. Spread into the tin, pressing down firmly.

Bake for 25 to 30 minutes. Remove from the oven and allow to cool in the tin, then cut into bars 2 cm × 11 cm (1 in × 4 in).

Jewish Poppy Seed Tricorns

Makes about 60

Dough:
2½ cups (10 oz) flour, sifted
½ teaspoon salt
3 teaspoons baking powder
½ cup (4 oz) sugar
¼ cup (2fl oz) milk
1 egg, lightly beaten
½ cup (4fl oz) melted butter
Filling:
1 tablespoon sugar
1 tablespoon poppy seeds
1 egg, lightly beaten

Preheat the oven to 180°C (350°F/Gas 4). Grease the baking trays.

Make a dough by mixing together all the ingredients and kneading well. Roll the dough out thinly and cut into 5 cm (2 in) rounds.

Make the filling by mixing together all the ingredients—you will not need all the egg. Place a spoonful of filling in the centre of each round and fold up the edges so that it forms a tricorn. Pinch them together to seal.

Bake for 20 minutes. Cool on wire racks.

Chocolate Mint Fingers

Cuts into 28 pieces

250 g (8 oz) butter, melted
2 cups (2 oz) cornflakes, crushed
2 cups (6 oz) desiccated coconut
1 cup (4 oz) self-raising flour, sifted
3 tablespoons cocoa
1 teaspoon vanilla essence
1 teaspoon peppermint essence
1 cup (7 oz) caster (powdered) sugar

Preheat the oven to 180°C (350°F/Gas 4). Thoroughly grease a shallow slab tin.

Combine all ingredients in a bowl, mixing well. Turn the mixture into the slab tin and press it in firmly.

Bake for 25 to 30 minutes. With a sharp knife, mark into fingers whilst hot, then set in refrigerator.

Coffee Lace Wafers

Makes about 20

90 g (3 oz) butter
1/3 cup (3 oz) sugar
1 tablespoon flour
2 tablespoons milk
2 teaspoons instant coffee powder
1/2 cup (2 oz) ground almonds

Preheat the oven to 160°C (325°F/Gas 3). Grease and flour the baking trays.

Combine all the ingredients in a saucepan and heat slowly until the mixture is well combined. Drop spoonfuls onto the baking trays, allowing about 10 cm (4 in) around each, for spreading.

Bake for 5 to 10 minutes until lightly browned. Remove from the oven, allow to stand for 30 seconds, then roll each wafer very carefully around the handle of a wooden spoon. Allow to cool on wire racks.

Basic Petits Fours

Makes about 30

2 cups (8 oz) flour, sifted
1/2 teaspoon baking powder
1/2 cup (4 oz) sugar
125 g (4 oz) butter
1/2 teaspoon vanilla essence
2 eggs, lightly beaten
Decoration: coloured sugar, halved or ground nuts, candied fruit, desiccated coconut, etc., or glacé icing (see recipe, page 130)

Sift the flour and baking powder together. In a separate bowl, combine sugar, butter, vanilla essence and eggs until well mixed, then add the flour to make a dough. Cover, and chill for several hours in the refrigerator.

Preheat the oven to 180°C (350°F/Gas 4). Grease the baking trays.

Roll the dough out thinly and cut into small fancy shapes. Decorate with coloured sugar, nuts, candied fruit, coconut, etc.

Bake for 15 minutes. Cool on a wire rack, and decorate with icing if baked plain.

Right: **Clockwise from bottom right: Chocolate Mint Fingers (see above); Petits Fours (see above); Coffee Lace Wafers (see above).**

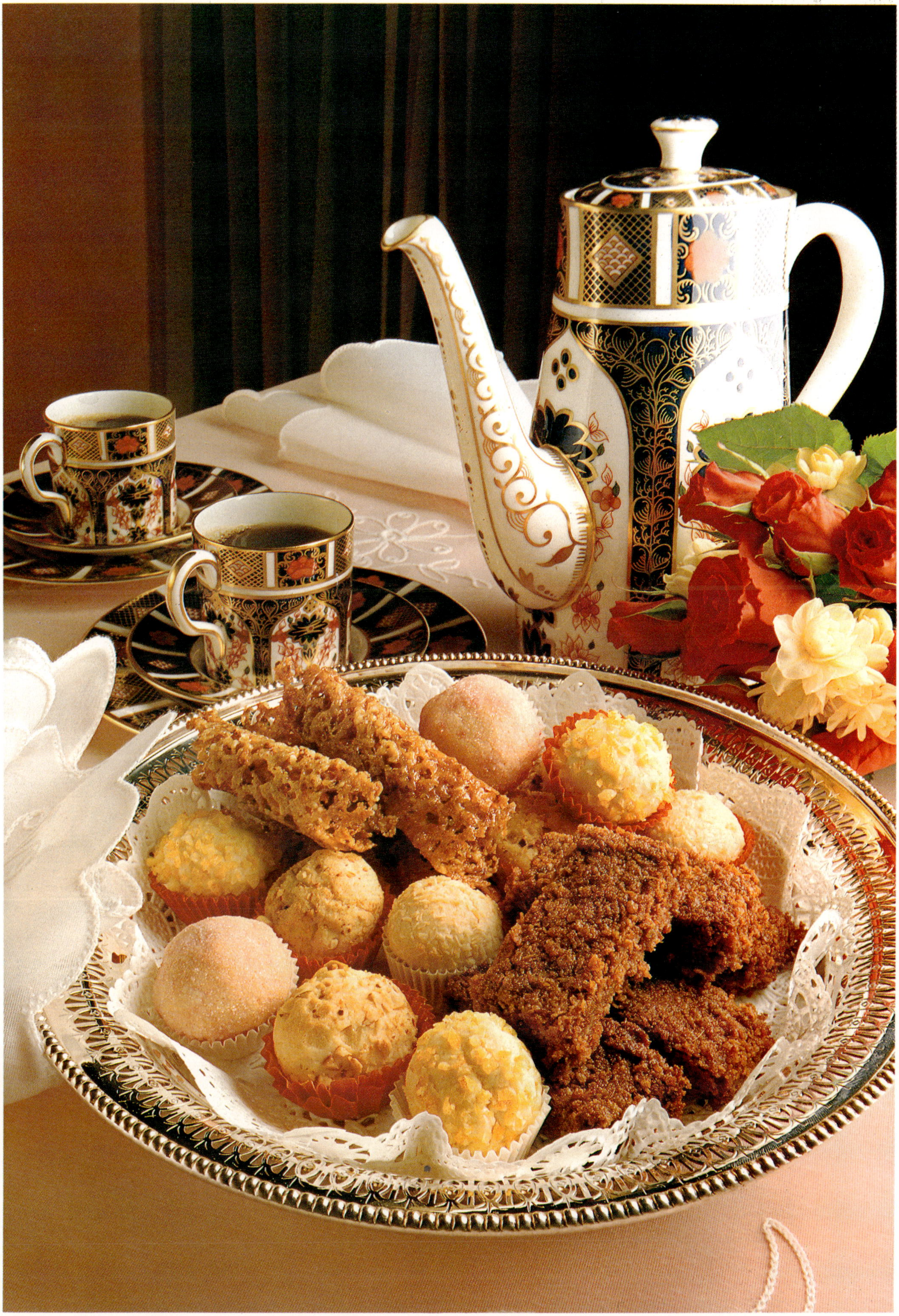

Raspberry Meringue Twirls

Makes about 20

1½ cups (6 oz) self-raising flour, sifted
pinch of salt
¼ cup (2 oz) sugar
½ cup (2 oz) ground almonds
125 g (4 oz) butter
2 egg yolks, lightly beaten
a little milk, if necessary
Topping: 2 egg whites
½ cup (4 oz) caster (powdered) sugar
raspberry jam (jelly), heated

Sift the flour and salt together into a bowl; add the sugar and ground almonds. Rub in the butter until the mixture resembles fine breadcrumbs. Add the egg yolks to bind the mixture into a firm dough—if necessary, adding a little milk. Cover, and chill thoroughly.

Preheat the oven to 190°C (375°F/Gas 5). Grease the baking trays.

Roll the dough out thinly and cut into rounds, about 5 cm (2 in) in diameter.

To make the meringue, beat the egg whites until stiff and gradually incorporate the caster sugar; beat until the mixture holds its shape. Pipe a spiral topping of meringue onto each round.

Bake for 20 to 25 minutes. Allow to cool on wire racks. When cold, trickle the heated and thinned raspberry jam over the top.

Chocolate Marshmallow Biscuits

Makes about 25

½ cup (4 oz) sugar
125 g (4 oz) butter, softened
1 egg, lightly beaten
2 cups (8 oz) self-raising flour, sifted
Marshmallow Topping: 1 tablespoon gelatine
1 cup water
1 cup (8 oz) sugar
2 tablespoons chocolate topping (sauce)

Preheat the oven to 220°C (425°F/Gas 7). Grease the baking trays.

Cream the sugar and butter together. Then beat in the egg. Add the flour, and mix well to make a stiff dough. Form into balls about 2.5 cm (1 in) in diameter and place on the baking trays; flatten with a fork. Bake for 12 to 15 minutes. Turn onto wire racks to cool.

Marshmallow Topping
Soak the gelatine in 2 tablespoons of the water. Heat the rest of the water with the sugar, and boil for 20 minutes. Remove from the heat, add the softened gelatine, place the saucepan in a bowl of ice and whisk continuously until thick and white. Add the chocolate topping, blending well. Spoon the topping onto cooled biscuits, and allow to set. Biscuits may be decorated with nuts or glacé icing.

Mixed Nut Bars

Makes about 18

125 g (4 oz) butter, softened

2 tablespoons icing (confectioners') sugar

2 teaspoons vanilla essence

½ cup cornflour (cornstarch), sifted

½ cup (2 oz) flour

30 g (1 oz) ground almonds

Topping:
30 g (1 oz) very finely chopped hazelnuts

30 g (1 oz) very finely chopped unsalted peanuts

30 g (1 oz) dark chocolate

Preheat the oven to 180°C (350°F/Gas 4). Grease the baking trays.

Beat the butter, sugar and vanilla together until fluffy and light textured. Sift the cornflour, flour and ground almonds together, then fold into the butter-sugar mixture and mix well. Spoon the mixture into a piping bag fitted with a 1 cm (½ in) serrated nozzle. Pipe 'sticks' of the mixture 8 cm (3 in) long, allowing room between them for spreading, on the baking trays. Carefully top with a light layer of hazelnut-peanut mixture.

Bake for 15 minutes. Cool on wire racks. Melt the chocolate in a double boiler and carefully coat half of each stick; allow to set.

Cognac Drops

Makes about 20

3 tablespoons sugar

2 egg yolks

1 tablespoon fresh white breadcrumbs

1 tablespoon cognac

1 cup (4 oz) ground hazelnuts

1 egg white, lightly beaten

Preheat the oven to 180°C (350°F/Gas 4). Grease the baking tray.

Beat together the egg yolks and sugar until creamy. Moisten the breadcrumbs with cognac and add to the egg yolk-sugar mixture along with the nuts. Fold in the beaten egg white. Drop teaspoonfuls on the baking tray.

Bake for 15 minutes. Allow to cool on a wire rack.

FILLED BISCUITS

A filled biscuit can be made by sticking together two cooked biscuits with a filling such as Jam (jelly) or Butter Cream (see recipes below).

Another method of filling is by placing a spoonful of the filling near one edge of a large round uncooked biscuit and folding the other edge over, then sealing the two edges; or by placing the filling in the centre and crimping up the edges around the filling. Square biscuits can be folded up over the filling to make tricorns.

Two shapes (uncooked) could be stuck together with a filling and their edges sealed all the way around.

A basic biscuit recipe is given below.

Basic Filled Biscuit

Makes about 20 filled biscuits

125 g (4 oz) butter

1 cup (7 oz) sugar

1 teaspoon vanilla essence

1 egg

2¾ cups (11 oz) flour, sifted

1½ teaspoons baking powder

¼ teaspoon bicarbonate of soda (baking soda)

½ cup (4 fl oz) milk

Cream together the butter and sugar with the vanilla essence. Add the egg, beating the mixture well. Sift together the dry ingredients and add alternately with the milk, beating well, to make a dough. Cover and chill the dough.

Preheat the oven to 180°C (350°F/Gas 4). Roll the dough out thinly and cut into rounds. Fill the rounds, seal their edges and prick their tops. Bake on a greased sheet for 10 minutes. Turn onto a wire rack to cool.

Butter Cream Filling

For cooked biscuits
Makes enough to fill 20 two-layer biscuits

2 tablespoons softened butter
1 cup (5 oz) icing (confectioners') sugar, sifted
½ teaspoon vanilla essence
2 tablespoons condensed milk

Beat together half of the icing sugar and the softened butter. Add the vanilla essence and then the condensed milk. Beat in the remaining icing sugar.

Chocolate Butter Cream
Add 2 teaspoons of cocoa powder to the first batch of icing sugar; and leave out 1 tablespoon of butter in the above recipe.

Jam (Jelly) Cream Filling

For cooked biscuits
Makes enough to fill 20 two-layer biscuits

1 tablespoon jam (jelly)—such as raspberry jam (jelly)
4 tablespoons (1 oz) icing (confectioners') sugar
2 teaspoons softened butter

Combine ingredients together to make a smooth, spreadable filling.

Brandy Cottage Cheese Filling

For uncooked biscuits
Makes enough to fill about 20 biscuits

1 cup (6 oz) cottage cheese
2 tablespoons finely chopped nuts
3 tablespoons currants
4 tablespoons sugar
¼ teaspoon finely grated lemon rind
¼ teaspoon ground nutmeg
¼ teaspoon ground cinnamon
2 tablespoons brandy or fruit juice
1 egg

Combine all the ingredients into a spreadable filling.

Dried Fruit Filling

For uncooked biscuits
Fills about 20 biscuits

1 cup (5 oz) chopped dried fruit (raisins, apricots, prunes, dates or figs)
½ cup (2 oz) chopped nuts, candied peel or desiccated coconut
½ cup (4 oz) sugar
½ cup (4 fl oz) water
1 teaspoon lemon juice
1 tablespoon flour

Combine the ingredients in a saucepan and simmer until thickened, stirring often. Cool before use.

Right: Clockwise from top left: Butter Cream Filling (see above); Brandy Cottage Cheese Filling (see above); Jam Cream Filling (see above); Dried Fruit Filling (see above).

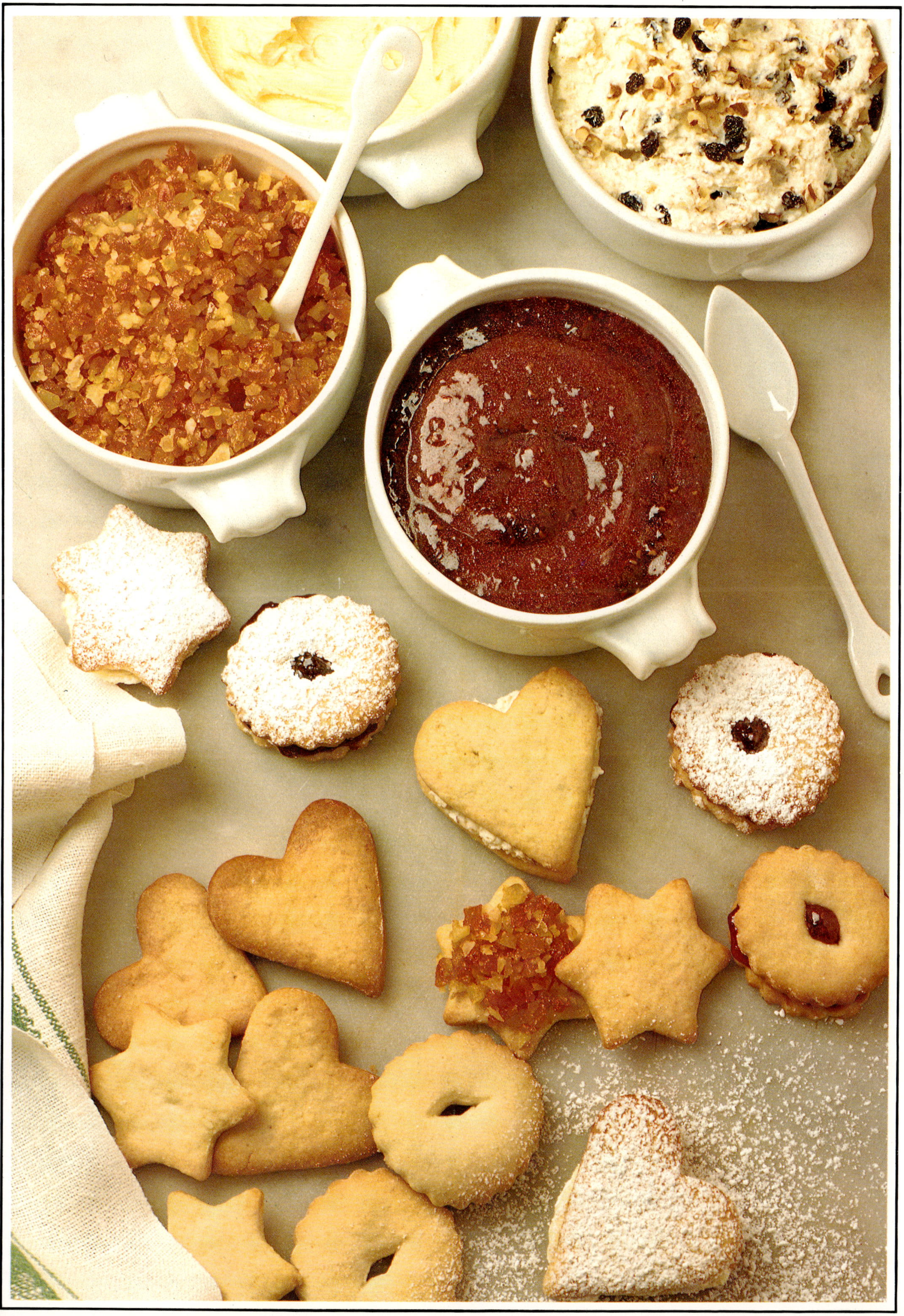

AMERICAN COOKIES

American Peanut Butter Cookies

Makes about 40

2¼ cups (9 oz) flour, sifted
2 teaspoons bicarbonate of soda (baking soda)
¼ teaspoon salt
250 g (8 oz) butter
1 cup (8 oz) peanut butter
1 cup (5 oz) brown sugar, firmly packed
½ cup (4 oz) caster (powdered) sugar
2 large eggs, lightly beaten
1 cup (5 oz) unsalted peanuts, coarsely chopped

Preheat the oven to 180°C (350°F/Gas 4).

Sift the flour, bicarbonate of soda and salt together into a bowl. In a separate bowl, cream together the butter, peanut butter and sugar. Beat in the eggs until well combined, then gradually incorporate the flour mixture to make a dough. Fold in the peanuts. Form into balls about 2 cm (¾ in) in diameter and place on an ungreased tray; flatten them with a fork.

Bake for 12 to 15 minutes, or until their edges are brown. Remove from the oven and allow to cool on the tray.

Yankee Brownies

Cuts into 16 squares

60 g (2 oz) bitter chocolate
125 g (4 oz) butter
1 cup (7 oz) sugar
2 eggs, well beaten
1 cup (4 oz) flour, sifted
2 teaspoons vanilla essence
1 cup (4 oz) finely chopped pecan nuts

Preheat the oven to 180°C (350°F/Gas 4). Grease and flour a shallow square slab tin.

In a double boiler, melt the chocolate and butter with the sugar. Pour this gradually onto the well-beaten eggs, beating after each addition. Add the flour and vanilla essence, mixing well. Spread into the slab tin and sprinkle the top with the nuts.

Bake for 20 to 25 minutes. Cut into squares, and allow to cool on wire racks.

Sugar Cookies

Makes about 36

125 g (4 oz) butter
¾ cup (6 oz) sugar
1 egg
1½ teaspoons vanilla essence
2¼ cups (9 oz) flour
1½ teaspoons baking powder
pinch of salt
extra sugar

Cream the butter, sugar, egg and vanilla essence until the mixture is light and fluffy. Add the sifted flour, baking powder and salt gradually, mixing well. Chill the mixture for 1 hour.

Roll out small portions of the dough on a floured board to 3 mm (⅛ in) thick. Cut into shapes, place on greased baking trays and sprinkle thickly with extra sugar.

Bake in a preheated over 190°C (375°F/Gas 5) for 12 to 15 minutes or until golden.

Old Fashioned Chocolate Cookies

Makes about 30

2 cups (8 oz) flour
½ teaspoon bicarbonate of soda (baking soda)
pinch of salt
125 g (4 oz) butter
60 g (2 oz) unsweetened chocolate
1 cup (5 oz) dark brown sugar, firmly packed
1 egg
1 teaspoon vanilla essence
½ cup (4 fl oz) milk
Chocolate Glaze: 30 g (1 oz) unsweetened chocolate
1 tablespoon butter
1½ tablespoons hot water
2 tablespoons cream
1 cup (5 oz) icing (confectioners') sugar
pecan nuts

Sift together the flour, bicarbonate of soda and salt and set aside. Cut the butter into pieces and place in a heavy saucepan. Add the chocolate and cook over low heat until melted. Remove from the heat and stir in the sugar. Add the egg and the vanilla to the warm chocolate mixture and stir until smooth. Stir in half of the sifted dry ingredients. Then, very gradually, just a few drops at a time at first, stir in the milk. Add the remaining dry ingredients and stir briskly until completely smooth.

Use a dessertspoon of dough for each cookie. Place them in even mounds 5 cm (2 in) apart on greased baking trays.

Bake in a preheated oven 180°C (350°F/Gas 4) for 12 to 15 minutes, turning the trays around to ensure even baking. The cookies are done when the tops spring back firmly if lightly touched with a fingertip.

Leave to stand for a moment then turn out into a wire rack to cool.

To make the glaze, melt the chocolate with the butter in the top of a small double boiler over hot water. Remove the saucepan from the heat and stir in the hot water and cream. Add the icing sugar and stir until smooth. If necessary, adjust with a bit more water or sugar to make the consistency similar to a heavy cream sauce.

With a small metal spatula, smooth the glaze over the tops of the cookies, staying about 1 cm (½ in) away from the edges.

Let stand for a few hours to dry. Top each cookie with a pecan nut.

Chocolate Chip Cookies

Makes about 30

125 g (4 oz) butter
⅔ cup (5 oz) brown and white sugar mixed
1 egg
¾ cup (3 oz) flour
½ teaspoon bicarbonate of soda (baking soda)
salt
1 tablespoon water
1 teaspoon vanilla essence
1½ cups (7 oz) quick cooking oats
1¼ cups chocolate chips

Cream the butter and sugar until light. Mix in the eggs and add half the flour, the bicarbonate of soda, the salt, water and vanilla. Beat well. Stir in the remaining flour, the oats and the chocolate chips.

Drop teaspoons of the mixture on greased baking trays and bake in a preheated oven 180°C (350°F/Gas 4) for 10 minutes. Cool on wire racks.

Oatmeal Carrot Cookies

Makes about 24

185 g (6 oz) butter
¾ cup (6 oz) sugar
1 cup grated raw carrot
1 egg
2 teaspoons lemon rind
1¼ cups (5 oz) flour
½ teaspoon salt
2 teaspoons baking powder
1 cup (5 oz) rolled oats

Cream the butter, cream in the sugar, beat in the carrot and egg, and blend well. Mix in the lemon rind and the flour, salt and baking powder sifted together. Stir in the rolled oats. Place teaspoons of dough onto a buttered baking sheet. Bake in a preheated oven 190°C (375°F/Gas 5) for 10 to 12 minutes or until the cookies are a delicate brown around the edges. Loosen from the pan while still warm, cool on a rack, and store in airtight containers. They freeze well.

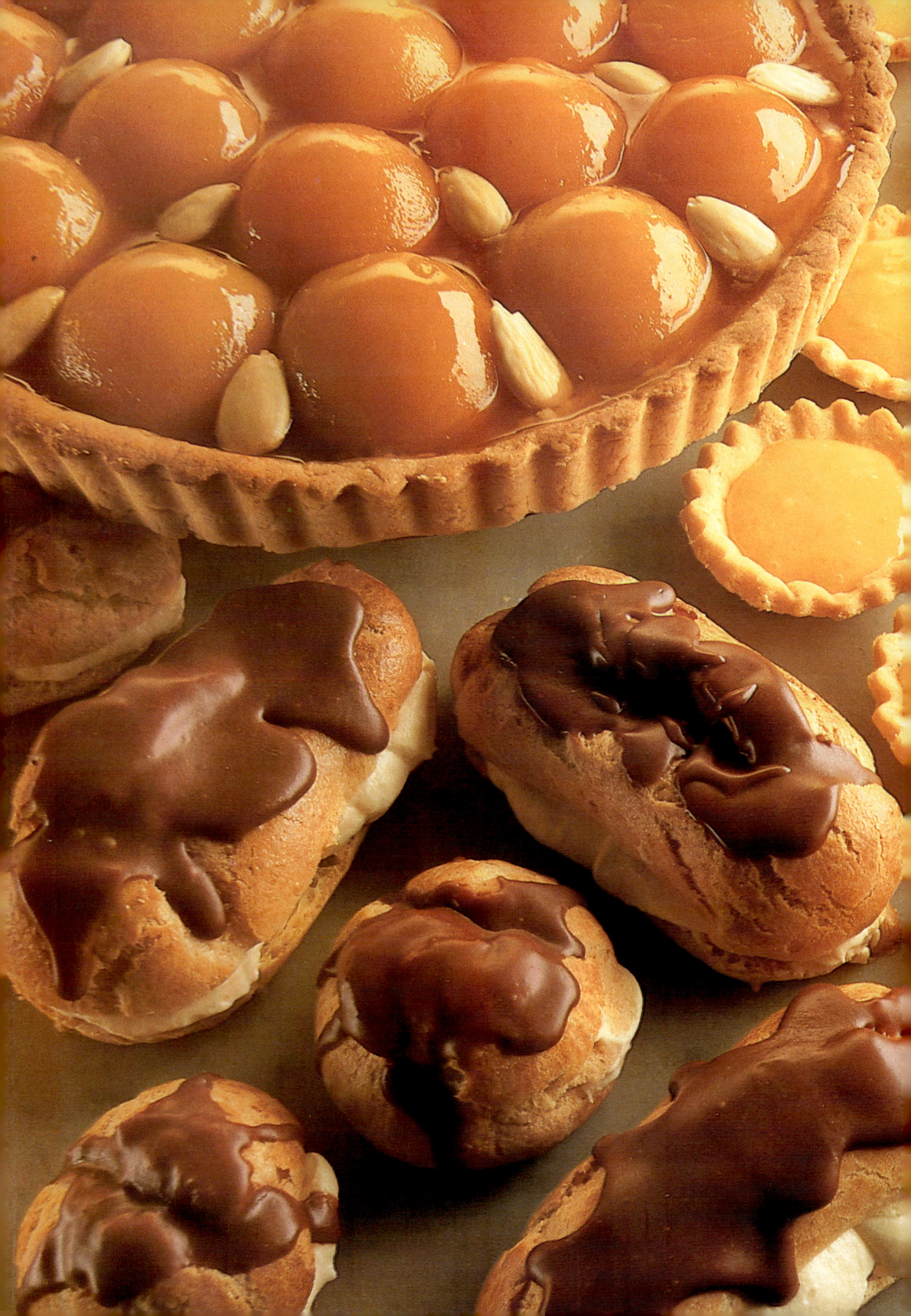

Pastry

Pastry

In the Constance Spry Cookery Book, the recognised textbook of the Cordon Bleu School in London, the Pastry chapter begins like this: 'Pastry-making would sometimes seem to be invested with a halo'. How true this statement still is, despite the advent of electric mixers and food processors in most kitchens today, for pastry-making remains a skill in which one must practise patiently to achieve the ultimate standard of constant perfection. This is quite discouraging to some cooks, particularly those who have had a go with disastrous results. However, there are some rules which, if understood and practised, will help you develop your skill in pastry-making.

The best way to teach pastry-making is by the demonstration method, followed by the students putting into practice what they have just observed so that they learn about textures and how to handle them, how to roll out correctly, which is most important, and how to shape and finish pastry dishes, thus building up confidence in their own skill. This is how I teach Pastry-Making in the special course at my Cookery School, but as this is impossible in a cookery book, I will attempt to help you with the following advice.

Anne Marshall

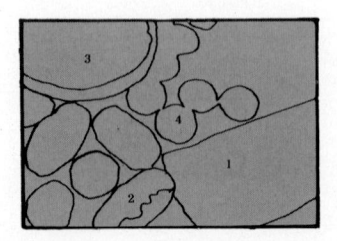

1. French Apple Slice (see p. 225)
2. Chocolate Éclairs (see p. 225)
3. Apricot and Almond Tart (see p. 233)
4. Tartlets filled with Lemon Sauce (see p. 140)

Pastry-making

- Work in a cool kitchen in cool weather for best results. Pastry is difficult to handle in hot, humid conditions. However, air-conditioning, an electric fan or cross-ventilation help create better conditions in hot weather.
- Use cool equipment. Chill bowls and rolling pins in the refrigerator in hot weather.
- The ingredients should also be cold. Chill fat in the refrigerator if using a mixer or food processor, but stand at room temperature for 30 minutes if rubbing in by hand. Use iced water.
- If rubbing fat in by hand, dip the fat into the flour, then cut it into small pieces with a round-bladed knife, then rub it in by lifting the mixture from the bottom of the bowl with both hands, palms upwards, and rub the thumbs forward over the fingertips, two or three times, before returning the hands to the bowl for more mixture.
- Keep the hands cold by holding them under cold running water for a few seconds.
- Test that the fat has been completely rubbed into the flour by shaking the bowl; the law of gravity means that any lumps of fat rise to the surface. Squeeze any lumps and if they are greasy, continue rubbing in or mixing, but if they are dry, it is ready for the next stage.
- Add the liquid gradually—too much makes the dough sticky to handle and tough when baked; too little makes the pastry crumbly and difficult to roll out. Mix the liquid in with a cold, round-bladed knife when making pastry by hand, using a cutting rather than a stirring movement.
- Toss the completed dough lightly in flour (as for a scone dough), then knead very lightly but firmly to compress the dough, just until it is smooth underneath. Only 6–10 kneading actions should be required; over-kneading will result in a tough, hard pastry when baked. Turn the compressed dough over and pat it into a round cake 1–2.5 cm (½–1 inch) thick, then wrap securely in greaseproof paper and chill before rolling out. Clear plastic wrap should be avoided since it makes the dough sweat.
- Chill the dough for 15 minutes in cold weather, and for 30 minutes in hot weather, before rolling out. If dough has been chilled for a long time, stand it at room temperature until it is soft enough to roll out without cracking. A well-chilled hard dough may be softened up quickly in a microwave oven, set at defrost, testing the texture after each single revolution, or after every 8 seconds, until it is soft enough for rolling out.
- Roll out on a marble slab preferably, as it is cold, smooth and hygienic, otherwise roll out on a clear, cold, dry laminated or formica topped kitchen bench. Pastry boards are good in cold climates but tend to sweat in hot climates.
- Use a traditional long, smooth wooden rolling pin, sprinkled lightly with flour and rub the flour into the wood with a cool hand to prevent sticking. I prefer this to all the gimmicky rolling pins.
- Before rolling out, press across the round cake of dough 3 times with the rolling pin, then turn dough around and press 3 times more at right angles, to give a thinner round of dough.
- Roll the pastry dough out on a lightly-floured surface with the rolling pin 'drill' action of 'down, forward, back and up' thus giving firm, quick and even pressure.
- When rolling, move the pastry around constantly; not the direction of rolling, to achieve evenly thinner dough, i.e. never roll sideways.
- If the pastry starts to stick to the surface or the rolling pin, sprinkle on more flour. If the pastry sticks to the surface, loosen with a palette knife and sprinkle flour under it before continuing.
- Never turn pastry over during rolling, but since the rolled side is the best, turn it over if lining a flan tin but do not turn over if topping a pie.
- Bake pastry in an electric oven in preference to a gas oven, because it has a dry radiant heat which gives a crisp pastry, whereas burning gas gives off water vapour as a by-product so the pastry is not as crisp.

Storage of pastry

Pastry dough should be wrapped in greaseproof paper, then sealed in a plastic bag for storage overnight in the refrigerator. In an efficient refrigerator it may be kept in this way for up to five days.

To freeze pastry dough, wrap it in greaseproof, then place in a freezer bag, extract the air, then seal well and store in the freezer. It will keep frozen successfully for up to three months.

Flour and fats

Always use plain household white flour for pastry unless otherwise stated in recipe. Self-raising flour results in a spongy rather than a short, crisp pastry. Flours vary from state to state and from continent to continent, so select a well-known national brand, avoiding both light cake flours, for they absorb less liquid, and high-gluten flours, for they absorb more liquid.

Fats vary in type and proportion from pastry to pastry, but in general, butter is used for its colour and flavour, lard is used for its shortening qualities, firm margarine for its colour, shortening properties and economy, polyunsaturated margarine is used for its health advantages. while suet is used for its flavour and texture in traditional suet crust pastry.

Liquids

The liquid usually used to bind pastry together is cold or iced water. Sometimes egg yolk or eggs are used to enrich. Milk may be used to achieve a softer textured pastry. An approximate measurement only can be given for the liquid used in most pastry recipes, for it varies according to the softness or hardness of the wheat grain used to make the flour. It also varies according to the temperature of the surroundings and to the amount of humidity in the atmosphere.

Shortcrust Pastry

Short refers to the crumbly, melt-in-the-mouth texture of this pastry, similar to the texture of good shortbread. Shortening is the American name of a white fat used to give this short texture to pastries. To cover and decorate a 1 litre (32fl oz) oval pie dish or a 23 cm (9 in) round pie dish, novice pastrycooks may need the full quantity, but experienced pastrycooks will need only three-quarters of this quantity. This pastry dough freezes well. It may also be stored for a few days in greaseproof paper inside a plastic freezer bag in the refrigerator.

Makes 250 g (8 oz)

2 cups (8 oz) flour
pinch of salt, optional
60 g (2 oz) chilled butter or firm margarine
60 g (2 oz) lard or white shortening
approx. 4 tablespoons cold water, to mix

Sift the flour into a cold mixing bowl. Cut the butter and lard into the flour with a round-bladed knife and coat the small pieces of fat with the flour. Rub the fat into the flour with the cool fingertips of both hands, lifting the mixture up and rubbing from a height, moving the thumbs from the little fingertips to the fore-fingertips, palms uppermost, to lighten and aerate the pastry.

Continue rubbing in until the mixture resembles breadcrumbs. To test for complete rubbing-in, shake the bowl gently and the lumps will rise to the surface, squeeze them—if they are dry, the fat is rubbed in sufficiently, but if the lumps feel greasy, you must continue rubbing in until you get a positive result to this test.

Sprinkle the cold water over gradually and mix in with a round-bladed knife (an English dinner knife) or a palette knife, until the mixture begins to form lumps which leave the side of the bowl cleanly. Knead the dough together lightly with a clean, cool hand.

Using an electric mixer: Sift the flour and salt into the bowl of the electric mixer then add butter and lard, cut into small cubes. Using a K-beater or pastry mixers, turn the machine on at minimum speed and increase gradually to Speed 2 as the fats break up, then continue mixing at Speed 2 until the mixture resembles fine breadcrumbs (about 2 minutes). Add cold water gradually, and mix at Speed 2 until the mixture forms a dough that leaves the sides of the bowl clean; switch off immediately.

Using a food processor: Mix the flour, salt, butter and lard together in the food processor, fitted with a steel blade, for 30 seconds or until the mixture resembles breadcrumbs. Add the cold water gradually, and process until the mixture forms a dough that leaves the sides of the bowl cleanly.

Turn the dough onto a lightly-floured pastry board or marble slab and knead very lightly with clean, cool hands until smooth underneath. Then turn it over and pat into a round cake shape 1–2.5 cm (½–1 in) thick. Wrap in greaseproof paper, and chill in the refrigerator for at least 30 minutes before use.

One-stage Shortcrust Pastry

If you do not have an electric mixer or a food processor, this is a simple method for making shortcrust pastry which eliminates the rather messy rubbing-in stage with the fingertips.

Makes 250 g (8 oz)

170 g (5½ oz) soft margarine chilled
5 teaspoons cold water
2 cups (8 oz) flour, sifted

Place the soft margarine, water and 2 tablespoons of the measured flour into a mixing bowl and mix to a smooth paste using a fork. Add the remaining flour, and continue mixing with the fork until the mixture forms a stiff dough and leaves the sides of the bowl cleanly. Press the dough together in the bowl with a clean cool hand, then turn it onto a lightly-floured marble slab and knead very lightly until smooth underneath. Turn over, pat into a thin, round cake shape, wrap in greaseproof paper and chill in the refrigerator for at least 30 minutes before use. If difficult to handle, roll out between two sheets of greaseproof paper.

Note: This pastry may also be made in a food processor fitted with a steel blade, by placing all ingredients in together and mixing until a dough is formed which leaves the sides of the bowl cleanly. Knead, shape and chill as above, before use.

Shortcrust Pastry

1. Sift flour and salt into bowl.

2. Rub in fat using fingertips until mixture resembles fine breadcrumbs.

3. Stir in water and draw dough together using a knife.

4. Knead dough lightly until smooth.

5. Roll out on a lightly floured marble slab or pastry board.

6. Use to line tartlet tins or as required.

1

2

3

4

5

6

Rich Shortcrust Pastry

Sufficient to line or cover and decorate a 23 cm (9 in) round pie dish, but three-quarters of this quantity is sufficient to line a 20 to 23 cm (8 or 9 in) flan tin. May be refrigerated or frozen (as for shortcrust pastry, above).

Makes 250 g (8 oz)

2 cups (8 oz) flour
125 g (4 oz) unsalted butter, chilled
1 tablespoon caster (powdered) sugar
pinch of salt, optional
1 egg yolk
2 teaspoons lemon juice
1–2 tablespoons cold water

Sift the flour into a cold mixing bowl. Cut the butter into the flour with a round-bladed knife, then rub the butter into the flour with the fingertips until the mixture resembles breadcrumbs. Stir in the sugar and salt if used, with a round-bladed knife. Stir the egg yolk and lemon juice together and sprinkle over the mixture, then mix together with the knife. Gradually mix in sufficient cold water until the mixture forms lumps which leave the sides of the bowl cleanly. Knead the dough together lightly with a clean, cool hand.

Using an electric mixer: Sift the flour into the bowl of the electric mixer. Add the butter cut into small cubes, the sugar and salt, switch to minimum speed and gradually increase the speed to 2 as the butter mixture breaks up. Mix until the mixture resembles fine breadcrumbs (about 1½ minutes). Stir the egg yolk, lemon juice and water together; add this to the mixture and mix at Speed 1 for about 30–50 seconds until the mixture leaves the sides of the bowl. Switch off as soon as the ingredients are incorporated.

Using a food processor: Mix the flour, butter, sugar and salt together in the food processor for 30 seconds or until the mixture resembles breadcrumbs. Add the egg yolk, lemon juice and sufficient water gradually, and process until the mixture forms a dough that leaves the sides of the bowl cleanly.

Turn the dough onto a lightly-floured board or marble slab and knead until smooth underneath. Turn over and pat into a round cake shape 1–2.5 cm (½–1 in) thick. Wrap in greaseproof paper and chill for 30 minutes in the refrigerator before use.

Sweet Shortcrust Pastry

This pastry is popular in the north of England, where it is used for fruit pies, particularly the traditional pastry 'top and bottom' apple pie.

Makes 250 g (8 oz)

2 cups (8 oz) flour
pinch of salt, optional
60 g (2 oz) chilled butter or firm margarine
60 g (2 oz) lard or white shortening
1 tablespoon caster (powdered) sugar
approx. 4 tablespoons cold water

Make as for Shortcrust Pastry, and add sugar at the 'breadcrumb' stage.

Low-cholesterol Shortcrust Pastry

This pastry should be used for those on a low-cholesterol diet. Its characteristic short texture can make it difficult to handle; if so, roll it out between two sheets of greaseproof paper.

Makes 250 g (8 oz)

170 g (5½ oz) polyunsaturated margarine, chilled
5 teaspoons cold water
2 cups (8 oz) flour, sifted

Make as for One-stage Shortcrust Pastry.

Wrap in greaseproof paper, and chill in the refrigerator for at least 30 minutes before use.

Cheese Pastry

This delicious pastry is ideal for melt-in-the-mouth cheese straws or cheese pastry canapés. If used for pies or flans, when it is necessary to roll it out thinly, it may be rolled out between two sheets of greaseproof paper to prevent crumbling.

Makes 185 g (6 oz)

125 g (4 oz) mature Cheddar cheese, finely-grated
2 tablespoons finely-grated Parmesan cheese, fresh or vacuum packed
125 g (4 oz) butter or firm margarine
1½ cups (6 oz) flour
pinch of salt
pinch of ground white pepper
pinch of cayenne pepper
2 egg yolks

Place the finely-grated cheeses and the butter in a mixing bowl and beat with the back of a wooden spoon until it is soft and creamy. Add the flour, salt, white pepper, cayenne pepper and beaten egg yolks and mix together with a round-bladed knife until the mixture forms lumps which leave the sides of the bowl cleanly. Knead lightly to form a dough with clean, cool hands.

Using an electric mixer: Place the finely-grated cheeses and the butter in the bowl of the electric mixer and mix with a K-beater or pastry mixers at Speed 2 until creamy. Sift the flour and seasonings onto a square of greaseproof paper. Add the sieved flour and the egg yolks to the creamed mixture, and mix at Speed 2 until the mixture forms a stiff dough (about 2 minutes).

Using a food processor: Mix the finely-grated cheeses with the butter in the food processor, fitted with a steel blade, until creamy. Add all the remaining ingredients and process until the mixture forms a dough that leaves the sides of the bowl cleanly.

Turn the dough onto a lightly-floured pastry board or marble slab and knead lightly until smooth. Then turn over and shape into a round cake shape 1 cm (⅜ in) thick. Wrap it in greaseproof paper and chill for 30 minutes before use.

Cream Cheese Pastry

This versatile pastry can be used for either savoury or sweet dishes and is easy to handle

Makes 250 g (8 oz)

250 g (8 oz) butter or margarine
250 g (8 oz) cream cheese, softened
½ teaspoon salt
2 cups (8 oz) flour

Using an electric mixer: Place the butter, cream cheese and salt into the bowl of the electric mixer and beat with a K-beater or pastry mixers until smooth and evenly combined. Sieve the flour onto a square of greaseproof paper, then add it to the bowl and mix at Speed 2 until the dough leaves the sides of the bowl cleanly.

Using a food processor: Cut the butter and cream cheese into 1 cm (⅜ in) cubes. Place all the ingredients together into the food processor, fitted with a steel blade, and process until the mixture forms a dough that leaves the sides of the bowl clean.

Turn the dough onto a lightly-floured marble slab and knead lightly until smooth underneath. Then turn over and pat into a round cake shape 1–2.5 cm (½–1 in) thick. Wrap in greaseproof paper and chill in the refrigerator for 30 minutes before rolling out.

American Pastry

This pastry is used for making fruit pies in America, and has a very short, melt-in-the-mouth texture.

Makes 250 g (8 oz)

155 g (5 oz) lard
3 tablespoons cold water
2 cups (8 oz) self-raising flour

Using an electric mixer: Place the lard and water in the bowl of the electric mixer, and mix at Speed 2 until soft and creamy. Add the sifted flour, them mix at minimum speed, gradually increasing to Speed 2 until the mixture resembles breadcrumbs (about 1½–2 minutes). Continue mixing until the mixture forms a dough.

Using a food processor: Place all the ingredients together in the food processor and mix until a dough forms which leaves the sides of the bowl cleanly.

Turn the dough onto a lightly-floured board, and knead lightly. Pat into a round cake shape, then wrap securely in greaseproof paper and chill in the refrigerator for at least 30 minutes.

Puff Pastry

The most difficult of the 'family' of puff pastries to make, this recipe nevertheless gives the best result, because after rolling and folding seven times, there are so many layers of pastry to puff up during baking.

Makes 250 g (8 oz)

250 g (8 oz) unsalted butter
2 cups (8 oz) flour
pinch of salt, optional
1 teaspoon lemon juice
cold water, to mix

Shape the butter into a flat square pat 5 mm (¼ in) thick, and squeeze and press it between two pieces of muslin to absorb excess moisture from the butter. Place it in the refrigerator until cool and firm.

Sieve the flour (and salt, if used) into a large mixing bowl or the bowl of an electric mixer. Using a round-bladed knife or a K-beater or pastry mixers, mix in the lemon juice and sufficient cold water, on minimum speed, to form an elastic dough.

Alternatively, mix the flour, lemon juice and sufficient cold water together in a food processor to form a dough.

Turn the dough onto a floured pastry board or marble slab, and knead lightly until the paste is smooth and elastic and not sticky.

Roll the dough out on a lightly-floured surface to a rectangle twice as big as the butter pat. Place the butter on the top half of the dough, and fold the bottom half over. Roll it out evenly to a long strip, taking care that the butter does not break through. Fold the strip of pastry in three—folding the bottom third up and the top third down. Allow to cool in the refrigerator for 10–15 minutes.

Place the pastry on the rolling surface, with the folded edge to the right. Roll and fold into three twice, placing the folded edge alternately to the left. Then return to the refrigerator to cool.

Repeat the rolling and folding processes until the pastry has had seven rolls and folds, chilling whenever necessary. Wrap the dough in greaseproof paper and chill well before use.

Note: The pastry dough stores overnight in greaseproof paper, inside a plastic bag, in the refrigerator. It also freezes well.

Rough Puff Pastry

A simplified, quicker version of the original Puff Pastry, which is not as rich and does not puff as well. Sufficient to cover and decorate a 1 litre (32 fl oz) oval pie dish.

Makes 250 g (8 oz)

90 g (3 oz) butter or firm margarine
90 g (3 oz) lard
2 cups (8 oz) flour
pinch of salt
3 tablespoons cold water

Mix the butter and lard together on an enamel plate with a round-bladed knife until well blended, then chill until firm.

Sift the flour and salt into a large mixing bowl or into the large bowl of an electric mixer. Cut the fat into even-sized pieces the size of a walnut and drop them into the flour, tossing each piece well to coat it. Add the cold water and, using a round-bladed knife or the K-beater or pastry mixers, mix at minimum speed for 15 seconds, or until a dough forms.

Turn the dough onto a lightly-floured board and roll out to an oblong about 25 × 15 cm (10 × 6 in). Fold in three and make a half turn so that an open end faces you. Repeat rolling, folding and turning twice more, turning alternately to the right then to the left. Refrigerate the dough at any stage when it becomes too soft and greasy to handle. Wrap in greaseproof paper and refrigerate for at least 30 minutes before use.

Note: The pastry dough stores well for a few days in greaseproof paper, in a plastic bag, in the refrigerator. It also freezes well.

Puff Pastry

1. Beat the butter into a flat rectangle between sheets of greaseproof paper.

2. Knead dough lightly until smooth and elastic.

3. Roll out dough on a lightly floured surface. Place chilled butter on the top half of dough, fold bottom half over.

4. Roll dough out evenly into a long strip.

5. Fold pastry into three.

6. Between folding, press dough firmly with rolling pin to evenly distribute the butter, then roll, fold and repeat (see recipe).

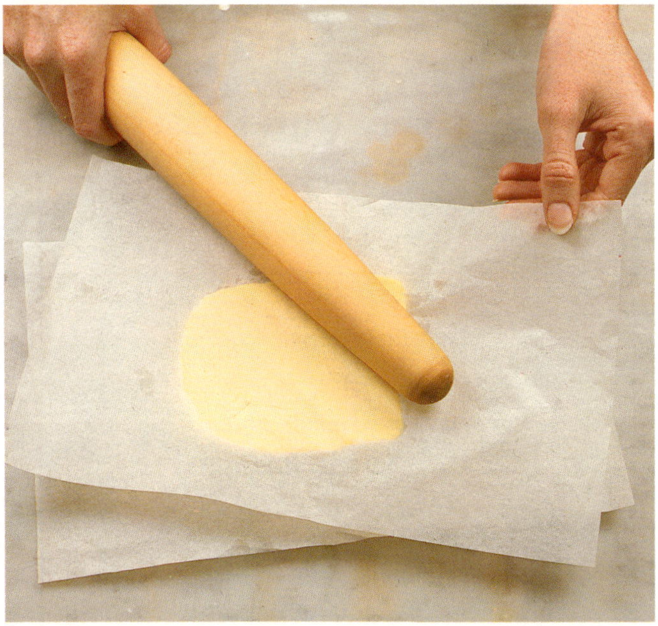
1

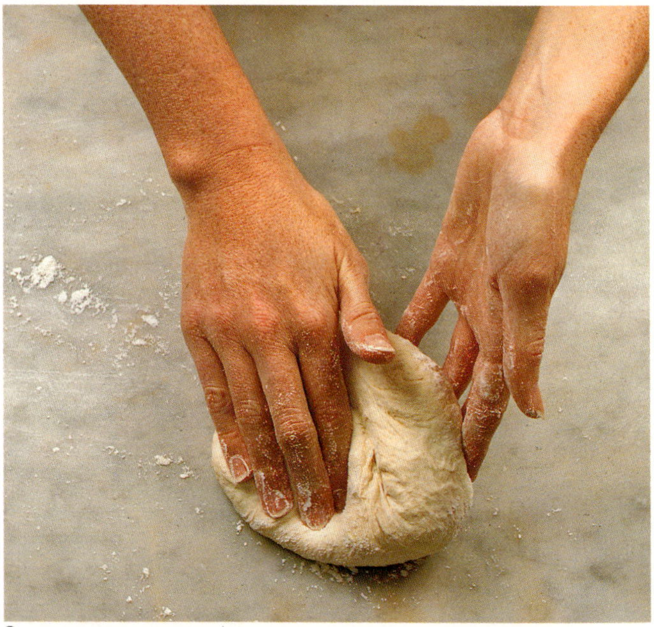
2

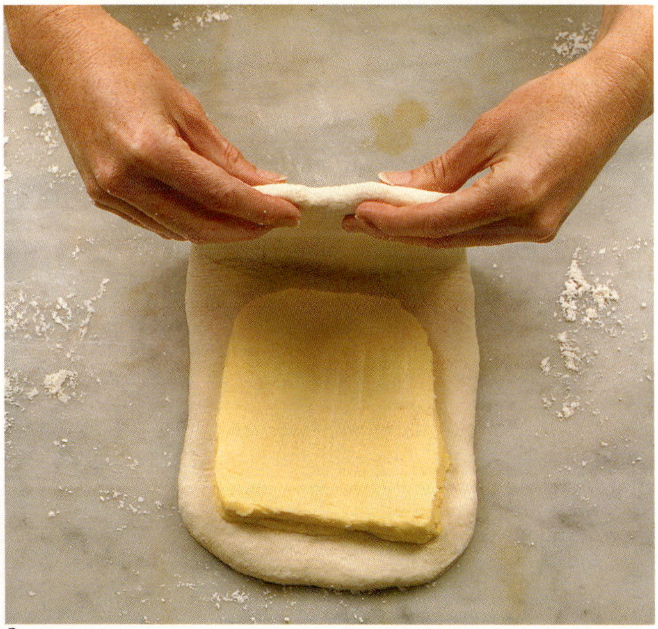
3

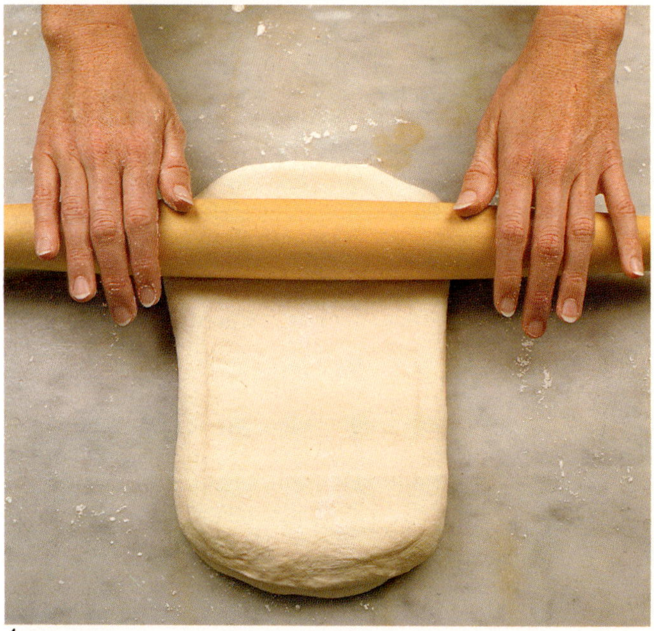
4

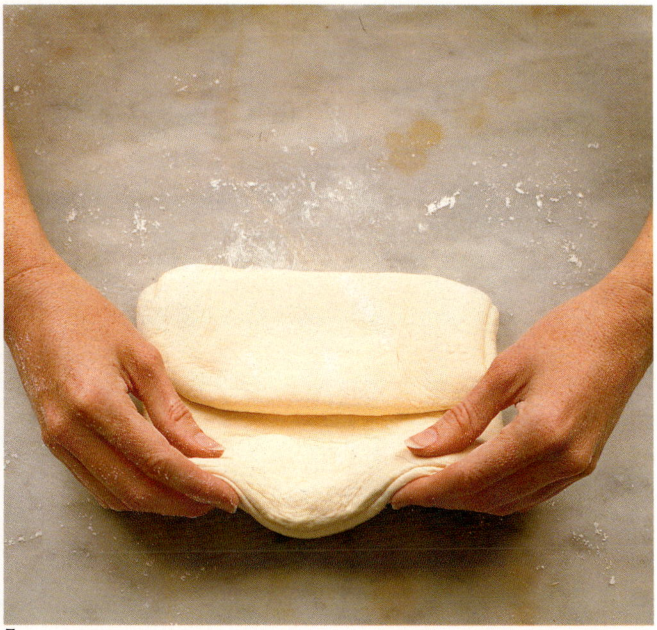
5

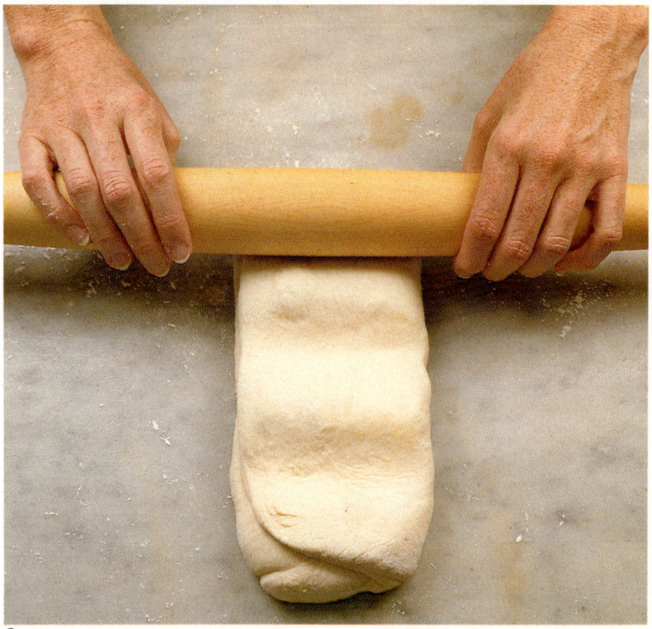
6

Flaky Pastry

Another simplified version of the original Puff Pastry which gives a better result than Rough Puff Pastry.

Makes 250 g (8 oz)

2 cups (8 oz) flour
pinch of salt
90 g (3 oz) butter or firm margarine
90 g (3 oz) lard
½ cup (4 fl oz) cold water

Sift the flour and salt into a mixing bowl. Mix the fats together on an enamel plate with a round-bladed knife and shape into a square block. Place a quarter of the mixed fat into the flour, coating it well, then cut it into small pieces with the round-bladed knife. Rub the fat into the flour with cool fingertips until the mixture resembles breadcrumbs. Sprinkle the cold water over and mix with a knife to form a dough which leaves the sides of the bowl cleanly.

Using an electric mixer: Sift the flour and salt into the bowl of an electric mixer. Mix the fats together on an enamel plate with a round-bladed knife and shape into a square block. Add a quarter of the mixed fat to the flour; mix at minimum speed, then increase to Speed 2 and mix until the mixture resembles fine breadcrumbs (about 2 minutes). Stop the mixer, add the water, then mix at Speed 2 to a firm dough that leaves the sides of the bowl cleanly—adding more water if necessary.

Turn the dough onto a lightly-floured board and knead it lightly until smooth. Roll out to an oblong about 25 × 15 cm (10 × 6 in). Put another quarter of the mixed fat, in flakes or small pieces, on the top two-thirds of the dough. Fold into three—folding the bottom third up and the top third over it. This gives you even layers of dough and fat. Half-turn the pastry (so that an open end faces you, and the top is now on the right side) and roll out again to an oblong.

Repeat flaking, folding and rolling of dough twice more. Refrigerate the dough at any stage when it becomes too soft and greasy to handle. Fold pastry into three once more. Wrap in greaseproof paper and refrigerate until required.

Note: This pastry dough will keep well for a few days in the refrigerator, in greaseproof paper in a plastic bag. It also freezes well.

Chocolate Puff Pastry

A delicious chocolate puff pastry for an exotic chocolate mille-feuille.

Makes 250 g (8 oz)

2 cups (8 oz) flour
4 tablespoons cocoa
4 tablespoons icing (confectioners') sugar
¼ teaspoon salt, optional
250 g (8 oz) unsalted butter
approx. ½ cup (4 fl oz) cold water

Sift the flour, cocoa and icing sugar (and salt, if used) into the large bowl of an electric mixer. Add 60 g (2 oz) of the butter, cut into 1 cm (⅜ in) cubes. Mix at Speed 2 for 2 minutes or until the mixture resembles breadcrumbs. Sprinkle the water in, then mix at Speed 2 until the mixture forms a dough that leaves the sides of the bowl cleanly.

Place the dough on a lightly-floured marble slab or cold surface, and knead lightly until smooth underneath. Then turn over and pat into a square shape 1 cm (⅜ in) thick. Wrap in greaseproof paper and chill in the refrigerator for 10–15 minutes.

Knead and squeeze the remaining 190 g (6 oz) butter into a square, 5 mm (¼ in) thick, between two pieces of muslin, in order to absorb excess moisture. Chill well until firm but not hard.

Roll the dough out on a floured marble slab or cold surface to a rectangle twice as big as the square of butter. Place the butter on the top half of the dough, and fold the bottom half over. Roll it out evenly to a long strip, taking care that the butter does not break through. Fold strip of pastry in three—folding the bottom third up and the top third down. Cool in the refrigerator for 10–15 minutes.

Roll and fold seven times (as for Puff Pastry), then chill well before use.

Sour Cream Pastry

Delicate to handle but has a melt-in-the-mouth texture when baked. May be used for savoury or sweet recipes.

Makes 250 g (8 oz)

---

2 cups (8 oz) flour

125 g (4 oz) chilled butter or firm margarine

165 ml (5½ fl oz) sour (soured) cream

Sift the flour into a cold mixing bowl. Cut the butter into the flour with a round-bladed knife. Rub the butter into the flour with the fingertips until the mixture resembles breadcrumbs. Add the sour cream and mix with the knife until the mixture begins to form lumps which leave the sides of the bowl. Knead the dough together lightly with a clean, cool hand.

Using an electric mixer: Sift the flour into the bowl of the electric mixer. Cut the butter into small cubes and add it to the flour. Beat with a K-beater or pastry mixers at Speed 2 for 1 minute 30 seconds. Increase the speed to 4 for a further 15 seconds or until the mixture resembles coarse breadbrumbs. Add the sour cream and beat at Speed 1 for 25 seconds or until the dough leaves the sides of the bowl clean.

Using a food processor: Place the flour and cubes of butter into the food processor, fitted with a steel blade, and mix for 30 seconds. Add the sour cream and mix until the dough leaves the sides of the bowl clean.

Turn the dough onto a lightly-floured pastry board or a marble slab, and knead very lightly into a smooth, round cake shape. Wrap in greaseproof paper and chill for at least 30 minutes before use.

Wholemeal Pastry

Pastry made with wholemeal flour contains more nutrients and fibre than pastry made with white flour. However, it absorbs more liquid and tends to 'crumble, so is more difficult to handle.

Makes 250 g (8 oz)

1¾ cups (8 oz) wholemeal flour, medium or coarse ground

1 teaspoon salt

125 g (4 oz) butter or firm margarine

cold water, to mix

Place the wholemeal flour and salt into a mixing bowl, and continue as for Shortcrust Pastry (page 182).

Note: The pastry dough stores well in greaseproof paper in a plastic bag in the refrigerator for a few days. It also freezes well.

Low-cholesterol Wholemeal Pastry

Wholemeal pastry made with polyunsaturated margarine is good for people on low-cholesterol diets.

Makes 250 g (8 oz)

---

125 g (4 oz) polyunsaturated margarine

2 tablespoons cold water

1¾ cups (8 oz) wholemeal flour, fine or medium ground

Make as for One-stage Shortcrust Pastry (page 182).

Note: The pastry dough freezes well. It may also be stored for a few days in greaseproof paper, in a plastic bag, in the refrigerator.

Suet Crust Pastry

This pastry may be used for savoury and sweet baked roly-polys. One cup (60 g) fresh white breadcrumbs may be substituted for ½ cup (60 g) flour to give a lighter crust.

Makes 250 g (8 oz)

---

250 g (2 cups) self-raising flour or 250 g (2 cups) plain flour and 1 teaspoon baking powder

pinch of salt

125 g (4 oz) suet, finely chopped

cold water to mix

Sift the flour and salt into a mixing bowl. Remove the tissues from the suet and chop the suet finely in a food processor or blender. Add the suet to the flour and mix well, then mix in sufficent cold water to form a soft, light dough, cutting it in with a roundbladed knife. Knead the dough on a lightly-floured surface until it is smooth and use immediately.

Pâte Brisée

The high proportion of butter to flour in this French pastry gives a good golden colour and a crisp, short texture. It is mainly used in savoury flans or quiches and should be baked 'blind' to give the best result. Sufficient for a 30 cm (12 in) flan tin.

Makes 250 g (8 oz)

170 g (5½ oz) chilled butter
2 cups (8 oz) flour
¼ teaspoon salt, optional
approx. 4–6 tablespoons iced water

Cut the butter into the sifted flour in a cold mixing bowl. Rub the butter into the flour with cold fingertips until the mixture resembles fine breadcrumbs. Add the salt, if used. Sprinkle iced water over, a tablespoon at a time, and mix with a round-bladed knife or a palette knife until the dough forms small lumps which leave the side of the bowl cleanly. Knead the dough together lightly with a clean, cold hand.

Using an electric mixer: Cut the butter into 1 cm (⅜ in) cubes and place in the bowl of the electric mixer. Sift flour and salt together onto a square of greaseproof paper. Add a little flour to the butter and mix with a K-beater or pastry mixers at minimum speed until mixture begins to break up. Then gradually add the remaining flour, increase the speed to 2, and mix for 2 minutes. Increase the speed to 3 for ½–1 minute more, or until the mixture resembles fine breadcrumbs. Add 4 tablespoons of the iced water all at once, and mix at Speed 3 for 10 seconds. If the dough has not come together, add the remaining water gradually on minimum speed until the mixture leaves the sides of the bowl clean.

Using a food processor: Place the butter, flour and salt into the food processor, fitted with a steel blade, and mix for 30 seconds or until the mixture resembles breadcrumbs. Then add 3 tablespoons of the iced water and mix for 5 seconds. If the dough does not leave the sides of the bowl cleanly, add 1 tablespoon of iced water and mix for a further 5 seconds; repeat until the dough leaves the sides of the bowl cleanly.

Turn the dough onto a lightly-floured marble slab or board and knead lightly with the fingertips until smooth. Turn over and pat into a round cake shape 1–2.5 cm (½–1 in) thick, then wrap in greaseproof paper and chill in the refrigerator for 30 minutes or until firm.

Note: This pastry dough freezes well. It also stores well in greaseproof paper, inside a plastic bag, in the refrigerator for a few days.

Pâte Sucrée

This is the most popular French pastry used for making sweet flans and fruit tarts. Sufficient for a 30 cm (12 in) flan tin.

Makes 250 g (8 oz)

125 g (4 oz) unsalted butter, chilled
2 cups (8 oz) flour
60 g (½ cup) icing (confectioners') sugar
2 egg yolks or 1 egg
1 teaspoon iced water, only if necessary

Sift flour onto marble slab. Using the cushion of your hand, sweep a large ring. Sift icing sugar into centre of ring and make a well. Place butter and egg yolks in the well, then, using a pecking motion with your fingertips, combine butter and egg yolks.

Gather in flour and icing sugar to combine dough. Knead very lightly until a smooth ball. Chill if necessary.

Using an electric mixer: Cut the butter into 1 cm (⅜ in) cubes, and place in the bowl of the electric mixer. Sift the flour and icing sugar together onto a square of greaseproof paper. Add a little flour to the butter and mix with a K-beater or pastry mixers at minimum speed until the butter begins to break up. Gradually add the remaining flour; increase the speed to 2 for 2 minutes, then increase the speed to 3 for a further 30 seconds or until the mixture resembles fine breadcrumbs. Reduce the speed to 1, add the egg, and mix until the dough comes together. If the dough is too dry and will not come together, add water and mix to bind.

Using a food processor: Place the butter, flour and icing sugar into the food processor, fitted with a steel blade, and mix for 30 seconds or until the mixture resembles breadcrumbs. Add egg yolks or beaten egg, and process until the mixture forms a dough that leaves the sides of the bowl cleanly. It is normally unnecessary to add the water when mixing in a food processor.

Turn the dough onto a lightly-floured marble slab or pastry board, and knead lightly just until smooth. Turn over and pat into a round cake shape 1–2.5 cm (½–1 in) thick, then wrap in greaseproof paper and chill in the refrigerator for 30 minutes until firm.

Pâte Sucrée

1. Place butter and sugar into a well in flour/sugar mixture.

2. Using a pecking motion with your fingertips, combine butter and egg yolks.

3. Gather in flour and icing sugar to combine dough.

4. Knead very lightly until smooth. Chill if necessary.

5. Roll out dough and carefully lift onto flan ring.

6. Roll away excess dough.

1

2

3

4

5

6

Wholemeal Wheatgerm Pastry

An exceptionally healthy pastry with a delicious nutty flavour.

Makes 250 g (8 oz)

1¼ cups (5½ oz) plain wholemeal flour, fine or medium ground
75 g (2½ oz) wheatgerm
125 g (4 oz) butter or polyunsaturated margarine
4 tablespoons iced water

Place the wholemeal flour in a large, cold mixing bowl and add the wheatgerm. Cut the butter into the flour and the wheatgerm with a round-bladed knife, coating each piece well. Rub the butter into the flour and wheatgerm with the fingertips until the mixture resembles breadcrumbs.

Sprinkle iced water over gradually and mix in with the round-bladed knife until the mixture begins to form lumps which leave the sides of the bowl cleanly. Knead the dough with a cold, clean hand to compress together lightly.

Using an electric mixer: Mix the flour and wheatgerm together in the bowl of the electric mixer. Add the butter or margarine and mix at Speed 2 for about 1 minute or until the mixture resembles fine breadcrumbs. Add the iced water, 1 tablespoon at a time, still mixing at Speed 2 for about 45–60 seconds or until the mixture leaves the sides of the bowl clean and forms a ball around the beater.

Using a food processor: Place the flour, wheatgerm and butter or margarine in the food processor and mix for 30 seconds. Add the iced water and mix until a dough forms which leaves the sides of the bowl clean.

Turn the pastry onto a lightly-floured board or marble slab, and knead until smooth. Then turn over and shape into a round cake shape. Wrap in greaseproof paper and chill in the refrigerator for at least 30 minutes.

Hot Water Crust Pastry

One of the oldest pastries created, and still used for traditional English pork pies, veal and ham pies and game pies.

Makes 375 g (12 oz)

3 cups (12 oz) flour
1 teaspoon salt
125 g (4 oz) lard
1 cup (8 fl oz) water
1 egg yolk

Sift the flour and salt into a large, warm mixing bowl or the warm bowl of an electric mixer. Heat the lard and water together in a saucepan, then bring rapidly to the boil. Quickly pour the boiling lard and water mixture onto the flour; and using a wooden spoon or a K-beater or pastry mixers, mix gently or at minimum speed for 15 seconds. Add the egg yolk and continue to beat for a further 15 seconds. Beat quicker with the wooden spoon or increase to Speed 2 and beat for a further 30 seconds or until the mixture leaves the sides of the bowl clean and forms a smooth ball around the beater.

Knead very lightly, then wrap in greaseproof paper and allow to rest at room temperature for 20–30 minutes before use.

Note: This pastry must be kept warm at all times, not cold.

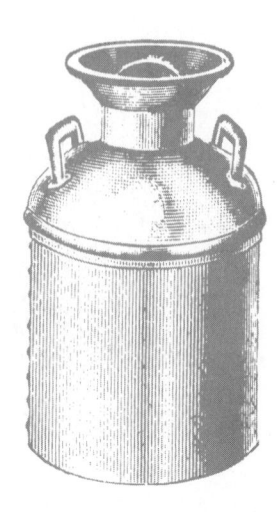

Crumb Crust

Crumb crusts are easier and quicker to make than pastry, and simpler to handle in hot weather. This basic recipe may be varied by adding 1 teaspoon of your favourite ground spice.

Makes 1 crumb crust

---
1 packet 225 g (8 oz) wholemeal or plain sweet biscuits
125 g (4 oz) butter

Break the biscuits in half into a blender, about a third at a time, then mix at maximum speed for 20 seconds or until the biscuits are crushed. This can also be done in one process in a food processor. Pour the biscuit crumbs into a bowl.

Melt the butter in a saucepan over a low heat; add it to the biscuit crumbs and mix thoroughly. Allow to cool slightly, then press into a 20 or 23 cm (8 or 9 in) pie plate, flan ring or springform tin. Refrigerate until firm (about 1 hour), or bake according to the instructions in a particular recipe.

Note: Less butter may be needed if the biscuits are rich.

Baked Crumb Crust

1¼ cups (4 oz) crushed plain sweet biscuits (cookies)
1 tablespoon caster (powdered) sugar
75 g (2½ oz) butter, melted

Preheat the oven to 190°C (375°F/Gas 5). Mix together the crumbs and the sugar. Blend in the butter and press the mixture into a greased 23 cm (9 in) pie plate, taking the crumbs up the sides to form a small rim. Bake for 8 to 10 minutes. Allow to cool, before topping.

Note: For a spicy crumb crust, ½ teaspoon of ground cinnamon or nutmeg may be added with the sugar.

Lard Pastry

Another extremely rich American pastry with a large proportion of fat to flour. Delicious when used for topping hot savoury pies or in traditional dessert pies.

Makes 155 g (5 oz)

1¼ cups (5 oz) flour
1 teaspoon sugar
pinch of salt
60 g (2 oz) lard
75 g (2½ oz) butter
2–3 tablespoons iced water

Sift the flour, sugar and salt into a cold mixing bowl. Cut the lard and butter into the flour mixture with a round-bladed knife. Rub the fats into the flour mixture with the fingertips until it resembles breadcrumbs. Sprinkle the iced water over gradually and mix in with the knife until the mixture starts to form lumps which leave the sides of the bowl cleanly. Knead the dough together lightly with a clean, cool hand.

Using an electric mixer: Sift the dry ingredients into the bowl of the electric mixer. Cut the lard and butter into small pieces and add to the dry ingredients. Mix at Speed 1, increasing to Speed 2 for 30 seconds, then increase to Speed 3 for a further 30 seconds or until the mixture is combined but resembles coarse crumbs. Add the iced water, 1 tablespoon at a time, mixing at Speed 3 until the mixture comes together to form a dough (about 15 seconds).

Using a food processor: Place the flour, sugar, salt, lard and butter into the food processor and mix for 30 seconds. Add the water, and mix until a dough forms.

Turn the dough onto a lightly-floured board and knead gently until smooth. Shape into a round cake, wrap in greaseproof paper and chill in the refrigerator for 30 minutes or until required.

Choux Pastry

Another unusual pastry, which needs heat to prepare the paste. **Choux** *is French for 'cabbage'.*
Makes 60 g (2 oz)

½ cup (2 oz) flour
⅛ teaspoon salt
½ cup (4 fl oz) water
60 g (2 oz) butter
2 large eggs
drops of vanilla essence

Sift the flour and salt together onto a square of greaseproof paper.

Place the water and butter in a ceramic-lined, cast iron saucepan and bring to boiling point over a medium heat. Remove immediately from the heat to prevent evaporation. Quickly stir in the sifted flour and salt all at once, using a wooden spoon. Beat the mixture until it forms a smooth paste which leaves the sides of the saucepan clean. Cool.

Beat the eggs; then beat them into the mixture in four stages, beating well after each addition until no trace of egg remains. Finally beat in a few drops of vanilla essence.

Use the pastry according to a given recipe, and bake immediately.

Cheese Choux Pastry

Makes 125 g (4 oz)

1 cup (8 fl oz) water
90 g (3 oz) butter
1 cup (4 oz) flour
pinch of salt
3 large eggs
3 tablespoons grated Parmesan cheese
salt and pepper
mustard powder

Prepare as for Choux Pastry, but beat the beaten eggs into the mixture in six stages, beating well after each addition, until no trace of egg remains and the mixture is smooth and shiny.

Finally beat in the Parmesan cheese and season to taste with salt, pepper and mustard powder. Use and bake immediately for best results.

Chocolate Choux Pastry

Delicious when used for cream puffs or éclairs.
Makes 75 g (2½ oz)

150 ml (5 fl oz) water
60 g (2 oz) butter or firm margarine
½ cup (2 oz) flour
1 tablespoon (¼ oz) cocoa
2 large eggs

Place the water and butter in a ceramic-lined cast iron saucepan and bring to boiling point over a medium heat. Meanwhile, sift the flour and cocoa together onto a square of greaseproof paper. Remove the saucepan from the heat immediately the mixture boils and stir in the sifted flour and cocoa all at once, using a wooden spoon. Return the saucepan to a low heat and beat for 1 minute, until the mixture is shiny and leaves the sides of the saucepan clean. Remove from the heat and allow to cool slightly.

Beat the eggs well with a fork; then beat them into the mixture in four parts, beating well after each addition until the mixture is smooth an shiny.

Use according to a particular recipe, and bake immediately for best results.

Choux Pastry

1. Tip sifted flour all at once into butter/water mixture.

2. Stir with wooden spoon.

3. Stir until mixture leaves the sides of the pan, cool.

4. Add eggs gradually.

5. Beat well until mixture is smooth and shiny.

6. Spoon or pipe onto greased baking trays.

1

2

3

4

5

6

Biscuit Pastry

Makes 375 g (12 oz)

125 g (4 oz) butter
⅓ cup (3 oz) sugar
1 egg
½ teaspoon vanilla essence
3 cups (12 oz) self-raising flour
¼ teaspoon salt

In a mixing bowl, cream the butter and sugar until light and fluffy. Add the egg and vanilla essence and mix well. Stir in the sifted flour and salt, form the dough into a ball and knead lightly. Wrap in greaseproof paper until you are ready to use it.

Almond Crust

A delicious crust for light, creamy tarts. Makes enough for a 25 cm (10 in) tart

2 egg whites
pinch of cream of tartar
pinch of salt
¼ teaspoon vanilla essence
½ cup (4 oz) sugar
1½ cups (5½ oz) finely chopped blanched almonds

Preheat the oven to 190°C (375°F/Gas 5). Beat the egg whites until foamy. Add cream of tartar, salt and vanilla. Gradually add the sugar and continue beating until the mixture is stiff and glossy. Fold in the almonds.

Spread the mixture over the bottom and sides of an oiled pie dish. Bake for 15 to 20 minutes or until lightly browned. Cool.

Pecan or Walnut Pastry

This is a good pastry for fruit tarts, especially pear tart. Makes 315 g (10 oz)

2½ cups (10 oz) flour
½ teaspoon salt
90 g (3 oz) butter, cut into small pieces
60 g (2 oz) vegetable fat
½ cup (4 oz) caster (powdered) sugar
¼ cup (1½ oz) pecans or walnuts, finely chopped
2 egg yolks, lightly beaten
3 tablespoons iced water

Sift the flour and salt into a large mixing bowl. Add the butter and vegetable fat and cut them into small pieces in the flour. Rub the fats into the flour with your fingertips until the mixture resembles coarse breadcrumbs. Add the sugar and pecans or walnuts and mix well.

Add the egg yolks and half the water and mix together with a round-bladed knife until the mixture forms lumps which leave the sides of the bowl cleanly. Add more water if the dough is too dry. Knead the dough lightly until it is smooth, then form it into a ball, flatten it slightly and wrap in greaseproof paper. Chill for 30 minutes before use.

Rosemary's Pastry

This is a very unorthodox way of making pastry, but surprisingly it works very well, provided you use it while it is warm. It is excellent for fruit pies and tarts. Makes 250 g (8 oz)

| 60 g (2 oz) butter |
| 1/4 cup (2 oz) caster (powdered) sugar |
| 1/4 cup (2 fl oz) milk |
| 1 egg |
| 2 cups (8 oz) self-raising flour |

Put the butter, sugar and milk in a saucepan and heat until the butter has melted and the sugar has dissolved. Beat the egg in a bowl and stir in the butter-sugar mixture. Sift in the flour and beat with a wooden spoon until the mixture forms a soft dough. Use while still warm.

Orange Pastry

A good pastry for fruit or cream cheese tarts. Makes 155 g (5 oz)

| 1 1/4 cups (5 oz) flour |
| 1/4 teaspoon salt |
| 75 g (2 1/2 oz) butter |
| juice and grated rind of 1/2 cold orange |

Sift the flour and salt into a bowl. Cut the butter into small pieces and rub them into the flour with your fingertips until the mixture resembles coarse breadcrumbs. Add the orange rind and mix well.

Gradually add the orange juice until the mixture begins to stick together. Gather into a ball, flatten lightly with the palm of your hand, wrap in greaseproof paper and chill for 30 minutes before use.

Oil Pastry

Oil pastry is heavier than butter pastry and should be chilled before it is rolled out, otherwise it can be difficult to handle. Makes 250 g (8 oz)

| 2 cups (8 oz) flour |
| 1 teaspoon salt |
| 2/3 cup (5 fl oz) vegetable oil |
| 3 tablespoons water or milk |

Sift the flour into a mixing bowl with the salt. Mix together the oil and water or milk and stir it into the flour. Form the dough into a ball, then pat it into a round cake shape 1–2.5 cm (1/2–1 in) thick. Wrap in greaseproof paper and chill in the refrigerator for at least 30 minutes before use.

Turnover Pastry

Excellent for all sweet and savoury turnovers. Makes 315 g (10 oz)

| 2 1/2 cups (10 oz) flour |
| 1/2 teaspoon salt |
| pinch of cream of tartar |
| 125 g (4 oz) butter |
| 3 tablespoons pure lard, cut into pieces |
| 1/2 cup (4 fl oz) iced water |

Sift the flour, salt and cream of tartar into a bowl. Cut the butter into small pieces and rub them into the flour with your fingertips until the mixture resembles coarse breadcrumbs. Add the iced water. Toss until the mixture is blended and form it into a ball.

Knead lightly with the heel of your hand and add the lard, blending it evenly through the dough.

Form into a ball and roll out on a lightly floured board into a rectangle 25 × 12 cm (10 × 5 in). Fold into thirds with the open side facing you. Roll out and repeat the process 3 more times. Chill the dough for at least 1 hour.

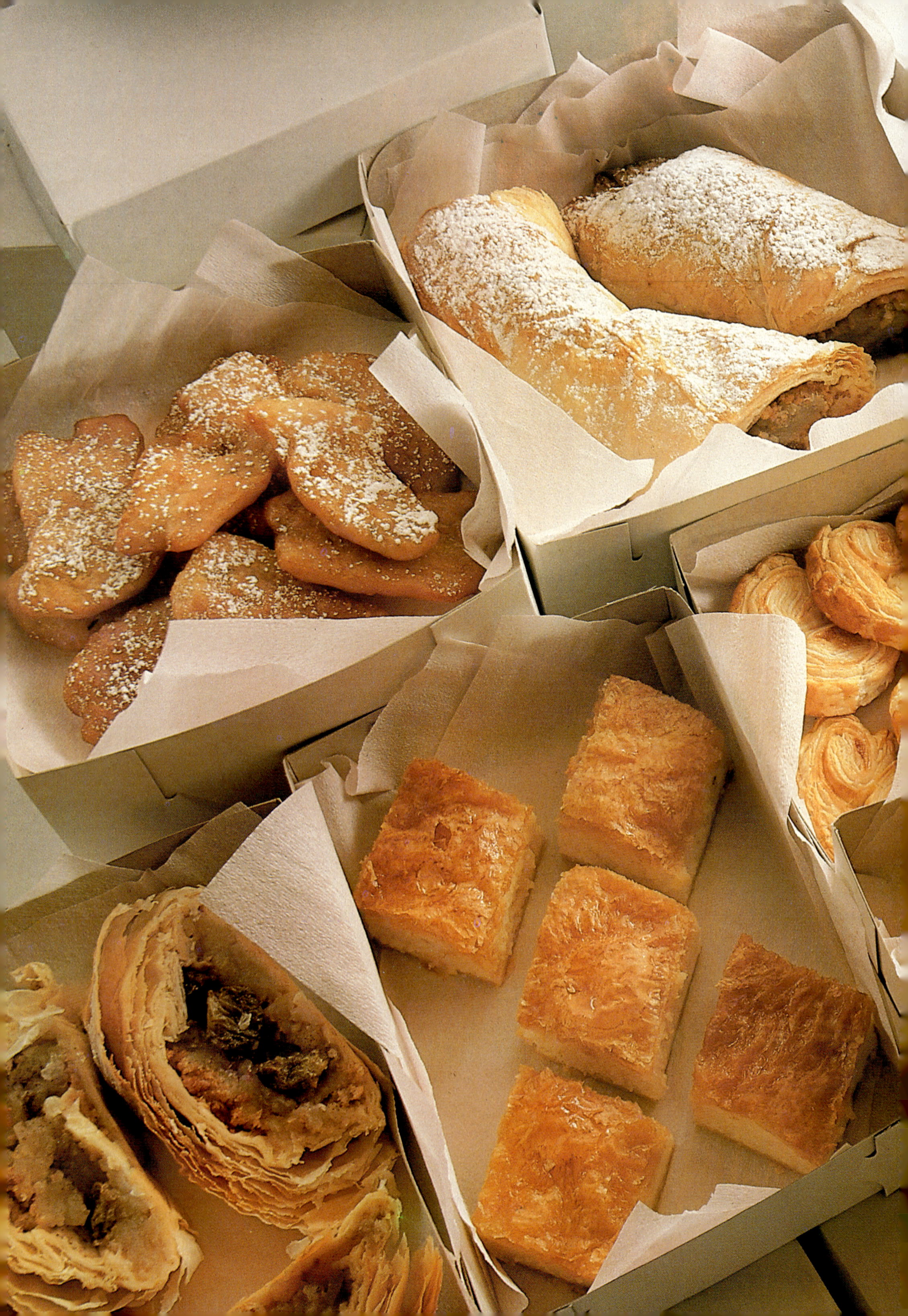

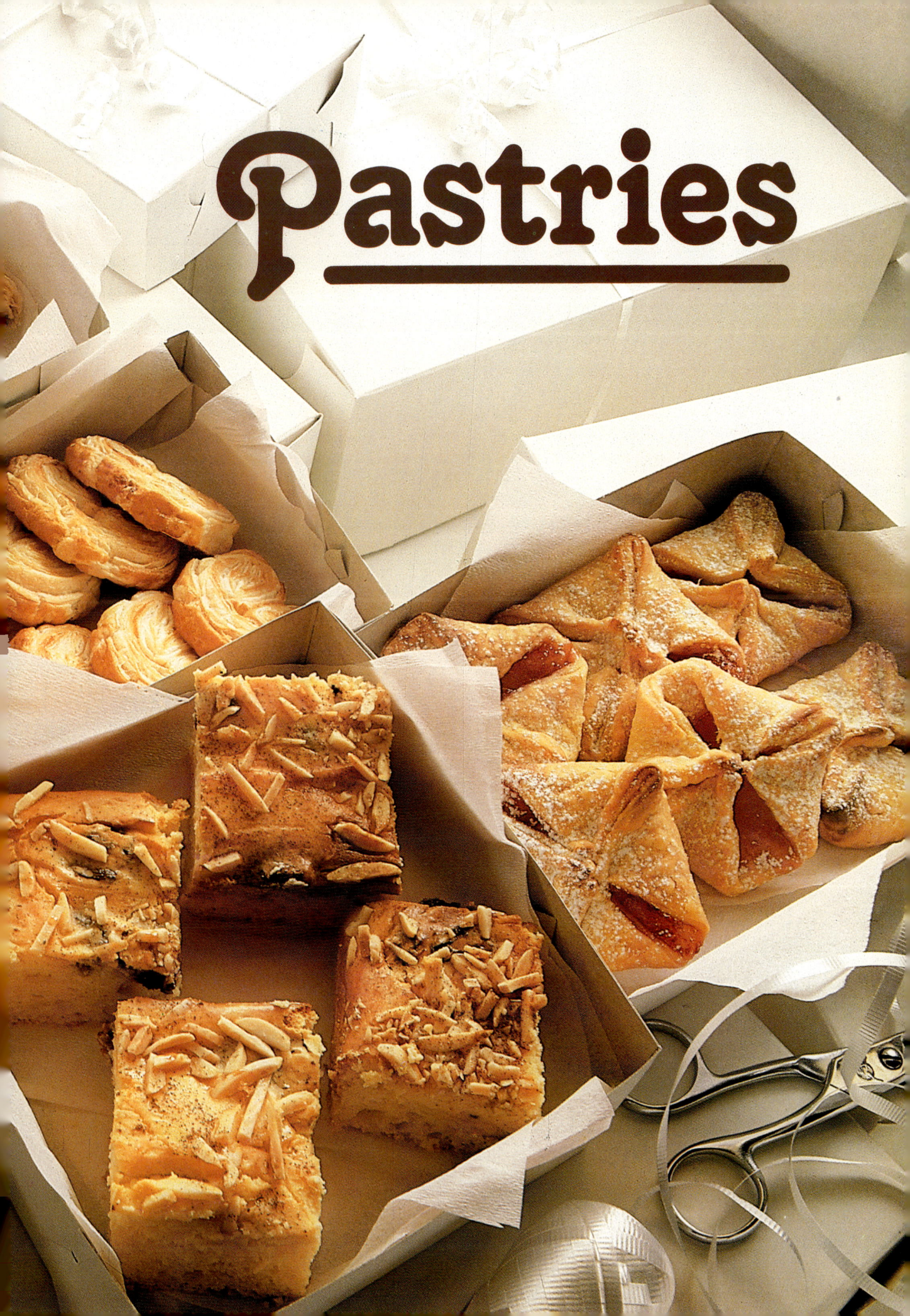

Pastries

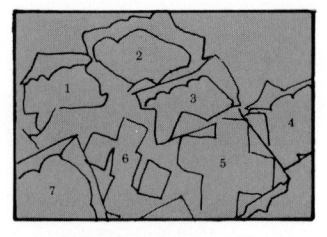

Pastries

1. Honey-sweet Fried Pastries (see p. 220)
2. Traditional Apple Strudel (see p. 208)
3. Palmiers (see p. 213)
4. Cream Cheese and Jelly Puffs (see p. 216)
5. Golden Cheesecake Pastry Squares (see p. 220)
6. Semolina Custard Slice (see p. 201)
7. Traditional Apple Strudel (see p. 208)

The description 'sweet pastries' conjures up different images for different people. Sweet pastries can be crispy-crunchy and feather-light, as in the delicately layered pastry matchsticks, or heavy and lushly sweet in pastries such as baklava.

I have found the written history of sweet pastries to be sketchy. It is not easy even to establish when they first became popular, but it seems reasonable to assume that an unprocessed sweetener, such as honey, would have been used before sugars became readily available.

Over the centuries, each country seems to have established its own particular pièce de résistance among pastries. Baklava is perhaps the best known traditional Greek sweet pastry, but do have a look in the window of a Greek cake shop some time, you'll be dazzled by the lush selection from which to choose. And all at about two thousand kilojoules each, I suspect!

The fame of Danish pastry is, of course, legendary and it is well worth mastering the art of making it. As you'll see, it provides the basis for a whole range of delectable, buttery indulgences. Similar to puff pastry in its ingredients and 'construction', it obviously has its origins in the same source.

One important point to remember in handling these buttery pastries is to keep ingredients, pastry board, rolling pin and hands as cool as possible. One of the old fashioned rolling pins which can be filled with ice cubes or iced water is ideal for pastry making.

Another interesting sweet pastries variation is the fried pastry. The Italian crostini is an example of this type of pastry, and I feel the traditional American doughnut would also have to be included in this category.

An early description of what sounds rather like fried sweet pastries mentions 'lozenges'. Apparently the dough consisted of flour, water, sugar and saffron. It was rolled very thinly, cut into shapes and fried in hot oil. These pastries were served with a syrup made from various alcoholic beverages, dried fruits and generous quantities of spices,—which doesn't sound too different from recipes still in favour today.

Perhaps the most delicate of all sweet pastries is the French millefeuille. This exquisite puff pastry, not sweet in itself, may enclose a variety of delectable fillings, often with whipped cream or custard as one of the components. It is not easy to establish when these delicacies were first introduced to the English table, but reference is made to puff pastry as early as the beginning of the 17th century. Certainly the great French chef, Câréme, did much to enhance the sophisticated presentation—and the popularity—of sweet pastries when he was coaxed to England early in Queen Victoria's reign.

Ann Creber

Sweet Pastry Doughs

Many of the doughs used in sweet pastries are actually made without sweetening. The sweetness is added by the addition of glazing, icing, syrup or by the filling itself. Choux pastry is an example of this. The same basic mixture may be used to create savoury puffs or sweet treats, and of course these versatile puffs are often presented very simply with cream and a dusting of icing sugar or, in the extreme, as the main components in the splendid croquembouche.

Choux pastry is often piped to create decorative shapes, such as swans, which are then filled with a savoury or sweet mixture. However, I must confess that I am not fond of that style of cookery which presents food in another guise, so dear reader, I fear you'll find no choux pastry swans in this chapter!

Far removed from the delicate and fragile French pastries we have already talked about is the sturdy Scottish Black Bun. Despite dipping into a wide range of my Scottish cookbooks, I have not found many recipes which could be described as sweet pastries, but having often eaten 'the Bun' during my childhood, I felt it had to have a place in this chapter.

Many traditional recipes have been altered in their journey down the years, and of course the sweet mince pie we know today is one of these. As in these recipes, many small pastry shapes were baked originally with a filling of sweet ingredients, combined with finely chopped meats. Dates and raisins are frequently mentioned, together with startling ingredients such as bone marrow and finely chopped kidneys.

Banbury cakes, still sold in some suburban cake shops and for which we include a recipe, were served in the 17th century. The name Banbury conjures up evocative word picture of places like Banbury Cross and Banbury Fair, doesn't it? And to me, this is a fascinating dimension of food and cookery. I love to think that those cooks of four centuries ago were preparing and eating the same sweet pastries that I am able to include in a recipe book of the 20th century. Comforting to know that some things don't change, despite the changes in society and cooking implements.

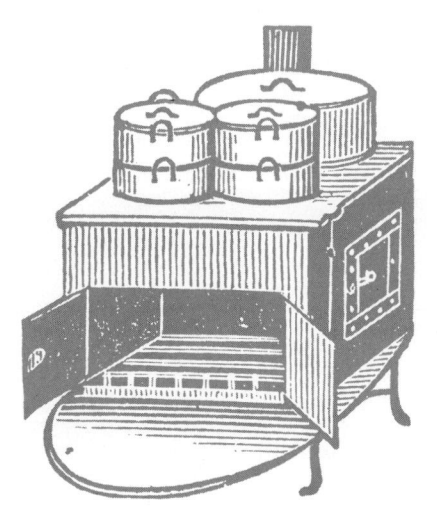

Semolina Custard Slice

500 g (1 lb) filo pastry
185 g (6 oz) unsalted butter, melted
Custard: *8 cups (2 litres) milk*
1½ cups (8 oz) semolina
4 eggs
1 cup (7 oz) sugar
1½ teaspoons vanilla essence
a little grated lemon peel
Syrup: *1¼ cups (9 oz) sugar*
1½ cups (12 fl oz) cold water
rind of ½ lemon
¼ cup (2 fl oz) lemon juice
2 tablespoons honey

Unwrap the filo pastry and spread it flat. (To prevent filo pastry drying out, cover with a damp teatowel whilst using it.) Using an upturned 28 × 25 cm (10 × 11 in) baking tray as a guide, trim pastry to fit into the tray. Grease the baking tray, place a sheet of pastry into the base and brush well with melted butter. Using half the quantity of pastry continue layering and buttering. Set this aside and prepare the custard.

To make the custard, heat the milk in a large saucepan to simmering point, then reduce the heat. Gradually sprinkle the semolina onto the milk, stirring constantly, until the mixture boils and thickens. Reduce the heat to very low, and allow the semolina mixture to simmer gently for 5 minutes, stirring constantly. Remove from the heat and cool slightly.

Beat the eggs thoroughly, with the sugar and vanilla. Gradually add to the semolina mixture and blend in thoroughly.

Allow the mixture to become cold, then pour or spoon it onto the pastry base in the baking tray. Spread evenly. Place a sheet of pastry on the custard, brush well with butter, then continue adding pastry and brushing with butter until all the pastry has been used. Chill until the custard has thickened and is very cold.

Preheat the oven to 220°C (325°F/Gas 7). Bake for 15 minutes, then reduce the oven temperature to 160°C (325°F/Gas 3) and cook for another 40 minutes.

In the meantime, place all the ingredients for the syrup into a large saucepan; stir over a low to moderate heat until the sugar dissolves. Bring to the boil, uncovered, and cook for several minutes. Allow to cool; discard lemon rind.

When the pastry is removed from the oven, cut into squares or diamond shapes. Spoon the syrup over the hot pastry, ensuring that it seeps between the squares or diamond shapes. Cool, then refrigerate until serving time.

Raspberry Crescents

Makes 24

1 cup (4 oz) flour

90 g (3 oz) cream cheese, softened

½ cup (2 oz) soft butter or margarine

¼ cup (3 oz) raspberry conserve

icing (confectioners') sugar, for sprinkling

Sift the flour into a bowl; add the cream cheese and butter, and knead to form a manageable dough. Divide the dough in half, and form into two balls. Wrap and chill overnight.

Next day: On a lightly-floured board, roll out each ball to a circle about 23 cm (9 in) in diameter. Cut each into 12 wedges. Place ½ teaspoon of raspberry conserve on the wide end of each wedge. Roll towards pointed end and shape into a crescent. Arrange crescents on a lightly-greased baking tray.

Bake in a preheated oven at 200°C (400°F/Gas 6) for 10 to 15 minutes or until golden brown. Cool on wire racks, sprinkle with icing sugar. Store in an airtight container (may be frozen for up to 6 months).

Maids of Honour

Makes 24 little cakes

1 quantity shortcrust pastry (see recipe, page 182)

raspberry jam (jelly)

½ cup (2 oz) ground almonds or desiccated coconut

⅓ cup (3 oz) caster (powdered) sugar

60 g (2 oz) ground rice

2 tablespoons self-raising flour

1 large egg

4 tablespoons milk

2 teaspoons honey

¼ teaspoon vanilla essence

Preheat the oven to 160°C (325°F/Gas 3). Grease the patty pans. Roll the pastry out to a thickness of 6 mm (¼ in), and cut to line each patty pan cavity. Place a little jam in each.

Blend together the ground almonds, sugar, ground rice and flour. Beat together the egg, milk, honey and vanilla essence, and combine this with the dry ingredients to form a soft mixture. Spoon the mixture into the pastry-lined patty pans.

Bake for 15 to 20 minutes. Turn out onto wire racks to cool.

Bohemian Pastry Roll

Serves 12–16

Pastry:
250 g (8 oz) cottage cheese

90 g (3 oz) raw sugar

6 tablespoons oil (preferably grapeseed oil)

6 tablespoons milk

1 teaspoon vanilla essence

3 cups (12 oz) self-raising flour

pinch of salt

60 g (2 oz) butter, melted

Filling:
90 g (3 oz) sultanas

60 g (2 oz) currants

60 g (2 oz) blanched, slivered almonds

Lemon Glacé Icing (optional) (see recipe, page 130)

To make the pastry, beat the cheese with the sugar, oil, milk and vanilla essence. Add half the flour and the salt, stir in, then knead in the remainder of the flour. If the dough is sticky, add a little more flour. Roll out into a rectangle about 50 × 30 cm (20 × 12 in) and brush lavishly with the melted butter.

Preheat the oven to 200°C (400°F/Gas 6). Grease a couple of scone trays.

Combine the sultanas, currants and almonds, and sprinkle over the pastry; roll the pastry up. Cut into slices about 2 cm (¾ in) thick. Slightly flatten each slice and place onto the greased tray. Bake for about 15 minutes. Turn onto a wire rack and allow to cool before icing the slices (if desired).

Right: Clockwise from top left: Bohemian Pastry Roll (see above); Raspberry Crescents (see above); Hazelnut Yeast Pastry Roll (see p. 221); Bread Cheesecakes (see p. 209).

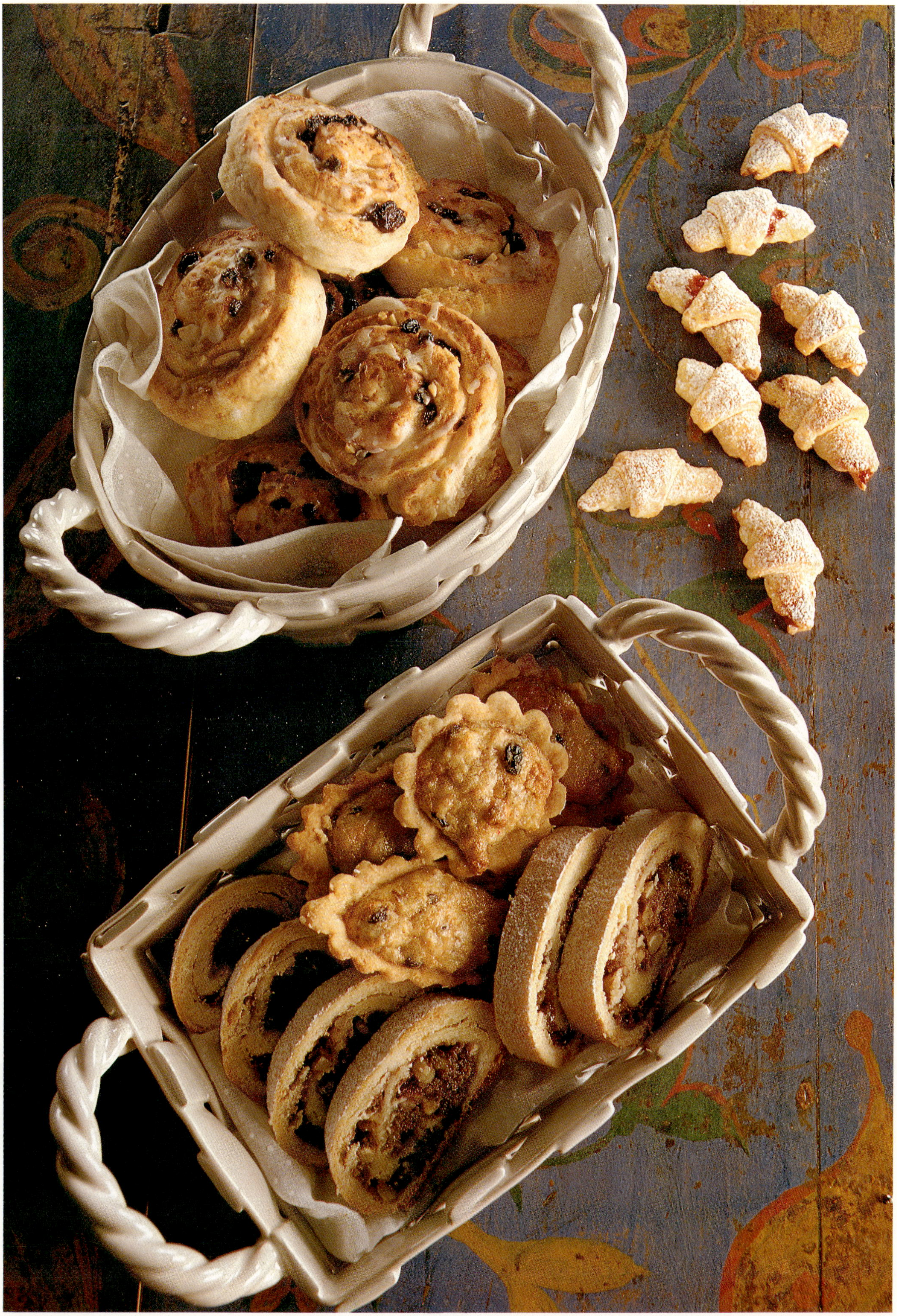

Apricots in Nightdress

Makes 6

500 g (1 lb) puff pastry (see recipe, page 186)

3 medium-sized apricots

2 tablespoons sugar

1 egg white, lightly beaten

icing (confectioners') sugar, for dusting

Preheat the oven to 230°C (450°F/Gas 8). Thoroughly grease a baking tray. Divide the pastry into six portions; roll out to about 3 mm (1/8 in) thick. Cut into squares.

Peel, halve and remove the stones from the apricots. Place an apricot half in the centre of one square of pastry and sprinkle with a little of the sugar. Brush the edges of the pastry with egg white and wrap tightly to encase the apricot half firmly in the pastry. Place on the baking tray, pastry seams down, and brush the top of the pastry with egg white.

Bake for 40 minutes or until golden brown in colour. Dust with icing sugar whilst hot, then allow to cool on a wire rack. Serve warm as a dessert or cold with afternoon tea or coffee.

Boiled Treacle (Molasses) Roly

An old favourite, economical to make and good to eat. The secret of success is to ensure that the water keeps boiling during the cooking time.
Serves 8

250 g (8 oz) suet crust pastry (see recipe, page 189)

4 tablespoons golden syrup (light corn syrup) or treacle

1/4 cup (1 oz) dry breadcrumbs

Roll out the suet crust pastry into an oblong shape about 30 × 20 cm (12 × 8 in). Spread the syrup or treacle over the pastry, leaving a 3 cm (1 in) margin around the border. Sprinkle the syrup with the breadcrumbs. Brush the edges with boiling water, then carefully roll up the pastry, pressing the edges together.

Roll the pastry into a prepared pudding cloth (which has been scalded with boiling water and sprinkled with flour) and tie at each end with string. The centre may be secured by stitching or fastening with a safety pin. Place into boiling water in a saucepan and boil steadily for 1½–2 hours.

When cooked, remove from the pan and carefully release the pastry from the pudding cloth. Allow to cool slightly, then slice into serving portions. Serve with custard or cream.

Apple Rings in Pastry

Makes 8

2 tablespoons butter

2 tablespoons sugar

2 tablespoons currants

2 medium-sized cooking apples

500 g (1 lb) puff pastry (see recipe, page 186)

1 egg white, lightly beaten

Cream the butter and sugar together until pale and fluffy; add the currants and mix thoroughly.

Roll out the pastry to a thickness of about 3 mm (1/8 in).

Peel and core the apples. Slice them crosswise into rings about 1 cm (1/2 in) thick. Place one of the slices onto a 25 × 13 cm (10 × 5 in) strip of pastry, towards one end of the strip. Fill the apple-core cavity with a spoonful of the butter-currant mixture. Wrap the pastry round the apple slice, folding the edges in and sealing with the egg white as it is rolled end-over-end. Make three slashes in the top of the rolled pastry and brush the top and sides with egg white. Repeat until all ingredients are used.

Preheat the oven to 230°C (450°F/Gas 8) and bake for 40 minutes or until rich golden brown in colour. Serve warm with cream or custard.

Peanut Crunch Pastry Slice

Cuts into 16 pieces

125 g (4 oz) sweet shortcrust pastry (see recipe, page 184)

125 g butter (4 oz)

1/3 cup (4 oz) honey

1/3 cup (3 oz) raw sugar

5 cups (4 oz) rice bubbles

2/3 cup (2 oz) desiccated coconut

1/3 cup (2 oz) roasted peanuts

Preheat the oven to 160°C (325°F/Gas 3). Roll the pastry out thinly and fit it into the base of a 23 cm (9 in) square tin; prick all over with a fork. Bake for about 20 minutes. Leave it in the tin to cool.

Peanut Crunch: Melt the butter in a large saucepan. Add the honey and sugar, bring to the boil, then reduce the heat a little and cook for 3 minutes. Mix in the rice bubbles, coconut and peanuts, coating them thoroughly.

Spread the mixture over the cool pastry, pressing firmly in place. Allow it to set, then cut into fingers. When slices are cold, store in an airtight container.

Baked Jam (Jelly) Roly

One of the simple but delicious sweet pastry dishes my Nanna used to make. When the old fruit trees were laden and we were desperate to find ways of using plums, she would sometimes pop a few whole plums in with the plum jam (jelly) she had already made (and used in every possible recipe!).
Serves 6

250 g (8 oz) sweet shortcrust pastry (see recipe, page 184)
6 tablespoons plum jam (jelly)
1 tablespoon caster (powdered) sugar
pure cream
Sweet Glaze: 2 tablespoon water
2 tablespoon sugar

Roll the pastry into a rectangle about 30 × 20 cm (12 × 8 in). Spread with the jam, leaving a 1 cm (½ in) rim all around. Brush the edges lightly with water, roll up like a swiss roll. Place onto a lightly greased oven tray, joined edges underneath.

Preheat the oven to 200°C (400°F/Gas 6).

To make the glaze, combine the sugar and water in a small saucepan, bring to the boil, then cook until of syrupy consistency. Brush the glaze over the unbaked jam roly.

Bake for 15 to 20 minutes, or until golden and crisp. Sprinkle with a little caster (powdered) sugar, if desired, and serve each portion with a spoonful of pure cream. Bliss!

Apricot Delights

Makes 24

1 quantity sweet short pastry (see recipe, page 184)
Filling: 60 g (2 oz) butter
⅓ cup (3 oz) sugar
1 egg
1 cup (4 oz) finely-chopped apricots

Preheat the oven to 190°C (375°F/Gas 5). Roll out the pastry thinly, cut out rounds, and press these into patty pans. Reserve small strips of pastry.

Cream the butter and sugar together, then beat in the egg. Mix in the chopped apricots.

Place a small spoonful of the filling into each pastry-lined patty pan. Place a cross of pastry on the top of each patty. Bake for 20 to 25 minutes. Serve warm or cold.

Bakewell Squares

This is an old favourite, which most people seem to enjoy; a useful standby to have in the cake tin.
Cuts into 12–16 squares

Pastry: 125 g (4 oz) butter
1¾ cup (7 oz) flour
pinch of baking powder
25 ml (1 tablespoon + 1 teaspoon) cold water
½ egg yolk
¼ cup (2 oz) caster (powdered) sugar
Filling: 60 g (2 oz) butter
¼ cup (2 oz) caster (powdered) sugar
1½ eggs
almond essence
½ cup (2 oz) ground almonds
½ cup (2 oz) sponge or white breadcrumbs
raspberry jam (jelly)
icing (confectioners') sugar

Pastry: Blend the butter and 1 cup (4 oz) of flour. Mix the water, egg yolk and sugar together; add to the flour and butter. Work in the remaining flour and baking powder, turn out onto a floured surface and work the mixture together. Refrigerate for 10 to 20 minutes.

Filling: Cream the butter and sugar together thoroughly. Continue mixing and add the beaten eggs gradually. Flavour with the almond essence. Lightly mix in the almonds and crumbs.

To Assemble: Preheat the oven to 180°C (350°F/Gas 4).

Roll out the pastry to 5 mm (¼ in) thick and line a small slice tin. Spread the pastry with the raspberry jam. Place the almond mixture on top and spread evenly.

Bake for 15 to 20 minutes. Dredge with icing sugar, or brush lightly with lemon-glacé icing (see recipe, page 130). Portion into serving slices. Serve cold.

Cream Horns

Makes 12

250 g (8 oz) rough puff pastry (see recipe, page 186)

1 egg white, beaten

¾ cup (6 oz) cream

2 teaspoons caster (powdered) sugar

vanilla essence

strawberry jam (jelly)

pistachio nuts, finely chopped

Lightly grease 12 cream horn moulds and a baking tray. Preheat the oven to 240°C (475°F/Gas 9).

Roll out the pastry to 3 mm (¼ in) thick, cut into strips 2.5 cm (1 in) long; brush these lightly with beaten egg white. Wind the pastry around the cream horn moulds, starting at the point and overlapping each round. Trim the tops, brush again with the egg white, set on the lightly-greased baking tray.

Cook in the preheated oven for 7 to 8 minutes until crisp and golden brown. Remove the horns from the tin.

Whip the cream with the sugar and drops of vanilla essence. When the horns are cold, place ½ teaspoon of jam at the bottom of each horn and fill with the whipped cream. Decorate each horn with a sprinkle of pistachio nuts.

Million Leaves Cake (Match-sticks)

Makes 8 cakes

3 sheets puff pastry, each about 25 × 12 cm (10 × 5 in)

2 tablespoons raspberry jam (jelly)

1 cup (8fl oz) fresh cream

drops of vanilla essence

1 cup (5 oz) icing (confectioners') sugar

water, to mix

Prick each sheet of puff pastry thoroughly with a fork. Cook the three sheets of pastry on separate baking trays in the middle of a moderate oven, 180°C (350°F/Gas 4), until a rich brown colour (20 to 30 minutes). Allow to cool on wire cake racks.

Spread one sheet of pastry with the raspberry jam and place a second sheet on top.

Flavour the fresh cream with a few drops of vanilla essence and whip until stiff. Spread the cream down the length of the pastry. Place the third sheet of pastry on top and press lightly, to spread the encased cream to the edges.

Prepare a spreadable but not over-soft water icing by combining a little water with the icing sugar. (Colour, as required.) Spread over the top layer of pastry and allow to set. Using a serrated knife, slice into serving portions. This is delicious served with afternoon tea or for suppers.

Cream Puffs

Makes 16

½ cup (2 oz) self-raising flour

¼ teaspoon salt

60 g (2 oz) butter

½ cup (4fl oz) water

½ teaspoon sugar

2 eggs

⅔ cup (5fl oz) cream

icing sugar

Sift the flour and salt onto a square of paper and leave in a warm dry place until required.

Preheat the oven to 220°C (425°F/Gas 7). Cut up the butter and place in a saucepan with the water and sugar; bring quickly to a boil. Tip the flour in all at once while the pan is still on the heat. Stir to mix and remove the pan from the heat. Beat the mixture thoroughly until it leaves the sides of the saucepan, then allow it to cool until the hand can be held comfortably against the side of the pot.

Lightly mix the eggs and beat in gradually. When the eggs have been added, the choux paste should appear thick and glossy and just stiff enough to hold its shape when piped. Place the mixture in a piping bag fitted with a 1 cm (½ in) tube and pipe 16 small mounds onto a lightly greased baking tray, allowing 8 cm (3 in) between mounds.

Bake for 20 minutes, then reduce the oven temperature to 180°C (350°F/Gas 4) and cook for a further 10 minutes until golden brown and crisp. Remove from the oven and pierce the bottom of the puffs. Allow to cool on a wire rack.

While the puffs are cooling make the filling. Whip the cream until almost stiff. Do not overbeat.

When the puffs are cold and just before serving, make a slit in each puff, fill with the cream, and dust with icing sugar.

Right: **Cream Horns** (see above); **Match-sticks** (see above).

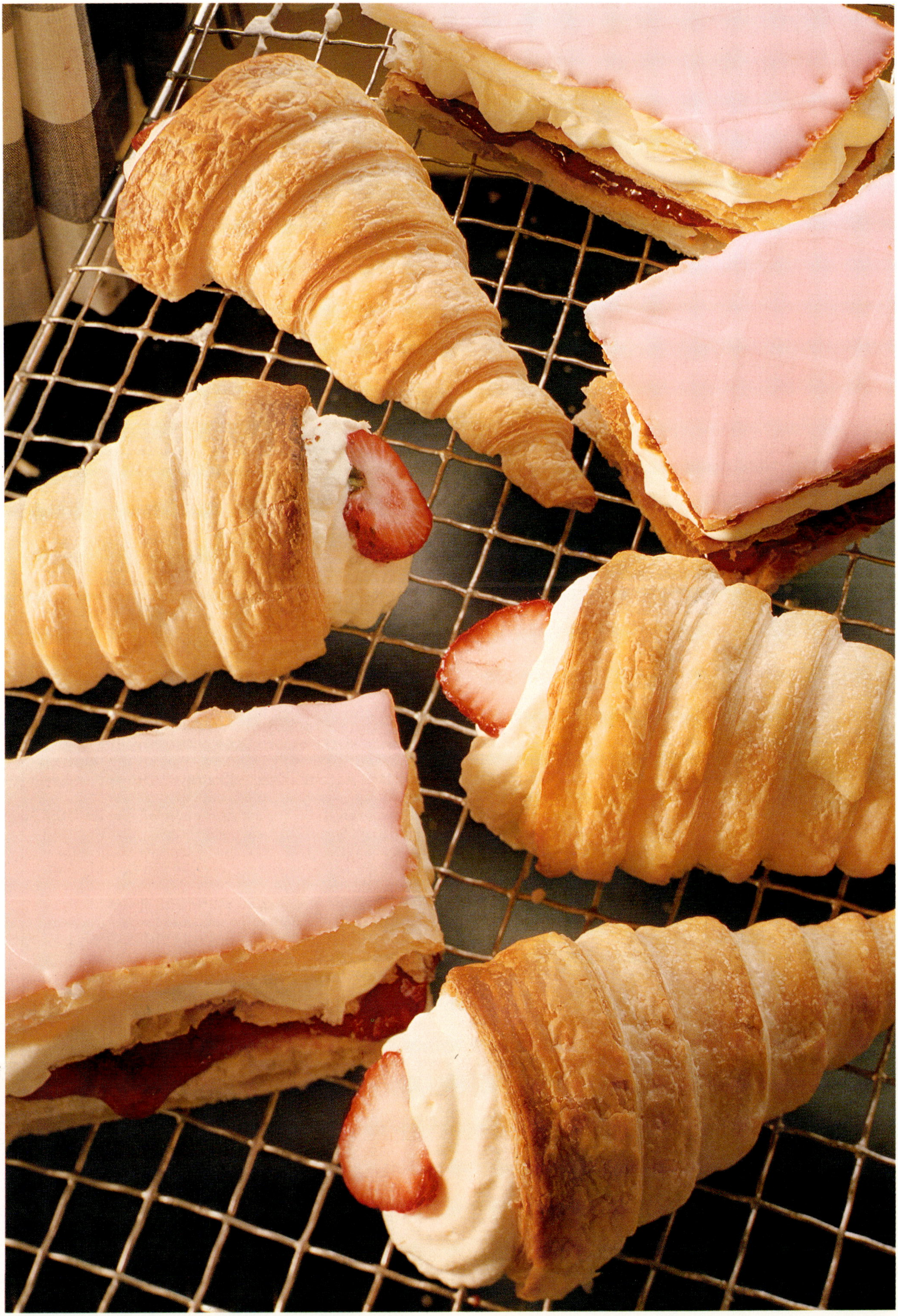

Traditional Apple Strudel

Nowadays we often take advantage of the convenience offered with filo pastry and use it to make our strudels. However, the culinary purists still consider it sacrilege to use any but the authentic dough—so we offer this to the dedicated cooks who have the time and devotion to make this beautiful pastry.

Serves 8–10

Strudel Pastry:
2 cups (8 oz) flour
pinch of salt
1 tablespoon melted butter
1 egg
2/3 cup (5 fl oz) warm water
1 teaspoon lemon juice
additional 3 tablespoons melted butter
icing (confectioners') sugar, for sprinkling
Filling:
15 g (1/2 oz) butter
2 tablespoons fresh white breadcrumbs
500 g (1 lb) cooking apples
1/4 cup (2 oz) sugar
1/2 cup (3 oz) raisins
1 level teaspoon ground cinnamon
finely grated rind of 1/2 lemon

To make the dough, sift the flour and salt into a bowl, and make a well in the centre. Mix 1 tablespoon of melted butter with the egg, warm water and lemon juice, and pour into the dry ingredients. Stir with a wooden spoon, gradually drawing the flour into the well. When well blended, turn the dough onto a lightly-floured board. The dough will be sticky, but flour both hands liberally and knead until it is smooth and elastic. From time to time, slap the dough sharply onto the board. Sprinkle the dough with a little flour and cover it with a large, warmed inverted bowl for 30 minutes (do not allow the bowl to actually touch the dough).

Prepare the Filling: Melt the butter in a pan, stir in the breadcrumbs and fry until golden; set aside. Peel, core and thinly slice the apples; mix with the sugar, raisins, cinnamon and lemon rind; set aside.

After 30 minutes the dough will be 'stretchable'. Place a clean cloth on the bench and sprinkle with flour. Place the dough, floured side down, in the centre of the cloth and carefully roll out thinly. Brush with a little melted butter, then gently slip both hands under the dough and carefully pull it outwards, being very careful not to tear it (always work from the centre outwards). When the dough is paper thin, brush with a little more melted butter and leave for 10 minutes.

Preheat the oven to 190°C (375°F/Gas 5).

To fill the strudel, sprinkle buttered breadcrumbs onto the pastry and arrange the apple mixture evenly ontop. Brush the edges with water, and roll it up like a swiss roll, using the cloth to support it. Very carefully lift it onto a greased baking tray and gently form into a horseshoe shape. Brush with melted butter.

Bake for about 50 minutes. When cold, or at least warm, dredge with icing sugar and cut into slices.

Black Cherry Strudel

Serves 6–8

1 quantity strudel dough (see recipe, page 208)
750 g (1 1/2 lb) black cherries, stoned and drained
125 g (4 oz) soft breadcrumbs, fried in butter
60 g (2 oz) currants
1/2 cup (4 oz) sugar
1/2 teaspoon ground cinnamon
grated rind of 1/2 lemon
125 g (4 oz) butter, melted

Make up the strudel dough, and while it is 'resting' prepare the filling.

Dice the stoned cherries, and gently mix them with all the other ingredients except the butter. When the pastry is ready, trim off any hard or thick outside edges and spread with the cherry filling, leaving approximately 2 cm (3/4 in) uncovered all around the outer edges. Roll the dough and filling very gently and carefully, and pinch the edges together. Carefully place onto a large, buttered baking tray. Brush lavishly with the melted butter.

Preheat the oven to 220°C (425°F/Gas 7). Bake the strudel for 20 minutes, then reduce the oven temperature to moderate, 160°C (325°F/Gas 3), and bake for a further 30 minutes. Brush with melted butter several times during baking.

Serve hot or cold with whipped, slightly sweetened cream.

Cherry Rolls

Makes about 8 rolls

250 g (8 oz) puff pastry (see recipe, page 186)
1 can 425 g (15 oz) red cherries, stones removed and drained
1 tablespoon sugar
egg white
icing (confectioners') sugar

Preheat the oven to 230°C (450°F/Gas 8). Grease a baking tray.

Roll out the puff pastry to about 3 mm (⅛ in) thick. Cut into squares 13 × 13 cm (5 × 5 in); and brush all four edges of each square with egg white.

Place a single row of cherries in the centre of each pastry square. Roll the pastry to sufficiently cover the cherries, and secure the side edges by folding in and pressing firmly. Continue to roll until the pastry forms a neat tight roll. Brush the top and edges generously with egg white.

Bake for about 20 minutes. When golden brown, remove from the oven and dust with icing sugar. Serve warm or cold. Cherry Rolls are best eaten the day they are baked.

Bread Cheesecakes

Makes 12 little cakes

125 g (4 oz) short or rough puff pastry (see recipes, page 182 and 186)
125 g (4 oz) white breadcrumbs
60 g (2 oz) sugar
pinch of grated nutmeg
150 ml (5 fl oz) milk
30 g (1 oz) butter
60 g (2 oz) currants
grated lemon rind
2 eggs
2 tablespoons jam (jelly)

Roll out the pastry. Cut into rounds, large enough to line the cavities in a small patty pan tin. Line each cavity. Preheat the oven to 200°C (400°F/Gas 6).

Combine the breadcrumbs, sugar and nutmeg. Heat the milk and butter in a small saucepan until boiling, then add to the breadcrumb mixture. Add the currants and a little lemon rind, and mix thoroughly.

Separate the yolks from the whites of the egg. Lightly whisk the yolks and add to the breadcrumb-currant mixture.

Put a little jam in the bottom of each pastry case.

Beat the egg whites to a firm peak; fold into the mixture using a metal spoon. Put a generous teaspoonful of the prepared mixture into each pastry case.

Bake for 20 minutes or until the centre is firm and golden in colour. Remove the cakes from the oven, slightly, then carefully turn onto a wire rack to cool completely. Serve cold.

Coconut Apple Slice

Cuts into about 16 fingers

Pastry Base: 125g (4 oz) butter or margarine
½ cup (4 oz) raw sugar
1 cup (4 oz) flour
1 teaspoon mixed spice
Topping: 2 eggs
1 cup (7 oz) raw sugar
1 cup (4 oz) roughly chopped walnuts
½ cup (1½ oz) desiccated coconut
1 tablespoon flour
1 teaspoon vanilla essence
1–1½ cups (2–3 oz) dried apples, lightly cooked in water and drained

Preheat the oven to 180°C (350°F/Gas 4). Thoroughly grease a baking tin 28 × 18 cm (11 × 7 in).

To make the pastry, cream the butter and sugar together; stir in the flour and spice. Spread the mixture into the prepared baking tin. Bake for 20 minutes. Remove from the oven and allow to cool for 10 minutes.

In the meantime, prepare the topping. Beat together the eggs and sugar; stir in the walnuts, coconut, flour and vanilla essence.

Spoon the cooked and drained apples in an even layer onto the semi-cooked pastry base. Spread the topping mixture over the apples.

Bake in the preheated oven for about 25 minutes or until the topping is brown. May be cut into fingers and served as biscuits, or cut into large squares and served warm, with cream or custard, as a dessert.

Danish Pastry

Variation 1

Some recipes seem to maintain a certain mystique—soufflés, breads and most yeast pastries such as brioche and croissants fall into this category. So too do Danish pastries and timid cooks avoid them, which is a pity. They aren't difficult to make and the satisfaction of producing these Danish delights is equalled only by the bliss of eating them.

Basic recipe which makes about 12 crescents

2½ cups (10 oz) flour
pinch of ground cardamom
15 g (½ oz) butter
pinch of salt
⅔ cup (5 fl oz) milk
6 teaspoons (1 oz) sugar
½ lightly-beaten egg
30 g (1 oz) fresh yeast or 15 g (½ oz) dried yeast
220 g (7 oz) cooking margarine
egg white, for glazing
caster (powdered) sugar, for sprinkling

Rub the cardamom-scented flour and butter together. In a separate bowl, mix the salt, milk, sugar, egg and yeast together. Combine the dry mixture and the liquid mixture, being careful not to overmix.

Soften the margarine slightly, and encase the margarine with the dough. Roll out and fold in three. Roll out again, and fold into two. Place the two halves together and roll again. Fold in three. Allow to rest for 15 minutes.

Danish Pastry Crescents: Preheat the oven to 200°C (400°F/Gas 6).

Roll the pastry out thinly and cut into triangle shapes. Moisten the edges with water; and roll each pastry piece, starting from the long edge on the bottom of the triangle, towards the point at the top. Curve into a crescent shape. Brush the surface with egg white and dust with caster sugar. Place on ungreased baking trays.

Bake for 15 to 20 minutes. Serve warm or allow to cool on wire racks.

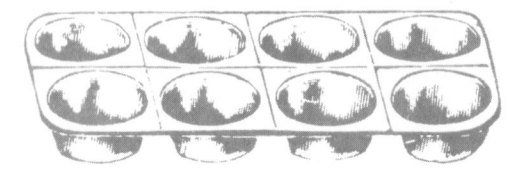

Danish Pastry

Variation 2

Basic recipe which makes about 15 small pastries

3 cups (12 oz) flour
pinch of salt
30 g (1 oz) fresh yeast or 15 g (½ oz) dried yeast
2 tablespoons caster (powdered) sugar
¾ cup (6 fl oz) lukewarm milk
1 egg, beaten
250 g (8 oz) butter: 60 g (2 oz) melted, and the remainder chilled

Sift the flour and salt into a large bowl. In a smaller bowl, cream together the yeast and 1 teaspoon of the sugar; add the beaten egg, milk and 60 g of the melted butter. (Chill the rest of the butter.) Make a well in the centre of the flour and add the liquid ingredients slowly. Mix to a smooth dough and knead lightly. Cover and leave at room temperature for 1 hour or until doubled in bulk.

Punch down the dough and turn onto a floured board; knead lightly. Roll out to an oblong shape. Cut one-third of the chilled butter into small pieces and spread these over two-thirds of the dough.

Fold into three, folding the bottom third up and the top third over it. Half turn the dough (so that an open end faces you and the top is now on the right side) and roll out again to an oblong. Spread with the second quantity of butter, fold and leave for 15 minutes. Repeat with the last portion of the butter, roll out and fold in half. Cover with cling film and refrigerate for several hours or overnight.

Fillings and cooking methods are included in the recipes that follow.

Right: Danish Pastries. Top basket left: Danish Cockscombs (see p. 213); Danish Crème Buns (see p. 213). Top basket right: Danish Cartwheels (see p. 212); Danish Crescent Moons (see p. 213). Bottom Basket: Danish Whirlygigs (see p. 212).

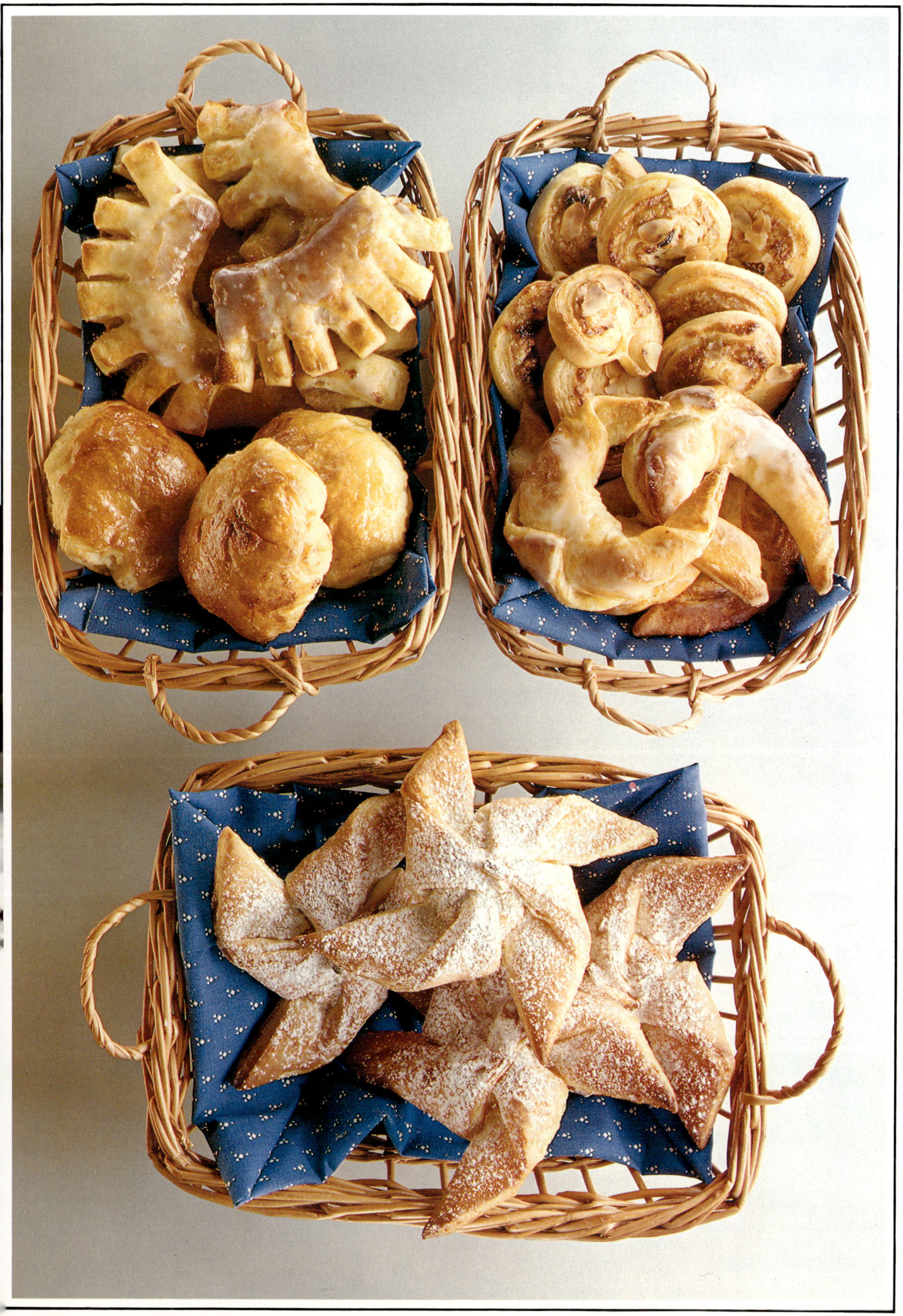

DANISH PASTRY FILLINGS

Almond Filling

60 g (2 oz) ground almonds

3 tablespoons caster (powdered) sugar

½ lightly-beaten egg

2 drops almond essence

Mix all the ingredients in a bowl, ready for use.

Apple Marmalade

500 g (1 lb) Granny Smith apples

strip of lemon peel

good squeeze of lemon juice

½ cup (4 oz) raw sugar

Cut cored but unpeeled apples into very thick wedges, and place into a well-buttered saucepan. Add lemon rind and juice. Cover the saucepan with a lid and cook over very low heat, stirring often, until the apples are soft. Put through a sieve or blender.

Rinse out the saucepan, return the apple mixture to it, add the sugar, and cook over a moderate heat, stirring often, until thick. Spoon into a bowl and chill before use.

Crème Pâtissière

1 egg, separated

1 extra egg yolk

¼ cup (2 oz) caster (powdered) sugar

1½ tablespoons flour

1 flat tablespoon cornflour (cornstarch)

1½ cups (12 fl oz) milk

2–3 drops vanilla essence

In a basin, blend the two egg yolks with the caster sugar, flour and cornflour to make a smooth paste. (If necessary, add a tablespoon of cold milk.) In a saucepan, bring the 1½ cups of milk to the boil; add to the egg yolk mixture, whisking constantly. Add the vanilla essence and pour the mixture back into the saucepan. Cook gently, stirring constantly, until the mixture thickens.

Whisk the egg white until stiff; fold into the custard mixture.

Danish Whirlygigs

Makes about 12

1 quantity Danish pastry (see recipe, page 210)

⅔ quantity almond filling (see recipe, page 212)

beaten egg, for glazing

icing (confectioners') sugar, for sprinkling

Preheat the oven to 220°C (425°F/Gas 7). Grease the baking trays.

Roll the pastry into a large rectangle. Cut into 13 cm (5 in) squares. Snip from each corner to within 1 cm (⅜ in) of the centre of each square. Place a spoonful of almond filling in the middle, then take alternate points to the centre. Place on the prepared tray(s) and allow to stand at room temperature for about 15 minutes. Brush the pastry with the beaten egg.

Bake for 20 to 25 minutes. Turn onto wire racks to cool. To serve, dust with icing sugar.

Danish Cartwheels

Makes about 12

1 quantity Danish pastry (see recipe, page 210)

1 quantity almond filling (see recipe, page 212)

⅓ cup (2 oz) raisins, chopped

beaten egg, for glazing

30 g (1 oz) flaked almonds, for sprinkling

Roll the pastry out to a large rectangle 35 × 23 cm (14 × 9 in). Spread with the almond filling and sprinkle with the chopped raisins. Roll the pastry up (like a swiss roll) and cut into slices 6 mm (1 in) thick. Place cut-side down on a greased baking tray. Allow to stand at room temperature for 15 to 20 minutes.

Preheat the oven to 220°C (425°F/Gas 7). Glaze the 'cartwheels' with beaten egg, and sprinkle with almonds. Bake for 20 to 25 minutes. Turn onto wire racks to cool.

Danish Cockscombs

Makes about 12

1 quantity Danish pastry (see recipe, page 210)
1 quantity apple marmalade, or almond filling (see recipes, page 212)
beaten egg, for glazing
2 tablespoons caster (powdered) sugar, for sprinkling

Roll out the pastry and cut into rectangles 13 × 9 cm (5 × 3½ in). With the long side facing you, spoon the filling along the lower edge. Brush the top edge with the beaten egg and fold over. Make about 6 incisions along the uncut edge and form the rectangles into crescent shapes. Place onto a greased baking tray and allow to stand at room temperature for 15 minutes.

Preheat the oven to 220°C (425°F/Gas 7). Glaze the pastries with the beaten egg and sprinkle with the caster sugar. Bake for 20 to 25 minutes. Turn on to wire racks to cool.

Danish Crescent Moons

Makes about 12

1 quantity Danish pastry (see recipe, page 210)
1 quantity apple marmalade (see recipe, page 212)
beaten egg, for glazing

Roll the pastry into a large circle about 3 mm (½ in) thick. Cut into wedge shapes, about 8 cm (3 in) at the outer edge. Place a teaspoon of apple marmalade filling at the base; roll up from the base towards the tip. Gently bend into crescents and arrange on a greased baking tray. Allow to stand at room temperature for about 15 minutes.

Preheat the oven to 220°C (425°F/Gas 7). Glaze the pastries with the beaten egg. Bake for 20 to 25 minutes. Turn onto wire racks to cool.

Danish Crème Buns

Makes about 12

1 quantity Danish pastry (see recipe, page 210)
⅔ quantity Crème Pâtissière (see recipe, page 146)
beaten egg, for glazing
Glacé Icing: 1½ cups (3 oz) icing (confectioners') sugar
2 tablespoons (approx.) warm water, or orange juice
flavouring and colouring to taste

Roll the pastry out into a rectangle, and cut into 15 cm (6 in) squares. Place a generous teaspoonful of Crème Pâtissière in the centre of each. Fold four corners around the filling, ensuring it is completely covered. Place on a greased baking tray, with folds underneath. Allow to stand at room temperature for 15 minutes.

Preheat the oven to 220°C (425°F/Gas 7). Glaze the pastry with the beaten egg, and bake for 15–20 minutes.

To prepare the glacé icing: Sift the icing sugar. Mix with warm liquid, adding sufficient liquid to make the icing coat the back of spoon without slipping off too easily. Beat well. Add flavouring and colouring to taste.

(*Note:* 1 tablespoon of butter or margarine may be added, if desired.)

Ice the buns while they are still warm.

Palmiers

Makes 8

250 g (8 oz) puff pastry (see recipe, page 186)
1 egg, beaten
¼ cup (2 oz) caster (powdered) sugar
⅔ cup/150 ml (5fl oz) cream, whipped

Roll out the pastry to a thickness of 3 mm (⅛ in) and a rectangle 30 cm (12 in) long. Brush with some of the beaten egg and sprinkle with some caster sugar. Fold over the pastry 5 cm (2 in) at each end, and then fold again so that the folds meet in the middle. Fold again to make a roll of 6 folds thickness.

Preheat the oven to 200°C (400°F/Gas 6). Cut the pastry roll into 1 cm (⅜ in) wide slices. Dip each side into the remaining beaten egg and then dust with caster sugar.

Place the slices on a greased baking tray and pinch the end of each to make a heart shape. Bake for 15 minutes. Allow to cool, and serve with the whipped cream.

Ecclefechan

Another of my Scottish Nanna's old-fashioned delights!
Makes 24

1 quantity sweet shortcrust pastry (see recipe, page 184)
2 eggs
125 g (4 oz) butter, melted
1 cup (6 oz) soft brown sugar
1 tablespoon vinegar
250 g (8 oz) mixed dried fruits
½ cup (2 oz) chopped walnuts

Preheat the oven to 190°C (375°F/Gas 5).
Roll the pastry out thinly and cut to fit into small patty pan tins. Grease the patty pans before lining them with the pastry.
Beat the eggs, add the melted butter, the sugar and vinegar. Mix thoroughly, then stir in the mixed fruits and nuts. Place a generous spoonful of the mixture into each pastry-lined patty pan.
Bake for about 20 minutes. Serve warm or cold.

Eccles Cakes

Makes 12

250 g (8 oz) puff pastry (see recipe, page 186)
60 g (2 oz) butter
¼ cup (2 oz) sugar
⅓ cup (2 oz) sultanas
⅓ cup (2 oz) candied peel
⅓ cup (2 oz) currants
pinch of mixed spice
grated rind and juice of 1 lemon
extra sugar and water, or 1 egg white, for glazing

Preheat the oven to 200°C (400°F/Gas 6). Roll the pastry out and cut into large rounds about the size of a saucer.
Cream the butter and sugar together and add the remaining ingredients. Place a spoonful of this mixture into the centre of each pastry round, then pick up all the edges. Seal the edges with water, then turn the round upside down and flatten with a rolling pin. Cut two or three slashes on the top and brush the surface with water and sugar, or egg white, to glaze.
Place on greased baking trays and bake for about 20 minutes or until golden brown. Allow to cool on wire racks.

Coconut Slice

Almost an Australian classic—as familiar to most households as the beloved 'pav' and lamingtons.
Cuts into about 16 squares

Pastry: 90 g (3 oz) butter
¼ cup (2 oz) sugar
1 egg
1¼ cups (5 oz) plain flour
¼ cup (1 oz) self-raising flour
Topping: 2 egg whites
1 cup (7 oz) sugar
½ teaspoon vanilla essence
3 cups (9 oz) desiccated coconut
raspberry jam (jelly)

Pastry: Beat the butter until creamy; add the sugar and beat until combined. Add the egg; beat well. Add the sifted flours; mix well. Press into a greased 23 cm (9 in) slab tin; prick the surface lightly. Refrigerate for 15 minutes.
Preheat the oven to 180°C (350°F/Gas 4).

Topping: Beat the egg whites until soft peaks form. Gradually add the sugar, beating well after each addition. Stir in the vanilla essence and coconut; mix well.
Spread a thin layer of raspberry jam over the pastry. Spoon the coconut mixture over this, spreading out evenly.
Bake for 25 to 30 minutes, or until the coconut topping is golden brown. Allow to cool in the tin, then cut into serving portions.

Right: **Clockwise from top: Eccles Cakes (see above); Vanilla Slices (see p. 216); Coconut Slice (see above).**

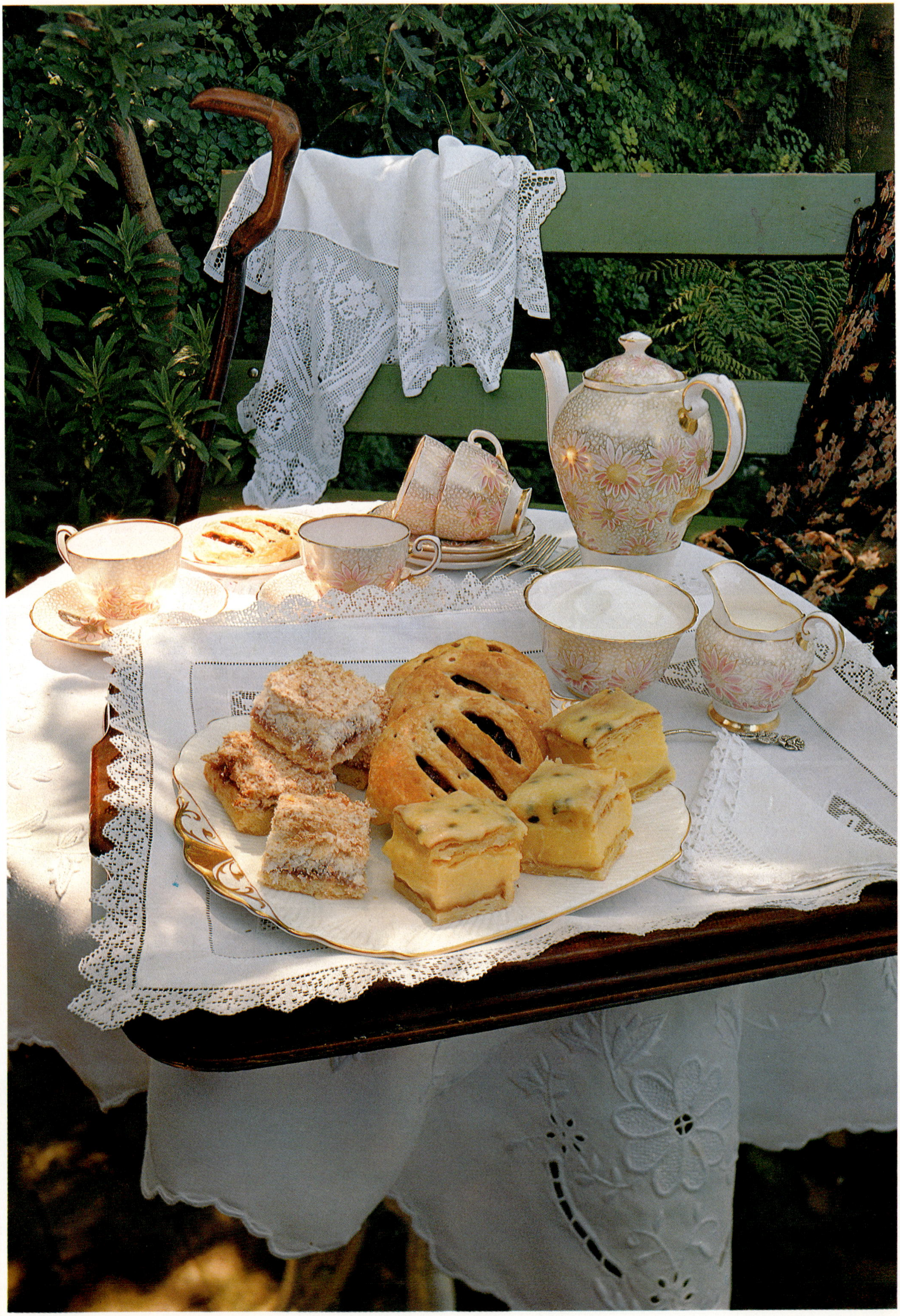

Vanilla Slices

Cuts into about 16 pieces

500 g (1 lb) puff pastry (see recipe, page 186)
1 cup (7 oz) sugar
¾ cup (3 oz) cornflour (cornstarch)
½ cup (2 oz) custard powder
1 litre (32fl oz) milk
60 g (2 oz) butter
2 egg yolks, beaten
2 teaspoons vanilla essence
Passionfruit Icing: *1 cup (5 oz) icing (confectioners') sugar*
1 teaspoon softened butter
pulp of 1 passionfruit
1 teaspoon water (approx.)

Bring the pastry to room temperature. Divide it in half, and roll each piece to a 33 cm (13 in) square; then with a sharp knife, trim each to a 30 cm (12 in) square.

Place one pastry square on a large ungreased oven tray, and bake in a preheated oven at 240°C (475°F/Gas 9) for 5 to 10 minutes, or until well browned. Trim the pastry with a sharp knife to 23 cm (9 in) square. Bake and trim the other pastry square in the same way. Flatten the 'puffy' side of both pieces of pastry with your hand.

Line a 23 cm (9 in) square slab tin with aluminim foil, bringing the foil up over the sides (this makes it easy to remove the vanilla slice when set). Place one piece of pastry into the base of the tin, flattened side uppermost.

Place the sugar, cornflour and custard powder in a heavy-based saucepan, mixing well to combine. Blend with a little of the milk until smooth, then stir in the remaining milk and add the butter. Stir the mixture constantly over heat until the custard boils and thickens; then reduce the heat, and simmer for 3 minutes. Remove from heat, quickly stir in the vanilla essence then stir in the beaten egg yolks. Pour the hot custard immediately over the pastry in the tin. Place the other pastry square ontop of the custard so that the flattened side touches the hot custard. Press the pastry firmly with your hand. Allow to cool.

To prepare the passionfruit icing: Sift the icing sugar into a small bowl. Add the softened butter and passionfruit pulp. Add enough water (about 1 teaspoonful) to make an icing of a thick spreading consistency; beat well. Spread over the pastry surface when the custard filling has cooled.

Refrigerate for several hours (or overnight) until set. Cut into serving portions.

Coconut Cheesecakes

Makes 12 little cakes

125 g (4 oz) rough puff pastry *(see recipe, page 186)*
60 g (2 oz) butter
¼ cup (2 oz) caster (powdered) sugar
1 egg
30 g (1 oz) rice flour
⅔ cup (2 oz) desiccated coconut
¼ teaspoon baking powder
jam (jelly)

Preheat the oven to 200°C (400°F/Gas 6). Roll out the pastry very thinly and cut rounds to line 12 buttered patty pans.

Cream the butter and sugar together. Add the egg and rice flour, beat well; and finally add the coconut and baking powder. Put a little jam on the pastry in each patty case and half-fill the cases with the mixture.

Bake for 20 minutes or until the centre of each little cake is firm and golden in colour.

Cream Cheese and Jelly Puffs

Makes 12

1 cup (4 oz) flour
125 g (4 oz) butter
125 g (4 oz) cream cheese
⅓ cup (4 oz) jam or fruit jelly
a little chopped fresh mint
icing sugar, for sprinkling

Preheat the oven to 220°C (425°F/Gas 7). Grease a couple of baking trays.

Sift the flour onto a pastry board (a marble slab is wonderful, if you own such a treasure). Cut the butter into small cubes; then lightly 'crumble' the cream cheese and butter cubes into the flour, handling as lightly and as little as possible. Press lightly into a ball, using fingertips only.

Roll the dough out to 6 mm (¼ in) thickness and cut into about 12 squares. Spoon a portion of the jam or fruit jelly into the centre of each, sprinkle with a little chopped mint. Gather up the four corners of the pastry, twist on top and press the edges firmly together. Place on the lightly-greased baking tray(s). Bake for 15 minutes. Serve hot, sprinkled with icing sugar.

Currant Fingers

Cuts into about 18 pieces

Pastry:
2½ cups (10 oz) flour

pinch of salt

185 g (6 oz) butter

½ cup (4fl oz) iced water (approx.)

1 egg white, for glazing

caster (powdered) sugar

Filling:
90 g (3 oz) butter

⅓ cup (2 oz) brown sugar, firmly packed

1 tablespoon golden syrup (light corn syrup)

1 tablespoon marmalade

1 tablespoon flour

1 teaspoon powdered cinnamon

2½ cups (12 oz) currants

Pastry: Sift the flour and salt into a basin. Grate the butter over the flour, stir in with a knife. Stir in enough iced water with a knife to give a firm, pliable dough. Refrigerate for 30 minutes.

Filling: Combine all the filling ingredients in a saucepan, stir over low heat until the butter is melted and the ingredients are combined. Allow the mixture to become cold.

To Assemble: Preheat the oven to 190°C (375°F/Gas 5). Grease a 28 × 18 cm (11 × 7 in) shallow tin.

Roll out two-thirds of the pastry to line the base and sides of the greased tin. Spread this evenly with the cold filling; top with the remaining pastry. Glaze the surface lightly with beaten egg white and sprinkle with caster sugar.

Bake for 25 minutes or until golden brown. When cold, remove from the tin and cut into fingers.

Date Oatmeal Pastry Slices

A nutritious treat for lunch boxes.
Cuts into about 36 slices.

Filling:
2¾ cups (14 oz) chopped dates

⅔ cup (5fl oz) water

2 tablespoons lemon juice

grated peel of 1 lemon

grated peel of ½ orange

Pastry:
155 g (5 oz) butter or margarine

1 cup (7 oz) raw sugar

2 cups (8 oz) wholemeal flour

1 heaped teaspoon bicarbonate of soda (baking soda)

pinch of salt

2½ cups (7 oz) rolled oats

Filling: Mix all the ingredients. Cook for 5 minutes over low heat, stirring constantly until the mixture is smooth and thick. Allow to cool before putting onto pastry.

Preheat the oven to 180°C (350°F/Gas 4).

To Make the Pastry: Work the butter (or margarine), sugar, flour, soda and salt into a crumbly mixture. Add the rolled oats, and mix well. Press half of the mixture into a well-greased baking tin and pat lightly into place.

Spread the cooled date filling onto the pastry. Top with a layer of the rest of the pastry mixture, pressing gently into place.

Bake in the preheated oven for about 35 minutes. Allow to cool, then cut into 8 × 3 cm (3 × 1 in) bars.

Healthy Baklava

We owe much to the culture of ancient Greece but we must also give contemporary Greece credit for having added so many culinary delights to our cuisine. Greek migrants have introduced us to many 'new' foods, and the wickedly delicious Baklava must be included in this category. I developed this 'healthy' version for my Health Food Cooking class, and it proved very popular.

Cuts into about 20 pieces

---

1 cup (4 oz) chopped walnuts

1 cup (4 oz) chopped almonds or hazelnuts

60 g (2 oz) lecithin meal

2¼ tablespoons/45 g (1½ oz) raw sugar

2 tablespoons toasted wheat germ

1 teaspoon ground cinnamon

pinch of ground cloves

about 17–18 sheets filo pastry

185 g (6 oz) unsalted butter, melted

Honey Syrup:
1 cup (8fl oz) water

¾ cup (9 oz) honey

1–2 tablespoons lemon juice

piece of cinnamon stick

3 whole cloves

Mix together the walnuts, almonds, lecithin meal, sugar, wheat germ, cinnamon and cloves.

Lightly butter the base of a large shallow oven dish or baking tin. Place a sheet of filo pastry into the dish, brush with melted butter and repeat with seven more sheets, brushing each with butter. Spread half the nut mixture over this.

Cover with two more sheets of pastry, brushing each with butter. Spread the remainder of the nut mixture onto the pastry. Place seven or eight more sheets of pastry on top, brushing each with butter, including the top layer.

Using a very sharp knife, neatly trim away any pastry overlapping the edges of the dish. Mark diamond patterns in the surface, cutting through the top couple of layers of pastry. Sprinkle with a little cold water (this creates a crispy, delicious surface).

Bake on a low shelf in the oven 160°C (325°F/Gas 3) for about 30 minutes, then move the dish up to a higher shelf and bake for another 30 minutes. Remove from the oven and cut the Baklava into diamond shapes. Whilst still hot, spoon the honey syrup over the top.

To make the honey syrup: In a saucepan mix together all the ingredients, bring to the boil, then simmer for about 10 minutes. Strain, and pour over the Baklava.

Allow to stand for at least 4 hours before serving with coffee or as a dessert.

Fruit Cream Puffs

Makes 24

---

1 quantity choux pastry
(see recipe, page 194)

⅔ cup (5½fl oz) cream, whipped

sliced bananas, strawberries or blackberries

icing (confectioners') sugar, for dusting

Place small mounds of choux pastry onto a greased baking tray. Cook in a preheated oven at 190°C (375°F/Gas 5) for 10 minutes, then reduce the oven temperature and continue baking until dry and crisp (about 30 minutes).

Split each puff as soon as it is cooked, in order to allow the steam to escape.

When cold, fill with the whipped cream blended with the sliced bananas, strawberries or blackberries. Dust the surface with icing sugar; or alternatively, pour a thin soft icing over the puffs and decorate with a piece of fruit rolled in caster (powdered) sugar.

Honey Nut Pastry Rolls

Makes 20

---

1 quantity short pastry (see recipe, page 182) to which ½ teaspoon cinnamon has been added

2 tablespoons honey

¼ cup (1 oz) chopped walnuts or almonds

⅓ cup (2 oz) raisins

⅓ cup (2 oz) sultanas

2 tablespoons (1 oz) mixed peel

½ teaspoon mixed spice

beaten egg, or milk, for glazing

Preheat the oven to 190°C (375°F/Gas 4).

Roll the pastry out thinly into an oblong shape. Spread with the honey. Sprinkle with the nuts, fruits, peel and spice. Roll up; cut into slices 4 cm (1½ in) thick. Place on a greased baking tray and glaze with the egg or milk.

Bake for 15 to 20 minutes.

Right: **Healthy Baklava** (see above).

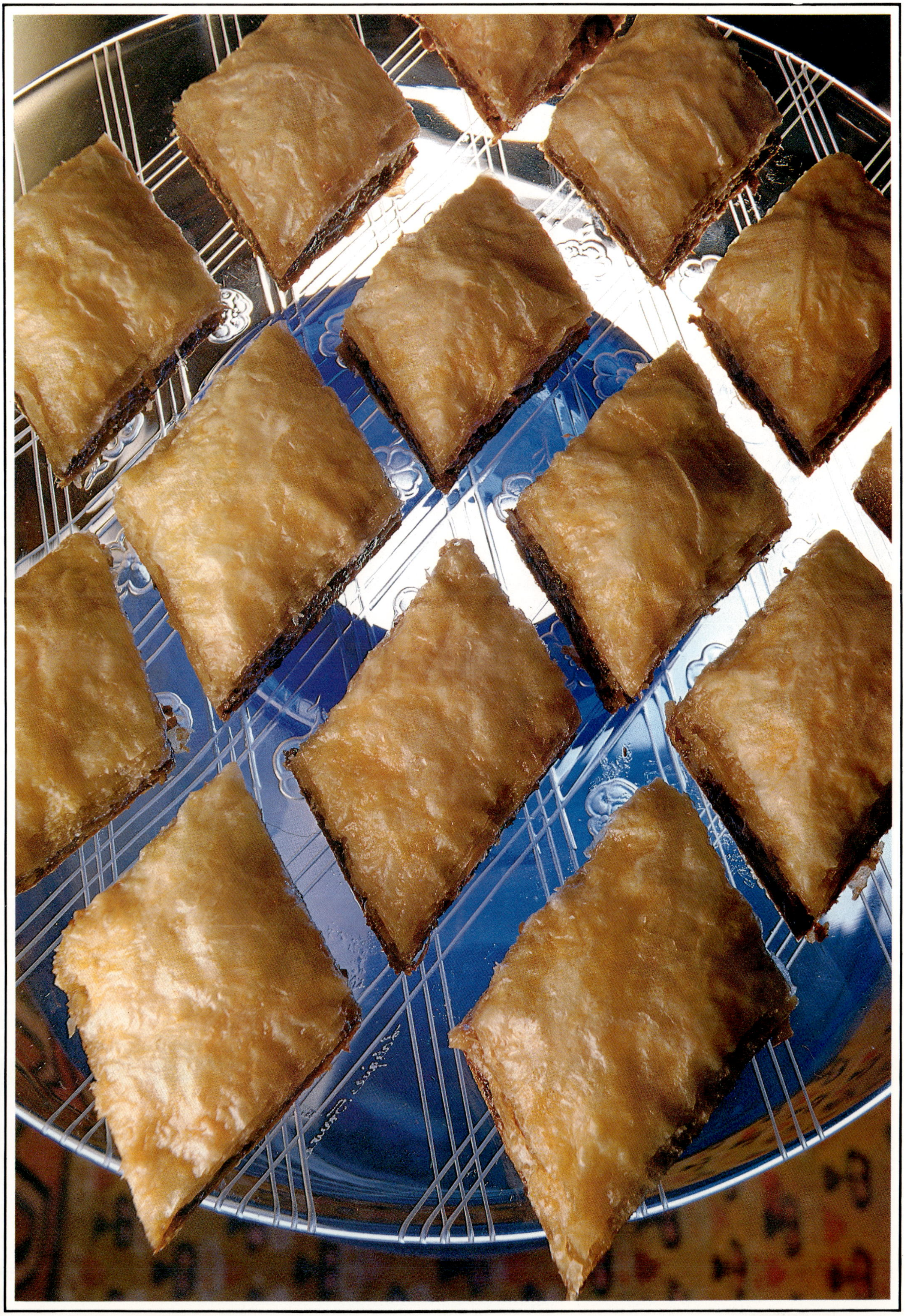

Honey-sweet Fried Pastries

These pastries are definitely for the sweet-tooths (or is it sweet-teeth?) among us. Spanish in origin, they are closely related to the sweet, fried Greek and Italian pastries which they resemble. Although often served cold, I feel they are at their best when eaten warm—they reheat well if placed on a wire rack set into a baking tin in a moderate oven. Makes about 45.

⅔ cup (5fl oz) oil
⅓ cup (2½fl oz) dry white wine
⅓ cup (2½fl oz) sweet white wine
3 tablespoons Grand Marnier (or preferred orange liqueur)
juice of 1 orange (approximately 3 tablespoons)
1 tablespoon toasted sesame seeds
2 teaspoons caraway seeds (optional)
3½–4 cups (14 oz – 1 lb) flour
oil, for frying
1 cup (10 oz) honey
¼ cup (2fl oz) water
icing (confectioners') sugar, for sprinkling
ground cinnamon, for sprinkling

Combine the oil, sweet and dry wines, Grand Marnier, orange juice, sesame seeds and (if using) caraway seeds in a large bowl. Sift the flour, and gradually work the mixture into the flour until a soft, sticky dough forms. Knead on a lightly-floured board until pliable; cover, and allow to stand for 30 minutes.

Divide the mixture into about 45 walnut-sized balls. Flatten each between fingers and thumb to rectangles about 7 × 4 cm (3 × 1½ in).

Heat 1 cm (⅜ in) of oil in a deep frying pan. Add three or four pastries at a time. Cook each for about 1½ minutes, turning once with tongs. Drain on kitchen paper.

Combine the honey and water in a saucepan; simmer until the honey melts. Using tongs, dip each pastry into the honey mixture, coating both sides; place onto a wire rack over a basin, so that excess honey drips through. Before serving, sprinkle with icing sugar and cinnamon.

These pastries actually improve if made two or three days before they are to be used. To store, allow to become cold, then place into an airtight container lined with greaseproof paper. Sprinkle with sugar and cinnamon just before serving. Delicious served with black coffee.

Golden Cheesecake Pastry Squares

Serves 8

Pastry:
2 cups (8 oz) self-raising flour (all wholemeal, all white, or half & half)
pinch of salt
125 g (4 oz) butter, melted
¾ cup (6fl oz) milk
½ cup (4 oz) sugar
2 eggs
grated peel of ½ lemon
Topping:
375 g (12 oz) cream cheese
2 egg yolks
1 teaspoon vanilla essence
½ cup (4 oz) raw sugar
¾ cup (4 oz) raisins, chopped
grated peel of 1 lemon
2 egg whites
1 cup (4 oz) slivered almonds
1 teaspoon ground cinnamon
2 tablespoons honey, slightly warmed

To make the pastry base, place the flour and salt into a large bowl. In a separate bowl, blend together the melted butter, milk, sugar and eggs; stir this into the flour. Blend in the lemon peel. Press the pastry into a greased tin 28 × 18 cm (11 × 7 in).

Preheat the oven to 180°C (350°F/Gas 4).

Topping: Beat the cream cheese, and add the egg yolks, vanilla and sugar. Beat until smooth. Stir in the raisins and lemon peel. Beat the egg whites until stiff; fold into the cream cheese mixture. Spread carefully onto the pastry base. Combine the almonds and cinnamon, and sprinkle over the surface of the cheese mixture; drizzle over the honey, which has been warmed.

Bake on a low shelf in the preheated oven at 180°C (350°F/Gas 4) for about 30 minutes. Reduce the oven temperature to 150°C (300°F/Gas 2) and bake for another 10 minutes. Topping should be set and golden brown.

Allow to cool slightly, then cut into squares. Serve each slice with a little whipped cream into which a teaspoon of freshly grated orange peel has been folded.

Hungarian Poppyseed Yeast Pastry Roll

Makes 2 rolls (plus sufficient pastry for the Hazelnut Yeast Pastry Roll recipe, below)

Filling: 185 g (6 oz) poppyseeds
½ cup (4 oz) sugar
⅔ cup (5 fl oz) milk
3 tablespoons chopped prunes
finely grated rind of ½ orange
finely grated rind of ½ lemon
2 tablespoons blackcurrant jelly
Sweet Yeast Pastry: 15 g (½ oz) compressed yeast
1 teaspoon sugar
3 tablespoons barely warm milk
4 cups (1 lb) flour
⅓ cup (3 oz) sugar
250 g (8 oz) butter
1 egg yolk
¼ cup sour cream
a little milk (at room temperature), for glazing
icing (confectioners') sugar, for sprinkling

Grind the poppy seeds in a blender. Combine all the ingredients for the filling in a saucepan; bring to the boil, stirring constantly, then simmer for 15 minutes or until the mixture becomes thick and smooth. Allow to cool.

To make the pastry, cream the yeast with the sugar and milk in a small bowl; blend until the yeast liquifies. Sift the flour into a large bowl, and add the sugar. Chop the butter into small pieces, add to the flour, and rub in; mix until the mixture is the consistency of coarse breadcrumbs. Blend together the egg yolk and sour cream, add to the flour and mix to form a soft, pliable dough. Allow to stand for 30 minutes.

Preheat the oven to 230°C (450°F/Gas 8).

Knead the dough gently on a lightly-floured board. Leave to stand for a further 30 minutes; divide the dough into three portions. (Retain one portion for Hazelnut Yeast Pastry Roll, see recipe below.) Roll out the two remaining dough portions into squares about 33 × 33 cm (13 × 13 in).

On one square, spread half the filling mixture. Roll the dough very carefully, like a swiss roll, starting at one wide edge. Transfer gently to a greased baking tray, with the seam on the underside. Repeat with the second portion of the pastry and the remainder of the filling. Brush the surface with a little milk, for glazing.

Bake for 10 minutes, then reduce the oven temperature to 180°C (350°F/Gas 4) and bake for another 20 minutes or until golden. Allow to cool on the baking tray before removing to a wire rack. Before serving, sprinkle generously with icing sugar, and serve with coffee.

Hazelnut Yeast Pastry Roll

Makes 1 roll

Filling: 125 g (4 oz) ground roasted hazelnuts
1 teaspoon sugar
a little ground cinnamon
⅓ cup (3 oz) raw sugar
½ cup (4 fl oz) milk
2 tablespoons chopped raisins
1 teaspoon finely grated lemon rind
Pastry: Portion reserved from Hungarian Poppyseed Yeast Pastry Roll (see recipe above)

Combine all the filling ingredients in a small saucepan, bring to the boil, then simmer, stirring constantly, for 15 minutes. Allow to cool.

Spread the filling onto the rolled-out pastry and make up as in the recipe for Hungarian Poppyseed Yeast Pastry Roll.

Bake in a preheated oven at 230°C (450°F/Gas 8) for 10 minutes, then reduce the oven temperature to 180°C (350°F/Gas 4) and bake for another 20 minutes or until golden.

Scottish Black Bun

King George IV is quoted as having offered in Edinburgh, 1822, the toast: 'Health to the Chieftains and Clans, and God Almighty bless the Land of Cakes.'

I have to admit that the glorious Scottish Black Bun is not exactly a sweet pastry, but neither is it a bun! However, as the descendant from a long line of McLeods, I cannot resist including this noble offering (and make no apologies for it!). Traditionally served at Hogmanay, it is made several weeks in advance and allowed to mature in an airtight tin.

Makes 1 cake

Pastry:
2 cups (8 oz) flour
1½ teaspoons baking powder
pinch of salt
185 g (6 oz) butter
water, to mix
Fruit Cake Mixture:
125 g (4 oz) butter
⅓ cup (2 oz) dark sugar
3 eggs
1 cup (4 oz) flour
1 teaspoon cream of tartar
½ teaspoon baking powder
pinch of salt
500 g (1 lb) currants
500 g (1 lb) raisins
500 g (1 lb) sultanas
125 g (4 oz) chopped mixed peel
2 teaspoons ground cinnamon
2 teaspoons mixed spice
½ teaspoon ground nutmeg
½ teaspoon ground ginger
½ teaspoon ground cloves
125 g (4 oz) chopped almonds

Pastry: Sift together the flour, baking powder and salt. Rub in the butter. Add just enough water to make a firm pastry. Roll out very thinly and line a greased 23 cm (9 in) round or square cake tin, reserving enough pastry for a lid.

Fruit Cake Mixture: Cream together the butter and sugar. Beat in the eggs, one at a time. Sift together the flour, cream of tartar, baking powder and salt and stir this into the creamed mixture. Add the fruits, spices and chopped almonds; mix thoroughly.

Spoon the cake mixture into the pastry-lined tin. Top with the pastry lid; moisten the edges, press firmly together, and crimp.

Preheat the oven to 150°C (300°F/Gas 2) and bake for 3 hours on a middle shelf in the oven. Allow to cool in the baking tin, before removing for storage.

Wholemeal Date Slice

Cuts into about 16 pieces

Filling:
400 g (14 oz) dates
½ cup (4 fl oz) water
2 teaspoons grated lemon rind
2 tablespoons lemon juice
Pastry:
1¼ cups (5 oz) wholemeal flour
1¼ cups (5 oz) self-raising flour wholemeal
pinch of salt
125 g (4 oz) butter
1 tablespoon honey
1 egg
⅓ cup (2½ fl oz) milk
extra milk, for glazing
sugar, for sprinkling

Filling: Chop and pit the dates. Place them in a saucepan with the water, lemon rind and lemon juice and, constantly stirring, cook until the mixture is thick and smooth. Allow to cool.

Pastry: Preheat the oven to 190°C (375°F/Gas 5).

Sift the flours and salt into a bowl. Rub in the butter until the mixture resembles fine breadcrumbs. Combine the honey, egg and milk; add to the dry ingredients and mix to a firm dough. Knead lightly on a floured surface.

Divide the dough in half. Roll out one portion to fit the base of a greased 28 × 18 cm (11 × 7 in) tin. Spread with the cold date mixture. Cover with the remaining rolled-out pastry, glaze with a little milk (or water), and sprinkle with sugar.

Bake for 25 to 30 minutes. Allow to cool in the tins, before cutting into squares.

Right: Scottish Black Bun (see above).

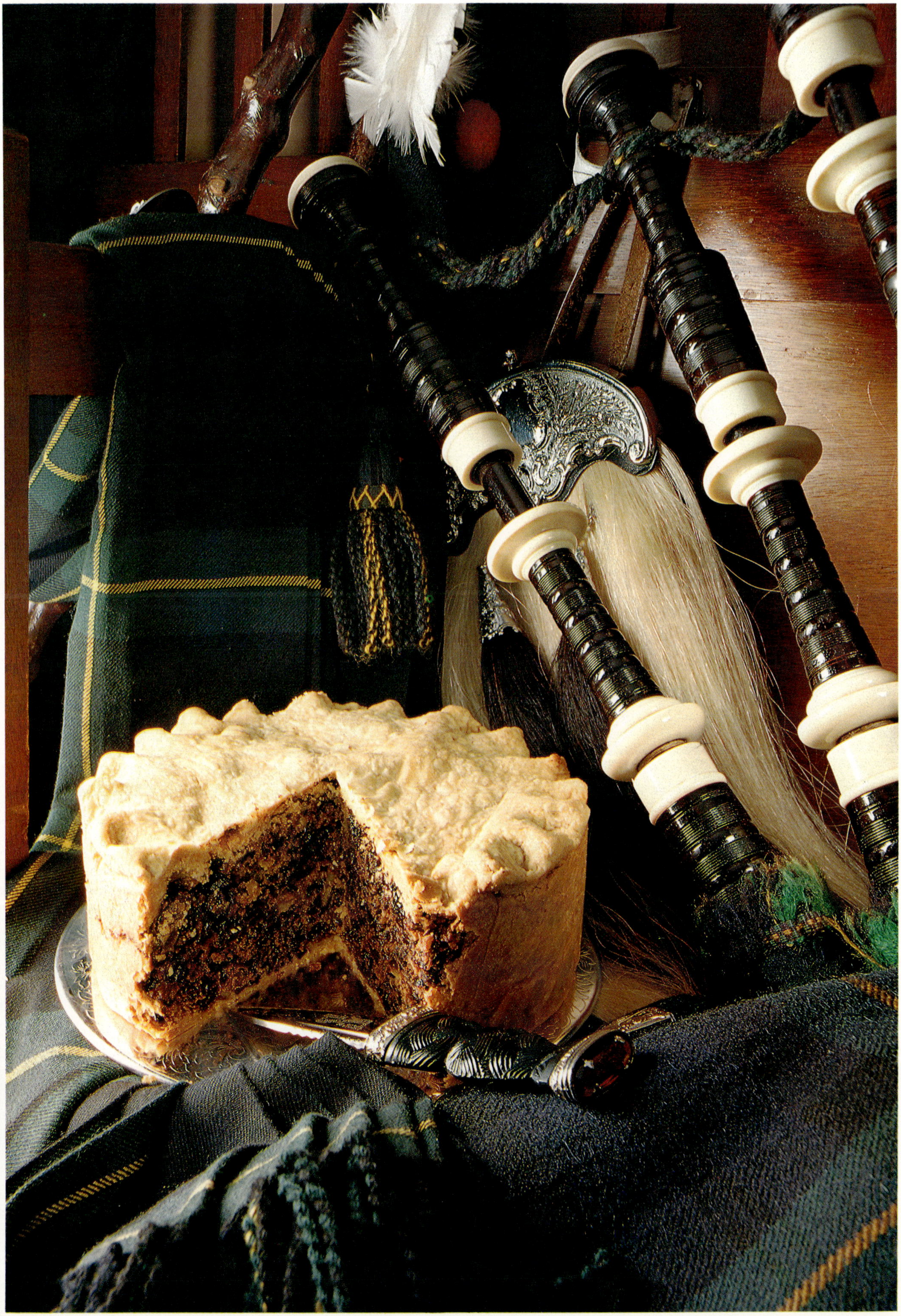

Shortcut Mille-Feuille with Strawberries

This delicious 'pastry of a thousand leaves' is easily made with filo pastry instead of the strudel-type pastry that is usually used. It is important that pastries be assembled only just before serving.
Serves 6

¼ cup (2fl oz) water
⅔ cup (5 oz) granulated sugar
2 punnets ripe strawberries, sliced (reserve 6 whole berries)
2 tablespoons Grand Marnier or Framboise
6 sheets filo pastry
30 g (1 oz) unsalted butter, melted
1⅓ cups (10fl oz) whipping cream
2–3 teaspoons caster (powdered sugar)
½ teaspoons vanilla essence
icing (confectioners') sugar, for sprinkling

In a medium-sized saucepan, combine the water and sugar. Stir until the sugar dissolves, then bring to the boil, and cook for 3–4 minutes. Remove from heat, cool and stir in the sliced strawberries and the Grand Marnier or Framboise. Cover and refrigerate for 1 to 2 hours.

Preheat the oven to 200°C (400°F/Gas 6). Cut each filo sheet into six 10 cm (4 in) circles. Place the pastry circles onto lightly-greased oven trays; brush each lightly with a little melted butter. Bake only until golden, probably about 2 minutes. Using a spatula or egg slide, remove the filo circles onto kitchen paper; allow to cool.

Lightly whip the cream until soft peaks form, then gradually beat in the caster sugar and vanilla. Beat until the cream is stiff.

To serve, set aside six of the filo circles. Spread each of the remainder with about 1½ tablespoons of whipped cream. Place one creamed pastry circle on each of six small serving plates; spoon 1 tablespoon of the strawberry mixture (without juice) over each. Continue layering with the remaining creamed circles; then a spoonful of the strawberry mixture. Top each serving with the reserved uncreamed pastry circles. Sprinkle each with icing sugar. Spoon the remaining strawberry mixture and juice onto each serving plate. Garnish each with a whole berry, and serve.

Strawberry Shortcake

Serves 4–6

Pastry:
2 cups (8 oz) flour
⅓–½ cup (3½–4 oz) caster (powdered) sugar
pinch of salt
100 g (3½ oz) butter
3 egg yolks
½ teaspoon grated orange peel
Filling:
3 egg yolks
½ cup (4 oz) sugar
½ cup (2 oz) flour
2 drops almond essence
1½ cups (12fl oz) milk
1½ cups hulled strawberries, lightly sweetened
¼ cup apple jelly or redcurrant jelly

Sift the flour, sugar and salt together onto a pastry board; make a well in the centre of the flour. Cut the butter into small cubes and add to the flour with the egg yolks and orange peel. Knead lightly with the fingertips. Do not over-work—knead only until smooth and manageable. Chill for 30 minutes.

Preheat the oven to 180°C (350°F/Gas 4).

Roll the pastry out lightly into a circle. Place over a lightly-greased 23 cm (9 in) flan tin and press into the tin. Prick the base of the pastry several times with a fork. Bake for about 20 minutes. Allow the pastry to cool, and then remove it carefully from the flan tin.

Filling: In a saucepan, beat together the egg yolks, sugar, flour and almond esence until well blended. Heat the milk, and add to the mixture in the saucepan in small quantites, beating constantly over low heat until the mixture thickens. Do not allow to boil.

Spread this creamy mixture onto the cooked pastry. Arrange the strawberries over the entire surface. Melt the jelly over low heat, and brush generously over the strawberries.

French Apple Slice

Serves 4–6

250 g (8 oz) puff pastry (see recipe, page 186)

egg white

4 large Granny Smith (green cooking) apples

¼ cup (2 oz) caster (powdered) sugar

spice, to flavour

juice of ½ lemon

icing (confectioners') sugar, for sprinkling

Roll out the pastry to not less than 5 mm (¼ in) thick and 30 cm (12 in) long. Cut two side strips 30 cm (12 in) long × 1 cm (⅜ in) wide; one base strip 30 cm long × 10 cm (4 in) wide; and one top strip 30 cm long × 14 cm (5½ in) wide. Set the top strip aside for the moment.

Brush the edges of the base strip with egg white and place on a greased baking tray. Place the side strips in position, along the two longer sides of the base strip.

Peel the apples and grate them into a bowl. Mix the spices into the sugar, and add to the grated apple; mix in the lemon juice. Spoon the flavoured apple onto the base pastry and spread evenly. Brush the top edges of the side strips of pastry with the egg white. Fold the top strip of pastry lengthways; every 1 cm (⅜ in) down the length of the fold, cut angled 1 cm incisions. Unfold the top strip and place it on top of the apple, so that it slightly overlaps the side strips of pastry. Make sure all edges are sealed. Allow it to stand for 30 minutes.

Preheat the oven to 200°C (400°F/Gas 6). Glaze the pastry surface by brushing with the egg white, and dredge with the icing sugar. Bake for about 45 minutes. Slice, and serve hot.

Chocolate Éclairs

Makes 30

1 quantity choux pastry (see recipe, page 194)

2½ cups (20fl oz) cream

125 g (4 oz) dark cooking chocolate

Preheat the oven to 200°C (400°F/Gas 6). Lightly grease a baking tray. Place a 1 cm (½ in) plain or star pipe into a forcing bag.

Put the choux pastry mixture into the bag and pipe the éclairs on the baking tray, 5–8 cm (2–3 in) long and 8 cm (3 in) apart. Sprinkle the éclairs and the tray liberally with water.

Bake for 15 minutes, then reduce the oven temperature to moderate, 160°C (325°F/Gas 3), and bake for a further 5 minutes. Turn the oven off and leave for 5 more minutes if not cooked enough. The éclairs should be crisp, light and golden colour. Remove from the baking tray to wire racks. When cool, cut open lengthways with a sharp knife.

To fill, pipe the whipped cream into the éclairs with a piping bag; set aside. Place the chocolate in the top of a double boiler, melt slowly and stir well to remove all lumps; *do not overheat*. Dip the top of each éclair into the chocolate and allow to set.

Lemon Passionfruit Slice

Makes 16–18 slices

Pastry:
1¼ cups (5 oz) self-raising flour

1¼ cups (5 oz) plain flour

pinch of salt

125 g (4 oz) butter

1 teaspoon lemon juice

⅓ cup (2½fl oz) water (approx.)

Filling:
2½ cups (20fl oz) water

1¼ cups (10 oz) sugar

2 tablespoons grated lemon rind

½ cup (2 oz) cornflour (cornstarch)

additional ½ cup (4fl oz) water

2 eggs, beaten

60 g (2 oz) butter

⅓ cup (2½fl oz) lemon juice

pulp of 4 passionfruit

milk, for glazing

sugar, for sprinkling

Make the filling first: Put the water, sugar and lemon rind in a saucepan, bring to the boil, stirring. Blend the cornflour with the extra ½ cup (4fl oz) of water; stir this into the lemon mixture. Cook over heat until the mixture boils and thickens, stirring constantly.

Remove from the heat, add the beaten eggs, butter, lemon juice and passionfruit pulp; blend well. Return to the heat and simmer for a further 2 minutes. Allow to cool.

Preheat the oven to 180°C (350°F/Gas 4). Lightly grease a 28 × 18 cm (11 × 7 in) tin.

To make the pastry: Sift the flours and salt into a bowl. Rub in the butter, and mix to a firm dough with the lemon juice and water. Press together lightly.

Roll out two-thirds of the pastry to fit the base and up the sides of the tin.

Spread the filling on this. Cover with the remaining rolled-out pastry; pinch the edges of the pastry lightly together. Brush the surface carefully with a little milk; sprinkle with a little extra sugar. Bake for 40 minutes or until golden brown. Allow to cool, then refrigerate until the filling has set. Cut into slices before serving.

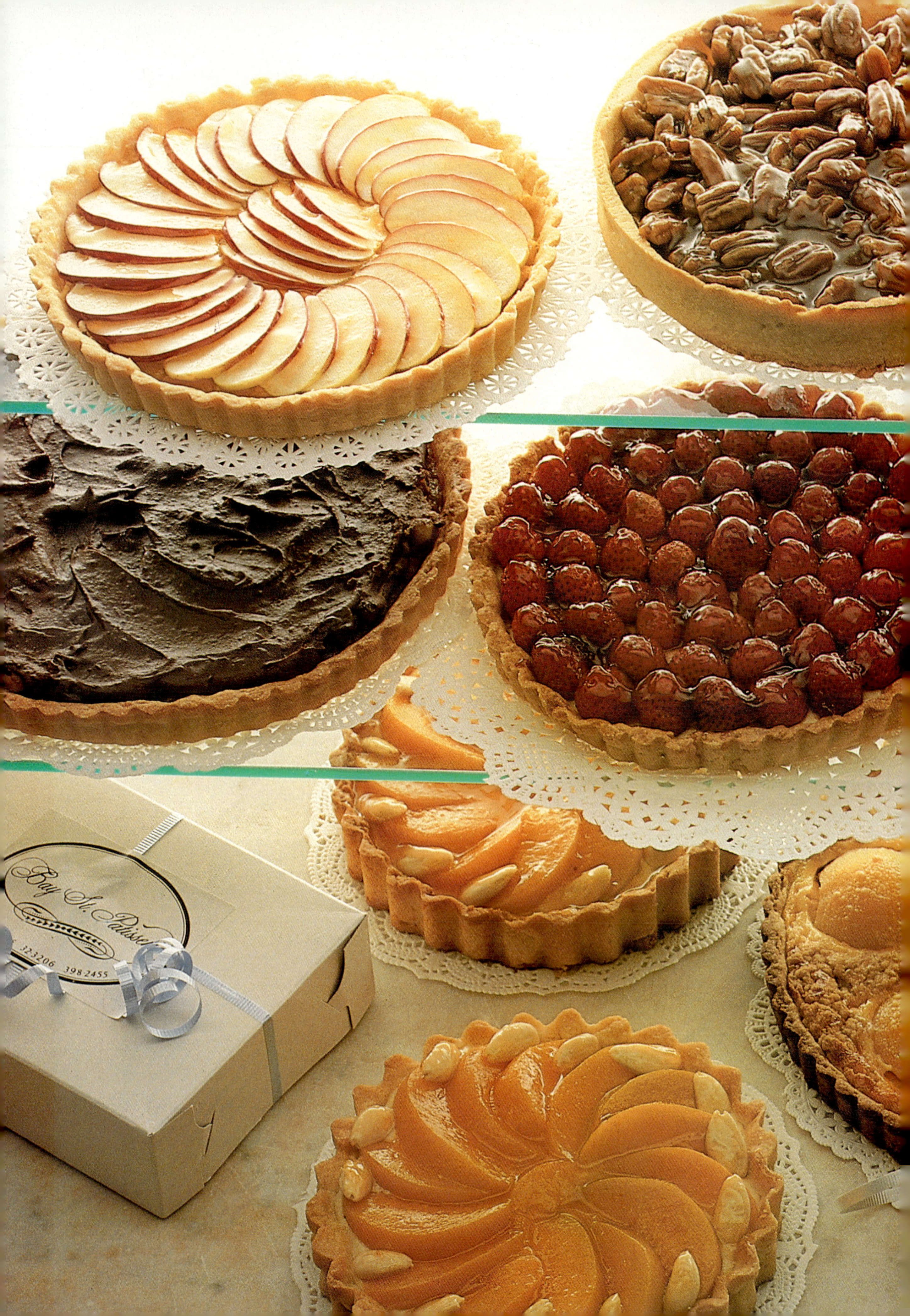
Bay St.
323206 398-2455

Tarts & Tartlets

Tarts & Tartlets

Can anything delight the eye and tease the tastebuds as much as a dessert trolley laden with a delicious selection of home-made tarts and tartlets, brimful of seasonal fruits, tempting nuts, sugary sweetness, light-as-air custards, rich chocolate and melt-in-the-mouth creams? I doubt it. Although it involves skill and patience to make them, it is surprisingly easy to produce tarts and tartlets in your own kitchen that will rival those of your nearest pâtisserie shop.

Firstly, it is essential to master the art and skill of making pâte sucrée and pâte brisée, the rich French pastries widely used in the making of tarts and tartlets. Pâte sucrée has a proportion of half butter to flour and is sweetened with icing (confectioners') sugar and enriched with egg yolk, whereas pâte brisée has a higher proportion of three-quarters butter to flour, is not usually sweetened and is bound with water. Pâte sucrée is sweet and short-textured and melts in the mouth, pâte brisée is very crisp and a darker brown because of its extra butter. Both are delicious, so experiment and use whichever you like best.

For the fillings, make sure that only top quality ingredients are used, the freshest butter and cream, eggs, nuts and fruit, then the accolades will be yours. Some fillings use creams, icings or toppings which require a little more in organisation, but patience will bring its own reward.

Anne Marshall

1. Normandy Apple Tart (see p. 232)
2. Pecan Caramel Tart (see p. 245)
3. Jam Meringue Tarts (see p. 253)
4. Chocolate Walnut Tart (see p. 244)
5. Strawberry Tart (see p. 236)
6. Sliced Almond Tart (see p. 246)
7. Peach Tart with Almond Cream (see p. 248)
8. French Pear Tart (see p. 236)
9. Filbert Tarts (see p. 252)

Baking Blind

A little advice here to aspiring bakers of pâtisserie on the lining of flan tins and the mystery of baking 'blind'. When lining a flan tin, roll the pastry out to a round, large enough to line the base and side of the tin and allow at least 5 mm (¼ inch) extra. The rolled side of the pastry is the best side, so lift the pastry over the rolling pin, then unroll the pastry into the flan tin, turning it over and in doing so the rolled side of the pastry will be on the outside of the flan (or tart). Working quickly, press the pastry from the centre of the tin into the sides of the tin with the back of the fingers, then ease the edges of pastry down to counteract shrinkage and finally roll over the top edge of the flan tin with the rolling pin, trimming off the excess pastry. Prick the bottom of the pastry well, but not all the way through, with the tines of a fine fork. Take a square of greaseproof paper, large enough to line the bottom and side of the flan tin and crumple it in the hands (this prevents pulling a skin of pastry off when removing the blind filling), then spread it smoothly into the pastry case. Pour some baking beans (haricot beans, dried peas or rice) into the paper, making a single layer over the bottom but pile up around edge to prevent edges of pastry falling in. Finally trim off excess greaseproof paper to prevent scorching.

To bake blind, the pastry case is put into a hot oven for 10 minutes, then the greaseproof paper and baking beans or the 'blind filling', is removed and the pastry case is returned to the oven for 10 minutes, or until set, sometimes at a reduced temperature. This is known as baking 'blind'.

If the pastry case rises in a bubble at this stage, prick it delicately while it is still soft with a darning needle, and allow the air bubble to escape.

The filling is then put in, or the empty pastry case is cooked completely according to the particular recipe.

The recipes that I have selected for you which follow are quite delicious and I had a lovely time testing and sometimes re-testing them. There is a big selection of fresh fruit tarts and I have tried to use every fruit possible: apples and pears, stone fruits, tropical fruits, berries and some unusual fruits like kiwi fruit and prunes or figs and a few luxury canned fruits. There are rich nut tarts with unusual toppings, light-as-a-feather custard tarts, sweet sugary tarts and a couple of gelatine dessert tarts which are handy hot weather recipes. In the tartlet selection there are delicate inspired recipes from France, England, Wales, Sweden and America, to serve at all occasions.

I hope you enjoy making, serving and eating these tarts and tartlets.

TARTS

Apple and Cider Tart

A delicious tart, popular at Simpson's-in-the-Strand in London, where it is better known as Hereford Flan.
Serves 6–8

¾ *quantity (6 oz) pâte sucrée or brisée (see page 190)*
Filling:
1½ *cups (12fl oz) cider*
2 *large green cooking apples*
3 *eggs*
½ *cup (4 oz) caster (powdered) sugar*
¼ *cup (1 oz) flour*

Preheat the oven to 220°C (425°F/Gas 7). Roll the pastry out thinly on a lightly-floured surface. Line a 23 cm (9 in) flan tin with the pastry, and with a fork prick the pastry that is on the base. Line the pastry case with greaseproof paper and weigh the paper down with dried beans. Bake near the top of the preheated oven for 10 minutes, then remove paper and beans and bake for a further 10 minutes until golden. (This process is known as 'baking blind'.) Place on a wire rack to cool; when the pastry case has become firm and has shrunk slightly (after a few minutes), remove from the flan tin.

Filling: Place the cider in a ceramic-lined or stainless steel saucepan. Cut each apple into eight, then remove the peel and core neatly. Add the apple segments to the cider and simmer, covered, for 5 to 7 minutes or until the apple is just tender. With a slotted spoon, transfer the apple segments and set aside to cool. Reserve the cider.

Beat the eggs and sugar together until thick and creamy; then beat in the flour and the reserved cider. Place the mixture in a saucepan and stir continuously over a medium heat for 4 to 5 minutes or until thickened.

To Finish the Tart:
Reduce the oven to 180°C (350°F/Gas 4). Arrange the apple in circles in the pastry case; pour the cider mixture over and spread smooth. Bake for 20 minutes. Serve warm or cold, with whipped cream or Simpson's style with cider syllabub.

Black Cherry Tart

Black cherries on a creamy custard base reminiscent of Créme Brûlée make this tart unforgettably delicious.
Serves 6–8

¾ quantity (6 oz) Pâte sucrée or brisée (see page 190)

Filling:
4 egg yolks

⅓ cup (3 oz) caster (powdered) sugar

2 cups (16 fl oz) cream

½ teaspoon vanilla essence

1 can/425 g (approx. 14 oz) black cherries

3 teaspoons arrowroot

1 tablespoon cold water

2 tablespoons Kirsch

whipped cream, for decoration (optional)

Roll out the pastry thinly and line a deep-sided 20 cm (8 in) flan tin. Prick the base of the pastry case with a fork (and line with greaseproof paper and baking beans). Bake 'blind' near the top of a preheated oven at 220°C (425°F/Gas 7) for 10 minutes. Remove the 'blind' filling and bake for a further 10 minutes until golden. Allow to cool on a wire rack.

Filling: Beat the egg yolks with sugar, then stir in the cream and vanilla.

Drain the cherries, remove their stones and reserve ¾ cup (6 fl oz) of syrup. Blend the arrowroot smoothly with water, add the reserved syrup, then bring to the boil in a saucepan, stirring continuously, and simmer for 2 minutes. Remove from the heat, stir in the Kirsch and allow to cool to room temperature.

To finish the tart: Reduce the oven to 190°C (375°F/Gas 5). Pour the custard mixture into the pastry case. Bake in the middle of the preheated oven for 30 minutes, then cover the tart lightly with foil and bake for a further 20 to 30 minutes or until the custard is set. Allow to cool on a wire rack.

When cold, spread the cherries on top of the custard and cover with the thickened syrup. Chill until set. Serve at room temperature, decorated with whipped cream if liked.

French Cherry Tart

Serves 6–8

¾ quantity (6 oz) pâte sucrée (see recipe, page 190)

Filling:
500 g (1 lb) fresh cherries (or 2 × 425 g) (approx. 14 oz) cans cherries, drained

¼ cup (2 oz) sugar

2 tablespoons Kirsch

1 large egg

2 tablespoons caster (powdered) sugar

1 teaspoon vanilla essence

3 tablespoons cream

icing (confectioners') sugar, for decoration

Roll out the pastry thinly and line a 23 cm (9 in) flan tin. Prick the base and chill for ½–1 hour.

Stone the cherries (with a cherry stoner or pointed knife), place in a bowl, sprinkle with the sugar and Kirsch, and let them stand for 1–2 hours. (If using canned cherries, sprinkle with Kirsch only and stand for 30 minutes.)

Beat the egg with the caster sugar, vanilla and cream.

Preheat the oven to 200°C (400°F/Gas 6).

If using fresh cherries, transfer them with a slotted spoon to the pastry case, and bake in the middle of the preheated oven for 25 minutes. Remove the tart from the oven, pour the egg mixture over, then bake in the bottom half of the oven for a further 20 minutes until the custard is set. (If using canned cherries, place them in the pastry case, pour the egg mixture over immediately and bake in the bottom of the oven for 20 minutes or until the custard is set.) Remove the tart from the oven, stand on a wire rack and sift icing sugar over while still warm. Serve warm or chilled with whipped cream.

Right: **French Cherry Tart** (see above).

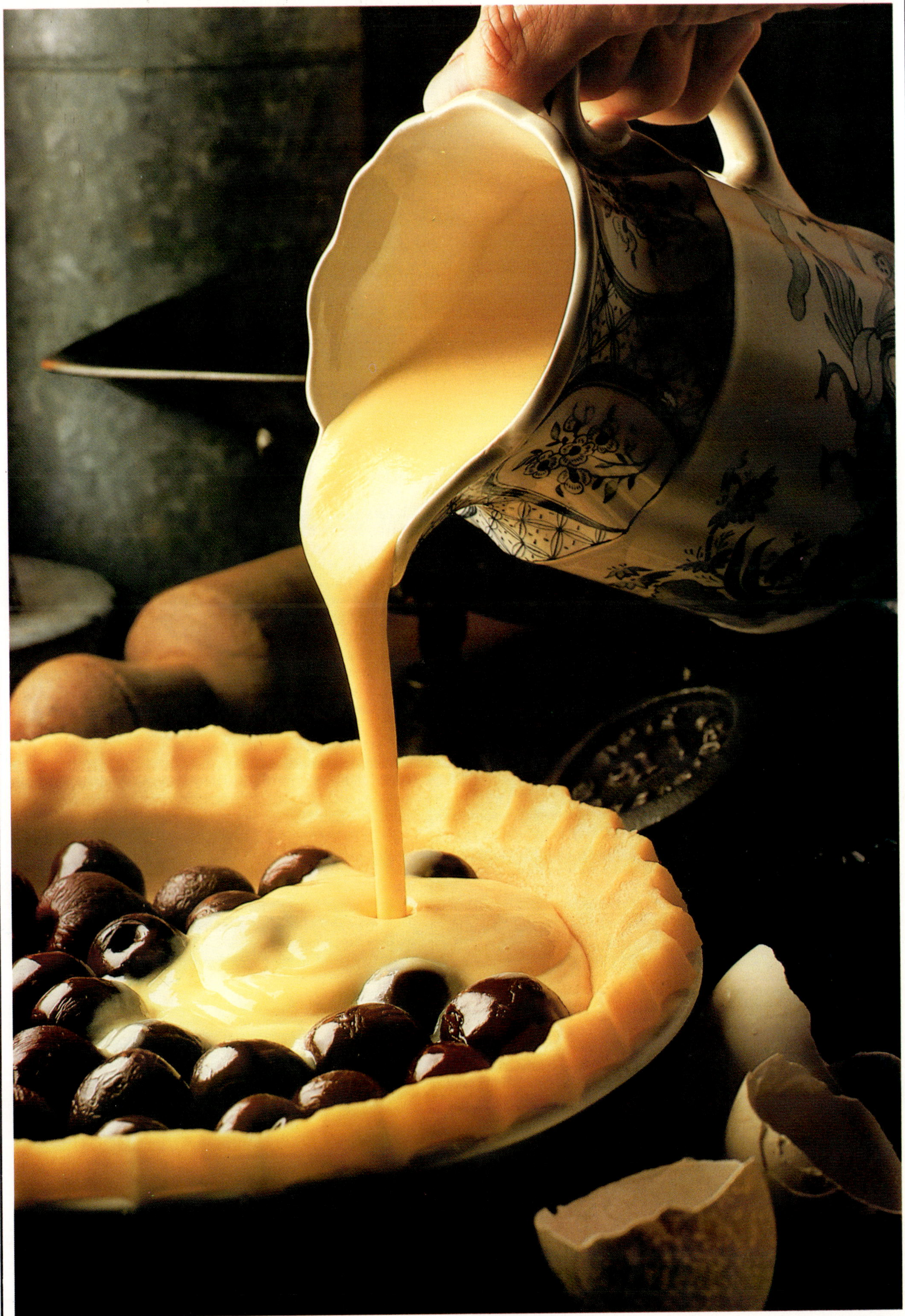

Banana and Pineapple Tart

Very rich, so serve in small portions
Serves 8–10

1 quantity (8 oz) pâte sucrée or sweet shortcrust pastry
(see recipes, page 184 and 190)

Filling:
⅔ cup (5 oz) sugar

⅔ cup (5 fl oz) water

½ cup (4 fl oz) rum

5 ripe bananas

1 quantity vanilla pastry cream
(see recipe, page 146)

750 g (1½ lb) fresh pineapple (or 1 can 825 g) (1¾ lb) unsweetened canned pineapple, drained)

¼–½ cup (2–4 oz) caster (powdered) sugar

Roll the pastry out thinly and line a 25 cm (10 in) flan tin. Bake 'blind' near the top of a preheated oven at 220°C (425°F/Gas 7) for 10 minutes, then remove the 'blind' filling and bake for a further 10 minutes or until cooked and golden. Cool on a wire rack, remove from flan tin when firm, and allow to cool completely.

Filling: Place the sugar, water and rum in a large, heavy-based frying pan and bring to the boil, stirring occasionally. Peel the bananas and cut into slices 1 cm (⅜ in) thick; add to the rum syrup and simmer for 10 minutes. Peel the pineapple, remove the core, and chop the fruit coarsely; mix to a purée in a blender or food processor. Add ¼–½ cup of caster sugar, to taste.

To finish the tart: Spread the vanilla pastry cream into the pastry case. Cover neatly with the drained banana slices. Spoon some pineapple purée over the banana, until well coated, using a pastry brush if necessary to coat evenly.

Serve immediately, accompanied by the remaining pineapple purée served in a jug.

Normandy Apple Tart

A most attractive eye-catching tart from Normandy province in France.
Serves 6–8

¾ quantity (6 oz) pâte sucrée
(see recipe, page 190)

Filling:
4 large green cooking apples

2 tablespoons sugar

2 tablespoons cold water

2 red apples

juice of 2 lemons

30 g (1 oz) butter, melted

3 tablespoons apricot jam (jelly)

Make the pastry, and chill well.

Peel, core and slice the cooking apples into a heavy-based saucepan. Add the sugar and water, cover the pan, and stew gently until tender and thick. Allow to cool, then mix the apples to a purée in an electric blender or food processor.

Roll the pastry out on a lightly-floured board to a round shape and line a flan tin: 20 cm (8 in) if deep-sided, or 23 cm (9 in) if shallow-sided. Prick the base of the pastry with a fork, and chill for 30 minutes.

Preheat the oven to 220°C (425°F/Gas 7). Bake 'blind' towards the top of the oven for 10 to 15 minutes or until the base is firm. Remove the 'blind' filling.

Core and slice the red apples very thinly and dip into lemon juice.

Spread apple purée in the flan case, and cover neatly with circles of overlapping slices of red apple. Brush the apples with melted butter, and return to the oven for a further 15 to 20 minutes or until the apple is golden. Allow to cool on a wire rack for 5 to 10 minutes, then remove the side and base of the flan tin when the pastry is firm.

Warm the apricot jam, and brush it ontop of the flan to coat the apples completely. Serve cold, with whipped cream.

Apricot and Almond Tart

Serves 6–8

¾ quantity (6 oz) rich shortcrust pastry or pâte sucrée (see recipes, page 184 and 190)

4 tablespoons (1 oz) ground almonds

Filling:
300 ml (10fl oz) cream

1 can/825 g (1¾ lb) apricot halves

6 tablespoons (6 oz) apricot jam (jelly)

2 teaspoons arrowroot, or cornflour (cornstarch)

blanched toasted almonds, for decoration

Make the pastry according to the recipe but adding ground almonds with the sugar. Chill well.

Roll the pastry out thinly and line a 20 cm (8 in) deep-sided flan tin or a 23 cm (9 in) shallow-sided flan tin. Bake 'blind' in the top of a preheated oven at 220°c (425°F/Gas 7) for 10 to 15 minutes or until the pastry is set in shape. Remove the 'blind' filling, reduce the oven temperature to 190°C (375°F/Gas 5), and bake for a further 10 to 15 minutes or until the pastry is cooked. Cool on a wire rack; after a few minutes remove the pastry from the flan tin, then leave until cold.

Filling: Whip the cream until thick. Drain the canned apricots well and reserve ½ cup (4fl oz) of juice. Place the apricot juice and the jam in a saucepan and dissolve the jam over a medium heat. Strain the juice and jam mixture and return to the saucepan. Blend the arrowroot (or cornflour) smoothly with a little extra apricot juice, add to the saucepan and bring to the boil, stirring continuously until the glaze clears and thickens. Cool, but do not allow to set.

To Finish the Tart: Spread whipped cream over the bottom of the pastry case, then top it neatly with apricot halves. Decorate with toasted almonds placed between the apricot halves. Brush the glaze over the fruit, and allow to set before serving.

Note: Canned peaches may be used instead of apricots.

Fruit Tart

A popular basic tart that can be filled with any variety or combination of fresh fruit in season. May be assembled a few hours before serving.
Serves 6–8

¾ quantity (6 oz) Pâte sucrée (see recipe, page 190)

Filling:
1 quantity vanilla pastry cream (see page 146)

500 g (1 lb) fresh fruit such as sliced ripe apricots, blackberries, blackcurrants, blueberries, stoned cherries, pitted chopped dates, peeled seedless grapes, peeled sliced kiwi fruit (Chinese gooseberries), mango balls, melon balls, mandarin or orange segments, passionfruit pulp, sliced peeled peaches, pawpaw (papaya) balls, peeled sliced pineapple, sliced stoned plums, raspberries, redcurrants, sliced strawberries

allow 250 g (8 oz) extra if fruit has stones or thick skin

½ cup (4fl oz) strained apricot jam (jelly) to glaze yellow fruits or ½ cup (4fl oz) redcurrant jelly to glaze red fruits

1 tablespoon water, strained orange juice, sweet sherry or liqueur

---

Roll the pastry out thinly and line a deep-sided 20 cm (8 in) or shallow-sided 23 cm (9 in) flan tin. Prick the base of pastry case and line with greaseproof paper and baking beans, for baking 'blind'. Bake near the top of a preheated oven at 220°C (425°F/Gas 7) for 10 minutes, then remove the 'blind' filling and bake for a further 10 minutes or until golden and cooked. Cool on a wire rack until firm, then remove the flan tin and leave the pastry case to cool completely.

Prepare the vanilla pastry cream and leave to cool. Prepare the fresh fruit accordingly (peeling, slicing, pitting, chopping).

Melt the jam or jelly with water or orange juice or sherry or liqueur in a small pan, bring to the boil, stirring, and simmer for 1 minute. Allow to cool to room temperature

Spread the vanilla pastry cream carefully in the pastry case and cover neatly with an attractive but simple arrangement of fresh fruit. Spoon the glaze over and brush over all the fruit and custard to seal well, using a pastry brush. Allow the glaze to set. Serve with whipped cream, if liked.

Prune Tart

Serves 8

¾ *quantity (6 oz) pâte brisée or sucrée (see page 190)*

Filling:
1 cup (6 oz) pitted prunes

2 large egg yolks

¼ cup (2 oz) sugar

1 tablespoon flour

½ cup (4 fl oz) milk or cream

2 tablespoons Kirsch

1 tablespoon orange flower water

Roll the pastry out thinly and line a 23 cm (9 in) flan tin. Prick the base of the pastry case and chill for 10 minutes.

Bake 'blind' near the top of a preheated oven at 220°C (425°F/Gas 7) for 10 minutes, then remove the 'blind' filling and bake for a further 10 minutes. Let it stand on a wire rack.

Filling: Cut the prunes into quarters. Mix all the remaining ingredients together in a bowl with a balloon-shaped whisk.

To finish the tart: Reduce the oven to 190°C (375°F/Gas 5). Arrange the prunes evenly in the pastry case; pour the egg mixture over. Bake in the middle of the oven for 20 to 30 minutes or until the filling is firm and golden. Cool the tart on a wire rack. Serve warm or cold accompanied by whipped cream.

Fig Tart: Fresh figs could be used in this delicious tart instead of the prunes. Use 8 ripe figs and cut them into quarters or smaller segments.

Tarte Tatin

This famous upside-down French tart has caramelised apples on top.
Serves 8

¾ *quantity (6 oz) flaky pastry (see recipe page 188)*

Topping:
125 g (4 oz) unsalted butter

1 cup (8 oz) sugar

4 large green cooking apples

Roll the pastry out thinly on a lightly-floured surface to a 25 cm (10 in) round. Place on a plate or board, prick well with a fine fork, and chill in the refrigerator.

Preheat the oven to 200°C (400°F/Gas 6). Peel, core, and halve the apples.

Use a round cast-iron enamel-lined ovenproof casserole or cake tin, 23 cm (19 in) in diameter and at least 5 cm (2 in) deep. In this melt the butter and sugar over a low heat. Place the apple halves in, very close together, and cook very slowly until the sugar just begins to caramelise (about 20 minutes).

Place the casserole in the preheated oven for 5 minutes. Remove from the oven, increase the oven temperature to 230°C (450°F/Gas 8), cover the apple mixture with the round of pastry, then return to the oven and bake for 20 minutes or until the pastry is cooked.

To turn out of the casserole, loosen the pastry around the edge with a round-bladed knife, place a serving dish ontop of the casserole and, holding firmly, turn both over to turn out the tart. Serve warm, with whipped cream.

Bakewell Tart

A favourite old English recipe
Serves 6

¾ *quantity (6 oz) sweet shortcrust pastry (see recipe, page 184)*

Filling:
90 g (3 oz) soft butter or margarine

⅓ cup (3 oz) caster (powdered) sugar

2 large eggs

½ cup (2 oz) ground almonds

½ cup (2 oz) self-raising flour, sifted

drops of almond essence

3 tablespoons raspberry jam (jelly)

6 split almonds, for decoration

icing (confectioners') sugar, for sprinkling

Prepare the pastry according to the recipe, and chill well.

Roll the pastry out thinly to a round, and line a deep-sided 20 cm (8 in) flan tin. Reserve the pastry trimmings; and prick the base of the pastry case.

Filling: Place all the ingredients except the jam and split almonds in a mixing bowl and beat well with an electric mixer or in a food processor until well mixed (about 1–2 minutes).

To finish the tart: Preheat the oven to 180°C (350°F/Gas 4). Spread the jam over the base of the pastry case, then spread with the filling mixture. Roll the pastry trimmings into a long strip and cut strips which are 1 cm (⅜ in) wide; place on the tart in a lattice pattern, and trim neatly. Decorate the top of the tart with split almonds.

Bake in the middle of the oven for 45 to 50 minutes, until cooked. Allow to cool on a wire rack. Serve warm sprinkled with icing sugar for a dessert, accompanied by custard or pouring cream.

Right: **Clockwise from left: Bakewell Tart (see above); Tarte Tatin (see above); Prune Tart (see above).**

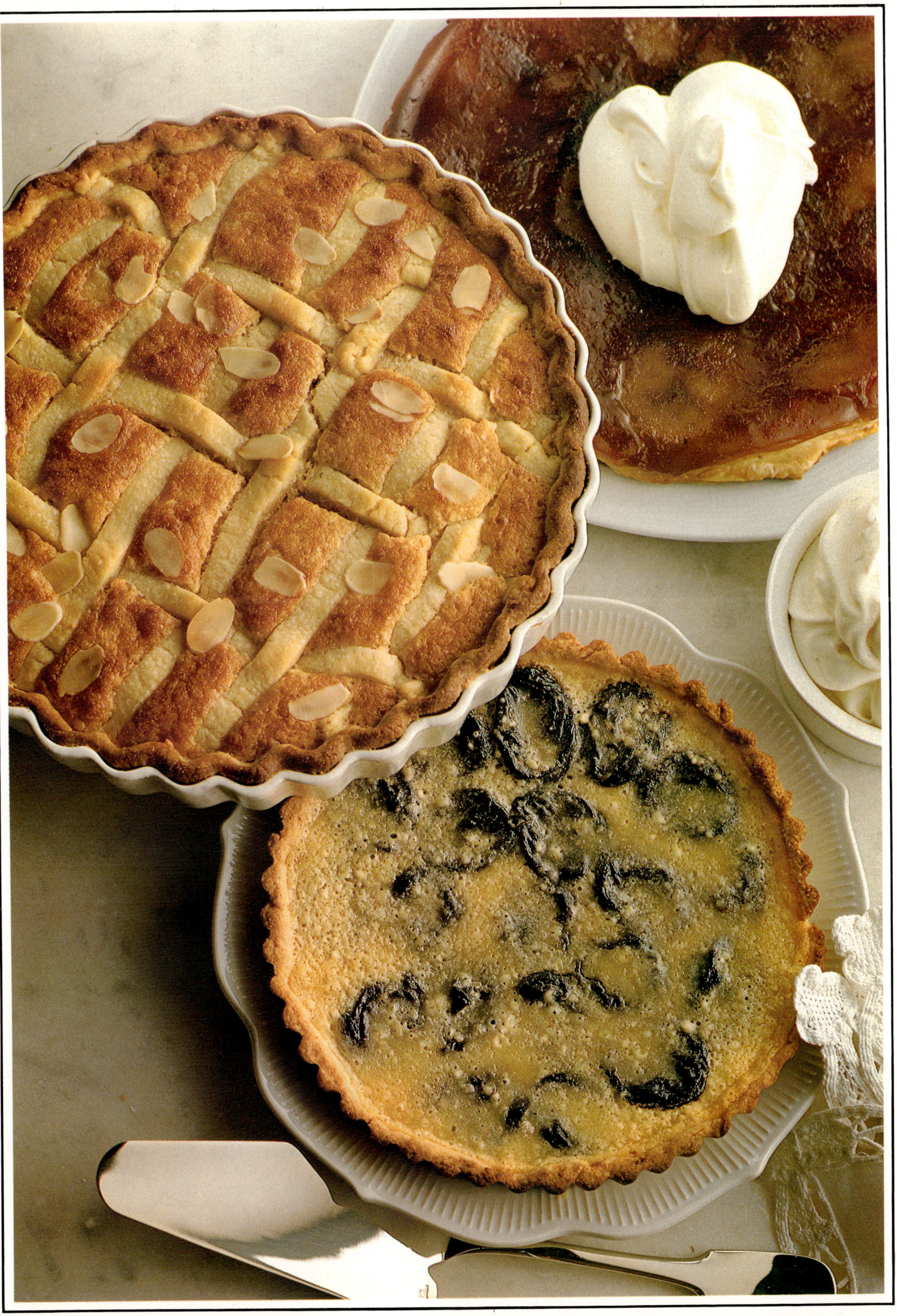

Strawberry Tart

Serves 6–8

¾ quantity (6 oz) rich shortcrust pastry or pâte sucrée (see recipes, page 184 and 190)

Filling:
500–750 g (1–1½ lb) strawberries, depending on size of berries

300 ml (10 fl oz) cream

6 tablespoons redcurrant jelly

2 teaspoons arrowroot, or cornflour (cornstarch)

1 tablespoon cold water

approx. 3 tablespoons orange juice

Prepare the pastry according to the recipe, and chill well.

Roll the pastry out thinly and line a 23 cm (9 in) flan tin. Bake 'blind' in the top of a preheated oven at 220°C (425°F/Gas 7) for 10 to 15 minutes or until the pastry is set in shape. Remove the 'blind' filling, reduce the oven temperature to 190°C (375°F/Gas 5), and bake for a further 10 to 15 minutes or until the pastry is cooked. Cool on a wire rack; after a few minutes remove the pastry from the flan tin, then leave until cold.

Filling: Hull the strawberries and check them to make sure they are clean; slice or halve large berries. Whip the cream until thick.

Heat the redcurrant jelly in a saucepan until melted and smooth. Blend the arrowroot or cornflour with cold water until smooth; stir this into the redcurrant jelly and bring to the boil, stirring continuously until the mixture is thick, clear and smooth. Stir in sufficient orange juice to give a smooth consistency.

To finish the tart: Spread the cream evenly over the bottom of the pastry case. Arrange the strawberries attractively on top of the cream, then spread or brush the redcurrant glaze over and allow to set. Serve the tart slightly chilled.

Variations:
The whipped cream may be replaced with vanilla pastry cream. And try substituting raspberries for strawberries.

French Pear Tart

A different but delicious tart to serve in cold weather.
Serves 6–8

¾ quantity (6 oz) rich shortcrust pastry or pâte sucrée (see recipes, page 184 and 190)

Filling:
3 ripe dessert pears

1 large egg

2 tablespoons caster (powdered) sugar

¼ teaspoon salt

⅛ teaspoon ground ginger

⅛ teaspoon ground nutmeg

finely grated rind of 1 lemon

1 cup (8 fl oz) sour cream

Topping:
2 tablespoons flour

3 tablespoons brown sugar

60 g (2 oz) chilled butter

¼ teaspoon ground nutmeg

Roll the pastry out thinly and line a 23 cm (9 in) flan tin. Trim and decorate the edge, and prick the base. Chill the pastry case while preparing the filling.

Filling: Peel the pears, cut in half lengthways and remove the core. Beat the egg, sugar, salt, spices, lemon rind and sour cream together.

Topping: Mix all the ingredients together in a food processor or blender until the mixture resembles coarse breadcrumbs.

To finish the tart: Preheat the oven to 200°C (400°F/Gas 6). Place the pears neatly into the pastry case, narrow tops towards the centre. Pour the egg and sour cream mixture over, and sprinkle with the topping. Bake in the centre of the oven for 25 minutes or until the filling is set. Allow to cool on a wire rack until firm, then remove from the flan tin. Serve warm with whipped cream.

Pineapple Hazelnut Tart

A delicious combination of flavours.
Serves 12

*1 quantity (8 oz) pâte sucrée
(see recipe, page 190)*

¼ cup (1 oz) ground hazelnuts

*Filling:
2 quantities (2 cups) (16fl oz) vanilla pastry cream (see recipe, page 146)*

½ cup (2 oz) ground toasted hazelnuts

1 tablespoon rum

1 large pineapple

125 ml (4fl oz) sieved apricot jam (jelly)

1 tablespoon water

hazelnuts for decoration

Make the pastry according to the recipe but adding ground hazelnuts with the egg. Chill well.

Roll the pastry out thinly and line a 30 cm (12 in) flan tin. Prick the base with a fork and bake 'blind' near the top of a preheated oven at 220°C (425°F/Gas 7) for 10 minutes. Remove the 'blind' filling, and bake for a further 10 minutes or until cooked. Allow to cool on a wire rack.

Filling: Mix the vanilla pastry cream with the ground, toasted hazelnuts and rum. Peel and core the pineapple and cut into slices 1 cm (⅜ in) thick.

To finish the tart: Spread the vanilla pastry cream in the bottom of the cold pastry case. Cover neatly with slices of pineapple. Heat the apricot jam with water, then spoon it over the pineapple, brushing the entire surface of the tart to seal. Decorate with the hazelnuts, and chill until firm. Serve with whipped cream.

Plum Tart Moulin de Mougins

This delicious tart comes from Roger Vergé's famous restaurant in Mougins, near Nice in France.
Serves 12

*1 quantity (8 oz) pâte sucrée
(see recipe, page 190)*

*Filling:
1 kg (2 lb) ripe plums*

¼ cup (1 oz) ground almonds

4 tablespoons vanilla sugar

2 large eggs

5 tablespoons cream

4 tablespoons brandy

1 tablespoon orange flower water

30 g (1 oz) unsalted butter, melted

Prepare the pastry according to the recipe and chill well.

Roll the pastry out thinly and line a 30 cm (12 in) flan tin. Trim and decorate the edge; prick the base of the pastry case. Chill until the filling is ready.

Filling: Cut the plums in half and remove the stones. Mix the ground almonds, vanilla sugar, eggs, cream, brandy and orange flower water together with an electric mixer or a whisk. Add the melted butter and mix well.

To finish the tart: Preheat the oven to 220°C (425°F/Gas 7). Arrange the plums, overlapping, in circles in the pastry case, starting around the edge and finishing in the centre. Pour the egg mixture over the plums. Bake near the top of the oven for 25 minutes or until the fruit is cooked and the filling is set. Serve warm or cold, with whipped cream.

Note: Fresh apricots could be used instead of the plums.

Vanilla sugar is made by placing one vanilla bean in 500 g (1 lb) sugar and allowing it to infuse for at least 5 days before use.

Black Bottom Tart
(Photograph below)

A favourite dessert in the southern states of North America
Serves 8

¾ quantity (6 oz) pâte sucrée (see recipe, page 190)
Filling: 60 g (2 oz) dark cooking chocolate
1¾ cups (14 fl oz) milk
3 large eggs, separated
½ cup (4 oz) sugar
1 tablespoon cornflour (cornstarch)
1 tablespoon gelatine
¼ cup (2 fl oz) cold water
1 tablespoon rum
pinch of cream of tartar
¼ cup (2 oz) caster (powdered) sugar
grated chocolate, for decoration

Roll the pastry out thinly and line a 25 cm (10 in) flan tin. Bake 'blind' near the top of a preheated oven at 220°C (425°F/Gas 7) for 10 minutes. Remove the 'blind' filling and bake for a further 10 minutes or until cooked. Allow to cool on a wire rack.

Filling: Melt the chocolate over gently simmering water in the top of a double boiler. Scald the milk. Mix the egg yolks with ½ cup sugar and the cornflour; stir in the hot milk, then transfer to a saucepan and bring to the boil, stirring continuously. Remove from the heat. Measure out 1 cup (8 fl oz) of this custard and stir into the melted chocolate.

Soak the gelatine in ¼ cup cold water, then add this to the remaining custard to dissolve. Add the rum and leave to cool.

Whisk the egg whites with cream of tartar until soft peaks form; add the caster sugar gradually, whisking continuously. Fold the egg whites into the remaining custard.

To finish the tart: Pour the chocolate custard into the pastry case and chill until set. When firm, swirl the rum-flavoured custard mixture on top, then chill again until firm. Serve decorated with grated chocolate sprinkled on top.

Wet Bottom Shoofly Tart
(Photograph below)

I like to substitute black treacle for molasses in this satisfying, traditional American tart
Serves 8

¾ quantity (6 oz) pâte brisée or sucrée (see page 190)
Filling: ¾ cup (6 fl oz) unsulphured molasses
¾ cup (6 fl oz) boiling water
½ teaspoon bicarbonate of soda (baking soda)
2 cups (8 oz) plain flour
¾ cup (4 oz) dark brown sugar
125 g (4 oz) unsalted butter
icing (confectioners') sugar, for decoration

Roll the pastry out thinly and line a 25 cm (10 in) flan tin. Chill, while preparing the filling.

Preheat the oven to 180°C (350°F/Gas 4). Place the molasses, boiling water and bicarbonate of soda together in a mixing bowl, stir together and allow to foam.

Place the flour, brown sugar and butter, previously cut into 1 cm (⅜ in) cubes, into a food processor or electric mixer, and mix until mixture resembles breadcrumbs.

To finish the tart: Pour the molasses mixture into the pastry case, then sprinkle the flour mixture evenly over the top. Bake in the middle of the preheated oven for 30 to 40 minutes or until the filling is firm. Allow to cool on a wire rack. Sieve icing sugar generously over the top before serving. Serve with thick soured cream or ice-cream.

Daiquiri Tart
(Photograph below)

A light, refreshing tart from New Orleans
Serves 8

¾ *quantity (6 oz) pâte brisée or sucrée (see page 190)*
Filling: 1 tablespoon gelatine
1 cup (7 oz) caster (powdered) sugar
½ teaspoon salt
3 large eggs, separated
¼ cup (2 fl oz) water
½ cup (4 fl oz) juice of fresh limes
1 teaspoon finely grated lime rind
2–3 drops green food colouring
4 tablespoons white rum
whipped cream, for decoration
grated chocolate, for decoration

Prepare the pastry according to the recipe, and chill well.

Roll the pastry out thinly and line a 23 or 25 cm (9 or 10 in) flan tin. Prick the base and chill well.

Bake 'blind' near the top of a preheated oven at 220°C (425°F/Gas 7) for 10 minutes. Remove the 'blind' filling and bake for a further 10 minutes or until golden. Allow to cool on a wire rack.

Filling: Place the gelatine, two-thirds of the sugar, salt, egg yolks and water in the top of a double boiler. Cook over boiling water, stirring constantly, for about 20 minutes or until the mixture has thickened slightly. Remove from the heat, and stir in the lime juice, lime rind, food colouring and rum. Pour into a bowl and chill until just beginning to set, stirring occasionally.

In a clean, dry bowl, whisk the egg whites until stiff, then gradually whisk in the remaining sugar. Fold into the rum mixture.

To finish the tart: Pour the filling into the pastry case and refrigerate for 2 to 3 hours. Serve decorated with whipped cream and grated chocolate.

Kiwi Fruit Tart

A delicious recipe from the Three Star chefs, the Troisgros brothers, whose restaurant is near Lyons in France.
Serves 12

*1 quantity (8 oz) pâte sucrée
(see recipe, page 190)*

Filling:
10 large kiwi fruit (Chinese gooseberries)

250 ml (8 fl oz) cream

1 cup (4 oz) icing (confectioners') sugar, sifted

2 large eggs

¼ cup (2 fl oz) brandy or Cointreau

additional ¼ cup (2 oz) icing (confectioners') sugar, for dusting

Make the pastry according to the recipe and chill well.

Roll the pastry out thinly and line a 30 cm (12 in) flan tin. Bake 'blind' near the top of a preheated oven at 220°C (425°F/Gas 7) for 10 minutes or until the pastry is set in shape. Remove the 'blind' filling, reduce the oven temperature to 180°C (375°F/Gas 5) and bake for a further 10 to 15 minutes or until the pastry is golden. Stand the flan tin on a wire rack, to cool.

Filling: Peel the kiwi fruit, and cut into slices 5 mm (¼ in) thick. In a bowl, combine the cream, icing sugar, eggs and brandy, and beat until well mixed.

To finish the tart: Reduce the oven to 180°C (375°F/Gas 5). Arrange the slices of kiwi fruit to overlap in circles in the pastry case. Pour the egg mixture over, then brush over all the fruit. Bake for 40 minutes.

Preheat the griller (broiler). Cover the pastry edge with foil, sieve extra icing sugar over, and place under the griller for 3 to 5 minutes or until the top is lightly caramelised. Remove the foil and remove the tart from the flan tin. Serve hot or at room temperature with whipped cream.

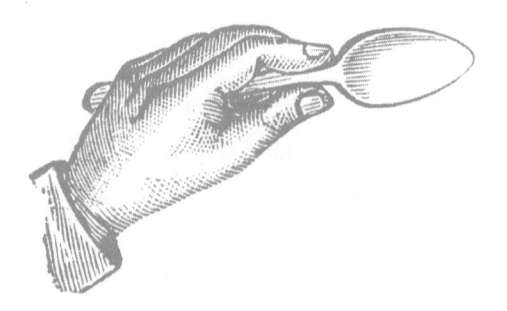

Apple and Rum Custard Tart

A delicious tart to take on a picnic.
Serves 8–10

*¾ quantity (6 oz) pâte brisée
(see recipe, page 190)*

Filling:
⅓ cup (1½ oz) currants

3 tablespoons rum

3 small cooking apples

¼ cup (½ oz) fresh white breadcrumbs

30 g (1 oz) butter melted

Custard:
2 large eggs

2 egg yolks

⅓ cup (2½ oz) sugar

500 ml (16 fl oz) cream

Topping:
1 tablespoon sugar, mixed with 1 tablespoon melted butter

Make the pastry according to the recipe and chill for ½–1 hour or until firm. Place the currants in a small bowl, pour the rum over and leave to soak for at least 20 minutes.

Preheat the oven to 200°C (400°F/Gas 6). Roll the pastry out thinly to a round, and line a 20 cm (8 in) springform cake tin. Peel and core the apples, and cut into slices 5 mm (¼ in) thick.

Mix the breadcrumbs with the melted butter, and sprinkle this over the base of the pastry case. Cover with the sliced apples. Drain the currants (reserve the rum) and sprinkle the currants over the apples. Bake in the centre of the oven for 15 minutes.

Prepare the custard mixture during this first baking. Beat the eggs, egg yolks and sugar together with a rotary beater until they are thick and lemon coloured. Beat in the reserved rum and the cream.

Remove the tart from the oven and, working quickly, pour half of the custard mixture evenly over the apples in the partly baked pastry case. Reduce the oven temperature to 190°C (375°F/Gas 5), and cook the tart for 20 to 30 minutes or until the custard is set.

Then pour the rest of the liquid custard in, and bake for a further 30 minutes or until set.

Sprinkle the top of the tart with the sugar mixed with melted butter. Bake in the top third of the oven for about 15 to 20 minutes, or until the top of the tart browns lightly.

Remove the tart from the oven and allow to cool completely before removing the outer frame of the flan tin. Slide the tart onto a cake plate, and serve accompanied by whipped cream.

Linzertorte

A delicious dessert given to us by the Austro-Hungarian empire.
Serves 6–8

Pastry:
1 cup (4 oz) flour

¼ cup (2 oz) caster (powdered) sugar

½ teaspoon baking powder

½ teaspoon ground cinnamon

pinch of ground cloves

1 cup (4 oz) ground almonds

finely grated rind of 1 lemon

125 g (4 oz) butter

milk or Kirsch

Filling:
1½ cups (12 fl oz) jam (jelly) (raspberry, redcurrant or strawberry)

beaten egg, for glazing

fresh raspberries, to decorate (optional)

Sift the flour, sugar, baking powder and spices into a mixing bowl. Mix in the almonds and lemon rind. Rub in the butter with the fingertips, or use an electric mixer or food processor. Add the milk or Kirsch, if required, to form a dry dough. Knead only until combined. Wrap in greaseproof paper and chill in the refrigerator for 30 minutes.

Roll out two-thirds of the pastry and press onto the base of a 20 cm (8 in) greased springform tin. Spread the jam on top. Roll out the remaining pastry, cut it into 1 cm (3/8 in) strips and arrange crossways on top, using the last strip as an edging around the side of the tart. Press down lightly. Chill the tart well.

Preheat the oven to 190°C (375°F/Gas 5). With beaten egg, brush the pastry only. Bake for 35 to 40 minutes. Allow to cool in the tin, then remove it carefully. Serve decorated with fresh raspberries, if available, and accompany with whipped cream.

Raspberry and Apple Tart

Serves 12

1 quantity (8 oz) pâte sucrée

1 egg white

Filling:
750 g (1½ lb) green cooking apples

250 g (8 oz) raspberries

¼ cup (2 oz) sugar

2 tablespoons quick-cooking sago

2 mandarins (or small oranges)

4 tablespoons red currant jelly

whipped cream, for decoration

Roll the pastry out thinly to a round, and line a 30 cm (12 in) flan tin. Prick the base with a fine fork and chill for 10 minutes.

Bake 'blind' near the top of a preheated oven at 220°C (425°F/Gas 7) for 10 minutes, then remove the 'blind' filling and brush the base of the pastry case with lightly-beaten egg white. Bake for a further 10 minutes or until pastry is cooked. Allow to cool on a wire rack.

Filling: Reduce the oven to 200°C (400°F/Gas 6). Peel the apples, cut each into sixteen segments and remove the core. Into an enamel-lined casserole, place the apples, raspberries, sugar, sago and finely grated rind of mandarins. (Reserve the mandarins themselves.) Cover the casserole and cook in the preheated oven for 20 minutes. Allow to cool slightly.

To finish the tart: Leave the oven on at 200°C (400°F/Gas 6). Spread the filling into the pastry case, return to the oven and bake for a further 20 minutes. Allow to cool on a wire rack.

Peel the mandarins neatly and cut them into segments; arrange neatly on top of the filling. Warm the red currant jelly, brush it over the tart, and leave to set. Serve decorated with rosettes of cream.

Raspberry and Rhubarb Tart: Instead of the apple, try using rhubarb in this light, delectable tart. Use 750 g (1½ lb) rhubarb, wash and trim the stems and cut them into 2.5 cm (1 in) lengths. Place in the enamel-lined casserole with the raspberries, sugar, sago and mandarin rind, and cook as in the recipe above.

Mince Tart

A Christmas favourite, quicker to make than little mince pies
Serves 8

¾ *quantity (6 oz) sweet shortcrust pastry (see recipe, page 184)*

Filling:
2 cups (16fl oz) fruit mincemeat (see recipe page 274)

1 cup (8fl oz) stewed apple

beaten egg and caster (powdered) sugar, for glazing

icing (confectioners') sugar, for decoration

Make the pastry according to the recipe, and chill well.

Roll three-quarters of the pastry out thinly to a round, and line a 23 or 25 cm (9 or 10 in) flan tin, trim and neaten the edge, prick the base and chill for 30 minutes.

Mix the fruit mincemeat with the stewed apple.

Bake the pastry case 'blind', near the top of a preheated oven at 220°C (425°F/Gas 7) for 10 minutes. Remove the 'blind' filling, and spread the fruit-mince filling in the pastry case. Roll the remaining pastry out thinly to a rectangle then cut into strips 1 cm (⅜ in) wide; place these on the tart in a lattice pattern and trim the edges. Glaze the pastry with the beaten egg and sprinkle with sugar. Bake near the top of a moderate oven at 180°C (350°F/Gas 4) for 25 minutes or until cooked. Serve warm or cold sifted generously with icing sugar, accompanied by whipped cream or ice cream.

English Custard Tart

A delicious tart, far too good to use in slap-stick comedy.
Serves 6–8

¾ *quantity (6 oz) rich shortcrust pastry (see recipe, page 184)*

egg white, for sealing

Filling:
3 large eggs

1 tablespoon caster (powdered) sugar

1¼ cups (10fl oz) milk

½ teaspoon vanilla essence

freshly grated nutmeg

Make the pastry according to the recipe, and chill well.

Roll the pastry out thinly and line a deep-sided 20 cm (8 in) flan tin. Press the base of the pastry case down firmly, then chill while preparing the filling.

Break the eggs into a mixing bowl and beat with a whisk until the eggs run smoothly through the wires of the whisk. Add the sugar, milk and vanilla, and stir well.

Preheat the oven to 200°C (400°F/Gas 6). Place the flan tin on a baking tray and bake 'blind' for 10 to 15 minutes, until set in shape.

Leave the oven on at 200°C (400°F/Gas 6). Brush the base of the pastry case with lightly-whisked egg white, then strain the filling into it. Sprinkle grated nutmeg on top. Place the tart in the top of the oven for 7 minutes, then reduce the temperature to 180°C (350°F/Gas 4) and bake for a further 7 to 12 minutes or until the custard is set.

Allow the custard to cool before removing the tart from the flan tin. Serve cold, as a dessert or for afternoon tea.

Lemon Tart René Verdon

A delightful tart, from ex-White House French chef René Verdon, now served at his superb down-town San Francisco restaurant, Le Trianon.
Serves 12

1 quantity (8 oz) Pâte sucrée (see recipe, page 190)

Filling:
4 large eggs

1¼ cups (10 oz) sugar

1 cup (8fl oz) lemon juice (or passionfruit pulp, or half and half)

⅔ *cup (5fl oz) orange juice*

finely grated rind of 3 lemons

½ *cup (4fl oz) cream*

2 tablespoons unsalted butter

whipped cream and chocolate curls or slices of Chinese gooseberry for decoration

Roll the pastry out thinly and line a shallow-sided 30 cm (12 in) flan tin; press the pastry into the tin, then roll off the excess and neaten the edges. Prick the base of the pastry case with a fine fork, and bake 'blind' near the top of a preheated oven at 220°C (425°F/Gas 7) for 10 minutes. Remove the 'blind' filling, and bake for a further 10 minutes or until golden.

Filling: Beat the eggs lightly; place in a saucepan, add the sugar, lemon juice, orange juice and lemon rind, Stir the mixture continuously over low–medium heat until thick, but do not allow to boil. Remove from the heat and stir in the cream and butter until absorbed. Transfer the lemon mixture to a mixing bowl set in a larger bowl of iced water and leave to cool, stirring occasionally.

Preheat the oven to 160°C (325°F/Gas 3).Pour the now-cold lemon mixture into the pastry case. Bake in the top of the oven for 25 minutes or until a skin forms ontop. Allow to cool on a wire rack.

Right: Clockwise from top: English Custard Tart (see above); Mince Tart (see above); Lemon Tart René Verdon (see above).

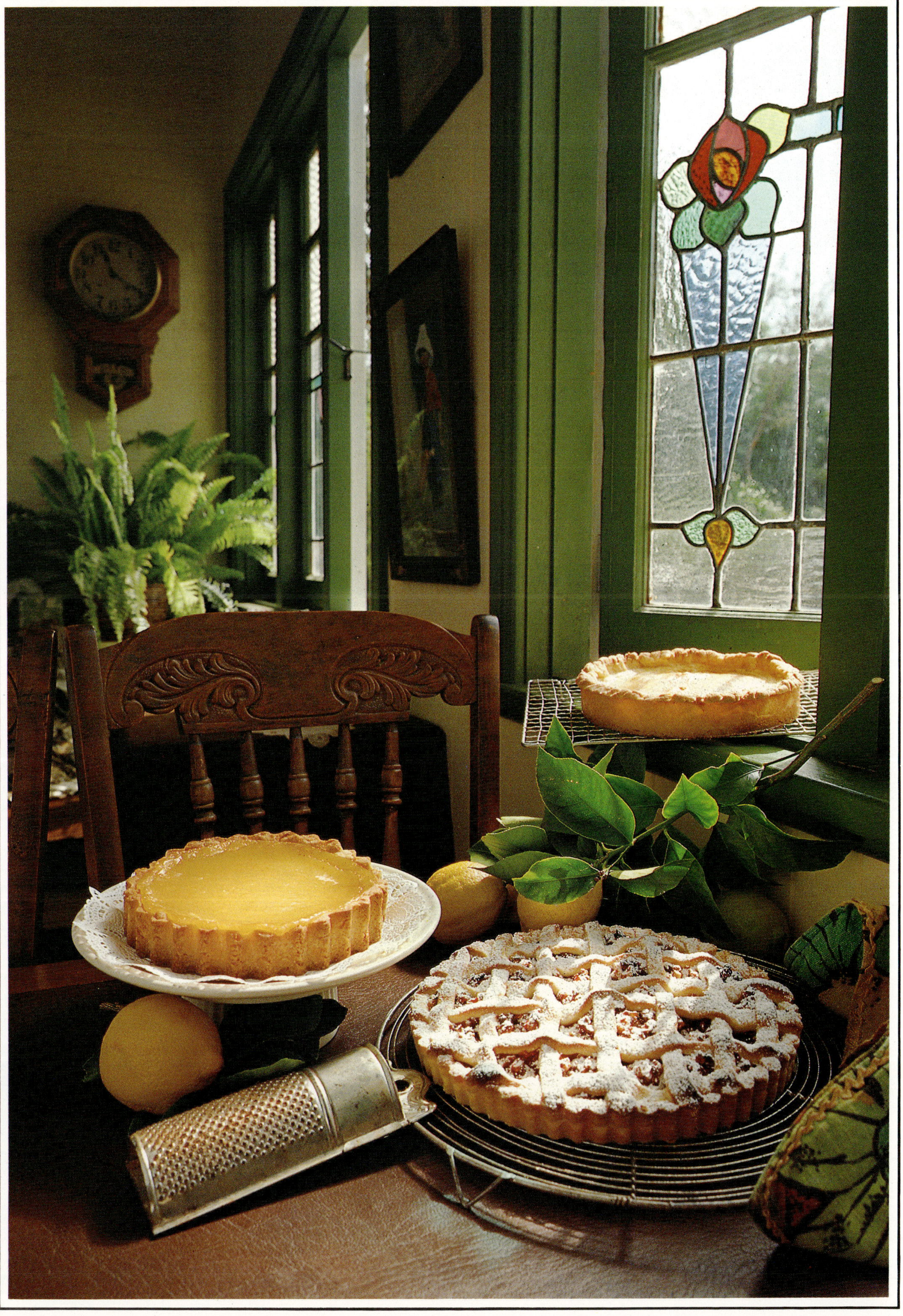

Chocolate Walnut Tart

One of the richest tarts I have ever tasted
Serves 8

¾ quantity (6 oz) pâte sucrée
(see recipe, page 190)

Filling:
½ cup (4 oz) sugar

3 tablespoons water

pinch of cream of tartar

1 cup (2 oz) coarsely chopped walnuts

½ cup (4fl oz) honey

1 cup (8fl oz) cream

2 large eggs, lightly beaten

125 g (4 oz) fresh or dessert dates,
seeded and chopped

3 tablespoons dry sherry

Chocolate Icing:
185 g (6 oz) dark cooking chocolate

½ cup (4fl oz) sour cream

raspberry or blackberry purée, for serving

Make the pastry according to the recipe, and chill well.

Roll the pastry out thinly to a round, and line a 23 cm (9 in) flan tin. Bake 'blind' near the top of a preheated oven at 220°C (425°F/Gas 7) for 10 minutes. Remove the 'blind' filling, reduce the oven temperature to 190°C (375°F/Gas 5) and bake for a further 10 to 15 minutes or until the pastry is light golden and cooked. Allow to cool on a wire rack.

Filling: Place the sugar, water and cream of tartar in a heavy-based saucepan. Bring slowly to the boil over a low heat, stirring and washing down any sugar crystals clinging to the sides of the pan with a brush dipped in cold water, until the sugar is dissolved. Increase the heat to medium, and cook the syrup until it is a deep caramel colour. Add the chopped walnuts, honey and cream, and cook over a high heat for 2 to 3 minutes or until slightly thickened. Reduce the heat to low, stir in the eggs and cook gently for 2 minutes.

Chocolate icing: Melt the chocolate over simmering water in the top of a double boiler, then stir in the sour cream.

To finish the tart: Pour the filling into the pastry case, and leave to firm. Then cover with chocolate icing, and chill for a further 1 to 2 hours. Allow the tart to return to room temperature before serving, and accompany it with raspberry or blackberry purée.

Coffee and Bran Tart

Add some fibre to your diet with this healthy recipe
Serves 6

¾ quantity (6 oz) rich shortcrust pastry
(see recipe, page 184)

Filling:
90 g (3 oz) soft butter or margarine

⅓ cup (3 oz) caster (powdered) sugar

1 large egg

1 cup (2 oz) bran cereal

¼ cup (1 oz) chopped hazelnuts

1 cup (4 oz) self-raising flour, sifted

2 teaspoons instant coffee dissolved in
3 teaspoons hot water

¼ cup (2fl oz) milk

4 tablespoons apricot or raspberry jam (jelly)

1 cup (8fl oz) sour cream or natural yoghurt

Make the pastry according to the recipe, and chill well.

Roll the pastry out thinly on a lightly-floured board to a round, and line a deep-sided 20 cm (8 in) flan tin. Prick the base of the pastry case. Chill while preparing the filling.

Filling: Cream the butter and sugar together in mixing bowl with an electric mixer until light and fluffy. Add the egg gradually, beating well after each addition. Stir in the bran cereal and hazelnuts, then fold in the sifted flour alternately with the dissolved coffee and milk.

To finish the tart: Preheat the oven to 200°C (400°F/Gas 6). Spread the jam over the base of the pastry case, then spread the coffee mixture over the jam. Bake in the middle of the oven for 10 minutes, then reduce the temperature to 160°C (325°F/Gas 3) and bake for a further 20 minutes. Remove the tart from the oven, quickly spread the sour cream (or yoghurt) over the top and return to the oven for 2 minutes. Serve warm.

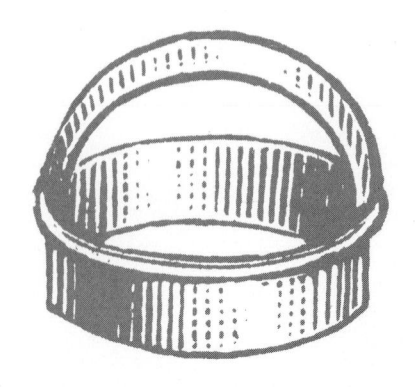

Pecan Caramel Tart

A delicious pastry to serve with coffee or, for a rich dessert, add whipped cream and chilled grapes
Serves 12

---

1 quantity (8 oz) pâte sucrée
(see recipe, page 190)

Filling:
125 g (4 oz) unsalted butter

2 cups (12 oz) light brown sugar

⅓ cup (2½ fl oz) corn syrup

4 cups (12 oz) pecan halves

½ cup (4 fl oz) cream

¼ teaspoon mixed spice

2 tablespoons brandy or rum

Roll the pastry out thinly and line a 30 cm (12 in) flan tin, prick the base of the pastry case and chill for 10 minutes.

Bake 'blind' near the top of a preheated oven at 220°C (425°F/Gas 7) for 10 minutes. Remove the 'blind' filling and bake for a further 5 to 10 minutes or until golden. Allow to cool on a wire rack.

Melt the butter in a heavy-based saucepan. Add the sugar and corn syrup, and cook over a medium-low heat, stirring continuously with a wooden spoon, for 8 to 10 minutes or until a sugar (candy) thermometer registers 130°C (260°F).

Remove from the heat and stir in the pecans, cream and mixed spice. Stir over a low heat for 5 minutes or until a thermometer registers 100°C (200°F). Cool for 5 minutes, then stir in the brandy. Spread the mixture in the tart case, and chill for at least 2 hours before serving.

Treacle Tart

An old English favourite, still popular with children
Serves 6

---

1 quantity (6 oz) sweet shortcrust pastry
(see recipe, page 184)

Filling:
8 tablespoons golden syrup (light corn syrup)

6 tablespoons fresh white breadcrumbs (or crushed cornflakes)

finely grated rind of 1 lemon

1 tablespoon lemon juice

1 grated apple (optional)

Prepare the pastry according to the recipe, and chill well.

Roll the pastry out to a round, and line a 20 cm (8 in) ovenproof (enamel is best) plate. Trim off excess pastry.

Filling: Mix all the ingredients together. Dip the measuring spoon into very hot water before measuring the golden syrup, or soften the syrup in a microwave oven.

To finish the tart: Preheat the oven to 220°C (425°F/Gas 7). Spread the filling over to within 2.5 cm (1 in) of the edge of the pastry case. Roll the remaining scraps of pastry out and cut into thin strips. Twist the strips and place in a lattice pattern over the filling, sealing the ends with water. Bake towards the top of the oven for 20 to 30 minutes or until the pastry is cooked. Serve warm with custard or cream.

Brown Sugar Tart

A little of this delicious French-Canadian tart goes a long way as it is very sweet, but ideal for a cold night treat
Serves 8

¾ quantity (6 oz) pâte sucrée
(see recipe, page 190)

Filling:
2½ cups (1 lb) brown sugar

1 cup (8 fl oz) cream

2 teaspoons unsalted butter

½ teaspoon vanilla essence

2 eggs, beaten

Roll the pastry out thinly and line a 23 cm (9 in) flan tin; reserve and chill the trimmings for decoration. Prick the base of the pastry case and bake 'blind' in a preheated oven at 220°C (425°F/Gas 7) for 10 minutes, then cool on a wire rack until the filling is ready.

Filling: Place the sugar and cream in a heavy-based saucepan, bring to the boil and simmer for 15 minutes, stirring frequently. Remove from the heat, stir in the butter and vanilla, then allow to cool until lukewarm. Beat the eggs into the warm mixture until well mixed.

To finish the tart: Reduce the oven to 200°C (400°F/Gas 6). Pour the filling into the pastry case. Roll the remaining pastry out to a long thin shape and cut into strips 1 cm (⅜ in) wide. Arrange the strips lattice-fashion on the tart, pressing the ends into the pastry case to seal. Bake in the lower half of the oven for 20 to 25 minutes or until the filling is set. Serve warm or cold, accompanied by a 'dollop' of Mascarpone (Italian cream cheese) or natural yoghurt.

Orange Almond Tart

Serves 6–8

¾ *quantity (6 oz) pâte sucrée (see recipe, page 190)*

4 *tablespoons ground almonds (optional)*

Filling:
125 g (4 oz) unsalted butter

⅓ *cup (3 oz) caster (powdered) sugar*

2 large eggs

1 cup (5 oz) blanched almonds, ground in a blender or food processor

2 tablespoons flour

5 large navel oranges

1 tablespoon Cointreau or Grand Marnier

2 tablespoons icing (confectioners') sugar

½ *cup (4fl oz) sieved orange marmalade*

1 tablespoon toasted sliced almonds, for decoration (optional)

Make the pastry according to the recipe, but if using ground almonds, add them with the egg. Chill well.

Roll the pastry out thinly and line a 23 cm (9 in) flan tin. Prick the base of the pastry case, and bake 'blind' near the top of a preheated oven at 220°C (425°F/Gas 7) for 10 minutes. Remove the 'blind' filling and bake for a further 10 minutes, until golden, then allow to cool on a wire rack.

Cream the butter and sugar together with an electric mixer. Add the eggs one at a time and beat well. Stir in the ground almonds and flour until evenly mixed.

Peel the oranges, working on a plate, with a small serrated knife; remove all the white pith and discard the rind. Cut the orange segments away from the membrane, then squeeze juice from the membrane over the orange segments. Sprinkle the liqueur and icing sugar over them; cover and leave to macerate for 30 minutes.

Reduce the oven to 180°C (350°F/Gas 4). Spread the almond mixture into the pastry case and bake in the middle of the oven for 20 to 25 minutes or until golden and a skewer comes out fairly dry. Allow to cool on a wire rack. Transfer the orange segments to a plate with a slotted spoon and pat dry with kitchen paper towels; reserve the liquor.

Place the sieved marmalade and 2 tablespoons of reserved liquor in a saucepan; bring to the boil, stirring continuously, simmer for 1 minute, then cool for 1 minute. Brush the marmalade glaze over the top of the tart, arrange the orange segments in circles on it, then brush with more glaze. Decorate the tart with toasted sliced almonds, if liked. Serve immediately, or store in the refrigerator and serve chilled, plain or with whipped cream.

Sliced Almond Tart

This nutty tart has a dual role—as a dessert or as a delicious pastry to serve with afternoon tea or coffee
Serves 8

¾ *quantity (6 oz) pâte sucrée (see recipe, page 190)*

Filling:
1 *cup (4 oz) sliced (flaked) blanched almonds*

¾ *cup (6 oz) caster (powdered) sugar*

¾ *cup (6fl oz) cream*

1 teaspoon orange-flavoured liqueur

¼ *teaspoon almond essence*

pinch of salt

Roll the pastry out thinly and line a 23 cm (9 in) flan tin. Bake 'blind' near the top of a preheated oven at 220°C (425°F/Gas 7) for 10 minutes.

Filling: Place all the ingredients together in a mixing bowl, stir until evenly mixed, then leave to stand for 15 minutes.

To finish the tart: Spoon the filling into the pastry case and bake in the lower half of a preheated oven at 200°C (400°F/Gas 6) for 30 to 40 minutes or until the top is caramelised and golden brown. It is advisable to protect the edge of the pastry case with foil after 15 minutes to prevent over-browning. Allow the tart to cool on a wire rack. Serve with vanilla ice-cream or whipped cream.

Right: **Orange Almond Tart** (see above).

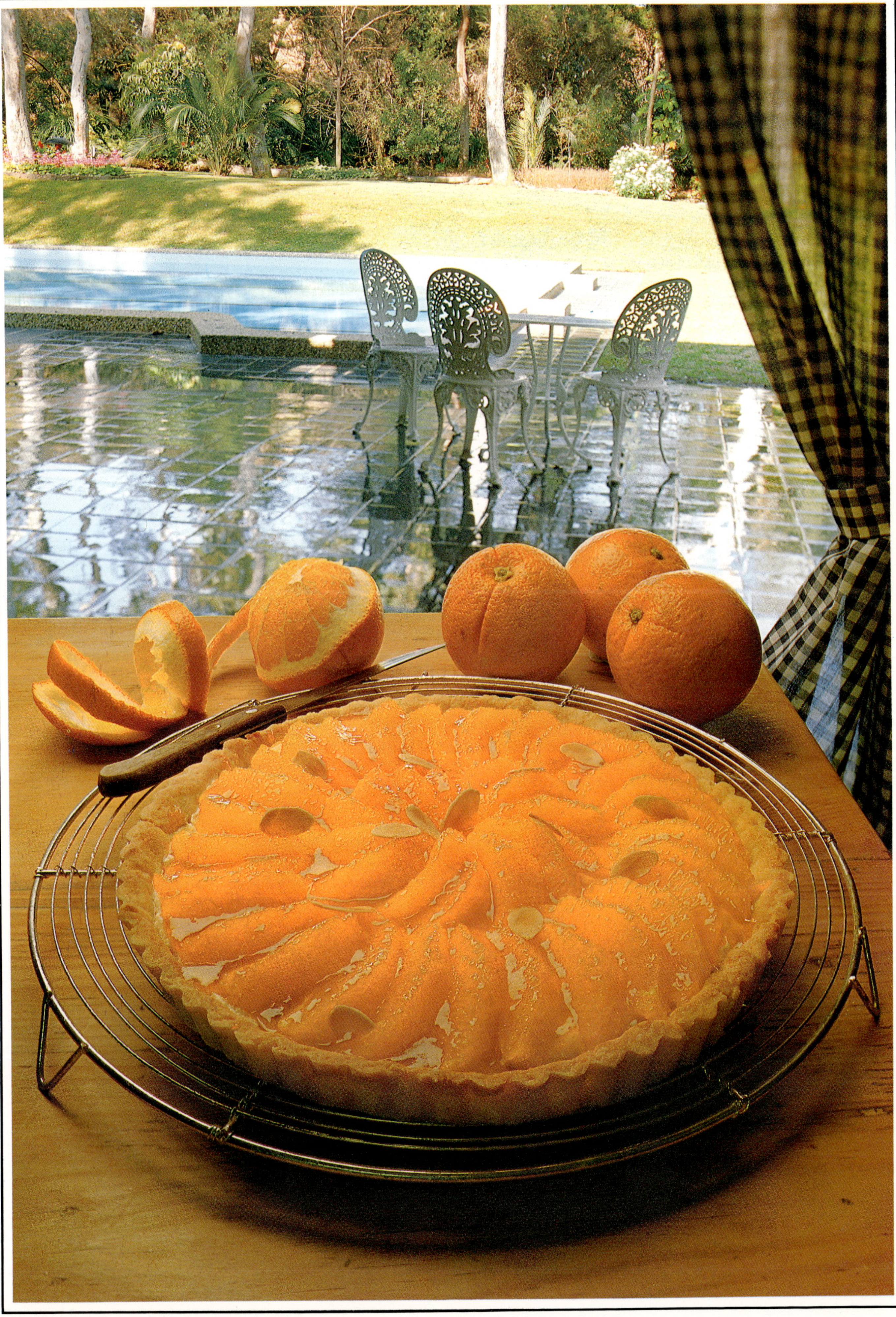

Peach Tart with Almond Cream

The almond cream may be made in advance and stored in the refrigerator for up to a week.
Serves 8–10

1 quantity (8 oz) Pâte sucrée (see recipe, page 190)

1 quantity (2 cups) (16fl oz) almond cream (see recipe, page 146)

4 large fresh peaches (or 8 canned peach halves)

125 ml (4fl oz) sieved apricot jam (jelly)

1 tablespoon water

Make the pastry according to the recipe and chill well.

Roll the pastry out thinly and line a 25 cm (10 in) flan tin. Prick the base of the pastry case, and bake 'blind' near the top of a preheated oven at 220°C (425°F/Gas 7) for 10 minutes. Cool for 10 minutes on a wire rack.

Filling: Prepare the almond cream according to the recipe. Halve the fresh peaches, then remove their stones and peel. (If using canned peaches, drain well.) Cut each peach half into thin slices crossways.

To finish the tart: Reduce the oven to 220°C (425°F/Gas 7). Spread the almond cream in the pastry case. Place one sliced peach half in the centre, then arrange the other sliced peach halves radiating in a star shape from the centre peach. Bake near the top of the oven for 30 minutes or until the cream is set. Allow to cool on a wire rack.

When cold, brush the top with the apricot jam that has been warmed with 1 tablespoon of water. Serve with whipped cream.

Cuba Libre Tart

Better known to some as Rum and Coke Pie, this is a popular recipe from Louisiana, U.S.A.
Serves 8

¾ quantity (6 oz) pâte brisée or sucrée (see page 190)

Filling:
1 tablespoon gelatine

250 ml (8fl oz) Coca-Cola, heated

125 ml (4fl oz) rum

¼ cup (1½ oz) brown sugar

125 ml (4fl oz) undrained, crushed, unsweetened pineapple (fresh or canned)

½ cup (3 oz) seedless raisins or sultanas

½ cup (2 oz) pecan nuts, roughly chopped

300 ml (10fl oz) cream, whipped

¼ cup (1 oz) icing (confectioners') sugar

2 teaspoons cocoa

grated chocolate, for decoration

Roll the pastry out thinly and line a 25 cm (10 in) flan tin.

Prick the base and chill well.

Bake the pastry case 'blind' near the top of a preheated oven at 220°C (425°F/Gas 7) for 10 minutes. Remove the 'blind' filling and bake for a further 10 minutes or until cooked. Cool on a wire rack until firm, then remove from the tin and cool completely.

Filling: Dissolve the gelatine in hot Coca-Cola. Allow to cool. Add the rum, brown sugar, pineapple, raisins and pecan nuts; mix well and refrigerate until it begins to set.

To finish the tart: Pour the filling mixture into the pastry case and refrigerate until well set. Decorate with whipped cream mixed with the icing sugar and cocoa. Sprinkle with grated chocolate.

TARTLETS

Almond Frangipane Tartlets

Eye-catching pastries to serve with afternoon tea
Makes 12

1 quantity (8 oz) pâte sucrée (see recipe, page 190)
Filling: 60 g (2 oz) butter
¼ cup (2 oz) caster (powdered) sugar
1 large egg
½ cup (2 oz) ground almonds
1½ tablespoons (½ oz) flour, sifted
lemon juice (or vanilla essence), to flavour
½ cup (2 oz) flaked almonds
sieved apricot jam (jelly), to glaze

Make the pastry and chill as directed. Roll the pastry out thinly and line twelve tartlet tins 8 cm (3 in) round. Prick the base of each pastry case with a fine fork.

Preheat the oven to 190°C (375°F/Gas 5). Cream the butter and sugar together until light and fluffy. Beat the egg in well. Stir in the ground almonds and flour, then flavour to taste with either lemon juice or vanilla.

Divide the filling between the pastry cases and spread smooth. Sprinkle the flaked almonds on top. Stand the tartlet tins on a baking tray and bake near the top of the preheated oven for 10 to 15 minutes or until firm and golden.

Have the apricot jam glaze ready and hot, and as soon as the tartlets come out of the oven, remove them from the tins and brush the tops generously with the apricot glaze.

Strawberry Cream Tartlets

Makes 12

¾ quantity (6 oz) rich shortcrust pastry (see recipe, page 184)
Filling: 185 g (6 oz) packaged cream cheese
¼ cup (2 oz) caster (powdered) sugar
1 teaspoon Kirsch
250 g (8 oz) small strawberries
½ cup (4fl oz) redcurrant jelly

Make the pastry according to the recipe, and chill well.

Roll the dough out thinly and line twelve 6 cm (2½ in) tartlet tins. Prick the base of each pastry case, place the tins on a baking tray, and bake near the top of a preheated oven at 200°C (400°F/Gas 6) for 10 to 12 minutes or until cooked. Allow to cool on wire racks.

Filling: Mix the cream cheese with the sugar and Kirsch with an electric mixer or in a food processor. Hull the strawberries, and halve or quarter them if large.

To finish the tartlets: Place 1 heaped teaspoon of filling in each cold tartlet case, then top neatly with strawberries.

Heat the redcurrant jelly until melted in a saucepan or microwave oven; brush it over the berries and filling, then leave to set. Serve for afternoon tea.

Strawberry Rhubarb Tartlets

Elegant tartlets ideal for a buffet reception
Makes 12

1 quantity (8 oz) pâte sucrée or brisée (see page 190)
Filling: 500 g (1 lb) ripe pink rhubarb
½ cup (4 oz) sugar
2 tablespoons cold water
1 cup (8fl oz) redcurrant jelly
1 tablespoon Kirsch
500 g (1 lb) strawberries
icing (confectioners') sugar, for decoration

Roll the pastry out thinly and line twelve boat-shaped tartlet tins arranged close together (as for Fruit Tartlets, on page 250). Prick the base of each pastry case and chill for 20 to 30 minutes.

Bake 'blind' near the top of a preheated oven at 200°C (400°F/Gas 6) for 10 minutes. Remove the 'blind' filling and bake for a further 5 minutes or until golden and cooked. Allow to cool on wire racks.

Trim and wash the rhubarb stems, and cut them into 1 cm (⅜ in) pieces. Place the rhubarb, sugar and water into a stainless steel or enamel-lined pan, bring to the boil, then simmer uncovered for 30 minutes, stirring occasionally, to form a thick purée. Cool, then chill until required.

Melt the redcurrant jelly with the Kirsch, then bring to the boil and simmer for 1 minute.

Hull and slice the strawberries.

To finish the tartlets: Brush the pastry cases with redcurrant glaze. Spread 2 tablespoons of rhubarb purée into each tartlet, top neatly with strawberry slices, then brush with more redcurrant glaze. Sift with icing sugar before serving. Serve with whipped cream, if liked.

Ricotta Tarts

Delightful tarts inspired by the Sicilian Cassata. Serve for afternoon tea, or for a dessert accompanied by chilled peaches or grapes
Makes 12

¾ *quantity (6 oz) sweet rich shortcrust pastry or pâte sucrée (see recipes, page 184 and 190)*

Filling:
500 g (1 lb) fresh Ricotta cheese

1 tablespoon cream

½ cup (4 oz) caster (powdered) sugar

¼ cup (1½ oz) mixed peel or chopped crystallised fruit

60 g (2 oz) dark cooking chocolate, grated

1 tablespoon Grand Marnier

Roll the pastry out thinly and line twelve tartlet tins. Prick the base of each pastry case, then chill for 10 to 15 minutes.

Bake the tartlet cases in the middle of a preheated oven at 220°C (425°F/Gas 7) for 8 to 10 minutes or until golden and cooked. Allow to cool on wire racks.

Filling: Mix the Ricotta cheese with the cream and sugar until well combined, then fold in the mixed peel or crystallised fruit, grated chocolate and Grand Marnier. Spoon the filling mixture into the pastry cases just before serving.

Lemon Chess Tartlets

A delightful winter dessert
Makes 4

¾ *quantity (6 oz) pâte sucrée (see recipe, page 190)*

Filling:
2 large eggs

4 tablespoons melted unsalted butter

¾ cup (6 oz) caster (powdered) sugar

2 tablespoons lemon juice

2 tablespoons cornmeal

2 teaspoons finely grated lemon rind

Roll the pastry out thinly and line four 8 cm (3 in) tartlet tins. Prick the base of each pastry case, and chill while preparing the filling.

Filling: Beat the eggs lightly in a bowl. Add the remaining ingredients, and mix until well combined.

To finish the tartlets: Preheat the oven to 150°C (300°F/Gas 2). Divide the filling between the pastry cases and spread smooth. Bake in the middle of the oven for 20 to 30 minutes until the filling is bubbling and the pastry is cooked. Allow to cool on wire racks (the filling will firm on cooling). Serve with whipped cream and strawberry purée.

Fruit Tartlets

Delightful to look at, delicious to eat
Makes 12

1 quantity (8 oz) pâte sucrée or brisée (see page 190)

Filling:
1 cup (8 fl oz) vanilla pastry cream (see recipe, page 146)

2 teaspoons brandy or liqueur (optional)

assorted fresh fruit, such as sliced apricots, sliced banana dipped in lemon juice, blueberries, blackcurrants, blackberries, stoned cherries, sliced Chinese gooseberries, seedless skinned grapes, ripe gooseberries, melon balls, mandarin and orange segments, pawpaw (papaya) balls, sliced plums or peaches, raspberries, redcurrants, sliced stawberries

½ cup (4 fl oz) apricot jam (jelly)

1 tablespoon water, brandy, liqueur or orange juice

Roll the pastry out thinly on a lightly-floured surface to a rectangle. Arrange twelve 8 cm (3 in) tartlet tins close together in rows, three by four. Drape the pastry loosely over the tins, allowing it to fall generously into each one, and press in with the fingers if necessary. Then roll over the top edge of the tins with the rolling pin to cut off the excess pastry. Press the pastry firmly into each tin with the tops of bent fingers, shaping to an even thickness around the sides. Prick the base of each pastry case with a fine fork, then chill for 20 to 30 minutes.

Line the pastry cases with greaseproof paper and baking beans or identical tins, and bake 'blind' near the top of a preheated oven at 200°C (400°F/Gas 6) for 10 minutes. Then remove the paper and beans or tins, and bake for a further 5 minutes or until golden and cooked. Allow to cool on wire racks.

Filling: Mix the vanilla pastry cream with the brandy. Prepare the fruit accordingly. Heat the jam; then strain, and stir in the water.

To finish the tartlets: Brush each pastry case with apricot glaze. Place 1 tablespoon of the vanilla pastry cream mixture into each pastry case, and top neatly with an attractive arrangement of prepared fresh fruit. Brush the fruit carefully with apricot glaze, making sure that the glaze seals to the edge of the pastry. Serve for afternoon tea or with whipped cream for dessert.

Right: **Fruit Tartlets** (see above).

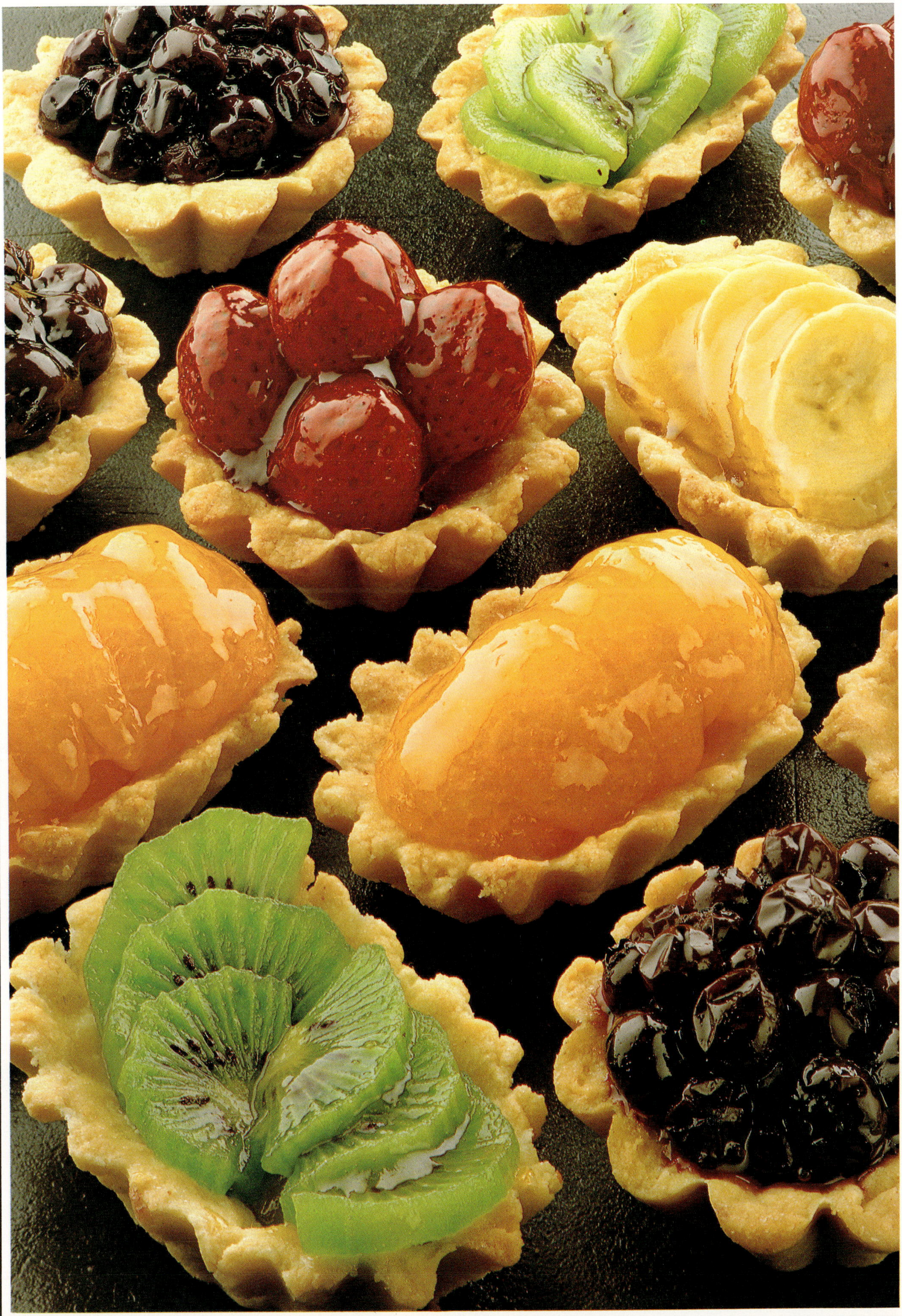

Filbert Tarts

Ideal for a special occasion, such as a Christening tea or a shower tea
Makes 12

Pastry:
1¼ cups (5 oz) flour
pinch of salt
90 g (3 oz) butter
¼ cup (2 oz) caster (powdered) sugar
¼ cup (1 oz) finely chopped hazelnuts
½ beaten egg
Filling:
60 g (2 oz) butter
¼ cup (2 oz) sugar
1 egg, beaten
1 teaspoon coffee essence
1 teaspoon honey
4 tablespoons (1½ oz) finely chopped hazelnuts
¼ cup (1 oz) cake or biscuit crumbs
1 tablespoon flour
1 tablespoon milk
raspberry jam (jelly)
Coffee Icing:
90 g (3 oz) soft butter or margarine
2 cups (10 oz) icing (confectioners') sugar, sifted
1 tablespoon coffee essence
crystallised mimosa or flower petals, for decoration

Pastry: Sift the flour and salt into the bowl of an electric mixer. Cut the butter into small pieces, then mix until mixture resembles fine breadcrumbs.

Add the sugar and hazelnuts, then mix to a stiff dough with the beaten egg. All ingredients may be mixed together in a food processor for 30 seconds. Wrap the dough in greaseproof paper and chill in the refrigerator for at least 30 minutes.

Filling: Cream the butter and sugar together in a food processor until light and fluffy. Add the remaining ingredients except the raspberry jam and mix well to a smooth consistency.

To finish the tartlets: Preheat the oven to 200°C (400°F/Gas 6). Roll the pastry out thinly on a lightly-floured board and line a tray of 12 tartlet tins. Place ½ teaspoon of raspberry jam in each pastry case and cover neatly with a heaped teaspoon of filling. Bake near the top of the oven for 15 to 20 minutes until cooked. Allow to cool on wire racks.

Coffee icing: Place all the ingredients in a bowl and mix with an electric mixer until soft and fluffy (like whipped cream). Pipe small rosettes of coffee icing on top of the tartlets, and decorate with crystallised mimosa.

Swedish Mazarin Tarts

Found in most pastry shops in Sweden, where they are popular with morning coffee
Makes 12

¾ quantity (6 oz) rich shortcrust pastry (see recipe, page 184)
Filling:
250 g (8 oz) marzipan or almond paste
2 tablespoons sugar
2 tablespoons flour
2 large eggs
1 egg white
¼ teaspoon almond essence
Icing:
1 cup (5 oz) icing (confectioners') sugar, sifted
2 tablespoons milk

Make the pastry according to the recipe, and chill well.

Break the almond paste into small pieces into a food processor or into the bowl of an electric mixer, and mix smoothly with the sugar and flour. Add the eggs and egg white separately, and mix until blended. Stir in the almond essence.

Preheat the oven to 160°C (325°F/Gas 3). Roll the pastry out thinly and line a tray of 12 tartlet tins. Prick the base of each pastry case. Spoon an equal quantity of filling into each. Bake near the top of the oven for 30 minutes or until the pastries are richly browned on top. Allow the tarts to cool for about 5 minutes in the tartlet tins, before removing and transferring to a wire rack.

Icing: Blend the sifted icing sugar smoothly with milk. Spoon equal quantities of icing onto each cooled mazarin, spread to coat evenly and leave to set.

The tarts can be stored in an airtight container for up to two days at room temperature. Freeze for longer storage.

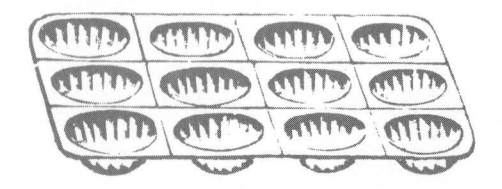

Redcurrant Tartlets

An original French recipe
Makes 12

¾ *quantity (6 oz) rich shortcrust pastry or pâte sucrée (see recipes, page 184 and 190)*

Filling:
185 g (6 oz) packaged cream cheese or Mascarpone (Italian cream cheese)

4 tablespoons cream

1 tablespoon caster (powdered) sugar

250 g (8 oz) redcurrants or blackcurrants (or mixed)

1 cup (8fl oz) redcurrant jelly

Make the pastry according to the recipe, and chill well.
  Roll the dough out thinly, cut into rounds and line twelve 6 cm (2½ in) tartlet tins. Press the pastry into the tins, and prick the base of each pastry case. Place the tins on a baking tray, and bake near the top of a preheated oven at 200°C (400°F/Gas 6) for 10 to 12 minutes or until cooked. Allow to cool on wire racks.

Filling: Mix the cream cheese with the cream and sugar in a food processor or with an electric mixer until smooth. Remove the stalks from the currants, and 'top and tail' them.

To finish the tartlets: Spread 1 tablespoon of cream cheese filling neatly in each cold pastry case. Sprinkle currants on top of the cream cheese, covering neatly.
  Heat the redcurrant jelly gently in a saucepan until clear and runny; spoon it over the currants and leave to set. Serve cold as a dessert or with coffee.

Variation: Try substituting fresh raspberries for currants.

Jam (Jelly) Meringue Tarts

Makes 12

¾ *quantity (6 oz) sweet rich shortcrust pastry or pâte sucrée (see recipes, page 190)*

Filling:
4 tablespoons raspberry or strawberry jam (jelly)

2 tablespoons redcurrant jelly

2 large egg whites

pinch of cream of tartar

½ cup (4 oz) caster (powdered) sugar

½ cup (2 oz) ground hazelnuts or walnuts (optional)

Roll the pastry out thinly and line twelve tartlet tins. Prick the base of each pastry case and chill well. Bake in the middle of a preheated oven at 200°C (400°F/Gas 6) for 10 minutes.

Filling: Mix the jam with the redcurrant jelly. Whisk the egg whites with the cream of tartar until stiff, then add the sugar slowly, whisking continuously. Fold in the ground nuts (if used).

To finish the tarts: Reduce the oven to 180°C (350°F/Gas 4). Place 2 teaspoons of jam and jelly mixture into each tartlet case, then pipe or spoon the meringue mixture neatly on top, covering the jam completely. Bake for 10 to 15 minutes until the meringue is lightly browned. Allow to cool on wire racks.

Variations: Substitute lemon butter (curd) or orange butter for the jam and jelly.

Honey Boats

Serve these elegant boat-shaped pastries at a special celebration.
Makes 12

---

1 quantity (8 oz) pâte sucrée (see recipe, page 190)

Filling:
90 g (3 oz) unsalted butter

⅓ cup (3 oz) caster (powdered) sugar

¾ cup (3 oz) ground almonds

1 tablespoon honey

coffee essence, to taste

Icing:
1 cup (5 oz) icing (confectioners') sugar

water, to mix

coffee essence

angelica and sugared mimosa balls, for decoration

Prepare the pastry and chill as directed. Roll the pastry out thinly, line twelve boat-shaped tartlet tins and bake 'blind' in a preheated oven at 190°C (375°F/Gas 5) for 5 to 7 minutes or until cooked. Allow to cool on wire racks.

Filling: Cream the butter and sugar until light and fluffy. Stir in the ground almonds and honey, then flavour with coffee essence to taste.

To finish the tartlets: Spread the filling neatly into the pastry cases, shaping it into a neat dome or peak with a small round-bladed knife. Place the filled boats on wire racks, and leave until the filling is firmly set.

Icing: Sift the icing sugar into a bowl, then stir in sufficient water to mix to a smooth, thick, coating consistency. Add a few drops of coffee essence, and mix to the desired colour. Spread the icing neatly over the honey boats, and decorate with tiny angelica leaves and sugared mimosa balls.

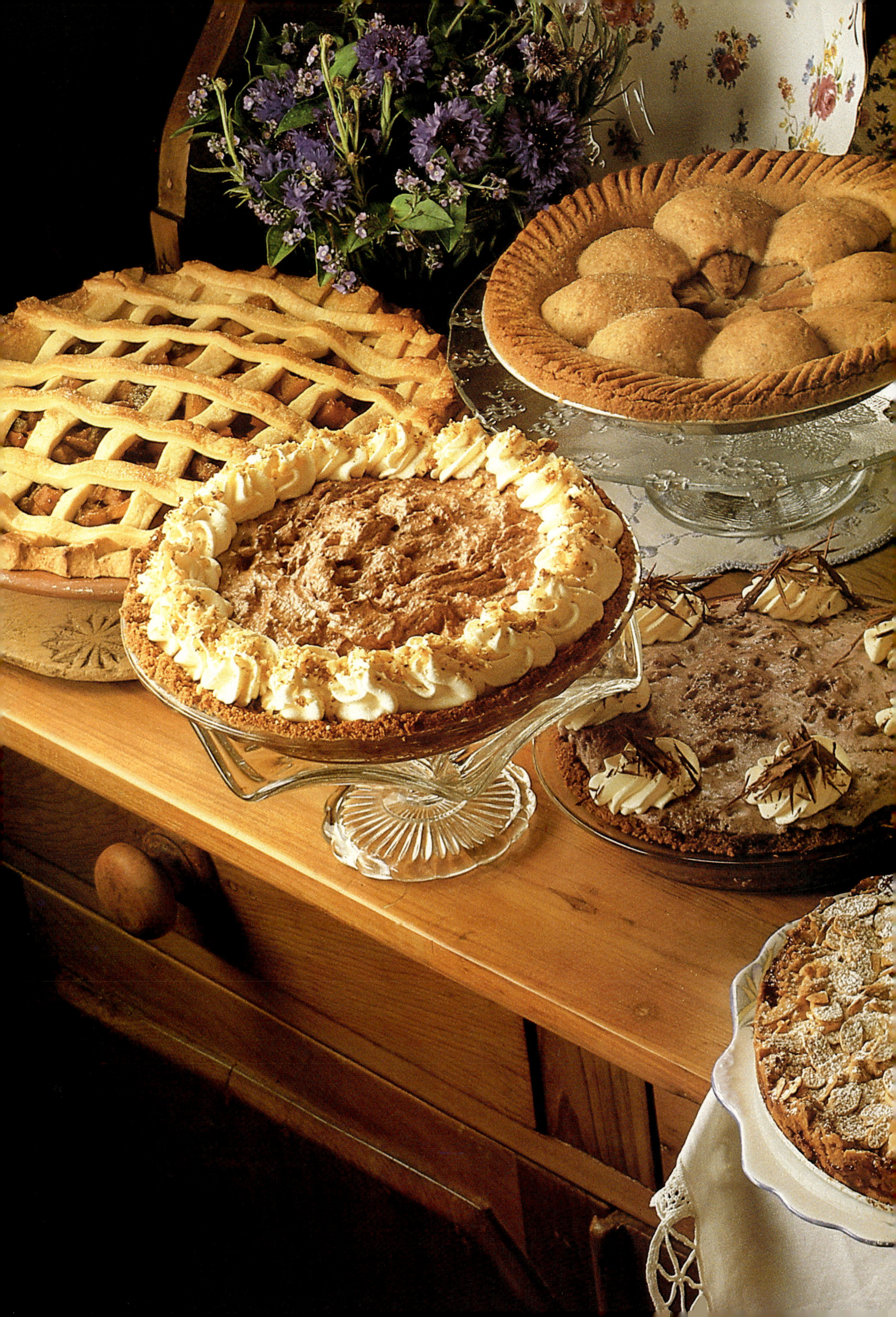

Sweet Pies

Sweet Pies

Simple Simon met a pieman,
Going to the fair;
Says Simple Simon to the pieman,
Let me taste your ware.

Says the pieman to Simple Simon,
Show me first your penny;
Says Simple Simon to the pieman,
Indeed I have not any.

If you met Simple Simon and the pieman going to the fair nowadays, you would probably find the look of his pies has not changed much—although he would certainly have a wider selection, as international influences would have intermingled with his traditional English fare.

A brief look at the history of the pie reveals that it has been popular since the time of Ancient Rome. The Romans after conquering the Greeks took back with them the Grecian art of pastry-making and combined it with their beautiful fruits, to create delicious desserts and puddings. From Rome, pie-making spread through Europe and the pie took on the flavour and the look of the host country.

From Europe, the Pilgrims introduced the art of pie-making to America, and there its development has been so closely related to the traditions and customs of the nation that we hear such sayings as: 'As American as Blueberry Pie'. Some two hundred years ago, cooks on the First Fleet took with them to Australia the traditional English pie.

The traditional pie, as we now know it, has altered little since those early times and is still high on the list of favourites. But with the ease of communication and travel, the flavour and techniques of any country's recipe that we wish to follow are at our fingertips.

Janice Baker

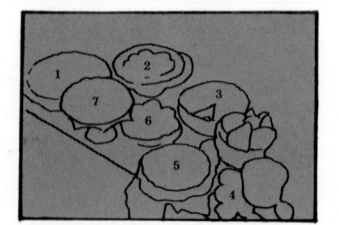

1. Gramma Pie (see p. 273)
2. Pear and Hazelnut Pie (see p. 258)
3. Lemon Meringue Pie (see p. 262)
4. Mincemeat Pies (see p. 274)
5. Shortbread Pie (see p. 278)
6. Raspberry Cream Pie (see p. 277)
7. French Mint Pie (see p. 264)

SWEET PIES

Tips for Better Pie-making

It is not always necessary to chill the pastry if it is handling well. Tests show that there is little difference in the shrinkage and shortness of the pastry if it has not been chilled. But if the weather is warm and the pastry is soft and oily looking, do chill the pastry for at least 15 minutes before rolling and baking.

Rolling Pastry to Fit a Pie Dish:
Place the ball of dough on a lightly-floured surface. Pound it lightly with the rolling pin to flatten it, then roll it out working from the centre to the edge in a quick stroke away from you.

Using a large palette knife, slide under the dough to release it from the working surface, and give the dough a half-turn clockwise.

Roll out in the same manner as before, rolling the dough with the end shape required in mind. Even up the edges with the palms of your hands, pushing the dough back towards the centre.

Roll out the pastry to about 3 mm (⅛ in) thick and about 5 cm (2 in) larger than the dish to be lined.

To line the pie plate: Slide the palette knife under the dough to release it. Gently roll the dough over the rolling pin and lay the pastry over the centre of the dish. Ease the dough into the dish and press the dough against the base and sides.

Trim off surplus edges of the dough, using a sharp knife and drawing the knife against the rim in a downwards action in short swift strokes. Or, roll the surplus pastry back under itself to form a thicker rim. Pinch or crimp the edges as desired.

If a double crust is desired, do not trim any overhang. Brush the bottom and sides well with beaten egg white if the filling is extra juicy and let it dry for a few minutes. Add the filling to pie shell, mounding it up in the centre. Roll out the top crust, making it slightly thinner if you like. Brush the pastry rim with a little water or egg, and fit the top crust over the filling. Trim both crusts evenly, press to seal the edges, and crimp. Decorate the top with pastry shapes, if liked, and cut decorative steam vents in the top crust.

To Bake 'Blind':
Line the pie tin first with pastry. Using soft apple paper or crumpled greaseproof paper, line the pastry. Cut surplus paper close to the rim of the pie. Fill with uncooked dried beans or rice to two-thirds fill the pie. Bake 'blind' in a preheated moderately hot oven, 180°C (375°F/Gas 5), for about 10 minutes for the larger pies and about 6 minutes for the smaller pies. Remove the baking beans and paper. Continue baking if the recipe requires; or put in the filling, then continue baking.

The reason for baking the pie blind with the beans or rice is to hold the pastry in place during the initial baking, as the actual filling would.

About Baking Pies:
Always preheat the oven before baking, so that the pastry starts to cook immediately it is placed in the oven.

Baking the pie on a baking tray that has been heated through in the oven, gives the bottom crust instant and even heat. It sets the bottom crust, so that the filling does not seep through the pastry and make the base crust soggy.

When baking more than one pie at a time, stagger the pie tins on the oven rack(s), leaving plenty of room between them for heat to circulate.

If the crust is browning too fast, cover it with a piece of aluminium foil. Crimped edges, in particular, brown faster than the rest; these may be covered with strips of aluminium foil to protect them.

If the pie is juicy and you wish it to have a crisp base crust, dry out the base over a very low heat on a heat-dispersing ring or mat for 15 minutes or so. (This can only be done if the pie plate is metal.)

Cutting Pies:
Most pies should be cooled for a few minutes on a wire rack before being cut.

Divide the pie mentally into the number of pieces required, before making the first cut. Use a very sharp thin-bladed knife. After cutting, lift the segment out of the tin with the flat of the knife or with a pie slice.

Meringue pies:
Use a sharp knife dipped into hot water after each cut, to stop the meringue from sticking to the knife.

Pear and Hazelnut Pie

This is an unusual pie using hazelnut and cinnamon-flavoured pastry which encases fresh quartered pears. Use the small dessert pears, if available. Serve warm with lightly-whipped cream. It makes a delightful dessert for a luncheon.
Serves 4–6

Pastry:
2 cups (8 oz) flour
pinch of salt
½ cup (2 oz) ground hazelnuts
2 teaspoons ground cinnamon
155 g (5 oz) butter
½ cup (4 oz) caster (powdered) sugar
2–3 drops vanilla essence
1 egg
1 tablespoon water
Filling:
3–4 ripe dessert pears
approx. 1 tablespoon caster (powdered) sugar
whipped cream, for serving

Pastry: Sift the flour and salt onto a working surface. Make a large well in the centre. Sprinkle the ground hazelnuts and cinnamon into the centre, and make another well using the cushion of your hand. Place the butter in the centre of the well and make a depression in the slab. Sprinkle over the sugar and break the egg on top; add the vanilla essence. Pinch the butter, sugar and egg together using the tips of your fingers only, until combined. Draw the ground hazelnuts and flour into the centre using a spatula. Add the tablespoon of water to the dough if needed. Gather the dough together and wrap in a sheet of greaseproof paper. Chill for 15 minutes.

Preheat the oven to 190°C (375°F/Gas 5).

Filling: Peel and quarter the pears, and remove the core.

To finish the pie: Roll out two-thirds of the pastry on a lightly-floured surface and use to line a shallow 20 cm (8 in) pie plate. Arrange the pear quarters over the base and sprinkle with some caster sugar. Roll the remaining pastry into a round, large enough to cover the pie; and cut a 6 cm (2½ in) circle out of the centre. Lay the pastry over the pears, and trim the edges. Press the edges together using the back of a fork or knife. Bake for 35 minutes or until evenly golden brown. Sprinkle with a little more caster sugar, and return to the oven for a few minutes. Cook on a rack. Serve warm, with lightly-whipped cream.

Cherry Pie

Serves 6–8

Pastry:
2 cups (8 oz) self-raising flour
125 g (4 oz) lard
5 tablespoons water
pinch of salt
Filling:
2½ cups (1¼ lb) stoned, stewed, drained cherries
1 cup (8 fl oz) cherry juice
½ cup (4 oz) sugar
½ teaspoon salt
2 drops almond essence
1 tablespoon fine tapioca
1 tablespoon melted butter
egg white, for glazing
caster (powdered) sugar, for glazing

Pastry: Sift the flour into a bowl and cut in the lard; rub in until the mixture resembles fine breadcrumbs. Add the water, and mix in with a knife until a rough dough forms. Refrigerate the dough for 30 minutes.

Filling: Combine all the ingredients for the filling, and allow to stand for 15 minutes.

Preheat the oven to 190°C (375°F/Gas 5). Line a deep 20 cm (8 in) pie dish with two-thirds of the pastry. Fill with the cherry mixture. Roll out the remaining pastry and use to cover the pie. Pinch the edges, and make four slits on the top of the pastry. Glaze the pastry with egg white, and sprinkle caster sugar over the top. Bake for 35 minutes.

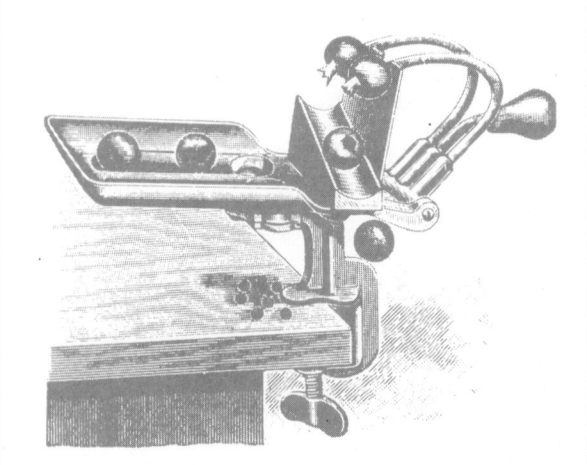

Right: **Cherry Pie** (see above).

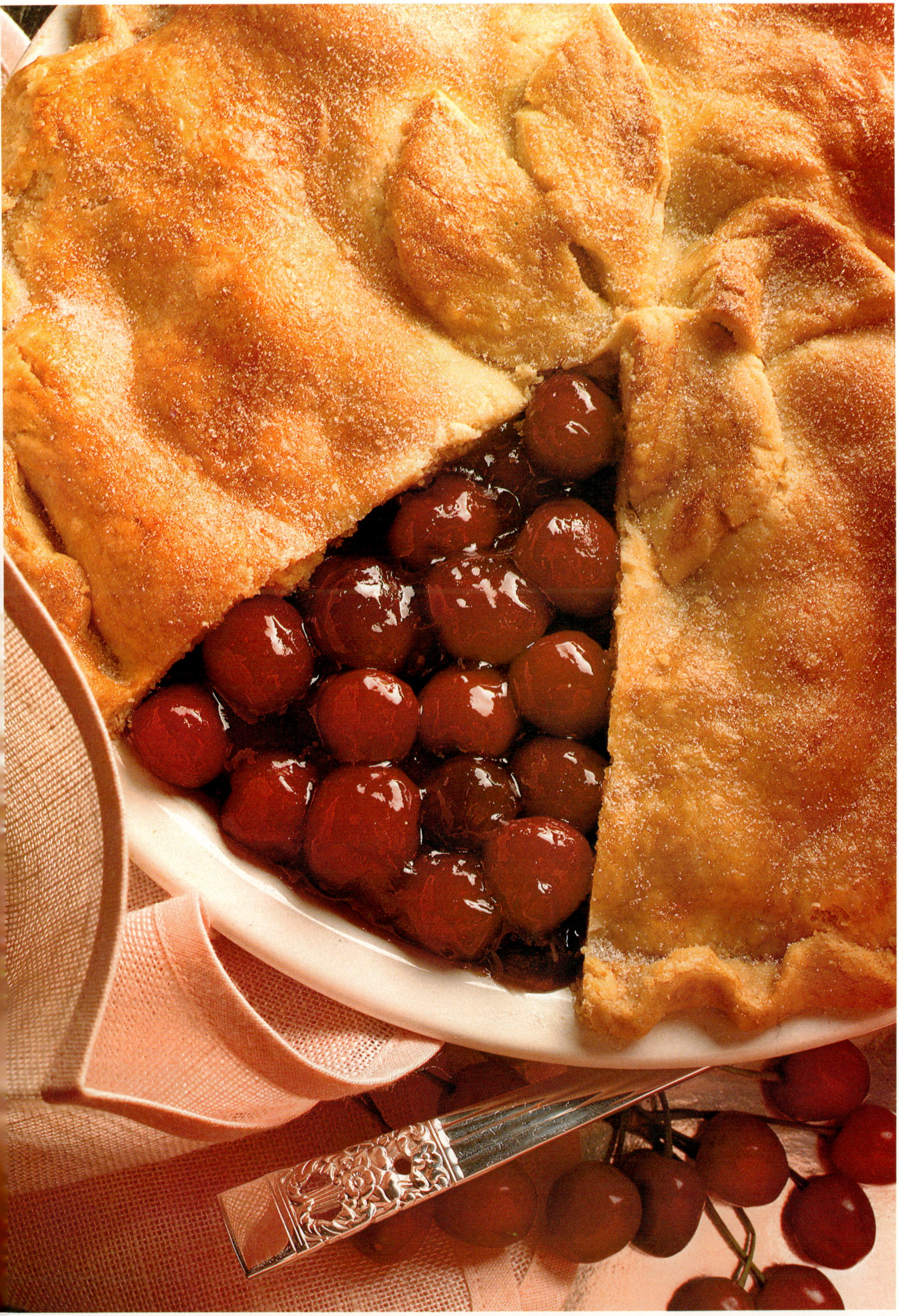

Custard Pie

Serves 6

185 g (6 oz) rich short crust pastry (see recipe, page 184)

Filling:
2½ cups (20fl oz) milk, or half milk/half cream

vanilla pod

3 eggs

1 egg yolk

2 tablespoons caster (powdered) sugar

nutmeg

Make the pastry according to the recipe, and chill. Use to line a 23 cm (9 in) pie plate.
Preheat the oven to 200°C (400°F/Gas 7).

Filling: Heat the milk with the vanilla pod (slit open to release the black seeds) until scalding. Beat the eggs and caster sugar together, and pour over the scalded milk. Strain into a jug, and allow to cool. (Dry out the vanilla pod and store it in sugar.)

To finish the pie: Bake the pastry case 'blind' in the preheated oven for 10 minutes. Remove the 'blind' filling (the baking beans and paper). Pour the now-cool custard over, and sprinkle with freshly grated nutmeg. Reduce the oven temperature to 180°C (350°F/Gas 4), return the pie to the oven and continue baking for 25 minutes or until the custard is set and the pastry is golden. Allow to cool on a wire rack.

Note: Be careful not to over-bake, as this makes the custard watery. If the custard begins to rise, remove from the oven at once.

Egg Nog Pie

Serves 6–8

250 g (8 oz) rich shortcrust pastry (see recipe, page 184)

Filling:
1¼ cups (10fl oz) milk

½ cup (4 oz) sugar

4 large eggs, separated

1 tablespoon gelatine

¼ cup (2fl oz) hot water

¾ cup (6fl oz) cream

1 tablespoon brandy

1 tablespoon caster (powdered) sugar

dark chocolate, for decoration

Make the pastry according to the recipe, and chill. Preheat the oven to 190°C (375°F/Gas 5). Roll out the pastry and use to line a 23 cm (9 in) pie plate. Decorate the edge and bake 'blind' for 10 minutes. Remove the baking beans and paper, and bake for a further 15 minutes or until the pastry is evenly golden brown and crisp. Allow to cool.

Filling: Heat the milk until lukewarm. Lightly beat the sugar and egg yolks together, and pour over the milk. Return the milk-eggs mixture to the top of a double boiler and cook, stirring until the custard coats the back of a spoon. Leave to cool, with a piece of wet greaseproof paper on top to prevent a skin forming.

Dissolve the gelatine in the hot water, and stir through the custard. Leave until just on setting point.

Whip the cream until it holds its shape, and then fold it through the custard with the brandy. Whisk the egg whites until stiff and beat in 1 tablespoon of caster sugar. Fold through the custard mixture. Pour the filling into the prepared pastry case, and chill.

When ready to serve, decorate with rosettes of whipped cream and grated curls of chocolate.

Buttermilk Chess Pie

Serves 6–8

155 g (5 oz) lard pastry or shortcrust pastry (see recipes, page 182 and 193)

Filling:
60 g (2 oz) butter

1 cup (7 oz) caster sugar

3 large eggs, beaten

¼ cup (1 oz) flour

pinch of salt

1 cup (8fl oz) buttermilk

1 teaspoon vanilla essence

ground nutmeg, for sprinkling

Make the pastry according to the recipe, and chill.
Preheat the oven to 200°C (400°F/Gas 6).

Filling: Cream the butter and sugar until light and creamy. Add the beaten eggs gradually, beating well after each addition. Fold in the sifted flour with the salt, beating well. Add the buttermilk and vanilla.

To finish the pie: Roll out the pastry on a lightly-floured surface and use to line a 23 cm (9 in) pie plate. Bake 'blind' in the preheated oven for 10 minutes. Remove the baking beans and paper, reduce the oven temperature to 190°C (375°F/Gas 5) and continue baking for 10 minutes. Remove from the oven, carefully spoon in the filling mixture, then return to the oven and bake for 30 minutes or until the filling is set.

Serve warm or cold, sprinkled with grated nutmeg and with a bowl of whipped cream.

Christmas Cottage Cheese Pie

Serves 8

250 g (8 oz) shortcrust pastry (see recipe, page 182)
Filling: 1 cup (8 oz) cottage cheese
2 large eggs
¼ cup (2 oz) caster (powdered) sugar
1 teaspoon vanilla essence
1 cup (8 oz) fruit mince
icing (confectioners') sugar, for dusting

Make the pastry according to the recipe, and chill.
Preheat the oven to 200°C (400°F/Gas 6).

Filling: Beat the cottage cheese, eggs, caster sugar and vanilla essence together.

To finish the pie: Roll out the pastry on a lightly-floured surface and use to line a 23 cm (9 in) pie plate. Bake 'blind' for 10 minutes in the preheated oven. Remove the 'blind' filling, and allow to cool.

Spread the fruit mince over the base of the pastry case, and spoon the cottage cheese mixture over. Bake in a preheated oven at 190°C (375°F/Gas 5) for 25 minutes. Allow to cool, and serve dusted with icing sugar and a sprig of holly.

Cream Cheese Peach Pie

Serves 6

185 g (6 oz) filo pastry
125 g (4 oz) butter, melted
Filling: 500 g (1 lb) fresh peaches (or canned peaches, drained)
½ cup (4 oz) sugar
1 tablespoon apricot jam (jelly)
1 tablespoon lemon juice
125 g (4 oz) cream cheese
grated rind of 1 lemon
sour cream
icing (confectioners') sugar, for sprinkling

Peel the peaches and remove their stones; chop roughly. Place in a heavy saucepan, and add the sugar, apricot jam and lemon juice. Simmer over a low heat until the mixture is quite thick (about 20 minutes). Allow to cool.

Preheat the oven 180°C (350°F/Gas 4).

Beat the cream cheese with the grated lemon rind and 1 tablespoon of sour cream.

To finish the pie: Brush a sheet of filo pastry with the melted butter; lay butter-side down in a 23 cm (9 in) pie plate. Brush with melted butter, and lay over another sheet of filo pastry. Brush with melted butter, and repeat with about three more layers of pastry.

Spoon the cream cheese mixture over, and smooth the top. Spoon the cooled peach filling over. Top the filling with about five sheets of pastry, brushing each one (as before) with the melted butter. Trim off the edges of the pastry with a sharp knife.

Bake for 30 to 40 minutes or until crisp and golden. Sprinkle with icing sugar and serve warm with sour cream.

Ricotta Pie

Serves 8

185 g (6 oz) pâte brisée (see recipe, page 190)
Filling: 3 tablespoons pine nuts
2 tablespoons slivered almonds
2 tablespoons chopped mixed peel
2 tablespoons currants
1 tablespoon flour
4 eggs
¾ cup (6 oz) sugar
750 g (1½ lb) Ricotta cheese
1 teaspoon vanilla essence

Make the pastry according to the recipe, and chill.

Preheat the oven to 190°C (375°F/Gas 5). Roll out the pastry on a lightly-floured surface and use to line a deep 23 cm (9 in) pie dish; crimp the edges. Bake 'blind' for about 10 minutes. Remove the baking beans and paper, and allow to cool while preparing the filling. Reset the oven temperature to 180°C (350°F/Gas 4).

Filling: Toast the pine nuts in a dry frying pan until just beginning to brown. Remove, and mix with the almonds, mixed peel, currants and flour.

Beat the eggs until light and fluffy, and gradually add the sugar. Beat the Ricotta cheese until creamy with the vanilla, and then beat in the egg mixture. Stir through the nut and fruit mixture.

Pour the filling into the prepared pie case, and bake in the preheated oven for about 40 minutes. Allow to cool.

Chocolate Praline Pie

Praline is a French confection made with almonds toasted in caramelised sugar. It can be made beforehand (a recipe is given below), and stored until ready for use in the pie.
Serves 4–6

185 g (6 oz) pâte sucrée (see recipe, page 190)
Filling: 3 tablespoons cocoa
⅓ cup (3 oz) sugar
2 cups (16 fl oz) water
1 tablespoon flour
4 tablespoons cornflour (cornstarch)
½ cup (4 fl oz) milk
2 egg yolks, lightly beaten
60 g (2 oz) butter
Topping: 3 tablespoons ground praline (see recipe below)
½ cup (4 fl oz) cream
1 teaspoon caster (powdered) sugar
drops of vanilla essence

Make the pastry according to the recipe, and chill.
 Preheat the oven to 190°C (375°F/Gas 5). Roll out the pastry on a lightly-floured surface and use to line a 20 cm (8 in) pie plate. Bake 'blind' for 7 minutes. Remove the 'blind' filling, and bake for a further 15 minutes or until the pastry is crisp and evenly golden. (Do not bake the pastry too dark or it will be bitter.)

Filling: Place the cocoa and sugar in a saucepan and mix in the water; bring to the boil, and simmer for 10 minutes. Mix the flours together with the milk until it forms a smooth paste; and add to the chocolate mixture, stirring over the heat until the mixture boils. Pour a little of the hot mixture over the egg yolks, mix in, and then pour this into the saucepan. Stirring constantly, add the butter a small piece at a time, until the butter is melted and the mixture is smooth. Allow it to cool a little, and pour into the prepared pie case. Chill.

Topping: Whip the cream with the sugar until it holds its shape, flavouring it with a couple of drops of vanilla. Spread over the chilled pie top, and sprinkle with ground praline.

Praline: Place ⅓ cup (2 oz) whole unblanched almonds and ¼ cup (2 oz) sugar in a small heavy saucepan. Cook over a very low heat until the sugar begins to caramelise and the nuts begin to toast. Tip the pan from side to side to coat the nuts in the liquid caramel; or use a metal spoon just to prod the nuts into the caramel. Do not stir. When a good deep caramel, turn the mixture out into a greased baking tin and leave to set. When it is set, crush with a rolling pin or in a food processor. Store immediately in an airtight jar until ready to use.

Lemon Meringue Pie

Serves 4–6

185 g (6 oz) rich shortcrust pastry (see recipe, page 184)
1 egg white
Filling: 4 tablespoons cornflour (cornstarch)
¾ cup (6 oz) sugar
1½ cups (12 fl oz) water
4 tablespoons lemon juice
grated rind and juice 1 lemon
2 eggs, separated
60 g (2 oz) butter
4 tablespoons caster (powdered) sugar, for meringue

Make the pastry according to the recipe, and chill.
 Preheat the oven to 190°C (375°F/Gas 5). Roll out the pastry thinly and use to line a 20 cm (8 in) pie plate. Crimp the edges well, bringing the pastry up quite high on the rim. Prick the base of the pastry well with a fork and brush with beaten egg white. Bake for 20 minutes.
 Leave the oven on, at 190°C (375°F/Gas 5).

Filling: Place the cornflour, sugar and water in a saucepan. Blend well and bring to the boil, stirring until the mixture thickens. Lower the heat, and cook for a few minutes longer. Stir in the lemon juice, lemon rind, egg yolks and butter. Beat well until smooth and shiny, then pour immediately into the prepared pie case.
 Whip the egg whites with a pinch of salt until stiff. Add the sugar gradually, making a stiff meringue. Spread the meringue over the lemon filling, sealing right to the edge of the pastry, and swirling peaks in the meringue.
 Bake in the preheated oven for 15 minutes. Allow to cool before cutting.

Right: **Chocolate Praline Pie** (see above).

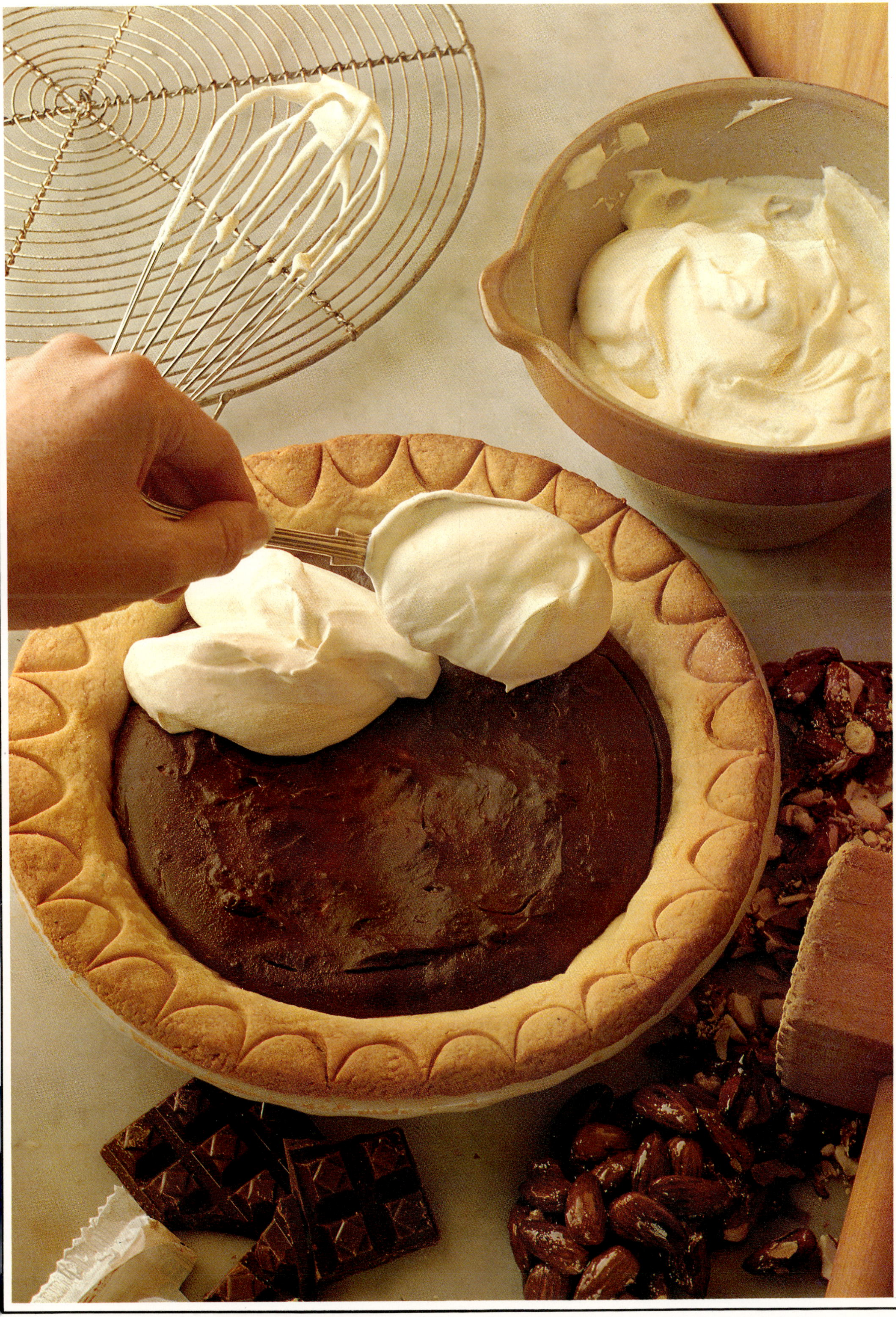

Gravel Pie

Serves 6

185 g (6 oz) rich shortcrust pastry (see recipe, page 184)
Filling: 1 cup (8 oz) sugar or honey
½ cup (4fl oz) water
3 eggs, lightly beaten
½ cup (3 oz) seedless raisins
1 cup (4 oz) cake crumbs
⅓ cup (1½ oz) flour
1 teaspoon cinnamon
pinch of ground nutmeg
pinch of ground ginger
90 g (3 oz) butter

Make the pastry according to the recipe, and chill.

Filling: Place the sugar (or honey), water and eggs in a bowl over a pan of simmering water. Stir until the sugar has dissolved and the mixture thickens. Allow to cool.

When cool, stir the raisins into the mixture.

Mix the cake crumbs, flour and spices together. Rub in the butter as you would for pastry.

To finish the pie: Preheat the oven to 180°C (350°F/Gas 4). Roll out the pastry on a lightly-floured surface and use it to line a 20–23 cm (8–9 in) pie dish. Crimp or decorate the edges. Pour in the raisin mixture, sprinkle the cake crumb mixture over the top, then sprinkle with the nutmeg and ginger. Bake for 30 minutes or until the topping is golden brown and the pastry is crisp.

Allow to cool, and serve with ice-cream or whipped cream.

French Mint Pie

Serves 6–8

1 quantity Crumb Crust (see recipe, page 193)
Filling: 60 g (2 oz) dark chocolate
90 g (3 oz) unsalted butter
1½ cup (8 oz) icing (confectioners') sugar
2 large eggs
2½ cups (20fl oz) cream
drops of peppermint essence
chopped walnuts, to decorate

Make the Crumb Crust according to the recipe, and use to line a 20 cm (8 in) pie plate. Bake in a preheated oven at 190°C (375°F/Gas 5) for 10 minutes. Allow to cool.

Melt the chocolate on a plate over a pan of simmering water. Allow to cool.

Beat the butter and icing sugar together until light and creamy. Beat the cooled chocolate into the butter mixture with the eggs until the mixture is light and fluffy.

Whip the cream until it holds its shape; fold half into the chocolate mixture. Stir through a couple of drops of peppermint essence to taste, and spoon the mixture into the prepared pie case. Chill until the filling is firm.

When ready to serve, decorate with remaining cream and the chopped walnuts.

Coconut Cream Pie

Serves 4–6

125 g (4 oz) shortcrust pastry (see recipe, page 182)
Filling: ½ cup (4 oz) caster (powdered) sugar
1 tablespoon arrowroot
pinch of salt
¾ cup (6fl oz) water
drops of almond essence
drops of vanilla essence
2 egg whites
¾ cup (6fl oz) cream
¾ cup (2½ oz) desiccated coconut

Make the pastry according to the recipe, and chill.

Preheat the oven to 190°C (375°F/Gas 5). Roll out the pastry and use to line an 18 cm (7 in) pie plate. Crimp the edges and bake 'blind' for 7 minutes. Remove the baking beans and paper, and bake for a further 15 minutes or until the pastry is evenly golden and crisp. Allow to cool on a wire rack.

Filling: Place 5 tablespoons of the measured sugar, and the arrowroot, salt and water into a small saucepan; cook over low heat until smooth and clear. Add 1 drop of almond essence and 2 drops of vanilla essence to flavour. Allow to cool.

Beat the egg whites stiffly and stir into the sugar mixture. Pour into the cooled pie shell.

Whip the cream and sweeten it with the remaining 1¼ tablespoons of caster sugar and add a drop each of almond essence and vanilla essence. Fold in half of the coconut, and spread over the pie. Sprinkle the top with the remaining coconut.

Set in the freezer for 30 minutes, then remove to the refrigerator. Serve chilled.

Frangipane Pie

Serves 6–8

185 g (6 oz) rich shortcrust pastry (see recipe, page 184)

First Layer of Filling:
¾ cup (6fl oz) evaporated milk

½ cup (4fl oz) water

¼ cup (2 oz) sugar

pinch of salt

2 tablespoons cornflour (cornstarch)

1 cup (3 oz) desiccated coconut

30 g (1 oz) butter

1 teaspoon vanilla essence

Second Layer of Filling:
450 g (1 lb) canned crushed pineapple

2 tablespoons cornflour

¼ cup (2fl oz) water

2 egg yolks

Meringue:
2 egg whites

4 tablespoons caster (powdered) sugar

Make the pastry according to the recipe, and chill.

Preheat the oven to 190°C (375°F/Gas 5). Roll out the pastry on a lightly-floured surface and use to line a 20 cm (8 in) pie dish. Crimp the edges, and bake 'blind' for 10 minutes. Remove the 'blind' filling, and bake for a further 20 minutes or until the pastry is golden and crisp. Allow to cool on a wire rack.

Filling: *First layer:* Place the evaporated milk, half the water, the sugar and salt in a heavy-based saucepan. Stir over a low heat until the mixture comes to the boil and the sugar has dissolved. Blend the remaining water and the cornflour together to a smooth paste. Add to the milk mixture, stirring until the mixture thickens. Remove from the heat, stir in the coconut, butter and vanilla, and allow to cool slightly.

Second Layer: Place the pineapple and juice from the can in a heavy-based saucepan, and bring to the boil. Blend the cornflour, water and egg yolks to a smooth paste; add to the pineapple, and stir over a low heat until thick. Allow to cool slightly.

Preheat the oven to 180°C (350°F/Gas 4).

Pour the first layer into the prepared pie dish. Then pour the second layer in.

Meringue: Whisk the egg whites until stiff. Gradually add the sugar, beating well after each addition; beat until it is the texture of a smooth stiff meringue. Spoon over the pie top, taking it right to the edge of the pastry.

Bake in the preheated oven for 15 minutes or until the meringue is golden. Serve warm or cold.

Rum Pie

Serves 6

185 g (6 oz) pâte brisée (see recipe, page 190)

Filling:
2 cups (16fl oz) milk

pinch of ground nutmeg

2 eggs, separated

1 egg yolk

¼ cup (2 oz) sugar

1 teaspoon cornflour (cornstarch)

2 teaspoons gelatine

2 tablespoons rum (preferably dark Jamaican rum)

Topping:
90 g (3 oz) dark chocolate

2 tablespoons water

½ cup (4fl oz) cream

1 tablespoon rum

Make the pastry according to the recipe, and chill.

Preheat the oven to 190°C (375°F/Gas 5). Roll out the pastry on a lightly-floured surface and use to line a 20 cm (8 in) pie plate. Bake 'blind' for 10 minutes. Remove the 'blind' filling, and bake for a further 15 minutes or until the pastry is evenly golden and crisp. Allow to cool on a wire rack.

Filling: Heat the milk and nutmeg. Beat the egg yolks and sugar together until pale, and add the cornflour. Pour a little of the hot milk into the mixture and mix well, then pour this into the rest of the hot milk; stir over a low heat until thickened. Dissolve the gelatine in a little hot water and add to the custard mixture; mix well. Allow to cool. When just on setting point, beat the egg whites until stiff and fold them through the custard mixture with 2 tablespoons of rum. Spoon into the pie shell, and chill while making the topping.

Topping: Melt the chocolate with the water. Allow to cool.

Whip the cream, and add the cooled chocolate and the rum. Pour over the pie top and chill again, until ready to serve. Serve with extra whipped cream.

Gâteau de Pithiviers Feuilleté

This buttery rich pie is a favourite among the French. Especially for holidays, the pâtisserie windows display rows of different-sized pies to tempt passers-by.
Serves 6–8

375 g (12 oz) puff pastry (see recipe, page 186)
Filling:
125 g (4 oz) butter
½ cup (4 oz) caster (powdered) sugar
1 egg
1 egg yolk
1¼ cups (4 oz) ground almonds
2 teaspoons flour
1 teaspoon vanilla essence
beaten egg, for glazing
extra caster sugar, for glazing

Make the pastry according to the recipe, and chill.

Filling: Cream the butter and sugar until pale and creamy. Beat in the egg and egg yolk. Stir in the ground almonds, flour and vanilla essence.

To finish the pie: Preheat the oven to 220°C (425°F/Gas 7). Roll out half of the pastry on a lightly-floured surface, into a round 28 cm (11 in) across. Using a saucepan lid, cut a circle 25 cm (10 in) across, angling the knife away from the lid slightly. Roll out the remaining pastry slightly thicker than for the first, and cut into a 25 cm (10 in) round. Place the thinner of the circles on a baking tray, and mound the filling in the centre, leaving a 2.5 cm (1 in) border. Brush the edge with water and place the second pastry round over the filling. Press the edges together firmly. Scallop the edge of the pie with the back of a knife, pulling it in at intervals. Brush the pie with beaten egg glaze and, working from the centre, score the top in curves like the petals of a flower. Chill for 15 minutes.

Bake for 30 to 35 minutes or until firm and puffed. Sprinkle the top with caster sugar and place the pie under a hot griller (broiler) until the sugar has caramelized and the surface is shiny. Allow to cool on a wire rack.

Variation: Mound 4–5 dessert pears, peeled, cored and sliced, in the centre of the pastry circle. Sprinkle with a little sugar and cinnamon or ground cardamom, and continue as above. Serve warm with whipped cream.

Almond and Poppy Seed Pie

This pie may be made in a pie dish or made like a strudel, by laying leaves of filo pastry on a baking tray and wrapping them around the filling. Ground poppy seeds are available from continental delicatessens.
Serves 4–6

Filling:
1 apple
¾ cup (3 oz) ground almonds
¾ cup (3 oz) ground poppy seeds
½ cup (4 fl oz) milk
¼ cup (2 fl oz) cream
¼ cup (1½ oz) currants
¼ cup (2 oz) sugar
1 tablespoon honey
30 g (1 oz) butter
1 teaspoon ground cinnamon
grated rind of ½ lemon
grated rind of ½ orange
Pastry:
185 g (6 oz) filo pastry
125 g (4 oz) butter, melted
icing (confectioners') sugar, for sprinkling

Filling: Peel and grate the apple into a bowl. Add the remaining ingredients for the filling, and place the bowl over a pan of simmering water. Cook, stirring continuously, over simmering water until very thick (about 20 minutes). Remove from the heat and allow to cool.

To finish the pie: Preheat the oven to 180°C (350°F/Gas 4). Brush a sheet of filo pastry with the melted butter. Lay butter side down in a 23 cm (9 in) pie plate. Brush with melted butter and lay another sheet of filo pastry over it. Brush with melted butter and repeat with three more layers of pastry. Spoon the filling into the prepared pie base, and smooth the surface. Top the filling with about five more sheets of pastry, brushing each one (as before) with the melted butter. Trim off the edges of the pastry with a sharp knife.

Bake in the preheated oven for 30 to 40 minutes or until crisp and golden. Sprinkle with icing sugar, and slice with a serrated knife. Serve warm or at room temperature.

Right: Almond and Poppy Seed Pie (see above); Gâteau de Pithiviers Feuilleté (see above).

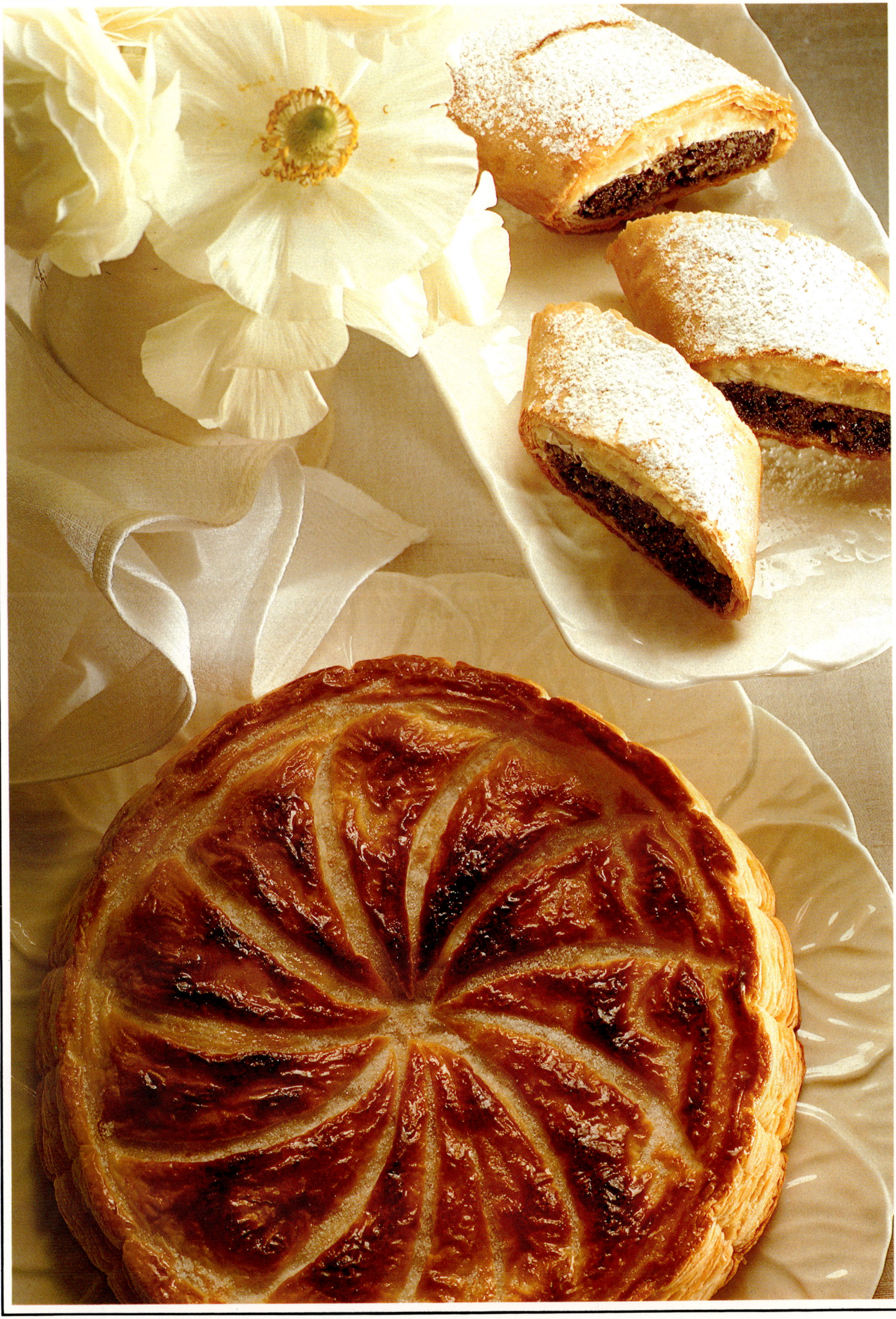

Key Lime Pie

If you are lucky enough to have your own lime tree growing in the garden, then you are set for this pie. Otherwise, look for the limes in larger fruit markets when in season. Limes are distinctly different to lemons in that their perfume is very heavily citrus sweet, but the juice is sharp. The action of the lime juice on the milk is the thickening agent in this pie's filling.
Serves 4–6

---
185 g (6 oz) shortcrust pastry (see recipe, page 182)

Filling:
2 cups (16 oz) sweetened condensed milk
---
1 tablespoon grated lime rind

½ cup (4fl oz) lime juice
---
pinch of salt
---
2 egg yolks

Meringue:
2 eggs whites
---
2 tablespoons sugar

Make the pastry according to the recipe, and chill.
Preheat the oven to 190°C (375°F/Gas 5). Roll out the pastry on a lightly-floured surface and use to line a 23 cm (9 in) pie plate. Bake 'blind' for 10 minutes. Remove the baking beans and paper, and bake for a further 20 minutes or until the pastry is crisp and golden. Allow to cool.
Set the oven temperature at 180°C (350°F/Gas 4).

Filling: Beat the sweetened condensed milk, lime rind, lime juice and salt together until thickened. Beat in the egg yolks. Pour into the prepared pie case and smooth the top.

Meringue: Whisk the egg whites until stiff, and beat in the sugar until stiff. Spoon the meringue over the top of the lime filling and bake for 10 minutes or until golden. Allow to cool.

Lemon Curd Pie

Serves 6–8

---
185 g (6 oz) pâte brisée (see recipe, page 190)

Filling:
6 egg yolks
---
1 cup (8 oz) caster (powdered) sugar
---
grated rind and juice of 4 lemons
---
185 g (6 oz) butter
---
2 teaspoons cornflour (cornstarch)
---
cream

Make the pastry according to the recipe, and chill.
Filling: Place the egg yolks and sugar in a bowl over a pan of simmering water. Add the lemon rind and lemon juice. Beat with a wooden spoon until smooth and the sugar is dissolved. Gradually add the butter in small pieces, slipping it through your fingers to soften it; stir until melted before adding the next lot of butter. Mix the cornflour with a little cream, and add to the lemon curd mixture. Cook over simmering water until thick and smooth. Then allow to cool.

To finish the pie: Preheat the oven to 190°C (375°F/Gas 5). Roll out the pastry on a lightly-floured surface and use to line a 23 cm (9 in) pie plate. Bake 'blind' for 10 minutes. Remove the baking beans and paper, pour the cooled lemon curd filling in, and return to the oven for a further 25 to 30 minutes. Serve warm or cold, with pouring cream.

Crème Brûlée Pie

Crème Brûlée, or Burnt Cream, is such a luxury. Although it is usually served in individual ramekins, this recipe takes the burnt cream and makes it into a pie filling. The filling may be varied by adding half a cup of chopped walnuts, almonds or pistachio nuts to the cream before pouring it into the shell. Or it may be used to fill a meringue shell and served with poached fresh fruit.
Serves 6

---
185 g (6 oz) pâte sucrée (see recipe, page 190)

Filling:
2 cups/500 ml (16fl oz) cream
---
6 tablespoons soft brown sugar
---
5 egg yolks

Make the pastry according to the recipe, and chill.
Preheat the oven to 190°C (375°F/Gas 5). Roll out the pastry and use to line a shallow 23 cm (9 in) pie dish. Bake 'blind' for 15 minutes. Remove the baking beans and paper, and bake for a further 10 to 15 minutes or until evenly golden brown. Remove from the oven and allow to cool.
Scald the cream and 3 tablespoons of the brown sugar. Leave this mixture to cool a little.
Beat the egg yolks in a heatproof bowl until pale, then pour in the cream mixture, stirring constantly. Place the bowl over a pan of simmering water and cook until the mixture thickens, stirring constantly. When the custard coats the back of the spoon, remove from the heat and allow to cool slightly.
Pour the custard into the pie shell and chill in the refrigerator.
Half an hour before serving, sprinkle the top of the pie with the remaining 3 tablespoons of brown sugar. Place strips of aluminium foil over the edge of the pie crust. Preheat the griller (broiler) and place the pie under the hot griller to caramelise the brown sugar. Allow to cool before serving.

CHIFFON PIES

Pointers for chiffon pies:

- Beat the egg yolks with the sugar over simmering water, not boiling.
- Do not let the gelatine and egg mixture go beyond 'just beginning to set' before adding the whipped cream-egg whites, otherwise they will not combine smoothly and the filling will be lumpy. If the gelatine mixture does set before adding the egg whites, gently warm the gelatine mixture to soften it and allow it to cool once again before adding the beaten egg whites or cream.
- 'Just beginning to set' is when the mixture will stay apart for a few seconds when the spoon is pulled through it.
- Beat the egg whites until stiff but not dry. They lose their elasticity and therefore hold less air when beaten until dry.
- Whip the cream until it will hold its shape—but not too stiffly as it would then be difficult to fold through the gelatine mixture.
- Make sure the pastry case or crumb crust is cold before spooning in the chiffon mixture.

Prune Chiffon Pie

Serves 6–8

185 g (6 oz) rich shortcrust pastry (see recipe, page 184)

Filling:
1 cup (8 oz) stoned stewed prunes

¾ cup (6 fl oz) prune juice

½ cup (4 oz) sugar

pinch of salt

finely grated rind and juice of 1 lemon

1½ tablespoons gelatine

3 tablespoons hot water

2 egg whites

Make the pastry according to the recipe, and chill.
Preheat the oven to 220°C (425°F/Gas 7). Roll out the pastry on a lightly-floured surface and use to line a 23 cm (9 in) pie plate. Bake 'blind' in a hot oven for 10 minutes. Remove the 'blind' filling, and bake for a further 10 minutes or until the pastry is golden and crisp. Allow to cool on a wire rack.

Filling: Place the stewed prunes and prune juice in a blender or food processor and blend until smooth. Add the sugar, salt, lemon rind and lemon juice; blend again. Pour into a small saucepan and stir over moderate heat to dissolve the sugar. Allow to cool.
Dissolve the gelatine in the 3 tablespoons of hot water, and add to the prune mixture. Chill until just beginning to set.

Whisk the egg whites until stiff, and fold them through the prune mixture. Spoon the filling into the prepared pie case, and chill until ready to serve.
Serve with whipped cream or fresh yogurt.

Macadamia Rum Chiffon Pie

Serves 12

185 g (6 oz) rich shortcrust pastry (see recipe, page 184)

Filling:
2 teaspoons gelatine

4 eggs, separated

2 tablespoons caster (powdered) sugar

½ cup boiling water

3 tablespoons rum

finely grated rind of 1 lemon

additional 2 tablespoons caster (powdered) sugar

½ cup (2 oz) chopped macadamia nuts

300 ml (10 fl oz) thickened cream

Prepare the pastry according to the recipe, and chill.
Preheat the oven to 220°C (425°F/Gas 7). Roll out the pastry on a lightly-floured surface and use to line a 23 cm (9 in) pie plate. Bake 'blind' for 10 minutes. Remove the 'blind' filling and return to the oven for a further 10 minutes or until golden and crisp. Allow to cool.

Filling: Dissolve the gelatine in a little hot water. Place the egg yolks and sugar in a mixing bowl over a pan of simmering water, and beat until thick and pale. Pour in the boiling water and beat until thick. Add the dissolved gelatine, and allow to cool.
When just beginning to set, stir in the rum and lemon rind.
Whisk the egg whites until stiff and gradually add the 2 tablespoons of caster sugar, whisking until it is the texture of a smooth meringue. Carefully fold through the rum mixture along with the macadamia nuts. Pour into the cold pastry shell and refrigerate until set.
Whip the cream, with an extra tablespoon of rum if liked, and pipe rosettes of cream to decorate the top of the pie. Sprinkle with extra macadamia nuts if liked. Serve lightly-chilled with coffee or as a dessert.

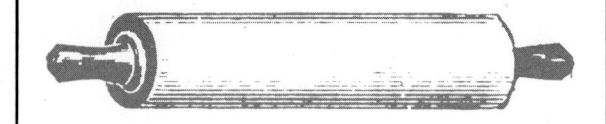

Jaffa Chiffon Pie
(Photograph right)

Serves 6–8

185 g (6 oz) rich shortcrust pastry
(see recipe, page 184) or

1 quantity Crumb Crust using plain sweet
chocolate biscuits (see recipe, page 193)

Filling:
1 teaspoon gelatine

1 tablespoon hot water

3 eggs, separated

1/3 cup (3 oz) caster (powdered) sugar

1 tablespoon orange juice

90 g (3 oz) dark chocolate

grated rind of 1 orange

2 tablespoons whipped cream

Make the pastry according to the recipe, and chill.
Preheat the oven to 190°C (375°F/Gas 5). Roll out the pastry on a lightly-floured surface and use to line a 23 cm (9 in) pie plate. Bake 'blind' for 10 minutes. Remove the baking beans and paper, and bake for a further 10 minutes or until evenly golden and crisp. Allow to cool.

If using Crumb Crust, make according to the recipe and use to line a 20 cm (8 in) deep pie plate. Bake for 10 minutes. Allow to cool.

Filling: Dissolve the gelatine in the hot water. Whisk the egg yolks, half of the caster sugar and the orange juice in a bowl over simmering water; beat until thick and pale, then remove from the heat.

Melt the chocolate on a plate over simmering water; and stir into the egg yolk mixture with the orange rind and the dissolved gelatine. Whisk the mixture until thick and light and just on the point of setting.

Whisk the egg whites with the remaining sugar, and fold through the chocolate and orange mixture with the whipped cream. Spoon into the prepared pie case, and chill until ready to serve.

Serve with extra whipped cream, if liked, and gratings of chocolate.

Lemon Chiffon Pie
(Photograph right)

Serves 4–6

185 g (6 oz) rich shortcrust pastry or
pâte sucrée
(see recipes, page 184 and 190)

Filling:
2 teaspoons gelatine

2 tablespoons hot water

3 large eggs, separated

1/2 cup (4 oz) caster (powdered) sugar

pinch of salt

grated rind and juice of 1 juicy lemon

2 tablespoons whipped cream

Make the pastry according to the recipe, and chill.
Preheat the oven to 190°C (375°F/Gas 5). Roll out the pastry on a lightly-floured surface and use to line a 23 cm (9 in) pie plate. Bake 'blind' for 10 minutes. Remove the baking beans and paper, and bake for a further 10 to 15 minutes or until the pastry is evenly golden and crisp. Allow to cool.

Filling: Dissolve the gelatine in the hot water. Place the egg yolks, half (i.e. 1/4 cup) of the sugar, salt, lemon rind and lemon juice in a small bowl. Set the bowl over a pan of simmering water, and whisk until thick and pale. Remove the bowl from the heat and add the dissolved gelatine. Continue whisking until the mixture is light and fluffy and on the point of setting.

Whisk the egg whites with the remaining 1/4 cup of sugar, and fold into the lemon mixture with the whipped cream. When it will hold its shape, pile the filling into the prepared pastry case. Chill until ready to serve.

Serve with extra whipped cream, if liked.

Banana Chiffon Pie
(Photograph left)
Serves 6–8

---

185 g (6 oz) rich shortcrust pastry (see recipe, page 184)

Filling:
1½ teaspoons gelatine

2 tablespoons hot water

¾ cup mashed banana (approx. 2 large bananas)

grated rind and juice of 1 lemon

2 eggs, separated

½ cup (4 oz) caster (powdered) sugar

Make the pastry according to the recipe, and chill. Preheat the oven to 220°C (425°F/Gas 7). Roll out the pastry on a lightly-floured surface and use to line a 23 cm (9 in) pie plate. Bake 'blind' for 10 minutes. Remove the baking beans and paper, reduce the oven temperature to 190°C (375°F/Gas 5) and bake for a further 10 minutes. Allow to cool on a wire rack.

Filling: Sprinkle the gelatine over the 2 tablespoons of hot water to dissolve. Place the bananas in a blender or food processor and blend until mashed—but not puréed. Place ¾ cup of the mashed bananas in a heavy-based saucepan. Add the lemon rind and lemon juice. Stir in the egg yolks and 3 tablespoons of the sugar and cook, stirring constantly, over a moderate heat until the mixture thickens. Remove from the heat and add the dissolved gelatine. Cool the mixture until just beginning to set.

Whisk the egg whites until stiff. Gradually add the remaining sugar and beat until it is the texture of smooth meringue. Fold into the banana mixture, and spoon into the prepared pie case. Chill until ready to serve.

Decorate with whipped cream, if liked.

Chocolate Crunch Pie

Serves 6

Biscuit Base:
185 g (6 oz) plain sweet biscuits (cookies)

60 g (2 oz) butter

2 tablespoons caster (powdered) sugar

Filling:
30 g (1 oz) butter

3 tablespoons cornflour (cornstarch)

1 tablespoon caster (powdered) sugar

1½ cups (12fl oz) milk

90 g (3 oz) dark cooking chocolate

cream, for decoration

extra chocolate for decoration

Biscuit base: Preheat the oven to 180°C (350°F/Gas 4). Crush the biscuits but not too finely (this would make the crust rather dense). Melt the butter and stir it into the crushed biscuits with the sugar. Press the mixture into a 20 cm (8 in) pie plate and bake for 10 minutes. Allow to cool.

Filling: Melt the butter in a saucepan. Blend in the cornflour and sugar, and gradually add the milk, stirring continuously while bringing it to the boil; cook for a few minutes, then remove the saucepan from heat.

Break the chocolate into pieces and stir into the hot milk sauce until melted. Cool a little, then pour into the prepared pie base. Leave until set.

Whip the cream and decorate the pie top with swirls of whipped cream and grated chocolate.

Honey Yoghurt Pie

Serves 4–6

185 g (6 oz) shortcrust pastry
(see recipe, page 182)

Filling:
1 cup (8fl oz) natural yoghurt

1 cup (8 oz) cottage cheese or farm cheese

1 teaspoon vanilla essence

1 tablespoon honey

ground cinnamon, for sprinkling

Make the pastry according to the recipe and use to line a 20 cm (8 in) pie dish. Bake 'blind' in a preheated oven at 190°C (375°F/Gas 5) for 10 minutes. Remove the 'blind' filling and bake for a further 20 minutes or until evenly golden brown. Remove from the oven and allow to cool.

Filling: Blend the yoghurt, cottage cheese (or farm cheese) and vanilla in a food processor until smooth. Warm the honey by placing its jar in hot water to allow easier mixing; add 1 tablespoon to the yoghurt mixture, and blend. Spoon into the prepared pie shell and refrigerate for 2 to 3 hours.

Dust with cinnamon, and serve with poached fruit if liked.

Variations: Fold whole strawberries or sliced banana or ½ cup (1 oz) broken walnuts through the filling, mixing before spooning it into the pie shell.

Butterscotch Meringue Pie

Serves 6–8

185 g (6 oz) rich shortcrust pastry
(see recipe, page 184)

Filling:
¾ cup (4 oz) soft brown sugar

¼ cup (2 oz) sugar

3 tablespoons cornflour (cornstarch)

pinch of salt

2½ cups (20fl oz) milk

3 egg yolks, beaten

30 g (1 oz) butter

1 teaspoon vanilla essence

Meringue:
3 egg whites

pinch of cream of tartar

½ cup (4 oz) caster (powdered) sugar

Make the pastry according to the recipe, and chill.

Preheat the oven to 200°C (400°F/Gas 6). Roll out the pastry on a lightly-floured surface and use to line a 23 cm (9 in) pie plate. Bake 'blind' for 10 minutes. Remove the baking beans and paper, and bake for a further 10 minutes.

Set the oven temperature at 190°C (375°F/Gas 5).

Filling: Combine the sugars, conflour and salt together in a saucepan. Gradually stir in the milk and mix until smooth. Bring to the boil, stirring constantly, and allow to simmer for 1 minute. Pour half of the mixture on to the beaten egg yolks, mix, and then pour this into the saucepan. Cook, while stirring, for a few minutes longer. Add the butter and vanilla essence, mix well, and pour into the pie shell.

Meringue: Beat the egg whites with a pinch of cream of tartar until stiff but not dry. Gradually add the caster sugar, beating well after each addition; beat until stiff peaks form. Spread the meringue over the pie top, taking it right to the edge of the pastry. Bake in the preheated oven for 7 to 10 minutes or until the meringue is golden. Allow to cool before serving.

Gramma Pie

This pie is uniquely Australian and quite different in flavour and texture from the American Pumpkin Pie. If Gramma, a member of the squash family, is not available, use pumpkin or the smaller Butternut pumpkin.

Serves 6–8

---

250 g (8 oz) rich shortcrust pastry
(see recipe, page 184)

Filling:
1 kg (2 lb) gramma or pumpkin

---

pinch of salt

¾ cup (4 oz) brown sugar

½ cup (3 oz) sultanas

---

1 teaspoon ground cinnamon

½ teaspoon grated nutmeg

---

1 tablespoon flour

---

grated rind and juice of 1 lemon

---

30 g (1 oz) butter

---

egg white, for glazing

---

caster (powdered) sugar, for glazing

Make the pastry according to the recipe, and chill. Preheat the oven to 200°C (400°F/Gas 6).

Filling: Peel the gramma and remove its seeds. Cut into small cubes and place in a saucepan with water and salt. Bring to the boil and simmer for 5 minutes or until just tender. Drain well. Combine the sugar, sultanas, cinnamon, nutmeg, flour, lemon rind and lemon juice with the drained gramma.

To finish the pie: Roll out two-thirds of the pastry on a lightly-floured surface and use to line a deep 23 cm (9 in) pie plate. Spoon in the filling, and dot with the butter.

Roll the remaining pastry into a round, large enough to cover the pie; cut into strips and use to form a lattice pattern on the pie.

Brush the lattice with a little egg white and dust with caster sugar. Bake in the preheated oven for 10 minutes, then reduce the heat to 180°C (350°F/Gas 4) and bake for a further 30 minutes or until the pastry is crisp and the gramma cooked. Serve warm or cold, with lashings of whipped cream.

Pumpkin Pie

Serves 6–8

---

185 g (6 oz) rich shortcrust pastry or wholemeal shortcrust
(see recipes, page 184 and 189)

Filling:
2 cups (16fl oz) cooked or canned pumpkin

1½ cups (12fl oz) evaporated milk or cream

¾ cup (6 oz) brown sugar

---

pinch of salt

---

1 teaspoon ground cinnamon

½ teaspoon ground ginger

---

pinch of ground nutmeg

---

pinch of cloves

---

2 eggs

Make the pastry according to the recipe, and chill.

Place all the filling ingredients in the container of a food processor and blend until smooth. Or blend together in a bowl until smooth.

Preheat the oven to 200°C (400°F/Gas 6). Roll out the pastry on a lightly-floured surface and use to line a 23 cm (9 in) pie plate; crimp the edges. Pour the filling into the pie shell and bake in the hot oven for 10 minutes. Reduce the oven temperature to moderate, 180°C (350°F/Gas 4), and bake for a further 40 minutes or until the filling is set and the pastry is a good golden colour. Allow to cool. Serve with extra whipped cream and a sprinkling of nutmeg.

Mincemeat Pies

These delightful little pies are a joy to see—cooling on a rack, just warm from the oven. They make lovely Christmas presents, bundled up in coloured cellophane with the recipe handwritten on a card. (Or if time is getting short, give a jar of home-made mincemeat with a recipe for the pies.)
Makes 12 pies

250 g (8 oz) rich shortcrust pastry (see recipe, page 184)
1 cup (5 oz) mincemeat (see recipe below)
1 egg
beaten egg, for glazing
caster (powdered) sugar, for sprinkling

Make the pastry according to the recipe, and chill.

Preheat the oven to 190°C (375°F/Gas 5). Assemble twelve small (individual-serving), deep pie tins, and line six of them at a time. Roll out half of the pastry into a rectangle. Gently lift it and lay it over six pie tins. Press the pastry into the tins lightly, and roll the rolling pin over to cut the edges; gather pastry off-cuts into a ball and set aside for the pie tops. Roll out the second half of the pastry and line the other six tins. (Alternatively, cut the pastry into rounds using a cutter, and line the pie tins.)

Spoon about 2 teaspoons of mincemeat into each pie.

Roll out the ball of off-cuts and, using a tiny star cutter, cut twelve pastry stars for each pie top. Lay a top over each pie and brush with beaten egg. Sprinkle with caster sugar and place the pie tins on a baking tray.

Bake in the preheated oven for 25 minutes or until pale golden brown. Serve warm or cold.

Home-made Mincemeat

Mincemeat may be made well in advance and stored in airtight jars. Preferably leave the mincemeat to mature for about a month before using. The suet may be replaced with 250 g (8 oz) butter if a lighter mincemeat is preferred. Keeps well for about 6 months. Once jars are opened keep in the refrigerator.
Makes 14 cups

125 g (4 oz) blanched almonds
500 g (1 lb) raisins
500 g (1 lb) currants
500 g (1 lb) sultanas
185 g (6 oz) glacé fruit, such as apricot, pineapple or fig
125 g (4 oz) glacé cherries
250 g (8 oz) candied peel
2 Granny Smith apples (cooking apples)
375 g (12 oz) raw or brown sugar
½ teaspoon each cinnamon, mixed spice, nutmeg and cardamom
315 g (10 oz) fresh suet, grated
grated rind and juice 2 oranges
¾ cup brandy or rum

Chop the nuts, dried and glacé fruit roughly. Mix in candied peel. Peel and grate the apples and mix into the dried fruit and nut mixture with the sugar, spices, suet and orange rind. Pour over the orange juice and brandy or rum. Mix thoroughly and pack into clean sterilised jars. Cover with a circle of waxed paper and seal with a lid.

Apricot Pie

Serves 8

375 g (12 oz) rich shortcrust pastry (see recipe, page 184)
Filling:
1 kg (2 lb) fresh apricots, halved and stoned, or 825 g (1 lb 10 oz) canned apricot halves
1 cup (8 oz) apricot jam (jelly)
1 lemon
egg white, for glazing
caster (powdered) sugar, for glazing

Make the pastry according to the recipe, and chill.

Preheat the oven to 220°C (425°F/Gas 7). Place a baking tray on a shelf ready for baking. Roll out half of the pastry on a lightly-floured surface and use to line a 23 cm (9 in) pie plate.

Drain the apricots if using canned fruit. Place the apricot halves into the pastry case, cover with the apricot jam, then grate the lemon rind over the top. Sprinkle the lemon juice over.

Roll out the remaining pastry to a round, and cover the pie. Pinch the edges. Brush with the lightly-beaten egg white, and sprinkle with the caster sugar.

Place the pie plate on the baking tray and bake for 20 to 30 minutes or until the pastry is cooked and golden brown. Serve warm, with whipped cream, custard or ice-cream.

Right: **Mincemeat Pies** (see above).

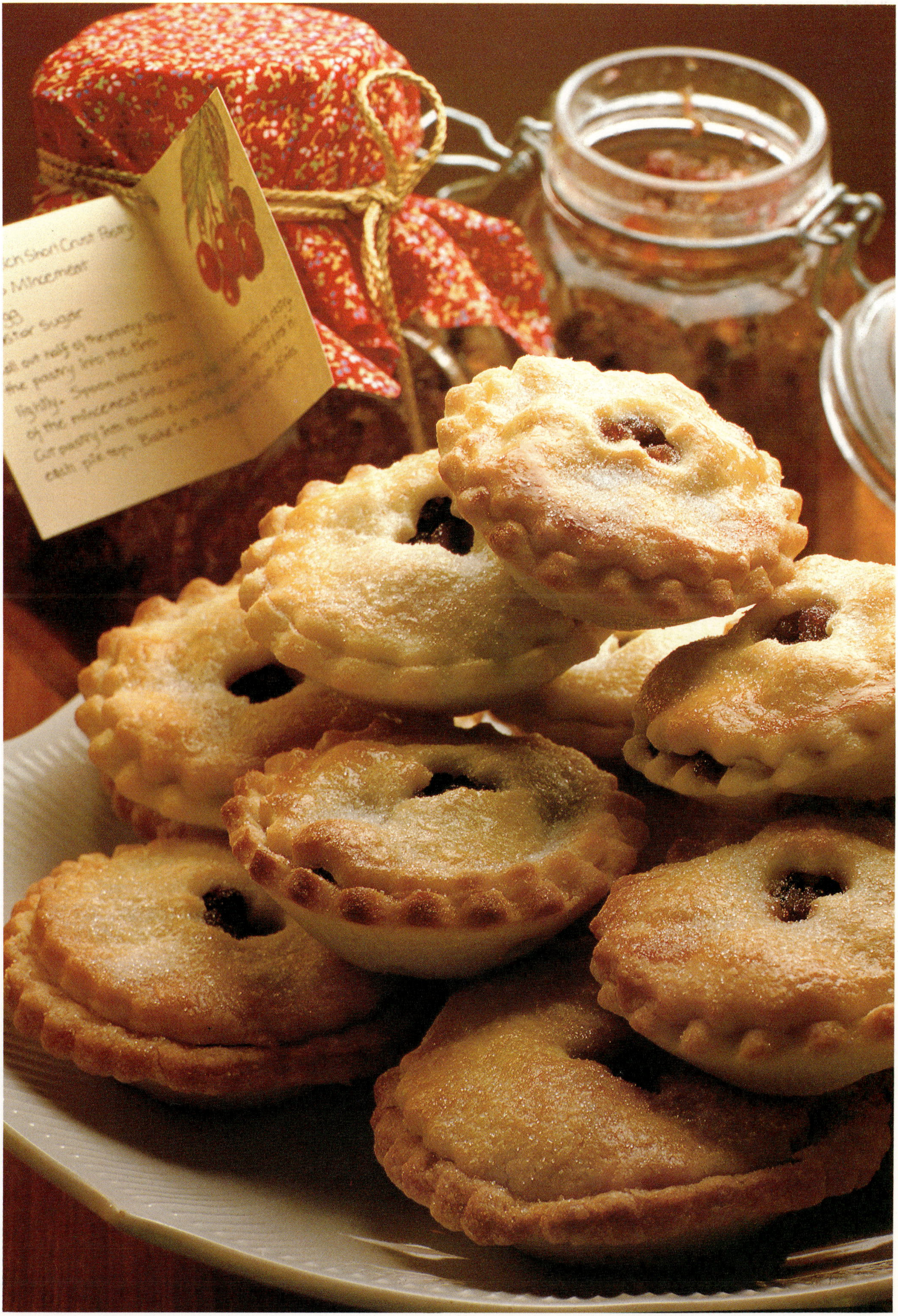
Mincemeat

Peach Pie

Serves 4–6

---
185 g (6 oz) wholemeal pastry, or rich shortcrust pastry (see recipes, page 184 and 189)

Filling:
8 fresh peaches, peeled and sliced, or 825 g (1 lb 10 oz) canned sliced peaches
---
2 tablespoons tapioca
---
egg white, for glazing
---
caster (powdered) sugar, for glazing

Prepare the pastry according to the recipe, and chill.

Preheat the oven to 200°C (400°F/Gas 6). If using canned peaches, drain the peaches and reserve the juice. Layer the sliced peaches with the tapioca in a 4-cup (1 litre) oval pie dish and pour over a little of the reserved juice.

Roll the pastry out to an oval shape 2.5 cm (1 in) larger than the top of the dish. Cut a 1 cm (3/8 in) rim off the pastry. Brush the rim of the pie dish with cold water, place the 1 cm (3/8 in) pastry strip around the rim of the dish, and press it down; trim the ends of the pastry strip where they meet, so that they meet without overlapping. Brush this pastry rim with cold water. Place the oval pastry top over the peach filling, easing it in carefully to avoid shrinkage during baking. Press around the rim to seal the pastry, and trim away any overhanging pastry with a sharp knife. Scallop or flute the edges, and make a few slits to allow the steam to escape during baking. Brush the pastry with the egg white, and sprinkle with the caster sugar.

Stand the pie dish on a baking tray and bake in the preheated oven for 20 to 30 minutes or until the pastry is cooked. Serve hot or cold, with whipped cream, custard or ice-cream.

Peach Cream Pie

Serves 6

Crumb Crust:
1 1/4 cups (4 oz) crushed plain sweet biscuits (cookies)
---
1 tablespoon sugar
---
75 g (2 1/2 oz) butter, melted

Filling:
3 egg yolks

1/3 cup (3 oz) caster (powdered) sugar
---
1 lemon
---
1 1/4 cups/300 ml (10 fl oz) cream

3–4 peaches, depending on their size

Crumb crust: Preheat the oven to 190°C (375°F/Gas 5). Mix together the crumbs and sugar. Blend in the butter, and press into a greased 23 cm (9 in) pie plate, taking the crumbs up the sides to form a small rim. Bake for 8 to 10 minutes. Allow to cool.

Filling: Beat the egg yolks and sugar together in a small bowl until pale. Blend in the finely-grated rind and the juice of the lemon. Place the bowl over a saucepan of simmering water, and cook, stirring until the mixture forms a smooth thick cream. Allow to cool.

Beat the cream until it holds its shape, and fold most of it into the cold lemon mixture.

Skin the peaches by plunging them into boiling water for a minute or so, then slipping the skins off. Slice the peaches and fold them into the cream mixture, reserving a few slices for decoration. Pile the cream and peach mixture into the prepared pie crust, and chill. Decorate with the reserved cream and sliced peaches.

Rhubarb Pie

Serves 6

---
185 g (6 oz) rich shortcrust pastry or flaky pastry (see recipes, page 184 and 188)

Filling:
3/4 cup (6 oz) sugar

4–5 cups cut fresh rhubarb
---
2 tablespoons tapioca
---
grated rind and a little juice from 1 lemon
---
egg white, for glazing
---
caster (powdered) sugar, for glazing

Make the pastry according to the recipe, and chill.

Filling: Combine the sugar, rhubarb, grated rind and juice from the lemon and the tapioca in the base of a deep pie dish or ovenproof dish; dome the fruit in the centre. Leave for 15 minutes.

To finish the pie: Preheat the oven to 200°C (400°F/Gas 6). Roll out the pastry on a lightly-floured surface slightly larger than the top of the pie dish. Trim off 1 cm (3/8 in) of the pastry and press this strip onto the rim of the pie dish. Dampen the pastry rim with a little water. Lay the pastry cover over the filling and rim, and press edges together with the back of a fork or knife. Cut a few slits to allow the steam to escape during baking. Brush the pastry with the egg white, and sprinkle with caster sugar.

Bake in the preheated oven for 10 minutes, then reduce the oven temperature to 180°C (350°F/Gas 4) and cook for a further 25 minutes or until the pastry is golden and the rhubarb is cooked. Serve warm, with custard or pouring cream.

Variation: Use half apple and half rhubarb.

Raspberry Cream Pie

Serves 6

1 quantity Biscuit Crumb Crust made with plain sweet chocolate biscuits (cookies) (see recipe, page 193)
Filling: 3 eggs
2 egg yolks
¼ cup (2 oz) caster (powdered) sugar
1 tablespoon gelatine
¼ cup hot water
juice of ½ lemon
⅔ cup raspberry purée
⅔ cup (5 fl oz) cream
grated chocolate, to decorate
extra cream, for decoration

Make the biscuit crumb crust according to the recipe, and use to line a 20 cm (8 in) pie dish. Bake in a preheated oven at 190°C (375°F/Gas 5) for 10 minutes. Allow to cool.

Filling: Combine the eggs, egg yolks and sugar in a bowl over a pan of simmering water, and whisk until thickened. Remove from the heat, and continue whisking until cool. Dissolve the gelatine in the hot water; and stir it through the egg mixture with the lemon juice and raspberry purée. Chill until just on setting point.

Whip the cream until it holds its shape, and fold it through the raspberry mixture. Spoon into the prepared pie case, and chill until set. Serve decorated with extra whipped cream and grated chocolate.

Note: Raspberry Purée can be made by processing fresh, frozen or canned raspberries in a food processor or blender until smooth.

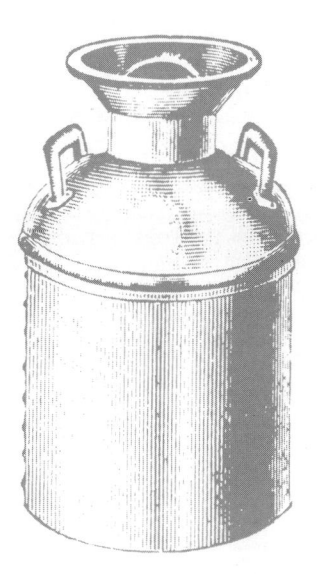

Pineapple Meringue Pie

Serves 6

185 g (6 oz) rich shortcrust pastry (see recipe, page 184)
Filling: 1 medium-sized fresh pineapple
3 tablespoons cornflour (cornstarch)
pinch of salt
½ cup (4 oz) sugar
2 tablespoons water
juice of ½ lemon
2 egg yolks
Meringue: 2 egg whites
4 tablespoons caster (powdered) sugar

Make the pastry according to the recipe, and chill.

Preheat the oven to 190°C (375°F/Gas 5). Roll out the pastry on a lightly-floured surface and use to line a 20 cm (8 in) pie dish. Bake 'blind' for 10 minutes. Remove the baking beans and paper, and return to the oven for a further 10 minutes. Allow to cool while making the filling.

Reset the oven temperature at 160°C (325°F/Gas 3).

Filling: Peel the pineapple and cut the flesh into chunks. Use a food processor or blender to purée the pineapple. Place the puréed pineapple in a heavy-based saucepan. Blend the cornflour, salt, sugar and water together, and stir into the pineapple. Bring to the boil and stirring constantly, simmer for 10 minutes. Add the lemon juice and egg yolks, and stir until the mixture is thickened without boiling. Pour into the prepared pie case.

Meringue: Whisk the egg whites until stiff, then gradually add the sugar until it is the texture of a smooth stiff meringue. Pile the meringue on top of the filling, taking it right to the edge of the pastry.

Bake for 15 minutes or until the meringue is golden. Serve warm or cold.

Shortbread Pie

Serves 6

1½ cups (6 oz) flour
pinch of salt
220 g (7 oz) butter
⅓ cup (2 oz) icing (confectioners') sugar
2 egg yolks
drops of vanilla essence
1⅓ cups (5 oz) ground almonds
¾ cup (8 oz) raspberry or blackberry jam (jelly), slightly warmed
¼ cup (1 oz) flaked almonds
icing sugar, for sprinkling

Sift the flour and salt onto a board. Make a well in the centre, and put in the butter, icing sugar, egg yolks and vanilla essence. Sprinkle the ground almonds onto the flour. Work the ingredients in the centre with the fingertips until thoroughly blended. Using a metal spatula, quickly draw in the flour and ground almonds. Knead the dough lightly, then chill for at least 1 hour.

Preheat the oven to 160°C (325°F/Gas 3).

Grate the dough on a coarse grater into a greased 20 cm (8 in) springform tin or pie dish, using about two-thirds of the quantity to cover the base thickly with dough. Spread with the slightly warmed jam, then grate the remaining dough over the jam. Press lightly into the tin, and sprinkle with the flaked almonds. Bake for 1¼ hours. Allow to cool.

When cold, sprinkle the top thickly with icing sugar. If using a springform tin, turn the pie out of the tin; if using a pie dish, serve straight from the dish. Serve with whipped cream.

Orange and Pine Nut Pie

Serves 4

185 g (6 oz) pâte sucrée (see recipe, page 190)
Filling: 125 g (4 oz) unsalted butter
⅓ cup (3 oz) caster (powdered) sugar
3 tablespoons cream
½ cup (3 oz) candied orange peel (see recipe below)
¾ cup (3 oz) pine nuts

Make the pastry according to the recipe, and chill.

Roll out the pastry on a lightly-floured surface and use to line a 20 cm (8 in) pie plate. Preheat the oven to 190°C (375°F/Gas 5).

Filling: Melt the butter and sugar in a small heavy pan. Bring to the boil and add the cream, candied orange peel and pine nuts. Return to the boil, then remove the pan from the heat.

To finish the pie: Bake the prepared pie case 'blind' in a moderately hot oven for 10 minutes. Remove the baking beans and paper, and spoon the warm filling into the pastry case. Return the pie to the oven and bake for a further 20 to 25 minutes or until the pastry is golden and the filling is lightly caramelised.

To Make Candied Orange Peel: Peel the rind from 1 orange and cut into strips. Place in a saucepan with 3 tablespoons of sugar and ½ cup (4fl oz) water. Bring to the boil and cook over a moderate heat until the water has evaporated and the orange zest is slightly candied but still moist. Remove from the saucepan and set aside on wax paper or on a rack.

Pecan Pie

This great southern American pie is delicious and very simple to make. Best served warm with a jug of pouring cream. The pecans are quite rich, so offer smallish portions to start—I'm sure they'll be back for seconds.

Serves 6

185 g (6 oz) rich shortcrust pastry (see recipe, page 184)
Filling: 90 g (3 oz) butter
1 cup (8fl oz) light corn syrup (golden syrup)
½ teaspoon salt
1 cup (7 oz) sugar
4 eggs
2 cups (8 oz) pecan halves
1 teaspoon vanilla essence

Roll out the pastry on a lightly-floured surface and use to line a 23 cm (9 in) pie plate. Chill while making the filling.

Preheat the oven to 190°C (375°F/Gas 5).

Filling: Melt the butter and stir in the corn syrup, salt, sugar and eggs. Mix well to combine. Add the nuts and vanilla essence. Pour the filling into the prepared pie case, arranging the pecan nuts face upwards. Bake for 35 to 40 minutes or until the filling is cooked and the pastry golden brown. Serve warm or cold, with pouring cream.

Right: **Pecan Pie** (see above).

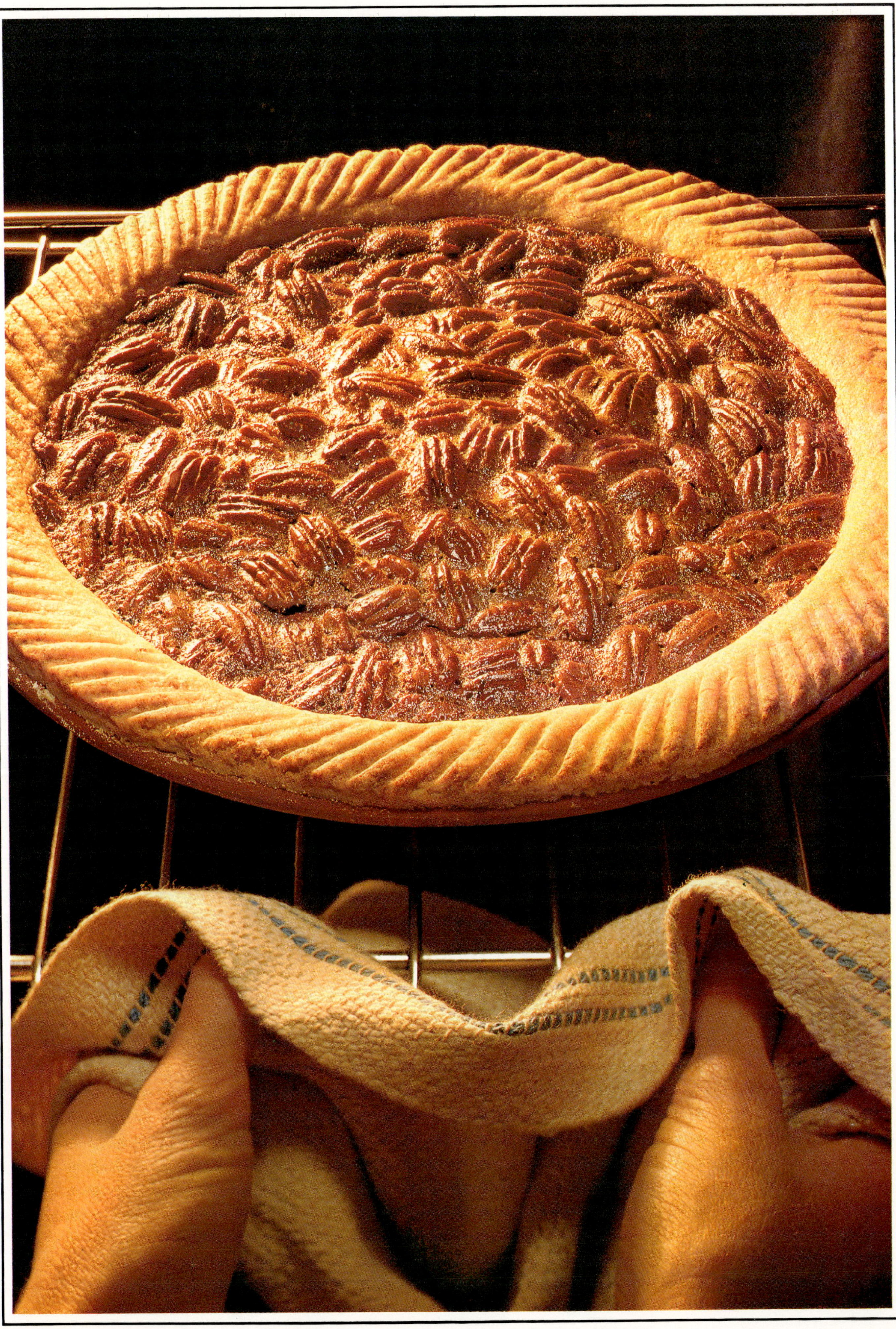

Cherry Almond Pie

Serves 6

Pastry:
1 cup (4 oz) flour

½ teaspoon baking powder

pinch of salt

30 g (1 oz) butter

¼ cup (2 oz) sugar

1 egg, lightly beaten

Filling:
4 cups (1½ lb) fresh ripe cherries

3 tablespoons fine breadcrumbs

2 tablespoons ground almonds

½ cup (4 oz) sugar

1 egg

pinch of salt

¼ cup (2 fl oz) cream

Preheat the oven to 230°C (450°F/Gas 8).

Pastry: Sift the flour, baking powder and salt into a bowl. Rub in the butter, until the mixture resembles fine breadcrumbs. Stir in the sugar and egg to form a smooth dough. Gather in a ball, and chill for 5 minutes.

Roll out the pastry on a floured surface to line a 23 cm (9 in) pie plate.

Filling: Wash and pit the cherries, reserving any juice that runs out of the cherries. Sprinkle the breadcrumbs and ground almonds over the base of the pastry. Spread the cherries over the crumb mixture, and sprinkle with the sugar. Beat the egg, salt and cream together until combined, and add the cherry juice. Pour the mixture over the cherries.

Bake in the preheated oven for 10 minutes, then reduce the heat to 180°C (350°F/Gas 4) and continue baking for 25 minutes or until the crust is golden brown and the filling is cooked. Serve warm, with whipped cream if liked.

Meringue-topped Cherry Pie: Whisk 2 egg whites until stiff, then whisk in 4 tablespoons of caster (powdered) sugar gradually until it is the texture of a stiff meringue. Swirl the meringue on top of the baked pie and return the pie to the oven at 160°C (325°F/Gas 3) for 15 minutes or until the meringue is golden. Serve warm or cold.

Sultana Oatmeal Pie

Serves 8

Pastry:
185 g (6 oz) wholemeal self-raising flour

pinch of salt

90 g (3 oz) margarine

1 tablespoon brown sugar

1–2 tablespoons water

Filling:
750 g (1½ lb) cooking apples

½ cup (4 oz) sugar

¾ cup (4 oz) sultanas

2 teaspoons ground cinnamon

60 g (2 oz) butter

2 tablespoons golden syrup
(light corn syrup)

1 cup (4 oz) rolled oats

Preheat the oven to 200°C (400°F/Gas 6).

Pastry: Sift the flour and salt into a bowl. Rub in the margarine until the mixture resembles breadcrumbs. Stir through the brown sugar and enough water to make a stiff dough. Roll out the pastry and use to line a 23 cm (9 in) pie plate.

Filling: Peel and core the apples; slice them thinly and mix with the sugar, sultanas and cinnamon. Fill the pie dish with the apple mixture.

Melt the butter with the golden syrup and stir in the rolled oats. Spread this mixture over the apples.

Bake in the preheated oven for 10 minutes, then lower the oven temperature to 180°C (350°F/Gas 4) and bake for a further 40 minutes. Serve hot or cold, with natural yoghurt and honey.

Variation: Reduce the quantity of rolled oats by 2 tablespoons, and substitute 2 tablespoons of desiccated coconut.

Chocolate Cream Pie

Serves 6

---

185 g (6 oz) pâte sucrée (see recipe, page 190)

Filling:
2 cups (16fl oz) milk

¼ cup (2 oz) caster (powdered) sugar

90 g (3 oz) dark sweet chocolate

4 egg yolks

1 cup (8fl oz) thickened cream

1 teaspoon vanilla essence

2 tablespoons brandy

2 tablespoons broken walnut pieces

whipped cream, for decoration

chopped walnuts, for decoration

Make the pastry according to the recipe, and chill.

Preheat the oven to 190°C (375°F/Gas 5). Roll out the pastry on a lightly-floured surface and use to line a 20 cm (8 in) pie plate. Bake 'blind' for 15 minutes. Remove the 'blind' filling and continue baking until evenly golden brown and crisp (about 10 minutes).

Filling: Place the milk and caster sugar in a heavy saucepan, bring to the boil, and stir until the sugar has dissolved. Grate the chocolate and stir into the hot milk, stirring until dissolved. Beat the egg yolks in a bowl and pour in a little of the hot milk. Return this liquid to the saucepan and heat over very low heat, stirring until thickened. Pour into a bowl as soon as the mixture coats the back of a spoon. Chill.

Beat the cream until it holds its shape, and fold the vanilla and brandy through. Fold the cream through the cold custard along with the broken walnut pieces. Spoon the filling into the prepared pie shell and chill until set.

When ready to serve, decorate with extra whipped cream and walnuts.

Coffee Cream Pie

This pie looks very special if decorated with chocolate coffee beans which are dark chocolates in the shape of coffee beans filled with a coffee liqueur.
Serves 6

---

185 g (6 oz) pâte sucrée (see recipe, page 190)

Filling:
2 cups (16fl oz) milk

1 vanilla pod

1½ tablespoons instant coffee powder

3 egg yolks

¼ cup (2 oz) caster (powdered) sugar

1 tablespoon + 1 teaspoon gelatine

¼ cup (2fl oz) hot water

⅔ cup (5fl oz) thickened cream

chocolate coffee beans, to decorate,
or grated chocolate

Make the pastry according to the recipe, and chill.

Preheat the oven to 190°C (375°F/Gas 5). Roll out the pastry on a lightly-floured surface and use to line a 23 cm (9 in) pie plate. Bake 'blind' for 10 to 15 minutes. Remove the baking beans and paper, and bake for a further 10 minutes or until the pastry is evenly golden and crisp. Allow to cool.

Scald the milk with the vanilla pod (split open). Leave to infuse for 10 minutes. Stir in the instant coffee. Remove the vanilla pod (store it in sugar).

Beat the egg yolks and sugar together until pale. Pour the hot milk over them, then return the liquid to the saucepan. Cook, stirring, without boiling, until thickened.

Dissolve the gelatine in the hot water, and stir it through the custard mixture. Pour the mixture into a bowl set over crushed ice, and stir it until just thickening.

Whip the cream, and fold half of the cream into the custard. Spoon the custard filling into the prepared pie shell, and chill until ready to serve.

Mask the top of the pie with the remaining cream, and decorate with the sweet coffee beans or grated chocolate.

Mrs Simpson's Apple Pie

Maureen (to be exact) makes this pie in a well-used metal pie plate about 4–5 cm (1½–2 in) deep. She says this keeps the undercrust crisp—and it certainly does. When we devoured this pie it brought back childhood memories of Grandma's apple pie. I don't think Grandma would mind if I said that Maureen's was marginally better. It's been a long time!
Serves 6–8

Pastry:
1 cup (4 oz) flour
1 cup (4 oz) self-raising flour
pinch of salt
155 g (5 oz) margarine
1 egg
3 tablespoons caster (powdered) sugar
Filling:
6–7 large apples
3 tablespoons sugar
15 g (½ oz) butter

Pastry: Sift the flours and salt into a large mixing bowl. Rub in the margarine until the mixture resembles coarse breadcrumbs. Beat the egg with the sugar and add to the flour, mixing quickly into a dough. Wrap and chill for 30 minutes.
   Preheat the oven to 190°C (375°F/Gas 5).

Filling: Peel, quarter and core the apples. Cut into slices, and toss them in the sugar.

To finish the pie: Roll out two-thirds of the pastry on a lightly-floured surface to line a deep 20 cm (8 in) pie tin (use a metal one for a crispy undercrust). Fill with the apple slices and dot with the butter. Brush around the rim of the pastry with a little water. Roll out the remaining pastry and use it to cover the pie. Trim the excess pastry, and seal the edges by pressing them down with a fork. Make a few slits to allow the steam to escape, brush over with water, and sprinkle with a little extra sugar.
   Bake in the preheated oven for about 1 hour. Serve warm, with whipped cream or ice-cream.

Note: The apples may be cooked till fluffy in a saucepan with just enough water to stop them sticking. Drain off any liquid, then stir in sugar to taste. Cook, then use to fill the pie. Or a large can of pie apple is also very good for apple pie.

Apple Amber

Serves 6–8

185 g (6 oz) rich shortcrust
Filling:
500 g (1 lb) Granny Smith apples (green cooking apples)
3 tablespoons (3 oz) brown sugar
1 lemon
1 tablespoon water
45 g (1½ oz) butter
2 eggs, separated
2 tablespoons caster (powdered) sugar for meringue
extra caster sugar, for sprinkling

Make the pastry according to the recipe, and chill. Preheat the oven to 180°C (350°F/Gas 4).

Filling: Peel, core and slice the apples. Place the apples, sugar, strips of lemon rind and water in a saucepan; cover, and cook gently until the apple is very soft. Remove the lemon rind strips, and purée the apple in a food processor. Cut the butter into small pieces and add with the egg yolks and lemon juice to the hot purée. Blend well.

To finish the pie: Roll out the pastry and use to line a deep 23 cm (9 in) pie dish. Crimp the edges or, using the cut-off scraps of pastry, decorate the edges with small circles of pastry placed overlapping all around the rim of the pie. Brush the pastry case with a little lightly-beaten egg white. Pour in the apple mixture. Bake for 30 minutes or until the pastry is crisp and golden.
   Prepare the meringue topping in the meantime. Whisk the egg whites until stiff, then fold in the caster sugar gently, using a large metal spoon. When the pastry is cooked and golden, remove the pie from the oven, and increase the oven temperature to 190°C (375°F/Gas 5). Pile the meringue on top of the apple, taking the meringue right to the edge of the pastry. Sprinkle with a little extra caster sugar. Bake for 15 minutes or until the meringue is golden. Serve warm or cold.

Right: **From top:** Apple Amber (see above); Dutch Apple and Mincemeat Pie (see p. 284; Mrs Simpson's Apple Pie (see above).

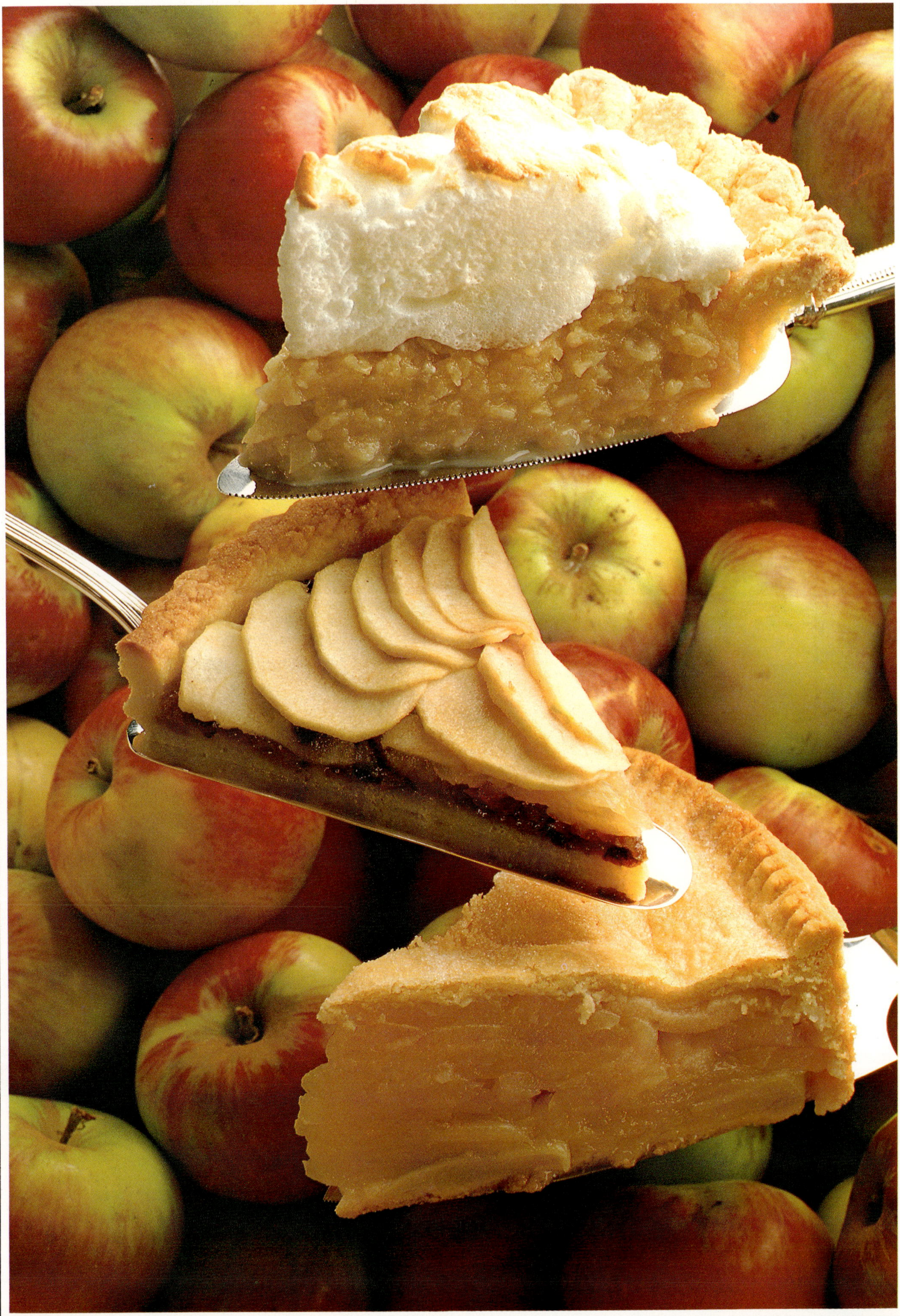

Dutch Apple and Mincemeat Pie

Serves 6–8

185 g (6 oz) pâte sucrée (see recipe, page 190)
Filling: 5 Granny Smith apples (green cooking apples)
rind from 1 lemon
pinch of ground cinnamon
pinch of ground cloves
1 tablespoon caster (powdered) sugar
1 tablespoon water
4 tablespoons mincemeat (see recipe, page 274)
2 tablespoons soft brown sugar

Make the pastry according to the recipe, and chill.

Preheat the oven to 190°C (375°F/Gas 5). Roll the pastry out thinly and use to line a 23 cm (9 in) pie dish. Trim off excess pastry and crimp the edges. Bake 'blind' for 10 to 12 minutes or until the pastry is a golden brown. Remove the 'blind' filling, and set the pie aside while making the filling.

Reset the oven temperature at 180°C (350°F/Gas 4).

Filling: Peel and core three of the apples and slice them into a small saucepan. Add the lemon rind, spices, caster sugar and water, and stew until soft.

Spread the base of the prepared pie case with the mincemeat, then spoon the stewed apples on top. Peel and core the two uncooked apples, slice them very thinly and arrange them over the stewed apples in concentric circles. Sprinkle with the soft brown sugar, and bake for 25 minutes. Serve warm, with whipped cream or ice-cream.

Apple Streusel Pie

Serves 8

Pastry: 1½ cups (6 oz) flour
pinch of salt
125 g (4 oz) butter
½ cup (1½ oz) rolled oats
2 tablespoons sugar
finely grated rind of 1 lemon
1 egg yolk
2–3 tablespoons water
egg white, for glazing
Filling: 1 kg (2 lb) cooking apples
1 tablespoon lemon juice
½ cup (3 oz) sultanas
½ cup (3 oz) brown sugar
½ teaspoon ground cinnamon
Topping: 30 g (1 oz) butter
2 tablespoons brown sugar
2 tablespoons flour
½ cup (1½ oz) rolled oats

Pastry: Sift the flour and salt into a bowl. Rub in the butter until the mixture resembles fine breadcrumbs. Stir in the rolled oats, sugar and grated lemon rind. Mix the egg yolk with water, and then stir it into the flour mixture to form a smooth dough. Knead lightly and wrap in greaseproof paper. Chill for 15 minutes.

Preheat the oven to 200°C (400°F/Gas 6).

Filling: Peel, core and slice the apples. Place in a bowl and sprinkle with the lemon juice. Add the sultanas, brown sugar and cinnamon; mix gently.

Topping: Place all the ingredients in a food processor and blend briefly, just until crumbly.

To finish the pie: On a lightly-floured surface, roll out the pastry to a thin round and line a 23 cm (9 in) pie plate. Decorate the edges by crimping or with the back of a knife or fork. Prick the base of the pastry with a fork, and brush all over with the lightly-beaten egg white. Place the filling carefully into the pastry case, shaping it into a dome in the centre. Sprinkle the topping over the filling.

Bake in the preheated oven for 10 minutes, then reduce the oven temperature to 180°C (350°F/Gas 4) and continue baking for a further 40 minutes or until the apples are just tender and the topping is crisp. Serve hot or cold, with whipped cream or ice-cream.

BERRY PIES

Fresh berry pies are something quite special. The harvesting season is all too short, so fresh berries are justifiably treated with reverence when they are available. Berry pies are often made with canned or bottled fruit—these are delicious, but can you imagine what a fresh fruit berry pie must be like.

About 4 cups of fresh fruit (3 cups of cooked fruit) will fill a 23 cm (9 in) pie. Sweetening is a matter of taste, but for this amount ½ cup (4 oz) of sugar will usually be sufficient for the sweeter fruits and 1–1½ cups (8–12 oz) of sugar for the tarter fruits such as gooseberries.

Thickening, too, depends on the fruit. For this quantity, ¼ cup (1 oz) of plain flour is about right. However, if the fruit is quite acid then use 2 tablespoons of tapioca mixed with the sugar or 2 tablespoons of cornflour (cornstarch) blended with ¼ cup (2fl oz) of juice or water; leave these to stand with the fruit for 15 minutes.

Use strawberries, raspberries, blueberries, mulberries, loganberries, blackberries or gooseberries.

Berry Pie

Serves 6–8

Pastry:
1 cup (4 oz) plain flour

1 cup (4 oz) self-raising flour

pinch of salt

155 g (5 oz) butter

2 tablespoons caster (powdered) sugar

1 egg, lightly beaten

1 tablespoon water

Filling:
4 cups fresh berries

¼–1½ cups (2–12 oz) sugar depending on the fruit

¼ cup (1 oz) flour (see note on thickening above), depending on the fruit

pinch of salt

1½ tablespoons lemon juice

grated lemon rind

egg white, for glazing

Pastry: Sift the flours and salt into a bowl. Rub in the butter until the mixture resembles fine breadcrumbs. Mix in the sugar until combined. Stir in the egg using a knife, and adding the water to make a smooth dough. Chill for about 10 minutes.

Preheat the oven to 200°C (400°F/Gas 6). Set a baking tray on a shelf ready for baking.

Roll out two-thirds of the pastry on a lightly-floured surface and use to line a 23 cm (9 in) pie dish or shallow cake tin.

Filling: Pick over the berries and hull or remove any stems. Rinse, and dry well on absorbent kitchen paper. Combine the berries with the sugar, flour, salt, lemon juice and lemon rind. (See the note in the introduction, above, if using tapioca or cornflour for thickening.) Spoon into the prepared pie dish.

Roll out the remaining pastry and cover the pie. Press the edges to seal and crimp the edges. Cut two vents in the pie. Brush with lightly-beaten egg white, and sprinkle with sugar. Bake in the preheated oven for 10 minutes on the baking tray set on the shelf. Reduce the oven temperature to 180°C (350°F/Gas 4) and bake for a further 35 to 40 minutes or until the pastry is golden brown and the berries are cooked.

Mulberry Pie

Serves 6

---

250 g (8 oz) rich shortcrust pastry (see recipe, page 184)

Filling:
3 cups fresh mulberries

1 cup (8 oz) sugar

1 tablespoon flour

1 tablespoon lemon juice

pinch of salt

15 g (½ oz) butter

egg white, for glazing

caster (powdered) sugar, for glazing

Make the pastry according to the recipe, and chill.

Preheat the oven to 200°C (400°F/Gas 6). Place a baking tray on a shelf ready for baking. Roll out two-thirds of the pastry and line a 20 cm (8 in) pie dish.

Filling: Pick over the mulberries and remove the stems. Combine the berries with the sugar, flour, lemon juice and salt. Spoon the berry mixture into the pastry case and dot with butter.

Roll out the remaining pastry and use to cover the pie. Trim off surplus pastry using a sharp knife. Crimp the edges and cut vents in top. Brush with the egg white, and sprinkle with the caster sugar. Place the pie dish on the baking tray, and bake in the preheated oven for 10 minutes, then reduce the oven temperature to 180°C (350°F/Gas 4) and bake for a further 40 minutes or until the berries and pastry are cooked.

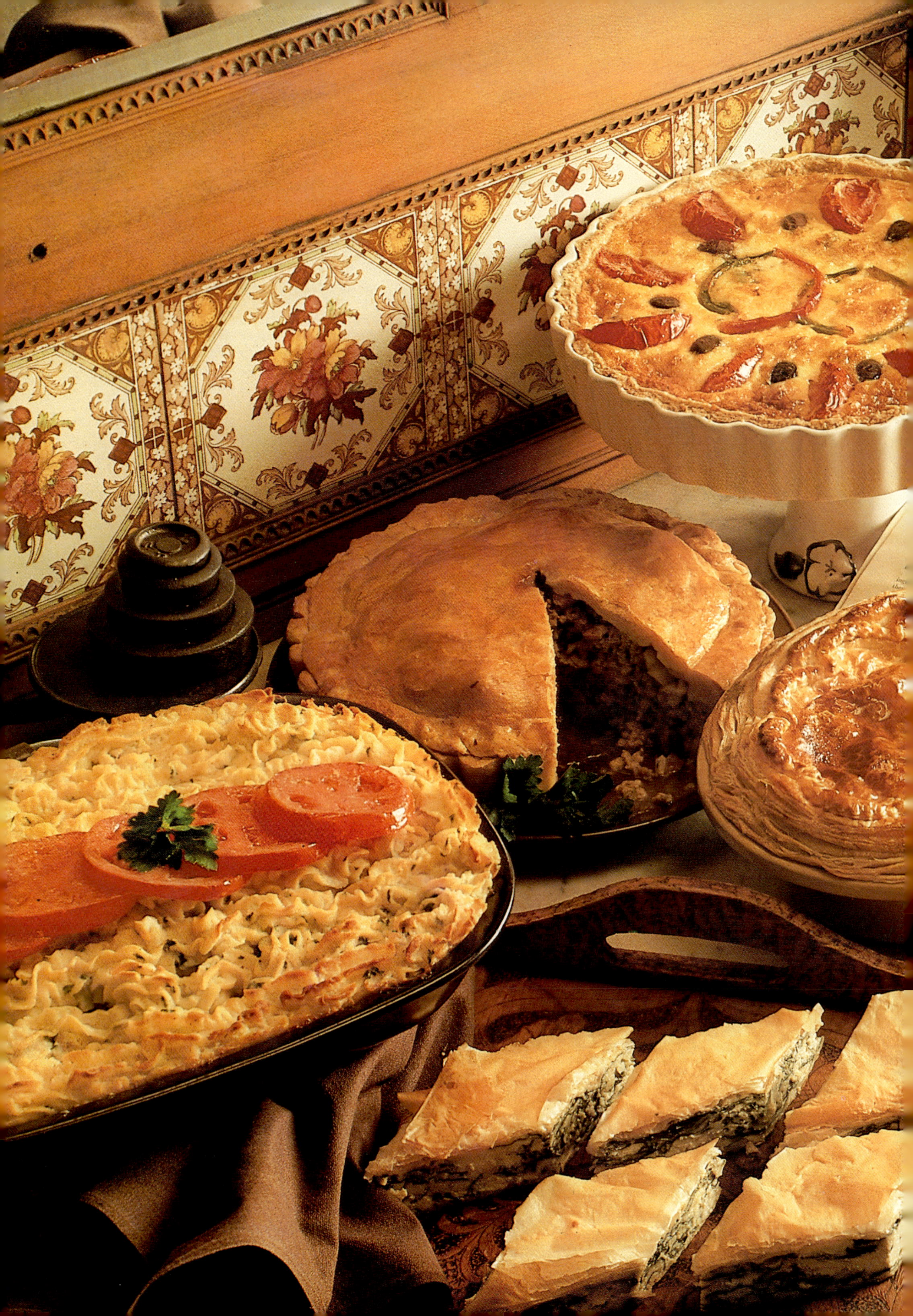

Savoury Pies

Savoury Pies

Meat pies have appeared in the cuisine of almost every country in one form or another, but in Australia 'pie 'n' sauce' is sometimes described—unkindly—as the national dish. And the ubiquitous meat pie is fine in its place. Even the most superior food writer would be hard-pressed to deny that at some time, in the right circumstances, he or she had actually *enjoyed* a commercial meat pie. (Mind you, they might have to go back some years, to those halcyon days when there was actually more meat than gravy in a 'shop-bought' pie!)

But there is considerably more to a pie than the ones to which I have referred. These pies have descended from a long and honourable line of pastry shells, many of which were filled with what we would consider strange mixtures.

For example, our mince pies, rich and succulent with dried fruits and spirits and now regarded as a traditional Christmas dessert, once featured minced meats, combined with apples, spices, honey and other sweet ingredients. Interestingly, one still finds American cookbooks featuring this recipe in very much its original form. Obviously it has changed little since the time the Pilgrim Fathers escaped to a new life in America, no doubt with the Pilgrim Mothers clutching their precious recipes as they fled. (I know my cherished old recipes would be one of the first items I'd reach for at the sound of the fire alarm!)

Ann Creber

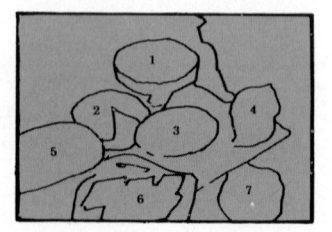

1. Neapolitan Quiche (see p. 297)
2. Tourtière (see p. 313)
3. Chicken and Parsley Pie (see p. 304)
4. Raised Veal and Ham Pie (see p. 309)
5. 'Old Faithful' Shepherd's Pie (see p. 309)
6. Cheese and Spinach Slice (see p. 296)
7. Economical Steak and Kidney Pie (see p. 308)

The History of the Pie

References to foods being encased in pastry of a kind go right back in history, and there is written evidence to suggest that this practice existed in Roman times. Pastries then would have been very crude and probably were meant to be discarded, rather than eaten. Presumably this was a refinement of the previously employed method of encasing food in a clay and water 'dough' which retained the juices during cooking, then was broken open and discarded when the food was cooked.

I believe Australian Aboriginals used this technique to cook small animals such as echidnas and lizards, so though the cooking medium was new to the Romans, the technique itself probably goes back into the culinary history of our origins.

If one believes the history books—both culinary and academic—it was England which turned the baking of pies into an art form. From the King's banquet table to the humblest cottage, the pie has its place in history.

And think how many expressions relating to pies have crept into our language—'a finger in every pie', 'promises like pie crusts', 'pie in the sky', 'eating humble pie' to name just a few. Incidentally, the 'humble pie' expression actually refers to Umble Pie, a pie made from the offal and entrails of game meat and birds. The superior flesh of the game was used in the pies served at the nobleman's table and the rejected portions in the pies eaten by his servants.

Hannah Glasse, Eliza Acton and Mrs. Beeton all featured grand pies among their recipes, including of course the most decorative of them—the raised pie. There is a lovely story about perhaps the most famous of these—the Melton Mowbray Raised Pie. Legend has it that a certain baker at Melton Mowbray, famed for the distinctive flavour of his raised pies, was the envy of all other bakers in neighbouring towns. 'Tis said that one wily fellow managed to have his niece employed by the Melton Mowbray baker and he, an easy victim to a pretty maiden, disclosed to her the secret of the mystery ingredient. It was, of course, anchovy sauce! (Perhaps the story is apocryphal, but I like to believe it.)

But perhaps the pie reached its pinnacle under the guidance of the great French chef Câréme, brought to England to preside over the kitchens of the Royal Pavilion at Brighton. With his French background very much in evidence, he introduced sophistications such as feuilletes, vol-au-vents and croustades. The renowned Italian Francatelli, personal chef to Queen Victoria—who obviously appreciated the good life—gave a new splendour to traditional regional pies, and no doubt helped contribute to that substantial girth we see depicted in the Royal portraits of Her Majesty's later years!

My own grandmother, whose family had come to Australia from Scotland, was employed as governess-housekeeper to a Tasmanian doctor, and she was one of the great pie-makers. Give Nanna a bit of flour, any kind of shortening and a few pieces of fruit or meat—and, lo, a wonderful pie would emerge from the oven, seemingly without any effort. She was proud of her skills and her resourcefulness. Every pie, no matter how simple or how quickly prepared, would be decorated with 'her' pastry design. She used to tell me that in the part of Scotland where her family had lived, each cook had a particular design she (and other members of the family) used to decorate pie crusts. This was carried on from one generation to the next, and there would have been great resentment had any outsider used that same design! In this way, it was immediately obvious to an observer, whose pie was which! On my own pies I still use the leaf and berry design which was used by my grandmother and, presumably, by all the pie-making McLeod women who went before her.

Of course nowadays we include a great diversity of pastries under the generic term 'pie'. Flans, savoury tarts, and quiche are all accepted in this category. Perhaps fortunately we no longer refer to 'coffins', an early name for pie cases.

To define a pie is not easy. How about a Shepherd's Pie?—not a scrap of pastry in sight. And what about the Italian pizza? That's another version of a pie!

In this chapter we will explore the realms of both prosaic and exotic pies. We will encounter the Cornish pastie—originally developed as a convenient lunchtime meal for a miner to carry to work in his pocket. We will also meet the Greek spinach pie, layered in its wafer thin leaves of filo pastry. So, put down that bottle of tomato sauce, pick up your rolling pin and we will set about investigating my savoury pie.

VEGETABLE PIES

Wholemeal Pizza Pie

The ever-popular pizza, consisting of pastry and filling is, of course, yet another form of pie. This version is wholesome and delicious.
Serves 6

Dough:
15 g (½ oz) fresh yeast or 7 g (¼ oz) dried yeast

2 teaspoons molasses or honey

1 cup (8 fl oz) lukewarm water

2 cups (8 oz) plain flour

2 cups (8 oz) wholemeal flour

pinch of salt

1 tablespoon soft margarine

Topping:
1 can/825 g (1 lb 14 oz) tomatoes

2 white onions, finely chopped

½ clove garlic, crushed

1 teaspoon raw sugar

½ teaspoon dried basil or 1 teaspoon fresh chopped basil

½ teaspoon oregano or 1 teaspoon fresh chopped oregano

salt and pepper

½ cup (4 oz) cooked soya beans

1 tablespoon oil, for brushing

185 g (6 oz) tasty cheese, grated

125 g (4 oz) mushrooms, sliced

6 green or black olives, pitted and slivered

125 g (4 oz) Mozzarella cheese, sliced

In a medium-sized bowl, blend together the yeast and molasses or honey. Stir in the warm water, and leave in a warm place until the mixture froths.

In a large bowl, combine the flours and salt. Rub in the margarine. Make a well in the centre, and pour in the yeast liquid, stirring until mixed. Tip the dough onto a lightly-floured board and knead for 5 minutes. Return it to the bowl, cover with a teatowel, and leave it to rise until it doubles in size.

Preheat the oven to 200°C (400°F/Gas 6).

While the dough is rising, prepare the filling. Chop the tomatoes and spoon them into a saucepan with the liquid from the can. Add the onions, garlic, sugar, herbs, salt and pepper, and simmer gently until the mixture thickens. Stir in the soya beans.

Punch the dough down with your fist, and roll it to fit a lightly-greased pizza tray. Prick the surface in several places, then brush with the oil. Sprinkle the pizza dough with the grated cheese, then spoon the tomato mixture over it, spreading evenly. Arrange the mushroom slices and slivered olives, then arrange the sliced Mozzarella cheese in a circle on top. Bake for about 30 minutes.

Hearty Wholemeal Vegetarian Pie

Another popular recipe from my cooking classes.
Serves 6–8

---

1 quantity wholemeal shortcrust pastry for double crust pie
(see recipe, page 189)

First Layer:
½ cup (4 oz) cooked brown rice

4 spring onions or shallots, chopped

2 tablespoons unflavoured yoghurt

2 tablespoons grated Parmesan cheese

2 tablespoons chopped parsley

freshly ground pepper

Second Layer:
250 g (8 oz) Ricotta cheese

1 cup cooked and chopped spinach or silver beet

3 tablespoons grated Parmesan cheese

salt and pepper

Preheat the oven to 180°C (350°F/Gas 4). Roll out two-thirds of the pastry and line a 23 × 20 cm (9 × 8 in) pie or flan dish.

Mix together all the ingredients for the first layer, and spoon into the pastry shell.

Cream the Ricotta cheese. Stir in the spinach or silver beet, Parmesan cheese, salt and pepper. Spread over the rice layer. (A little grated cheddar cheese may be added for extra flavour and nutrition.)

Roll out the remainder of the pastry and place it on top of the filling. Pinch the pastry edges together and cut a few vents in the top crust. (If desired, brush the surface with a little milk and add a sprinkle of Parmesan cheese.)

Bake for about 50 minutes. Remove from the oven and cut into squares for serving. This is a delicious 'pie' to serve as part of a buffet and, provided it is not overcooked initially, it reheats quite well.

Right: From top: Wholemeal Pizza Pie (see above); Hearty Wholemeal Vegetarian Pie (see above); Wholemeal Onion Tart (see p. 293).

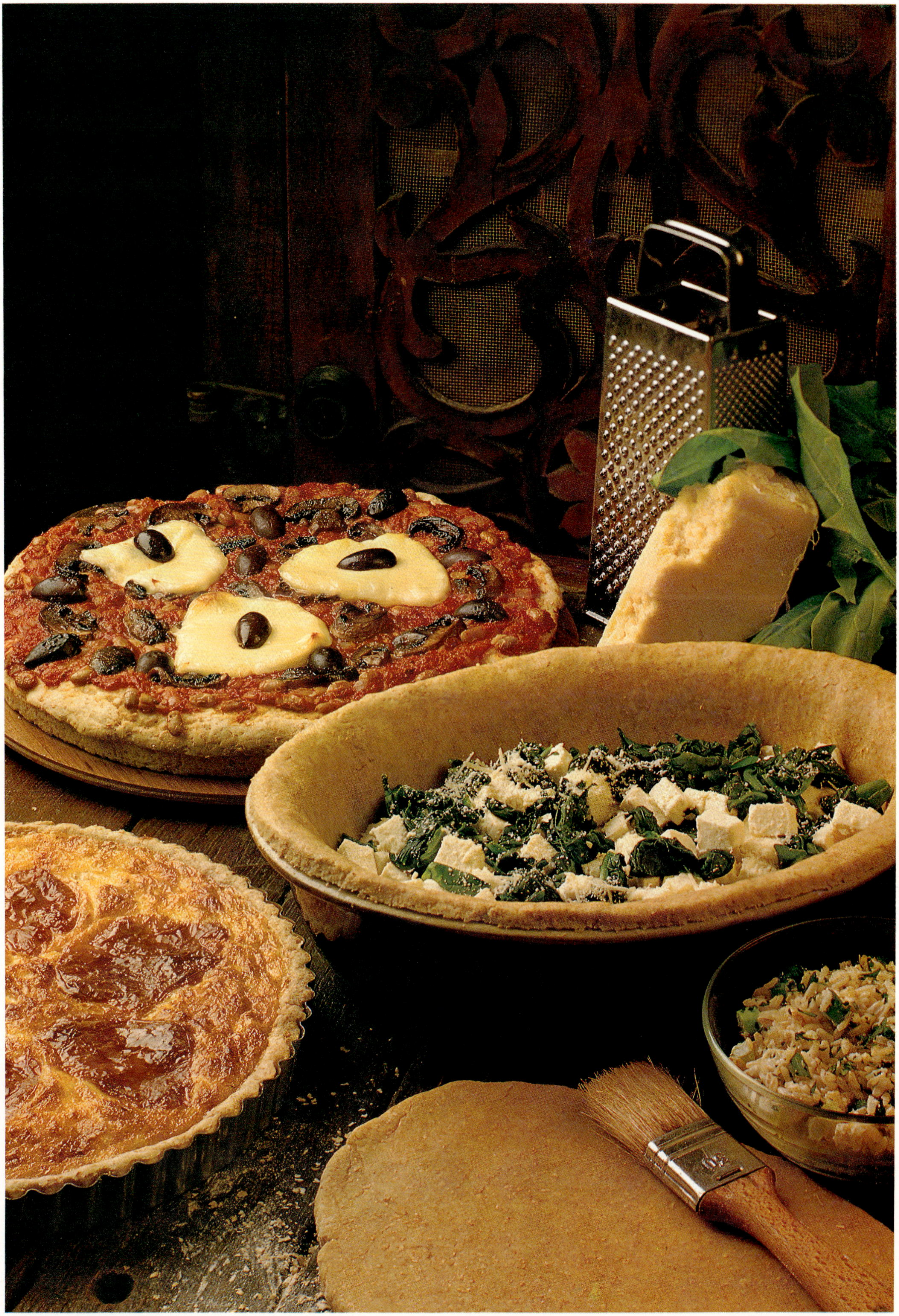

Carrot Flan

Serves 4–5

1 quantity wholemeal shortcrust pastry (see recipe, page 189)

Filling:
500 g (1 lb) young carrots, cooked and mashed

2 egg yolks

⅓ cup (2½fl oz) reduced cream

4 tablespoons grated tasty cheese

3 tablespoons finely chopped chives (or onion greens)

½ teaspoon finely chopped fresh rosemary

salt and pepper

Make the pastry according to the recipe. Roll it out and use it to line a 20 cm (8 in) flan tin. Bake 'blind' in a preheated oven at 150°C (300°F/Gas 3) for 20 minutes.

Leave the oven on at 180°C (350°F/Gas 4).

When the carrots have been cooked and mashed, beat in the egg yolks, cream, cheese, chives, rosemary and salt and pepper. Spoon the mixture into the pastry case. Bake for about 30 minutes or until the filling is firm. Serve warm, with a green salad.

This provides a lovely, light luncheon dish, which may be varied by adding a couple of bacon rashers, crisply cooked and crumbled.

Corn 'n' Cheese Flan

Serves 6

1 quantity shortcrust pastry (see recipe, page 182)

Filling:
1 cup sweetcorn (fresh, frozen or canned)

1 cup (8fl oz) reduced cream

¾ cup (6fl oz) milk

2 eggs

125 g (4 oz) tasty cheese, grated

2 rashers bacon, grilled and crumbled

½ teaspoon French mustard

2 tablespoons finely-chopped parsley

salt and pepper

Make the pastry according to the recipe. Roll it out and use it to line a deep 20 cm (8 in) flan tin. If using fresh corn, cook it lightly and then drain. Allow frozen corn to thaw. Or if using canned corn, drain it well.

Preheat the oven to 180°C (350°F/Gas 4). Place the cupful of corn into a large bowl. Lightly mix together the cream, milk and eggs, and add to the corn. Add the cheese, bacon, mustard, parsley, salt and pepper, and mix in. Spoon the mixture into the pastry case and bake for about 45 minutes.

(If preferred, use ½ cup (4fl oz) of cream, 1¼ cups (10fl oz) of milk and an extra egg.)

Cheese and Mushroom Potato Pastry Flan

Serves 6

Pastry:
60 g (2 oz) butter, softened

1 cup (4 oz) flour

1 cup (4 oz) warm mashed potatoes

2 tablespoons finely chopped parsley

salt and pepper

Filling:
3 eggs

½ cup (4fl oz) reduced cream or evaporated milk

90 g (3 oz) tasty cheese, grated

1 teaspoon dried mixed herbs or 3 teaspoons fresh chopped herbs

salt and pepper

90 g (3 oz) button mushrooms, sliced

2 tomatoes, sliced

Preheat the oven to 190°C (375°F/Gas 5).

To make the pastry, rub the butter into the flour; then work in the mashed potatoes, parsley, salt and pepper. Roll out thinly and line a 20 cm (8 in) flan tin. Reserve any pastry scraps.

Filling: Beat the eggs and cream together, then stir in the cheese, herbs, salt and pepper. Pour or spoon the mixture into the flan case. Arrange the sliced mushrooms and tomatoes over the egg-cream mixture.

Roll out the reserved pastry scraps, cut into thin strips, and arrange decoratively over the top of the filling. Bake on a lower shelf in the preheated oven for 35 to 45 minutes or until the filling has set and the pastry is golden brown. Serve warm or cold.

Onion and Edam Cheese Flan

Serves 6

1 quantity shortcrust pastry (see recipe, page 182)
Filling: 250 g (8 oz) Edam cheese, grated
2 tablespoons flour
1 tablespoon butter
1 large onion, finely sliced
4 eggs
1 cup (8 fl oz) cream
1 cup (8 fl oz) milk
¼ teaspoon grated nutmeg
drops of Tabasco sauce
freshly ground pepper

Make the pastry and use it to line a 23 cm (9 in) flan tin. Bake 'blind' in a preheated oven at 150°C (300°F/Gas 3) for 20 minutes. Remove the 'blind' filling.

Set the oven temperature at 200°C (400°F/Gas 6).

Filling: Mix the cheese and flour together, and sprinkle into the pastry case. Heat the butter in a pan and sauté the onion until it is transparent; arrange over the cheese-flour. Beat the eggs lightly and add the cream, milk, nutmeg, Tabasco sauce and salt and pepper to taste; pour the mixture carefully over the onion.

Bake for 30 to 35 minutes or until the filling is set and the top is golden brown. Serve hot or cold.

Wholemeal Onion Tart

Serves 6

1 quantity wholemeal shortcrust pastry (see recipe, page 189)
Filling: 60 g (2 oz) butter
250 g (8 oz) white onions, sliced
½ cup (4 fl oz) milk
½ cup (4 fl oz) cream
3 eggs
90 g (3 oz) tasty cheese, grated
salt and pepper
185 g (6 oz) Mozzarella cheese

Make the pastry according to the recipe. Roll it out thinly and line a 20 or 23 cm (8 or 9 in) flan tin.

Preheat the oven to 180°C (350°F/Gas 4).

Filling: Melt the butter and sauté the onions until soft and golden. Beat together the milk, cream and eggs; stir in the grated cheese, salt and pepper. Combine with the onions, then spoon the mixture into the pastry case. Thinly slice the Mozzarella cheese, and arrange it gently on top of the onion filling.

Bake for about 45 minutes. If the filling is firm and golden after this time, remove the flan from the oven; otherwise continue cooking for a little longer. Serve hot or cold.

Potato Galette with Savoury Layer

Serves 6

750 g (1½ lb) potatoes
4 tablespoons grated tasty cheese
2 tablespoon butter
2 tablespoons milk
1 teaspoon English mustard powder
salt and pepper
Savoury Layer: 250 g (8 oz) small mushrooms, sliced
1 tablespoon butter
4 lean rashers of bacon, fried or grilled
2 stalks celery, chopped
1 medium-sized onion, chopped
2 tablespoon chopped parsley
1 teaspoon chopped fresh herbs or ½ teaspoon dried herbs
2 tablespoon melted butter
parsley sprigs, for garnish

Preheat the oven to 200°C (400°F/Gas 6).

Peel and cube the potatoes, and cook them in salted water until tender. Mash whilst still hot, and beat in the cheese, butter, milk, mustard, salt and pepper.

While the potatoes are cooking, prepare the savoury layer. Sauté the mushrooms in butter; add the bacon, celery, onion, parsley and herbs. Sauté until the vegetables are tender.

Line a greased pie dish or cake tin with half of the hot mashed potatoes. Spoon the savoury layer mixture over the top. Then cover with the remainder of the potatoes. Roughen the surface with a fork, and brush generously with the melted butter. Bake for about 35 minutes or until the top is golden brown. Serve hot, garnished with sprigs of parsley.

Quiche with Olives

Serves 6

1 × 23 cm (9 in) shortcrust flan shell, partially cooked and cooled
Filling: 1½ cups (12fl oz) light cream
½ cup (4fl oz) buttermilk
4 eggs, lightly beaten
125 g (4 oz) bacon, grilled and crumbled
125 g (4 oz) Edam cheese, grated
8 spring onions, finely chopped
125 g (4 oz) black or green olives, pitted and slivered

Beat together the cream, buttermilk and eggs. Fold in the bacon, cheese, onions, and olives, and pour into the partially-baked pastry shell. Bake in a preheated oven at 190°C (375°F/Gas 5) for about 35 minutes or until the custard is golden and lightly set. Serve warm or cold.

Pumpkin Pasties

Makes 6

1 quantity shortcrust pastry (see recipe, page 182)
egg wash (1 egg with 2 tablespoon cream), for glazing
2 tablespoons sesame seeds, for sprinkling
Filling: 30 g (1 oz) butter or margarine
1 white onion, grated or finely chopped
1 cup (4 oz) finely shredded cabbage
1 cup (5 oz) frozen peas
½ teaspoon mixed dried herbs or thyme
125 g (4 oz) butternut pumpkin, grated
125 g (4 oz) tasty cheese, grated
1 tablespoon finely chopped parsley
salt and pepper

Preheat the oven to 200°C (400°F/Gas 6).
Make the pastry, roll it out thinly and cut into six saucer-sized rounds.

Filling: Melt the butter or margarine in a saucepan, add the onion, cabbage, peas and herbs, and sauté for 5 minutes. Remove from the heat and stir in the pumpkin, cheese, parsley and salt and pepper.

Place equal portions of the filling onto the centre of each pastry round. Dampen the outside edges of the pastry and bring them together over the filling (like a Cornish pastie), crimping the joined edges into a frill. Place on a greased baking tray, brush over each pastie with the egg glaze, and sprinkle with a few sesame seeds.

Bake in the preheated oven for 8 to 10 minutes, then reduce the oven temperature to 180°C (350°F/Gas 4) and continue baking for a further 25 to 30 minutes. Serve hot or cold.

Savoury Pumpkin Pie

Serves 6–8

Pastry: 125 g (4 oz) butter or margarine, softened
2 tablespoons hot water
250 g (8 oz) wholemeal self-raising flour
pinch of salt
3 tablespoon crushed nuts
Filling: 1½ cups cooked dry pumpkin
2 eggs, separated
⅔ cup (5fl oz) sour cream
⅔ cup (5fl oz) milk
½ teaspoon ground ginger
salt and pepper
90 g (3 oz) tasty cheese, grated
6 spring onions, finely chopped
2 teaspoons finely grated lemon peel
2 teaspoons Worcestershire sauce
½ teaspoon dried mustard
1 tablespoon finely chopped parsley

Preheat the oven to 160°C (325°F/Gas 3). Place the butter in a bowl, pour on the hot water, and mash well with a fork. Add the flour and salt, add the nuts and work together until it is a soft dough. Allow to firm up in the refrigerator if necessary. Roll out and line (or press into) a 23 cm (9 in) pie dish. Prick the base of the pastry well with a fork and bake 'blind' for 10 to 15 minutes. Remove the 'blind' filling and allow to cool.

Preheat the oven to 220°C (425°F/Gas 7).

Filling: Mash the pumpkin, and beat in the egg yolks, cream, milk, ginger, salt and pepper. Stir in the cheese, chopped spring onions, lemon peel, Worcestershire sauce, dried mustard and parsley. Beat the egg whites and fold into the mixture. Pour into the cold pastry shell and bake in the preheated oven for 15 minutes, then reduce the temperature to 160°C (325°F/Gas 3) and continue baking for a further 35 minutes. Serve warm, with a crisp green salad.

Right: **Savoury Pumpkin Pie** (see above).

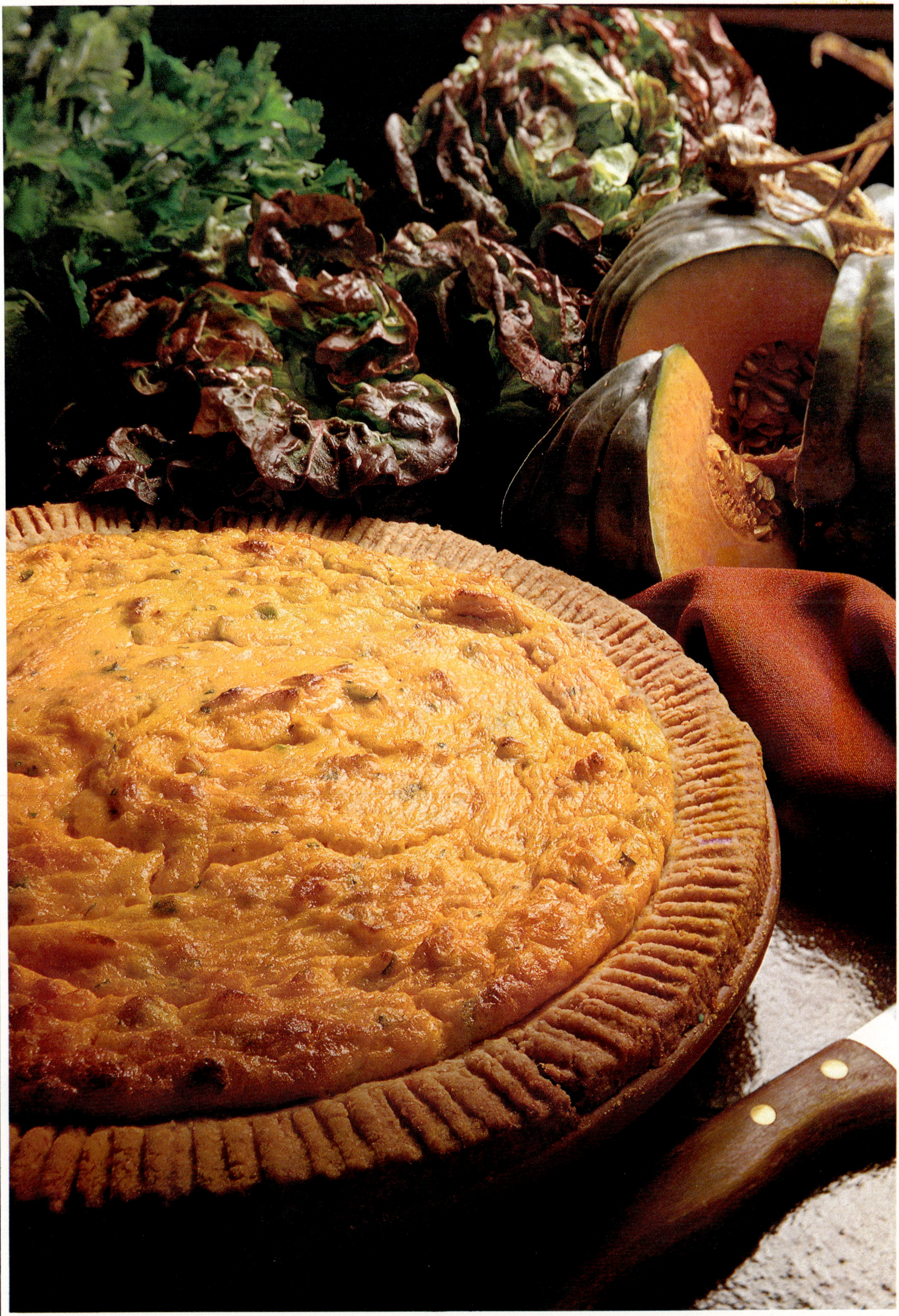

Cheese and Spinach Slice

A recipe that was popular in my cooking classes. Based on the traditional Greek recipe, this slice is nutritious as well as tasty.

Serves 6–8

250 g (8 oz) bunch of spinach
15 g (½ oz) butter
2 medium onions, chopped
½ clove garlic, crushed
185 g (6 oz) cream cheese
185 g (6 oz) Feta cheese
125 g (4 oz) tasty cheese
1 tablespoon chopped parsley
2 tablespoons chopped fresh dill or ¾ teaspoon dried dill
3 eggs, lightly beaten
good pinch of ground nutmeg
salt and pepper
16 sheets filo pastry
155 g (5 oz) butter, melted

Wash the spinach well, remove coarse stems, shred or coarsely chop the green leaves, and drain well in a colander.

Preheat the oven to 160° (325°F/Gas 3).

Melt the 15 g butter in a frying pan, and sauté the onions and garlic until golden. Combine the onions-garlic and chopped spinach in a large bowl.

In another bowl, mash the cream cheese, grate the feta cheese and tasty cheese, and mix in the parsley and dill. Stir this cheese mixture into the spinach and onion. Add the lightly-beaten eggs, nutmeg, salt and pepper, and blend thoroughly.

Place a sheet of the filo pastry into a greased baking dish, brush with melted butter. Repeat with another seven sheets of the pastry, brushing each one with the butter. Spread the spinach and cheese mixture evenly onto the top layer of pastry. Cover with another eight layers of pastry, brushing between each with the melted butter. Using a sharp knife, trim off excess pastry around the edges of the baking dish, and slightly score the top layer of the pastry—this ensures a crisp and flaky topping.

Bake for about 50 minutes, or until golden brown.

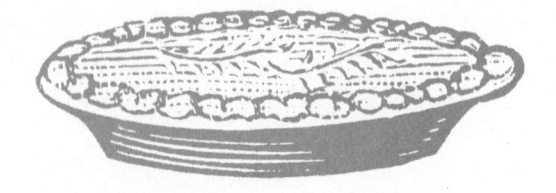

Vegetable Pie

Serves 6–8

500 g (1 lb) potatoes
1 small cauliflower
1 small bunch of celery, finely sliced
1 small parsnip, chopped
1 white onion, sliced
1 carrot, chopped
3 tablespoons finely chopped parsley
freshly ground pepper
Sauce:
30 g (1 oz) butter
1 tablespoon flour
1¼ cups (10 fl oz) milk
3 tablespoons grated cheese
salt and pepper

Prepare the potatoes and boil them in lightly-salted water until tender. Break the cauliflower into small florets and boil in lightly-salted water until tender. Combine the celery, parsnip, onion and carrot in a saucepan, cover with salted water and simmer until tender.

Preheat the oven to 180°C (350°F/Gas 4).

Drain the potatoes and mash them with a little milk until quite smooth. Line a buttered casserole with two-thirds of the potato mixture.

Drain the cauliflower well. Drain the other vegetables (save the stock to use in soups). Combine the vegetables with the parsley and pepper, and spoon half of the quantity into the potato-lined casserole.

Sauce: Melt the butter in a small saucepan, add the flour, and cook for 3 minutes, stirring with a wooden spoon. Add the milk, and whisk constantly until the sauce thickens. Remove from the heat, stir in the cheese, and add salt and pepper to taste.

Pour half of the sauce over the vegetables in the potato case, add the remainder of the vegetables, and top with the rest of the sauce. Cover with the remaining potatoes.

Bake for 40 minutes or until golden brown.

Neapolitan Quiche

Serves 4–6

1 quantity wholemeal pastry (see recipe, page 189)

Filling:
2 tablespoons butter

1 white onion, chopped

½ clove garlic, crushed

2 tablespoons finely chopped red or green pepper

3 tomatoes, sliced

1 teaspoon fresh basil or ½ teaspoon dried basil

salt and pepper

90 g (3 oz) tasty cheese, grated

3 eggs

1 cup (8 fl oz) milk

2 slices green pepper

3 small tomatoes, quartered

8 black olives, pitted and slivered

Preheat the oven to 190°C (375°F/Gas 5). Line a 23 cm (9 in) flan tin with the pastry.

Heat 1 tablespoon of the butter and sauté the onion, garlic and chopped pepper until tender. Remove from the pan.

Add the second tablespoon of butter to the pan, and add the tomato slices; fry gently until just tender, then drain and arrange in the base of the pastry case. Sprinkle with the basil and salt and pepper. Spoon the sautéed onion-garlic-peppers into the flan case. Then add the grated cheese. Beat the eggs lightly and add the milk; pour carefully into the flan case. Arrange the green pepper slices, quartered tomatoes and slivered olives on top.

Bake for 35 to 40 minutes or until the filling is set and golden brown. May be eaten hot or cold.

Tarte Niçoise

Serves 4–6

Pastry:
1¾ cups (7 oz) flour

pinch of salt

1 teaspoon baking powder

100 g (3½ oz) butter

1 egg yolk

1 teaspoon lemon juice

1 tablespoon iced water

Filling:
6 small tomatoes

½ cup (2 oz) grated tasty cheese

¼ cup (1 oz) dried breadcrumbs

1 tablespoon butter

salt

pinch of cayenne pepper

grated nutmeg

2 teaspoons chopped fresh basil or 1 teaspoon dried basil

2 eggs

1½ cups (12 fl oz) cream

salt and black pepper

6 black olives, stoned and halved

To make the pastry, sift the flour, salt and baking powder into a bowl. Rub in the butter until the mixture resembles breadcrumbs (a food processor may be used). Beat the egg yolk, lemon juice and water, and stir into the flour. Mix lightly with a knife blade to form a smooth but rather dry dough. (If necessary add a little more water—but not unless essential.) Knead as little as possible. Allow to stand for 30 minutes.

Preheat the oven to 160°C (325°F/Gas 3). Roll out the pastry and line a 23 cm (9 in) flan tin or tart tin. Line with greaseproof paper and baking beans, and bake 'blind' for 12 to 15 minutes, or until just set but not browned.

Reset the oven temperature at 190°C (375°F/Gas 5).

Filling: Cut the tomatoes in half and gently scrape out the seeds and juice. Combine the cheese, breadcrumbs, butter, salt, cayenne pepper, nutmeg and basil and stuff the mixture into the cavities of the tomatoes. Arrange them (cut side up) in the base of the flan.

Beat together the eggs, cream, salt and black pepper, and pour into the flan case around the tomatoes. Arrange the olives between the tomatoes.

Bake for about 35 minutes, reducing the heat slightly if the top is browning too quickly. Serve warm or cold.

Asparagus Flan

Serves 4–6

1 quantity shortcrust pastry
(see recipe, page 182)

Filling:
1 tablespoon butter

1 onion, finely chopped or grated

2 eggs, lightly beaten

½ cup (4fl oz) cream

125 g (4 oz) tasty cheese, grated

½ teaspoon French mustard

salt and black pepper

12 canned or cooked asparagus spears, drained

Make the pastry according to the recipe. Roll it out and use it to line a 20 cm (8 in) flan tin.
Preheat the oven to 200°C (400°F/Gas 6).
Heat the butter and sauté the onion until soft. Beat the eggs and cream together, stir in the cheese, mustard, salt and pepper, then the cooled onion. Pour into the pastry case, and arrange the asparagus spears on top.
Bake in the preheated oven for 10 minutes, then reduce the oven temperature to 190°C (375°F/Gas 5) and continue baking for a further 30 minutes or until set. Serve warm or cold.

Herbed Vegetable Flan

Serves 4–6

1 quantity wholemeal shortcrust pastry
(see recipe, page 189)

Filling:
1 tablespoon butter

2 tablespoons wholemeal flour

1 can (15fl oz) vegetable juice

2 small zucchini (courgettes) thinly sliced

2 small carrots, grated

1 small onion, thinly sliced

1 clove garlic, crushed

1 teaspoon chopped fresh herbs

60 g (2 oz) mushrooms, sliced

Topping:
45 g (1½ oz) butter

1 clove garlic, crushed

1 cup (2 oz) fresh wholemeal breadcrumbs

½ cup (2 oz) grated tasty cheese

2 tablespoons chopped parsley

Roll out the pastry thinly and line a 25 cm (10 in) flan tin. Bake 'blind' in a preheated oven at 180°C (350°F/Gas 4) until golden.

Filling: Melt the butter in a saucepan. Add the flour and cook for several minutes, stirring constantly. Gradually stir in the vegetable juice and whisk until smooth. Add the zucchini, carrots, onion, garlic and herbs. Simmer over low heat until the vegetables are just tender and the mixture has thickened. Add the mushrooms and cook for another minute or two. Allow to cool.
Preheat the oven to 190°C (375°F/Gas 5). Spoon the now-cool filling into the pastry case.

Topping: Melt the butter, add the crushed garlic, and sauté for a minute or two. Add the breadcrumbs and stir until the crumbs are coated with butter. Remove from the heat; stir in the cheese and parsley. Spread onto the vegetable filling. Bake for 10 to 15 minutes or until the crumb topping is crisp and brown. Serve hot or warm.

Gourmet Seafood Flan

Serves 6

1 quantity rich shortcrust pastry
(see recipe, page 184)

Filling:
30 g (1 oz) butter

2–3 white onions, sliced

2 tablespoons flour

⅔ cup (5fl oz) reduced cream or milk

2 eggs, beaten

500 g (1 lb) mixed cooked seafood meat
(oysters, scallops, yabbies, prawns, crayfish)

2 teaspoons dried green dill tips

salt and pepper

45 g (1½ oz) grated cheese

Roll out the prepared pastry and line a lightly-greased 18 cm (7 in) flan tin. Chill.
Preheat the oven to 190°C (375°F/Gas 5).
Melt the butter in a frying pan, add the onions and sauté until softened. Add the flour and continue cooking, stirring constantly, for about 3 minutes. Pour the cream or milk into the pan, simmer, stirring for 3 minutes or until the mixture thickens. Cool to lukewarm.
Beat the eggs into the mixture. Add the chopped seafood, dill, nutmeg, salt and pepper. Pour the filling into the pastry case, and sprinkle with the cheese. Bake for 30 minutes, or until set. Serve warm.

Right: Clockwise from top: Herbed Vegetable Flan (above); Gourmet Seafood Flan (above); Asparagus Flan (above).

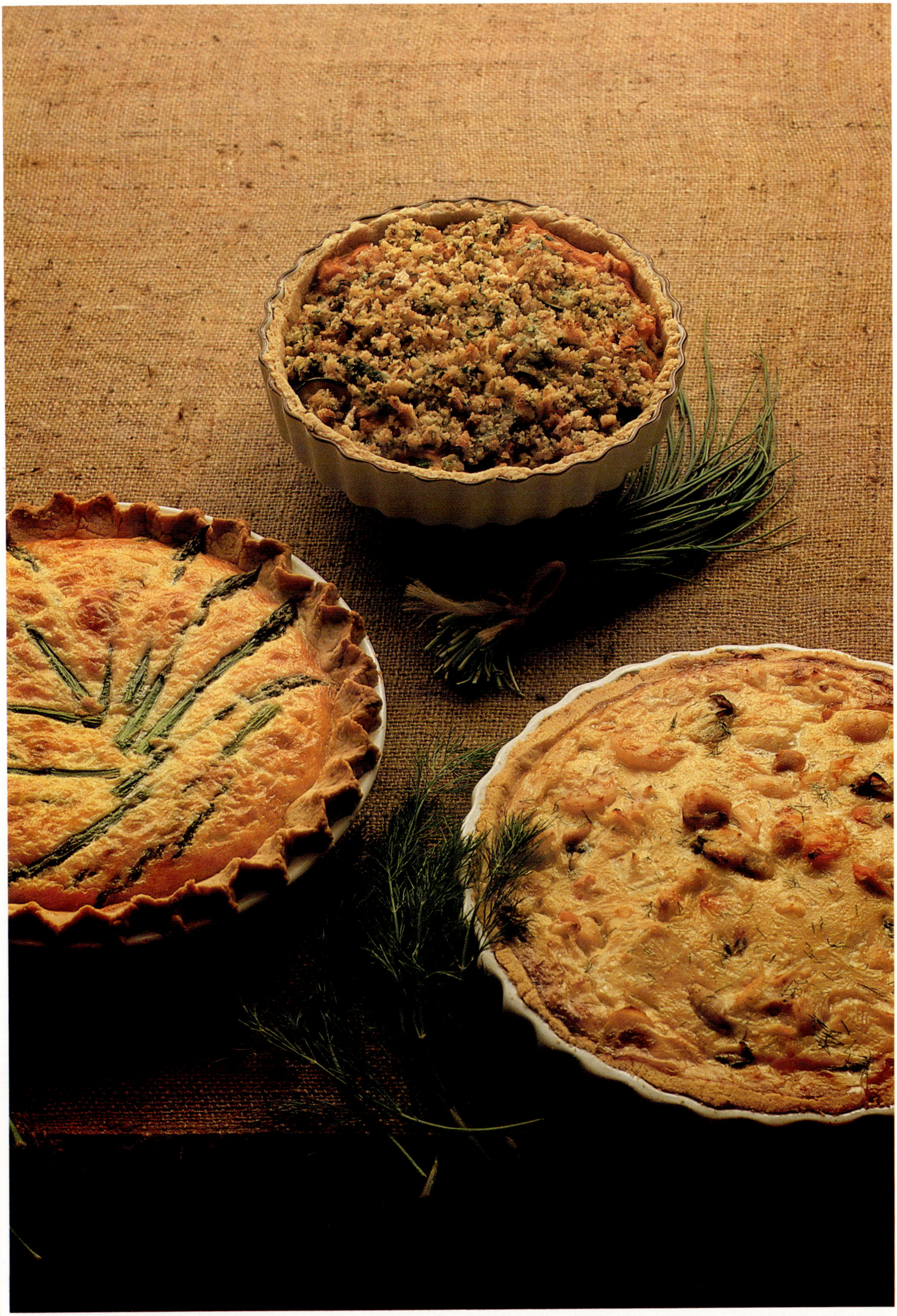

CHEESE PIES

Tyropita

*This tasty cheese slice is quickly and easily made using pre-rolled puff pastry. Different, but do try it.
Cuts into about 34 pieces*

2 sheets pre-rolled puff pastry
Filling:
250 g (8 oz) cottage cheese
60 g (2 oz) blue vein cheese, crumbled
60 g (2 oz) cheddar cheese, grated
2 eggs
2 tablespoons dry breadcrumbs
2 teaspoons chopped fresh mint or ½ teaspoon dried mint
salt
pinch of cayenne pepper
egg yolk beaten with a little water, for glazing

Preheat the oven to 190°C (375°F/Gas 5). Place 1 layer of pastry into a lightly-greased baking pan.

Beat the cottage cheese; then add the blue vein cheese, cheddar cheese and eggs, and beat until smooth. Stir in the breadcrumbs, mint, salt and cayenne pepper. Spread the mixture over the pastry, and top it with the remaining dough. Brush over with the egg yolk and water.

Bake for 35 to 40 minutes or until the pastry is golden. Cut into diamond shapes and serve hot.

Doctor's Favourite Savoury Tarts

*This recipe, taken from my Nanna's old hand-written cookbook, has been a great favourite with students in my cooking classes.
Makes 12 small tarts*

1 quantity puff pastry (see recipe, page 186)
Filling:
125 g (4 oz) tasty cheese, grated
1 egg yolk
½ teaspoon dry mustard
salt and pepper
15 g (½ oz) butter, softened
60 g (2 oz) finely chopped walnuts
2 egg whites, stiffly beaten

Preheat the oven to 160°C (325°F/Gas 3).

Prepare the pastry, roll it out thinly and line twelve greased patty pans or small tartlet tins.

Blend together the grated cheese and the egg yolk; season with the mustard, salt and pepper. Stir in the soft butter and the walnuts, then lightly fold in the stiffly-beaten egg whites. Place a generous portion into each pastry-lined patty tin.

Bake for about 20 minutes or until the filling is puffed and the pastry is golden. Serve at once, as the lovely soufflé-like texture of the filling will drop as it cools. A delicious accompaniment for pre-dinner drinks.

Rich Bacon and Cheese Pie with Bran Crust

Serves 6

Pastry:
1 cup (4 oz) processed bran (such as All-Bran)
½ cup (4fl oz) milk
1½ cups (6 oz) self-raising flour
salt
125 g (4 oz) butter or margarine
Filling:
6 lean bacon rashers, grilled and crumbled
250 g (8 oz) tasty cheese, grated
1¾ cups (14fl oz) light cream
2 eggs, beaten
salt and pepper
1 spring onion, chopped
2 tablespoons chopped parsley

Preheat the oven to 190°C (375°F/Gas 5).

Soak the bran in the milk for about 5 minutes. Sift the flour and salt together, then rub in the butter. Combine the two mixtures and knead lightly until smooth. Roll the pastry out, and line a 23 cm (9 in) flan dish.

Combine all the filling ingredients, and pour the mixture into the pastry case. Bake for about 40 minutes or until golden brown.

This nutritious but rich flan may be lightened by substituting evaporated milk for the cream. This also reduces the cost of making it.

SEAFOOD PIES

Salmon and Mushroom Pie

Serves 4–6

1 quantity shortcrust pastry (see recipe, page 182)
Filling: 250 g (8 oz) mushrooms, sliced
²⁄₃ cup (5 fl oz) milk
30 g (1 oz) butter
30 g (1 oz) flour
1½ cups (12 fl oz) reduced cream
salt and black pepper
½ teaspoon dried dill tips or 1½ teaspoons fresh chopped dill
grated rind of ½ lemon
1 can/425 g (15 oz) salmon (or tuna), drained and flaked

Preheat the oven to 200°C (400°F/Gas 6).

Simmer the mushrooms in the milk, then drain, and retain the milk.

Melt the butter in a heavy saucepan, add the flour and cook over moderate heat for 3 to 4 minutes, stirring with a wooden spoon. Pour in the milk from the mushrooms; and add the cream, salt and pepper and dill, and whisk until the sauce is smooth and thick. Add the lemon rind.

Combine the mushrooms and salmon in a large bowl, blend in the white sauce, and spoon the mixture into a pie dish. Roll out the pastry and place it over the filling. Press the pastry firmly onto the edges of the pie dish and cut several vents in the pastry top.

Bake for about 40 minutes. Garnish with lemon wedges, and serve with a green salad.

Emergency Pie

This is for those occasions when the cook is faced with the need to produce a quick meal from ingredients in the cupboard. Most of us can put our hands on the odd tin or two...
Serves 4–5

1 can/425 g (15 oz) tuna
1½ cups (12 fl oz) cream of celery soup
½ cup chopped celery (if available)
½ cup frozen peas
1 tablespoon chopped parsley
salt and pepper
375 g (12 oz) potatoes, boiled and mashed

Preheat the oven to 160°C (325°F/Gas 3). Combine the drained tuna with the soup, chopped celery, frozen peas, parsley and salt and pepper. Spoon into a pie dish, and cover with a layer of mashed potatoes. Bake for 30 minutes or until heated through.

Cheesy Tuna Puffs

Makes 12

Choux Pastry: ½ cup (2 oz) self-raising flour
½ cup (4 fl oz) water
60 g (2 oz) butter
pinch of salt
2 eggs
Filling: 1 can/425 g (15 oz) tuna, drained
45 g (1½ oz) tasty cheese, grated
1 cup chopped celery
2 spring onions, finely chopped
½ small red pepper, finely chopped
½ cup mayonnaise
2 tablespoons finely chopped parsley
salt and pepper

Preheat the oven to 220°C (425°F/Gas 7).

To make the pastry, sift the flour and salt onto a piece of paper. Combine the water and butter in a saucepan, bring to a rapid boil, and pour all the flour into the boiling liquid. Cook for a couple of minutes, stirring constantly until the mixture leaves the sides of the saucepan. Transfer the mixture to a bowl and allow to cool to lukewarm, then beat in the eggs.

Beat the eggs into the mixture, one at a time; beat until it is smooth and shiny. Spoon twelve rounds onto a lightly-greased oven tray and bake in the preheated oven for 20 minutes, then reduce the oven temperature to 190°C (375°F/Gas 5) for a further 10 minutes. Remove from the oven and prick the bottom of each puff so that steam may escape. Allow to cool on wire racks.

To make the filling, drain and flake the tuna, and combine with all the other ingredients. Split the puffs when cool, fill with the tuna mixture, and serve. (If preferred, heat the pastry shells; gently heat the filling in a small saucepan and spoon into the split heated shells.)

Smoked Cod Pie

Serves 4

250 g (8 oz) shortcrust pastry (see recipe, page 182)

Filling:
250 g (8 oz) smoked cod, cooked, well drained and flaked

2 hard-boiled eggs, sliced

125 g (4 oz) cooked rice

2 spring onions, finely chopped

grated peel of ½ lemon

2 tablespoons chopped parsley

salt and pepper

egg wash (1 egg with 2 tablespoons cream)

Preheat the oven to 230°C (450°F/Gas 8). Roll out the pastry to about 25 cm (10 in) square and place onto a greased baking tray.

In a large bowl, mix together the flaked smoked cod, sliced eggs, rice, onion, lemon peel, parsley and salt and pepper. Spoon the mixture along the centre of the pastry shape. Brush the edges with water and fold over the two flaps to overlap. Brush the pastry surface with the egg wash.

Bake for about 30 minutes.

'Tater-topped Fish Pie

Serves 4

250 g (8 oz) white fish fillets

2 cups (16fl oz) milk

6 scallops

45 g (1½ oz) butter

1 heaped tablespoon flour

185 g (6 oz) mushrooms, sliced

185 g (6 oz) shelled cooked prawns, chopped

6 oysters, chopped

salt and pepper

Topping:
500 g (1 lb) potatoes, cooked and still hot

2 tablespoons finely chopped parsley

salt and pepper

little melted butter

Preheat the oven to 220°C (425°F/Gas 7).

Cut the fish fillets into chunks, and poach in the milk until tender enough to flake. Add the scallops for the last 3 or 4 minutes while the fish is cooking. Drain, and reserve the liquid; place the fish into a bowl.

Melt 30 g of the butter in a saucepan, blend in the flour and cook for 3 minutes. Gradually whisk in the poaching liquid, stirring constantly until the mixture thickens.

Melt the remaining 15 g of butter and sauté the mushrooms until just tender. Fold them into the fish mixture, add the chopped prawns and oysters and salt and pepper.

Butter a pie dish and spoon in a layer of the fish and mushroom mixture. Cover with a layer of sauce, then the remainder of the fish mixture, then the remaining sauce.

Mash the hot potatoes, stir in the parsley and salt and pepper. Spread evenly over the mixture in the pie dish. Pour the melted butter over, and roughen the surface. Bake for 15 to 20 minutes.

Tuna Cobbler

Serves 5

1 can/450 g (1 lb) chunky tuna in brine

approx. 1 cup (8fl oz) milk

60 g (2 oz) butter

1 medium-sized onion, chopped

⅓ cup (1½ oz) flour

4 tomatoes, peeled and chopped

2 stalks celery, finely sliced

1 tablespoon chopped parsley

salt and pepper

1 teaspoon lemon juice

½ teaspoon grated lemon rind

Scone Topping:
1½ cups (6 oz) self-raising flour

salt and pepper

2 teaspoons butter

½ cup (4fl oz) milk (or little less)

Preheat the oven to 220°C (425°F/Gas 7). Drain the tuna; measure the liquid, and make up to 300 ml (9fl oz) with milk.

Melt the butter in a saucepan, add the onion and sauté until tender. Stir in the flour and cook for a few minutes. Gradually add the liquid, stir constantly, bringing to the boil. Add the tuna, tomatoes, celery, parsley, salt and pepper, lemon juice and lemon rind. Heat the mixture through, and spoon into a pie dish.

To make the scone topping, sift the flour into a bowl, add the salt and pepper and rub in the butter. Stir in the milk gradually, and mix into a light, soft dough. Cut into rounds and arrange in a single layer on top of the tuna mixture.

Bake for 10 to 15 minutes or until the scones are golden brown. Serve with a French salad.

Right: 'Tater-topped Fish Pie (see above); Smoked Cod Pie (see above).

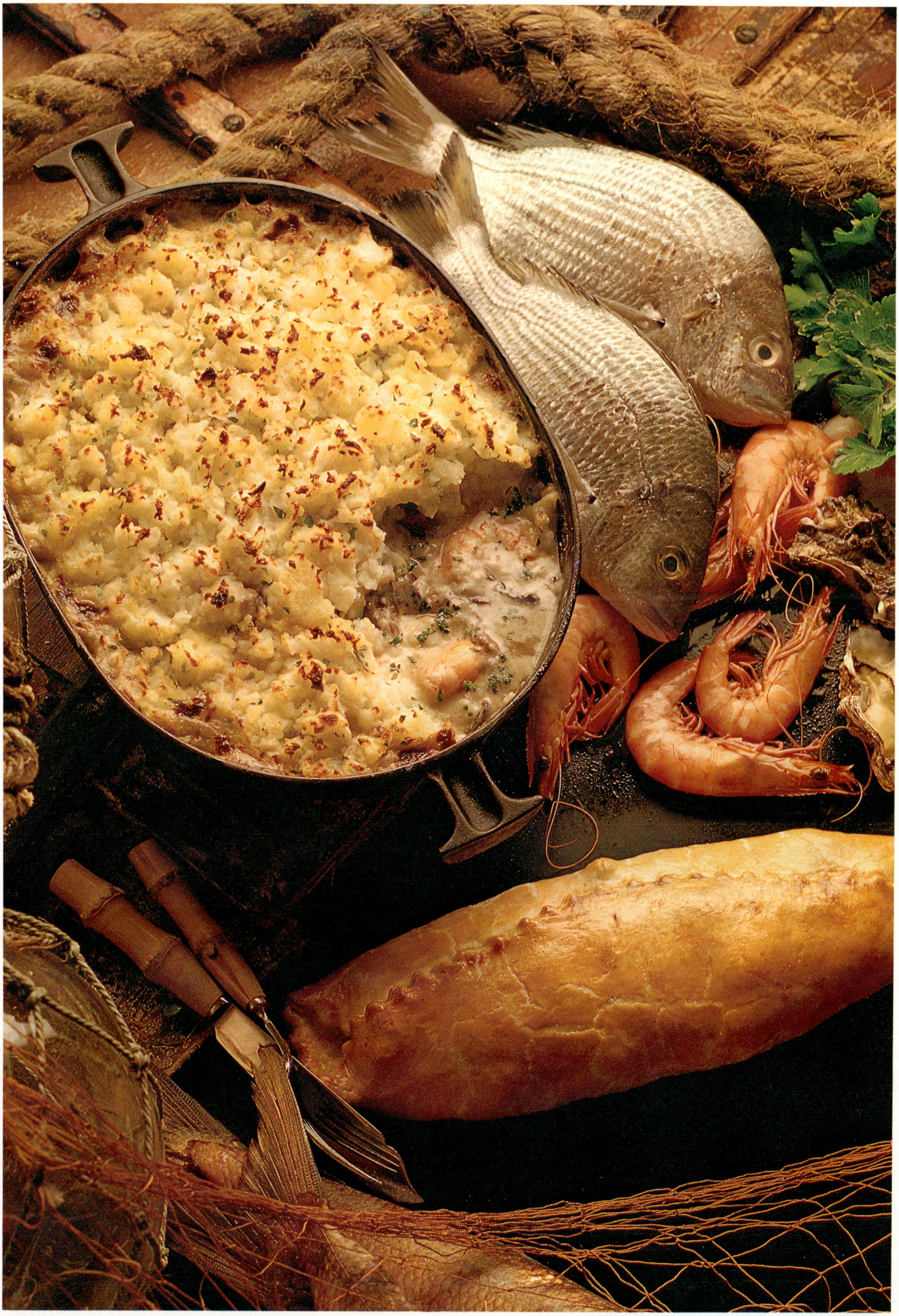

CHICKEN PIES

Chicken and Asparagus Flan

Serves 4–6

1 quantity rich shortcrust pastry (see recipe, page 184)
2 chicken breasts
salt and peppercorns
sprig of thyme
sprig of parsley
small can of green asparagus cuts, drained
1½ cups (12fl oz) commercial sour cream
2 eggs

Roll out the pastry to line a 23 cm (9 in) flan tin. Trim the edges, and refrigerate until ready to use.

Place the chicken breasts into a small saucepan with a little salt, a few peppercorns, and sprigs of thyme and parsley; add sufficient water to cover. Cover the saucepan and cook gently until the chicken is tender.

Preheat the oven to 190°C (375°F/Gas 5). Finely chop the chicken meat. (Reserve the stock for soups, etc.) Sprinkle the diced chicken over the base of the pastry case, cover with the well-drained asparagus pieces.

Lightly beat together the sour cream, eggs and (if necessary) salt and pepper. Pour very carefully into the flan case.

Bake in the preheated oven for 10 minutes, then reduce the oven temperature to 160°C (325°F/Gas 3) and continue baking for another 25 to 30 minutes or until the custard is set. Serve warm.

Chicken and Parsley Pie

Serves 6

1 quantity puff pastry (see recipe, page 186)
6 chicken breasts, skinned and trimmed
salt and peppercorns
sprig of thyme
sprig of parsley
30 g (1 oz) butter
6 shallots (or spring onions), finely-chopped
125 g (4 oz) button mushrooms, sliced
1 cup finely-chopped parsley
salt and pepper
2 tablespoons wholemeal flour
3 hard-boiled eggs, sliced
egg white, for glazing

Place the chicken breasts into a saucepan with a little salt, a few peppercorns, and sprigs of thyme and parsley; add sufficient water to cover. Cover the saucepan and cook gently for about 30 minutes.

Preheat the oven to 200°C (400°F/Gas 6).

Strain off and reserve the chicken stock. Dice the chicken meat.

Heat the butter in a frying pan, add the shallots, mushrooms, parsley, and salt and pepper, and sauté for 5 minutes. Stir in the flour and cook for a few minutes. Pour in ½ cup (4fl oz) of chicken stock and continue whisking until the mixture has thickened. Mix in the chicken meat and adjust the seasonings.

Place half of the mixture in the base of a deep pie dish. Arrange the sliced eggs on top, then cover with the remainder of the chicken mixture. Cover with the rolled puff pastry. Crimp around the edges and cut three or four vents in the pastry. Cut remnants of pastry into leaf shapes and arrange on top. Brush lightly with a little beaten egg white.

Bake in the preheated oven for 15 minutes, then reduce the oven temperature to 160°C (325°F/Gas 3) and continue baking for about 30 minutes. Serve hot.

If desired, 2 rashers of bacon may be grilled, then crumbled and added to the filling.

MEAT PASTIES & SMALL PIES

Sausages in Cream Cheese Pastry

Makes 10

2½ cups (10 oz) flour
250 g (8 oz) cream cheese
250 g (8 oz) butter, softened
¼ cup (2 fl oz) cream
salt
10 pork sausages
1 cup (8 fl oz) dry white wine
1 cup (8 fl oz) water
2 teaspoons French mustard
egg yolk beaten with water, or milk, for glazing

Place the flour in a bowl, add the chopped cream cheese, butter, cream and salt. Using the fingertips, lightly work into a paste by blending the cream cheese, cream and butter into the flour. When the dough is smooth, wrap it in plastic and refrigerate.

Place the sausages in a heavy saucepan with the wine and water, and simmer gently for approximately 20 minutes or until the sausages are cooked. Drain the sausages and remove their skins; allow to cool.

Preheat the oven to 230°C (450°F/Gas 8).

On a lightly-floured board, roll out the dough to 6 mm (¼ in) thickness, and cut into 10 rectangles, each large enough to encase a sausage. Place a sausage on each pastry portion; spread each with mustard. Wrap the pastry around each sausage and press the pastry edges together. Brush with egg glaze or milk, and prick the pastry with a fork. Arrange the sausage rolls on a lightly-buttered baking tray.

Bake in the preheated oven for 10 minutes, then reduce the oven temperature to 180°C (350°F/Gas 4) and cook for another 20 minutes or until the pastry is golden brown.

Homestead Pasties

Makes 8

750 g (1½ lb) shortcrust pastry (see recipe, page 182)
750 g (1½ lb) ripe tomatoes
750 g (1½ lb) sausage meat
salt and pepper
1 tablespoon chopped parsley
½ teaspoon mixed dried herbs or 1½ teaspoons fresh chopped herbs

Prepare the pastry according to the recipe, and chill. Preheat the oven to 200°C (400°F/Gas 6).

Pour boiling water over the tomatoes, remove their skins and cut into slices. Roll out the pastry and cut into eight rounds. Spread a portion of the sausage meat onto half of each pastry round, then place a slice of tomato on each. Sprinkle with salt and pepper and herbs. Fold the pastry over the filling, moisten the edges and press together. Place the pasties on a baking tray and bake for about 25 minutes.

The pasties may be glazed with a little milk (at room temperature) before cooking.

Traditional Cornish Pasties

Makes 6

500 (1 lb) shortcrust pastry (see recipe, page 182)
500 g (1 lb) steak, finely chopped
125 g (4 oz) kidney, finely chopped
250 g (8 oz) mixed, diced potatoes, turnips, onions and carrot
salt and pepper
beaten egg, for glazing

Prepare the pastry according to the recipe, and chill.

Preheat the oven to 190°C (375°F/Gas 5). Chop the meats and vegetables, and mix with the salt and pepper. Roll out the pastry and cut six saucer-sized circles. Place a portion of the filling mixture onto the centre of each round. Dampen the outside edges of the pastry and bring them together over the filling, crimping the joined edges into a decorative frill. Place on a greased baking tray. Prick each pastie several times with a fork and glaze with the beaten egg.

Bake in the preheated oven for about 15 minutes, then reduce the oven temperature to 160°C (325°F/Gas 3) and continue baking for another 40 minutes. Serve hot or cold.

Little Lambie Pies

An old Scottish recipe, hence the dripping in the pastry. Butter or margarine may be substituted.
Serves 6

Pastry:
125 g (4 oz) dripping
1½ cups (12 fl oz) water
4 cups (1 lb) flour
salt
Filling:
375 g (12 oz) lean lamb, finely diced or minced (ground)
1 small onion, chopped
salt and pepper
chopped parsley
1–2 tablespoons rich stock
milk or beaten egg, for glazing

Preheat the oven to 180°C (350°F/Gas 4).

To make the pastry, place the dripping and water in a saucepan and bring to the boil. Sift the flour and salt into a bowl; make a well in the centre, and pour in the hot liquid. Mix to a soft dough with a knife blade, and then knead on a board until the dough is smooth.

Cut off a quarter of the dough and keep it warm. Line six small tartlet tins with the larger quantity of pastry.

Filling: Combine the chopped lamb with the onion, salt, pepper and parsley; add a little stock to moisten. Fill the pastry cases with the meat mixture.

Roll out the remainder of the pastry and cut lids for the pies. Moisten the edges and press onto the filled pastry cases, pinching the edges together. Cut a small air vent in the top of each, then brush the pastry surfaces with a little milk or beaten egg.

Bake for 40 minutes. Serve hot. If desired, make up a little rich gravy and spoon in through the vent holes before serving.

Bedfordshire Clanger

This traditional recipe from Bedfordshire has an interesting history. Farmers' wives originally made these pastries for their menfolk to take as lunch when they worked in the fields. One end of the pastry was filled with a savoury mixture, the other end with a sweet filling—a savoury main course and a dessert, all in one pastry parcel! Fun to make, and fun for the family to eat. What a bit of one-upmanship to produce a Clanger for lunch at the football!
Makes 3

500 g (1 lb) shortcrust pastry (see recipe, page 182)
Savoury Filling:
30 g (1 oz) butter
1 small carrot, finely diced
2–3 tablespoons frozen peas
1 spring onion, chopped
185 g (6 oz) very finely diced or minced (ground) lamb or beef
1 teaspoon dried mixed herbs
2 teaspoons Worcestershire sauce
salt and pepper
Sweet Filling:
1 Granny Smith apple (green cooking apple), peeled and diced
1 tablespoon caster (powdered) sugar
generous pinch of cinnamon or cloves
beaten egg, for glazing

Roll the pastry to 4 mm (¼ in) thickness and cut it into six saucer-sized rounds. Roll out the trimmings and cut three strips about 15 × 1 cm (6 × ½ in). Melt the butter in a pan and sauté the carrot, peas and onion for several minutes. Add the meat, herbs, sauce and salt and pepper, cover the pan and cook very gently until the meat is tender. (If necessary, add 1 tablespoon of water or stock to prevent browning.) Allow to cool.

Preheat the oven to 180°C (350°F/Gas 4).

Mix together the diced apple, sugar and spice.

Brush the centre of each pastry round with the beaten egg; and set three rounds aside for the moment. Place a pastry strip across each round, spoon a portion of the meat filling onto one end of each pastry round, then spoon a portion of the apple onto the other end (the pastry strip acts as a divider). Place the three reserved pastry rounds on top of the fillings; seal the outer edges and lightly press down the pastry over the strip. Prick the tops in several places and glaze with the beaten egg.

Bake for about 30 minutes.

Right: Clockwise from top: Tarte a l'Ancienne (see p. 308); Carrot Flan (see p. 392); Bedfordshire Clanger (see above).

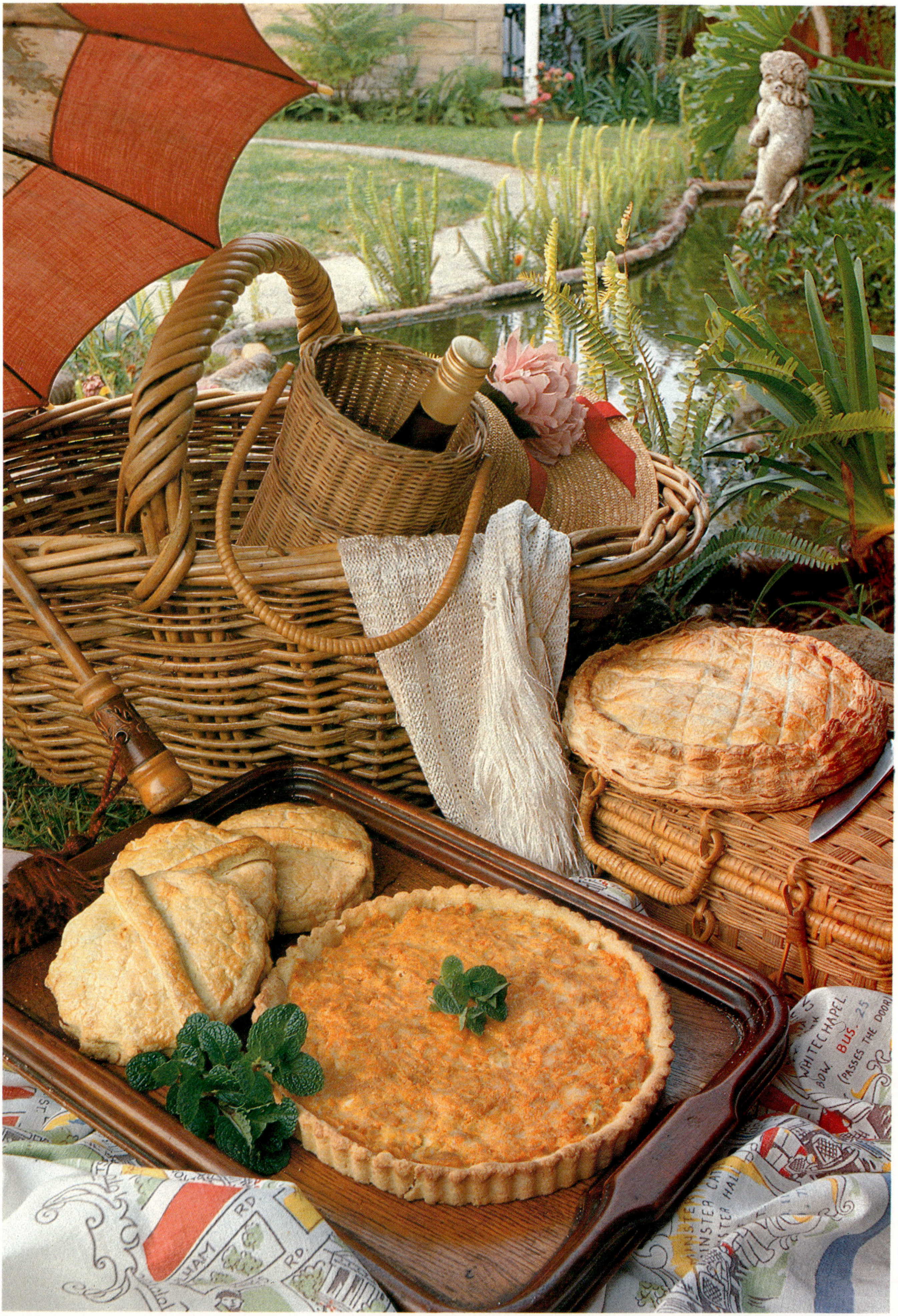
WHITECHAPEL
BOW
BUS. 25
(PASSES THE DOOR)

MEAT PIES

Economical Steak and Kidney Pie

Serves 6

1 kg (2 lb) bladebone or chuck steak
125 g (4 oz) ox kidney, or 2 sheep kidneys
1 tablespoon flour
salt and pepper
2 tablespoons oil
1 medium-sized onion, chopped
½ cup (4 fl oz) stock
2 teaspoons flour
2 teaspoons butter
1 quantity puff pastry (home-made or commercial)
beaten egg, for glazing

Cut the meat into small cubes. Discard the skin and tubes from the kidney and dice it. Toss the meat and kidney in the flour mixed with the salt and pepper. Heat the oil and sauté the onion until golden. Add the meat and kidney, and cook until browned. Transfer the onions and meats to a small saucepan, add the stock, cover the saucepan and simmer gently for 1½ hours or until the meat is tender.

Preheat the oven to 240°C (475°F/Gas 9).

Blend together 2 teaspoons of flour and 2 teaspoons of butter, and drop this into the simmering liquid in tiny pieces, stirring constantly until the liquid thickens. Spoon the meat and liquid into a pie dish.

Roll out the pastry and use it to cover the pie dish. Trim the edges to the shape of the dish. Cut several steam vents in the pastry surface and garnish with shapes cut from pastry scraps. Brush with the beaten egg.

Bake in the preheated oven for 20 minutes, then reduce the oven temperature to 180°C (350°F/Gas 4) and bake for a further 40 minutes or until the crust is crisp and golden.

Tarte à l'Ancienne

This traditional French meat pie is distinctive in flavour and presentation. Coax a marrow bone from your butcher—it is an important ingredient in this very special pie.
Serves 6

500 g (1 lb) puff pastry (see recipe, page 186)
Filling:
250 g (8 oz) veal steak
250 g (8 oz) pork fillet
2 ox kidneys
30 g (1 oz) pork fat, finely chopped
½ teaspoon mixed dried herbs
generous pinch of ground nutmeg
salt and freshly ground black pepper
1 marrow bone, about 10 cm (4 in) long
1 egg yolk
½ cup (4 fl oz) dry white wine
béchamel sauce (see recipe, below)
45 g (1½ oz) butter
30 g (1 oz) flour
½ cup (4 fl oz) milk
egg white or water, for sealing
egg white or milk, for glazing

Preheat the oven to 160°C (325°F/Gas 3).

Filling: Mince (grind) the veal, pork and kidneys together, and combine with the pork fat, herbs, nutmeg, and salt and pepper. Scoop out the marrow from the bone, and add to the meat mixture. Beat the egg and egg yolk together, and add to the meat mixture, together with the wine and béchamel sauce. Blend thoroughly.

Roll out the pastry into two rounds, one about 30 cm (12 in) in diameter, and the other about 25 cm (10 in). Place the smaller round on a greased baking tray. Pile the filling into a dome shape on it, leaving a 2.5 cm (1 in) border of pastry uncovered. Brush the border with a little egg white or water. Place the second pastry round over the filling and press the edges firmly together. Pinch into a frill around the edges. Using a sharp knife, lightly cut a criss-cross pattern into the pastry. Make a small hole in the centre of the dome and insert a small foil cylinder (made by rolling a piece of foil around a wooden spoon handle). Brush the pie with the beaten egg white or milk.

Bake for about 1 hour.

Béchamel Sauce: Melt the butter in a saucepan, add the flour, and cook for several minutes, stirring constantly. Remove from the heat, and add the milk. Return to the heat and stir constantly until the mixture boils and thickens. Use as directed.

Raised Veal and Ham Pie

Serves 5–6

1 quantity Hot Water Crust pastry
(see recipe, page 192)

Filling:
375 g (12 oz) veal steak

1¼ cups (10 fl oz) water

bouquet garni

¼ teaspoon dried thyme

125 g (4 oz) ham, diced

1 spring onion, chopped

salt and pepper

2 hard-boiled eggs

beaten egg, for glazing

Jelly:
2½ teaspoons gelatine

1¼ cups (10 fl oz) veal stock

salt and pepper

Filling: Place the veal steak in a saucepan and add the water. Bring to the boil, skim, add the bouquet garni and thyme; simmer for 15 minutes. Remove the veal from the liquid and allow to cool. Strain the veal stock and place in a small saucepan. Boil the stock rapidly until it reduces to 1 tablespoon. Cool and reserve.

Preheat the oven to 200°C (400°F/Gas 6). Cut the veal into 1 cm (⅜ in) cubes; mix with the ham, onion, salt and pepper.

Make the pastry and press two-thirds of it into a greased raised-pie mould; reserve the remainder for a pastry lid. Fill the pastry case with the meat mixture, and arrange the hard-boiled eggs in the centre of the meat. Spoon the reserved veal stock over the meat.

Roll out the remaining pastry to fit the top of the pie. Place it over the filling and press the edges of the pastry together to seal. Brush the top of the pie with the beaten egg. Trim the surplus pastry edge with scissors. Roll out left-over scraps of pastry, cut out four decorative leaves and mould a decorative flower bud. In the top of the pie, cut two slits crosswise in the centre and fold back the four pieces of pastry. Brush the folded-back pastry with the egg. Arrange the pastry leaves on top and place the flower bud in the centre of the leaves. Brush all over with the egg.

Bake in the preheated oven for 30 minutes, then reduce the oven temperature to 160°C (325°F/Gas 3), cover the pie with greaseproof paper if becoming overbrown, and bake for a further 60 minutes. Remove the greaseproof paper, unmould the pie and allow to cool.

To make the jelly, dissolve the gelatine in the stock, and add the seasoning. When the pie is cool and the jelly has thickened, pour the jelly into the pie through the vent. Allow to set. Serve cold.

'Old Faithful' Shepherd's Pie

My son always describes this as 'Poverty Pie'! Economical it might be, but it is still jolly good eating on a wintry night.
Serves 4

1 tablespoon butter or margarine

500 g (1 lb) lean minced (ground) steak

6 spring onions, chopped

3 teaspoons flour

½ teaspoon mixed dried herbs or 1 teaspoon fresh herbs

1 tablespoon tomato sauce

2 teaspoons Worcestershire sauce

salt and pepper

Topping:
500 g (1 lb) potatoes, cooked and mashed with milk

2 tablespoons chopped parsley

salt and pepper

a little extra butter, melted

1 tomato, sliced

Melt the butter or margarine in a pan or saucepan, add the minced meat, onions and flour and cook gently, stirring occasionally, until the meat is lightly cooked. Remove from the heat, and stir in the herbs, tomato sauce, Worcestershire sauce, salt and pepper. Spoon into a slightly-greased deep enamel pie dish.

Prepare the mashed potatoes, add the parsley and salt and pepper. Spread onto the meat mixture, roughen the surface and brush with the butter. Arrange the tomato slices on top.

Place into a preheated oven at 220°C (425°F/Gas 7) for about 25 minutes or until the top is well browned.

Pizza Siciliano

A family favourite, this pizza is quick and easy to prepare using scone dough as a base. The pizza has become part of our national cuisine and deserves a place in any pie book.
Serves 4–6

Scone Dough:
90 g (3 oz) plain flour

90 g (3 oz) self-raising flour

½ teaspoon dry mustard

salt and cayenne pepper

60 g (2 oz) butter or margarine

1 egg

3 tablespoons milk

1 tablespoon oil

Topping:
1 tablespoon oil

250 g (8 oz) lean minced (ground) steak or ham

1 white onion, chopped

½ clove garlic, crushed

3 medium-sized tomatoes, peeled and chopped

125 g (4 oz) tasty cheese, grated

2 teaspoons anchovy essence (optional)

1 tablespoon chopped parsley

Preheat the oven to 190°C (375°F/Gas 5).

To make the scone dough, sift together the flours, mustard, salt and cayenne. Rub in the butter or margarine. Beat together the egg and milk, add to the dry ingredients and stir in. Mix to a firm dough. Knead lightly only until the dough is smooth. Roll it out to 3 mm (⅛ in) thickness and place onto a greased pizza tray. Brush liberally with the oil.

Topping: Heat the oil in a large pan, add the minced steak, onion and garlic. Sauté until the meat changes colour and the onion is tender. Spoon the mixture into a bowl and allow to cool.

Add the remaining ingredients to the mixture, mix well, and spread onto the pizza crust. Bake in the preheated oven for about 30 minutes. Cut into wedges, and serve hot.

Pissaladière

Another traditional recipe from the Nice region, this savoury flan provides an attractive and interesting luncheon dish.
Serves 6–8

Pastry:
185 g (6 oz) flour

pinch of salt

90 g (3 oz) butter

approx. 2 tablespoons water

Topping:
2 tablespoons olive oil

2 medium-sized white onions, thinly sliced

freshly ground pepper

3 tablespoons freshly grated Parmesan cheese

5 large tomatoes, peeled and chopped

1 tablespoon tomato paste or tomato granules

8 anchovy fillets

8 black olives, stoned and halved

Sift the flour and salt into a bowl and rub in the butter. Add enough water to make a firm dough; knead lightly. Roll on a lightly-floured board and place onto a greased pizza tray. Pinch the edges to form a decorative border and prick the base all over with a fork. Refrigerate for 1 hour.

Preheat the oven to 180°C (350°F/Gas 4). Bake for 15 minutes, then remove the pastry from the oven but leave the oven on.

In the meantime, prepare the topping. Heat the olive oil in a frying pan, and sauté the onions for about 10 minutes or until tender. Remove from the pan, allow to cool slightly, then arrange them on the pastry. Sprinkle with the pepper and grated Parmesan cheese.

Place the chopped tomatoes and tomato paste or granules in the frying pan; cook for about 10 minutes or until the moisture has evaporated. Spoon the tomato over the cheese and sprinkle with a little more pepper. Arrange the anchovies in a lattice design on top of the tomatoes and place half an olive in each diamond.

Bake in the preheated oven for 10 minutes. Serve hot, with a green salad.

Note: If the anchovies are very salty, soak them for an hour or so in milk. Pat dry before using. (Your cat will be in a state of ecstasy if you give it the anchovy-flavoured milk.)

Right: Pizza Siciliano (see above); Pissaladière (see above).

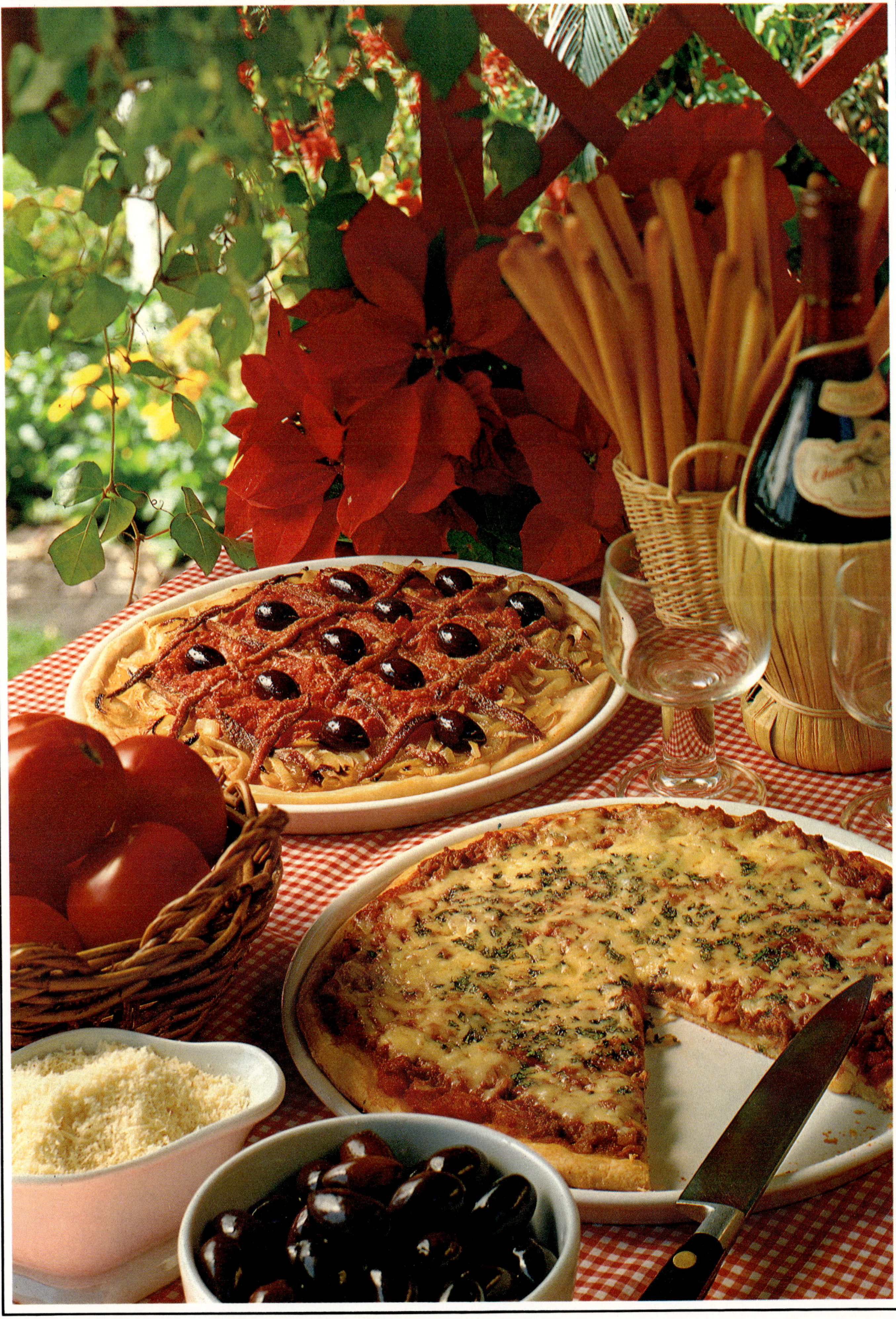

Family-Style Meat Pie

Serves 5

1 quantity pâte brisée (see recipe, page 190)
Filling:
500 g (1 lb) bladebone
2 small carrots, sliced
2 white onions, chopped
½ medium-sized parsnip, peeled and cubed
chopped parsley
1 cup (8fl oz) rich beef stock
salt and pepper
generous pinch of dried thyme
1 level tablespoon flour
milk, for glazing

Make the pastry and set aside until ready to use.

Remove the fat and sinew from the meat; cut into small cubes. Combine the meat, vegetables, and parsley in a saucepan; pour in the stock, add the salt and pepper and thyme. Cover the saucepan and simmer gently for about 1½ hours or until the meat is tender. Allow to cool, then stir in the flour.

Preheat the oven to 190°C (375°F/Gas 5).

Roll out two-thirds of the pastry to fit a 23 cm (9 in) pie dish. Spoon in the cooled meat, then cover with the remainder of the pastry. Pinch the edges of the pastry together to seal; cut several steam vents in the top. Brush with a little milk.

Bake for about 45 minutes or until the crust is crisp and golden. Serve hot or cold.

Toad-in-the-Hole

Not truly a pie, but it does have a delicious batter topping and I feel it earns its place in any section dedicated to the study of the noble pie. This is a luxury version, but blanched sausages are often substituted, with good results.
Serves 4

500 g (1 lb) rump steak, cut into 2.5 cm (1 in) cubes
freshly ground pepper
1 cup (4 oz) flour
approx. 1½ cups (12fl oz) milk
1 egg, beaten
salt and pepper
1 tablespoon dripping

Chop the meat and sprinkle it with the pepper; set aside. Mix the flour, milk (added gradually), beaten egg, salt and pepper to make a smooth and not-too-thick batter. Leave it to stand for 30 minutes.

Preheat the oven to 190°C (375°F/Gas 5).

Heat the dripping in an ovenproof casserole or small baking tin until smoking hot, then pour in a quarter of the batter mixture. Bake in the preheated oven for about 10 minutes or until the batter is set.

Arrange the meat on the batter, pour the remaining batter over it, and bake for about 25 minutes until well risen. Reduce the oven temperature to 160°C (325°F/Gas 3) and continue baking for another 20 minutes. Serve piping hot, garnished with grilled bacon rolls.

Exotic Shepherd's Pie

The flavour of this South American Shepherd's Pie bears little resemblance to the traditional one we know, but is excitingly different and interesting.
Serves 8–10

2 tablespoons olive oil
30 g (1 oz) butter
3 large onions, chopped
1 kg (2 lb) lean minced (ground) beef
¾ cup (4 oz) sultanas
90 g (3 oz) green olives, stoned and sliced
¼ teaspoon ground cloves (more if preferred)
½ teaspoon ground cumin
1 clove garlic, crushed
salt and pepper
1 can/425 g (15 oz) tomatoes, drained and chopped
4 hard-boiled eggs
1.5 kg (3 lb) potatoes, boiled and mashed with milk
30 g (1 oz) butter, melted

Preheat the oven to 190°C (375°F/Gas 5).

Heat the oil and butter in a saucepan or deep frying pan, and sauté the onions until softened. Add the beef, sultanas, olives, spices, garlic and salt and pepper; simmer for 10 minutes, then add the chopped tomatoes. Simmer gently until most of the liquid has evaporated; adjust the seasoning, if necessary.

Turn the mixture into an ovenproof casserole. Cut the eggs into quarters and lightly fold them through the meat mixture. Cover with the prepared mashed potatoes, roughen the surface, and pour melted butter over the top.

Bake for about 40 minutes or until golden brown. The pie may be successfully reheated.

Tourtière

This traditional French Canadian pork pie takes its name from the deep, fluted 'tourtière' in which it is baked. Equally good to eat either hot or cold, the filling may be baked in a hot water crust in a raised pie mould tin.
Serves 6

2 quantities pâte brisée
(see recipe, page 190)

Filling:
3 tablespoons butter

2 onions, chopped

1 clove garlic, crushed or finely chopped

750 g (1½ lb) minced (ground) lean pork

¼ cup (2 fl oz) boiling water

1 teaspoon salt

freshly ground black pepper

¼ teaspoon ground nutmeg

¼ teaspoon ground ginger

½ teaspoon thyme

1 bay leaf

2 lean rashers of bacon, chopped

egg wash (1 egg with 2 tablespoons cream)

Prepare the pastry. Roll out two-thirds of it into a 30 cm (12 in) round. Drape the pastry round over the rolling pin and fit it neatly into a greased fluted tourtière 20 cm (8 in) in diameter and 5 cm (2 in) deep. Press the pastry firmly into the tourtière, and trim off any excess pastry around the edge. Chill the pastry shell and the remaining pastry for 30 minutes.

In a heavy pan, melt the butter and sauté the onions and garlic. Add the minced pork and sauté until the meat changes colour. Reduce the heat, add the boiling water, salt, pepper, spices and herbs; cover the pan and cook for 10 minutes over moderate heat. Spoon the mixture into a bowl and allow to cool.

Preheat the oven to 230°C (450°F/Gas 8).

Spoon the meat mixture into the pastry shell and sprinkle chopped bacon on top. Roll out the remainder of the pastry, cover the pie, and trim the edges. Firmly crimp the edges together. Cut a vent in the centre of the pastry.

Bake in the preheated oven for 10 minutes. Brush the crust with egg wash, reduce the oven temperature to 180°C (350°F/Gas 4) and bake for a further 50 minutes or until the pie crust is well browned.

Simple Upside-down Pie

Serves 5–6

Crust:
2 tablespoons butter

500 g (1 lb) minced (ground) steak

1 medium-sized onion, grated or finely chopped

2 cups (4 oz) soft breadcrumbs

1 tablespoon Worcestershire sauce

1 tablespoon tomato sauce

2 tablespoons chopped parsley

1 egg

salt and pepper

Filling:
2 tablespoons butter

3 tablespoons flour

2½ cups (20 fl oz) milk

1 bay leaf, slightly crushed

salt

a little white pepper

½ teaspoon dry mustard

1 cup mixed cooked vegetables (such as peas, carrots, celery, parsnips)

60 g (2 oz) cheddar cheese

Preheat the oven to 190°C (375°F/Gas 5).

To make the crust, melt the butter in a large frying pan, add the minced steak and onion, and sauté until the meat changes colour. Combine the meat and onion with all the other ingredients for the crust, and press the mixture into a deep, lightly-greased pie dish.

Filling: Melt the butter in a saucepan, stir in the flour and cook for 2 to 3 minutes. Gradually add the milk, whisking constantly to prevent lumps from forming.

Add the bayleaf, salt, pepper and mustard, bring the sauce to a simmer, reduce the heat and stir constantly until smooth and thick. Remove the bayleaf.

Stir the vegetables into the sauce with half of the cheese. Spread this into the pie dish. Sprinkle the remainder of the cheese over the filling.

Bake on a low shelf in the preheated oven for about 45 minutes. Serve with salad or green vegetables.

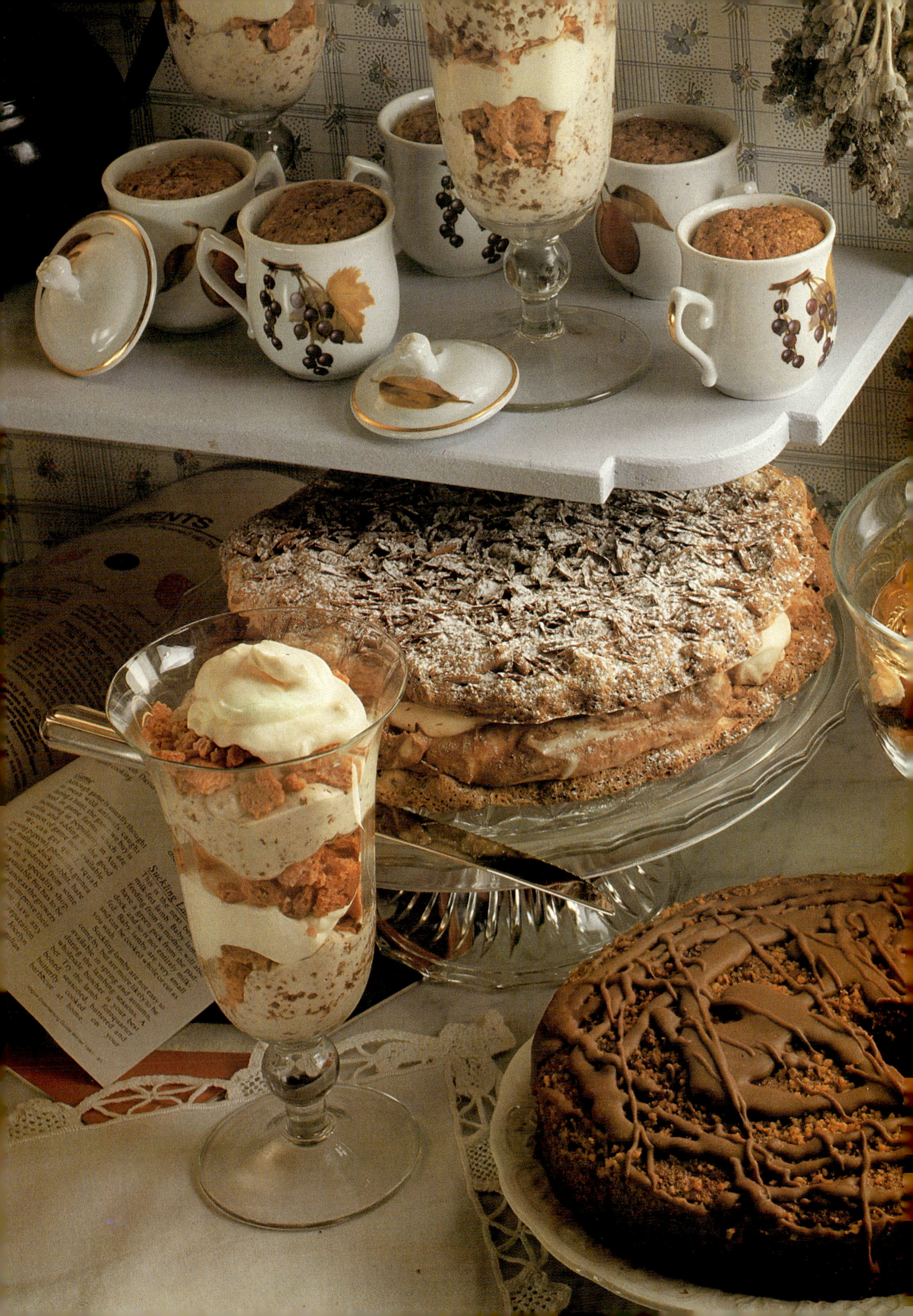

Desserts

Desserts

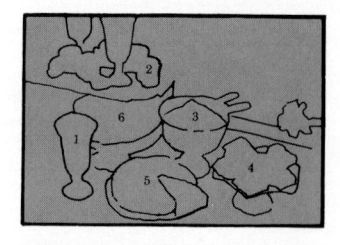

1. Mocha Macaroon Parfaits (see p. 353)
2. Chocolate Marsala Creams (see p. 357)
3. Rhubarb Apple Crunch (see p. 328)
4. Peach Kuchen Squares (see p. 348)
5. Chocaroon Torte (see p. 356)
6. Gâteau Elizabethe (see p. 344)

What should they be called ... sweets, confections, desserts or puddings? Generally speaking, interpretations depend upon upbringing, education or experience and fashion. Light and airy chilled concoctions are referred to as sweets, small morsels for serving with coffee are known as confections, those that are hot and hearty or sustaining are called puddings and the more elaborate, both in preparation and in presentation, become desserts.

In a lighter vein perhaps one could say that small children talk lovingly of sweets, the not-so-small and the figure-conscious speak enviously of desserts, the old-fashioned or food-loving person reminisces fondly about puddings, and the fashionable hostess serves her guests confections. Then of course the health and food fanatic dismisses them all as not only unessential but downright detrimental to good nutrition!

Serving sweet food as a separate part of a meal was not in vogue until about the early nineteenth century. Manufactured sugar in a refined form did not replace the natural honey and syrup sweetmeats until well into the fifteenth century. Even then it was scarce and very costly—as were the sweet spices used for flavouring—so that only members of the nobility, wealthy landowners and such were able to afford the elaborately decorated bread and cake centrepieces which decorated their tables. These were usually made by the famous bakers, pâtissiers or chefs of the times.

More general households had to make do with various fresh and preserved fruits, marzipans and nuts which were scattered around the tables along with the roast meats, fish, etc., to be eaten at any time according to the guests' fancy.

Practical and economical methods of preserving and chilling foods were not available to the general households and this, as well as the colder climates, no doubt contributed to the vast range of hot substantial puddings which were the mainstay of the sweet course on European, English and American menus.

Many of the more elegant desserts that have since become world-wide classics were invented by the great French and Italian chefs of their day. The very word 'dessert' is derived from the French phrase meaning to clear the table. A tradition still practised in classic restaurants throughout the world is that the cutlery, cruets, bread plates, etc., used with preceding courses are removed before the sweet course is introduced.

Betty Dunleavy

DESSERTS

Soufflé

Antonin Câreme is claimed as the originator of the baked soufflé, a dessert which for some reason or other has achieved the reputation of being difficult to make. This is not necessarily true. All that is needed is a light mixing hand and a consistent oven, plus the patience not to peek during the first three-parts of the baking time. For further sure success, the soufflé must be eaten within minutes of being removed from the oven. Far from being a special guest occasion masterpiece, soufflés are light, nutritious and economical when compared to other sweet desserts—and can be quickly and easily prepared. (Recipes for soufflés are included in this chapter.)

Pavlova

One popular dessert which seems to have 'collected' a number of inventors is the Pavlova. A chef in Perth, a hostess in Melbourne and a pastry cook in New Zealand are but a few who have laid claims to the origin of this meringue confection made to honour the famous Russian ballerina. However, if one looks at the basic method for making a Vacherin, a Meringue Torte or several other Continental classics, they are remarkably similar.

There are two recipes for Pavlova—a delicious confection which has become an Australian national dessert and an international classic—in the following pages, one that is more often prepared in home-style kitchens, the other now commercially prepared for restaurants and take-away consumption.

Prepared Pudding Mixes

Prepared pudding mixes, available in many varieties, not only are great time-savers but also reduce the risk of failure through mistakes in ingredient measurement, incorrect preparation or ingredient variation (or sheer carelessness or forgetfulness of the cook). Prepared mixes are of necessity fairly basic or standard in taste and texture, so that once the cook has mastered the simple mix she may desire to become more innovative and make many new and interesting desserts. For the inexperienced cook, however, it is of utmost importance to follow the manufacturer's instructions implicitly when first attempting a new brand or variety.

Baked Milk Custards

Baked milk custards and their variations are an invaluable standby in many households. The ingredients are almost always on hand, they are economical and, also of importance, they are good, wholesome fare for growing families. Another great advantage is that they can be cooked whilst the main-course roast is in the oven, or they can be baked ahead of time whilst the oven is in use for other baking, then refrigerated for a day or so until they are served.

Fruit Desserts

Fruit in all its forms—fresh, canned, dried or preserved in other ways—has come to represent an integral part of the final food for a meal. Its versatility for use in almost any type of dessert, plus its multitude of delicious yet different flavours, ensures that it is well represented in all sections of this chapter on baked desserts.

Rice, cereal and pasta desserts, shortcakes, babas, cobblers, crumbles, crunches, and the currently popular cheesecake desserts, all feature in this chapter—recipes for desserts that are guaranteed to bring forth compliments and constant pleas for yet another slice!

Wines

Wines, particularly sweet table and fortified wines, play an important role in the flavour of many desserts. They help to provide a subtle yet distinguished taste which transforms a simple dessert into a delightful finale to the meal. The serving of wines as a beverage with the dessert is, of course, a matter of personal choice, and today there are many sweet table and fortified dessert wines which can only bring added pleasure to the overall taste of the food itself. Should a wine be used in the preparation then a suggestion would be to use the same wine for the beverage. Otherwise, choose a wine which you yourself feel would complement the tastes of the ingredients used for the dish.

The qualities that go to making a memorable dessert are imagination, care in preparation and attractive presentation.

The choice of a dessert to serve with a meal should be made to provide good balance, depending on the number and substance of preceding courses. Light and delicate sweet foods are more acceptable after a many-course complex or lavish dinner, whereas the more substantial or hearty pudding types may be best appreciated after a simple one- or two-course meal containing few filling accompaniments.

Colour, texture, flavour, repetition, seasonal changes, the occasion and (last but not least) the needs, tastes and/or preferences of those partaking of the meal must all be part of the final consideration. There are no hard and fast rules—simply cook what you feel your family, your guests and you yourself most enjoy.

From the large selection of baked sweets, desserts and puddings which are offered in the following pages you can surely make a good selection. Ones that you would like to try yourself! Particular flavour tastes to satisfy the sweet tooth members of the family! Next-to-no-time delights for extra busy days and, of course, many special creations which will grace the table and create that lasting impression of a successful guest occasion.

FRESH, DRIED AND CANNED FRUITS

Snow Peak Peaches

Serves 4–6

12 large canned peach halves
1 cup (3 oz) crushed macaroons (see recipe, page 158)
¼ cup (1 oz) chopped almonds or walnuts
¼ cup (1½ oz) chopped glacé cherries
2 eggs, separated
1–1¼ cups (8–10fl oz) canned peach syrup
2 tablespoons brandy
2 teaspoons lemon juice
¼ cup (2 oz) sugar
slivered almonds, for decoration

Preheat the oven to 150°C (300°F/Gas 2). Drain the peaches and place them in a single layer, hollow side uppermost, in a well-greased shallow casserole.

Combine the macaroon crumbs with the almonds, cherries and egg yolks. Spoon the mixture into the hollow of each peach half.

Heat the peach syrup, brandy and lemon juice with a little of the sugar in a small saucepan until boiling and pour it over and around the peaches.

Beat the egg whites until stiff and glossy; gradually add the remaining sugar. Roughly pile this meringue mixture over each peach and spike with the slivered almonds.

Bake for 20 to 25 minutes. Serve warm.

Spiced Orange Delite

Serves 5–6

5–6 large oranges—one for each serving
90 g (3 oz) butter or margarine, melted
¼ cup (3 oz) golden syrup (light corn syrup)
½ cup (3 oz) brown sugar
2–3 tablespoons sweet sherry
½ cup (3 oz) raisins or sultanas
1 teaspoon ground cinnamon
ice-cream, for serving

Preheat the oven to 190°C (375°F/Gas 5). Peel the oranges, removing as much of the white pith as possible; cut into rings and arrange over the base of a well-greased casserole.

Combine the melted butter, golden syrup, sugar, sweet sherry, raisins and cinnamon, and spoon over the orange slices. Cover loosely with aluminium foil.

Bake for 15 to 20 minutes. Arrange scoops of ice-cream on each serving plate and spoon the hot orange slices over. Serve at once.

Fruited Apple Charlotte

Serves 5–6

4–5 large cooking apples, peeled and cored
1 lemon
2 tablespoons (2 oz) golden syrup (light corn syrup) or honey
¼ cup (2fl oz) water
½ teaspoon ground cinnamon or cloves
1 cup (5 oz) sultanas
8–10 slices white bread, crusts removed
125 g (4 oz) butter or margarine, melted
additional 1 tablespoon (1 oz) golden syrup or honey
whipped cream, for serving

Thinly slice the apples and place in a small saucepan with 2–3 strips of lemon peel, the juice of the lemon, the golden syrup and water; cover and cook over low heat until the apples are softened.

Allow to cool, remove the lemon peel, and beat until the apples form a pulp. Add the spice and sultanas, and mix through.

Preheat the oven to 190°C (375°F/Gas 5).

Cut the bread into finger-sized pieces; brush each piece generously with melted butter all over and arrange over the base and sides of a casserole; press down firmly. Fill the centre with the fruited apple pulp, and cover the top with the remaining bread slices (buttered). Drizzle the extra golden syrup over the surface.

Bake for 50 to 55 minutes. Remove from the oven and allow to stand for 25 to 30 minutes. Serve with whipped cream, if desired.

Right: **Fruited Apple Charlotte** (see above).

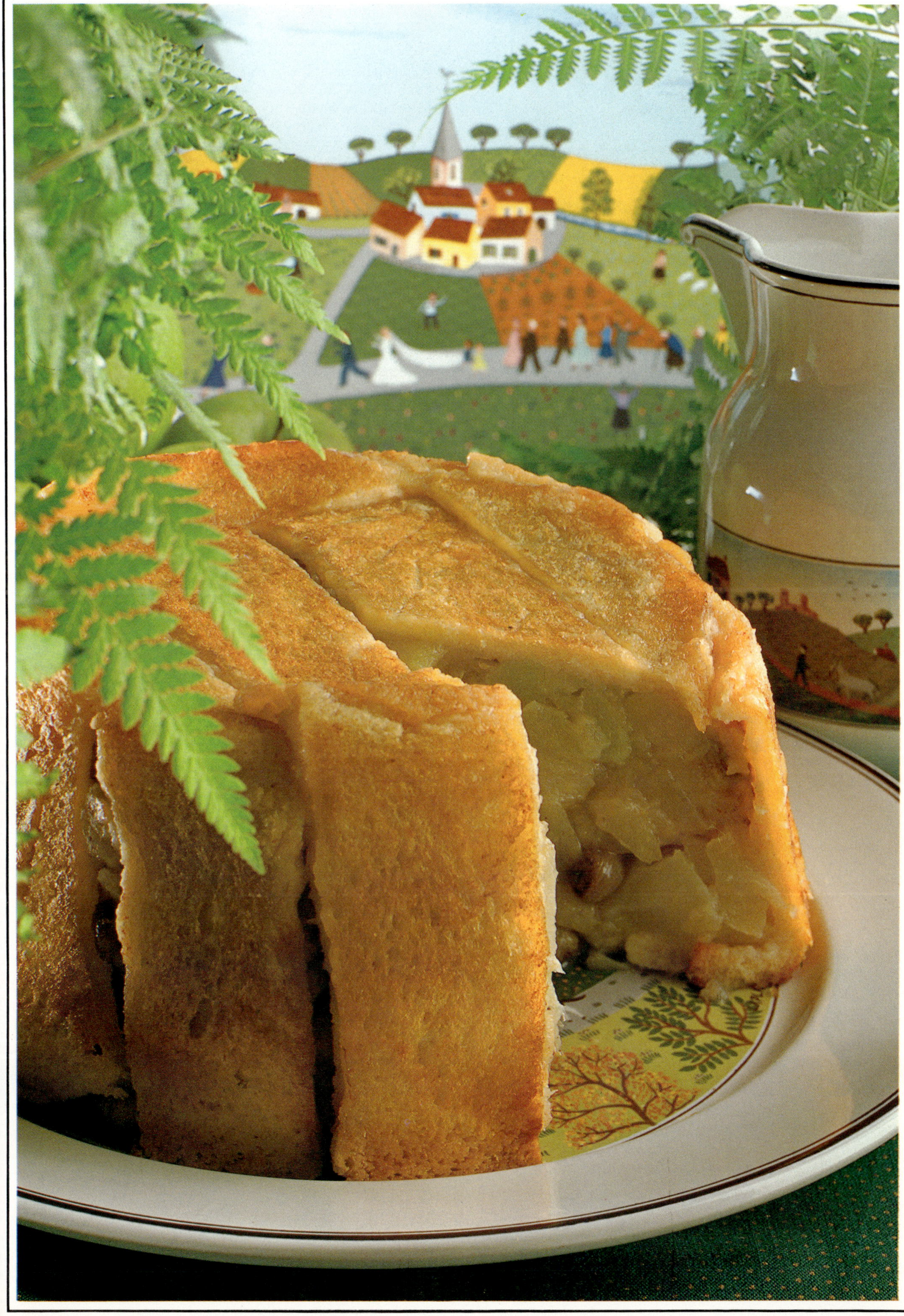

Sliced Apple Pudding

Serves 5–6

4 large cooking apples
60 g (2 oz) butter or margarine, melted
1 tablespoon cornflour (cornstarch)
¾ cup (6 oz) caster (powdered) sugar
1–2 teaspoons grated lemon rind
½ teaspoon cinnamon
¾ cup (4 oz) raisins, chopped
125 g (4 oz) cream cheese, softened
3 eggs, beaten
¾ cup (6fl oz) evaporated milk
2 tablespoons (1 oz) icing (confectioners') sugar
whipped cream, for serving

Preheat the oven to 180°C (350°F/Gas 4). Peel and core the apples and cut into thick slices or rings. Brush each piece with the melted butter; and coat with the combined cornflour, half of the caster sugar, lemon rind and cinnamon. Arrange the apple slices in a well-greased casserole; scatter the raisins over the surface.

Beat the cream cheese, remaining sugar, eggs and evaporated milk together, and pour over the apples and raisins.

Bake in the preheated oven for 15 to 20 minutes, then reduce the oven temperature to 150°C (300°F/Gas 2) and cook until the apples are softened and the custard mixture is set (about 30 minutes). Remove from the oven, and dust the icing sugar over the surface. Serve warm, with whipped cream.

Pineapple Ginger Dessert

Serves 5–6

1 can/450 g (1 lb) crushed pineapple
water
¾ cups (6 oz) sugar
1¼ cups (10fl oz) evaporated milk
2 teaspoons grated lemon rind
3 tablespoons (1 oz) cornflour (cornstarch)
2 eggs, separated
30 g (1 oz) butter or margarine, melted
⅓ cup (2 oz) glacé ginger in syrup
6–7 macaroons, crushed
additional ½ cup (4 oz) sugar

Preheat the oven to 180°C (350°F/Gas 4).

Drain the canned pineapple, reserving the syrup. Arrange the pineapple in the base of a greased casserole dish. Measure the drained syrup, and make up the quantity to 1¼ cups (10fl oz) with the water (set aside ¼ cup for later use).

Combine the sugar, 1 cup of pineapple water, evaporated milk and lemon rind in a thick-based nonstick saucepan. Heat, beating slowly, until just commencing to simmer. Beat the cornflour, reserved pineapple water, egg yolks and butter together; gradually add to the saucepan, stirring constantly. When thickened and starting to bubble, lower the heat and simmer for 1 to 2 minutes, stirring frequently. Remove from the heat and add the ginger. Allow to cool slightly.

Pour the cooled mixture over the crushed pineapple; scatter the macaroons over.

Beat the egg whites to meringue consistency; gradually beat the sugar through and pile roughly over the casserole contents.

Bake for 12 to 15 minutes. Serve warm.

Brazilian Bananas

Serves 5–6

6 large firm bananas
1–2 tablespoons rum or coffee liqueur
1–2 tablespoons lemon juice
60 g (2 oz) butter or margarine, melted
2 tablespoons (1 oz) brown sugar
¾ cup (4 oz) chopped dates
½ cup (2 oz) sliced Brazil nuts
60 g (2 oz) marshmallows, halved
coffee-flavoured ice-cream, for serving

Preheat the oven to 180°C (350°F/Gas 4). Peel the bananas and diagonally slice each into four pieces; brush all over with the combined rum and lemon juice.

Pour the melted butter into a casserole, and sprinkle the brown sugar over. Layer the banana slices, dates, Brazil nuts and marshmallows over the top, finishing with marshmallows.

Bake for 20 to 25 minutes. Serve hot over scoops of coffee ice-cream.

Flambé: For a special dramatic effect, slightly warm a little extra rum or coffee liqueur, set alight, and carefully spoon over the banana dessert.

Cherry Mallow 'Pie'

Serves 6–8

5–6 thin slices milk bread
melted butter or margarine
750 g (1½ lb) ripe tart cherries
¼ cup (2 oz) sugar
14–16 marshmallows, halved
¾ cup (3 oz) flaked almonds
icing (confectioners') sugar, for topping
whipped cream, for serving

Preheat the oven to 190°C (375°F/Gas 5). Cut the crusts off the bread slices and cut each slice into halves or quarters. Brush both sides generously with melted butter, and arrange over the base and sides of a 23 cm (9 in) pie dish to resemble a pastry crust.

Remove the stems and stones from the washed cherries, and mix with the sugar; scatter over the bread 'crust'. Place the marshmallow halves on top and sprinkle with the flaked almonds. Cover loosely with aluminium foil.

Bake for 15 minutes; remove the foil and continue baking for a further 15 to 20 minutes. Remove from the oven and dust the surface with a little icing sugar. Allow to stand until just warm, then slice and serve with whipped cream if desired.

Note: Cherry stoners may be purchased at most specialty kitchenware stores.

Honeyed Rhubarb Crunch

Serves 4–5

4–5 cups diced rhubarb
½ cup (5 oz) honey, warmed
2 tablespoons lemon juice
½ cup (2½ oz) chopped dates
½ cup (2 oz) chopped pecans or walnuts
6–8 macaroons, coarsely crushed (see recipe, page 158)
whipped cream, chilled

Arrange the washed rhubarb pieces over the base of a well-greased non-metal casserole. Drizzle the honey over the surface, then sprinkle with the lemon juice. Cover loosely with aluminium foil. Cook in a preheated oven at 180°C (350°F/Gas 4) for 25 to 30 minutes. Remove the foil, carefully fold the dates and nuts through, and continue cooking for a further 5 minutes.

Remove from the oven, allow to cool and then chill. Just before serving, spoon into dessert glasses or bowls, sprinkle the macaroon crumbs over each serving, and top with a dollop of whipped cream.

Fruit Pudding Cups

Serves 8–10

3 cups (1 lb) mixed dried fruits
½ cup (2½ oz) chopped dates
2–3 teaspoons grated orange rind
125 g (4 oz) butter or margarine
1 cup (8 oz) sugar
¾ cup (6fl oz) water
2 eggs, beaten
½ cup (4fl oz) sweet sherry
2 cups (8 oz) flour
1 teaspoon baking powder
1 teaspoon mixed spices
½ teaspoon bicarbonate of soda (baking soda)

Combine the dried fruits (chopping, if required), dates, orange rind, butter, sugar and water in a saucepan; bring slowly to the boil, stirring frequently, then simmer for 2 minutes. Remove from the heat and allow to cool.

Preheat the oven to 180°C (350°F/Gas 4).

Add the beaten eggs and sweet sherry to the fruit mixture and mix through. Sift the dry ingredients into a bowl; add the fruit mixture and mix well.

Spoon the mixture into 8–10 well-greased large custard or breakfast coffee cups, to two-thirds fill. Cover each cup with greased aluminium foil, pressing the foil tightly around each cup. Place the cups into a large baking pan half-filled with boiling water, and carefully place the pan into the moderate oven to steam-bake for 1¼–1½ hours.

Remove from the oven and carefully lift the cups from the water; loosen and remove the aluminium foil covers, and unmould the puddings into bowls. Serve with custard, cream or ice-cream, as desired.

Creamy Peach Roll

Serves 6–8

---
3 eggs

¾ cup (6 oz) caster (powdered) sugar

½ teaspoon almond essence

¾ cup (4 oz) packaged pancake mix
---
icing (confectioners') sugar, for dusting
---
1 can/425 g (15 oz) sliced peaches, drained well

½ cup (2 oz) flaked almonds
---
approx. 2 cups vanilla ice-cream
---
300 ml (10fl oz) thickened cream
---
2 teaspoons caster (powdered) sugar, for sweetening cream
---
flaked almonds, for decoration

Preheat the oven to 200°C (400°F/Gas 6). Prepare a 30 × 25 cm (12 × 10 in) swiss (jelly) roll tin by lining it with greaseproof paper and greasing thoroughly.

Beat the eggs until thick and frothy; gradually add the sugar, beating well after each addition. Add the essence, then fold in the pancake mix. Spread the batter into the prepared tin, and bake for 8 to 10 minutes.

Prepare a rolling surface with aluminium foil or greaseproof paper; dust generously with icing sugar. When the roll is baked, carefully loosen the sides and turn it out onto the prepared foil or paper. Roll up, let stand for 20 minutes and then unroll.

Meanwhile, reserving 3–4 peach slices, chop the remainder and combine with the almonds and ice cream. Quickly spread over the roll, re-roll carefully, and wrap in the foil. Freeze for 2 to 3 hours.

Just before serving, remove the foil from the frozen roll and coat all over with the whipped sweetened cream. Place on a serving plate, and decorate with the reserved peach slices and extra flaked almonds. Serve, cut in slices whilst the roll is still partially frozen.

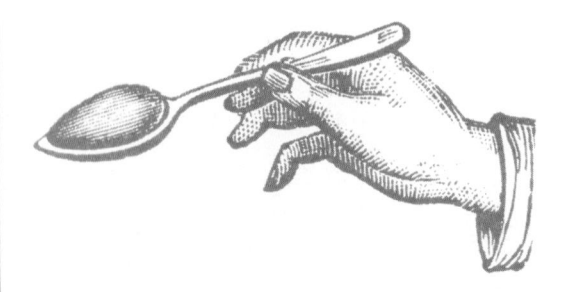

Stuffed Apples

Serves 4–5

4–5 large cooking apples
---
lemon juice
---
apple stuffing—see the variations below

½ cup (4 oz) sugar

1½ cups (12fl oz) sweet white wine

1½ cups (12fl oz) water
---
whipped cream, for serving

Preheat the oven to 180°C (350°F/Gas 4).

Remove the core from each apple, and remove the peel from the top half of each; brush the peeled section with the lemon juice to prevent browning.

Prepare the apple stuffing by combining all the ingredients. Fill the core cavity of each apple and pile the filling high over the top.

Place the apples into a small casserole or baking pan. Combine the sugar, wine and water, and drizzle this around the apples in the casserole. Cover loosely with aluminium foil, and bake for 30 to 40 minutes until the apples are just soft. Lift the apples onto the serving plates, and reduce the liquid in the casserole by boiling briskly; spoon over the apples and serve hot with whipped cream.

Apple Stuffings:
The quantities of the ingredients are approximate only, as the amount required depends on the size of the apples and the core cavity.
- ½ cup (5 oz) apricot jam, ¼ cup (2 oz) brown sugar, ¼ cup (1 oz) chopped almonds, and 1 tablespoon rum or brandy.
- ½ cup (3 oz) chopped raisins, ¼ cup (2 oz) brown sugar, ¼ cup (1 oz) chopped walnuts, 1 teaspoon mixed spices, and 1 tablespoon sweet sherry.
- ½ cup (3 oz) chopped dates, ¼ cup (2 oz) brown sugar, ¼ cup (1 oz) chopped orange flesh, and ¼ teaspoon cinnamon.
- ¾ cup (6 oz) prepared fruitmince, and 1 tablespoon brandy or sweet sherry.
- ¾ cup (4 oz) chopped banana, 2 tablespoons golden syrup (light corn syrup); and 1 tablespoon lemon juice.

Right: **Stuffed Apples** (see above).

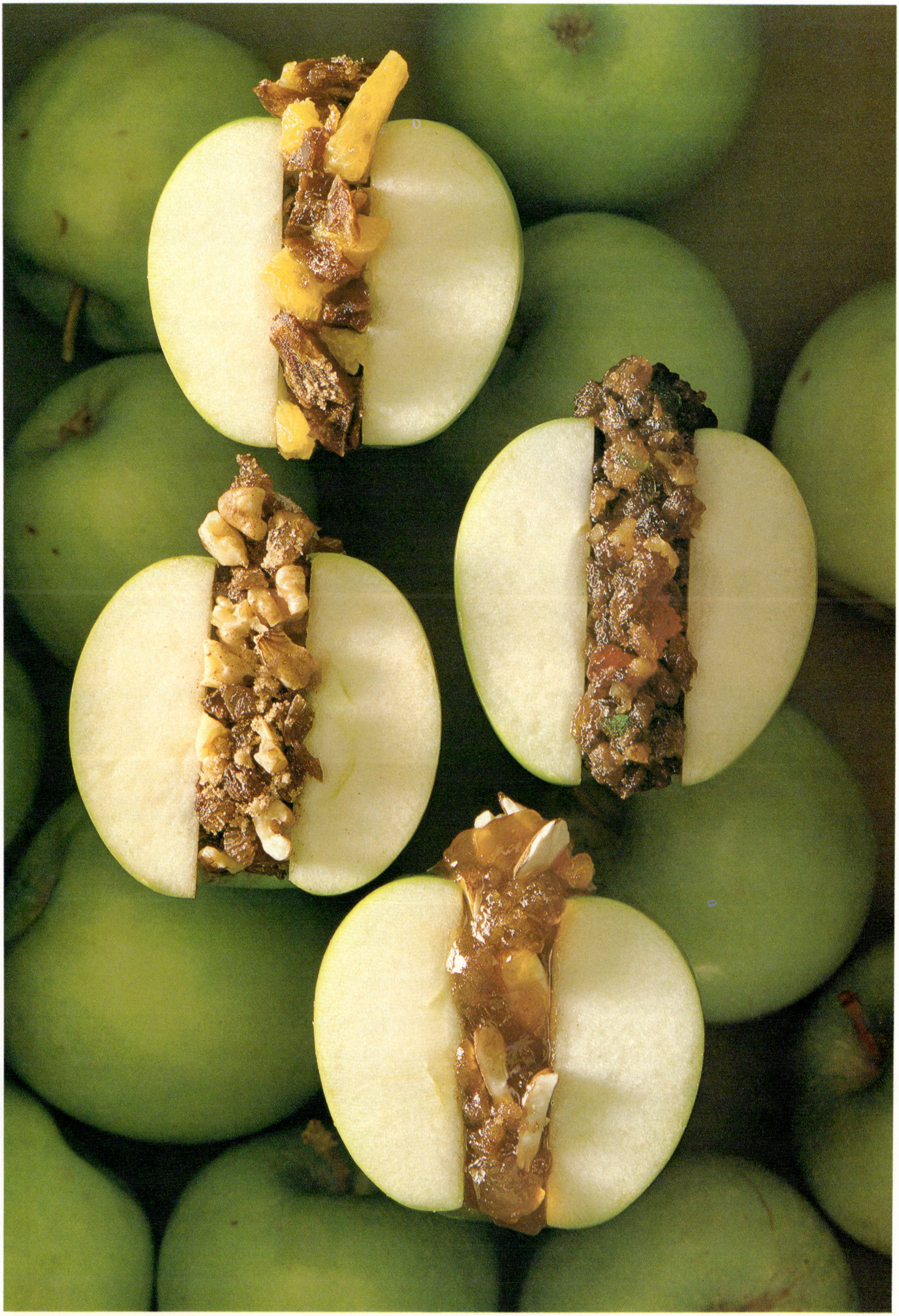

Strawberry Crêpes Royale

Serves 5–6

Crêpes: Makes 10–12
1¼ cups (5 oz) flour

¼ teaspoon salt

½ teaspoon baking powder

2 teaspoons sugar

2 eggs

1 teaspoon vanilla, rum or brandy essence

2 tablespoons light vegetable oil

2 cups (16 fl oz) milk

water—as required, see method

butter or oil for frying

Filling:
2 tablespoons sweet sherry

250 g (8 oz) full cream cheese, softened

2 tablespoons (1 oz) icing (confectioners') sugar

1½ teaspoons grated orange rind

¼ cup (2 fl oz) orange juice

20–24 strawberries, hulled and sliced

¾ cup (6 fl oz) apricot conserve

additional 2 tablespoons sweet sherry

30 g (1 oz) butter or margarine, melted

½ cup (2 oz) flaked almonds

sour cream, for serving

Sift the flour, salt, baking powder and sugar into a bowl; make a well in the centre.

Beat the eggs with the essence, oil and milk; add to the flour mixture gradually, whisking until the mixture is a smooth creamy consistency.

Set aside for at least 30 minutes then whisk in sufficient water to produce a thin cream consistency.

Heat a shallow crêpe or omelette pan and grease lightly with butter or oil; pour in 2 to 3 tablespoons of the batter and tilt the pan to coat the base—pour off any excess batter.

Place over medium-high heat and cook until the underside is lightly browned; carefully flip or turn over and cook a further minute.

Lift out and place on a plate; make remaining crêpes in a similar way, placing a strip of greaseproof paper between each while stacking to complete the required number.

Preheat the oven to 180°C (350°F/Gas 4).

Lightly brush one side of each crêpe with the sweet sherry. Combine the cream cheese, icing sugar, orange rind and orange juice, and spoon about 2 tablespoons across each crêpe. Roll up loosely, and arrange in a single layer in a well-greased shallow casserole.

Spoon the sliced strawberries over the crêpes. Combine the apricot conserve, extra sweet sherry and melted butter, and spoon this over the top. Scatter with almonds, and loosely cover with aluminium foil.

Bake for 15 to 20 minutes. Serve at once, with a spoonful of sour cream on top.

Flambé Crêpes: Carefully pour a little flaming brandy over the crêpes just before serving.

Danish Apple Dessert

Serves 5–6

3 large cooking apples

water and lemon juice

¼ cup (2 fl oz) cherry brandy liqueur

¼ cup (2 oz) sugar

20–24 macaroons (see recipe, page 158)

½ teaspoon ground cinnamon or nutmeg

90 g (3 oz) butter or margarine

½ cup (3 oz) chopped glacé cherries

whipped cream, for serving

Preheat the oven to 180°C (350°F/Gas 4).

Peel and core the apples, cut into thin slices and place in the water and lemon juice to prevent discolouration. Drain, and place in a saucepan with the cherry liqueur and sugar. Cover tightly and place over low heat; cook slowly, stirring occasionally, until just softened.

Coarsely crush the macaroons and mix with the cinnamon. Heat the butter in a small pan, and sauté the macaroon crumbs, tossing constantly until lightly browned.

Place layers of apples, macaroons and cherries in a well-greased casserole and bake in the preheated oven for 20 to 25 minutes. Serve warm or cold, with whipped cream.

COBBLERS, CRUMBLES AND CRUNCHES

Rhubarb Apple Cobbler

Serves 5–6

2½–3 cups diced, fresh rhubarb
2 cooking apples, cored and thinly sliced
2 teaspoons grated orange rind
½ cup (4fl oz) orange juice
2 cups (8 oz) flour
3 teaspoons baking powder
60 g (2 oz) butter or margarine
¼ cup (2 oz) sugar
1 egg
¾ cup (6fl oz) milk
1 tablespoon desiccated coconut
extra sugar for sprinkling over

Arrange the rhubarb pieces in the base of a well-greased casserole and top with a layer of the apple slices; sprinkle the orange rind over and drizzle the juice over the surface.

Cover loosely with aluminium foil and bake in a moderately hot oven 190°C (375°F/Gas 5) until the fruits are softened—15–20 minutes.

Meanwhile sift the flour and baking powder into a bowl; rub in the butter with the fingertips and sprinkle the sugar over.

Beat the egg with half the milk and stir into the mixture; add sufficient of the remaining milk to mix to a firm cake consistency.

Add the coconut and drop the mixture in rough spoonfuls over the hot fruit; sprinkle the surface with sugar and return to the oven for a further 30 to 35 minutes.

Serve hot, warm or cold.

Rosy Apple Crumble

Serves 6–7

6–7 firm, red apples
lemon-water, for soaking
¾ cup (3 oz) self-raising flour
½ cup (2 oz) quick-cooking oats
2 teaspoons grated lemon rind
1 tablespoon lemon juice
125 g (4 oz) butter or margarine, chilled
½ cup (3 oz) brown sugar
Sauce:
2 egg yolks
1 tablespoon sugar
1 tablespoon brandy
½ teaspoon ground cinnamon
1 cup (8fl oz) cream or evaporated milk

Preheat the oven to 160°C (325°F/Gas 3). Halve the apples, remove the core and cut each half into 6–7 wedges; drop into the lemon water to prevent discolouration.

Place the flour, quick-cooking oats, lemon rind, lemon juice and chopped butter in a processor and cut until well combined (or rub the butter through with the fingertips). Add the sugar, and mix through.

Drain the lemon-water off the apples and, holding the skin edge, dip each wedge into the crumble mixture. Arrange in overlapping pieces in a generously-greased round shallow casserole or quiche dish. Drizzle 1–2 tablespoons of the lemon-water over, and scatter any remaining crumble over the top.

Bake for 30 to 35 minutes; if desired, cover loosely with aluminium foil to prevent drying out or overbrowning the sauce. Combine the egg yolks, sugar brandy and cinnamon in the top half of a double saucepan; stir the cream through and cook over simmering water, stirring constantly until thickened to a custard consistency. Serve the apple dessert warm with the sauce in a jug for individual use.

Apricot Sparkle
(Photograph below)
Serves 4–5

---
1 large can/825 g (1 lb 14 oz) apricot halves
---
2 cups (16fl oz) sparkling white wine
---
1 cinnamon stick 5–8 cm (2–3 in) long, broken into smaller pieces
---
½ cup (4 oz) sugar

3–4 whole cloves
---
2 egg whites

½ cup (4 oz) caster (powdered) sugar
---
1 cup (3 oz) desiccated coconut
---
glacé cherries, for decoration

Drain the apricots (reserving the syrup) and arrange, hollow side up, in a greased baking dish. Combine the wine, broken cinnamon stick, sugar and whole cloves, and pour this over and around the apricots. Place in a preheated oven at 180°C (350°F/Gas 4) and bake for 20 minutes.

Lift the apricots onto a heatproof platter with a slotted spoon and keep hot.

Add the apricot syrup to the liquid in the baking dish and boil briskly over a high heat until the quantity is reduced to about half. Strain into a jug.

Meanwhile beat the egg whites until stiff and glossy; gradually add the caster sugar, then fold the coconut through. Pile into the centre of each apricot, and place under a low griller (broiler); heat until golden-tipped. Pour the syrup over, top with a glacé cherry, and serve hot.

Variations:
Substitute canned peaches or pears if desired. Or use fresh fruits, though allow extra baking time to soften them.

Cathy's Magic Lemon Pie
(Photograph below)

This simple yet unusual dessert, when cooked, resembles a pie—there is a soft pastry layer on the base, a lemon-flavoured custard in the centre and a crunchy coconut topping.
Serves 6–8

---
4 eggs
---
60 g (2 oz) butter or margarine, softened
---
1 cup (8 oz) sugar

½ cup (2 oz) self-raising flour

¼ teaspoon salt
---
2 teaspoons grated lemon rind

½ cup (4fl oz) lemon juice

1½ cups (12fl oz) milk
---
1 cup (3 oz) desiccated coconut
---
ice-cream, for serving

Preheat the oven to 180°C (350°F/Gas 4).

Place all the ingredients in a large blender or food processor at the one time, and blend until well mixed together (1–1¼ minutes).

Pour into a well-greased 23–25 cm (9–10 in) pie dish and bake for 1 hour. Allow to stand for about 10 minutes before slicing, and serve warm with a scoop of ice-cream.

Variations:
Alternative flavours in place of lemon:
- ½ cup (4 oz) crushed pineapple, undrained
- ½ cup (4 oz) passionfruit pulp
- ½ cup (4 oz) soft mashed bananas
- ½ cup (4fl oz) orange juice or mango juice

Pear Crumble Cake
(Photograph below)

Serves 5–6

---

1 packet buttercake mix

1 or 2 eggs

water

5–6 cooked pear halves, drained well

Crumble Topping:
¾ cup (3 oz) self-raising flour, sifted

⅛ teaspoon salt

1 teaspoon mixed spices

2 tablespoons (1 oz) brown sugar

60 g (2 oz) butter or margarine

custard, for serving

Preheat the oven to 180°C (350°F/Gas 4).

Make up the cake mix as directed on the package, using the egg(s) as specified but only half the amount of water to make a firmer batter. Spread into a well-greased 20 cm (8 in) springform tin.

Arrange the pear halves over the cake mixture, hollow side uppermost and in a cartwheel pattern.

Topping: Combine the flour, salt, spices and brown sugar in a bowl; rub in the butter with the fingertips, then crumble over the top of each pear half.

Bake for 30 to 35 minutes. Remove from the oven, place on a cake rack and loosen the springform ring. Allow to stand for 10 to 15 minutes, then lift the dessert onto a serving plate. Cut into slices, and serve with hot custard if desired.

Rhubarb Apple Crunch

Serves 5–6

1 cup (8 oz) cooked sweetened apples, drained
2 cups (16 oz) cooked sweetened rhubarb, drained
1–2 tablespoons orange juice
½ teaspoon ground cinnamon
2 eggs, separated
2 tablespoons (2 oz) golden syrup (light corn syrup) or honey
1½ tablespoons (½ oz) custard powder
2 cups (16 fl oz) milk
2 tablespoons brown sugar
2 tablespoons (1 oz) rolled oats
2 tablespoons (½ oz) desiccated coconut
60 g (2 oz) butter or margarine, melted

Preheat the oven to 160°C (325°F/Gas 3). Layer the cooked apples and rhubarb in the base of a greased casserole. Drizzle the orange juice over, and sprinkle with the cinnamon.

Make a rich custard with the egg yolks, golden syrup, custard powder and milk, stirring over low heat until thickened; pour over the apples and rhubarb.

Beat the egg whites until stiff and glossy; add the brown sugar and beat well, before folding in the oats, coconut and cooled butter. Spoon this roughly over the custard. Bake for 20 to 25 minutes. Serve warm.

Note: Extra baking time may be required if the apples, rhubarb and custard are very cold before topping with the meringue crunch.

Layered Apricot Crumble

Serves 4–5

1 large can/825 g (1 lb 13 oz) apricot halves
2 tablespoons lemon juice
1 teaspoon almond essence
10–12 macaroons or tiny meringues, crumbled
⅓ cup (2 oz) brown sugar
½ teaspoon ground cinnamon
60 g (2 oz) butter or margarine, melted
whipped cream, for serving

Preheat the oven to 180°C (350°F/Gas 4). Drain the apricots (reserve the syrup), and slice the halves into 4–5 pieces. Arrange half of the apricots over the base of a well-greased casserole. Combine the lemon juice, almond essence and ½ cup (4 fl oz) of apricot syrup, and drizzle half of this liquid over the apricots. Combine the macaroon crumbs, brown sugar and cinnamon, and scatter half of the mixture over the apricots. Repeat each of the layers, then drizzle the melted butter over the surface. Loosely cover with aluminium foil.

Bake for 15 to 20 minutes; remove the foil cover and continue baking for a further 15 to 20 minutes or until the top is crusty. Serve warm, with whipped cream if desired.

Variation: Use canned peaches, pears, rhubarb or berry fruit in place of the apricots.

Crusted Peach Dessert

Serves 4–5

1 can/425 g (15 oz) sliced peaches
water
1 tablespoon lemon juice
1½ tablespoons cornflour (cornstarch)
½ teaspoon almond extract or essence
30 g (1 oz) butter or margarine
1 cup (4 oz) self-raising flour
¼ teaspoon salt
1 egg, beaten
additional 60 g (2 oz) butter or margarine, melted
¼ cup (2 oz) sugar
½ teaspoon ground cinnamon
whipped cream, for serving

Preheat the oven to 180°C (350°F/Gas 4). Drain the peaches and set ⅓ cup (2½ fl oz) of the syrup aside for the topping; measure the remaining syrup and make up to 1 cup (8 fl oz) with water.

Blend the lemon juice and cornflour together; combine this with the syrup-water and almond extract in a saucepan. Heat, stirring constantly, until thickened and bubbling, then add the butter and stir through.

Arrange the peach slices over the base of a well-greased casserole, and pour the thickened syrup mixture over the top.

Sift the flour and salt into a bowl. Combine the beaten egg, melted butter, reserved peach syrup and half of the sugar; add this to the flour and mix to a firm batter. Drop in rough spoonfuls over the peaches. Sprinkle the remaining sugar and cinnamon over the surface.

Bake for 30 to 35 minutes. Serve warm, with whipped cream if desired.

CHEESECAKES

Fruitmince Cheesecake

Serves 8–10

250 g (8 oz) ginger-flavoured biscuit crumbs
125 g (4 oz) butter or margarine, melted
1 egg, separated
1¾ cups (1 lb) prepared fruitmince (see recipe, page 274)
2 teaspoons Angostura bitters
500 g (1 lb) full cream cheese
300 ml (10 fl oz) thick sour cream
4 eggs, beaten
1 cup (8 oz) caster (powdered) sugar
2 teaspoons grated orange rind
1 tablespoon orange juice
½ teaspoon ground nutmeg
whipped cream, for topping

Combine the biscuit crumbs with the cooled, melted butter and egg yolk. Press firmly over the base and sides of a well-greased 23 cm (9 in) springform tin; brush lightly-beaten egg white over the surface. Chill for 1 hour.

Preheat the oven to 180°C (350°F/Gas 4). Mix the prepared fruitmince and bitters together, and spoon onto the crumb crust; press lightly.

Press the cream cheese and sour cream through a fine sieve into a bowl. Beat the eggs and sugar until thickened, then gradually add the cream cheese mixture, beating well between each addition. Flavour with the orange rind and orange juice, and spoon the mixture over the fruitmince.

Bake for 15 minutes, then reduce the oven temperature to 150°C (300°F/Gas 2) and continue baking for a further 20 to 25 minutes. Allow to stand in the oven with the door ajar for 15 minutes, then remove, allow to cool and refrigerate (preferably overnight). Just before serving, dust the surface of the cheesecake with nutmeg and decorate with whipped cream.

Continental Raisin Squares

Makes 9–12 dessert squares

Base:
1½ cups (6 oz) flour
½ cup (2 oz) cornflour (cornstarch)
1 teaspoon baking powder
¼ teaspoon salt
125 g (4 oz) butter or margarine
2 tablespoons (1 oz) icing (confectioners') sugar
1 egg
milk, as required
Topping:
250 g (8 oz) cream cheese
125 g (4 oz) butter or margarine
3 eggs
¼ cup (2 oz) caster (powdered) sugar
2 teaspoons grated lemon rind
½ cup (3 oz) chopped raisins
1 teaspoon cinnamon or nutmeg
whipped cream for serving

Sift the flour, cornflour, baking powder and salt together. Beat the butter until creamy, stir in the icing sugar and gradually beat in the eggs; mix in the flour mixture and add sufficient milk to make a soft dough. Press over the base of a greased 23 to 25 cm (9–10 in) square cake tin, prick the dough generously with a fork and bake in a moderate oven 180°C (350°F/Gas 4) for 10 minutes only; lift out and set aside.

Beat the cream cheese and butter together until very creamy; beat the eggs and sugar together and add to the creamed mixture gradually. Add the lemon rind and fold the raisins into the mixture; spoon over the partly-baked base and sprinkle the cinnamon over the top. Place the cake tin on a biscuit tray and return to the oven for a further 35 to 40 minutes; allow to stand in the oven with the door ajar for 10 minutes before removing to cook. Serve, cool or chilled, cut in squares with a dot of whipped cream for decoration.

Pineapple Ginger Cheesecake

Serves 8–10

250 g (8 oz) coconut-flavoured biscuits
60 g (2 oz) wholemeal biscuits
1 cup (9 oz) crushed, drained pineapple
1/3 cup (2 oz) chopped preserved ginger
2 eggs
1/2 cup (4 oz) sugar
1–2 teaspoons lemon juice
250 g (8 oz) packaged cream cheese, softened
375 g (12 oz) creamed cottage cheese
1 cup (8fl oz) sour cream
1/2 teaspoon ground cinnamon
1/2 teaspoon ground ginger

Crush the coconut and wholemeal biscuits, and scatter over the base of a well-greased 23 cm (9 in) springform tin. Cover with the combined crushed pineapple and ginger, pressing firmly into the crumbs. Chill for 30–40 minutes.

Preheat the oven to 160°C (325°F/Gas 3).

Beat the eggs, sugar and lemon juice together until thick and fluffy. Gradually beat in the cream cheese and cottage cheese. Pour into the springform tin on top of the crumb mixture.

Bake for 35 to 40 minutes. Carefully spread the combined sour cream and spices over the surface of the cheesecake, and return to the oven for a further 7 to 10 minutes. Open the oven door and allow the cheesecake to cool in the oven for 15 to 20 minutes. Remove and set in a draught-free area until cold. Chill for several hours or overnight before slicing.

Marbled Chocolate Cheesecake

Serves 10–12

250 g (8 oz) chocolate-flavoured biscuits, crushed finely
60 g (2 oz) coffee-flavoured biscuits, crushed finely
1/2 teaspoon ground cinnamon
155 g (5 oz) butter or margarine, melted
750 g (1 1/2 lb) packaged cream cheese, softened
1 cup (8 oz) caster (powdered) sugar
3 eggs, beaten
1/2 cup (4fl oz) cream
1 teaspoon brandy essence or rum essence
185 g (6 oz) pure cooking chocolate, melted
whipped cream, for decoration

Combine the crushed biscuits with the cinnamon and cooled butter; mix thoroughly and press onto the base and sides of a well-greased 23 cm (9 in) springform pan. Chill for 30 minutes.

Preheat the oven to 150°C (300°F/Gas 2).

Beat the cream cheese until well blended in a bowl. Gradually add the sugar, then the beaten eggs, beating well after each addition. Mix the cream and essence through. Spoon all but about 1 cup of the mixture into the crumb crust.

Combine the remaining mixture with the just-warm melted chocolate, and drizzle this over the plain mixture; with a thin-bladed knife or skewer, swirl the chocolate mixture through the plain mixture to create a marbled effect.

Bake for 35 to 40 minutes. Open the oven door and leave the cheesecake in the oven until cold. Chill for several hours or overnight, then decorate with the whipped cream and cut into slices for serving.

Right: From top: Fruitmince Cheesecake (see p. 329); Marbled Chocolate Cheesecake (see above); Pineapple Ginger Cheesecake (see above).

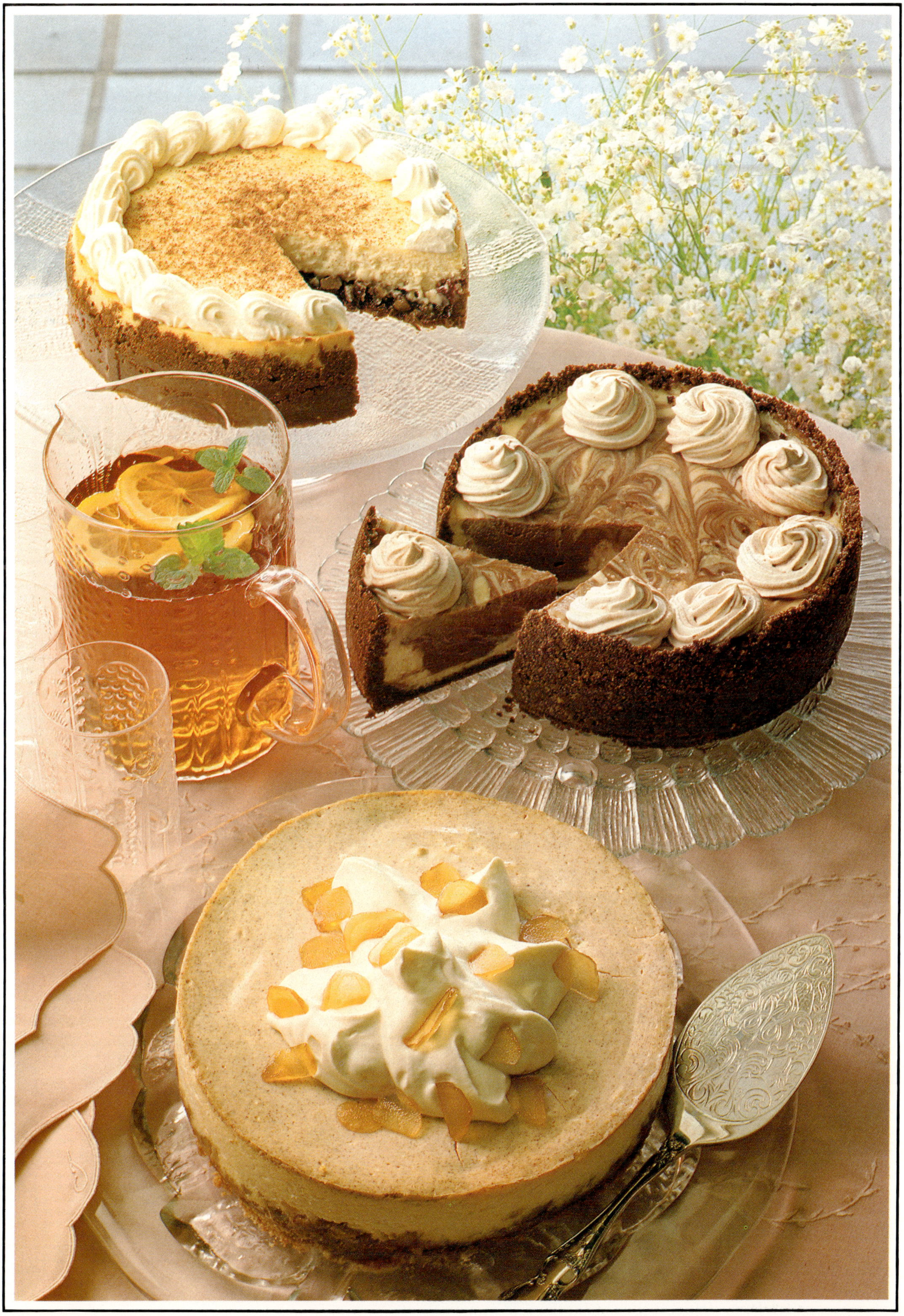

Golden Cheesecake Squares

Serves 9

2 cups (8 oz) self-raising flour
1½ teaspoons grated lemon rind
¼ teaspoon salt
125 g (4 oz) butter or margarine, melted
½ cup (4 oz) caster (powdered) sugar
2 eggs, beaten
¾ cup (6 fl oz) milk
250 g (8 oz) thinly sliced canned peaches, drained
Topping: 3 eggs, separated
½ cup (4 oz) sugar
375 g (12 oz) cream cheese, sieved
½ cup (4 fl oz) cream
1½ tablespoons cornflour (cornstarch)
½ cup (2 oz) flaked almonds
¼ teaspoon ground cinnamon

Preheat the oven to 180°C (350°F/Gas 4).

Combine the flour, lemon rind and salt in a bowl and make a depression in the centre; add the cooled butter, sugar, eggs and milk, and gradually work in to form a smooth mixture. Spread over the base of a well-greased 23 cm (9 in) square cake pan. Place the sliced peaches in a layer over the surface.

Topping: Combine the egg yolks, sugar, cream cheese, cream and cornflour, and beat briskly until smooth. Fold in the stiffly-beaten egg whites. Spoon the topping over the peaches.

Bake for 20 minutes. Quickly scatter the almonds and cinnamon over the surface, reduce the oven temperature to 150°C (300°F/Gas 2) and continue baking for a further 30 to 35 minutes. Allow to cool slightly, mark into squares, then cool and chill before serving.

PUDDINGS

Sour Cherry Cream Pudding

Serves 5–6

¾ cup (6 oz) caster (powdered) sugar
60 g (2 oz) butter or margarine, softened
2 eggs, separated
1 cup (4 oz) flour
1 teaspoon baking powder
¼ teaspoon salt
¼–⅓ cup milk
1 can/425 g (15 oz) sour red cherries
additional ¼ cup (2 oz) sugar
½ cup (4 fl oz) cherry syrup
whipped cream, for serving

Preheat the oven to 180°C (350°F/Gas 4).

Beat the sugar and butter until creamy; add the egg yolks and beat well. Sift the flour, baking powder and salt over the sugar-egg mixture. Drizzle ¼ cup of milk down one side of the bowl and lightly fold through; add extra milk, if required, to make a soft cake batter.

Whisk the egg whites until soft peaks form. Carefully fold through the cake batter—do not overmix. Spoon the mixture into a well-greased casserole.

Heat the cherries, extra sugar and cherry syrup until boiling, and carefully pour over the cake mixture.

Bake for 30 to 35 minutes. Remove from the oven and allow to cool slightly. Serve warm, with whipped cream if desired.

Mocha Walnut Pudding

Serves 5–6

1 packet chocolate cake mix
egg(s) and water (less 1 tablespoon), as directed
¼ cup (1½ oz) brown sugar
¼ cup (2 oz) white sugar
½ cup (2 oz) chopped walnuts
¼ cup (1 oz) chopped raisins
1 tablespoon cocoa powder
1 cup (8 fl oz) hot black coffee

Preheat the oven to 180°C (350°F/Gas 4). Prepare the chocolate cake mix with the egg(s) as directed on the package but using less water than specified. Spoon into a well-greased 20 cm (8 in) casserole.

Combine the sugars with the walnuts, raisins and cocoa, and scatter over the cake mixture. Carefully pour the hot coffee over the surface. Bake for 35 to 40 minutes. Serve hot or warm.

One-two-three Chocolate Pudding

Serves 4–5

1 cup (4 oz) self-raising flour
¾ cup (6 oz) sugar
¼ teaspoon salt
2 tablespoons (½ oz) cocoa powder
½ cup (4fl oz) milk
1–1½ tablespoons maize oil
1 teaspoon vanilla essence
½ cup (3 oz) chopped raisins
¼ cup (1 oz) chopped walnuts
¾ cup (4 oz) brown sugar
additional ¼ cup (1 oz) cocoa powder
1¾ cups (14fl oz) very hot water

Preheat the oven to 160°C (325°F/Gas 3). Sift the first four ingredients into a bowl. Add the next five ingredients, and mix well. Pour into a well-greased casserole. Combine the brown sugar and extra cocoa, and sprinkle it over the mixture. Carefully pour the hot water over the surface.

Bake for 40 to 45 minutes. Serve warm.

Lemon Honey Sponge

Serves 4–5

90 g (3 oz) butter or margarine, softened
1 cup (7 oz) caster (powdered) sugar
1 tablespoon (1 oz) honey
3 teaspoons grated lemon rind
¼ cup lemon juice
3 eggs, separated
1½ cups (12fl oz) milk (at room temperature)
⅓ cup (1½ oz) self-raising flour
¼ cup (1 oz) cornflour (cornstarch)

Preheat the oven to 150°C (300°F/Gas 2).

Beat the butter and sugar until white and creamy. Add the honey, lemon rind and lemon juice, and beat well. Add the egg yolks and gradually beat in the milk (the mixture will 'curdle' slightly). Fold in the sifted flour and cornflour.

Beat the egg whites until well foamed but not stiff; carefully fold into the batter mixture (pieces of egg white should still remain visible). Spoon the mixture into a well-greased casserole.

Bake for 55 to 60 minutes.

Note: The pudding may be baked at a slightly higher or lower temperature whilst a main-course roast is in the oven; adjust the timing as required. Serve warm, with ice-cream if desired.

Lemon Apple Sponge

Serves 4–5

125 g (4 oz) butter or margarine, softened
¼ cup (3 oz) caster (powdered) sugar
2 eggs, separated
3 teaspoons grated lemon rind
½ cup (4fl oz) lemon juice
2 cups (4 oz) stale sponge cake pieces
1 teaspoon baking powder
⅓ cup (3 oz) sugar
1 large apple

Preheat the oven to 160°C (325°F/Gas 3).

Beat the butter and caster sugar until creamy; add the egg yolks and lemon rind and beat well. Mix in the lemon juice and sponge cake pieces, and lastly scatter the baking powder over the surface and fold through.

Turn into a well-greased shallow casserole and place in the oven; loosely cover with a sheet of aluminium foil. Bake for 30 to 35 minutes. (When cooked, remove from the oven and increase the oven temperature to 200°C (400°F/Gas 6).)

Beat the egg whites until stiff and glossy; gradually add the sugar, beating well after each addition. Core the apple but do not peel; grate it coarsely and fold into the meringue mixture. Carefully spoon the meringue over the top of the lemon sponge and return it to the hotter oven to set the surface (about 7 minutes). Serve hot or warm.

One-dish Date Pudding

Serves 5–6

1 cup (5 oz) chopped dates
60 g (2 oz) butter or margarine, chopped
1 cup (8 fl oz) boiling water
1 teaspoon grated lemon rind
1 egg
1½ cups (6 oz) self-raising flour, sieved
½ cup (3 oz) brown sugar
¼ teaspoon ground cinnamon
¼ cup (1 oz) chopped walnuts
additional 1 cup (6 oz) brown sugar
additional 1 cup (8 fl oz) boiling water

Preheat the oven to 190°C (375°F/Gas 5). Scatter the dates over the base of a casserole 20 cm (8 in) round. Add the butter, then the boiling water, stirring to soften the dates.

Add the lemon rind, egg, flour and brown sugar with the cinnamon, and beat lightly until well blended; scrape the base and sides of the casserole occasionally whilst mixing. Scatter the combined walnuts and extra brown sugar over the surface. Carefully pour the extra boiling water over all.

Bake for 40 to 45 minutes. Serve hot or warm.

Oven-steamed Syrup Pudding

Serves 5–6

1 cup (4 oz) self-raising flour, sieved
1 cup (2 oz) soft white breadcrumbs
⅓ cup (3 oz) brown sugar
1 teaspoon grated lemon rind
125 g (4 oz) grated chilled suet or margarine
1 egg, beaten
⅓–½ cup (2½–4 fl oz) milk
¾ cup (9 oz) golden syrup (light corn syrup)
warm custard, for serving

Preheat the oven to 190°C (375°F/Gas 5).

Combine the flour, breadcrumbs, sugar and lemon rind in a bowl; add the grated suet and mix to a fairly soft dough with the beaten egg and enough milk as required.

Spread a little golden syrup over the base of a well-greased pudding basin. Add the dough and the remaining syrup in layers until the basin is about two-thirds filled. Cover with greased aluminium foil and press to seal around the sides. Lower the basin into a larger pan containing 2–3 cups of boiling water and place in the preheated oven.

Steam-bake for 30 minutes, then lower the oven temperature to 160°C (325°F/Gas 3) and cook for a further 1–1¼ hours, replenishing the boiling water as required. Remove and allow to stand for 5 to 6 minutes before unmoulding on to a serving plate; cut into slices, and serve with custard.

Steam-baked Carrot Ring

Serves 6–8

60 g (2 oz) butter or margarine, softened
½ cup (4 oz) sugar
2 eggs
1 teaspoon mixed spices
¼ teaspoon salt
¾ cup (3 oz) soft white breadcrumbs
⅓ cup (2 oz) sultanas
½ cup (2 oz) chopped walnuts
1 cup cooked, mashed carrots, cooled
2 tablespoons sweet sherry
2 tablespoons evaporated milk

Preheat the oven to 180°C (350°F/Gas 4).

Beat the butter and sugar until creamy. Add the eggs, one at a time and beat well, before adding the spices, salt and breadcrumbs. Mix in the sultanas, walnuts, mashed carrot, sherry and evaporated milk.

Turn the mixture into a well-greased and crumb-coated fluted ring mould (or 18 cm (7 in) ring tin) and cover securely with greased aluminium foil. Stand in a baking pan containing 2.5–4 cm (1–1½ in) boiling water, and steam-bake for 55 to 60 minutes. Serve hot with custard, cream or ice-cream.

Microwave Cooking:
The pudding mixture may be placed into a non-metal ring mould and cooked in a microwave oven for 8 to 10 minutes on medium heat. Allow to stand for 8 to 10 minutes before slicing and serving.

Right: Steam-baked Carrot Ring (see above).

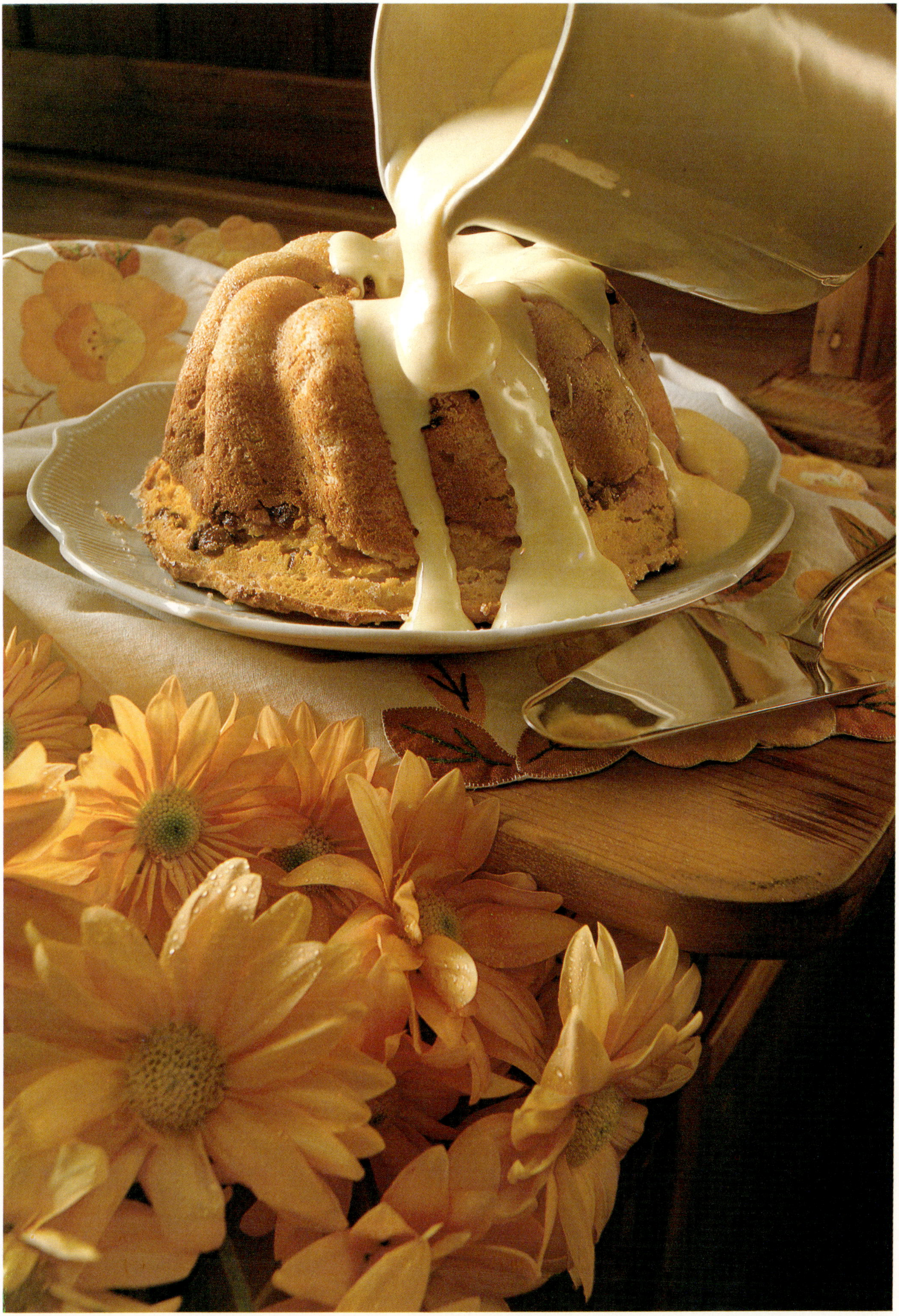

Chocolate Bread Pudding

Serves 6–8

3 cups (24fl oz) milk
1 cup (8fl oz) cream
1½ cups (3 oz) soft white breadcrumbs
125 g (4 oz) pure cooking chocolate, grated
additional 2 cups (16fl oz) milk
½ cup (4 oz) sugar
½ cup (3 oz) sultanas
1 teaspoon vanilla essence
4 eggs, separated

Heat the milk and cream in a nonstick saucepan until scalding. Add the breadcrumbs and set aside, loosely covered, for 30 minutes.

Preheat the oven to 150°C (300°F/Gas 2).

Melt the chocolate in the top half of a double saucepan, then add the extra milk and the sugar and stir over low heat until blended.

Stir the sultanas into the breadcrumb mixture, add the vanilla essence and egg yolks and beat well, gradually adding the chocolate milk.

Whisk the egg whites until well foamed and fold into the breaded milk. Carefully pour into a well-greased casserole.

Place the casserole dish on a biscuit tray and bake for 1 to 1¼ hours or until set. Remove from the oven, allow to stand for 10 to 15 minutes, and serve warm.

Swiss Apricot Trifle

Serves 6

¾ cup (3½–4 oz) dried apricots
½ cup (4fl oz) sweet sherry, warmed
1 sponge Swiss roll (jelly roll), home-made or purchased
3 eggs, separated
1½ tablespoons custard powder
½ cup (4 oz) sugar
1 teaspoon vanilla essence
600 ml (20fl oz) creamy milk
½ teaspoon grated nutmeg
glacé cherries, for decoration
glacé angelica, for decoration
whipped cream, for serving

Generously brush the apricots all over with the warmed sherry. Let them stand for 15 to 20 minutes, re-brushing from time to time.

Preheat the oven to 180°C (350°F/Gas 4). Cut the Swiss roll into slices and line the base and sides of a well-greased, shallow casserole. Place the apricots over the sponge slices; sprinkle any remaining sweet sherry over the top.

Beat the egg yolks with the custard powder, half of the sugar and the vanilla essence and with sufficient milk to blend to a creamy mixture. Heat the remaining milk in a nonstick saucepan until scalding. Gradually stir the egg mixture and the nutmeg through, and continue stirring over very low heat until thickened. Carefully spoon over the apricots and sponge slices.

Beat the egg whites and remaining sugar until it is the consistency of a meringue. Spoon it roughly over the custard.

Bake for 15 to 20 minutes. Press a few glacé cherries and angelica pieces into the meringue for decoration, and allow to stand for 15 to 20 minutes. Serve warm, with whipped cream if desired.

Speedy Chocolate Fudge Dessert

A delicious recipe for microwave cooking
Serves 6–8

1 packet chocolate cake mix
1 packet chocolate-flavoured instant pudding mix
1 cup (8fl oz) water, lukewarm
¼ cup (2fl oz) vegetable oil
whipped cream or creamy custard, for serving
shaved chocolate, for decoration

Empty the cake and pudding mixes into a bowl, and make a well in the centre; add the water and oil, and beat on the medium speed of an electric mixer for 4 minutes.

Line and generously grease a 25 cm (10 in) microwave-safe ring tin (or place a small glass in the centre of a cake tin); pour the mixture into the tin and cook in a microwave oven on medium heat (or according to manufacturer's directions for cake cooking) for 15 minutes.

Remove from the oven and cover loosely with a cloth; allow to stand for 15 minutes, then turn out. Serve warm, with whipped cream or custard as desired and a decoration of shaved chocolate.

Chocolate Snowdrift

Serves 4–5

1 cup (4 oz) flour
1 teaspoon baking powder
30 g (1 oz) butter or margarine
3 cups (24 fl oz) boiling milk
¼ cup (2 oz) sugar
2 eggs, separated
1 teaspoon vanilla essence
90 g (3 oz) cooking chocolate, coarsely grated
whipped cream, for serving

Preheat the oven to 200°C (400°F/Gas 6). Sift the flour and baking powder into a heatproof bowl, and rub the butter in; make a well in the centre, and pour in the boiling milk, whisking quickly and constantly.

Add the sugar, egg yolks and vanilla and beat well. Stiffly beat the egg whites and fold into the mixture—do not overmix. Spoon the mixture into a well-greased casserole and sprinkle the chocolate over the surface.

Bake for 15 to 17 minutes or until the mixture sets. Remove from the oven, allow to stand for 5 to 6 minutes, and serve warm with whipped cream if desired.

Old-fashioned Roly Poly

Serves 8

2 cups (8 oz) self-raising flour
1½ tablespoons (1 oz) sugar
½ teaspoon salt
1 tablespoon powdered milk
125 g (4 oz) shredded suet (or shredded chilled margarine)
water to mix, chilled
½–¾ cup (6–8 oz) raspberry jam (jelly)
2–3 firm bananas
creamy custard, for serving

Preheat the oven to 220°C (425°F/Gas 7).

Place the flour, salt and sugar in a bowl with the powdered milk and suet, and toss to mix well. Using a knife for mixing, add sufficient water to mix to a soft pliable dough. Turn onto a floured board and knead very lightly. Pat out to a rectangle about 2.5 cm (1 in) thick.

Spread the raspberry jam over the surface to within 2.5 cm (1 in) of the edge. Place the peeled bananas along one side; loosely roll up the dough, and lift onto a well-greased biscuit tray. Using a sharp knife, make three or four slashes along the surface of the roll; brush the surface with water.

Bake for 30 to 40 minutes. Serve hot, cut into slices, with creamy custard.

Sweet Syrup Puffs

Serves 4–5

1¼ cups (5 oz) self-raising flour, sifted
1 teaspoon grated lemon rind
¼ teaspoon salt
45 g (1½ oz) butter or margarine
1 egg, beaten
3 tablespoons milk
¾ cup (4 oz) brown sugar
additional 60 g (2 oz) butter or margarine
2 tablespoons (2 oz) golden syrup (light corn syrup)
2 cups (16 fl oz) boiling water
whipped cream, for serving

Combine the flour, lemon rind and salt in a bowl, and rub in the butter. Add the combined egg and milk, and mix to a soft dough. Turn onto a floured board and knead lightly. Shape into a long roll and cut into 8 to 10 slices; place these on a plate and chill for 10 to 15 minutes.

Preheat the oven to 190°C (375°F/Gas 5). Combine the brown sugar, butter, golden syrup and boiling water in a small baking pan, and place in the preheated oven for 5 to 7 minutes. Lift out, carefully drop in each of the dough slices, and quickly baste the pan liquid over them; return to the oven for 17–20 minutes.

Serve the puffs hot, with the syrup spooned over and an accompanying bowl of cream for individual use.

Baked Pancakes Jubilee

Serves 4

Filling:
2 green cooking apples, peeled, cored and sliced

---

60 g (2 oz) butter or margarine

¼ cup (1 oz) raisins

¼ teaspoon ground cinnamon

¼ teaspoon ground nutmeg

Pancakes:
¼ cup (1 oz) flour

⅛ teaspoon salt

---

1 egg, beaten

1½ tablespoons (1fl oz) strong made coffee

1½ tablespoons (1fl oz) milk

---

90 g (3 oz) butter or margarine, melted

---

icing (confectioners') sugar, for sprinkling

---

ice-cream, for serving

Pancakes: Preheat the oven to 230°C (450°F/Gas 8). Sift the flour and salt into a bowl; add the egg, coffee and milk and whisk lightly for 2 to 3 minutes.

Pour half of the melted butter into each of two deep 23 cm (9 in) enamel pie plates; tilt the plates to coat the base and sides. Heat the pie plates over a very low heat; and when the butter is gently sizzling, pour half of the pancake batter into each plate.

Immediately place into the preheated oven and bake for 10 to 12 minutes. After 2 or 3 minutes the batter will commence to bubble and puff up, so quickly open the oven door and prick or puncture with a skewer or fork; repeat this process once or twice more as the batter puffs up. Then reduce the oven temperature to 180°C (350°F/Gas 4) and continue baking for a further 8 to 10 minutes. The batter will gradually creep up the sides of the plates during the baking. When golden brown and crisp around the edges, remove from the oven and carefully drain off any surplus butter.

Filling: Cook the sliced apples in the heated butter over low heat until just softened. Add the raisins and spices, and mix through.

To assemble the pancakes, spoon half of the filling down the centre of each pancake and fold the sides over the centre; dust each liberally with icing sugar. Cut each roll in half, and serve with ice-cream if desired.

Upside-down Pudding

Serves 5–6

Butterscotch Layer:
½ cup (3 oz) brown sugar

---

90 g (3 oz) butter, softened

---

fruits and nuts—see below

Cake Layer:
90 g (3 oz) butter or margarine, softened

⅓ cup (3 oz) caster (powdered) sugar

---

1 teaspoon vanilla essence

---

2 eggs, beaten

¼ cup (2fl oz) milk

1½ cups (6 oz) self-raising flour

Preheat the oven to 180°C (350°F/Gas 4). Cream the brown sugar and butter together, and spread over the base of a well-greased 20 cm (8 in) round or square cake tin. Arrange the fruits and nuts over the surface in a pattern.

Cake layer: Beat the butter, sugar and vanilla essence together until creamy. Add the eggs and milk, and beat well. Fold in the sifted flour, and carefully spread over the arranged fruits and nuts.

Bake for 30 to 35 minutes. Allow to stand in the tin for 6 to 8 minutes, then invert onto a serving platter so that the fruit and nut pattern is uppermost. Serve hot in wedges or squares, with hot custard or ice-cream as desired.

Fruits and Nuts:
- Dried apricots, prunes and walnuts—lightly soaked and seeded as required.
- Pineapple, ginger and pecans—sliced—with glacé ginger pieces.
- Peaches, cherries and almonds—sliced—with glacé cherries halved.

Right: **Upside-down Pudding** (see above).

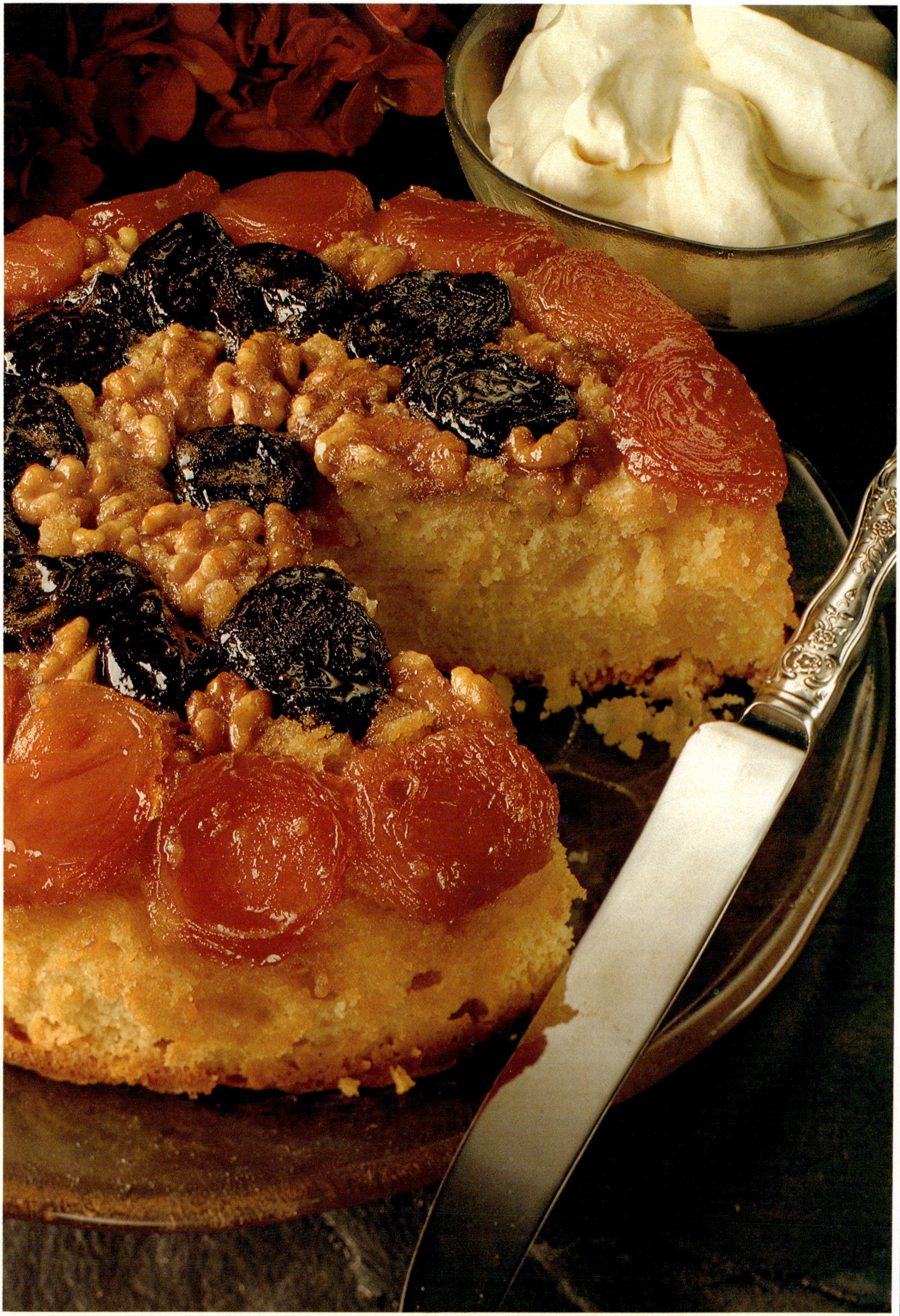

RICE, CEREAL AND PASTA DESSERTS

Raisin Rice Dessert

Serves 5–6

1½ cups (8 oz) long-grain rice
4 cups (32fl oz) milk, warmed
½ teaspoon salt
¾ cup (6fl oz) Marsala wine or sweet sherry
¾ cup (6 oz) sugar
½ teaspoon ground nutmeg
¾ cup (4 oz) chopped raisins
3 egg yolks, beaten
whipped cream, for serving

Wash the rice under running water for 1 to 2 minutes; drain very well. Place the rice into the top half of a double boiler and pour the milk and salt over, then let it stand for 30 to 40 minutes.

Add the Marsala wine and cook over boiling water for 15 minutes.

Preheat the oven to 180°C (350°F/Gas 4). Allow the rice to cool for 10 minutes, then add the sugar, nutmeg, raisins and egg yolks and stir through. Turn into a well-greased casserole.

Bake for 20 to 25 minutes. Remove from the oven and serve warm with whipped cream.

Variations: Use chopped dates, prunes, dried apricots or sultanas in place of the raisins.

Crusted Honey Rice

Serves 6–7

1¼ cups (8 oz) long-grain rice, washed
1 lemon
1¼ cups (10fl oz) evaporated milk
1 cup (8fl oz) fresh milk, heated
½ cup (4fl oz) water, boiling
¾ cup (8 oz) honey, warmed
¾ cup (4 oz) chopped raisins
60 g (2 oz) butter or margarine
½ teaspoon ground cinnamon
2 egg whites
¼ cup (2 oz) sugar
whipped cream, for serving

Place the rice, two or three strips of lemon peel, 2 tablespoons of lemon juice, the evaporated and fresh milk and the water in the top of a double boiler; cook over boiling water, stirring occasionally, for 30 minutes.

Preheat the oven to 180°C (350°F/Gas 4). Remove the lemon peel from the rice and add the honey, raisins, butter and cinnamon. Turn into a greased casserole.

Beat the egg whites until stiff and glossy; gradually add the sugar, beating well after each addition. Spoon the meringue roughly over the rice.

Bake for 20 to 25 minutes, to set the meringue. Serve warm with whipped cream.

Fruit Pasta Pudding

Serves 6–8

1½–2 cups (12–16 oz) cooked and drained fruit—see the variations below
½ teaspoon ground cinnamon or nutmeg
¼ cup (1 oz) chopped pecan or walnuts
1½–2 cups (7-10 oz) cooked pasta shapes (90 g (3 oz) uncooked)
60 g (2 oz) butter or margarine, melted
½ cup (4fl oz) sour cream
1 cup (8fl oz) cottage cheese, sieved
2 eggs, beaten
½ cup (4fl oz) fruit syrup—from the cooked fruit
2 tablespoons (1 oz) brown sugar
additional ½ teaspoon cinnamon or nutmeg

Preheat the oven to 180°C (350°F/Gas 4). Combine the fruit, spice and nuts and spread over the base of a well-greased casserole.

Toss the cooked pasta and melted butter together. Combine the sour cream, cottage cheese, eggs and fruit syrup, and mix into the pasta. Spoon the mixture into the casserole and sprinkle the combined brown sugar and extra spice over the surface.

Bake for 30 to 35 minutes. Remove from the oven and allow to stand for 10 minutes before serving hot. Or stand longer and serve warm or cold (but not chilled), if desired.

Fruit Variations:
• One of the following: apples, rhubarb, apricots, peaches, quinces or berry fruits—add sugar for desired sweetening.
• Combine apples with chopped dates, figs (or prunes), raisins, sultanas, currants.

Mock Strawberry Crisp

Serves 6

½ cup (4 oz) sugar
3 tablespoons (1 oz) cornflour (cornstarch)
⅛ teaspoon cardamom
⅛ teaspoon cloves
3½–4 cups diced rhubarb
2–3 teaspoons strawberry essence
¼ cup (2fl oz) orange juice
¾ cup (4 oz) brown sugar
¾ cup (3 oz) quick-cooking oats
1 tablespoon (¼ oz) desiccated coconut
½ cup (2 oz) self-raising flour, sifted
90 g (3 oz) butter or margarine, melted
2 egg whites, stiffly beaten
ice-cream or cream, for serving

Combine the sugar, cornflour and spices, and toss through the rhubarb; place in a well-greased casserole and mix the combined strawberry essence and orange juice through.

Place in a moderate oven, 180°C (350°F/Gas 4), and cook the rhubarb until it is softened; stir occasionally to distribute the thickening syrup.

Meanwhile combine the brown sugar, oats, coconut and sifted flour in a bowl; mix the melted butter through, then lightly fold in the beaten egg whites.

Roughly spoon this over the rhubarb mixture and return to the oven for a further 20 to 25 minutes until the topping is crisp. Serve warm, with ice-cream or cream if desired.

Honeyed Pineapple Rice

Serves 5–6

½ cup (3 oz) long-grain rice
3½ cups (28fl oz) creamy milk, warmed
30 g (1 oz) butter or margarine
½ teaspoon ground ginger
2 eggs, separated
½ cup (5 oz) honey
1 can/450 g (1 lb) pineapple pieces, drained well
whipped cream, for serving

Preheat the oven to 150°C (300°F/Gas 2). Wash the rice under running water; drain well.

Combine the rice and warm milk in a well-greased casserole; dot with pieces of butter, and sprinkle with the ground ginger. Bake for 1½ hours, stirring occasionally. Remove, and allow to cool slightly.

Reset the oven temperature at 180°C (350°F/Gas 4).

Beat the egg yolks with one-third of the honey, and fold into the rice custard. Arrange the pineapple pieces over the surface.

Whisk the egg whites until stiff and glossy; gradually add the remaining honey and beat until the meringue stands in peaks. Roughly pile it over the pineapple pieces and return the casserole to the oven for 20 to 25 minutes to set the top of the meringue. Serve warm or cold, with whipped cream.

Fruit Variations:
- Apricots with cinnamon flavour
- Peaches with nutmeg flavour
- Apples with clove flavour
- Raisins or sultanas with mixed spice flavour

Apricot Rice Caramel

Serves 5–6

125 g (4 oz) dried apricots
water to cover
60 g (2 oz) butter or margarine, melted
½ cup (3 oz) brown sugar
1½ cups cooked rice (⅔ cup (4 oz) uncooked)
1½ cups (12fl oz) milk, warmed
3 eggs, beaten
¼ cup (2 oz) sugar
½ teaspoon vanilla essence
½ cup (4fl oz) cream
¼ teaspoon ground nutmeg
whipped cream, for serving

Place the apricots in a small saucepan and just cover with water. Cover the pan, and cook slowly until just tender; then remove from heat, cool and drain.

Preheat the oven to 180°C (350°F/Gas 4).

Combine the melted butter and brown sugar, and spread over the base and about one-third of the way up the sides of an ovenproof pudding bowl. Press the apricots over the surface, and then press the cooked rice over the apricots.

To the warm milk, add the beaten eggs, sugar and vanilla; then beat the cream through. Carefully pour the mixture into the centre of the pudding basin, and sprinkle the nutmeg over the surface.

Lift the bowl into a baking pan containing 1–2 cups of hot water, place in the preheated oven and bake for 1 hour or until set. Remove, allow to cool and then chill well. Turn on to a serving platter and serve with whipped cream if desired.

Fruited Muesli Dessert

Serves 6

4 eggs, separated
1½ cups (12fl oz) milk
¾ cup (6fl oz) sweetened condensed milk
1½ tablespoons cornflour (cornstarch)
3–4 bananas
1 cup (5 oz) raisins
1½ cups (8 oz) toasted muesli cereal
⅓ cup (3 oz) sugar

Preheat the oven to 180°C (350°F/Gas 4). Grease a casserole.

Combine the egg yolks with the milk, condensed milk and cornflour in a nonstick saucepan and cook over low heat, stirring constantly, until the consistency is that of a thin custard.

Peel the bananas and cut into slices; arrange them in layers in the greased casserole with the raisins and the muesli cereal, spooning hot custard between each layer.

Beat the egg whites until stiff and glossy; gradually add the sugar, beating well between each addition. Spoon roughly over the layers of dessert in the casserole.

Bake until the meringue is tipped with golden brown (17 to 20 minutes). Serve warm or cold.

Note: If preparing the first section of the dessert ahead of time, place it in the oven to heat through before topping with the meringue.

DESSERT CAKES

Almond Cream Roll

Serves 8

3 eggs (at room temperature)
½ cup (4 oz) caster (powdered) sugar, slightly warmed
1 cup (4 oz) self-raising flour
¼ teaspoon almond essence
2–3 tablespoons milk or water
Filling:
125 g (4 oz) butter or margarine, softened
½ cup (4 oz) caster sugar
2 eggs, separated
1 cup (3½ oz) ground almonds
¼ cup (2fl oz) thickened cream, whipped
Topping:
2–3 tablespoons sweet sherry
1 tablespoon orange juice
1 cup (8fl oz) thickened cream, chilled
2–3 teaspoons icing (confectioners') sugar
2–3 teaspoons grated orange rind

Preheat the oven to 190°C (375°F/Gas 5). Prepare a 35 × 25 cm (14 × 10 in) swiss roll tin (jelly roll pan) by lining it with greaseproof paper and greasing thoroughly.

Place the eggs and sugar in a bowl and beat until very thick—about 12 to 15 minutes. Fold in the sifted flour, and add the almond essence with sufficient milk to mix to a soft sponge batter. Spread into the prepared tin, and bake for 12 to 15 minutes. Turn out onto greaseproof paper (lightly dusted with caster sugar), then carefully roll the sponge up with the greaseproof paper. Leave for 2 to 3 minutes then carefully unroll and remove the paper. Loosely re-roll, and allow to cool.

Filling: Cream the butter and sugar well. Gradually beat the egg yolks through; then add the ground almonds, mixing well.

Beat the egg whites until well foamed, add the cream and fold through; carefully fold into the butter mixture. Unroll the sponge and spread the filling over; re-roll.

Topping: Combine the sweet sherry and orange juice, and sprinkle it all over the outside of the sponge. Chill for 30 minutes.

Whip the cream until stiff. Add the icing sugar and orange rind. Spread over the outside of the sponge roll, swirling to form an attractive design on the surface. Chill until ready to slice and serve.

Right: **Fruited Muesli Dessert** (see above).

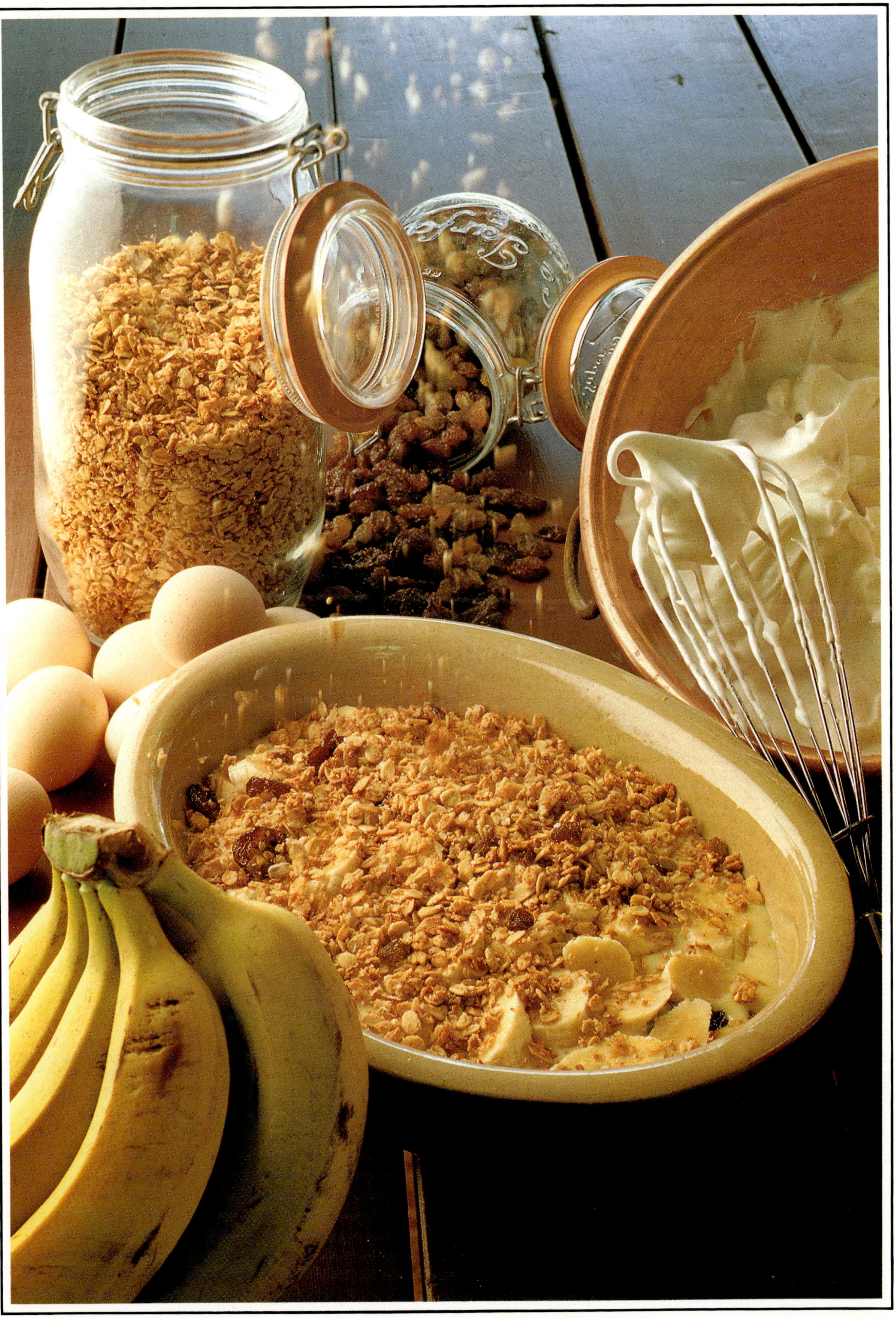

Chestnut Chocolate Ring

Serves 6–8

4 eggs, separated

1 cup (8 oz) sugar

90 g (3 oz) dark pure cooking chocolate, melted

250 g (8 oz) chestnut purée

1½ cups (6 oz) self-raising flour

*Chocolate Rum Cream:
90 g (3 oz) dark cooking chocolate, melted*

30 g (1 oz) butter or margarine, softened

1 tablespoon rum

200 ml (6½ fl oz) thickened cream, chilled

Preheat the oven to 190°C (375°F/Gas 5).
  Beat the egg yolks with half the sugar until thick. Beat the egg whites until stiff and glossy, and gradually add the remaining sugar, beating well.
  Add the cooled melted chocolate and the chestnut purée to the egg yolk mixture, mixing well; add the sifted flour, then fold in the egg white mixture, mixing lightly. Spoon the mixture into a greased and floured 20 cm (8 in) fluted ring tin, and bake for 30 to 35 minutes.
  Allow to stand for 3 to 4 minutes, then carefully turn out onto a cake rack to cool; transfer to a serving plate.
  Combine the melted chocolate, softened butter and rum, mixing well. Beat the cream until stiff, then carefully fold into the chocolate mixture. Pile into the centre of the chestnut ring, and chill before serving.

Gâteau Elizabethe

Serves 6–8

125 g (4 oz) butter or margarine

185 g (6 oz) pure cooking chocolate, chopped

½ cup (4 oz) caster (powdered) sugar

4 eggs, separated

1 teaspoon brandy or rum essence

½ cup (2 oz) potato flour, sifted

¾ cup (3 oz) finely chopped walnuts

chocolate flavoured Warm Glacé Icing (see recipe, page 000)

whipped cream, for serving

Melt the butter in a nonstick saucepan; add the chocolate and sugar, and stir over a low heat until blended well. Remove from the heat, add the egg yolks and essence, and beat briskly to combine. Allow to cool.
  Preheat the oven to 180°C (350°F/Gas 4).
  Fold the sifted potato flour into the chocolate mixture. Whisk the egg whites until stiff and glossy, and fold into the mixture—do not overmix.
  Prepare a 20 cm (8 in) springform tin by greasing it well and coating the base and sides with the walnuts. Carefully spoon in the chocolate-egg mixture, being careful not to disturb the walnuts on the sides. Scatter the remaining walnuts lightly over the surface.
  Bake for 40 to 45 minutes. Allow to stand for 5 to 6 minutes before loosening the springform ring. Allow to cool.
  Drizzle the chocolate icing over the top, carefully lift the cake onto a serving plate, and cut into slices for serving with whipped cream if desired.

Baked 'Saucer' Cakes

Serves 6–7

1 cup (8fl oz) milk

½ cup (4fl oz) water

strips of lemon peel

½ teaspoon ground nutmeg

60 g (2 oz) butter or margarine, softened

¼ cup (2 oz) sugar

2 eggs, separated

½ cup (2 oz) self-raising flour

¾ cup (3 oz) flaked almonds

¾ cup (6fl oz) apricot jam (jelly)

2–3 tablespoons brandy or sweet sherry

icing (confectioners') sugar, for sprinkling

Heat the milk, water, a few strips of lemon peel and nutmeg in a nonstick saucepan until scalding. Set aside to cool, then strain.
  Preheat the oven to 200°C (400°F/Gas 6). Beat the butter and sugar until creamy. Add the egg yolks and beat well; then fold in the flour. Gradually add the cooled milk mixture. Then beat the egg whites and lightly fold them in—do not overmix.
  Prepare six or seven old or ovenproof saucers or small edged plates by placing them on oven trays and heating in the hot oven for 5 to 6 minutes; remove from the oven and quickly grease each one. Divide the batter onto each saucer and scatter the flaked almonds over; replace in the oven and bake for 12 to 15 minutes.
  Combine the apricot jam with the brandy or sweet sherry, and heat until warm. Slip the 'saucer' cakes on to individual serving plates, and drizzle the apricot sauce over; sprinkle with icing sugar and serve hot.

SHORTCAKES AND BABAS

Mock Orange Babas

Serves 6–8

---

1 packet orange cake mix

water and egg(s) as directed on package

¾ cup (6 fl oz) water

¾ cup (6 oz) sugar

3 tablespoons sweet orange marmalade

1–2 tablespoons brandy

whipped cream, for serving

Make up the packet cake mix with the water and egg(s) as directed on the package; spoon into six to eight well-greased custard cups or small moulds, and place on a biscuit tray.

Bake in a preheated oven at 190°C (375°F/Gas 5) for 25 to 27 minutes. Carefully turn out onto individual serving plates.

Meanwhile heat the water and sugar in a small saucepan until boiling; add the marmalade and allow to boil briskly, without stirring, for 5 minutes. Remove from the heat, add the brandy and slowly spoon over the hot cakes, allowing the syrup to be absorbed.

Serve cool or chilled, with whipped cream spooned over each baba.

Orange Date Squares

Serves 8

---

3 cups (12 oz) chopped dates

¼ cup (2 oz) sugar

½ cup (4 fl oz) water

¾ cup (6 fl oz) orange juice

2–3 teaspoons grated orange rind

185 g (6 oz) butter or margarine, softened

1 cup (5 oz) brown sugar

1 egg

1 teaspoon vanilla essence

2 cups (8 oz) self-raising flour, sifted

1½ cups (5 oz) quick-cooking oats

¼ teaspoon mixed spices

warm custard, for serving

Combine the dates with the sugar, water, orange juice and orange rind in a saucepan; heat slowly, stirring constantly, until bubbling then lower the heat and simmer for 2 to 3 minutes. Allow to cool.

Preheat the oven to 190°C (375°F/Gas 5). Thoroughly grease a 20–30 cm (8–9 in) square cake tin.

Beat the butter and brown sugar until creamy. Add the egg and vanilla essence, and mix well. Add the flour, oats and spices, and stir thoroughly.

Press about two-thirds of the mixture into the prepared cake tin and spread the cooled date mixture over. Crumble the remaining oat mixture over the surface; press lightly.

Bake for 30 to 35 minutes. Cut into squares while still hot; serve warm, with custard spooned over each square.

Glazed Fruit Shortcake

Serves 8–10

Shortcake:
185 g (6 oz) butter or margarine, softened

¾ cup (6 oz) caster (powdered) sugar

2 eggs, beaten

2¼ cups (9 oz) self-raising flour, sifted

rind and juice of 1 small orange

Topping:
½ cup (3 oz) glacé cherries, chopped

½ cup (3 oz) raisins, chopped

½ cup (2 oz) slivered almonds

⅓ cup (3 oz) brown sugar

¼ cup (1 oz) self-raising flour

60 g (2 oz) butter or margarine, melted

¼ cup (3 oz) golden syrup (light corn syrup), warmed

Preheat the oven to 180°C (350°F/Gas 4).

Cream the butter and sugar together well. Add the eggs and beat thoroughly. Fold in the sifted flour. Then add the orange rind and sufficient orange juice to form a firm cake mixture.

Spread into a well-greased 20 cm (8 in) springform tin, and bake for 45 to 50 minutes.

While the cake is cooking, prepare the topping. Combine the cherries, raisins, almonds, sugar and flour in a bowl. Drizzle the melted butter over, and mix well.

Without removing the cake from the oven, carefully coat the surface with the fruit-nut mixture; drizzle the golden syrup over the top, and continue baking for a further 15–20 minutes.

Remove from the oven, allow to stand for 3 to 4 minutes, then lift off the springform ring and continue cooling for 10 to 15 minutes. Serve warm, with ice-cream, cream or custard.

Strawberry Shortcake
(Photograph below)
Serves 8

2½ cups (10 oz) flour
2 teaspoons baking powder
¼ teaspoon salt
90 g (3 oz) butter or margarine, chopped
⅓ cup (3 oz) sugar
1 cup (8 fl oz) milk
1 egg, beaten
20–24 strawberries
additional 30 g (1 oz) butter or margarine, melted
whipped cream or ice-cream, for serving

Preheat the oven to 200°C (400°F/Gas 6).

Sift the flour, baking powder and salt into a bowl; add the butter and rub through with the fingertips. Add two-thirds of the sugar and mix well. Combine the milk and egg; add almost all of it, mixing lightly to make a soft dough.

Divide into two sections, one slightly larger than the other, and knead each lightly into rounds about 15 cm (6 in) and 10 cm (4 in) across. Place each round on a well-greased biscuit tray and prick the surface with a fork. Brush the remaining milk-egg mixture over each round and sprinkle with the remaining sugar.

Bake for 15 minutes or until golden brown.

Meanwhile select 6-8 strawberries for the decoration and chop the remainder coarsely; drain off any juices and reserve.

Take the shortcakes from the oven, spoon the chopped strawberries over the larger round and place the other round on top; brush the extra butter over the entire surface and place the whole strawberries on the top—work as quickly as possible at this stage. Drizzle the reserved juice over the top, and return to the oven for a further 5 to 7 minutes.

Serve warm, with whipped cream or ice-cream as desired.

Tropical Fruit Recess
(Photograph below right)
Serves 6–8

60 g (2 oz) butter or margarine, softened
⅓ cup (3 oz) caster (powdered) sugar
2 eggs
3 bananas, mashed—approx. 1¼ cups (10 oz)
½ cup (4 fl oz) mixed orange juice and water
1½ cups (6 oz) self-raising flour
2 teaspoons custard powder
2 teaspoons full-cream milk powder
Passionfruit Cream:
2 tablespoons (2 oz) condensed milk
2 tablespoons fresh lemon juice
pulp of 6 passionfruit—approx. 1¼ cups
½ cup (4 fl oz) fresh cream, chilled

Preheat the oven to 180°C (350°F/Gas 4). Grease and flour a deep-sided 20 cm (8 in) recess tin.

Beat the butter and sugar to a cream. Add the eggs, one at a time, and beat well. Add the mashed bananas and orange juice mixture, beat well. Sift the dry ingredients together and fold into the butter-banana mixture. Spoon into tin.

Bake for 45 to 50 minutes. Allow to stand for 3 to 4 minutes, then cool on a cake rack.

Passionfruit Cream: Combine the condensed milk and lemon juice in a small bowl; add the passionfruit pulp and gradually stir in the cream, beating constantly. Refrigerate until thickened. Spoon into the banana cake recess, and refrigerate until ready for serving.

Grecian Dessert Cake

(Photograph left)
Serves 8–10

250 g (8 oz) butter or margarine, softened

1 cup (8 oz) caster (powdered) sugar

1 teaspoon vanilla essence

4 eggs separated

1½ cups (6 oz) self-raising flour

2 teaspoons mixed spices

2 teaspoons grated lemon rind

1½ cups (8 oz) fine semolina

Syrup:
½ cup (4 oz) sugar

½ cup (5 oz) honey

1 cup (8 fl oz) water

1 tablespoon lemon juice

whole cloves, for decoration

Preheat oven to 180°C (350°F/Gas 4). Line and grease a 23 cm (9 in) slab tin. Beat butter, sugar and vanilla until creamy; add egg yolks and beat well. Sift flour with spices; add the lemon rind and semolina, and mix well.

Whisk the egg whites well (do not beat stiffly). Into the butter-egg mixture, fold alternate batches of the dry ingredients and the beaten egg whites, about a third of each at a time. Spoon the mixture into the tin, and bake for 35 to 40 minutes.

Syrup: Combine ingredients, bring slowly to the boil, simmer 7 to 8 minutes.

Slowly spoon the cooled syrup over the cooked cake so that it is absorbed. Cut and allow to cool in the tin. Decorate with cloves.

Peach Kuchen Squares

Serves 9

1 packet plain cake mix
½ cup (1½ oz) flaked or desiccated coconut
125 g (4 oz) butter or margarine, chopped
1 can/825 g (1 lb 13 oz) sliced peaches, well drained
¼ cup (1½ oz) brown sugar
½ teaspoon cinnamon
300 ml (10 fl oz) sour cream
2 eggs, beaten
additional 1 tablespoon brown sugar, for topping
additional flaked or desiccated coconut, for topping

Preheat the oven to 180°C (350°F/Gas 4). Mix the contents of the cake mix package with the coconut. Cut the butter through until the mixture resembles coarse breadcrumbs, and press over the base of a well-greased 23 cm (9 in) square slab tin.

Bake for 15 to 20 minutes. Remove from the oven and allow to cool slightly (leave the oven on).

Arrange the peach slices over the partially baked base; sprinkle the combined brown sugar and cinnamon over the top. Beat the sour cream and eggs together until just blended; spoon over the peaches. Sprinkle the extra brown sugar and coconut over the surface.

Return to the oven and bake for a further 10 to 15 minutes until the topping is set. Serve warm, cut into squares.

MERINGUES AND TORTES

One-egg Meringue

Serves 6

1 egg white
1 cup (7 oz) caster (powdered) sugar
2 tablespoons boiling water
1 teaspoon vanilla essence
2 teaspoons baking powder
cornflour, for dusting
Filling:
1½–2 cups (12–16 oz) chopped fruit salad, well drained
300 ml (10 fl oz) thickened cream, chilled
1–2 teaspoons icing (confectioners') sugar

Lightly mix the egg white and all but 2 teaspoons of the caster sugar in the small bowl of an electric mixer. Cover loosely and set aside for several hours or overnight.

Next day: Re-beat the sugared egg white in the mixer for 2 minutes on medium speed; add the boiling water and vanilla essence, and beat on high speed for 15 minutes. Remove the beaters, sift the baking powder over the surface and fold in very lightly but thoroughly.

Preheat the oven to 120°C (250°F/Gas ½). Prepare a biscuit tray by greasing and dusting lightly with cornflour. Mark an 18 cm (7 in) circle in the centre and roughly cover with the meringue. Form a slight depression in the centre of the meringue, and dust the edges with the reserved 2 teaspoons of sugar.

Bake for 1 to 1¼ hours. Allow to stand in the oven with the door ajar for 30 minutes; then remove and allow to cool.

Just before serving, spoon the fruit salad onto the centre, and cover with whipped and sweetened cream. Cut into wedges to serve.

White Mountain Meringue

Serves 8–10

4 egg whites (at room temperature)
¼ teaspoon salt
¼ teaspoon cream of tartar or ½ teaspoon lemon juice
1¼ cups (9 oz) caster (powdered) sugar
1 teaspoon vanilla essence
cornflour (cornstarch), for dusting
Topping: *1 can 470 g (1 lb) chestnut purée*
2 tablespoons brandy liqueur
1 cup (8 fl oz) thickened cream, chilled
1 tablespoon icing (confectioners') sugar
60 g (2 oz) pure cooking chocolate, coarsely grated, or ¼ cup (1 oz) chopped walnuts

Preheat the oven to 150°C (300°F/Gas 2).

Whisk the egg whites with the salt until stiff and glossy but not dry. Beat in the cream of tartar (or lemon juice). Gradually add the sugar, a tablespoon at a time, beating well after each addition until about two-thirds has been added and the mixture resembles a thick marshmallow. Fold in all but 1 tablespoon of the remaining sugar, and the vanilla essence.

Cover a biscuit tray with aluminium foil and lightly grease the area of an 18 cm (7 in) circle; dust over the circle with cornflour. Spoon the meringue into a large piping bag fitted with a fluted or rose tube. Fill the prepared circle with a spiral of meringue. Then continue to pipe decreasing sizes of spiral circles—one on top of the other—until a cone shape is reached and the meringue is all used.

Place in the preheated oven and bake for 20 minutes. Lower the oven temperature *by* about 25°C (50°F) and continue baking for a further 45 to 50 minutes. Carefully remove the meringue from the foil whilst it is still warm and place on a serving plate to cool.

Meanwhile, combine the chestnut purée with the brandy liqueur, beating well. Whip the cream with the icing sugar until it is thick yet still soft, then chill well.

Drizzle the chestnut purée mixture from the top of the meringue cone so that it runs unevenly down the sides. Spoon the cream over in the same fashion but do not entirely cover the purée. Scatter the chocolate or walnuts over the top and serve.

Pavlova Plus

Serves 8

Meringue: *5 egg whites*
¼ teaspoon salt
1 cup (8 oz) sugar
2 teaspoons cornflour (cornstarch)
2 teaspoons vinegar
Filling: *300 ml (10 fl oz) thickened cream, chilled*
2–3 teaspoons icing (confectioners') sugar
1 teaspoon vanilla essence
Topping: *1 cup (4 oz) chopped canned fruits*
1 cup (5 oz) chopped dried fruits
1 cup (8 fl oz) canned fruit syrup
½ cup jam (jelly) or marmalade
¼–⅓ cup (2–2½ fl oz) brandy

Preheat the oven to 150°C (300°F/Gas 2).

Beat the egg whites with the salt until stiff and glossy. Add half of the sugar in small amounts, beating well after each addition. Combine the remaining sugar and cornflour, and fold through the egg whites. Sprinkle the vinegar over the surface, and fold in—do not overbeat.

Place a 23–25 cm (9–10 in) round of aluminium foil or greaseproof paper on a biscuit tray; grease lightly and dust a little cornflour over the surface. Spread the meringue over the foil or paper, scooping out the centre slightly to resemble a pie shell.

Bake for 60 to 70 minutes. Open the oven door and allow the meringue to cool slowly for 15 to 20 minutes, then remove to a draught-free area to stand until completely cold.

Filling: Whip the cream until thickened, add sugar (to taste) with the vanilla, and chill until required.

Topping: Combine the fruits, fruit syrup and jam or marmalade in a saucepan, and bring slowly to the boil over low heat; simmer for 3 to 4 minutes, then remove from the heat. Add the brandy and stir through. Then allow to cool, and chill until required.

To assemble the dessert: Carefully peel the foil or paper away from the base of the meringue; place on a flat serving plate. Spoon the cream filling into the recessed section of the meringue, and drizzle the brandied fruit sauce over the surface. Cut into slices for serving.

Note: Canned apricots, peaches, pineapple, etc., may be mixed with dried apricots, raisins, prunes, etc., in varying proportions as desired.

Passionfruit Pavlova

Serves 8–10

6 egg whites (at room temperature)
1/8 teaspoon cream of tartar
1 cup (8 oz) sugar
1 tablespoon cornflour (cornstarch)
2 teaspoons white vinegar
cornflour, for dusting
Topping:
300 ml (10fl oz) thickened cream, chilled
1 teaspoon vanilla essence
2 teaspoons icing (confectioners') sugar
pulp of 4 large passionfruit (or 1/2–3/4 cup canned passionfruit pulp)

Preheat the oven to 200°C (400°F/Gas 6).

Beat the egg whites (preferably in a large glass bowl) until stiff and glossy. Combine the cream of tartar, sugar and cornflour, and gradually add to the egg whites, beating well after each addition. Sprinkle the vinegar over the surface and fold in lightly—do not overmix.

Grease the base and sides of a 20 cm (8 in) springform tin and dust with cornflour; shake off any excess. Pile the meringue into the tin, spreading to form a slight depression in the centre.

Place into the preheated oven, close the door and immediately reduce the oven temperature to very slow, 120°C (250°F/Gas 1/2), and bake for 1 1/4 to 1 1/2 hours.

Open the oven door and leave the meringue standing in the oven for 15 minutes, before removing to a draught-free area; carefully loosen the springform tin rim and allow to cool (the meringue may sink slightly in the centre). Carefully lift the meringue onto a flat platter, removing the tin base.

Topping: Whip the cream, vanilla essence and icing sugar until thickened and firm. Spoon onto the meringue and lightly spread it. Spoon the passionfruit pulp over the cream, and chill until ready to serve.

Note: For ease of slicing, use a large knife constantly dipped into hot water.

Hazelnut Meringue

Serves 8

4 egg whites
1 cup (7 oz) caster sugar
1/2 teaspoon vinegar
1 teaspoon instant coffee powder
1 cup (3 1/2 oz) ground hazelnuts
Topping:
300 ml (10fl oz) thickened cream, chilled
2 teaspoons icing (confectioners') sugar
60 g (2 oz) grated chocolate
1–2 tablespoons whisky cream liqueur
60 g (2 oz) chocolate, melted
whole hazelnuts, for decoration

Preheat the oven to 190°C (375°F/Gas 5).

Beat the egg whites until stiff and glossy. Gradually add the sugar, beating constantly; then add the vinegar and coffee powder, and beat through. Fold in the ground hazelnuts. Spoon the mixture into two 20 cm (8 in) greased springform tins (or cake tins with removable bases).

Bake for 35 to 40 minutes. Remove from the oven, loosen the springform rings, and allow to cool.

Whip the cream until stiff. Sweeten with the icing sugar and fold the grated chocolate through.

Drizzle the whisky cream liqueur over each of the hazelnut meringues. Spread each with the whipped chocolate cream, and sandwich together. Drizzle the melted chocolate over the top layer of cream, and decorate with whole hazelnuts. Chill well before serving.

Right: **Hazelnut Meringue (see above);** **Passionfruit Pavlova (see above).**

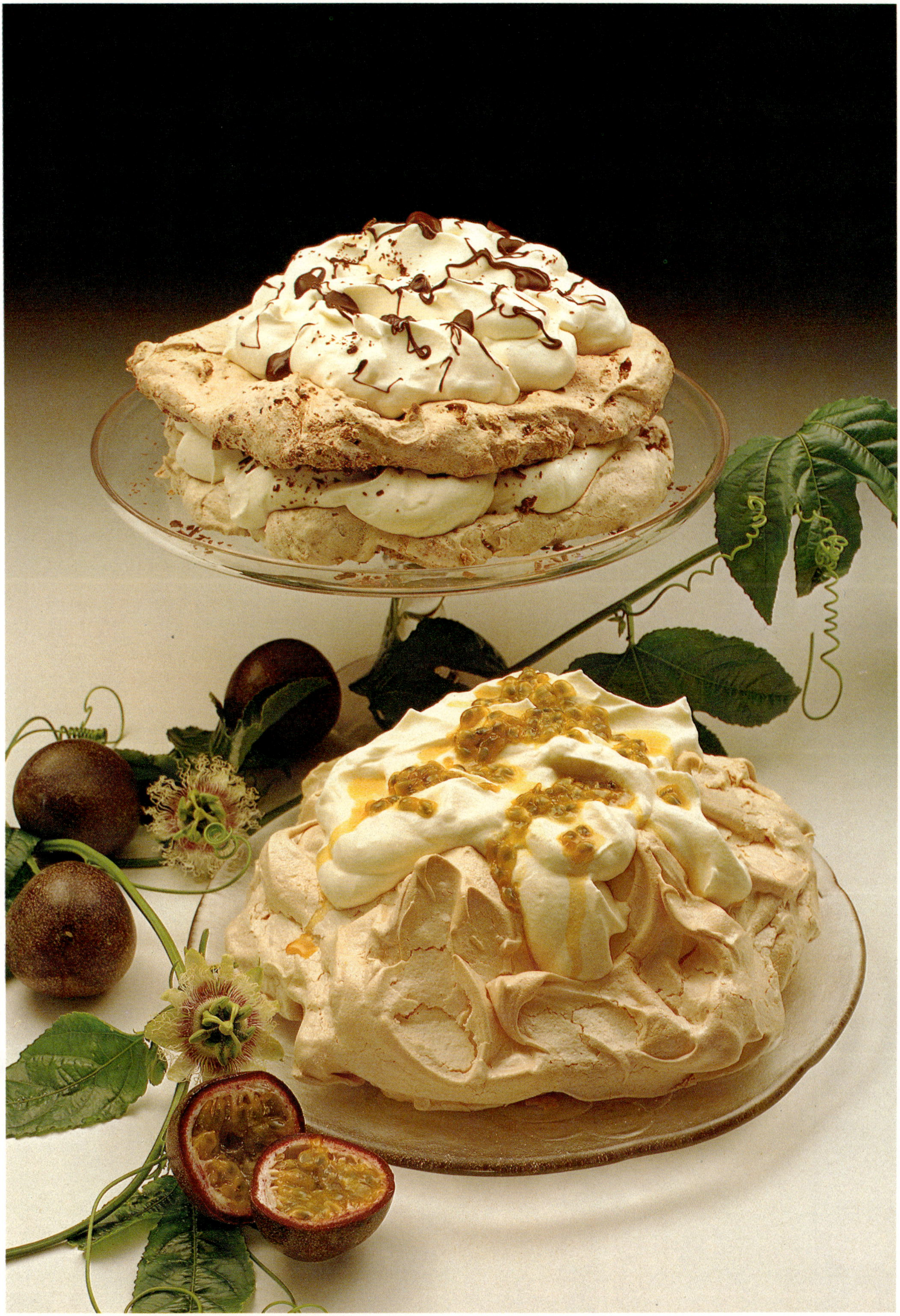

Orange Meringue Loaf

Serves 6–8

6 egg whites (at room temperature)
¼ teaspoon cream of tartar
¼ teaspoon salt
1 cup (8 oz) sugar
½ teaspoon orange essence
½ teaspoon brandy essence
Orange Sauce: 1 cup (8 oz) sugar
⅛ teaspoon salt
3 tablespoons (1 oz) cornflour (cornstarch)
2 teaspoons grated lemon rind
1 cup (8fl oz) orange juice
3 egg yolks, lightly beaten
15 g (½ oz) butter or margarine
1 cup (8fl oz) thickened cream, chilled
flaked, toasted almonds for topping

Preheat the oven to 180°C (350°F/Gas 4).

Beat the egg whites until stiff and glossy. Add the cream of tartar and salt, and beat through. Gradually add the sugar, beating well after each addition. Flavour with the essences.

Spoon the mixture into a greased and cornflour-dusted 23 × 13 × 8 cm (9 × 5 × 3 in) loaf tin. Set the tin in a baking pan containing 3–4 cups hot water.

Bake for 55 to 60 minutes. Remove from the oven and place the loaf tin on a wire rack in a draught-free area to cool.

Meanwhile combine the sugar, salt, cornflour and lemon rind in the top half of a double boiler; blend in the orange juice and egg yolks, and cook over boiling water until the sauce is of a thick custard consistency. Add the butter, brushing it across the surface to prevent a skin forming on the custard whilst it cools. Chill.

Whip the cream until soft peaks form; fold into the orange custard. Carefully turn the meringue onto a serving plate and spoon the orange sauce over. Scatter the almonds over the top, and cut into slices for serving.

Sauce Variations:
Use pineapple juice, crushed and sieved strawberries, passionfruit pulp, apricot or peach purée, etc., in place of the orange juice.

Butterscotch Meringue Sponge

Serves 6

1 cooked 20 cm (8 in) sponge (see recipe, page 73)
1–2 tablespoons sweet sherry
2 tablespoons cornflour (cornstarch)
½ cup (3 oz) brown sugar
2 eggs, separated
1¼ cups (10fl oz) creamy milk
½ cup (4 oz) sugar
60 g (2 oz) butter
½ teaspoon vanilla essence
½ cup (2 oz) chopped almonds or walnuts
whipped cream, for serving

Cut the sponge horizontally into halves, and sprinkle the sweet sherry over each half. Place the bottom half onto an ovenproof platter about 8 cm (3 in) wider than the cake.

Blend the cornflour, brown sugar, egg yolks and milk in a nonstick saucepan and cook over low heat, stirring constantly, until thickened and boiling; simmer for 1 minute, remove from the heat, and cover closely to avoid a skin forming on the surface.

Place half the sugar with the butter and vanilla essence in a small pan; heat until the mixture is bubbling and commencing to brown, then quickly beat it into the hot custard. Allow the butterscotch to cool.

Preheat the oven to 200°C (400°F/Gas 6). Spread the cooled butterscotch over the bottom sponge layer and place the top layer over to form a sandwich. Scatter the chopped almonds over the surface.

Beat the egg whites until stiff and glossy; gradually add the remaining sugar, beating well between each addition to form a meringue. Spoon the meringue over the top and sides of the filled sponge, swirling to form an attractive design.

Place the platter on a biscuit tray in the hot oven and bake for 4 to 5 minutes until the meringue crust is crisp. Remove from the oven, and carefully cut into wedges for serving with the accompanying whipped cream.

DESSERTS

Mocha Macaroon Parfaits

Serves 5–6

Macaroons:

3 egg whites, unchilled

1 cup (8 oz) sugar

½ cup (1 oz) instant potato flakes, dry

1 cup (3 oz) desiccated coconut

⅛ teaspoon salt

1 teaspoon instant coffee powder

Parfaits:

¼–⅓ cup Marsala wine, coffee-flavoured

300 ml (10 fl oz) cream

90 g (3 oz) semi-sweet chocolate, grated

1 teaspoon instant coffee powder

1 tablespoon icing (confectioners') sugar

Macaroons: Preheat the oven to 180°C (350°F/Gas 4). Beat the egg whites until stiff and glossy. Gradually add the sugar, beating well after each addition. Lightly fold the potato flakes, coconut, salt and coffee powder through. Place the mixture in heaped teaspoonfuls onto greased biscuit trays and bake for 20 to 22 minutes. Allow to cool on wire racks.

Parfaits: Coarsely crush the macaroons and mix with the Marsala wine. Whip the cream until firm; divide in half, flavouring one half with the grated chocolate and coffee powder, and the other with icing sugar.

Spoon alternate amounts of crushed macaroons, chocolate cream and sweetened cream into parfait glasses. Chill until ready for serving.

Alaskan Bombe Surprise

The basic Bombe Alaska dessert is a great favourite for both family parties and special dinners. The contrast in temperatures and textures in the dessert can be very pleasing to the palate.. the hot soft meringue exterior, the icy cold cream centre and the firmer sponge cake at the base.

It is a dessert which can be easily prepared by the novice cook, using commercially prepared sponge cake and ice cream, then all the cook has to do is quickly whisk up an egg white-sugar meringue. Secrets of success are the quickness in covering the ice cream with the meringue before it has a chance to soften and melt; then the quick baking in a hot oven.

If preparing the dessert for a party it can be pre-prepared and placed, uncovered in the freezer compartment whilst the first stages of the meal are eaten. Freezing time should not be longer than one hour, then leave at room temperature for five minutes for the outside meringue to thaw slightly before quickly setting it in a hot oven.

A dramatic touch can be added by pressing empty egg-shell halves—hollow sides out—into the meringue before placing it in the oven; upon removal pour a little brandy into the shells and set alight. Carry carefully to the table for serving.

Serves 6–8

3 egg whites

¾ cup (6 oz) caster (powdered) sugar

1 20 cm (8 in) sponge (see recipe, page 74)

1 can/410 g (14 oz) sliced peaches

2 tablespoons (⅔ oz) cornflour (cornstarch)

2 tablespoons sweet sherry

1 teaspoon grated lemon rind

1 small block (approx. 3 cups) ice-cream, flavour as desired, well frozen

Preheat the oven to 200°C (400°F/Gas 6).

Beat the egg whites until stiff and glossy. Gradually beat in one-third of the sugar, then fold in all but 1 tablespoon of the remainder.

Cut or break the sponge into large bite-sized pieces and arrange half in the base of a shallow casserole. Drain the sliced peaches (reserve the syrup) and scatter them over the sponge layer.

Sauce: Combine the cornflour, sherry, lemon rind and drained peach syrup in a small saucepan, bring slowly to the boil, stirring constantly, then allow to simmer for 1 to 2 minutes.

Top the peaches with scoops of frozen ice-cream (keeping it away from the sides of the dish) and place the remaining sponge pieces over the top.

Pile the meringue over all, allowing it to come right to the sides of the dish; and sprinkle the reserved sugar over.

Place the dish on a biscuit tray in the pre-heated oven and bake for 3 to 4 minutes. Serve immediately with the hot sherry sauce.

Chocolate Strawberry Japanais

Serves 6

¼ cup (1 oz) cornflour (cornstarch)

¾ cup (3 oz) finely chopped almonds

¾ cup (6 oz) caster (powdered) sugar

4 egg whites

1–2 teaspoons lemon juice

Topping:
18–20 strawberries

1 cup (8fl oz) thickened cream, chilled

2 teaspoons icing (confectioners') sugar

chocolate-flavoured Warm Glacé Icing (see recipe, page 130)

½ cup (2 oz) flaked or slivered almonds, toasted

Preheat the oven to 150°C (300°F/Gas 2).

Combine the cornflour, chopped almonds and caster sugar; mix thoroughly.

Beat the egg whites until stiff and glossy. Fold the almond mixture through as lightly as possible, adding lemon juice for flavour.

Cover two biscuit trays with aluminium foil. Mark out an 18 cm (7 in) circle on each, and lightly brush the areas with oil. Spread a layer of the almond meringue over each one.

Bake for 50 to 60 minutes. Lift the foil carefully onto cake racks and allow the meringues to cool. When cold, turn each over and peel the foil from underneath.

Hull and coarsely chop almost all the strawberries, reserving a few for decoration. Whip the cream until stiff, sweeten with the icing sugar, and fold the chopped strawberries through; use as a filling for the two almond meringues. Drizzle the chocolate icing over the top, and decorate with the flaked almonds and reserved strawberries. Chill well before serving.

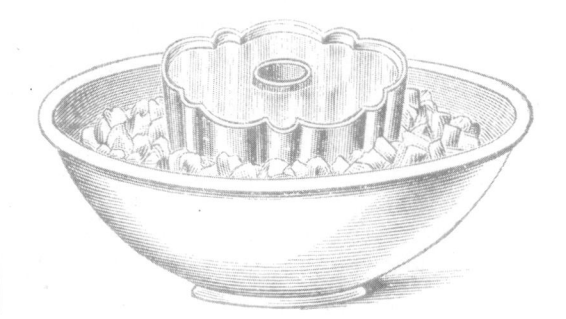

Choc-coffee Torte

Serves 8–10

5 egg whites (at room temperature)

1 cup (7 oz) caster (powdered) sugar

2 teaspoons cornflour (cornstarch)

1 packet/185 g (6 oz) chocolate chips

1 teaspoon coffee essence

Filling:
125 g (4 oz) cooking chocolate, chopped

2 egg yolks

¼ cup (2 oz) sugar

1 cup (8fl oz) made milk-coffee

1–2 tablespoons coffee liqueur

1 cup (8fl oz) thickened cream, chilled

1–2 teaspoons icing (confectioners') sugar

Preheat the oven to 140°C (275°F/Gas 1).

Beat the egg whites until stiff and glossy. Sprinkle one-third of the sugar over the surface, and beat again for 3 to 5 minutes. Combine the remaining sugar and the cornflour; sprinkle over the egg whites and fold in very gently but thoroughly—do not overmix. Fold the chocolate chips and coffee essence through.

Cover a biscuit tray with aluminium foil. Mark out a circle about 20–23 cm (8–9 in) round and brush this area with oil. Pile the meringue onto the greased foil, slightly depressing the centre of it to form a 'tart case'.

Bake in the preheated oven for 30 minutes, then reduce the oven temperature to 110°C (225°F/Gas ¼) and bake for a further 40 to 45 minutes. Remove to a draught-free area to cool.

Filling: Melt the chocolate in the top half of a double boiler over hot—not boiling—water. Combine the beaten egg yolks, sugar and milk-coffee; add this to the chocolate and cook, stirring constantly, until it is of a custard consistency. Flavour with the liqueur and set aside to cool.

Whip the cream and sweeten it with the icing sugar.

To assemble: Carefully peel the aluminium foil away from the base of the meringue and place it on a flat platter. Spoon the chocolate filling into the centre, and decorate with the whipped cream. Chill until ready to serve.

Right: Strawberry Crêpes Royale (see p. 324).

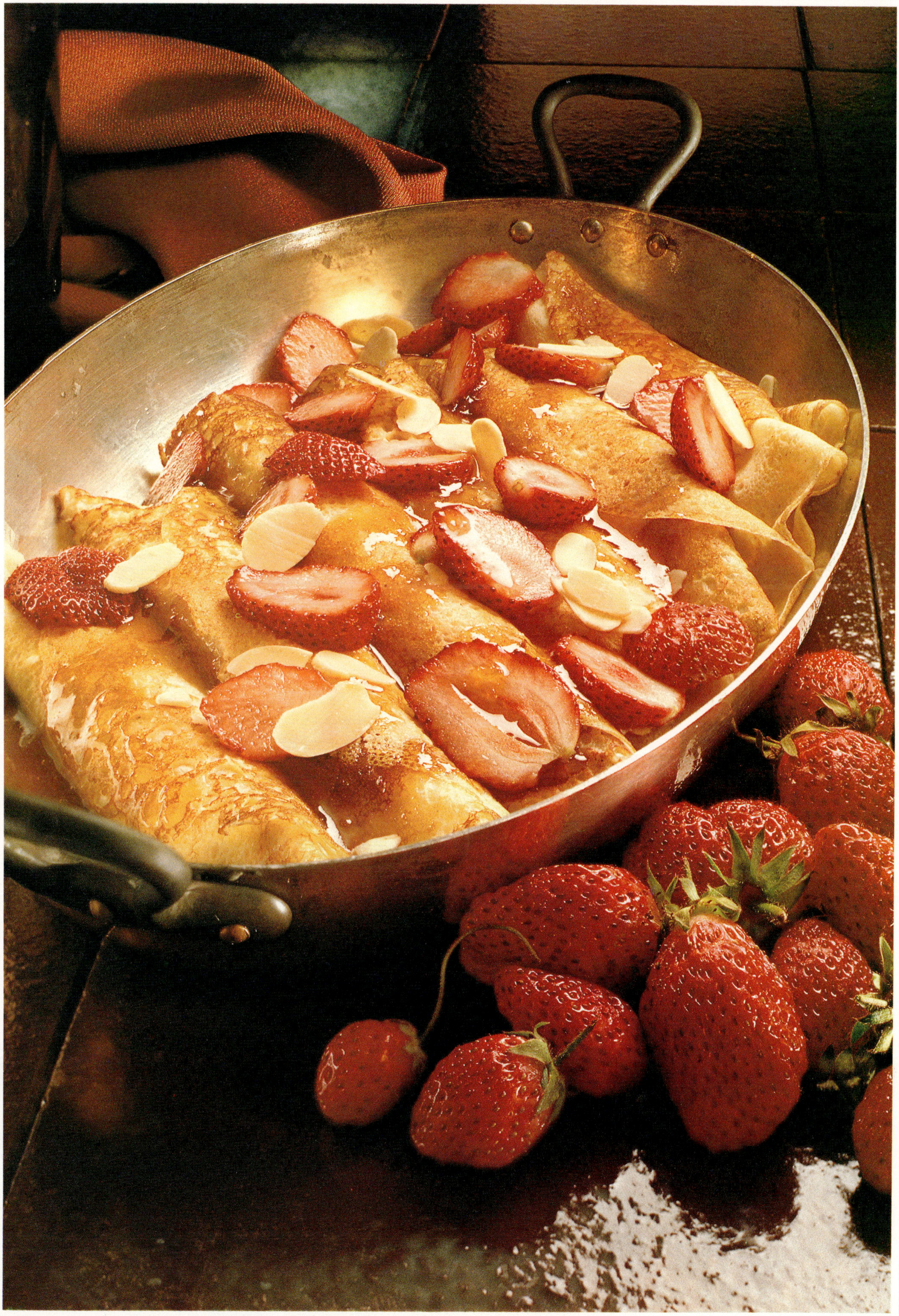

Apricot Almond Torte

Serves 6–8

1½ cups (6 oz) flour
½ teaspoon baking powder
¼ teaspoon salt
½ teaspoon ground cinnamon
125 g (4 oz) butter or margarine, chopped
¾ cup (4 oz) brown sugar
½ cup (2 oz) finely-chopped almonds
1 egg, beaten
water, if required
½ cup (6 oz) apricot conserve
1 tablespoon brandy
icing (confectioners') sugar, for dusting
whipped cream, for serving

Sift the flour, baking powder, salt and cinnamon into a bowl; add the butter and rub through with the fingertips to resemble coarse crumbs. Add the brown sugar and almonds, and mix to a dough with the egg and a little water (if required). Knead lightly into a ball, cover with aluminium foil and chill for 30 minutes.

Preheat the oven to 190°C (375°F/Gas 5). Roll out about two-thirds of the dough on a lightly-floured board to fit the base and sides of a 20–23 cm (8–9 in) flan tin. Spoon the combined apricot conserve and brandy over the surface. Roll out and cut narrow strips from the remaining dough with a pastry wheel or knife; arrange over the filling in a lattice pattern.

Bake for 30 to 35 minutes. Remove and allow to cool. Dust with icing sugar and serve in slices with whipped cream if desired.

Chocaroon Torte

Serves 8–10

185 g (6 oz) pure cooking chocolate, grated
3 egg whites
1 cup (6 oz) icing (confectioners') sugar, sifted
10–12 macaroons, crushed coarsely (see recipe, page 158)
1 teaspoon brandy or rum essence
Chocolate Filling: ¼ cup (2 fl oz) evaporated milk
3 tablespoons (¾ oz) cocoa
1 teaspoon brandy essence or rum essence
90 g (3 oz) butter or margarine, softened
1 cup (6 oz) icing (confectioners') sugar, sifted
½ cup (4 fl oz) whipped cream
Topping: chocolate curls or shavings, for decoration
icing (confectioners') sugar, for dusting

Preheat the oven to 180°C (350°F/Gas 4). Melt the chocolate over hot—not boiling—water; set aside to cool but not reset.

Beat the egg whites until soft peaks form. Gradually add the icing sugar and beat until the mixture stands in peaks. Fold in the macaroon crumbs, the cooled chocolate and the essence—do not overmix.

Cover two biscuit trays with aluminium foil. Lightly oil the areas of two 20 cm (8 in) circles, and spoon the meringue mixture onto each circle.

Bake for 20 to 22 minutes. Open the oven door and leave for 5 minutes, before removing to allow to cool slightly. Carefully peel the foil away from the meringues and set them aside until cold.

Combine the evaporated milk and cocoa in a nonstick saucepan and slowly heat, stirring constantly, until well blended. Add the essence, and remove from the heat to allow to cool slightly.

Cream the butter and icing sugar together. Gradually add the chocolate mixture, stirring well, then fold in the whipped cream.

Spread the filling onto one of the meringues and place the other meringue on top. Decorate the top with chocolate curls or shavings and dust a little icing sugar over. Chill until ready to serve.

SOUFFLÉS

Apricot Almond Soufflé

Serves 5–6

250 g (8 oz) dried apricots

1½ cups (12fl oz) water

2 tablespoons lemon juice

⅓ cup (3 oz) sugar

2 eggs, separated

3 egg whites

½ cup (2 oz) chopped, toasted almonds

extra sugar, for dusting

whipped cream, for serving

Cover the dried apricots with the water and lemon juice and stand for 30 minutes.

Preheat the oven to 180°C (350°F/Gas 4).

Bring the apricots slowly to the boil, then simmer until the apricots are softened. Remove from the heat, allow to stand for 10 minutes, then purée in an electric processor or press through a fine sieve. Whilst still warm, add half of the sugar and the egg yolks and beat well.

Whisk the 5 egg whites until soft peaks form. Add the remaining sugar and whisk well, then lightly fold into the apricot purée with the almonds—do not overmix.

Prepare a soufflé dish or straight-sided casserole by greasing well and dusting with extra sugar. Add the apricot mixture, being careful not to disturb the coating on the dish. Dust a little sugar over the surface.

Bake for 30 to 35 minutes. Serve at once, with whipped cream if desired.

Chocolate Marsala Creams

Serves 5–6

3 cups (7 oz) sponge cake crumbs

¼ cup Marsala wine or sweet sherry

¾ cup (6fl oz) cream

125 g (4 oz) butter or margarine, softened

4 eggs, separated

½ cup (4 oz) caster (powdered) sugar

½ cup (2 oz) ground almonds

125 g (4 oz) pure cooking chocolate, melted

whipped cream, for serving

Place the cake crumbs in a bowl and sprinkle the Marsala wine over; add the cream and stir to mix through, then stand for 30 to 40 minutes to soften the crumbs well.

Preheat the oven to 160°C (325°F/Gas 3).

Beat the butter until creamy. Add the egg yolks and half of the sugar, and beat well. Mix the ground almonds and cooled chocolate through.

Whisk the egg whites until soft peaks form. Add the remaining sugar and beat well, before lightly folding into the crumb-chocolate mixture—do not overmix. Divide the mixture into five or six small soufflé dishes or custard cups; place the dishes in a baking pan and add 3–4 cups of hot water into the pan.

Carefully place in the preheated oven and bake for 45 to 50 minutes until just set. Remove, allow to stand until just warm, and serve with whipped cream if desired.

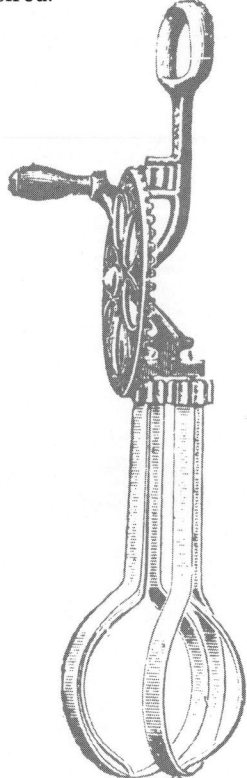

Miniature Fruit Soufflés

Serves 6–8

250 g (8 oz) ripe stoned fruit—peaches, apricots, etc.

½ cup (4 oz) caster (powdered) sugar

6 egg whites (at room temperature)

sweet biscuit crumbs, for coating

2 tablespoons brandy fruit liqueur

1–2 tablespoons icing (confectioners') sugar

Preheat the oven to 220°C (425°F/Gas 7).

Peel and chop the fruit coarsely, and rub through a sieve for a final weight of 185 g (6 oz); mix with the caster sugar. Beat the egg whites until very stiff and glossy. Fold in the sweetened fruit purée as lightly as possible.

Grease six to eight small soufflé dishes, and dust the insides with fine sweet biscuit crumbs. Spoon equal portions of the fruit mixture into each one. Place the dishes on a biscuit tray.

Bake for 8 to 9 minutes. Remove from the oven, and serve hot or cold with a sprinkling of brandy liqueur and a dusting of icing sugar over the top.

Note: If using canned stoned fruits, drain well (both before and after sieving) and decrease the sugar slightly for the sweetened varieties.

Hazelnut Puffs

Serves 4–5

3 eggs, separated

⅛ teaspoon salt

½ cup (4 oz) sugar

90 g (3 oz) pure cooking chocolate, melted

1 teaspoon brandy or rum essence

1 cup (4 oz) finely-chopped hazelnuts

¼ cup (2½ oz) chopped glacé cherries

additional finely-chopped hazelnuts, for coating

whipped cream, for decoration

chocolate curls, for decoration

Preheat the oven to 180°C (350°F/Gas 4).

Whisk the egg whites until stiff and glossy. Gradually add the salt and sugar, beating well after each addition.

Beat the egg yolks until thickened. Fold in the cooled chocolate, essence, hazelnuts and cherries; then lightly fold the egg white mixture through.

Prepare 4 or 5 custard cups or straight-sided moulds by greasing and then dusting with finely-chopped hazelnuts. Divide the dessert mixture into each one, being careful not to disturb the sides. Arrange the custard cups in a baking pan and pour 2–3 cups of hot water into the base.

Carefully place in the oven, cover loosely with aluminium foil and bake for 15 to 17 minutes. Serve warm, with a topping of whipped cream and chocolate curls for decoration.

Cream Cheese Soufflé

Serves 5–6

185 g (6 oz) packaged cream cheese, softened

¾ cup (6 fl oz) sour cream

2 tablespoons (2 oz) honey

½ teaspoon cinnamon or nutmeg

4 eggs, separated

1 egg white

1½ tablespoons (1 oz) sugar

1½ tablespoons finely chopped walnuts

additional 60 g (2 oz) packaged cream cheese

additional ¼ cup (2 fl oz) sour cream

additional 1 tablespoon (1 oz) honey

Preheat the oven to 160°C (325°F/Gas 3). Push the cream cheese and sour cream together through a fine sieve. Add the honey, cinnamon and egg yolks, and beat well.

Whisk all the egg whites until soft peaks form. Add the sugar and whisk well, then lightly fold into the cream cheese mixture—do not overmix.

Prepare a soufflé dish or straight-sided casserole by greasing well and dusting with the finely chopped nuts. Spoon the soufflé mixture into the dish, taking care not to disturb the coating on the sides.

Bake for 40 to 45 minutes. Serve at once, with a cream made by combining the extra cream cheese, sour cream and honey together.

Right: **Miniature Fruit Soufflés** (see above).

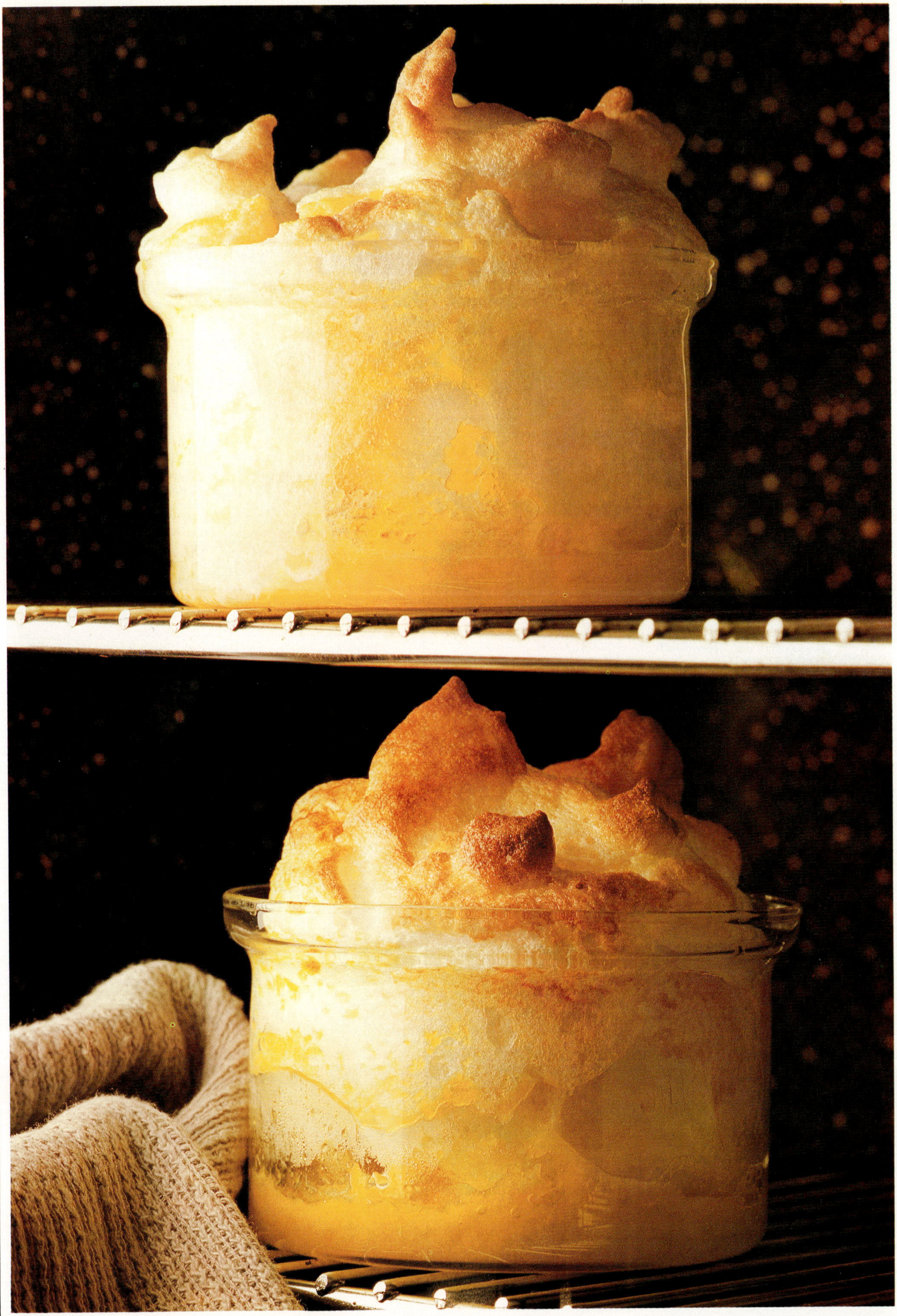

BAKED CUSTARDS, CREAMS

Fruity Rice Custard

Serves 5–6

2 cups cooked rice (³/₄ cup (5 oz) uncooked)
³/₄ cup (4 oz) stoned and chopped dates
¼ cup (3 oz) honey or golden syrup (light corn syrup)
½–1 teaspoon ground nutmeg
2 eggs, beaten
1¼ cups (10fl oz) milk
¼ cup (2fl oz) condensed sweetened milk
whipped cream, for serving

Preheat the oven to 160°C (325°F/Gas 3). Arrange the rice, dates and honey or golden syrup in layers in a well-greased casserole, beginning and ending with rice. Sprinkle nutmeg over the surface. Combine the beaten eggs with the fresh and condensed milks, and drizzle over the layered ingredients.

Bake for 40 to 50 minutes or until the custard is softly set. Remove from the oven and serve warm, with whipped cream.

Note: Baking time may be reduced by 10 to 15 minutes if the rice is freshly cooked and hot when arranged in the casserole.

Apricot Custard Cream

Serves 5–6

½–³/₄ cup (5–7 oz) thick apricot conserve
600 ml (20fl oz) milk
300 ml (10fl oz) evaporated milk
3 whole eggs
1 egg yolk
¼ cup (2 oz) sugar
1 teaspoon vanilla essence
1 cup (8fl oz) thickened cream, chilled
2–3 tablespoons grated chocolate
1–2 tablespoons flaked toasted almonds

Preheat the oven to 150°C (300°F/Gas 2). Spread the apricot conserve to a depth of about 1 cm (¼–½ in) over the base of a well-greased casserole.

Heat the milk and evaporated milk in a nonstick saucepan until scalding. Beat the whole eggs, egg yolk, sugar and vanilla essence well. Gradually add about one-quarter of the milk to the egg mixture, whisking constantly; pour all back into the remaining milk, stirring well.

Strain carefully over the apricot conserve; cover the casserole loosely with aluminium foil.

Bake for 1 hour or until the custard is set. Remove, allow to cool and chill.

Whip the cream until stiff, fold in the grated chocolate, and spoon it over the chilled custard. Scatter the toasted almonds over the surface, and serve.

Petits Pots de Crème

Serves 5–6

1½ cups (12fl oz) milk
½ cup (4fl oz) cream
4 egg yolks
1 whole egg
¼ cup (2 oz) sugar
1–1½ teaspoons brandy essence or rum essence
60 g (2 oz) pure cooking chocolate, grated
whipped cream, for decoration

Preheat the oven to 160°C (325°F/Gas 3).

Combine the milk and cream in a small nonstick saucepan and heat slowly until scalding. Strain into a bowl.

Beat the egg yolks, the egg and sugar well. Gradually add about one-quarter of the milk, then pour all back into the remaining milk, stirring constantly. Flavour with the essence and add the grated chocolate; stir to dissolve.

Pour the chocolate mixture into five or six small custard cups and stand these in a baking pan containing 3–4 cups of hot water; cover loosely with aluminium foil.

Bake for 50 to 60 minutes or until the custard is set. Remove, allow to cool and then chill. Serve with a rosette of whipped cream on each little pot.

DESSERTS

Cottage Cheese Cocottes

Serves 5–6

2 eggs, firm-cooked and cooled
375 g (12 oz) cottage cheese
3 eggs, separated
1 cup (7 oz) caster (powdered) sugar
60 g (2 oz) butter or margarine, melted
¼ cup (1 oz) self-raising flour
½ cup (3 oz) sultanas
1 teaspoon grated lemon rind
whipped cream, for serving

Preheat the oven to 160°C (325°F/Gas 3). Grease five or six individual cocotte or custard cups.

Shell the firm-cooked eggs and press through a fine sieve with the cottage cheese; mix well.

Beat the egg yolks and sugar until thick, add the cooled butter; mix into the cottage cheese, and beat well. Fold in the sifted flour, sultanas and lemon rind.

Beat the egg whites until well foamed and lightly fold through the cottage cheese mixture. Spoon the mixture into the prepared containers and arrange them on a biscuit tray.

Bake for 35 to 40 minutes, or until set. Remove, allow to stand for 2 to 3 minutes, then run a knife around the sides of each dish before carefully turning out onto a dessert plate. Serve warm, with cream if desired.

Cottage Custard Cream

Serves 6

3 eggs
¼ cup (1 oz) cornflour (cornstarch)
½ cup (4 oz) sugar
375 g (12 oz) creamed cottage cheese
1¼ cups (10 fl oz) milk
300 ml (10 fl oz) cream, whipped
2 teaspoons grated orange rind (optional)
18–20 strawberries

Preheat the oven to 180°C (350°F/Gas 4).

Beat the eggs with the cornflour and sugar until thick and fluffy. Gradually add the cottage cheese and milk, beating well. Fold in half of the whipped cream and the orange rind (or use other flavourings as desired). Pour into a greased casserole.

Place the casserole in a baking pan containing 2–3 cups of hot water and bake for 50 to 60 minutes until just set. Remove from the oven, allow to cool, and chill. Serve with the sliced strawberries and remaining whipped cream.

Apricot Yoghurt Custard

Serves 6–8

600 ml (20 fl oz) unflavoured yoghurt
3 eggs, beaten
1 cup (8 fl oz) milk
¼ cup (2 oz) sugar
1 tablespoon (⅓ oz) cornflour (cornstarch)
1¼ cups cooked and drained riced (90 g (3 oz) uncooked)
6 canned apricot halves, chopped coarsely
grated nutmeg, for sprinkling

Preheat the oven to 180°C (350°F/Gas 4). Combine the yoghurt, eggs and milk, beating well. Blend in the combined sugar and cornflour.

Spread the rice over the base of a well-greased casserole, and arrange the apricot pieces over; sprinkle with nutmeg as desired. Carefully spoon the yoghurt mixture over the top. Place the casserole in a baking pan containing 2–3 cups of hot water.

Bake for 55 to 60 minutes or until set. Serve warm or cold.

Old-fashioned Baked Custard

Serves 6

3 eggs, beaten

¼ cup (2 oz) sugar

1 tablespoon full-cream milk powder

1 teaspoon vanilla essence

2½ cups (20 fl oz) milk, warmed

½ teaspoon grated nutmeg

Preheat the oven to 160°C (325°F/Gas 3).

Beat the eggs, sugar, powdered milk and vanilla, only until well blended but not frothy in appearance. Add the milk and mix through.

Strain into a well-greased casserole and place the casserole in a baking pan containing 2–3 cups of hot water. Sprinkle the nutmeg over the surface.

Bake for 50 to 60 minutes, or until a knife inserted in the centre of the custard comes away clean. Remove, allow to cool and chill as desired.

Note: If baking the custard with other foods in the oven, the temperature may be varied slightly. Do not bake at a temperature higher than 180°C (350°F/Gas 4), or the custard may separate or curdle.

Variations

Rice:
Add 2–3 tablespoons of partially cooked, drained rice—omitting 1 egg.

Pasta:
Add 2–3 tablespoons of partially cooked, drained pasta—omitting 1 egg.

Chocolate:
Add ½ cup (½–1 oz) of grated chocolate or 2 tablespoons of drinking chocolate.

Dried Fruits:
Add ½ cup (3 oz) of sultanas, raisins or currants, or chopped dried apricots or dates, to the basic mixture.

Caramel:
Line the base of the casserole with a boiled caramel—1 cup (8 oz) sugar and ½ cup (4 fl oz) water—before pouring the custard mixture over. Unmould before serving.

Bread and Butter:
Arrange 2–3 slices of buttered bread over the surface of the custard before baking. Scatter extra sugar over the top if desired.

Golden Cream:
Replace 1 cup (8 fl oz) of the milk with evaporated milk or cream, and substitute golden syrup (light corn syrup) for the sugar.

Honey Spice:
Use honey in place of the sugar, and stir 1 teaspoon mixed spices through the custard before baking.

Coconut Superbe:
Substitute condensed sweetened milk for the sugar and add 2–3 tablespoons desiccated coconut to the milk mixture.

Custard Brûlée:
Bake the custard in a flameproof casserole as usual; allow to cool and then chill well. Sprinkle a generous layer of sugar over the top of the custard and place under a hot griller (broiler) until the sugar melts and forms a toffee glaze; serve at once.

Note: Insulate the edge of the casserole with a multiple layer of crushed aluminium foil if required.

Golden Custard Slice

Serves 8–10

250 g (8 oz) ginger-flavoured biscuits (cookies)

½ cup (1½ oz) desiccated coconut

185 g (6 oz) butter or margarine, melted

Custard:
½ cup (5 oz) golden syrup (light corn syrup)

1 teaspoon mixed spices

1½ cups cooked and mashed pumpkin (375 g (12 oz) raw)

½ cup (3 oz) sultanas

3 eggs, separated

2 tablespoons sweet sherry

250 ml (8 fl oz) sour cream

whipped cream, for serving

Crush the biscuits to fine crumbs, and combine with the coconut and cooled butter. Press onto the base and about halfway up the sides of a well-greased 20 cm (8 in) springform tin. Chill for 30 minutes.

Preheat the oven to 200°C (400°F/Gas 6). Combine the golden syrup, spices, cold pumpkin, sultanas and egg yolks and sweet sherry; mix well. Gradually add the sour cream. Then fold in stiffly beaten egg whites, mixing very lightly. Carefully pour into the biscuit crumb crust.

Bake in the preheated oven for 10 minutes, then reduce the oven temperature to 160°C (325°F/Gas 2) and bake for a further 50 to 55 minutes or until the custard is set. Remove, allow to cool and chill. For serving, cut into slices, and serving with whipped cream if desired.

Right: From top: Caramel Baked Custard (see above); Old-fashioned Baked Custard (see above); Spiced Orange Delite (see p. 318).

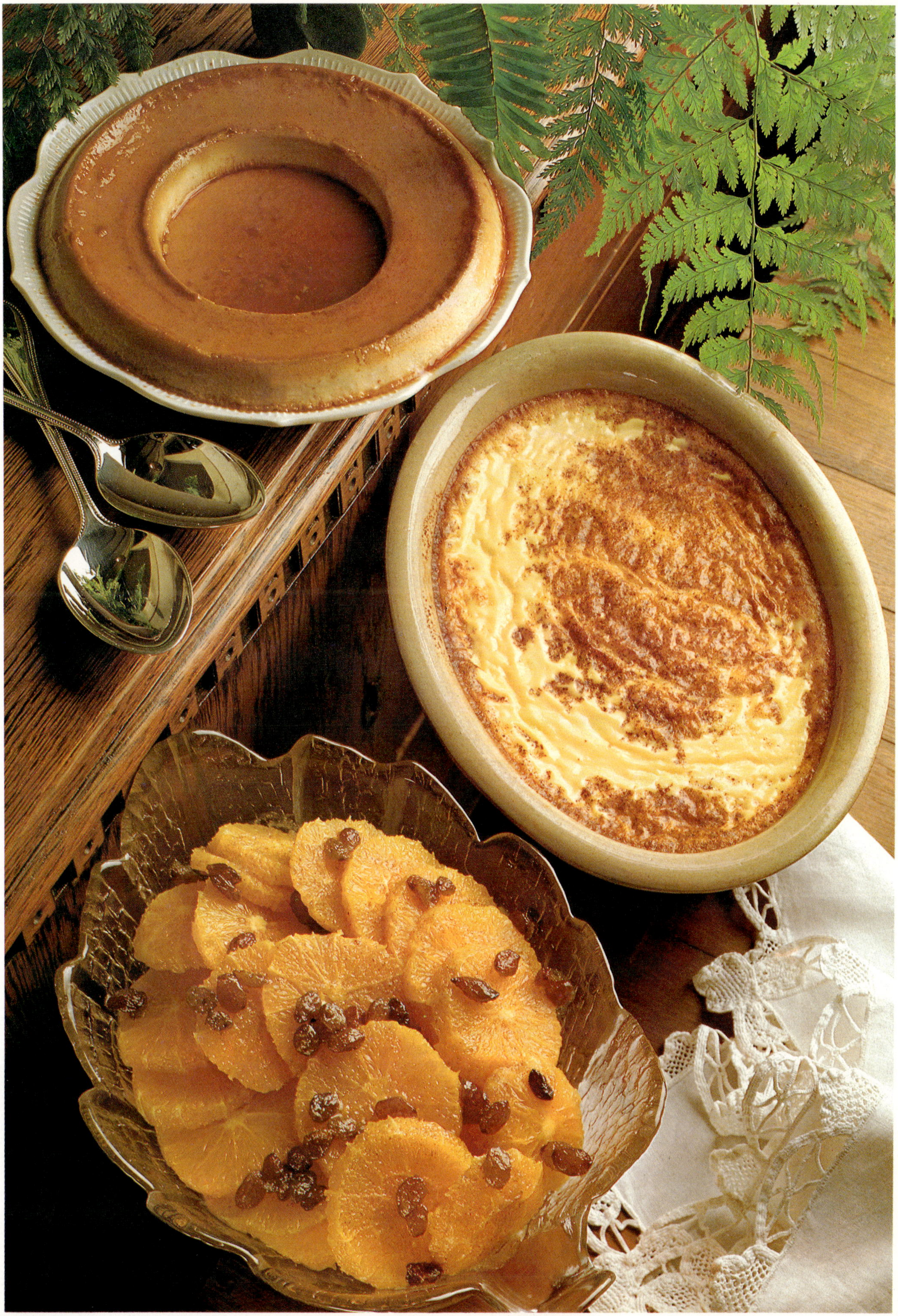

INDEX

A

Almond
 Almond Butter Ring, 78
 Almond Cream Roll, 342
 Almond Crust, 196
 Almond Filling, 212
 Almond and Orange Buns, 41
 Almond Pastry Cream, 146
 Almond and Poppy Seed Pie, 266
 Apricot Almond Soufflé, 357
 Apricot Almond Tart, 233
 Apricot Almond Torte, 356
 Cherry Almond Pie, 280
 Chocolate Almond Cream, 148
 Frangipane Tartlets, 249
 Gâteau de Pithiviers Feuilleté, 266
 Macaroons, 158
 Marzipan, 133
 Mock Almond Paste, 133
 Orange Almond Biscuits, 168
 Orange Almond Tart, 246
 Peach Tart with Almond Cream, 248
 Shortbread Pie, 278
 Sliced Almond Tart, 246
 Swedish Mazarin Tarts, 252
Anchovy Loaf, 26
Aniseed Cookies, German, 160
Anzac Biscuits, Val's, 163
Apple
 Apple Amber, 282
 Apple and Cider Tart, 229
 Apple Marmalade, 212
 Apple Rings in Pastry, 204
 Apple and Rum Custard Tart, 240
 Apple Streusel Pie, 284
 Apple Surprises, 162
 Bedfordshire Clanger, 306
 Coconut Apple Slice, 209
 Danish Apple Dessert, 324
 Dutch Apple and Mincemeat Pie, 284
 French Apple Slice, 225
 Fresh Apple Cake, 54
 Fruited Apple Charlotte, 318
 Granny's Apple Cake, 92
 Latticed Apple Cake, 102
 Lemon Apple Sponge, 333
 Mrs Simpson's Apple Pie, 282
 Normandy Apple Tart, 232
 Raspberry and Apple Tart, 241
 Rhubarb Apple Cobbler, 325
 Rhubarb Apple Crunch, 328
 Rosy Apple Crumble, 325
 Sliced Apple Pudding, 320
 Spicy Apple Drops, 117
 Stuffed Apples, 322
 Tarte Tatin, 234
 Traditional Apple Strudel, 208
Apricot
 Apricot Almond Soufflé, 357
 Apricot and Almond Tart, 233
 Apricot Almond Torte, 356
 Apricot Cream Bars, 96
 Apricot Crunchies, 122
 Apricot Custard Cream, 360
 Apricot Delights, 205
 Apricots in Nightdress, 204
 Apricot Nut Loaf, 89
 Apricot Pie, 274
 Apricot Rice Caramel, 341
 Apricot Sparkle, 326
 Apricot Tang Slice, 169
 Apricot Yoghurt Custard, 361
 Baked 'Saucer' Cakes, 344
 Brandied Apricot Glaze, 149
 Layered Apricot Crumble, 328
 Lemon and Apricot Bread, 58
 Swiss Apricot Trifle, 336
 Walnut Crumble Apricot Cake, 56
Asparagus
 Asparagus Flan, 298
 Chicken and Asparagus Flan, 304

B

Babas, Mopck Orange, 345
Bacon
 Bacon and Cheese Pie, 300
 Bacon Loaf, 26
Bagels, 36–7
Bakewell Squares, 205
Bakewell Tart, 234
Baking blind, hints, 229, 257
Baklava, Healthy, 218
Banana
 Banana-Bender's Biscuits, 160
 Brazilian Bananas, 320
 Banana Butter Cake, 76
 Banana Chiffon Pie, 271
 Banana Patty Cakes, 114
 Banana and Pineapple Tart, 232
 Frosted Banana Cream Cake, 80
 Glazed Banana Bread, 65
 Spiced Banana Scones, 62
Béchamel Sauce, 308
Bedfordshire Clanger, 306
Berry
 Berry Pie, 285
 see also Raspberry; Redcurrant; Strawberry
Biscuit(s)
 biscuit making hints, 153
 Biscuit Pastry, 196
 filled biscuits, 173–4
 savoury biscuits, 154–7
 sweet biscuits, 158–73
 see also Cookies
Bizcochos, 156
Black Bottom Tart, 238
Black Bun, Scottish, 222
Blue Ribbon Sponge Sandwich, 74
Bombe Surprise, Alaskan, 353
Bran
 Bran Crust, 300
 Coffee and Bran Tart, 244
 Fresh Pear and Bran Cake, 57
 Sultana Bran Cakes, 120
Brandy
 Brandied Apricot Glaze, 149
 Brandied Coffee Cream, 144
 Brandy Cottage Cheese Filling, 174
Brazil Nut Stars, 166
Bread, 12–45, 58, 62, 64–5
 Bread and Butter Custard, 362
 Bread Cheesecakes, 209
 Bread Knots, 16
 bread making, 13–15, 48
 Chocolate Bread Pudding, 336
 Flat Bread, 25, 29
 see also Buns; Rolls
Brioche, 37
Brownies, Yankee, 176
Buns
 Almond and Orange Buns, 41
 Chelsea Buns, 44–5
 Devonshire Splits, 34
 Hot Cross Buns, 34
 Scottish Black Bun, 222
Butter
 Brazilian Butter Cream, 148
 butter cakes, 49, 76–81
 Butter Cream Filling, 174
 Buttered Cottage Twists, 94
Butterfly Cakes, 114
Buttermilk
 Buttermilk Chess Pie, 260
 Buttermilk Fruit Loaf, 92
 Pennsylvania Buttermilk Cookies, 164
 Spiced Buttermilk Cake, 93
Butter Nut Frosting, 135
Butterscotch
 Butterscotch Meringue Pie, 272
 Butterscotch Meringue Sponge, 352
 Coconut Butterscotch Cookies, 161
 Crunchy Butterscotch Frosting, 136
 Upside-down Pudding, 338

C

Cakes
 cake baking, 48, 69–70
 butter cakes, 49, 76–81
 celebration cakes, 104–9
 chocolate and coffee cakes, 81–7
 dessert cakes, 342–4
 freezing cakes, 70, 113
 fruit cakes, 52–4, 58, 64–5, 104–9
 layer cakes, 73–4, 84, 96–102
 luncheon cakes, 88–96
 marble cakes, 76, 114
 package mixes, 69–70
 small cakes, 113–25
 sponges, 73–4
 tea cakes, 44, 49–60
 see also Gâteau
Candy Cups, 125
Caramel
 Apricot Rice Caramel, 341
 Caramel Custard, 362
 Caramel Frosting, 101
 Caramel Layer Cake, 101
 Caramel Walnut Frosting, 136
 Pecan Caramel Tart, 245
Caraway
 Caraway Muscatel Scones, 60
 Caraway Seed Cake, 52
 Russian Caraway Triangles, 156
Carrot
 Carrot Cream Cheese Frosting, 136
 Carrot Flan, 292
 Oatmeal Carrot Cookies, 177
 Steam-baked Carrot Ring, 334
 Wholemeal Carrot Cake, 95
Cereal desserts, 341–2
Challah Braid, 24
Cheese
 Cheese Bread, 28
 Cheese Choux Pastry, 194
 Cheese and Mushroom Potato Pastry Flan, 292
 Cheese Pastry, 185
 Cheese Pies, 261
 Cheese and Spinach Slice, 296
 Cheese Straws, 154
 Cheesy Tuna Puffs, 301
 Corn 'n' Cheese Flan, 292
 Doctor's Favourite Savoury Tarts, 300
 Onion and Edam Cheese Flan, 293
 Rich Bacon and Cheese Pie, 300
 Sesame Seed Cheese Buttons, 154
 Sri Lankan Curry Crisps, 154
 Tyropita, 300
Cheese, Cottage
 Brandy Cottage Cheese Filling, 174
 Christmas Cottage Cheese Pie, 261
 Cottage Cheese Cocottes, 361
Cheese, Cream
 Cream Cheese Frosting, 88, 136
 Cream Cheese and Jelly Puffs, 216
 Cream Cheese Pastry, 185
 Cream Cheese Peach Pie, 261
 Cream Cheese Soufflé, 358
Cheese, Ricotta
 Ricotta Pie, 261
 Ricotta Tarts, 250
Cheesecakes, 209, 216, 220, 329–32
Chelsea Buns, 44–5
Cherry
 Black Cherry Strudel, 208
 Black Cherry Tart, 230
 Cherry Almond Butter Cake, 76
 Cherry Almond Pie, 280
 Cherry Crystal Ring, 80
 Cherry Frosting, 134
 Cherry Lemon Ring, 93
 Cherry Liqueur Glaze, 149
 Cherry Mallow 'Pie', 321
 Cherry Patty Cakes, 114
 Cherry Pie, 258
 Cherry Rolls, 209
 Cherry Seed Cake, 80
 French Cherry Tart, 230
 Meringue-topped Cherry Pie, 280
 Sour Cherry Cream Pudding, 332
Chestnut Chocolate Ring, 344

INDEX

Chicken
  Chicken and Asparagus Flan, 304
  Chicken and Parsley Pie, 304
Chiffon pies, 269–71
Chocolate
  Aunty Mary's Chocolate Roll, 81
  Black Bottom Tart, 238
  Chestnut Chocolate Ring, 344
  Chocaroon Torte, 356
  Choc-Coffee Butter Cake, 77
  Choc-Coffee Cream, 144
  Choc-Coffee Rounds, 116
  Choc-Coffee Torte, 354
  Choc-nut Patty Cakes, 114
  Chocolate Almond Cream, 148
  Chocolate Bread Pudding, 336
  Chocolate Butter Cake, 49, 76, 78
  Chocolate Butter Cream, 144
  Chocolate Caraque, 84
  Chocolate Chip Cookies, 177
  Chocolate Choux Pastry, 194
  Chocolate Cream Cheese Frosting, 136
  Chocolate Cream Pie, 281
  Chocolate Cream Torte, 100
  Chocolate Crunch Pie, 272
  Chocolate Custard, 362
  Chocolate Éclairs, 225
  Chocolate frostings, 78, 134, 137
  Chocolate Fudge Cake, 84
  Chocolate Glacé Icing, 130
  Chocolate Glaze, 149
  Chocolate Liqueur Filling, 140
  Chocolate Marsala Creams, 357
  Chocolate Marshmallow Biscuits, 172
  Chocolate Mint Fingers, 170
  Chocolate Mock Cream Filling, 140
  Chocolate Peppermint Gloss, 137
  Chocolate Praline Pie, 262
  Chocolate Prune Cake, 54
  Chocolate Puff Pastry, 188
  Chocolate Rum Vienna Cream, 144
  Chocolate Snowdrift, 337
  Chocolate Strawberry Japanais, 354
  Chocolate Velvet Cake, 85
  Chocolate Vienna Cream, 144
  Chocolate Walnut Tart, 244
  Chocomallows, 121
  Coconut Chocolate Drop Cookies, 164
  French Mint Pie, 264
  Gâteau Elizabethe, 344
  Jaffa Chiffon Pie, 270
  Marbled Chocolate Cheesecake, 330
  Old Fashioned Chocolate Cookies, 177
  One-two-three Chocolate Pudding, 333
  Petits Pots de Crème, 360
  Rum Pie, 265
  Sherried Chocolate Ring, 82
  Special Crusted Chocolate Cake, 83
  Speedy Chocolate Fudge Dessert, 336
  Whisked Chocolate Slice, 83
Choux Pastry, 194
Christmas cakes, 104–9
Cider Honey Luncheon Cake, 90
Cinnamon
  Cinnamon Cream Cheese Frosting, 136
  Cinnamon Cream Frosting, 80
  Cinnamon Shapes, 166
  Cinnamon Tea Cake, 50
Citrus
  Citrus Biscuits, 168
  Citrus Butter Cake, 77
  see also Grapefruit; Lemon; Lime; Orange
Cloverleaf Rolls, 17
Cobbers, 325–8
Coconut
  Coco-Lemon Cakes, 117
  Coconut Apple Slice, 209
  Coconut Butter Cake, 76
  Coconut Butterscotch Cookies, 161
  Coconut Cake, 50
  Coconut Cheesecakes, 216
  Coconut Chocolate Drop Cookies, 164
  Coconut Cream Pie, 264
  Coconut Macaroons, 160
  Coconut Slice, 214
  Coconut Superbe, 362
  Coconut Topping, 138
  Coco-Pine Cream, 145
  Greek Coconut Cake, 64
Cod Pie, Smoked, 302
Coffee
  Brandied Coffee Cream, 144
  Caribbean Coffee Cake, 84
  Choc-Coffee Cream, 144
  Choc-Coffee Rounds, 116
  Choc-Coffee Torte, 354
  Coffee and Bran Tart, 244
  Coffee Cake, 52
  Coffee Cream Pie, 281
  Coffee Frosting, 134
  Coffee Fudge Frosting, 135
  Coffee Glacé Icing, 130
  Coffee Icing, 252
  Coffee Lace Wafers, 170
  Coffee Nut Cakes, 120
  Coffee Nut Cookies, 164
  Coffee and Peppermint Cake, 56
  Coffee Vienna Cream, 144
  Crumble Top Coffee Cake, 86
  Hazelnut Coffee Cake, 86
Cognac Drops, 173
Continental Butter Ring Cake, 77
Cookies
  American cookies, 176–7
  Swedish Christmas Cookies, 158
  see also Biscuits
Coriander Cakes, Sweet Shrewsbury, 161
Corn
  Corn Bread, 22
  Corn 'n' Cheese Flan, 292
  Cornflake Crisps, 114
  Cornish Pasties, Traditional, 305
Cottage Cheese, see Cheese, Cottage
Cottage Custard Cream, 361
Cottage Loaf, 18
Cracked Wheat Bread, 18
Crackers, 157, 161
Cranberry Bread, 41
Cream
  Continental Cream Sponge, 74
  cream desserts, 360–2
  cream fillings, 129, 144–8
  Cream Horns, 206
  Cream Puffs, 206, 218
  mock cream fillings, 140–1
  see also Crème
Cream, Sour
  Scandinavian Sour Cream Biscuits, 166
  Sour Cream Frosting, 136
  Sour Cream Pastry, 189
Cream Cheese see Cheese, Cream
Crème
  Crème Brûlée Pie, 268
  Crème Pâtissière, 146, 212
  Petits Pots de Crème, 360
  see also Cream
Crêpes Royale, Strawberry, 324
Crescent Rolls, 16
Croissants, 36
Crumbles, 325–8
Crumpets, 42
Crunches, 325–8
Crunchies, Queensland, 160
Crusts, Crumb, 193
Cuba Libre Tart, 248
Currant
  Currant Fingers, 217
  Currant Tea Loaf, 89
Curry Crisps, Sri Lankan, 154
Custards, 360–2
  baked custards, 317, 362
  Custard Brûlée, 362
  custard creams, 360–1
  Custard Pie, 260
  English Custard Tart, 242
  Golden Custard Slice, 362

D

Daiquiri Tart, 239
Damper, 62
Danish pastries, 210–13
Date
  Crusted Date Squares, 124
  Date Butter Cake, 76
  Date and Nut Slice, 85
  Date Oatmeal Pastry Slices, 217
  Date and Peanut Ragamuffins, 124
  Date Pillows, 163
  Date Surprise, 114
  Date and Walnut Filling, 141
  One-dish Date Pudding, 334
  Orange Date Square, 345
  Walnut Date Roll, 90
  Wholemeal Date Scones, 60
  Wholemeal Date Slice, 222
Devonshire Splits, 34
Dundee Cake, 105

E

Ecclefechan, 214
Eccles Cakes, 214
Éclairs, Chocolate, 225
Egg Nog Pie, 260
Emergency Pie, 301

F

Fairy Cakes 1.2.3., 125
Fan Tans, 38
Farmhouse Loaves, 18
Fig
  Fig Tart, 234
  Ginger Fig Scones, 60
  Greek Honey Fig Biscuits, 165
  Turkish Fig Bar, 57
Filbert Tarts, 252
Fillings, 129
  biscuit fillings, 174
  cake fillings, 140–1
  pastry fillings, 212–13
Fish pies, 302
Flower Pot Loaves, 22
Fondants, 129, 142
Frangipane Pie, 265
French Bread, 20
Frostings, 129, 134–7
  Caramel Frosting, 101
  Chocolate Frosting, 78
  Cinnamon Cream Frosting, 80
  Cream Cheese Frosting, 88
  Mocha Frosting, 100–101
  Orange Frosting, 95
  Peanut Butter Frosting, 102
Fruit
  A Light Fruit Cake, 53
  Brandied Ale Fruit Cake, 109
  Buttermilk Fruit Loaf, 92
  Canadian Fruit and Nut Drops, 165
  Dried Fruit Custard, 362
  Dried Fruit Filling, 174
  Dundee Cake, 105
  Easy Fruit Bread, 64
  Festive Fruit Wreath, 104
  fruit cakes, directions, 106–7
  Fruit Cream Puffs, 218
  fruit desserts, 317–28
  Fruited Muesli Dessert, 342
  Fruit and Nut Bread, 33
  Fruit Pasta Pudding, 340
  Fruit Pudding Cups, 321
  Fruit Tart, 233
  Fruit Tartlets, 250
  Fruit and Vegetable Cake, 108
  Glazed Fruit Shortcake, 345
  Golden Fruit Cake, 105
  Miniature Fruit Soufflés, 358
  Panettone, 40
  Rich Fruit Cake, 104
  Stollen, 45
  see also individual fresh and dried fruits

365

THE COMPLETE BOOK OF BAKING

Fruitmince
　Fruitmince Cheesecake, 329
　Fruitmince Pecan Ring, 109
　see also Mincemeat

G

Garlic Bread, 26
Gâteau
　Gâteau Elizabethe, 344
　Gâteau de Pithiviers Feuilleté, 266
　Genoise Gâteau, 98
　Rich Mocha Cream Gâteau, 100
　see also Cakes
Gem cakes, 120–1
Gem Scones, 61
Ginger
　Ginger Chocolate Cake, 85
　Ginger Fig Scones, 60
　Ginger Layer Cake, 73
　Ginger Pine Patties, 119
　Golden Ginger Gems, 121
　Lemon Ginger Cream, 145
　Pineapple Ginger Cheesecake, 330
　Pineapple Ginger Dessert, 320
　Pineapple Ginger Filling, 141
　Pine Ginger Cream, 145
Gingerbread, 53, 94
Glacé Icing, 130
Glazes, 129, 149, 177
Golden syrup
　Golden Cream Custard, 362
　Golden Fruit Cake, 105
　Golden Ginger Gems, 121
　see also Syrup
Gramma Pie, 273
Grapefruit Cream Cake, 96
Gravel Pie, 264
Grecian Dessert Cake, 347

H

Ham
　Hungarian Onion Ham Slice, 156
　Raised Veal and Ham Pie, 309
Hazelnut
　Hazelnut Coffee Cake, 86
　Hazelnut Custard Cream, 148
　Hazelnut Meringue, 350
　Hazelnut-Popcorn Macaroons, 161
　Hazelnut Puffs, 358
　Hazelnut Yeast Pastry Roll, 221
　Hungarian Hazelnut Filling, 140
　Pear and Hazelnut Pie, 258
　Pineapple Hazelnut Tart, 237
Herb Bread, 29
Homestead Pasties, 305
Honey
　Cider Honey Luncheon Cake, 90
　Crusted Honey Rice, 340
　Greek Honey Fig Biscuits, 165
　Honey Boats, 253
　Honeyed Chocolate Frosting, 137
　Honeyed Pineapple Rice, 341
　Honeyed Rhubarb Crunch, 321
　Honey Nut Pastry Rolls, 218
　Honey Spice Custard, 362
　Honey Spice Vienna Cream, 144
　Honey Strips, 165
　Honey-sweet Fried Pastries, 220
　Honey Yoghurt Pie, 272
　Lemon Honey Crackers, 161
　Lemon Honey Sponge, 333
　Spiced Honey Sponge, 73
Hot Cross Buns, 34
Household Bread, 17

I

Icing, 45, 129–32
　Coffee Icing, 252
　Boiled White Icing, 132
　directions for icing, 72
　Lamington Icing, 116

J

Jaffa
　Jaffa Chiffon Pie, 270
　Jaffa Gems, 120

Jam (Jelly)
　Baked Jam Roly, 205
　Baked 'Saucer' Cakes, 344
　Bakewell Squares, 205
　Bakewell Tart, 234
　Jam Cream Filling, 174
　Jam Meringue Tarts, 253
　Linzertorte, 241
　Old-fashioned Roly Poly, 337
　Shortbread Pie, 278

K

Kipferl, 157
Kiwi Fruit Tart, 240

L

Lambie Pies, Little, 306
Lamingtons, 116
Lemon
　Cathy's Magic Lemon Pie, 326
　Cherry Lemon Ring, 93
　Coco-Lemon Cakes, 117
　Lemallow Cream, 145
　Lemon Apple Sponge, 333
　Lemon and Apricot Bread, 58
　Lemon Butter Cream, 145
　Lemon Chess Tartlets, 250
　Lemon Chiffon Pie, 270
　Lemon Curd Pie, 268
　Lemon Frosting, 134
　Lemon Ginger Cream, 145
　Lemon Glacé Icing, 130
　Lemon Honey Crackers, 161
　Lemon Honey Sponge, 333
　Lemon Meringue Pie, 262
　Lemon Passionfruit Slice, 225
　Lemon Sauce Filling, 140
　Lemon Sponge, 74
　Lemon Tart René Verdon, 242
　Lemon Vienna Cream, 144
　Lemon Yoghurt Cake, 56
Lime Pie, Key, 268
Linzertorte, 241
Low Calorie Energy Biscuits, 164
Low-cholesterol pastries, 184, 189
Luncheon cakes, 88–96
Luncheon loaves, 88–93

M

Macadamia Rum Chiffon Pie, 269
Macaroons, 158–61
　Mocha Macaroon Parfaits, 353
Madeira
　Classic Madeira Butter Cake, 77
　Madeira Cake, 50
Maids of Honour, 202
Malt
　Malted Sultana Cake, 108
　Malt Fruit Loaf, 64
Maple Icing, Mock, 132
Marmalade, Apple, 212
Marshmallow, 121
　Cherry Mallow 'Pie', 321
　Chocolate Marshmallow Biscuits, 172
　Lemallow Cream, 145
　Marshmallow Topping, 172
Marzipan, 133
Match-sticks, 206
Mazarin Tarts, Swedish, 252
Meat
　meat pasties, 305–7
　meat pies, 308–9, 312–13
　see also individual meats
Melba Toast, 29
Meringue, 98, 348–54
　Butterscotch Meringue Pie, 272
　Frangipane Pie, 265
　Meringue Genoise, 97
　Lemon Meringue Pie, 262
　Meringue-topped Cherry Pie, 280
　One Egg Meringue, 348
　Pineapple Meringue Pie, 277
　Raspberry Meringue Twirls, 172
Micro Minis, 125
Milk Bread, 16
Mille-Feuille with Strawberries, 224

Million Leaves Cake, 206
Mincemeat, 274
　Apple and Mincemeat Pie, 284
　Mincemeat Pies, 274
　Mince Tart, 242
　see also Fruitmince
Mint Pie, French, 264
Mocha
　Mocha Butter Cake, 76
　Mocha Custard Filling, 141
　Mocha Frosting, 100–101
　Mocha Glacé Icing, 130
　Mocha Macaroons Parfait, 353
　Mocha Mock Cream Filling, 140
　Mocha Vienna Cream, 144
　Mocha Walnut Pudding, 332
　Rich Mocha Cream Gâteau, 100
　Rich Mocha Icing, 132
Molasses
　Wet Bottom Shoofly Tart, 238
　see also Treacle
Muesli Dessert, Fruited, 342
Muffins, 42, 117
Mulberry Pie, 285
Mushroom
　Cheese and Mushroom Potato Pastry Flan, 292
　Salmon and Mushroom Pie, 301

N

Naan, 25
Nut
　Apricot Nut Loaf, 89
　Canadian Fruit and Nut Drops, 165
　Coffee Nut Cakes, 120
　Coffee Nut Cookies, 164
　Date and Nut Slice, 85
　Fruit and Nut Bread, 33
　Honey Nut Pastry Rolls, 218
　Mixed Nut Bars, 173
　Nut Crunch, 134
　Nut Crunch Vienna Cream, 144
　Nut Pumpkin Gems, 122
　see also individual nuts

O

Oat Cake, Golden, 108
Oatmeal
　Country Oatmeal Bread, 20
　Date Oatmeal Pastry Slices, 217
　Oatmeal Carrot Cookies, 177
　Sultana Oatmeal Pie, 280
Olive(s)
　Olive and Feta Cheese Bread, 28
　Quiche with Olives, 294
One Bowl Butter Cake Supreme, 77
Onion
　Onion Bread, 26
　Onion and Edam Cheese Flan, 293
　Wholemeal Onion Tart, 293
Orange
　California Orange Cake, 81
　Jaffa Chiffon Pie, 270
　Mock Orange Babas, 345
　Orange Almond Biscuits, 168
　Orange Almond Tart, 246
　Orange Blossom Cake, 54
　Orange Butter Cake, 49, 76
　Orange Butter Cream, 145
　Orange Date Squares, 345
　Orange Frosting, 95, 134
　Orange Glacé Icing, 130
　Orange Jaffa Cream, 145
　Orange Meringue Loaf, 352
　Orange Pastry, 197
　Orange and Pine Nut Pie, 278
　Orange Raisin Loaf, 89
　Orange Vienna Cream, 144
　Spiced Orange Delite, 318

P

Palmiers, 213
Pancakes Jubilee, Baked, 338
Panettone, 40
Paprika Scone Round, 61
Parfaits, Mocha Macaroon, 353

INDEX

Passionfruit
  Lemon Passionfruit Slice, 225
  Passionfruit Butter Cream, 145
  Passionfruit Cream, 346
  Passionfruit Glacé Icing, 130
  Passionfruit Patty Cakes, 114
  Passionfruit Pavlova, 350
  Passionfruit Snow Cake, 101
  Passionfruit Sponge, 74
  Passionfruit Vienna Cream, 144
Pasta
  Pasta Custard, 362
  Pasta Dessert, 340
Pastes, 129, 133
Pasties, 294, 305
Pastries, 201–5
  Bohemian Pastry Roll, 202
  Cherry Rolls, 209
  Danish pastries, 210–13
  Honey Nut Pastry Rolls, 218
  pastry creams, 146
  Yeast Pastry Rolls, 221
Pastry
  Almond Crust, 196
  American Pastry, 185
  Biscuit Pastry, 196
  Cheese Pastry, 185
  Choux Pastry, 194
  Crumb Crust, 193
  Flaky Pastry, 188
  Hot Water Crust, 192
  Lard Pastry, 193
  low-cholesterol pastries, 184, 189
  making pastry, 181
  Oil Pastry, 197
  Orange Pastry, 197
  Pâte Brisée, 190
  Pâte Sucrée, 190
  Pecan Pastry, 196
  Puff Pastry, 186–8
  Rosemary's Pastry, 197
  Shortcrust Pastry, 182–4
  Sour Cream Pastry, 189
  Suet Crust Pastry, 189
  sweet doughs, 201
  Turnover Pastry, 196
  Walnut Pastry, 196
  Wholemeal Pastry, 189, 192
Patty Cakes, 113–14
Pavlovas, 317, 349–50
Peach
  Butter Cake with Peaches, 49
  Cream Cheese Peach Pie, 261
  Creamy Peach Roll, 322
  Crusted Peach Dessert, 328
  Peach Cream Pie, 276
  Peach Kuchen Squares, 348
  Peach Pie, 276
  Peach Tart with Almond Cream, 248
  Peanut-Peach Cookies, 168
  Snow Peak Peaches, 318
Peaches (small cakes), 118
Peanut
  American Peanut Butter Cookies, 176
  Butter Nut Frosting, 135
  Date and Peanut Ragamuffins, 124
  Frosted Peanut Butter Cake, 102
  Peanut Crunch Pastry Slice, 204
  Peanut-Peach Cookies, 168
  Raspberry Peach Squares, 92
Pear
  French Pear Tart, 236
  Fresh Pear and Bran Cake, 57
  Pear Crumble Cake, 327
  Pear and Hazelnut Pie, 258
Pecan
  Fruitmince Pecan Ring, 109
  Pecan Butter Cream Topping, 109
  Pecan Caramel Tart, 245
  Pecan Nut Buttons, 162
  Pecan Pastry, 196
  Pecan Pie, 278
  Pecan Prune Roll, 90
Petits Fours, 119, 170
Pineapple
  Banana and Pineapple Tart, 232
  Frangipane Pie, 265

  Ginger-Pine Patties, 119
  Honeyed Pineapple Rice, 341
  Pineapple Bread, 65
  Pineapple Coconut Cake, 50
  Pineapple Ginger Cheesecake, 330
  Pineapple Ginger Dessert, 320
  Pineapple Ginger Filling, 141
  Pineapple Hazelnut Tart, 237
  Pineapple Meringue Pie, 277
  Pine Ginger Cream, 145
Pine Nut
  Orange and Pine Nut Pie, 278
  Pine Nut Topping, 138
Pissaladière, 310
Pizza
  Pizza Siciliano, 310
  Wholemeal Pizza Pie, 290
Plum Tart Moulin de Mougins, 237
Pocket Bread, 25
Poppy Seed
  Hungarian Poppy Seed Yeast Pastry Roll, 221
  Jewish Poppy Seed Tricorns, 169
  Poppy Seed and Almond Pie, 266
  Poppy Seed Cake, 53
  Poppy Seed Layer Cake, 98
Potato
  Cheese and Mushroom Potato Pastry Flan, 292
  Kipferl, 157
  Potato Bread, 24
  Potato Galette with Savoury Layer, 293
  'Tater-topped Fish Pie, 302
Pound Cake, Wholemeal, 60
Pretzels, 38
Princess Cakes, 114
Prune
  Pecan Prune Roll, 90
  Prune Chiffon Pie, 269
  Prune Health Loaf, 64
  Prune Tart, 234
Pudding mixes, prepared, 317
Puddings, 332–8
Puffs, Cream, 206, 216, 218
Pumpkin
  Nut Pumpkin Gems, 122
  Pumpkin Nut Bread, 58
  Pumpkin Pasties, 294
  Pumpkin Pie, 273
  Savoury Pumpkin Pie, 294

Q

Quiche
  Neapolitan Quiche, 297
  Quiche with Olives, 294

R

Rainbow Cake, 76
Raised Veal and Ham Pie, 309
Raisin
  Continental Raisin Squares, 329
  Orange Raisin Loaf, 89
  Raisin Munchies, 117
  Raisin Rice Dessert, 340
  Tomato Raisin Loaf, 88
Raspberry
  Raspberry and Apple Tart, 241
  Raspberry Cream Pie, 277
  Raspberry Crescents, 202
  Raspberry Meringue Twirls, 172
  Raspberry Peanut Squares, 92
  Raspberry and Rhubarb Tart, 241
Redcurrant Tartlets, 253
Rhubarb
  Honeyed Rhubarb Crunch, 321
  Raspberry and Rhubarb Tart, 241
  Rhubarb Apple Cobbler, 325
  Rhubarb Apple Crunch, 328
  Rhubarb Pie, 276
  Strawberry Rhubarb Tartlets, 249
Rice
  Fruity Rice Custard, 360
  Rice Custard, 362
  rice desserts, 340–1
Ricotta, see Cheese, Ricotta

Rock Cakes, 113
Rocky Road Frosting, 137
Rolls, 16–17, 36–8
Roly
  Baked Jam (Jelly) Roly, 205
  Boiled Treacle (Molasses) Roly, 204
  Old-fashioned Roly Poly, 337
Rosewater Currant Ring, 58
Royal Icing, 130
Rum
  Brazilian Butter Cream, 148
  Cuba Libre Tart, 248
  Rum Pie, 265
Rye breads, 21–2

S

St Clements Cakes, 124
St Clements Rock Cakes, 113
Sally Lunns, 44
Salmon and Mushroom Pie, 301
Sand Cake, 49
Satin Icing, 132
'Saucer' Cakes, Baked, 344
Sausages in Cream Cheese Pastry, 305
Savoury Tarts, Doctor's Favourite, 300
Scones, 60–2
Seafood
  Gourmet Seafood Flan, 298
  Seafood Pies, 301–2
Seed Cake, Cherry, 80
Semolina
  Mediterranean Semolina Cake, 97
  Semolina Custard Slice, 201
Sesame Seed Cheese Buttons, 154
Shepherd's Pie, 309, 312
Sherry
  Sherry Cream, 144
  Sherry Nut Cream Cheese Frosting, 136
  Spanish Sherry Twists, 156
Shortbread
  Scottish Shortbread, 158
  Shortbread Pie, 278
Shortcakes, 224, 345–6
Slices, 83, 85, 169, 201–25
  see also Squares
Snow Frosting, 134
Soda Bread, 62
Soufflés, 317, 357–9
Sour Cream, see Cream, Sour
Sourdough breads, 21
Spice
  Spiced Plaited Loaf, 33
  Spice 'n' Sugar Swirls, 122
  see also Banana; Buttermilk; Cinnamon; Honey
Spinach and Cheese Slice, 296
Sponges, 73–4
Squares (biscuit), 92, 205, 220, 329, 332, 345, 348
  see also Slices
Steak and Kidney Pie, Economical, 308
Stollen, 45
Strawberry
  Chocolate Strawberry Japanais, 354
  Mock Strawberry Crisp, 341
  Strawberry Cream Cheese Frosting, 136
  Strawberry Cream Tartlets, 249
  Strawberry Crêpes Royale, 324
  Strawberry Rhubarb Tartlets, 249
  Strawberry Shortcake, 224, 346
  Strawberry Sparklets, 114
  Strawberry Sponge, 74
  Strawberry Tart, 236
Straws, Cheese, 154
Streusel Topping, 138
Strudel, 208
Sugar
  Brown Sugar Tart, 245
  Sugar Cookies, 176
  Sugar Tops, 113
Sultana
  Malted Sultana Cake, 108
  Spiced Sultana Patties, 114, 116

Sultana Bran Cakes, 120
Sultana Butter Cake, 76
Sultana Cake, 52
Sultana Oatmeal Pie, 280
Swiss (Jelly) Roll, 73
Syrup
  Oven-steamed Syrup Pudding, 334
  Sweet Syrup Puffs, 337
  see also Golden syrup

T
Tarte
  Tarte à l'Ancienne, 308
  Tarte Niçoise, 297
  Tarte Tatin, 234
Tartlets, 249–53
Tarts, 229–48
Thistledowns, 120
Toad-in-the-Hole, 312
Toffee
  Toffee Sponge, 74
  Toffee Topping, 138
Tomato
  Mexican Tomato Biscuits, 157
  Tomato Raisin Loaf, 88
Toppings, 109, 138, 172
Tortes, 100, 354–6
Tourtière, 313
Town and Country Loaves, 93
Treacle (Molasses)

Boiled Treacle Roly, 204
  Treacle Tart, 245
Tsoureki, 40
Tuna
  Cheesy Tuna Puffs, 301
  Emergency Pie, 301
  Tuna Cobbler, 302
Turnover Pastry, 196
Tyropita, 300

U
Upside-down Pie, Simple, 313
Upside-down Pudding, 338

V
Vanilla
  Vanilla Pastry Cream, 146
  Vanilla Slices, 216
Veal and Ham Pie, Raised, 309
Vegetable
  Fruit and Vegetable Cake, 108
  Hearty Vegetarian Pie, 290
  Herbed Vegetable Flan, 299
  vegetable pies, 290–9
  see also individual vegetables
Vienna Cream, 144

W
Walnut
  Caramel Walnut Frosting, 136
  Chocolate Walnut Tart, 244

Date and Walnut Filling, 141
  Mocha Walnut Pudding, 332
  Walnut Butter Cake, 49
  Walnut Crumble Apricot Cake, 56
  Walnut Date Roll, 90
  Walnut Pastry, 196
Wet Bottom Shoofly Tart, 238
White Mountain Meringue, 349
White Icing, Boiled 132
Wholemeal
  Hearty Vegetarian Pie, 290
  Wholemeal Bread, 17
  Wholemeal Carrot Cake, 95
  Wholemeal Date Scones, 60
  Wholemeal Date Slice, 222
  Wholemeal Onion Tart, 293
  Wholemeal Pastry, 189
  Wholemeal Pizza Pie, 290
  Wholemeal Pound Cake, 60
  Wholemeal Rock Cakes, 113
  Wholemeal Wheatgerm Pastry, 192
Wine
  dessert wines, 317
  Italian Wine Crackers. 157

Y
Yeast cooking, 32
Yoghurt
  Apricot Yoghurt Custard, 361
  Honey Yoghurt Pie, 272
  Lemon Yoghurt Cake, 56